Lecture Notes in Computer Science   **14655**

The series Lecture Notes in Computer Science (LNCS), including its subseries Lecture Notes in Artificial Intelligence (LNAI) and Lecture Notes in Bioinformatics (LNBI), has established itself as a medium for the publication of new developments in computer science and information technology research, teaching, and education.

LNCS enjoys close cooperation with the computer science R & D community, the series counts many renowned academics among its volume editors and paper authors, and collaborates with prestigious societies. Its mission is to serve this international community by providing an invaluable service, mainly focused on the publication of conference and workshop proceedings and postproceedings. LNCS commenced publication in 1973.

Marc Joye · Gregor Leander

Editors

Advances in Cryptology – EUROCRYPT 2024

43rd Annual International Conference on the Theory
and Applications of Cryptographic Techniques
Zurich, Switzerland, May 26–30, 2024
Proceedings, Part V

 Springer

Editors
Marc Joye ⓘ
Zama
Paris, France

Gregor Leander ⓘ
Ruhr University Bochum
Bochum, Germany

ISSN 0302-9743   ISSN 1611-3349 (electronic)
Lecture Notes in Computer Science
ISBN 978-3-031-58739-9   ISBN 978-3-031-58740-5 (eBook)
https://doi.org/10.1007/978-3-031-58740-5

This Springer imprint is published by the registered company Springer Nature Switzerland AG
The registered company address is: Gewerbestrasse 11, 6330 Cham, Switzerland

Paper in this product is recyclable.

Preface

EUROCRYPT 2024 is the 43rd Annual International Conference on the Theory and Applications of Cryptographic Techniques. It was held in Zurich, Switzerland, during May 26–30, 2024. EUROCRYPT is an annual conference organized by the International Association for Cryptologic Research (IACR).

EUROCRYPT 2024 received 501 submissions, out of which 469 formally went to the review process. Every submission was assigned in a double blind way to three program committee members and, in some cases, one or two extra reviewers were added. The IACR version of the HotCRP software was used for the whole review process. In total, 1436 reviews were produced and 5200+ comments were made during the whole process. After a first round, 290 papers were pre-selected by the program committee to enter the second round. These remaining papers were offered a rebuttal to answer questions and requests for clarification from the reviewers. After several weeks of subsequent discussions, the committee ultimately selected 105 papers for acceptance.

The program committee was made up of 110 top cryptography researchers, all expert in their respective fields. For some papers, external sub-referees were appointed by the committee members. We warmly thank all the committee members and their sub-referees for the hard work in the peer review and their active participation in the discussions. We greatly benefited from the help of the area chairs: Shweta Agrawal for "Public Key Primitives with Advanced Functionalities", Serge Fehr for "Theoretical Foundations", Pierre-Alain Fouque for "Secure and Efficient Implementation, Cryptographic Engineering, and Real-World Cryptography", María Naya-Plasencia for "Symmetric Cryptology", Claudio Orlandi for "Multi-Party Computation and Zero-Knowledge", and Daniel Wichs for "Classic Public Key Cryptography". They each led the discussions and the paper selection in their respective area. The previous program chairs for IACR flagship conferences were also very helpful; in particular, we are grateful to Carmit Hazay and Martijn Stam for sharing their experience with EUROCRYPT 2023.

The IACR aims to support open and reproducible research within the field of cryptography. For the first time for a flagship conference, authors of accepted papers were invited to submit artifacts associated with their papers, such as software or datasets, for review, in a collaborative process between authors and the artifact review committee. We thank Martin Albrecht for having accepted to chair the artifact committee.

Three papers were awarded this year. The Best Paper Awards went to Pierrick Dartois, Antonin Leroux, Damien Robert and Benjamin Wesolowski for their paper "SQIsignHD: New Dimensions in Cryptography" and to Itai Dinur for his paper "Tight Indistinguishability Bounds for the XOR of Independent Random Permutations by Fourier Analysis". The Early-Career Best Paper Award was given to Maria Corte-Real Santos, Jonathan Komada Eriksen, Michael Meyer, and Krijn Reijnders for their paper "AprèsSQI: Extra Fast Verification for SQIsign Using Extension-Field Signing".

In addition to the contributed papers, EUROCRYPT 2024 featured two invited talks: "Cryptography in the Wild" by Kenny Paterson and "An Attack Became a Tool: Isogeny-based Cryptography 2.0" by Wouter Castryck. The conference also included a panel discussion on the future of publications; the panel was moderated by Anne Canteaut. The traditional rump session featuring short and entertaining presentations was held on Wednesday 29th.

Several people were key to the success of the conference. Our two general chairs, Julia Hesse and Thyla van der Merwe, did a fantastic job with the overall organization of EUROCRYPT 2024. Kevin McCurley ensured everything went smoothly with the review software and in the collection of the final papers. The conference relied on sponsors to help ensure student participation and reduce costs. We gratefully acknowledge the financial support of (in alphabetical order): Apple, AWS, CASA, City of Zürich, Concordium, Cosmian, Ethereum Foundation, Fair Math, Google, Huawei, IBM, Input/Output, NTT Research, SandboxAQ, Swiss National Science Foundation, Starkware, TII, Zama, and ZISC.

May 2024

Marc Joye
Gregor Leander

Organization

General Co-chairs

Thyla van der Merwe   Google, Switzerland
Julia Hesse   IBM Research Zurich, Switzerland

Program Co-chairs

Marc Joye   Zama, France
Gregor Leander   Ruhr-University Bochum, Germany

Area Chairs

Shweta Agrawal   IIT Madras, India
Serge Fehr   CWI Amsterdam and Leiden University,
                               The Netherlands
Pierre-Alain Fouque   Université de Rennes, CNRS and Inria, France
María Naya-Plasencia   Inria, France
Claudio Orlandi   Aarhus University, Denmark
Daniel Wichs   Northeastern University and NTT Research, USA

Program Committee

Martin R. Albrecht   King's College London and SandboxAQ, UK
Diego F. Aranha   Aarhus University, Denmark
Nuttapong Attrapadung   AIST, Japan
Christof Beierle   RUB, Germany
Sonia Belaïd   CryptoExperts, France
Tim Beyne   KU Leuven, Belgium
Olivier Blazy   Ecole Polytechnique, France
Jeremiah Blocki   Purdue University, USA
Alexandra Boldyreva   Georgia Tech University, USA
Xavier Bonnetain   Inria, France
Jonathan Bootle   IBM Research Europe – Zurich, Switzerland
Christina Boura   University of Versailles, France

Stanislaw Jarecki	UC Irvine, USA
Jérémy Jean	ANSSI, France
Bhavana Kanukurthi	Indian Institute of Science, India
Shuichi Katsumata	PQShield LTD, UK, and AIST, Japan
Ilan Komargodski	Hebrew University of Jerusalem and NTT Research, Israel
Yashvanth Kondi	Aarhus University, Denmark
Venkata Koppula	IIT Delhi, India
Fabien Laguillaumie	Université de Montpellier, LIRMM, France
Wei-Kai Lin	University of Virginia, USA
Jiahui Liu	The University of Texas at Austin, USA
Chen-Da Liu-Zhang	HSLU and Web3 Foundation, Switzerland
Mark Manulis	Universität der Bundeswehr, Munich, Germany
Bart Mennink	Radboud University, The Netherlands
Pratyay Mukherjee	Supra Research, USA
Ruben Niederhagen	Academia Sinica, Taiwan, and University of Southern Denmark, Denmark
Svetla Nikova	KU Leuven, Belgium, and University of Bergen, Norway
Ryo Nishimaki	NTT Social Informatics Laboratories, Japan
Anca Nitulescu	Protocol Labs, France
Ariel Nof	Bar Ilan University, Israel
Kaisa Nyberg	Aalto University, Finland
Jiaxin Pan	University of Kassel, Germany and NTNU, Norway
Omer Paneth	Tel Aviv University, Israel
Arpita Patra	Indian Institute of Science, India
Duong Hieu Phan	Telecom Paris, France
Raphael C.-W. Phan	Monash University, Malaysia
Stjepan Picek	Radboud University, The Netherlands
Thomas Pornin	NCC Group, Canada
Manoj Prabhakaran	IIT Bombay, India
Carla Ràfols	Universitat Pompeu Fabra, Spain
Divya Ravi	Aarhus University, Denmark
Doreen Riepel	UC San Diego, USA
Matthieu Rivain	CryptoExperts, France
Mélissa Rossi	ANSSI, France
Adeline Roux-Langlois	CNRS, GREYC, France
Andy Rupp	University of Luxembourg, Luxembourg, and KASTEL SRL, Germany
Alessandra Scafuro	NC State University, USA
Peter Scholl	Aarhus University, Denmark

André Schrottenloher	Inria, Université de Rennes, IRISA, France
Peter Schwabe	MPI-SP, Germany, and Radboud University, The Netherlands
Yannick Seurin	Ledger, France
Mark Simkin	Ethereum Foundation, Denmark
Pratik Soni	University of Utah, USA
Akshayaram Srinivasan	University of Toronto, Canada
Damien Stehlé	CryptoLab, France
Siwei Sun	Chinese Academy of Sciences, China
Berk Sunar	Worcester Polytechnic Institute, USA
Yosuke Todo	NTT Social Informatics Laboratories, Japan
Junichi Tomida	NTT Social Informatics Laboratories, Japan
Serge Vaudenay	EPFL, Switzerland
Frederik Vercauteren	KU Leuven, Belgium
Ivan Visconti	University of Salerno, Italy
David Wu	UT Austin, USA
Mark Zhandry	NTT Research, USA

External Reviewers

Marius A. Aardal
Aysajan Abdin
Ittai Abraham
Damiano Abram
Hamza Abusalah
Anasuya Acharya
Léo Ackermann
Amit Agarwal
Ahmet Agirtas
Prabhanjan Ananth
Yoshinoro Aono
Ananya Appan
Nicolas Aragon
Arasu Arun
Gennaro Avitabile
Renas Bacho
Youngjin Bae
David Balbas
Marshall Ball
Fabio Banfi
Zhenzhen Bao
Manuel Barbosa

Augustin Bariant
Cruz Barnum
Khashayar Barooti
James Bartusek
Balthazar Bauer
Amit Behera
Shalev Ben-David
Shany Ben-David
Omri Ben-Eliezer
Loris Bergerat
Ward Beullens
Varsha Bhat
Ritam Bhaumik
Kaartik Bhushan
Alexander Bienstock
Alexander Block
Erica Blum
Jan Bobolz
Nicolas Bon
Charlotte Bonte
Carl Bootland
Joppe Bos

Katharina Boudgoust

Alexandre Bouez

Clemence Bouvier

Cyril Bouvier

Pedro Branco

Nicholas Brandt

Lennart Braun

Alessio Caminata

Matteo Campanelli

Sébastien Canard

Kevin Carrier

Ignacio Cascudo

Gaëtan Cassiers

Guilhem Castagnos

Wouter Castryck

Pierre-Louis Cayrel

André Chailloux

Debasmita Chakraborty

Hubert Chan

Anirudh Chandramouli

Rahul Chatterjee

Rohit Chatterjee

Mingjie Chen

Yanlin Chen

Yilei Chen

Yu Long Chen

Jesús-Javier Chi-Domínguez

Ilaria Chillotti

Hyeongmin Choe

Wonseok Choi

Wutichai Chongchitmate

Arka Ra Choudhuri

Hao Chung

Kai-Min Chung

Michele Ciampi

Sebastian Clermont

Benoît Cogliati

Daniel Collins

Brice Colombier

Sandro Coretti

Alain Couvreur

Daniele Cozzo

Wei Dai

Quang Dao

Debajyoti Das

Sourav Das

Pratish Datta

Emma Dauterman

Gareth T. Davies

Leo de Castro

Thomas De Cnudde

Paola de Perthuis

Giovanni Deligios

Cyprien Delpech de Saint Guilhem

Rafael del Pino

Amit Deo

Julien Devevey

Siemen Dhooghe

Zijing Di

Emanuele Di Giandomenico

Christoph Dobraunig

Rafael Dowsley

Leo Ducas

Jesko Dujmovic

Betül Durak

Avijit Dutta

Christoph Egger

Martin Ekera

Felix Engelmann

Simon Erfurth

Reo Eriguchi

Jonathan Komada Eriksen

Hülya Evkan

Thibauld Feneuil

Giacomo Fenzi

Rex Fernando

Valerie Fetzer

Rune Fiedler

Ben Fisch

Matthias Fitzi

Nils Fleischhacker

Pouyan Forghani

Boris Fouotsa

Cody Freitag

Sapir Freizeit

Daniele Friolo

Paul Frixons

Margot Funk

Phillip Gajland

Daniel Gardham

Rachit Garg
Francois Garillot
Gayathri Garimella
John Gaspoz
Robin Geelen
Paul Gerhart
Diana Ghinea
Satrajit Ghosh
Ashrujit Ghoshol
Emanuele Giunta
Kristian Gjøsteen
Aarushi Goel
Evangelos Gkoumas
Eli Goldin
Rishab Goyal
Adam Groce
Ziyi Guan
Zichen Gui
Antonio Guimaraes
Felix Günther
Kanav Gupta
Nirupam Gupta
Kamil Doruk Gur
Hosein Hadipour
Mohammad Hajiabadi
Ghaith Hammouri
Guillaume Hanrot
Keisuke Hara
Patrick Harasser
Dominik Hartmann
Keitaro Hashimoto
Rachelle Heim
Nadia Heninger
Alexandra Henzinger
Julius Hermelink
Julia Hesse
Hans Heum
Shuichi Hirahara
Taiga Hiroka
Marc Houben
James Hsin-Yu Chiang
Kai Hu
Yungcong Hu
Tao Huang
Zhenyu Huang

Loïs Huguenin-Dumittan
James Hulett
Atsunori Ichikawa
Akiko Inoue
Tetsu Iwata
Joseph Jaeger
Jonas Janneck
Dirmanto Jap
Samuel Jaques
Ruta Jawale
Corentin Jeudy
Ashwin Jha
Dan Jones
Philipp Jovanovic
Bernhard Jungk
Fatih Kaleoglu
Chethan Kamath
Jiayi Kang
Minsik Kang
Julia Kastner
Hannah Keller
Qiao Kexin
Mustafa Khairallah
Dmitry Khovratovich
Ryo Kikuchi
Jiseung Kim
Elena Kirshanova
Fuyuki Kitagawa
Michael Klooß
Christian Knabenhans
Lisa Kohl
Sebastian Kolby
Dimitris Kolonelos
Chelsea Komlo
Anders Konring
Nishat Koti
Mukul Kulkarni
Protik Kumar Paul
Simran Kumari
Norman Lahr
Russell W. F. Lai
Baptiste Lambin
Oleksandra Lapiha
Eysa Lee
Joohee Lee

Jooyoung Lee
Seunghoon Lee
Ryan Lehmkuhl
Tancrède Lepoint
Matthieu Lequesne
Andrea Lesavourey
Baiyu Li
Shun Li
Xingjian Li
Zengpeng Li
Xiao Liang
Chuanwei Lin
Fuchun Lin
Yao-Ting Lin
Fukang Liu
Peiyuan Liu
Qipeng Liu
Patrick Longa
Julian Loss
Paul Lou
George Lu
Steve Lu
Zhenghao Lu
Reinhard Lüftenegger
Vadim Lyubashevsky
Fermi Ma
Varun Madathil
Christian Majenz
Giulio Malavolta
Mary Maller
Nathan Manohar
Mario Marhuenda Beltrán
Ange Martinelli
Elisaweta Masserova
Takahiro Matsuda
Christian Matt
Noam Mazor
Pierrick Méaux
Jeremias Mechler
Jonas Meers
Willi Meier
Kelsey Melissaris
Nikolas Melissaris
Michael Meyer
Pierre Meyer

Charles Meyer-Hilfiger
Peihan Miao
Chohong Min
Brice Minaud
Kazuhiko Minematsu
Tomoyuki Morimae
Hiraku Morita
Mahnush Movahedi
Anne Mueller
Michael Naehrig
Marcel Nageler
Vineet Nair
Yusuke Naito
Varun Narayanan
Hugo Nartz
Shafik Nassar
Patrick Neumann
Lucien K. L. Ng
Ruth Ng
Dinh Duy Nguyen
Jérôme Nguyen
Khoa Nguyen
Ky Nguyen
Ngoc Khanh Nguyen
Phong Nguyen
Phuong Hoa Nguyen
Thi Thu Quyen Nguyen
Viet-Sang Nguyen
Georgio Nicolas
Guilhem Niot
Julian Nowakowski
Koji Nuida
Sabine Oechsner
Kazuma Ohara
Olya Ohrimenko
Jean-Baptiste Orfila
Astrid Ottenhues
Rasmus Pagh
Arghya Pal
Tapas Pal
Mahak Pancholi
Omkant Pandey
Lorenz Panny
Jai Hyun Park
Nikitas Paslis

Alain Passelègue
Rutvik Patel
Shravani Patil
Sikhar Patranabis
Robi Pedersen
Alice Pellet-Mary
Hilder V. L. Pereira
Guilherme Perin
Léo Perrin
Thomas Peters
Richard Petri
Krzysztof Pietrzak
Benny Pinkas
Guru-Vamsi Policharla
Eamonn Postlethwaite
Thomas Prest
Ludo Pulles
Kirthivaasan Puniamurthy
Luowen Qian
Kexin Qiao
Xianrui Qin
Willy Quach
Rahul Rachuri
Rajeev Raghunath
Ahmadreza Rahimi
Markus Raiber
Justin Raizes
Bhavish Raj Gopal
Sailaja Rajanala
Hugues Randriam
Rishabh Ranjan
Shahram Rasoolzadeh
Christian Rechberger
Michael Reichle
Krijn Reijnders
Jean-René Reinhard
Bhaskar Roberts
Andrei Romashchenko
Maxime Roméas
Franck Rondepierre
Schuyler Rosefield
Mike Rosulek
Dragos Rotaru
Yann Rotella
Lior Rotem

Lawrence Roy
Ittai Rubinstein
Luigi Russo
Keegan Ryan
Sayandeep Saha
Yusuke Sakai
Matteo Salvino
Simona Samardjiska
Olga Sanina
Antonio Sanso
Giacomo Santato
Paolo Santini
Maria Corte-Real Santos
Roozbeh Sarenche
Pratik Sarkar
Yu Sasaki
Rahul Satish
Sarah Scheffler
Dominique Schröder
Jacob Schuldt
Mark Schultz-Wu
Gregor Seiler
Sruthi Sekar
Nicolas Sendrier
Akash Shah
Laura Shea
Yixin Shen
Yu Shen
Omri Shmueli
Ferdinand Sibleyras
Janno Siim
Tjerand Silde
Jaspal Singh
Nitin Singh
Rohit Sinha
Luisa Siniscalchi
Naomi Sirkin
Daniel Slamanig
Daniel Smith-Tone
Yifan Song
Yongsoo Song
Eduardo Soria-Vazquez
Nick Spooner
Mahesh Sreekumar Rajasree
Sriram Sridhar

Srivatsan Sridhar
Lukas Stennes
Gilad Stern
Marc Stöttinger
Bing Sun
Ling Sun
Ajith Suresh
Elias Suvanto
Jakub Szefer
Akira Takahashi
Abdullah Talayhan
Abdul Rahman Taleb
Suprita Talnikar
Tianxin Tang
Samuel Tap
Stefano Tessaro
Jean-Pierre Tillich
Ivan Tjuawinata
Patrick Towa
Kazunari Tozawa
Bénédikt Tran
Daniel Tschudi
Yiannis Tselekounis
Ida Tucker
Nirvan Tyagi
LaKyah Tyner
Rei Ueno
Gilles Van Assche
Wessel Van Woerden
Nikhil Vanjani
Marloes Venema
Michiel Verbauwhede
Javier Verbel
Tanner Verber
Damien Vergnaud
Fernando Virdia
Damian Vizár
Benedikt Wagner
Roman Walch
Julian Wälde

Alexandre Wallet
Chenghong Wang
Mingyuan Wang
Qingju Wang
Xunhua Wang
Yuyu Wang
Alice Wanner
Fiona Weber
Christian Weinert
Weiqiangg Wen
Chenkai Weng
Ivy K. Y. Woo
Lichao Wu
Keita Xagawa
Aayush Yadav
Anshu Yadav
Saikumar Yadugiri
Shota Yamada
Takashi Yamakawa
Hailun Yan
Yibin Yang
Kevin Yeo
Eylon Yogev
Yang Yu
Chen Yuan
Mohammad Zaheri
Gabriel Zaid
Riccardo Zanotto
Arantxa Zapico
Maryam Zarezadeh
Greg Zaverucha
Marcin Zawada
Runzhi Zeng
Tina Zhang
Yinuo Zhang
Yupeng Zhang
Yuxi Zheng
Mingxun Zhou
Chenzhi Zhu

Contents – Part V

Multi-party Computation and Zero-Knowledge (I/II)

Efficient Arithmetic in Garbled Circuits

David Heath[✉][iD]

University of Illinois Urbana-Champaign, Champaign, USA
daheath@illinois.edu

Abstract. Garbled Circuit (GC) techniques usually work with Boolean circuits. Despite intense interest, efficient arithmetic generalizations of GC were only known from strong assumptions, such as LWE.

We construct symmetric-key-based arithmetic garbled circuits from circular correlation robust hashes, the assumption underlying the celebrated Free XOR garbling technique. Let λ denote a security parameter, and consider the integers $\mathbb{Z}_m$ for any $m \geq 2$. Let $\ell = \lceil \log_2 m \rceil$ be the bit length of $\mathbb{Z}_m$ values. We garble arithmetic circuits over $\mathbb{Z}_m$ where the garbling of each gate has size $O(\ell \cdot \lambda)$ bits. Contrast this with Boolean-circuit-based arithmetic, requiring $O(\ell^2 \cdot \lambda)$ bits via the schoolbook multiplication algorithm, or $O(\ell^{1.585} \cdot \lambda)$ bits via Karatsuba's algorithm.

Our arithmetic gates are compatible with Boolean operations and with Garbled RAM, allowing to garble complex programs of arithmetic values.

Keywords: Garbled Circuits · Arithmetic Circuits

1 Introduction

Yao's Garbled Circuit (GC) [25] is one of the main techniques for achieving secure multiparty computation (MPC). GC allows two parties, a garbler G and an evaluator E, to securely evaluate an arbitrary program over their joint private inputs. GC's crucial advantage is that it allows for protocols that run in only a constant number of rounds and that rely almost entirely on fast symmetric-key operations. Thus, GC is fast and flexible, making it a core tool in MPC.

While GC has steadily improved since Yao originally proposed the technique, GC still had a major weakness: arithmetic operations were expensive. This weakness is prominent because, by contrast, interactive secret-sharing-based MPC cost-efficiently generalizes from Boolean to arithmetic.

The Cost of GC. GC incurs three primary costs: (1) G's compute when garbling the program, (2) E's compute when evaluating the garbled program, and (3) the size of the garbled program. We refer to the bits of the garbled program as its *material*. The amount of material is the most interesting GC cost metric because it dictates communication cost, which is typically the performance bottleneck. We optimize GC material while keeping G's and E's compute reasonable.

Full version appears in IACR ePrint Archive: https://eprint.iacr.org/2024/139. This research was developed with funding from NSF grant CNS-2246353, and from USDA APHIS, under opportunity number USDA-APHIS-10025-VSSP0000-23-0003.

© International Association for Cryptologic Research 2024
M. Joye and G. Leander (Eds.): EUROCRYPT 2024, LNCS 14655, pp. 3–31, 2024.
https://doi.org/10.1007/978-3-031-58740-5_1

Let λ denote the computational security parameter. Classic GC demonstrates how to garble any n-gate Boolean circuit with $O(n \cdot \lambda)$ bits of material. Prior to this work, efficient arithmetic generalizations of GC were not known, except those that only efficiently handle addition/subtraction [3] or that use heavy cryptographic assumptions such as learning with errors or decisional composite residuosity [1,2].

1.1   Contribution

We demonstrate efficient arithmetic garbled circuits from an assumption underlying most of the recent advances in symmetric-key-based GC.

Consider the integers $\mathbb{Z}_m$ for arbitrary modulus $m \geq 2$, and let $\ell = \lceil \log_2 m \rceil$. Let C be an n-gate arithmetic circuit over $\mathbb{Z}_m$ with addition, subtraction, and multiplication gates. Our garbling of C uses at most $O(n \cdot \ell \cdot \lambda)$ bits of material. Thus, each multiplication gate uses only $O(\ell \cdot \lambda)$ bits of material. Compare this with Boolean-circuit-based arithmetic, requiring $O(\ell^2 \cdot \lambda)$ bits via the schoolbook multiplication algorithm, or $O(\ell^{1.585} \cdot \lambda)$ bits via Karatsuba's algorithm [17]. Our scheme assumes only circular correlation robust hashes, the assumption underlying the popular Free XOR technique [8,19].

We consider two classes of moduli: arbitrary moduli m and *short* moduli 2^k for $k = O(\log n)$. While our handling of long moduli m is admittedly expensive, our handling of short moduli is surprisingly practical. Multiplication on short moduli 2^k costs only $(4k - 1) \cdot \lambda$ bits of material. Compare this to the $\approx (1.5 \cdot k^2) \cdot \lambda$ bits needed by state-of-the-art Boolean garbling [23] with schoolbook multiplication. Our short integer arithmetic becomes *even cheaper* when considering complex computations, such as vector inner products.

Our arithmetic values are compatible with Boolean operations. We can translate a value from arithmetic to Boolean (and vice versa) at cost $O(\ell \cdot \lambda)$ bits. This, for example, implies that comparisons are compatible with our approach. Comparisons are often a challenge for arithmetic systems.

We formalize our techniques in a novel model of computation that we call the *switch system* model. Switch systems describe computations as systems of equations. Switch systems generalize the recently proposed tri-state circuit model [15], a model that enables efficient garbling of RAM programs. Switch systems unify many GC capabilities, including Free XOR [19], the half-gates technique [26], our arithmetic techniques, the one-hot garbling technique [14], and Garbled RAM [20].

1.2   Background and Related Work

Basic Garbling. The basic idea underlying GC is to encode each input of a small function as *keys*, and then to use these keys to encrypt each row of the function's truth table. These keys are often called *labels*. We can design protocols that ensure that the evaluator E will only obtain labels that allow decryption of a *single* row, and – with care – this allows E to correctly evaluate any small function while remaining oblivious to the function input.

This idea sensibly extends from individual functions to Boolean circuits: Boolean gates are small functions, and we can use gate input labels to encrypt output labels. This basic approach leads to a garbling of size $O(n \cdot \lambda)$ [25]. While many works subsequently improved the handling of Boolean gates – e.g. [10,18,19,21–23,26] – asymptotic cost has not changed.

Challenge of Arithmetic Garbling. The natural generalization from the Boolean domain to arithmetic domains is impractical, because as we increase the bit-width of the domain, function tables grow in size exponentially. One might hope, then, that we can find ways to garble functions *without* encrypting function tables, and perhaps this would lead to arithmetic generalizations.

The celebrated Free XOR technique [19] achieves one such result. Free XOR allows us to garble XOR gates by simply XORing the gate's input labels. [3] showed that Free XOR indeed generalizes to arithmetic domains, so we can garble the addition operation of finite fields "for free".

While [3]'s arithmetic garbling can add arithmetic labels "for free", multiplication incurs *exponential* cost. Other works demonstrated better multiplication, but only by making strong assumptions, such as learning with errors, decisional composite residuosity, or bilinear maps [1,2,9]. Such approaches are of great interest, but they discard basic GC's practicality, and they require that we work with large numbers; as an example, [2] estimate their approach is similar in performance to the symmetric-key-based GC [23] once arithmetic values are almost *four thousand bits long*.

Compiling Arithmetic to Boolean. The practical approach to garbling arithmetic circuits did not use custom cryptography. It was better to simply compile each arithmetic gate to Boolean gates. To keep the resulting Boolean circuit's size in check, this approach leverages multiplication algorithms. In practice, GC uses either the classic schoolbook method (see e.g. [24]) or Karatsuba's algorithm [16,17].

Asymptotically efficient multiplication algorithms do exist, particularly the breakthrough $O(\ell \cdot \log \ell)$ multiplication of [13], but such algorithms involve infeasible constants. Thus, the reasonable approach to arithmetic GC used Karatusba's algorithm, incurring $O(\ell^{1.585})$ Boolean gates per multiplication. This superlinear circuit size made arithmetic operations expensive.

Figure 1 compares our approach with prior arithmetic techniques. In short, powerful and general techniques for arithmetic GC remained elusive.

One-Hot Garbling. The one-hot garbling technique [14] challenges the GC paradigm of encrypting truth table rows, and it supports efficient garbling of a new class of functions. Let $\mathbf{x}$ denote a length-n Boolean vector. Given a garbling of $\mathbf{x}$, the technique allows to efficiently compute a garbling of the *one-hot encoding* $\mathcal{H}(\mathbf{x})$, a length-2^n vector that holds zero at each index except index $\mathbf{x}$ (interpreting $\mathbf{x}$ as an integer), where it holds one.

Scheme	+	×	<	Domain
This work (longs)	$O(\ell \cdot \lambda)$	$O(\ell \cdot \lambda)$	$O(\ell \cdot \lambda)$	$\mathbb{Z}_m$
This work (shorts)	$(2k-1) \cdot \lambda$	$(4k-1) \cdot \lambda$	$O(k \cdot \lambda)$	$\mathbb{Z}_{2^k}$
Schoolbook	$O(\ell \cdot \lambda)$	$O(\ell^2 \cdot \lambda)$	$O(\ell \cdot \lambda)$	$\mathbb{Z}_m$
Karatsuba [17]	$O(\ell \cdot \lambda)$	$O(\ell^{\log_2 3} \cdot \lambda)$	$O(\ell \cdot \lambda)$	$\mathbb{Z}_m$
CRT [1]	$O(\ell \cdot \lambda)$	$O(\ell \cdot \log \ell \cdot \lambda)$	✗	$\mathbb{Z}_N$
[3]	0	$O(2^\ell \cdot \lambda)$	$O(2^\ell \cdot \lambda)$	$\mathbb{Z}_p$
[3] w/ CRT	0	$O(\ell^2 / \log \ell \cdot \lambda)$	$O(\ell^3 / \log \ell \cdot \lambda)$	$\mathbb{Z}_N$

Fig. 1. Worst case GC material cost (in bits) of our approach as compared to other symmetric-key arithmetic GC that avoids practically infeasible algorithms. We highlight each column's most desirable asymptotic result. Low "<" cost demonstrates compatibility with Boolean operations. ℓ denotes the bit-length of values. m denotes an arbitrary modulus. p denotes a prime modulus. N is a product of pairwise coprime values, suitable for the Chinese Remainder Theorem (CRT, see Sect. 2.4).

These garbled one-hot encodings support two crucial operations. First, given a garbling of a bit y and a garbling of $\mathcal{H}(\mathbf{x})$, we can compute a garbling of the scaled vector $y \cdot \mathcal{H}(\mathbf{x})$ for only λ bits of material. This operation is limited in that it only works when the GC evaluator E knows $\mathbf{x}$ in cleartext, but in this case, it allows to compress the garbling of certain functions. Using basic GC, this operation would require $O(2^n \cdot \lambda)$ bits of material. Second, the one-hot garbling technique is compatible with Free XOR, meaning that for arbitrary affine function f, we can compute $f(\mathcal{H}(\mathbf{x}))$ for *no additional material*.

One-hot garbling is powerful because one-hot encodings are in a sense "fully homomorphic". Suppose we have a garbling of $\mathbf{x}$ where $\mathbf{x}$ is known to E, and suppose we wish to compute $f(\mathbf{x})$ for *arbitrary* f. [14] shows that we can (1) use $O(n \cdot \lambda)$ bits of material to compute $\mathcal{H}(\mathbf{x})$ and then (2) freely compute the linear operation $\langle \mathcal{T}(f) \cdot \mathcal{H}(x) \rangle$, where $\mathcal{T}(f)$ denotes the truth table of f and where $\langle \_ \cdot \_ \rangle$ denotes a vector inner product. This inner product "selects" the $\mathbf{x}$-th row of the truth table, computing a garbling of $f(\mathbf{x})$. Thus one-hot garbling can compute $f(\mathbf{x})$ for *any* f at material cost linear in $|\mathbf{x}|$.

Despite its power, one-hot garbling is limited: E must know $\mathbf{x}$ in cleartext, and (2) $\mathbf{x}$ must be relatively short, as the one-hot vector's length is exponential in $\mathbf{x}$'s length. When these constraints can be satisfied, the approach is useful.

One-hot garbling is a key ingredient in our approach. Indeed, we reconstruct the technique in our switch system formalism, and we demonstrate its compatibility with arithmetic values. We also optimize [14]'s technique, reducing by factor two the material cost to compute a one-hot encoding.

1.3   Summary of Our Approach

Our garbling of arithmetic circuits starts with a novel generalization of Free XOR [19]. Our new garbled labels encode integers in $\mathbb{Z}_{2^k}$ for any k. Unlike [3]'s generalization of Free XOR, our arithmetic labels are *not shorter* than a basic bit-by-bit garbling of an integer. However, our arithmetic labels have a crucial advantage over bit-by-bit garbling, because they allow us to add/subtract $\mathbb{Z}_{2^k}$ values "for free".

To multiply values, we demonstrate compatibility between our new labels and the one-hot garbling technique [14]. Let $x, y \in \mathbb{Z}_{2^k}$. We show how to multiply a garbled one-hot vector $\mathcal{H}(x)$ by an arithmetic label y yielding arithmetic label $x \cdot y \mod 2^k$ for only $k \cdot \lambda$ bits of material.

We also give gadgets that *convert* between (1) garbled binary encodings of $\mathbb{Z}_{2^k}$ values, (2) garbled arithmetic encodings of $\mathbb{Z}_{2^k}$ values, and (3) garbled one-hot encodings of $\mathbb{Z}_{2^k}$ values. All such conversions cost at most $O(k \cdot \lambda)$ bits of material. By combining our multiplication procedure with conversions and one-time pad masks, we achieve arithmetic circuits over *short* integers, i.e. integers modulo $\mathbb{Z}_{2^k}$ where k is at most logarithmic in the circuit size.

To achieve arithmetic over *long* integers (i.e. integers modulo m for arbitrary m), we leverage the classic Chinese Remainder Theorem (CRT), which roughly states that arithmetic on long integers reduces to arithmetic on short integers. To complete the approach, we show that we can convert between long integers in binary representation and long integers in CRT representation. These conversions, again, heavily leverage one-hot garbling and our new arithmetic labels' free operations. With this done, we can handle arbitrary arithmetic circuits while using at most linear material per gate.

On Our Presentation. Much of our handling is intricate. For example, our conversion from an arithmetic label x to a one-hot encoding $\mathcal{H}(x)$ is tricky, as it requires that the GC evaluator E iteratively and simultaneously refine (1) a garbled binary encoding $\mathsf{bin}(x)$ and (2) a garbled one-hot encoding $\mathcal{H}(x)$. At each step, E uses one bit of $\mathsf{bin}(x)$ to solve for half of the remaining bits of $\mathcal{H}(x)$, then uses these new bits to solve for the next bit of $\mathsf{bin}(x)$, and so on. This iterative refinement boils down to solving a system of equations.

In light of this intricacy, our presentation is modular. First, we introduce a model of computation that we call the *switch system* model. This model captures our arithmetic operations, and it specifies computations as a system of constraints that E can solve. Proving that we can securely garble (oblivious) switch systems is relatively straightforward. With this done, we focus on switch systems and ignore garbling-specific concerns. We formalize our arithmetic techniques as switch systems, and this leads to a natural proof of security.

2 Preliminaries

2.1 Cryptographic Assumption

We use a circular correlation robust hash (CCRH) function H [8,26]. Roughly speaking, a CCRH produces random-looking output, even when hashing strings related by some correlation Δ, and even when using the output of the hash to encrypt strings that also involve the same correlation Δ. The CCRH definition enables the Free XOR technique [19], which leverages GC labels related by Δ. We use the CCRH definition given by [26]:

Definition 1 (Circular Correlation Robustness). *We define two oracles that each accept as input a label $K \in \{0,1\}^{\lambda}$, a nonce i, and a bit b:*

- $\mathsf{circ}_{\Delta}(K, i, b) \triangleq H(K \oplus \Delta, i) \oplus b \cdot \Delta$ *where $\Delta \in \{0,1\}^{\lambda-1}1$.*
- $\mathcal{R}(K, i, b)$ *is a random function with λ-bit output.*

A sequence of oracle queries (K, i, b) is legal *when the same value (K, i) is never queried with different values of b. H is* **circular correlation robust** *if no poly-time adversary $\mathcal{A}$ issuing legal queries can distinguish circ_{Δ} and $\mathcal{R}$. I.e.:*

$$\left| \Pr_{\Delta} \left[\mathcal{A}^{\mathsf{circ}_{\Delta}}(1^{\lambda}) = 1 \right] - \Pr_{\mathcal{R}} \left[\mathcal{A}^{\mathcal{R}}(1^{\lambda}) = 1 \right] \right| < \mathsf{negl}(\lambda)$$

In practice, H is often instantiated using fixed-key AES [11].

2.2 Garbling Schemes

A *garbling scheme* [7] is a tuple of procedures that specify how to garble a class of circuits.

Definition 2 (Garbling Scheme). *A **garbling scheme** for a class of circuits $\mathbb{C}$ is a tuple of procedures:*

$$\{ \text{ Garble, Encode, Evaluate, Decode } \}$$

where (1) Garble maps a circuit $C \in \mathbb{C}$ to garbled circuit material $\hat{C}$, an input encoding string e, and an output decoding string d; (2) Encode maps an input encoding string e and a cleartext bitstring x to an encoded input; (3) Evaluate maps a circuit C, garbled circuit material $\hat{C}$, and an encoded input to an encoded output; and (4) Decode maps an output decoding string d and encoded output to a cleartext output string (or it outputs $\perp$ if the encoded output is invalid).

A garbling scheme must be **correct** and may satisfy any combination of **obliviousness**, **privacy**, and **authenticity** [7]. The most interesting of these is obliviousness, which informally states that the garbled material together with encoded inputs reveals nothing to the evaluator:

Definition 3 (Oblivious Garbling Scheme). *A garbling scheme is **oblivious** if there exists a simulator* Sim *such that for any circuit* $C \in \mathbb{C}$ *and for all inputs* x *the following indistinguishability holds:*

$$(\tilde{C}, \text{Encode}(e, x)) \overset{c}{=} \text{Sim}(1^\lambda, C) \qquad \text{where } (\tilde{C}, e, \cdot) \leftarrow \text{Garble}(1^\lambda, C)$$

For most GC techniques (including ours), authenticity and privacy follow from obliviousness in a standard manner. Our full version expands.

2.3 Modular Arithmetic

We work with integers under various moduli, so we provide relevant notation.

- We use $[x]_m$ to denote the remainder of x divided by m.
- We use $x \equiv_m y$ to denote the modular congruence *relation*. Namely, x is congruent to – but not necessarily equal to – y.

When introducing variables we sometimes write $[x]_m$ to denote x is an integer modulo m. We also extend $[\cdot]$. notation to vectors. If $\mathbf{x}$ is a vector, then $[\mathbf{x}]_m$ denotes element-wise remainders:

$$[\mathbf{x}]_m = [\mathbf{x}[0], \ldots, \mathbf{x}[n-1]]_m \triangleq [\mathbf{x}[0]]_m, \ldots, [\mathbf{x}[n-1]]_m$$

We recall relevant properties of modular arithmetic:

$$[[x]_m + [y]_m]_m = [x+y]_m \qquad [[x]_m \cdot [y]_m]_m = [x \cdot y]_m$$
$$[[x]_{c \cdot m}]_m = [x]_m \qquad [x]_m \equiv_m x$$

2.4 Chinese Remainder Theorem

Our handling of long integers relies on the *Chinese Remainder Theorem* (CRT). Our full version reviews CRT, and it includes a formula that converts integers in CRT representation to integers in binary reprentation. We implement this conversion as part of our realization of long integer operations.

2.5 Barrett's Modular Reduction

One challenge in computing over a ring $\mathbb{Z}_m$ is simplifying values modulo m. The naïve approach – which implements modular reduction by repeated subtraction – uses $O(\ell^2)$ Boolean operations, which is too expensive.

Barrett [4] demonstrated another approach to modular reduction. Consider a value x that is less than m^2, sufficient to simplify products of values mod m. Barrett's approach computes $[x]_m$ using two multiplications, a division by a public power of four, and a *conditional subtraction*:

$$x \ominus y \triangleq \begin{cases} x - y & \text{if } x \geq y \\ x & \text{otherwise} \end{cases} \tag{1}$$

Barrett's approach reduces modulo m as follows:

$$[x]_m = \left(x - \left\lfloor \frac{x \cdot \left\lfloor \frac{4^\ell}{m} \right\rfloor}{4^\ell} \right\rfloor \cdot m \right) \ominus m \qquad (2)$$

The crucial point of Equation (2) is that once we demonstrate a linear cost procedure for multiplying binary numbers, we obtain a linear cost procedure for multiplying numbers modulo m. This works because (1) division by public powers of four can be achieved by simply dropping least significant bits and (2) conditional subtraction can be implemented using well-known linear-sized Boolean circuits (see e.g. [24]). Therefore, it suffices to demonstrate a linear cost multiplication procedure for binary-encoded integers.

2.6   Miscellaneous Notation

- λ is a security parameter and can be understood as key length (e.g. 128 bits).
- 'msb' stands for 'most significant bit'; 'lsb' stands for 'least significant bit'.
- We use n to denote circuit size. We often consider values k that are at most logarithmic in n – i.e. $k = O(\log n)$ – such that 2^k is polynomial in n.
- We emphasize a value is a vector with bold: $\mathbf{x}$.
- $\mathbf{x}[0]$ is considered the msb of vector $\mathbf{x}$.
- We denote by $\mathbf{x} \sqcup \mathbf{y}$ the concatenation of $\mathbf{x}$ and $\mathbf{y}$.
- $x \triangleq y$ denotes that x is equal to y by definition.
- $x \overset{c}{=} y$ denotes that x is computationally indistinguishable from y.
- $x \leftarrow_\$ D$ denotes that x is sampled from distribution D. If D is a set, we mean that x is drawn uniformly from D.

We discuss the *binary encoding* of integers:

Notation 1 (Binary Encoding). *Let* $x \in \mathbb{Z}_{2^k}$ *be an integer and* $\mathbf{x} \in \{0,1\}^k$ *denote a vector.* $\mathbf{x}$ *is a **binary encoding** of* x, *written* $\mathbf{x} = \mathsf{bin}(x)$, *if:*

$$x = \mathsf{bin}^{-1}(\mathbf{x}) \triangleq \sum_{i \in [k]} 2^i \cdot \mathbf{x}[k - i - 1]$$

3   Garbled Switch Systems

This section introduces our switch system model of computation and demonstrates how to garble any switch system. Sections 4 and 5 implement arithmetic operations in this model.

Switch systems are inspired by the tri-state circuit model [15], which was recently formalized as a basis for Garbled RAM [20]. We discuss connections between switch systems and tri-state circuits in the full version.

Our switch system model unifies many capabilities of GC, as it captures our arithmetic techniques, as well as many other GC techniques including Free XOR, One-Hot Garbling, and Garbled RAM.

3.1   Generalizing Free XOR

Our starting point is Free XOR [19]. In classic GC, the garbler G associates with each wire w two uniformly chosen labels, K_w^0 and K_w^1. At evaluation, E only holds the particular label associated with the logical value on each wire.

Free XOR changes the format of labels by sampling only *one* label K_w^0 per wire, and then defining K_w^1:

$$K_w^1 \triangleq K_w^0 \oplus \Delta$$

Here, G uniformly[1] draws $\Delta \in \{0,1\}^{\lambda-1}1$. Δ is *global* to the circuit, meaning that *each* pair of labels is correlated by the same value Δ.

The upshot is that G and E now implement XOR gates without G sending *any* material – the gate is "free". To garble an XOR gate $z \leftarrow x \oplus y$, G computes the labels for wire z based on the labels for x and y:

$$K_z^0 \triangleq K_x^0 \oplus K_y^0 \qquad K_z^1 \triangleq K_z^0 \oplus \Delta$$

When evaluating (and overloading the name of each input wire with its value), E holds labels K_x^x and K_y^y. E simply locally XORs the input labels, correctly computing an output label $K_x^x \oplus K_y^y = K_z^{x \oplus y}$.

Our Generalization of Free XOR. Consider a Free XOR label $K_x^x = K_x^0 \oplus x \cdot \Delta$, and view K_x^0, Δ as λ-bit *vectors*:

$$K_x^0 \oplus x \cdot \Delta = \begin{bmatrix} K_x^0[0] \\ \vdots \\ K_x^0[\lambda-1] \end{bmatrix} \oplus x \cdot \begin{bmatrix} \Delta[0] \\ \vdots \\ \Delta[\lambda-1] \end{bmatrix}$$

Viewed this way, there is a natural generalization from labels that encode *bits* to labels that encode *words*. Let $K_x^0, \Delta \in \mathbb{Z}_{2^k}^\lambda$ now denote vectors of $\mathbb{Z}_{2^k}$ elements[2], and let $x \in \mathbb{Z}_{2^k}$ now denote a word. We consider labels of the form $[K_x^0 + x \cdot \Delta]_{2^k}$:

$$[K_x^0 + x \cdot \Delta]_{2^k} = \left[\begin{bmatrix} K_x^0[0] \\ \vdots \\ K_x^0[\lambda-1] \end{bmatrix} + x \cdot \begin{bmatrix} \Delta[0] \\ \vdots \\ \Delta[\lambda-1] \end{bmatrix} \right]_{2^k}$$

Remark 1 (On the Size of Arithmetic Labels.). At first glance, it seems that our new labels have not given us anything new. To encode a k-bit word, we still require an encoding of length $k \cdot \lambda$, exactly as if we were to encode the word bit by bit. However, our new labels enable new free operations, and these free operations ultimately enable efficient arithmetic circuits.

---

[1] Free XOR sets Δ's lsb to one, enabling the point-and-permute technique [6].

[2] In fact, we *could* generalize to *any* modulus m. We only consider moduli 2^k because they are sufficient and because this restriction allows security from Definition 1.

Free Operations on Arithmetic Labels. The first free operation is a direct generalization of Free XOR:

Lemma 1 (Free Affine Maps). *Let* $f : \mathbb{Z}_m^s \to \mathbb{Z}_m^t$ *denote an arbitrary affine map and let* $\mathbf{x} \in \mathbb{Z}_m^s$ *be a vector. Let* $\otimes$ *denote the* vector outer product *tensor:*

$$f([K_\mathbf{x}^0 + \mathbf{x} \otimes \Delta]_{2^k}) = [f(K_\mathbf{x}^0) + f(\mathbf{x}) \otimes \Delta]_{2^k}$$

Proof. Immediate by the fact that f is affine.   □

This implies that addition, subtraction, and multiplication by constants are free operations. For instance, to add two garbled words, just add the labels.

Our encoding also comes with a second free operation. Namely, we can in certain cases compute *modular reductions* for free. The following is immediate by properties of modular arithmetic:

Lemma 2 (Free Modular Reduction). *Let* $x \in \mathbb{Z}_{2^{k+c}}$ *be an integer.*

$$[[K_x^0 + x \cdot \Delta]_{2^{k+c}}]_{2^k} = [K_x^0 + x \cdot \Delta]_{2^k}$$

Said another way, if E holds a word label modulo 2^{k+c}, then E can freely simplify to a smaller word modulo 2^k by simply dropping msbs of each vector entry in the label. This allows us to extract labels encoding low bits of words, which is useful when converting from word labels to binary labels.

Remark 2 (Upcasting). Our modular reduction 'downcasts' large words to small words for free, but the other direction is not free. Our construction will require 'upcasting' binary labels to word labels, and this will require garbled material.

Finally, our word labels support a related operation that allows us to freely *discard* lsbs of labels, but only if they are known to be zero:

Lemma 3 (Free Division). *Let* $x \in \mathbb{Z}_{2^{k+c}}$ *be an integer such that* $[x]_{2^c} = 0$. *I.e.,* 2^c *divides* x. *Integer division by* 2^c *is a free operation. Namely:*

$$\left\lfloor \frac{[K_x^0 + x \cdot \Delta]_{2^{k+c}}}{2^c} \right\rfloor = \left[\left\lfloor \frac{K_x^0}{2^c} \right\rfloor + \frac{x}{2^c} \cdot \Delta \right]_{2^k}$$

Proof. Immediate by the fact that 2^c divides x.   □

Crucially, if the above values K_x^0, Δ are uniform in $\mathbb{Z}_{2^{k+c}}^\lambda$, then $\lfloor K_x^0/2^c \rfloor$ (resp. $\lfloor \Delta/2^c \rfloor$) is uniform in $\mathbb{Z}_{2^k}^\lambda$. Floored division by 2^c partitions the values in $\mathbb{Z}_{2^{c+k}}$ into 2^k size-2^c congruence classes. This means that the above operation is safe in the sense that if the input label is uniform, then so is the output label. On the other hand, it is *not safe* to interpret the resulting quotient as an element modulo 2^{k+c}: the label $\lfloor K_x^0/2^c \rfloor$ is *not* uniform over $\mathbb{Z}_{2^{k+c}}^\lambda$.

The upshot is that if E is working with a word label encoding x, and if it is statically deducible that the lsb of x is zero, then E can locally discard the lsb of x by simply discarding the lsb of each of the λ vector entries in the label.

Multidirectional Gates. Free XOR labels – and by extension our arithmetic labels – allow E to compute addition gates by simply adding labels. As a thought experiment, suppose E instead is missing one gate input label, but has somehow obtained a gate output label. E can *solve* for the missing input label.

In other words, each XOR/addition expresses a linear relation on three labels, and given *any* two labels, E can solve for the third. Thus, we need not restrict ourselves to gates that evaluate only in one direction. This insight underlies our switch system model, which views garbled computation as taking place in a *constraint system*, where E uses some labels to solve for others, and where the order in which the system is solved might vary from one execution to another.

As we will see, our formalization of computations as constraint systems allow us to capture and improve the capabilities of one-hot garbling [14].

3.2   Switch Systems

We introduce our switch system model. In short, switch systems formalize the capabilities of our arithmetic labels (Sect. 3.1), making explicit various available operations, including our free operations.

Switch systems are circuit-like objects that establish constraints on arithmetic wires holding values under moduli 2^k for various k. As the name suggests, switch systems focus on components that we call *switches*:

A switch is a component relating three wires: a mod 2 *control* wire ctrl, and two mod 2^k *data* wires x and y. If the control wire holds logical zero, then the switch closes, connecting wires x and y such that they hold the same value; otherwise the switch remains open, and x and y are free to hold distinct values.

In the GC setting, we implement switches via a call to our CCRH function H. Namely, suppose wire x has zero label $[K_x^0]_{2^k}$ while Boolean wire ctrl has zero label $[K_{ctrl}^0]_2$. G *defines* the zero label for wire y as follows:

$$K_y^0 \triangleq [K_x^0 + H(K_{ctrl}^0, \nu)]_{2^k}$$

Here, ν is a nonce, and we ensure H outputs $\lambda \cdot k$ bits (by calling H k times).

If E knows the value of ctrl, and if ctrl $= 0$, then E can use its ctrl label to compute $H(K_{ctrl}^0, \nu)$, allowing E to compute the difference between the x and the y label such that E can indeed "connect" these wires. Note the inherent bidirectionality of the switch: E can use the difference between labels to translate an x label to y label, or vice versa.

Switches require that E know in cleartext the control wire's value. This is inherent from the fact that E's behavior is conditional, connecting two data wires iff ctrl $= 0$. Of course, our goal is to handle arithmetic circuits that protect privacy, and so our handling must ultimately hide from E intermediate wire values. We achieve privacy-preserving computation via *oblivious* switch systems, which are explained later.

We now formalize the switch system model which captures the capabilities of our arithmetic representation. We show how to garble such systems shortly:

Definition 4 (Switch System). *A **switch system** is a system of constraints on wires (i.e., constrained variables) holding values over moduli 2^k for various k. The system is defined in terms of* gates. *Non-input wires in the system are initially **not set** (i.e., have no value), and as the system runs, wires become **set** according to the rules of each gate. The types of gates are as follows:*

- *A **switch** takes as input a binary control wire $\mathsf{ctrl} \in \mathbb{Z}_2$ and data wire $x \in \mathbb{Z}_{2^k}$. The gate outputs data wire $y \in \mathbb{Z}_{2^k}$, and it establishes the following implication constraint:*

$$\mathsf{ctrl} = 0 \implies x = y$$

We denote the output of a switch by writing $x \vdash \mathsf{ctrl}$.[3] Switches are bidirectional in the sense that the system ensures that if $\mathsf{ctrl} = 0$, then $x = y$, regardless of which data wire is set first.

- *A **join** takes input wires $x, y \in \mathbb{Z}_{2^k}$ and establishes an equality contraint:*

$$x = y$$

We denote a join by writing $x \bowtie y$. Joins are bidirectional in the sense that the system ensures $x = y$, regardless of which wire is set first.

- *An **affine gate** is parameterized by an affine map $f : \mathbb{Z}_{2^k}^{\mathsf{in}} \to \mathbb{Z}_{2^k}^{\mathsf{out}}$. It takes as input a vector of wires $\mathbf{x} \in \mathbb{Z}_{2^k}^{\mathsf{in}}$, and it outputs a vector of wires $\mathbf{y} \in \mathbb{Z}_{2^k}^{\mathsf{out}}$. The gate establishes the following constraint:*

$$f(\mathbf{x}) = \mathbf{y}$$

We denote affine gates by simply writing affine constraints of wires. Affine gates are multidirectional in the sense that the system uses the values of set wires to solve for unset wires.

- *A **modulus gate** takes as input a wire $x \in \mathbb{Z}_{2^{k+c}}$ for arbitrary c, k. It outputs a wire $y \in \mathbb{Z}_{2^k}$, and it establishes the following constraint:*

$$y = [x]_{2^k}$$

Modulus gates are one directional: the system uses x to solve for y.

- *A **division gate** takes as input a wire $x \in \mathbb{Z}_{2^{k+c}}$ where it is statically guaranteed that 2^c divides x. It outputs a wire $y \in \mathbb{Z}_{2^k}$, and it establishes the following constraint:*

$$y = [x/2^c]_{2^k}$$

Division gates are one directional: the system uses x to solve for y.

For convenience, we assume each gate has some unique identifier gid. *A switch system has **input wires** and **output wires**. For a switch system S, we denote by $S(\mathbf{x})$ the values on output wires after running with input wires $\mathbf{x}$.*

---

[3] $x \vdash \mathsf{ctrl}$ can be read 'x controlled by ctrl'. The symbol '$\vdash$' is meant to depict two vertical data wires connected at a point controlled by the horizontal control wire.

Remark 3 (Mismatched Moduli). Switch system joins/affine gates cannot combine values with different moduli. Indeed, corresponding operations on garbled words are only secure and correct when operating on matching moduli. Thus to, e.g., add a 1-bit value to a k-bit value, one must first "upcast" the 1-bit value to a k-bit value. Implementing such casts is a main challenge in our approach.

A crucial component of a switch system is its collection of control wires:

Definition 5 (Controls). *Let S be a switch system and let $\mathbf{x}$ be an assignment of input wires. The **controls of** S **on** $\mathbf{x}$, denoted $\mathsf{controls}(S, \mathbf{x}) \in \mathbb{Z}_2^*$, is the set of all switch control wire values (each labeled by its gate ID).*

As we discuss later, in a garbled switch system the controls of the switches are revealed to E; we introduce random masks as auxiliary input wires to ensure that all such revealed wires can be *simulated*.

Ruling Out Degenerate Systems. So far, it is not guaranteed that a switch system S with input $\mathbf{x}$ has only one possible configuration of wire values. For instance, using switches it is possible to introduce wires that, under particular inputs, are disconnected from the rest of the system. We are interested in well-formed systems where all wires are uniquely determined by the input wires:

Definition 6 (Legal Switch System). *A switch system S is **legal** if for any input $\mathbf{x}$, there exists only one assignment of circuit wires that satisfies the gate constraints. I.e., wire values are a function of the input wires.*

From here on, we only consider/construct legal switch systems.

Order of Gate Definition and the Need for Joins. It may seem strange that we specify gates as having inputs and outputs when gates are bidirectional.

We view such gates as producing their output wires because this is how the garbler G chooses wire labels. For example and as already discussed, for a switch gate, the label for wire y is computed from the labels for x and ctrl. Thus, we insist that switch system be written out as gates, each of which produces fresh output. This ensures G can compute all labels.

Joins provide a mechanism to connect two wires that are each the output of some gate. Joins may at first glance seem innocuous or even ad hoc. Not so. In our garbling, joins are the *only* significant source of garbled material. All other gates allow G and E to compute wire labels as a function of labels they already hold; joins require that G send to E the difference between two wire labels.

Crucially, switch system gates need not execute in the same order they are written down; E solves for unset wire labels as gate constraints become solvable.

Cost Metrics. The *size* of a switch system $|S|$ (the number of gates) is misleading as a cost metric, because switch systems allow wires over various moduli. Thus some wires carry more information than others, and, accordingly, some gates perform more work than others. To measure the complexity of a switch system, we measure the amount of information on wires. As we will see, the garbling of a switch system grows only from join gates. Other gates are are 'free'. Accordingly, our most important metric is the total *width* of joined wires:

Definition 7 (Switch System Join Width). *Consider a switch system S, and let $x \in \mathbb{Z}_{2^k}$ denote a wire modulo 2^k in S. We say that wire x has **width** k. We denote the width of wire x by writing* width(x). *Consider a join $x \bowtie y$. The* ***width*** *of $x \bowtie y$ is the width of wire x (which is equal to the width of y):*

$$\text{width}(x \bowtie y) \triangleq \text{width}(x)$$

*The **join width** of S is defined by summing the width of each of S's join gates. We denote the join width of S by* join-width(S). *Width is measured in bits; we often say that S joins* join-width(S) *bits.*

Remark 4 (Reducing Garbled Material). As we will see, the amount of material needed to garble a switch system S is almost exactly join-width$(S) \cdot \lambda$ bits. We can thus **reformulate our goal** of reducing material to reducing join-width(S).

Completeness. It may not be obvious that switch systems form a complete model of computation. To show that they are complete, and as a warm-up, we demonstrate switch systems are at least as powerful as Boolean circuits. (The following is similar to an argument about tri-state circuits [15]).

Theorem 1 (Emulating Boolean Circuits). *For any Boolean circuit C, there exists a switch system S such that:*

- *$|S| = O(|C|)$ and* join-width$(S) = O(|C|)$.
- *For all inputs $\mathbf{x}$, $S(\mathbf{x}) = C(\mathbf{x})$.*

Proof. By constructing Boolean gates from switch system gates. More specifically, we emulate the complete Boolean basis $\{\oplus, \wedge, 1\}$.

Other than AND gates, emulation is straightforward: we can respectively emulate Boolean 0 and 1 by wire value $[0]_2$ and $[1]_2$, and each XOR is trivially emulated by an affine gate that adds values modulo 2 (i.e., computes XOR). Similarly, NOT gates can be emulated via an affine gate that adds $[1]_2$ to its input. AND gates are more complex, but can be emulated as follows:

$$\text{AND}(x, y) \triangleq z \leftarrow x \vdash \neg y \quad ; \quad z \bowtie ([0]_2 \vdash y) \quad ; \quad \textbf{return } z$$

We sketch the emulated gate:

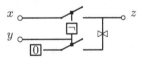

In our system, y and $\neg y$ are controls. If y holds 1, then only the top switch closes, connecting x to z; if y holds 0, then only the bottom switch closes, connecting 0 to z. Thus z is indeed the AND of x and y. We emphasize that we *must* include a join to properly set z. The system[4] joins only one bit. □

---

[4]   In the terminology of [26], this system implements a "half gate", where E learns the cleartext bit y.

Oblivious Switch Systems. As already mentioned, our garbling of switch systems reveals to E all controls (Definition 5). Of course, our goal is to build garbling that preserves privacy, so we must ensure that the controls reveal no *useful* information. To achieve this, we consider switch systems with auxilliary random inputs; these random inputs will act as masks on cleartext values:

Definition 8 (Randomized Switch System). *A randomized switch system is a pair consisting of a switch system S and a distribution D. The execution of a randomized switch system on input $\mathbf{x}$ is defined by randomly sampling $\mathbf{r} \leftarrow_\$ D$, then running S on $\mathbf{x}$ and $\mathbf{r}$:*

$$(S, D)(\mathbf{x}) \triangleq S(\mathbf{x}; \mathbf{r}) \qquad\qquad where \ \mathbf{r} \leftarrow_\$ D$$

As we will see, we garble randomized switch systems by having G locally sample the distribution $\mathbf{r} \leftarrow_\$ D$; E does not know $\mathbf{r}$.

By including randomized inputs, we can consider switch systems that are *oblivious*, meaning that their control wires can be simulated:

Definition 9 (Oblivious Switch System). *Consider a family of legal randomized switch systems (S_i, D_i) for $i \in \mathbb{N}$. This family is **oblivious** if the distribution of controls (Definition 5) of (S_i, D_i) can be simulated. I.e., there exists a simulator $\mathsf{Sim}_{\mathsf{ctrl}}$ such that for all inputs $\mathbf{x}$:*

$$\mathsf{Sim}_{\mathsf{ctrl}}(1^\lambda) \overset{s}{=} \{\ \mathsf{controls}(S_\lambda, (\mathbf{x}; \mathbf{r}))\ \mid\ \mathbf{r} \leftarrow_\$ D_\lambda\ \}$$

Here, $\overset{s}{=}$ denotes that the distributions are statistically close (wrt λ).

Like deterministic switch systems, oblivious switch systems also form a complete model of computation. Namely, for any Boolean circuit, there is an oblivious switch system computing the same function.

Theorem 2 (Obliviously Emulating Boolean Circuits). *For any Boolean circuit C, there exists an **oblivious** switch system (S, D) such that:*

- *$|S| = O(|C|)$ and $\mathsf{join\text{-}width}(S) = O(|C|)$.*
- *For all inputs $\mathbf{x}$, $(S, D)(\mathbf{x}) = C(\mathbf{x})$.*

Proof. Theorem 1 shows that switch systems are complete, but the resulting construction is not oblivious. We achieve obliviousness via the 'half-gates' technique [26]. Namely, to AND bits x and y, we include in our randomized switch system's distribution D a Beaver multiplication triple [5]:

$$\{\ \alpha, \beta, \alpha \cdot \beta\ \mid\ \alpha, \beta \leftarrow_\$ \mathbb{Z}_2\ \}$$

Then, we use two non-oblivious AND gates (Theorem 1) to compute:

$$x \cdot (y \oplus \beta) \oplus \beta \cdot (x \oplus \alpha) \oplus \alpha \cdot \beta = x \cdot y$$

Because non-oblivious AND reveals its second argument to E, E learns $y \oplus \beta$ and $x \oplus \alpha$. α and β are uniform, so $y \oplus \beta$, $x \oplus \alpha$ can be simulated by uniform bits. Thus, the half-gates technique can be embedded in switch systems (the resulting GC material cost will match [26]'s 2λ bits per AND). $\qquad\square$

We rely on Theorem 2 in parts of our construction of arithmetic circuits.

1 $\mathsf{Garble}(1^\lambda, (S_i, D_i))$:	1 $\mathsf{Sim}(1^\lambda, (S_i, D_i))$:
2 $\Delta \leftarrow_\$ \mathbb{Z}_{2^{\text{max-width}}}^{\lambda-1} \sqcup 1$	2 $\mathsf{ctrls} \leftarrow \mathsf{Sim}_{\mathsf{ctrl}}(1^\lambda)$
3 $\mathbf{r} \leftarrow_\$ D_\lambda$	3 **for** *each input* w *with width* k :
4 **for** *each input* w *with width* k :	4 $K_w \leftarrow_\$ \mathbb{Z}_{2^k}^\lambda$
5 $K_w^0 \leftarrow_\$ \mathbb{Z}_{2^k}^\lambda$	5 **for** *each random* $w : K_w \leftarrow 0$
6 **for** *each random* w *set to* $[\mathbf{r}[i]]_{2^k}$:	6 **for** $(g, \mathsf{gid}) \in S_\lambda$; **match** g :
7 $K_w^0 \leftarrow [(0 - \mathbf{r}[i]) \cdot \Delta]_{2^k}$	7 **case** $y \leftarrow x \vdash \mathsf{ctrl}$:
8 **for** $(g, \mathsf{gid}) \in S_\lambda$; **match** g :	8 **send** $\mathsf{lsb}(K_{\mathsf{ctrl}}) \oplus \mathsf{ctrls}[\mathsf{ctrl}]$
9 **case** $y \leftarrow x \vdash \mathsf{ctrl}$:	9 **if** $\mathsf{ctrls}[\mathsf{ctrl}] = 0$:
10 **send** $\mathsf{lsb}(K_{\mathsf{ctrl}}^0)$	10 $K_y \leftarrow K_x + H(K_{\mathsf{ctrl}}, \mathsf{gid})$
11 $K_y^0 \leftarrow K_x^0 + H(K_{\mathsf{ctrl}}^0, \mathsf{gid})$	11 **else** : $K_y \leftarrow_\$ \mathbb{Z}_{2^k}^\lambda$
12 **case** $x \bowtie y$: **send** $K_y^0 - K_x^0$	12 **case** $x \bowtie y$: **send** $K_y - K_x$
13 **case** $\mathbf{y} \leftarrow f(\mathbf{x}) : K_\mathbf{y}^0 \leftarrow f(K_\mathbf{x}^0)$	13 **case** $\mathbf{y} \leftarrow f(\mathbf{x}) : K_\mathbf{y} \leftarrow f(K_\mathbf{x})$
14 **case** $y \leftarrow [x]_{2^k} : K_y^0 \leftarrow [K_x^0]_{2^k}$	14 **case** $y \leftarrow [x]_{2^k} : K_y \leftarrow [K_x]_{2^k}$
15 **case** $y \leftarrow [x/2^c]_{2^k}$:	15 **case** $y \leftarrow [x/2^c]_{2^k}$:
16 $K_y^0 \leftarrow [K_x^0/2^c]_{2^k}$	16 $K_y \leftarrow [K_x/2^c]_{2^k}$

Fig. 2. Our procedure for garbling oblivious switch system families (left) and our simulator used to prove security (right). max-width denotes the maximum width of any system wire. f ranges over affine functions. gid denotes a gate-specific nonce. lsb outputs the lsb of a Boolean GC label. H is a CCRH (Definition 1). **send** indicates to attach a string to the garbled material. The crucial security argument is that for each switch with a one control (highlighted), we can simulate the gate's output label by a uniform string.

3.3 Garbling Switch Systems

Our approach to garbling oblivious switch systems is relatively straightforward. We use H to implement switches, G sends lsbs of control wire labels to reveal their values, G sends differences between labels to implement joins, and all other gates are implemented via arithmetic label free operations (Sect. 3.1). G locally samples the oblivious distribution $\mathbf{r} \leftarrow_\$ D$; E does not learn $\mathbf{r}$. Crucially, the garbling of a switch system uses only $\approx \lambda \cdot \mathsf{join\text{-}width}(S)$ bits of material.

One key point is that G garbles gates in a fixed order, but E evaluates gates in whichever order it can. This order can vary with the system input, depending on which switches close and which do not. We formalize our handling:

Construction 1 (Garbled Switch Systems). *We define our garbling scheme (Definition 2) for oblivious switch systems (Definition 9). In the following, each wire w has zero label K_w^0; we denote the runtime label held by E as $K_w = K_w^0 \oplus w \cdot \Delta$. For simplicity, assume system input/output wires are mod 2 wires:*

– Garble *is defined in Fig. 2.*
– Encode *encodes each input wire value* x *as an input label* $K_x = K_x^0 \oplus x \cdot \Delta$,
  where K_x^0 *and* Δ *are chosen by* Garble. *Namely, our scheme's input encoding
  string* e *includes for each input wire the pair of possible labels.*
– Evaluate *uses available labels to solve for further labels:*
  • *Consider a switch* $y \leftarrow x \vdash$ ctrl. *Suppose* K_{ctrl} *and* K_x *(resp.* K_y*) are
    available.* Evaluate *uses the lsb included by* Garble *to decrypt* ctrl. *If* ctrl $=$
    1, *the gate is solved. If* ctrl $= 0$, Evaluate *computes* $H(K_{\mathsf{ctrl}}, \mathsf{gid})$ *to find
    difference* $K_y^0 - K_x^0$. *It then adds (resp. subtracts) this difference to* K_x
    (resp. K_y*) to compute* K_y *(resp.* K_x*).*
  • *Consider a join* $x \bowtie y$. *Suppose* K_x *(resp.* K_y*) is available.* Evaluate
    fetches the material $K_y^0 - K_x^0$ *and adds (resp. subtracts) this difference to
    solve for* K_y *(resp.* K_x*).*
  • *Consider an affine gate* $\mathbf{y} \leftarrow f(\mathbf{x})$, *and suppose some set wires in* $\mathbf{x}, \mathbf{y}$
    fully determine some other wire. Evaluate *uses affine operations on labels
    to solve for the determined wire's label.*
  • *Consider modulus gate* $y \leftarrow [x]_{2^k}$. Evaluate *drops msbs of entries of the
    vector* K_x *to compute* $K_y \leftarrow [K_x]_{2^k}$.
  • *Consider division gate* $y \leftarrow [x/2^c]_{2^k}$ *where* x *is statically guaranteed to be
    a multiple of* 2^c. Evaluate *drops lsbs of entries of the vector* K_x *to compute*
    $K_y \leftarrow [K_x/2^c]_{2^k}$.
– Decode *decodes each output wire label* K_y *as follows:*

$$\mathsf{Decode}(K_y) = \begin{cases} 0 & \text{if } H(K_y, \nu) = H(K_y^0, \nu) \\ 1 & \text{if } H(K_y, \nu) = H(K_y^0 \oplus \Delta, \nu) \\ \bot & \text{otherwise} \end{cases}$$

Here, K_y^0 *and* Δ *are chosen by* Garble. *Namely, our scheme's output decoding
string* d *includes for each output wire the hash of the pair of possible output
labels. Note, hashing the output labels ensures even a malicious evaluator
cannot forge an output label that successfully decodes.*

Remark 5 (Revealing Control Bits). Construction 1 reveals control bits to E by
including in the GC material lsbs of control wires. These are individual bits, not
length-λ strings. Sending a bit for *every* switch is overkill, as the value of one
control bit is often deducible from other control bits. Rather than meticulously
accounting for this, we simply point out that in our constructions the number of
control bits that need to be revealed is small, and is not asymptotically relevant.
From here on and when counting material cost, we only count joined bits, which
are *significantly* more expensive than revealed control bits.

Construction 1 is correct, and it is also oblivious (Definition 3) so long as the
switch system is itself oblivious (Definition 9). Accordingly, the scheme can be
used to build GC protocols.

Theorem 3 (Obliviousness). *When (S_i, D_i) is an oblivious switch system family, Construction 1 is an oblivious garbling scheme. Namely, let H be a circular correlation robust hash function (Definition 1). There exists a simulator* Sim *such that for all inputs* $\mathbf{x}$ *the following indistinguishability holds:*

$$(\tilde{S}, \text{Encode}(e, \mathbf{x})) \overset{c}{=} \text{Sim}(1^\lambda, (S_\lambda, D_\lambda)) \quad \text{where } (\tilde{S}, e, \cdot) \leftarrow \text{Garble}(1^\lambda, (S_\lambda, D_\lambda))$$

The full version provides a detailed proof of Theorem 3. For now, we provide a detailed obliviousness simulator and sketch an argument of security.

Proof Sketch By construction of a simulator Sim (Fig. 2). In short, Sim produces a convincing view by using (1) the properties of H and (2) the switch system's control wire simulator Sim_{ctrl}.

The real garbling of (S_λ, D_λ) reveals to E the control bits $\text{controls}(S_\lambda, (\mathbf{x}; \mathbf{r}))$, and this string depends on the input $\mathbf{x}$. Sim does not know $\mathbf{x}$, so it cannot reveal the same values. Instead, it uses the obliviousness of (S_i, D_i) to call Sim_{ctrl}, allowing it to reveal values that are *statistically close* to the real world controls.

The remaining challenge is to simulate output labels from switches. For each switch, there are two cases. If the control holds zero (the switch is closed), Sim matches the real-world garbling. If the control holds one, Sim simulates the label with a uniformly random string; this is a good simulation because of the properties of the CCRH and because we know E will not learn the control wire zero label. There is some nuance in showing CCRH is sufficient to garble an inactive switch, since CCRH is defined for Boolean strings, but our labels are $\mathbb{Z}_{2^k}$ vectors. Resolving this mismatch is not hard; see the full proof for details. □

4   Generalized One Hot Garbling

The core of our approach uses switch systems to connect our arithmetic labels (Sect. 3.1) with the one-hot garbling technique [14]. Our handling of arithmetic circuits ultimately reduces to switch systems developed in this section.

Our new one-hot formalism is more efficient than the presentation of [14]. [14] uses $2(n-1) \cdot \lambda$ bits of material to garble a one-hot encoding (defined shortly) of a length-n string; we improve by factor two, achieving the same result at cost $(n-1) \cdot \lambda$ bits. Unwinding our handling of switch system gates, the following approach is similar to the GGM tree improvement of [12].

We start by defining one-hot encodings. The one-hot encoding of an integer x is a zero/one vector that – as the name suggests – is *one-hot*: it has exactly one non-zero entry, and the location of this entry encodes x:

Notation 2 (One-Hot Encoding). *Let* $x \in \mathbb{Z}_{2^k}$ *be an integer. The **one-hot encoding** of* x *is a length* 2^k *vector* $\mathcal{H}(x)$ *s.t. each* $\mathcal{H}(x)[i]$ *is a one iff* $x = i$:

$$\mathcal{H}(x) = \bigsqcup_{i \in [2^k]} (x \overset{?}{=} i)$$

Remark 6 (Arithmetic and Binary One-Hot Encodings). It will be convenient to consider one-hot encodings both where zero/one entries are in $\mathbb{Z}_2$ and where zero/one entries are in $\mathbb{Z}_{2^k}$. We refer to the former as a *binary* one-hot encoding and to the latter as an *arithmetic* one-hot encoding.

The crucial property of one-hot encodings is that they are 'fully homomorphic' in the sense that we can evaluate an arbitrary function via an affine map:

Lemma 4 (Evaluation via Truth Table [14]). *Let $x \in \mathbb{Z}_{2^k}$ and $f : \mathbb{Z}_{2^k} \to \mathbb{Z}_{2^k}$ denote a function.*

$$\langle \mathcal{T}(f) \cdot \mathcal{H}(x) \rangle = f(x)$$

Here, entries of $\mathcal{H}(x)$ are $\mathbb{Z}_{2^k}$ elements, $\mathcal{T}(f)$ denotes the truth table *of f expressed as a vector, and $\langle \_ \cdot \_ \rangle$ denotes the vector inner product operation.*

Thus, if we construct a one-hot encoding of a value x, then we can compute $f(x)$ for free. This is crucial throughout our approach.

Remark 7 (Obliviousness). In the remainder of this section, assume that all one-hot positions are known in the clear to the evaluator E. Our handling of arithmetic circuits later uses one-time pads to mask true values from E, achieving oblivious switch systems (Definition 9) and thus secure arithmetic GC.

4.1 Our Approach to One-Hot Garbling

Our first goal is to construct a switch system that on input a binary encoding $\mathbf{x} = \mathsf{bin}(x)$ outputs a binary one-hot encoding $\mathcal{H}(x)$. We approach this problem recursively, so assume that we have a one-hot encoding of the first i bits of $\mathbf{x}$; we wish to construct a one-hot encoding of the first $i + 1$ bits.

Our key tool for taking this step is a switch system that scales a one-hot vector $\mathbf{h}$ by some scalar $s \in \mathbb{Z}_{2^k}$ for arbitrary k:

$$\mathsf{scale}_k(\mathbf{h} = \mathcal{H}(x)) \triangleq \mathbf{y} \leftarrow \left(\bigsqcup_i [0]_{2^k} \vdash \mathbf{h}[i] \right) \; ; \; s \leftarrow \sum_i \mathbf{y}[i] \; ; \; \textbf{return } (s, \mathbf{y})$$

The system treats scalar s as an output, not as an input; this will be formally convenient later. As wires are bidirectional, s can be 'converted to an input' by joining it with some other wire. For reference, we draw an example of the above system both with symbolic inputs (left) and on a concrete input (right):

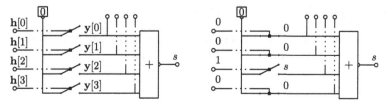

We construct each word of the output vector $\mathbf{y}[i]$ by switching data value $0 \in \mathbb{Z}_{2^k}$ with control $\mathbf{h}[i]$. Because $\mathbf{h}$ is one-hot, all except one switch closes. We add together the entries of $\mathbf{y}$, and we name the sum s.

Since all except one wire in $\mathbf{y}$ holds a zero, there is a unique wire assignment that satisfies the system: the single non-zero entry of $\mathbf{y}$ must be equal to s. In the context of garbling, this means that E can use available zero labels and a label that encodes s to solve for the single non-zero label in the encoding of $\mathbf{y}$. Thus, this system indeed scales the one-hot vector $\mathbf{h}$ by the scalar s. The scale system has no join gates, and hence it is "free".

We can use scale to construct a one-hot encoding of the binary vector $\mathbf{x}$ recursively. In the base case, the one-hot encoding of a single bit $\mathbf{x}[0]$ is simply the pair $(\neg\mathbf{x}[0], \mathbf{x}[0])$. In the recursive case, we take the one-hot encoding of the first i bits of $\mathbf{x}$ and scale it by the next bit of $\mathbf{x}$. From here, we extend the one-hot encoding with XORs (addition mod 2). The construction is as follows:

1   bin-to-hot($\mathbf{x} = \mathrm{bin}(x)$) $\triangleq$
2   **if** $(|\mathbf{x}| = 1)$:   **return** $(\neg\mathbf{x}[0], \mathbf{x}[0])$
3   **else** :
4        $\mathbf{h} \leftarrow$ bin-to-hot($\mathbf{x}[1..]$) ; $(s, \mathbf{h}') \leftarrow$ scale$_1(\mathbf{h})$; $s \bowtie \mathbf{x}[0]$
5   **return** $([\mathbf{h}' + \mathbf{h}]_2) \sqcup \mathbf{h}'$

Given a length-n input vector, each recursive call joins one bit, so bin-to-hot joins $n - 1$ total bits. Again, this is a factor two improvement over [14].

4.2   Half Multiplication

As a stepping stone to full multiplication of short arithmetic values, we build a 'half multiplier', similar in flavor to [26]'s half AND gate (see Theorem 1). The system takes as input one-hot-encoded x and word-encoded $y \in \mathbb{Z}_{2^k}$:

$$\text{half-mul}(\mathbf{h} = \mathcal{H}(x), y) \triangleq (s, \mathbf{h}') \leftarrow \text{scale}_k(\mathbf{h}) ; s \bowtie y ; \textbf{return} \sum_i i \cdot \mathbf{h}'[i]$$

half-mul observes that we can scale x's one-hot vector by y, then use affine operations to scale each entry of $\mathbf{h}'[i]$ by its index i (each i is a constant). After this, the one-hot location stores $[x \cdot y]_{2^k}$, and all other locations store zero. Summing these products computes $[x \cdot y]_{2^k}$. half-mul joins only k bits.

4.3   Conversions

To support general arithmetic operations, we need a variety of *conversion* operators that move between various data representations.

Conversions from One-Hot Encodings. It is useful to convert an arithmetic one-hot encoding $\mathcal{H}(x)$ to binary encoding $\mathrm{bin}(x)$ and/or word encoding x. These conversions are free, due to the 'fully homomorphic' nature of one-hot encodings.

In more detail, let $\mathrm{id} : \mathbb{Z}_{2^k} \to \mathbb{Z}_{2^k}$ denote the identity function.

$$\mathsf{hot\text{-}to\text{-}word}(\mathbf{h} = \mathcal{H}(x)) \triangleq \langle \mathcal{T}(\mathrm{id}) \cdot \mathbf{h} \rangle$$

By Lemma 4 this correctly computes the word encoding of x.

Similarly, we can extract a binary encoding of an arithmetic one-hot encoded value $\mathcal{H}(x)$. We simplify the one-hot indices modulo 2, then take an appropriate linear combination of the wires:

$$\mathsf{hot\text{-}to\text{-}bin}(\mathbf{h} = \mathcal{H}(x)) \triangleq \langle \mathcal{T}(\mathrm{bin}) \cdot [\mathbf{h}]_2 \rangle$$

Converting Words to One-Hots. We can now convert binary strings to one-hot vectors, and we can easily convert one-hot vectors to words/binary. The final conversion – words to one-hot vectors – is significantly more complex.

Our observation is that to compute a one-hot encoding of x, we first need a *binary* encoding $\mathrm{bin}(x)$. If we can achieve this, then we can apply bin-to-hot, scale the result by $[1]_{2^k}$, and the problem is solved. However, efficiently converting a word x to a binary encoding $\mathrm{bin}(x)$ is non-trivial.

Our mod gate allows us to freely extract from x the lsb $[x]_2$. However, higher bits are harder to extract. Our division gate *would* allow us to make progress, *if* we could ensure that the lsb of x was zero. Of course, x might have lsb one, so this does not yet work. To extract the second lsb of x, we need to first *subtract off* the lsb. We have this lsb $[x]_2$, but we cannot yet subtract it off, because its modulus 2 does not match x's modulus 2^k, and our linear operations require wires with matching moduli (Remark 3). Thus, to compute $[x - [x]_2]_{2^k}$, we first need to "upcast" the bit $[x]_2$ to a word $[[x]_2]_{2^k}$.

As a strawman solution to this upcast problem, consider the following system:

$$([0]_{2^k} \vdash [x]_2) \bowtie ([1]_{2^k} \vdash \neg[x]_2)$$

This strawman is correct: if $[x]_2 = 0$, then the joined wire hold $[0]_{2^k}$; otherwise, the joined wires hold $[1]_{2^k}$. *The problem* is that this system joins k bits, which is simply too expensive. To extract *all* bits of x, we would need to upcast *each* of its bits in turn, and each upcast would join $O(k)$ bits. In total we would join $O(k^2)$ bits, which is useless for linear cost arithmetic.

Still, the above template ultimately leads to an efficient solution: (1) use mod to obtain the lsb of x, (2) upcast the lsb to a word, (3) subtract the upcasted lsb from x, (4) now that the lsb of x is guaranteed to be zero, use division to remove the lsb, and (5) repeat. To instantiate this template efficiently, our system upcasts all of the lsbs of x *in batch*. The resulting solution is a single switch system that converts each bit of x to binary, and it simultaneously converts x to arithmetic one-hot representation. The full system joins only $2k - 1$ bits.

1   word-to-hot$_k(x) \triangleq$

2   $\mathbf{h}_{\mathsf{bin}} \leftarrow$ bin-to-hot(bin(x)) ; $\mathbf{h}_{\mathsf{arith}} \leftarrow \bigsqcup_i ([0]_{2^k} \vdash \mathbf{h}_{\mathsf{bin}}[i])$

3   $(\mathbf{h}^\ell, \mathbf{h}^r) \leftarrow$ halves($\mathbf{h}_{\mathsf{arith}}$) ; bin($x$) $\leftarrow$ solve-bin$_{k-1}(\mathbf{h}^\ell + \mathbf{h}^r)$

4   **return** $\mathbf{h}_{\mathsf{arith}}$

5   **where** solve-bin$_i(\mathbf{h} = \mathcal{H}([x]_{2^i})) \triangleq$

6   **if** $(i = 0)$: $\mathbf{h}[0] \bowtie [1]_{2^k}$; **return** $[x]_2$

7   **else** :

8         $[[x]_{2^i}]_{2^k} \leftarrow$ hot-to-word($\mathbf{h}$) ; msb $\leftarrow [(x - [x]_{2^i})/2^i]_2$

9         $(\mathbf{h}^\ell, \mathbf{h}^r) \leftarrow$ halves($\mathbf{h}$) ; lsbs $\leftarrow$ solve-bin$_{i-1}(\mathbf{h}^\ell + \mathbf{h}^r)$

10   **return** msb $\sqcup$ lsbs

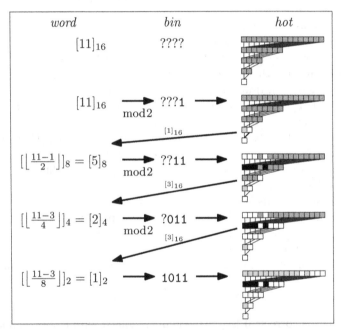

Fig. 3. (Top) our word-to-hot switch system converts an arithmetic word $[x]_{2^k}$ to an arithmetic one-hot vector $[\mathcal{H}(x)]_{2^k}$. halves splits a length-2^i vector at its middle, giving two length-2^{i-1} outputs. (Bottom) an example word-to-hot execution. The system maintains three encodings of its input x: a word encoding, a binary encoding, and an arithmetic one-hot encoding (as well as one-hot encodings of x modulo powers of two). Black squares represent logical zero; white squares represent one; gray squares represent an unknown value. At each step, the system uses mod to extract the lsb of x, yielding the next bit in the binary encoding. It then can refine its one-hot encodings. These one-hot encodings allow to linearly compute a word encoding of lsbs, which are subtracted from x, allowing us to repeat until we fully solve the one-hot encoding.

word-to-hot (see Fig. 3) is our most intricate construction. It leverages gate bidirectionality to solve for x's binary encoding and one-hot encoding *together*. Figure 3 sketches an example, and it show how E solves the constraints.

The system itself is circularly defined: the binary one-hot vector $\mathbf{h}_{\mathsf{bin}}$ is defined based on $\mathsf{bin}(x)$, which is not defined until the later call to solve-bin. This definition is nevertheless sensible: the system iteratively *refines* its solution for both $\mathsf{bin}(x)$ and $\mathbf{h}_{\mathsf{bin}}$. Note, the system can immediately solve for the lsb of x (base case of solve-bin) via a mod gate.

In a sense, we construct $\mathbf{h}_{\mathsf{bin}} = [\mathcal{H}(x)]_2$ by *imagining* that we already have $\mathsf{bin}(x)$. With $\mathbf{h}_{\mathsf{bin}}$ constructed, we use switches to cast the zero slots of $\mathbf{h}_{\mathsf{bin}}$ to words mod 2^k, yielding an arithmetic one-hot vector $\mathbf{h}_{\mathsf{arith}}$ whose one slot is initially unconstrained. We again *imagine* that this one slot is filled with $[1]_{2^k}$, in which case $\mathbf{h}_{\mathsf{arith}}$ would be a valid arithmetic one-hot encoding of x. Then, we repeatedly take left and right halves of $\mathbf{h}_{\mathsf{arith}}$ and sum them to a vector of half the length. This iteratively yields shorter and shorter arithmetic one-hot vectors:

$$[\mathcal{H}([x]_{2^k})]_{2^k} \quad [\mathcal{H}([x]_{2^{k-1}})]_{2^k} \quad \cdots \quad [\mathcal{H}([x]_2)]_{2^k} \quad [1]_{2^k}$$

The final singleton one-hot vector is degenerately equal to $[1]_{2^k}$, but only because we *imagined* that the one slot of $\mathbf{h}_{\mathsf{arith}}$ was filled, so in fact this final value is so far *unconstrained*. We *insist* that this final value is indeed $[1]_{2^k}$ by applying a join gate (base case of solve-bin).

If we can indeed solve for the one-hot encoding of x, then we can solve for intermediate arithmetic one-hot encodings by propagating $[1]_{2^k}$ *backwards* through the system (see Fig. 3). From here, we use the intermediate encodings to linearly compute word encodings of each bit of x.

Evaluation of the system proceeds as follows. Because the lsb of x is initially available, E can solve for *half* of the entries of $\mathbf{h}_{\mathsf{bin}}$. Specifically, E solves for each one-hot index whose lsb does *not* match that of x; see Fig. 3. This, in turn, lets E solve for a word encoding of x's lsb, which can be subtracted from x. Now x must have lsb zero, so we can iterate, extracting a binary encoding of x's second lsb, allowing E to refine the one-hot encoding of x, allowing E to obtain a word encoding of x's second lsb, and so on.

While intricate, word-to-hot is lean: it joins only $2k - 1$ bits. This low cost makes it affordable to convert arithmetic labels to arithmetic one-hot encodings.

5   Garbled Arithmetic from Switch Systems

We now have our core tools that combine one-hot garbling with arithmetic labels. From here, we assemble arithmetic garbling. We start by building switch systems for short integers; this handling is straightforward and practical. We use short integers to achieve long integers by applying the Chinese Remainder Theorem.

5.1   Short Integers

Based on our new one-hot operations (Sect. 4), we can construct oblivious switch systems (Definition 9) that operate on *short* integers (henceforth, "shorts"). Here, we consider integers modulo 2^k where $k = O(\log n)$ is at most logarithmic in the circuit size n. The fact that k is small allows us to write out one-hot encodings of integers in polynomial time. Later, we will use shorts as a building block to garble *long* integers, which have no restriction on the modulus.

Notation 3 (Short). *The **short encoding** of integer $x \in \mathbb{Z}_{2^k}$ – written $\mathsf{short}(x)$ – consists of (1) a uniform mask $\alpha \in \mathbb{Z}_{2^k}$ and (2) a length 2^k arithmetic one-hot encoding $\mathcal{H}(x + \alpha)$.*

Recall that in a one-hot encoding, the evaluator E knows the one-hot value in cleartext; the one-time pad mask α hides x. In the context of a randomized switch system, the mask α is part of the system's randomized inputs, and in GC the garbler G knows α in cleartext.

Conversions on Shorts. Before explaining how to add/subtract/multiply shorts, we need conversion operations on shorts. These operations are a straightforward consequence of conversion operations on one-hot encodings (Sect. 4.3).

For instance, to convert short encoding $\mathsf{short}(x)$ to word encoding x, we simply use the appropriate conversion on one-hot vectors, then subtract off α:

$$\mathsf{short\text{-}to\text{-}word}((\mathbf{h}, \alpha) = \mathsf{short}(x)) \triangleq \mathbf{return}\ \mathsf{hot\text{-}to\text{-}word}(\mathbf{h}) - \alpha$$

This system is free (i.e., has no joins).

Conversions from a word to a short and between shorts and binary are similar:

$$\mathsf{word\text{-}to\text{-}short}(x) \triangleq \alpha \leftarrow_\$ \mathbb{Z}_{2^k}\ ;\ \mathbf{return}\ (\mathsf{word\text{-}to\text{-}hot}(x + \alpha), \alpha)$$
$$\mathsf{short\text{-}to\text{-}bin}((\mathbf{h}, \alpha) = \mathsf{short}(x)) \triangleq \mathbf{return}\ \mathsf{hot\text{-}to\text{-}bin}(\mathbf{h}) - \alpha$$
$$\mathsf{bin\text{-}to\text{-}short}(\mathbf{x} = \mathsf{bin}(x)) \triangleq \alpha \leftarrow_\$ \mathbb{Z}_{2^k}\ ;\ \mathbf{return}\ (\mathsf{bin\text{-}to\text{-}hot}(\mathbf{x} + \mathsf{bin}(\alpha)), \alpha)$$

$\mathsf{word\text{-}to\text{-}short}$ joins $2k - 1$ bits, due to the call to $\mathsf{word\text{-}to\text{-}hot}$.

$\mathsf{short\text{-}to\text{-}bin}$ and $\mathsf{bin\text{-}to\text{-}short}$ requiring adding/subtracting uniform mask α *in binary representation*. Here, addition/subtraction is implemented by a ripple-carry adder built from oblivious Boolean gates (Theorem 2). It is crucial to use *oblivious* gates to hide x from E. A ripple-carry adder can be built from XORs and $k - 1$ oblivious ANDs (see e.g. [24]), so the full adder joins $2k - 2$ bits.

Operations on Shorts. We use our new conversions to operate on shorts. Addition/subtract/scaling by public constants are simple: convert arguments to word representation, perform the operation for free, then convert the result back to short representation. Let x, y be short encodings and let $s \in \mathbb{Z}_{2^k}$ be a constant:

$$x + y \triangleq \mathsf{word\text{-}to\text{-}short}(\mathsf{short\text{-}to\text{-}word}(x) + \mathsf{short\text{-}to\text{-}word}(y))$$
$$x - y \triangleq \mathsf{word\text{-}to\text{-}short}(\mathsf{short\text{-}to\text{-}word}(x) - \mathsf{short\text{-}to\text{-}word}(y))$$
$$s \cdot x \triangleq \mathsf{word\text{-}to\text{-}short}(s \cdot \mathsf{short\text{-}to\text{-}word}(x))$$

Each operation joins only $2k - 1$ bits, due to the call to $\mathsf{word\text{-}to\text{-}short}$.

Multiplication on shorts is more difficult, but can be achieved with two *half multipliers* (Sect. 4.2) and conversions. Consider two values $\mathsf{short}(x), \mathsf{short}(y)$, and suppose we wish to compute $\mathsf{short}(x \cdot y)$:

1 $((\mathbf{h}_x, \alpha) = \mathsf{short}(x)) \cdot ((\mathbf{h}_y, \beta) = \mathsf{short}(y)) \triangleq$

2 $\quad y \leftarrow \mathsf{short\text{-}to\text{-}word}(\mathsf{short}(y))$

3 $\quad (x + \alpha) \cdot y \leftarrow \mathsf{half\text{-}mul}(\mathbf{h}_x, y)$

4 $\quad (y + \beta) \cdot \alpha \leftarrow \mathsf{half\text{-}mul}(\mathbf{h}_y, \alpha)$

5 $\quad x \cdot y \leftarrow (x + \alpha) \cdot y - (y + \beta) \cdot \alpha + \alpha \cdot \beta$

6 $\quad \mathbf{return}\ \mathsf{word\text{-}to\text{-}short}(x \cdot y)$

Here, $\alpha \cdot \beta$ is part of the switch system's randomized input.

The full multiplication procedure joins only $4k - 1$ bits: k bits are joined per half-mul, and $2k - 1$ bits are joined as part of word-to-short.

Delayed Conversions and Inner Products. Our operations on shorts convert from words to shorts, joining $2k - 1$ bits. When handling more complex arithmetic expressions, we can as an optimization simply delay conversion back to short representation. For example, to compute the inner product of two length-n vectors of shorts, we can pointwise multiply the vector elements to obtain n words, add the words together, then perform only a single conversion back to short representation. This inner product operation thus uses $2n$ half multipliers and one word-to-short conversion, joining only $2nk + 2k - 1$ total bits.

Binary Multiplication; Modular Reduction. By using binary/short conversions with short multiplication, we can multiply k-bit binary numbers while joining only $O(k)$ bits. Because we can efficiently multiply short binary integers, we have the tools we need to apply Barrett's modular reduction algorithm (Sect. 2.5) to short integers. Namely, we can we can reduce short binary numbers modulo m while joining only $O(k)$ bits, so long as the binary number is less than m^2.

We now have all the tools we need to implement arithmetic circuits over $\mathbb{Z}_m$ for arbitrary *small* modulus $m \geq 2$. To garble an arithmetic operation over $\mathbb{Z}_m$, choose a modulus $2^k > m^2$, perform the operation on shorts in 2^k, then use Barrett reduction to simplify the result modulo m. This fact will be useful in constructing switch systems for long integers, see next.

5.2 Long Integers

All that remains is to upgrade our handling of words and shorts to handling of *long* integers, i.e. integers modulo arbitrary $m \geq 2$. Let $\ell = \lceil \log_2 m \rceil$. We show that for any choice of m, our arithmetic gates join at most $O(\ell)$ bits.

Before presenting our approach, we remark that our handling here is more theoretical than in Sect. 5.1. Our operations on longs require many conversions between representations, and this is concretely expensive. Accordingly, our presentation is less granular and less concerned with constants. Nevertheless, when garbling ℓ-bit integers, all operations join $O(\ell)$ bits. We believe our work will help lead to practically efficient garbling of long integers.

Our basic idea is to apply the Chinese Remainder Theorem (CRT, Sect. 2.4). To operate on arbitrary modulus $m \geq 2$, we consider a CRT modulus $N >$

m^2, large enough to support overflow from multiplication. We choose N as the product of the smallest distinct primes such that $N > m^2$ holds. Let r denote the number of distinct primes.

We represent a long as r shorts, where each j-th short computes operations over prime modulus p_j. We refer to each such short as a *residue*. Let P denote the largest prime modulus. Our shorts use as their word modulus the smallest modulus 2^k such that $2^k > \mathsf{max}(P^2, P \cdot \ell^2)$, sufficient to prevent overflow in all considered cases. P is at most $O(\ell)$, so $k = O(\log \ell)$; moreover, P is the $O(\ell/\log \ell)$-th prime.

Longs modulo N. To multiply/add/subtract longs modulo a CRT modulus N, we simply pairwise operate on the r residues, then reduce each j-th result modulo p_j (see discussion of modular reduction in Sect. 5.1). By the Chinese Remainder Theorem, this implements the corresponding operation modulo N. Morever, the total bit-length of all r residues is linear in $\ell = \lceil \log_2 N \rceil$, so this indeed joins only $O(\ell)$ bits per operation.

Longs modulo m; conversions to/from binary. To operate over an arbitrary modulus $\mathbb{Z}_m$, we operate over $\mathbb{Z}_N$ and simplify modulo m after each operation. To do so, we will apply Barrett's modular reduction (Sect. 2.5). However, Barrett's algorithm uses operations on *binary* integers, and our integers are currently in CRT representation. Thus, we must explain how to convert long integers to binary and vice versa. In the following, let $x \in \mathbb{Z}_N$ be the converted integer.

Converting from binary to long roughly proceeds as follows: (1) partition the bits of x into small chunks so that we can sensibly make a one-hot vector encoding each chunk, (2) use free operations on one-hot encodings to convert each chunk to CRT representation, and (3) use free addition to combine the CRT chunks into a CRT representation of x.

More precisely, we first sample a uniform mask $\alpha \in \mathbb{Z}_N$ and use oblivious Boolean gates (Theorem 2) to compute $(x+\alpha) \ominus N = [x+\alpha]_N$. Recall, $\ominus$ denotes conditional subtraction (Equation (1)), which can be achieved by a Boolean comparator and ripple-carry adder, joining only $O(\ell)$ bits.

Now that x is masked, we can reveal $[x+\alpha]_N$ to E, allowing us to use one-hot techniques. We partition the bits of $[x+\alpha]_N$ into *chunks* of $\lceil \log_2 \ell \rceil$ bits (we pad with msb zeros to ensure chunks have equal length). We use bin-to-hot and scale to convert each chunk to an arithmetic one-hot encoding (where one-hot vector entries are $\mathbb{Z}_{2^k}$ words).

Let $\mathcal{H}(c_i)$ be the i-th chunk, such that $x = \sum_i 2^{i \cdot \lceil \log_2 \ell \rceil} \cdot c_i$. We convert *each* chunk to r residue words. Computing each j-th residue is a free operation:

$$\langle \mathcal{T}(x \mapsto [2^{i \cdot \lceil \log_2 \ell \rceil} \cdot x]_{p_j}) \cdot \mathcal{H}(c_i) \rangle = [2^{i \cdot \lceil \log_2 \ell \rceil} \cdot c_i]_{p_j} \qquad \text{Lemma 4}$$

Now, for each chunk we have a word representing the residue of that chunk modulo each prime p_j. For each such j, we use free addition to sum all such residues. The result is a $\mathbb{Z}_{2^k}$ value *congruent to* – but not equal to – $[x + \alpha]_{p_j}$. Note that each sum is at most $(p_j - 1)$ times the number of chunks, which is $O(\ell/\log \ell)$. By our choice of k, this sum does not overflow $\mathbb{Z}_{2^k}$. To complete the conversion, we use short operations to subtract off α and reduce modulo p_j.

This full conversion joins only $O(\ell)$ bits. Its non-free operations involve (1) adding a uniform mask α, (2) converting chunks to arithmetic one-hot representation, and (3) simplification of the short residues.

Converting from long to binary leverages similar ideas. To start, G samples a uniform mask $\alpha \in \mathbb{Z}_N$ and adds $[\alpha]_{p_j}$ to each j-th residue. CRT supports the following conversion between residues $[x + \alpha]_{p_j}$ and $[x + \alpha]_N$

$$[x + \alpha]_N = \left[\sum_{i=0}^{r-1} s_j \cdot [(x + \alpha) \cdot s_j^{-1}]_{p_j} \right]_N \qquad \text{where } s_j = \frac{N}{p_j}$$

Roughly speaking, we implement this equation while using as many free operations as we can. Note that each s_j and $[s_j^{-1}]_{p_j}$ is a constant.

We use operations on shorts to compute $[(x + \alpha) \cdot s_j^{-1}]_{p_j}$ as a word. Next, we treat each constant s_j as an integer mod N, and we partition its bits into chunks of size $\lceil \log_2 \ell \rceil$. Let c_j^i denote the i-th such chunk, such that $s_j = \sum_i 2^{i \cdot \lceil \log_2 \ell \rceil} \cdot c_j^i$. We use free operations to scale the residue $[(x+\alpha) \cdot s_j^{-1}]_{p_j}$ by each chunk c_j^i. The result from each residue is $\lceil \ell / \log_2 \ell \rceil$ words, each with value at most $\lceil \log_2 \ell \rceil \cdot p_j$. These words together represent the product $s_j \cdot [(x+\alpha) \cdot s_j^{-1}]_{p_j}$. We refer to these words as the *radices* of this product.

Next, we sum each i-th radix of each residue. The result is $O(\ell / \log \ell)$ radices that jointly represent $\sum_{i=0}^{r-1} s_j \cdot [(x + \alpha) \cdot s_j^{-1}]_{p_j}$. Each sum has value at most $\lceil \ell / \log_2 \ell \rceil \cdot \ell \cdot P$. Our choice of k ensures that this does not overflow modulus 2^k.

We convert each radix to binary representation via the word-to-hot system. Note, this is oblivious due to the inclusion of uniform mask α. We use (non-oblivious) ripple-carry adders to add together all such binary integers. This may seem problematic, since we are adding $O(\ell / \log \ell)$ values, and ripple carry adders use linear gates. However, because each binary integer is only $O(\log \ell)$ bits long, we can with basic care achieve the sum while joining only $O(\ell)$ bits.

The sum of all these binary integers may be as high as $\lceil \ell / \log_2 \ell \rceil \cdot N$, and we need to simplify the result modulo N to complete the conversion. To do so, we strip the top $\lceil \log_2 \ell \rceil$ bits from the binary representation, convert these to one-hot via bin-to-hot, and use a free operation to compute a binary encoding of these bits modulo N. We then use a ripple-carry adder to recombine this with the unstripped low bits. The result is still congruent to $[x + \alpha]_N$, and now it must be lower than $2N$. Finally, we use more Boolean gates to (1) conditionally subtract off N and (2) subtract off α, resulting in a binary encoding of $[x]_N$.

Garbling Arithmetic Circuits. By combining constructions in this section, we achieve the following:

Theorem 4. *Let $m \geq 2$ be an arbitrary modulus, and let $\ell = \lceil \log_2 m \rceil$. For any n-gate arithmetic circuit C over $\mathbb{Z}_m$, there exists an oblivious switch system (S, D) that emulates C and such that* join-width$(S) = O(n \cdot \ell)$.

In the full version we prove that the system is oblivious; in short, the argument is straightforward from our inclusion of uniform masks on all values. Combining Theorem 4 with Construction 1, we achieve the following:

Corollary 1. (Arithmetic Garbled Circuits from Free XOR). *Let* $m \geq 2$ *be an arbitrary modulus, and let* $\ell = \lceil \log_2 m \rceil$. *Assuming circular correlation robust hashes (Definition 1), there exists a correct, oblivious, private, and authentic garbling scheme [7] for arithmetic circuits over* $\mathbb{Z}_m$. *For an* n-*gate circuit* C, *the scheme's* Garble *procedure outputs* $O(n \cdot \ell \cdot \lambda)$ *bits of material.*

References

1. Applebaum, B., Ishai, Y., Kushilevitz, E.: How to garble arithmetic circuits. In: Ostrovsky, R. (ed.) 52nd FOCS, pp. 120–129. IEEE Computer Society Press (2011). https://doi.org/10.1109/FOCS.2011.40
2. Ball, M., Li, H., Lin, H., Liu, T.: New ways to garble arithmetic circuits. In: Hazay, C., Stam, M. (eds.) EUROCRYPT 2023, Part II. LNCS, vol. 14005, pp. 3–34. Springer, Heidelberg (2023). https://doi.org/10.1007/978-3-031-30617-4_1
3. Ball, M., Malkin, T., Rosulek, M.: Garbling gadgets for Boolean and arithmetic circuits. In: Weippl, E.R., Katzenbeisser, S., Kruegel, C., Myers, A.C., Halevi, S. (eds.) ACM CCS 2016, pp. 565–577. ACM Press (2016). https://doi.org/10.1145/2976749.2978410
4. Barrett, P.: Implementing the Rivest Shamir and Adleman public key encryption algorithm on a standard digital signal processor. In: Odlyzko, A.M. (ed.) CRYPTO 1986. LNCS, vol. 263, pp. 311–323. Springer, Heidelberg (1987). https://doi.org/10.1007/3-540-47721-7_24
5. Beaver, D.: Efficient multiparty protocols using circuit randomization. In: Feigenbaum, J. (ed.) CRYPTO 1991. LNCS, vol. 576, pp. 420–432. Springer, Heidelberg (1992). https://doi.org/10.1007/3-540-46766-1_34
6. Beaver, D., Micali, S., Rogaway, P.: The round complexity of secure protocols (extended abstract). In: 22nd ACM STOC, pp. 503–513. ACM Press (1990). https://doi.org/10.1145/100216.100287
7. Bellare, M., Hoang, V.T., Rogaway, P.: Foundations of garbled circuits. In: Yu, T., Danezis, G., Gligor, V.D. (eds.) ACM CCS 2012, pp. 784–796. ACM Press (2012). https://doi.org/10.1145/2382196.2382279
8. Choi, S.G., Katz, J., Kumaresan, R., Zhou, H.S.: On the security of the "free-XOR" technique. In: Cramer, R. (ed.) TCC 2012. LNCS, vol. 7194, pp. 39–53. Springer, Heidelberg (2012). https://doi.org/10.1007/978-3-642-28914-9_3
9. Fleischhacker, N., Malavolta, G., Schröder, D.: Arithmetic garbling from bilinear maps. In: Sako, K., Schneider, S., Ryan, P.Y.A. (eds.) ESORICS 2019, Part II. LNCS, vol. 11736, pp. 172–192. Springer, Heidelberg (2019). https://doi.org/10.1007/978-3-030-29962-0_9
10. Gueron, S., Lindell, Y., Nof, A., Pinkas, B.: Fast garbling of circuits under standard assumptions. J. Cryptol. **31**(3), 798–844 (2018). https://doi.org/10.1007/s00145-017-9271-y
11. Guo, C., Katz, J., Wang, X., Yu, Y.: Efficient and secure multiparty computation from fixed-key block ciphers. In: 2020 IEEE Symposium on Security and Privacy, pp. 825–841. IEEE Computer Society Press (2020). https://doi.org/10.1109/SP40000.2020.00016
12. Guo, X., et al.: Half-tree: halving the cost of tree expansion in COT and DPF. In: Hazay, C., Stam, M. (eds.) EUROCRYPT 2023, Part I. LNCS, vol. 14004, pp. 330–362. Springer, Heidelberg (2023). https://doi.org/10.1007/978-3-031-30545-0_12

13. Harvey, D., van der Hoeven, J.: Integer multiplication in time $O(n \log n)$. Ann. Math. **193**(2), 563–617 (2021)
14. Heath, D., Kolesnikov, V.: One hot garbling. In: Vigna, G., Shi, E. (eds.) ACM CCS 2021, pp. 574–593. ACM Press (2021). https://doi.org/10.1145/3460120.3484764
15. Heath, D., Kolesnikov, V., Ostrovsky, R.: Tri-state circuits - a circuit model that captures RAM. In: Handschuh, H., Lysyanskaya, A. (eds.) CRYPTO 2023, Part IV. LNCS, vol. 14084, pp. 128–160. Springer, Heidelberg (2023). https://doi.org/10.1007/978-3-031-38551-3_5
16. Henecka, W., Kögl, S., Sadeghi, A.R., Schneider, T., Wehrenberg, I.: TASTY: tool for automating secure two-party computations. In: Al-Shaer, E., Keromytis, A.D., Shmatikov, V. (eds.) ACM CCS 2010, pp. 451–462. ACM Press (2010). https://doi.org/10.1145/1866307.1866358
17. Karatsuba, A., Ofman, Y.: Multiplication of many-digital numbers by automatic computers. In: SSSR Academy of Sciences (1962)
18. Kolesnikov, V., Mohassel, P., Rosulek, M.: FleXOR: flexible garbling for XOR gates that beats free-XOR. In: Garay, J.A., Gennaro, R. (eds.) CRYPTO 2014, Part II. LNCS, vol. 8617, pp. 440–457. Springer, Heidelberg (2014). https://doi.org/10.1007/978-3-662-44381-1_25
19. Kolesnikov, V., Schneider, T.: Improved garbled circuit: free XOR gates and applications. In: Aceto, L., et al. (eds.) ICALP 2008, Part II. LNCS, vol. 5126, pp. 486–498. Springer, Heidelberg (2008). https://doi.org/10.1007/978-3-540-70583-3_40
20. Lu, S., Ostrovsky, R.: How to garble RAM programs. In: Johansson, T., Nguyen, P.Q. (eds.) EUROCRYPT 2013. LNCS, vol. 7881, pp. 719–734. Springer, Heidelberg (2013). https://doi.org/10.1007/978-3-642-38348-9_42
21. Naor, M., Pinkas, B., Sumner, R.: Privacy preserving auctions and mechanism design. In: Proceedings of the 1st ACM Conference on Electronic Commerce, pp. 129–139. ACM (1999)
22. Pinkas, B., Schneider, T., Smart, N.P., Williams, S.C.: Secure two-party computation is practical. In: Matsui, M. (ed.) ASIACRYPT 2009. LNCS, vol. 5912, pp. 250–267. Springer, Heidelberg (2009). https://doi.org/10.1007/978-3-642-10366-7_15
23. Rosulek, M., Roy, L.: Three halves make a whole? Beating the half-gates lower bound for garbled circuits. In: Malkin, T., Peikert, C. (eds.) CRYPTO 2021, Part I. LNCS, vol. 12825, pp. 94–124. Springer, Heidelberg, Virtual Event (2021). https://doi.org/10.1007/978-3-030-84242-0_5
24. Wang, X., Malozemoff, A.J., Katz, J.: EMP-toolkit: efficient MultiParty computation toolkit (2016). https://github.com/emp-toolkit
25. Yao, A.C.C.: How to generate and exchange secrets (extended abstract). In: 27th FOCS, pp. 162–167. IEEE Computer Society Press (1986). https://doi.org/10.1109/SFCS.1986.25
26. Zahur, S., Rosulek, M., Evans, D.: Two halves make a whole - reducing data transfer in garbled circuits using half gates. In: Oswald, E., Fischlin, M. (eds.) EUROCRYPT 2015, Part II. LNCS, vol. 9057, pp. 220–250. Springer, Heidelberg (2015). https://doi.org/10.1007/978-3-662-46803-6_8

Can Alice and Bob Guarantee Output to Carol?

Bar Alon[1]([⊠]), Eran Omri[2], and Muthuramakrishnan Venkitasubramaniam[3]

[1] Department of Computer Science, Ben-Gurion University, Beersheba, Israel
alonbar08@gmail.com
[2] Department of Computer Science, Ariel Cyber Innovation Center (ACIC), Ariel
University, Ariel, Israel
omrier@ariel.ac.il
[3] Georgetown University, Washington, DC, USA
mv783@georgetown.edu

Abstract. In the setting of solitary output computations, only a single designated party learns the output of some function applied to the private inputs of all participating parties with the guarantee that nothing beyond the output is revealed. The setting of solitary output functionalities is a special case of secure multiparty computation, which allows a set of mutually distrusting parties to compute some function of their private inputs. The computation should guarantee some security properties, such as correctness, privacy, fairness, and output delivery. Full security captures all these properties together.

Solitary output computation is a common setting that has become increasingly important, as it is relevant to many real-world scenarios, such as federated learning and set disjointness. In the set-disjointness problem, a set of parties with private datasets wish to convey to another party whether they have a common input. In this work, we investigate the limits of achieving set-disjointness which already has numerous applications and whose feasibility (under non-trivial conditions) was left open in the work of Halevi et al. (TCC 2019).

Towards resolving this, we completely characterize the set of Boolean functions that can be computed in the three-party setting in the face of a malicious adversary that corrupts up to two of the parties. As a corollary, we characterize the family of set-disjointness functions that can be computed in this setting, providing somewhat surprising results regarding this family and resolving the open question posed by Halevi et al.

1 Introduction

Solitary output computations [20] consider a single central entity that wishes to compute a function over data that is distributed among several other entities while providing privacy of the data. Such computations are emerging as an important category and capture many real-world scenarios. Examples include service providers that wish to perform some analysis over their client's data, federated learning, federal regulatory agencies wishing to detect fraudulent

© International Association for Cryptologic Research 2024
M. Joye and G. Leander (Eds.): EUROCRYPT 2024, LNCS 14655, pp. 32–61, 2024.
https://doi.org/10.1007/978-3-031-58740-5_2

users/transactions among banks, researchers looking to collect statistics from users, or a government security agency wishing to detect widespread intrusions on different high-value state agencies. In cryptography, solitary output functionalities have been considered in privacy-preserving federated learning [7,9,10] on the practical side, in designing minimal communication protocols via Private Simultaneous Messages Protocols [15] and its robust variant [1,6], and in the setting of very large-scale computations for tech giants, recently introduced in [3].

From a theoretical perspective, solitary output computation is related to the question of fairness in secure multiparty computation, i.e., where it is required that either all parties obtain the output or none of them do. This may seem counterintuitive since in solitary output computation there is no issue of fairness. However, Halevi et al. [20] showed that the impossibility of computing a function f in the solitary output setting directly implies that f also cannot be computed with fairness. Our work strengthens this connection, where both our upper and lower bounds in the solitary output settings inherit ideas from the fairness literature. We believe that understanding fairness can benefit from analyzing solitary output computation.

Our work is further motivated by more practical applications. Specifically, we are interested in the special, yet important instance of implementing the *set disjointness* functionality, where one party (that has no input) wishes to learn whether a set of parties, each holding a private dataset, have a common element. Protocols for set disjointness are useful in several contexts:

1. Intelligence agencies from multiple countries trying to communicate to another country if they are all tracking the same individual (for say, deviant activities).
2. A federal health agency that wants to learn if a common disease is emerging among multiple hospitals.
3. Drug-enforcement agencies that wish to find if multiple drug stores have a common prescription.
4. A (financial) market maker that wishes to identify if two of its clients have matching orders.

We note that in most of these scenarios, it is reasonable to assume that some of the participating entities (including the central one) collude to break the privacy of honest parties' inputs or disrupt the computation. Still, it is necessary to guarantee that the central entity receives an output.

If we assume that a majority of the parties are honest, then we know since the 80s that *any* functionality can be computed with such guarantees of security [8,16,23]. The setting where a majority of the parties cannot be assumed to be honest is more challenging, yet an important one. The investigation of the set of solitary output functionalities that can be securely computed was initiated in the work of Halevi et al. [20]. They further considered the set disjointness functionality and showed certain parameters for which it is possible to securely compute. However, they left open the exact parameters for which the functionality can be securely computed.

We continue this line of investigation to understand the feasibility of set disjointness, but, more generally, arbitrary Boolean functionalities. We begin with understanding the already challenging three-party solitary output setting (i.e. two input parties and one output receiving party). More precisely, we ask the following concrete question:

What functions with solitary output admit full security in the three-party setting where the output receiving party has no input?

Slightly more formally, we are interested in the setting where a pair of parties Alice and Bob that hold n bit inputs x and y, respectively, with respect to a Boolean function $f : \{0,1\}^n \times \{0,1\}^n \rightarrow \{0,1\}$ and wish to securely disclose $f(x, y)$ to a third party Carol. The main question we address in this work is whether it is possible to guarantee that Carol receives an output even in the presence of an adversary that can corrupt up to any two of the parties Alice, Bob, and Carol. For the specific case of set-disjointness, Alice and Bob have inputs S and T, respectively, that are subsets of some universe, and Carol wishes to learn whether $S \cap T$ is empty or not. It turns out this admits essentially a "trivial" protocol if we allow the parties to input the empty set. The more interesting case, and one identified in [20] as an important one, is where the parties are restricted to sets of a certain size and left the following question open:

Under what input restrictions, can the set disjointness functionality be computed with full security?

This question is formalized via the notion of secure multiparty computation [8,11,16,24]. Secure multiparty computation or MPC allows a group of distrustful parties to jointly compute a function over their private inputs where nothing beyond the output is revealed. *Guaranteed output delivery* or *full security* is the strongest form of security one can demand and requires that parties learn their output in any execution. A weaker notion referred to as *fairness* only requires that no corrupted party can learn the output while simultaneously denying honest parties from receiving the output. As mentioned before, guaranteed output delivery is achievable for all functionalities if we assume an honest majority, and security hold against unbounded adversaries (with point-to-point channels and a broadcast channel) [23] or against computationally bounded adversaries (assuming a public-key infrastructure) [16,17].

A celebrated result due to Cleve [12] says that fairness is impossible to achieve for all functionalities without an honest majority. The seminal result of [19] showed that in the two-party setting, there are non-trivial functionalities that can be computed with full security. This led to a line of works [4,21] culminating in the work of [5] that characterized completely which Boolean functions can be computed with full security in the two-party setting (where both parties receive the same output). In the multiparty setting, much less is known when there is a dishonest majority, with only a few examples of functionalities that can be computed securely [13,18]. Halevi et al. [20] continued this line of research to understand if full security is achievable where only one (solitary) party receives an output. Note that in this case, fairness is not an issue. Despite this fact, it was shown in [20] that even in the setting of solitary output, not all functions can be computed with full security.

A special case of solitary output is the three-party setting with Boolean functions (considered in this work) where only two parties have inputs and the third party receives the output. As part of their work, Halevi et al. [20] investigated this useful case and were able to demonstrate several possibility results. Towards analyzing the landscape of Boolean functions for which full security is achievable, they heuristically (via experiments over random functions) measure the number of functions for which the known possibility results do not hold (i.e. the status for these functions are unknown). However, their work falls short of providing a (full) characterization.

1.1 Our Results

Our main contribution is a complete characterization of the set of Boolean solitary output three-party functionalities that can be computed in our setting with guaranteed output delivery. We then use this characterization to analyze the parameters which allow set disjointness to be securely computable (see Theorem 2 below). Before presenting the characterization, we first introduce a new notion. The notion strengthens the notion of *semi-balanced* functionalities taken from the two-party fairness literature [5,21].

Definition 1 (Strong semi-balanced, informal). *Let* $f : \mathcal{X} \times \mathcal{Y} \times \{\lambda\} \to \{0,1\}$ *be a solitary output Boolean three-party two-input functionality (we let* λ *denote the empty string), where* $|\mathcal{X}|$ *and* $|\mathcal{Y}|$ *are polynomial in the security parameter. We call* f *strong semi-balanced if there exist two vectors* $\mathbf{p}$ *and* $\mathbf{q}$ *over* $\mathbb{R}$, *such that*

$$\begin{cases} \mathbf{M}_f^T \cdot \mathbf{p} = 1, \\ \sum_{x \in \mathcal{X}} p_x < 1, \end{cases} \quad and \quad \begin{cases} \mathbf{M}_f \cdot \mathbf{q} = 1, \\ \sum_{y \in \mathcal{Y}} q_y < 1. \end{cases}$$

where $\mathbf{M}_f$ *is a matrix defined as* $\mathbf{M}_f(x,y) = f(x,y)$ *for all* x *and* y.

Intuitively, the vectors $\mathbf{p}$ and $\mathbf{q}$ encode strategies for the pairs (A, C) and (B, C) that include sampling an input and applying some local operation to the output of f. These strategies allow each pair to fix the output distribution for C. Additionally, as we show below, the constraints on the sum of entries in each vector bound how much information on the honest party's input an (ideal world) adversary can receive from the output alone (given that the honest party sampled its input according to the strategy). We stress that the vectors can have negative entries and for the case where the vectors only have non-negative entries, [20] showed how to securely compute the corresponding functionality.

We are now ready to state our characterization.

Theorem 1 (Informal, characterization of Boolean functionalities). *Let* $f : \mathcal{X} \times \mathcal{Y} \times \{\lambda\} \to \{0,1\}$ *be a solitary output Boolean three-party functionality,* *where $|\mathcal{X}|$ and $|\mathcal{Y}|$ are polynomial in the security parameter. Then, if f is strong semi-balanced, it cannot be computed securely. On the other hand, if f is not strong semi-balanced and a secure protocol for OT exists, then f can be securely computed.*

The formal statement appears in Sect. 3. In Sect. 3.1, we provide an additional characterization, which roughly states that f can be securely computed if and only if the all-one or the all-zero vectors can be described using a specific linear combination of either the rows or columns.

As an application of Theorem 1, consider the disjointness functionality disj, where the domain of both A and B is $\{\mathcal{S} \subseteq \{1,2,3\} : 1 \leq |\mathcal{S}| \leq 2\}$. It is given by the 6×6 matrix

$$
\mathbf{M}_{\mathsf{disj}} = \begin{pmatrix} 0\,1\,1\,0\,0\,1 \\ 1\,0\,1\,0\,1\,0 \\ 1\,1\,0\,1\,0\,0 \\ 0\,0\,1\,0\,0\,0 \\ 0\,1\,0\,0\,0\,0 \\ 1\,0\,0\,0\,0\,0 \end{pmatrix},
$$

where the inputs are ordered lexicographically. Observe that taking $\mathbf{p} = \mathbf{q} = (1,1,1,-1,-1,-1)^T$ satisfies the conditions for being strong semi-balanced. In other words, by Theorem 1, disj cannot be computed securely.

On the positive side, here is a function f that can be computed with full security given by the 5×5 matrix

$$
\mathbf{M}_f = \begin{pmatrix} 0\,0\,0\,0\,1 \\ 0\,0\,0\,1\,0 \\ 0\,0\,1\,0\,0 \\ 0\,1\,0\,0\,1 \\ 1\,0\,0\,1\,1 \end{pmatrix}.
$$

Since $\mathbf{M}_f$ is invertible, there is a unique solution to $\mathbf{M}_f \cdot \mathbf{q} = \mathbf{1}$, namely $\mathbf{q} = (-1,0,1,1,1)^T$. As $\sum_{y \in \mathcal{Y}} q_y = 2 > 1$, it follows that f is not strong semi-balanced, hence by Theorem 1, the functionality f can be computed with full security. We highlight that this function serves as an example of a function whose status was unknown, i.e. not captured by the results of [20]. Indeed, the positive results of [20] capture functionalities that can be computed fairly as a *two-party* functionality, or functionalities where one of the parties can fix the output distribution using an appropriate distribution over its inputs (a class of functions [20] referred to as *forced*). The latter clearly does not hold for the above example. Additionally, there is no affine combination[1] of the rows or columns that result in the all-zero or the all-one vector, hence it cannot be computed fairly as a two-party functionality [5].

Using Theorem 1 we are able to analyze the disjointness functionality $\mathsf{disj}_{k,n}$, where $1 \leq k < n/2$ and the domain of both A and B is $\{\mathcal{S} \subseteq [n] : k \leq |\mathcal{S}| \leq n -$

---

[1] An affine combination is a linear combination where the sum of coefficients is 1.

$k\}$.[2] We completely characterize the values of k and n for which the functionality can be computed securely, assuming the size of the domain is polynomial in the security parameter. Interestingly, this only depends on the parity of n.

Theorem 2. *The solitary output functionality* $\mathsf{disj}_{k,n}$ *can be computed securely if and only if n is even (the positive direction holds assuming a secure protocol for OT exists).*

Extensions to the Multiparty Setting. We also consider some natural extensions of our results to the multiparty setting with a dishonest majority. For the impossibility, it is possible to extend the result using a player partitioning argument. In more detail, let f be an $(m+1)$-party functionality, let P_0 denote the output receiving party (holding no input), and let $\mathcal{P} = \{\mathsf{P}_1, \ldots, \mathsf{P}_m\}$ denote the set of remaining parties. Then, if there exists a partitioning of $\mathcal{P}$ into two sets A and B of size $|\mathsf{A}|, |\mathsf{B}| \geq m/2$, such that the resulting three-party functionality is impossible to securely compute, then f cannot be computed with full security against a dishonest majority.

As a concrete example, suppose we take an $(m+1)$-party solitary output functionality that depends on only two inputs, say of P_1 and P_m. Suppose for simplicity that m is even. Then for the partition $\mathsf{A} = \{\mathsf{P}_1, \ldots, \mathsf{P}_{\frac{m}{2}}\}$ and $\mathsf{B} = \{\mathsf{P}_{\frac{m}{2}+1}, \ldots, \mathsf{P}_m\}$, if the resulting three-party functionality cannot be securely computed, it follows that the $(m+1)$-party functionality cannot be securely computed against $m/2$ corruptions. Stated differently, adding "dummy" parties does not provide any additional power if no honest majority can be guaranteed.

We note, however, that this argument does not rule out multiparty set disjointness (where all parties in $\mathcal{P}$ hold an input). This is because this problem reduces to a "degenerate" functionality in the three-party setting where one of the (input) parties can always fix the output, which we know can be computed securely [20]. In slightly more detail, after considering the partitioning of the m parties holding inputs into two parties, both parties hold many sets as input. This results in a function that can be securely computed since the parties can fix the output to be 1 by choosing two disjoint sets for their inputs.

On the positive side, we show an $(m+1)$-party protocol for disjointness that is secure against $m-1$ corruptions. In fact, this can be generalized to include all functions where any two parties among $\mathcal{P}$ can fix the output distribution by sampling their inputs accordingly. Moreover, the protocol is secure even if the output receiving party P_0 has an input, and the output of the function is not necessarily Boolean. The protocol can be further generalized to an $(m+1)$-party protocol that is secure against $m-t+1$ parties, assuming any $t \leq (m+1)/2$ parties[3] among those in $\mathcal{P}$ can fix the output distribution. Note that for $t = 1$ we get the *forced* condition, where any party among $\mathcal{P}$ can fix the output distribution. This was observed by [20] to be a sufficient condition for secure

---

[2] If the domain of either A or B includes $\emptyset$, or $[n]$, or it contains only sets all of which have the same size, then the functionality is known to be securely computable [20].

[3] Observe that for $t > (m+1)/2$ we get an honest majority.

computation for solitary output functionalities. Thus, we refer to the generalized set of functionalities we consider as *t-forced*. We show the following.

Theorem 3. *Let f be an $(m + 1)$-party solitary output t-forced functionality. Then, assuming a secure protocol for OT exists, f can be securely computed against $(m - t + 1)$ corruptions.*

The construction is a generalization of the protocol for forced functions due to [20]: The parties compute an $(m - t + 2)$-out-of-$(m + 1)$ Shamir's secret sharing of the output using a secure-with-identifiable-abort protocol. In case a party aborts, the remaining parties restart. Otherwise, all parties send their shares to P_0 to reconstruct the output. If at least t parties aborted, then P_0 sample their inputs accordingly in order to fix the output distribution.[4] Due to lack of space, we give the formal result in the full version.

1.2   Our Techniques

We now turn to describe our techniques. We begin with our lower bound followed by our upper bound. The formal statements and proofs of these results can be found in Sects. 4 and 5, respectively. Finally, we provide some high-level overview of the proof of Theorem 2.

General Proof Strategy for an Impossibility Result. We first present our proof strategy for the lower bounds. First, we recall a concept used in the fairness literature called *locking strategies* [14,22]. In the two-party setting, a locking strategy for party A is a pair (D_A, φ_A), where D_A is a distribution over the set of inputs $\mathcal{X}$, and $\varphi_A : \mathcal{X} \times \{0, 1\} \to \{0, 1\}$ is a function that determines the output of A. The function φ_A depends both on the input x of party A and on the value of $f(x, y)$ (which is Boolean in our setting). To be locking, the strategy is required to fix the distribution of A's output, regardless of the input y of B, i.e., the quantity $\Pr_{x \leftarrow D_A}[\varphi_A(x, f(x, y)) = 1]$ is independent of y. We will refer to the output of $\varphi(x, f(x, y))$ as the locked output of A. A locking strategy (D_B, φ_B) for B is defined analogously.

Locking strategies were used in prior works [14,21,22] to identify two-party functionalities f that imply fair sampling – a generalization of coin tossing. Specifically, in fair sampling, the goal for A and B is to sample correlated values from some fixed distribution. As this task is known to be impossible [2,12], this implies that f cannot be computed securely. Specifically, the functions that imply fair sampling are the ones where the locking strategies exist for both parties and generate correlated outputs.

Now, although fairness is not an issue in the solitary output setting, we are still able to show that under certain (additional) assumptions on the locking

---

[4] Note that a malicious party may send an incorrect share. To overcome this issue, we let the secure-with-identifiable-abort protocol also MAC the shares and give to P_0 the key. Thus, if a malicious party modifies its share, it will be caught except with negligible probability, and this can be viewed as an abort.

strategies, f cannot be computed as a three-party solitary output functionality as well. We do so by making the following observation: the pair (D_A, φ_A) defining the locking strategy of A, also defines some correlation between the input x and the (real) output $f(x, y)$. Similarly, (D_B, φ_B) defines some correlation between the input y of B and the output $f(x, y)$. Moreover, as the function is already assumed to imply fair sampling, there is a correlation between the two locked outputs of the two parties, i.e., between $\varphi_A(x, f(x, y))$ and $\varphi_B(y, f(x, y))$, where $x \leftarrow D_A$ and $y \leftarrow D_B$.

Intuitively, these correlations suggest that a real-world attacker can impose some "bias" on the locked output (with respect to the honest party's strategy). Note that this "biased" output is *not* given to the parties holding the inputs (i.e., A and B). However, if the adversary also corrupts C, then this can improve its chances of guessing whatever the "biased" output would have been. This in turn leaks to the adversary some information about the honest party's input. All that is left to obtain an impossibility is to identify the functionalities for which no ideal world simulator can obtain the same information. To make the above argument formal, we first use the fact that for Boolean functions, the locking strategy for each party can be encoded using some (normalized probability) vector [21]. Next, we reduce the non-simulatability condition to constraints on the locking strategy vectors for Alice and Bob (see Definition 1 for the constraints). We provide more details next. Before that, we remark that, quite surprisingly, we are able to show that these conditions are, in fact, sufficient by designing a secure protocol whenever the condition fails to hold.

Overview of the Impossibility Result. Let us fix a solitary output Boolean three-party functionality f that is strong semi-balanced. Namely, there exists vectors $\mathbf{p}$ and $\mathbf{q}$, where $\sum_{x \in \mathcal{X}} p_x < 1$ and $\sum_{y \in \mathcal{Y}} q_y < 1$, satisfying $\mathbf{M}_f \cdot \mathbf{q} = \mathbf{1}$ and $\mathbf{M}_f^T \cdot \mathbf{p} = \mathbf{1}$. Towards showing that f cannot be computed securely as a solitary output three-party functionality, it is illustrative to understand why it cannot be computed fairly as a two-party functionality.

Define vectors $\mathbf{p}'$ and $\mathbf{q}'$ to be $\mathbf{p}$ and $\mathbf{q}$ normalized with respect to the ℓ_1 norm, respectively. Then, for $\delta_1^{-1} := \sum_{x \in \mathcal{X}} |p_x|$ and for $\delta_2^{-1} := \sum_{y \in \mathcal{Y}} |q_y|$, it holds that

$$\begin{cases} \mathbf{M}_f^T \cdot \mathbf{p}' = \delta_1 \cdot \mathbf{1}, \\ \sum_{x \in \mathcal{X}} p_x' < \delta_1, \\ \sum_{x \in \mathcal{X}} |p_x'| = 1, \end{cases} \quad \text{and} \quad \begin{cases} \mathbf{M}_f \cdot \mathbf{q}' = \delta_2 \cdot \mathbf{1}, \\ \sum_{y \in \mathcal{Y}} q_y' < \delta_2, \\ \sum_{y \in \mathcal{Y}} |q_y'| = 1. \end{cases}$$

Makriyannis [21] used $\mathbf{p}'$ and $\mathbf{q}'$ to show that f cannot be computed fairly. This was done by constructing a protocol for fair sampling, which is known to be impossible [2,12]. We next explain the construction. The vector $\mathbf{p}'$ encodes the following strategy for A: Sample an input x with probability $|p_x'|$, send it to the hybrid functionality computing f, and flip the result received if and only if $p_x' < 0$. Similarly, $\mathbf{q}'$ encodes the following strategy for B respectively: Sample an input y with probability $|q_y'|$, send it to the hybrid functionality, and flip the result received if and only if $q_y' < 0$. With respect to these strategies, [21] proved that the output distribution of either of the parties is independent of the input sent by the other party. Specifically, regardless of the input y' that B sent, the output OUT_1 of A will be 1 with probability

$$\delta_1 + \Pr\left[\text{A flips the output}\right].$$

Similarly, the output OUT_2 of B is 1 with probability

$$\delta_2 + \Pr\left[\text{B flips the output}\right].$$

Finally, [21] showed that the assumptions $\sum_{x \in \mathcal{X}} p'_x < \delta_1$ and $\sum_{y \in \mathcal{Y}} q'_y < \delta_2$, imply that OUT_1 and OUT_2 are correlated.[5] This results in a secure fair sampling protocol, and thus we arrive at a contradiction.

Note that, as fairness is not an issue for solitary output functionalities, such a reduction from fair sampling is not applicable in our setting. To better explain how we overcome this issue, we next provide a direct proof that f cannot be computed fairly, and then show how to "lift" the argument to the solitary output three-party case. To simplify the discussion, we will consider perfect security.

Assume for the sake of contradiction that there exists an r-round fair two-party protocol π computing f securely (with perfect security). We let A and B sample their inputs according to the distributions encoded by $\mathbf{p}'$ and $\mathbf{q}'$, as was done in the previous construction. Define $\text{flip}(x) = 1$ if $p'_x < 0$ and $\text{flip}(x) = 0$ otherwise. Similarly, let $\text{flip}(y) = 1$ if $q'_y < 0$ and $\text{flip}(y) = 0$ otherwise.[6] First, observe that if B aborts after sending i messages to A, then the output a_i of A satisfies

$$\Pr\left[a_i \oplus \text{flip}(x) = 1\right] = \delta_1 + \Pr_x\left[\text{flip}(x) = 1\right].$$

This is due to the fact that in the ideal world, the output of A satisfies the above relation, as stated previously. Similarly, if A aborts after sending i messages to B, then the output b_i of B satisfies

$$\Pr\left[b_i \oplus \text{flip}(y) = 1\right] = \delta_2 + \Pr_y\left[\text{flip}(y) = 1\right].$$

Second, at the start of the protocol, before any message was sent, the random variables a_0 and b_0 are completely independent. Since x and y were sampled independently as well, it follows that $a_0 \oplus \text{flip}(x)$ and $b_0 \oplus \text{flip}(y)$ are independent. Finally, at the end of the protocol, it holds that $a_r = b_r = f(x, y)$. As stated previously, $a_r \oplus \text{flip}(x)$ and $b_r \oplus \text{flip}(y)$ are correlated. Thus, by an averaging argument, there exists a round where there is a "jump" in the correlation between $a_i \oplus \text{flip}(x)$ and $b_i \oplus \text{flip}(y)$. An adversary can then use this "jump" to bias the output of the other party. More concretely, the adversary either corrupts A and forces B to output a value $b \in \{0, 1\}$ satisfying

$$\left|\Pr\left[b \oplus \text{flip}(y) = 1\right] - (\delta_2 + \Pr_y\left[\text{flip}(y) = 1\right])\right| \geq \Omega(1/r),$$

---

[5] In fact, to show correlation it suffices to assume $\sum_{x \in \mathcal{X}} p'_x \neq \delta_1$ and $\sum_{y \in \mathcal{Y}} q'_y \neq \delta_2$.

[6] We abuse notation and define flip over both $\mathcal{X}$ and $\mathcal{Y}$.

or it corrupts B and forces A to output a value $a \in \{0,1\}$ satisfying

$$|\Pr\left[a \oplus \mathsf{flip}(x) = 1\right] - (\delta_1 + \Pr_x\left[\mathsf{flip}(x) = 1\right])| \geq \Omega(1/r).$$

We now show how to "lift" the above argument to the solitary output three-party case. As stated previously, we cannot construct an adversary that biases the output, since only one party receives it. Instead, we use the fact that there is a "jump" in the correlation between $a_i \oplus \mathsf{flip}(x)$ and $b_i \oplus \mathsf{flip}(y)$. This allows the adversary to improve the probability of guessing $\mathsf{flip}(\cdot)$ applied to the honest party's input. Specifically, assume without loss of generality that an adversary corrupting A and C that can force the output to be a value $b \in \{0,1\}$ satisfying

$$\Pr\left[b \oplus \mathsf{flip}(y) = 1\right] \geq (\delta_2 + \Pr_y\left[\mathsf{flip}(y) = 1\right]) + \Omega(1/r).$$

This can be done using a similar adversary to the two-party case, where A and C act honestly until the "jump", instruct A to abort depending on whether $a_i \oplus \mathsf{flip}(x) = 1$ or not, and instruct C to continue honestly until the termination of the protocol where it obtains b. Then, as the adversary holds b, it can guess $\mathsf{flip}(y) = b \oplus 1$, and it will succeed with a probability that is noticeably greater than $\delta_2 + \Pr_y\left[\mathsf{flip}(y) = 1\right]$.

To conclude the argument, we show that any ideal world simulator S cannot guess $\mathsf{flip}(y)$ with a probability that is greater than $\delta_2 + \Pr_y\left[\mathsf{flip}(y) = 1\right]$. Suppose that S sent an input x, and obtained the output $z = f(x,y)$. Let $\tilde{z} = z \oplus \mathsf{flip}(y)$. Then

$$
\begin{aligned}
\Pr\left[\mathsf{S}(z) = \mathsf{flip}(y)\right] &= \Pr\left[\mathsf{S}(z) \oplus z = \tilde{z}\right] \\
&= \Pr\left[\mathsf{S}(0) = 0, z = 0, \tilde{z} = 0\right] + \Pr\left[\mathsf{S}(1) = 1, z = 1, \tilde{z} = 0\right] \\
&\quad + \Pr\left[\mathsf{S}(0) = 1, z = 0, \tilde{z} = 1\right] + \Pr\left[\mathsf{S}(1) = 0, z = 1, \tilde{z} = 1\right] \\
&= \Pr\left[\mathsf{S}(0) = 0\right] \cdot \Pr\left[z = 0, \tilde{z} = 0\right] + \Pr\left[\mathsf{S}(1) = 1\right] \cdot \Pr\left[z = 1, \tilde{z} = 0\right] \\
&\quad + \Pr\left[\mathsf{S}(0) = 1\right] \cdot \Pr\left[z = 0, \tilde{z} = 1\right] + \Pr\left[\mathsf{S}(1) = 0\right] \cdot \Pr\left[z = 1, \tilde{z} = 1\right] \\
&\leq \max\{\Pr\left[z = 0, \tilde{z} = 0\right], \Pr\left[z = 0, \tilde{z} = 1\right]\} \\
&\quad + \max\{\Pr\left[z = 1, \tilde{z} = 0\right], \Pr\left[z = 1, \tilde{z} = 1\right]\}.
\end{aligned}
$$

Depending on which quantities are larger, the above expression is upper-bounded by one of the following.

- $\Pr\left[\tilde{z} = z\right] = \Pr_y\left[\mathsf{flip}(y) = 0\right]$,
- $\Pr\left[\tilde{z} \neq z\right] = \Pr_y\left[\mathsf{flip}(y) = 1\right]$,
- $\Pr\left[\tilde{z} = 0\right] = -\delta_2 + \Pr_y\left[\mathsf{flip}(y) = 0\right]$,
- $\Pr\left[\tilde{z} = 1\right] = \delta_2 + \Pr_y\left[\mathsf{flip}(y) = 1\right]$.

Recall that $\delta_2 > 0$ and $\delta_2 > \sum_{y:q'_y < 0} q'_y = \Pr_y\left[\mathsf{flip}(y) = 0\right] - \Pr_y\left[\mathsf{flip}(y) = 1\right]$. Thus, the largest quantity is $\delta_2 + \Pr_y\left[\mathsf{flip}(y) = 1\right]$, concluding the proof.

Overview of the Positive Results. For the positive direction, we assume that f is not strong semi-balanced. That is, either there is no vector $\mathbf{p}$ such that

$\mathbf{M}_f^T \cdot \mathbf{p} = 1$ and $\sum_{x \in \mathcal{X}} p_x < 1$, or there is no vector $\mathbf{q}$ such that $\mathbf{M}_f \cdot \mathbf{q} = 1$ and $\sum_{y \in \mathcal{Y}} q_y < 1$. We may further assume without loss of generality that f *cannot* be computed securely as a *two-party* functionality. This is due to the fact that the result of [20] implies that any f that can be securely computed as a two-party functionality, can also be computed as a solitary output three-party functionality.

We use the characterization of securely computable Boolean two-party functionalities provided by [5]. They showed that such a functionality *cannot* be securely computable if and only if there is a vector $\mathbf{p}'$ such that $\mathbf{M}_f^T \cdot \mathbf{p}' = 1$ and $\sum_{x \in \mathcal{X}} p_x' \neq 1$, and there is a vector $\mathbf{q}'$ such that $\mathbf{M}_f \cdot \mathbf{q}' = 1$ and $\sum_{y \in \mathcal{Y}} q_y' \neq 1$.[7] By our assumption that f is not strong semi-balanced, the sum of entries in either $\mathbf{p}'$ or $\mathbf{q}'$ cannot be smaller than 1. We assume the former without loss of generality and present a secure protocol for computing f. For the construction we next present, it suffices to assume there exists a vector $\mathbf{p}$ such that

$$\mathbf{M}_f^T \cdot \mathbf{p} = 1 \quad \text{and} \quad \sum_{x \in \mathcal{X}} p_x \geq 1.$$

We next present a protocol inspired by the protocols of [5,19], which follow the special round paradigm. Roughly, a special round i^* (whose value is unknown to all parties) is sampled at random according to a geometric distribution with a sufficiently small parameter $\alpha > 0$. Before round i^* is reached, each pair among (A, C) and (B, C) together learn a random independent value, while after i^* is reached they learn the output. Specifically, the values are held shared in a 2-out-of-2 secret sharing scheme. If A aborts at some round, then B helps C to recover the last value they received and have C output it. Similarly, if B aborts at some round, then A helps C to recover the last value they received. For this reason, these values are called *backup values*. Finally, we let the pair (A, C) learn the new (possibly random) value before the pair (B, C).

It is left to describe the distribution used to sample the random values before round i^*. For $i < i^*$ we give A and C the backup value $a_i = f(x, \tilde{y}_i)$, where $\tilde{y}_i \leftarrow \mathcal{Y}$. For B and C, if $i < i^* - 1$ then they receive $b_i = f(\tilde{x}_i, y)$, where $\tilde{x}_i \leftarrow \mathcal{X}$. If $i = i^* - 1$, then B and C receive a bit b_{i^*-1} sampled according to distribution independent of the parties' inputs.[8]

Intuitively, if the adversary corrupts C, then the only issue that could possibly arise is that of receiving two applications of f over the honest parties' input. Note, however, that in the above protocol, this will never occur, thus the protocol is private. The hardest case to analyze is when A is corrupted. Although the adversary's view consists of only random shares, it can force C to output the bit b_{i^*-1}, which is independent of y, with noticeable probability. Nevertheless, we are able to show that if α is sufficiently small, and if we take b_{i^*-1} to be 1 with probability $(\sum_{x \in \mathcal{X}} p_x)^{-1} \leq 1$, then there exists a distribution over the inputs A that causes C to output in the ideal world, a bit that is identically distributed to the output in the real world. We refer the reader to Sect. 5 for more details.

---

[7] Such functionalities were named semi-balanced functionalities [5,21].

[8] In the protocol of [5] this bit is fixed and depends only on the function.

Analyzing Set-Disjointness. As the proof is rather technical, we only provide a high-level overview of the analysis. The formal arguments can be found in Sect. 6. In order to apply Theorem 1 to the set-disjointness functionality $\mathsf{disj}_{k,n}$, we first solve the system

$$\mathbf{M}_{\mathsf{disj}} \cdot \mathbf{q} = (1, \ldots, 1)^T.$$

When the domain of both parties is $\{\mathcal{S} \subseteq [n] : k \leq |\mathcal{S}| \leq n - k\}$, we show that the (unique) solution is $\mathbf{q}_{\mathcal{T}} = (-1)^{k+|\mathcal{T}|} \cdot \binom{|\mathcal{T}|-1}{k-1}$. We do so by viewing each sum

$$\mathbf{M}_{\mathsf{disj}}(\mathcal{S}, \cdot) \cdot \mathbf{q} = \sum_{\mathcal{T}:\mathcal{S}\cap\mathcal{T}=\emptyset} q_{\mathcal{T}} = \sum_{m=k}^{n-|\mathcal{S}|} (-1)^{k+m} \cdot \binom{n - |\mathcal{S}|}{m} \binom{m - 1}{k - 1}$$

as a function of k, denoted $s(k)$. As it turns out, $s(k) - s(k + 1) = 0$ for all $1 \leq k < n - |\mathcal{S}|$. As $s(n - |\mathcal{S}|)$ is clearly 1, the proof follows. Finally, identifying when $\mathsf{disj}_{k,n}$ can be computed reduces to analyzing $\sum_{\mathcal{S}} q_{\mathcal{S}}$ which further reduces to bounding some expressions involving binomials. See Sect. 6 for the details.

1.3 Organization

The preliminaries and definition of the model of computation appear in Sect. 2. In Sect. 3 we state our results. Then, in Sects. 4 and 5 we prove the negative and positive results, respectively. Finally, in Sect. 6 we analyze the set-disjointness functionality.

2 Preliminaries

We use standard definitions and notations. We next provide the definitions that we find more essential for the readability of the bulk of the paper.

We let $\mathbf{1}_n$ and $\mathbf{0}_n$ denote the all-one and all-zero vectors, respectively, of dimension n. We will remove n when its value is clear from context. A vector is called *probability vector* if all of its entries are positive and sum up to 1. We will sometimes treat such vectors the same as treat distributions, e.g., we write $v \leftarrow \mathbf{v}$ to indicate that v is sampled according to the distribution that corresponds to $\mathbf{v}$. Finally, we let $|\mathbf{v}|$ denote the vector that is created by taking the absolute value in every entry of $\mathbf{v}$, i.e., its ith position is $|v_i|$.

The Model of Computation. In this paper we consider solitary output three-party functionalities. We further restrict the setting so that the output receiving party has no input. A functionality is a sequence of function $f = \{f_\kappa\}_{\kappa\in\mathbb{N}}$, where $f_\kappa \colon \mathcal{X}_\kappa \times \mathcal{Y}_\kappa \times \{\lambda\} \to \mathcal{Z}_\kappa$ for every value of the security parameter $\kappa \in \mathbb{N}$.[9]

---

[9] The typical convention in secure computation is to let $f : (\{0,1\}^*)^3 \to \{0,1\}^*$. However, we will mostly be dealing with functionalities whose domain is of polynomial size in κ, which is why we introduce this notation.

We denote the parties by A, B and C. We let C be the output receiving party, and let A and B hold inputs x and y. To alleviate notations, we will remove κ from f and its domain and range, and simply write it as $f : \mathcal{X} \times \mathcal{Y} \times \{\lambda\} \to \mathcal{Z}$. Furthermore, all of our results hold assuming $|\mathcal{X}|$ and $|\mathcal{Y}|$ are polynomial is κ. For brevity, we will not mention it in the statements.

We consider the standard ideal vs. real paradigm for defining security. We consider an ideal computation with *guaranteed output delivery* (also referred to as *full security*), where a trusted party performs the computation on behalf of the parties, and the ideal-world adversary *cannot* abort the computation. We say a protocol admits full security if it is fully secure against any number of corrupted parties.

We next define the notion of backup values, which are the values that C outputs in case a party aborts (after sending messages honestly). Note that this is well-defined for any fully secure protocol.

Definition 2 (Backup values). *Let f a solitary output three-party functionality, and let π be an r-round protocol computing f with full security. Let $i \in \{0, \ldots, r\}$, sample the randomness of the parties, and consider an honest execution of π with the sampled randomness until all parties sent i messages. The ith backup value of (A, C), denoted a_i, is the output of an honest C in case party B aborted after sending i messages honestly (and party A remains honest). Similarly, the ith backup value of (B, C), denoted b_i, is the output of an honest C in case party A aborted after sending i messages honestly.*

The Dealer Model. In the description of our positive results, it will be convenient to consider the dealer model. Here, the real world is augmented with a trusted dealer that can interact with the parties in a limited way. Additionally, the adversary is assumed to be fail-stop, namely, it acts honestly, however, it may decide to abort prematurely. Essentially, the dealer will compute the backup values for (A, C) and for (B, C). In each round, the dealer sends to each pair its corresponding backup value, held shared by the two parties using a 2-out-of-2 secret sharing. After receiving its shares, an adversary can decide whether to abort a (corrupted) party or not. If a party aborts, then the dealer notifies the other parties and halts. Note that removing the dealer can be done using standard techniques.

Definitions from the Fairness Literature. We will use certain notions that were defined in order to analyze fairness in the two-party setting. We first associate a matrix with any Boolean solitary output three-party functionality, where one of the parties has no input. Throughout the rest of the section, we fix $f : \mathcal{X} \times \mathcal{Y} \times \{\lambda\} \to \{0, 1\}$ to be a Boolean solitary output three-party function.

Definition 3 (The matrix associated with a function). *We associate with f an $|\mathcal{X}| \times |\mathcal{Y}|$ Boolean matrix $\mathbf{M}_f$, defined as $\mathbf{M}_f(x, y) = f(x, y)$ for all $x \in \mathcal{X}$ and $y \in \mathcal{Y}$.*

A function is called forced if either A or B can fix the output distribution using an appropriate distribution over their inputs.

Definition 4 (Forced function [20]). *We say that f is forced if either there exists a probability vector $\mathbf{p}$ such that $\mathbf{p}^T \cdot \mathbf{M}_f = \delta_1 \cdot \mathbf{1}^T$, for some $\delta_1 \geq 0$, or there exists a probability vector $\mathbf{q}$ such that $\mathbf{M}_f \cdot \mathbf{q} = \delta_2 \cdot \mathbf{1}$, for some $\delta_2 \geq 0$.*

The next definition describes locking strategies for Boolean functionalities. Roughly speaking, a locking strategy [14,22] for a party is a way for it to sample an input, and apply a local operation to the output of the function, such that the distribution of its final output is independent of the other party's input.

For Boolean functions, the local operation is to either flip or not, possibly depending on the input. Makriyannis [21] encoded these strategies (for each party) using a single vector, where the absolute value of each entry represents the weight of the corresponding input, and the sign represents whether or not the party should flip the output. Thus, for the Boolean case, a locking strategy is simply a vector that results in an output distribution that is independent of the other party's input. A nice and equivalent way to formalize this is to require that multiplying the vector by the matrix results in a constant vector (see [21, Lemma 6.5] and Lemma 7).

Definition 5 (Locking strategy for Boolean functionalities [14,21,22]). *A locking strategy for A is a vector $\mathbf{p} \in \mathbb{R}^{|\mathcal{X}|}$ satisfying $\mathbf{p}^T \cdot \mathbf{M}_f = \delta \cdot \mathbf{1}^T$, for some $\delta \in \mathbb{R}$. We call the locking strategy $\mathbf{p}$ normalized if $\sum_{x \in \mathcal{X}} |p_x| = 1$.[10] Similarly, a locking strategy for B is a vector $\mathbf{q} \in \mathbb{R}^{|\mathcal{Y}|}$ satisfying $\mathbf{M}_f \cdot \mathbf{q} = \delta \cdot \mathbf{1}$, for some $\delta \in \mathbb{R}$. We call $\mathbf{q}$ normalized if $\sum_{y \in \mathcal{Y}} |q_y| = 1$. Observe that the set of all locking strategies for A (and B) forms a linear subspace.*

We next define semi-balanced functionalities. These are functionalities where, in addition to both A and B having locking strategies, the resulting two (possibly flipped) outputs are correlated. As shown by Makriyannis [21], the latter condition have can be expressed as a condition on the total weight of the vectors representing the locking strategies.

Definition 6 (Semi-balanced functionalities [5,21]). *We call f semi-balanced if there exists locking strategies $\mathbf{p}$ and $\mathbf{q}$ for A and B, respectively, such that*

$$\begin{cases} \mathbf{p}^T \cdot \mathbf{M}_f = \mathbf{1}^T, \\ \mathbf{1}^T \cdot \mathbf{p} \neq 1, \end{cases} \quad \text{and} \quad \begin{cases} \mathbf{M}_f \cdot \mathbf{q} = \mathbf{1}, \\ \mathbf{1}^T \cdot \mathbf{q} \neq 1. \end{cases}$$

3   Statement of Our Results

Our main result is the complete characterization of the Boolean solitary output three-party functionalities that can be computed with full security. Roughly, our

---

[10] [14,22] defined locking strategies as the algorithm themselves, rather then their encodings.

characterization state that a functionality *cannot* be computed securely if and only if it is semi-balanced, where the locking strategies of both parties have weights less than 1. We call these functionalities strong semi-balanced.

Definition 7 (Strong semi-balanced). *Let* $f : \mathcal{X} \times \mathcal{Y} \times \{\lambda\} \rightarrow \{0,1\}$ *be a solitary output three-party functionality. Suppose that f is semi-balanced with associated locking strategies* **p** *and* **q**. *We call f strong semi-balanced if* $\mathbf{1}^T \cdot \mathbf{p} < 1$ *and* $\mathbf{1}^T \cdot \mathbf{q} < 1$.

Theorem 4. *Let* $f : \mathcal{X} \times \mathcal{Y} \times \{\lambda\} \rightarrow \{0,1\}$ *be a solitary output three-party functionality. Then, if f is strong semi-balanced, then it cannot be computed with full security. On the other hand, if a secure protocol for OT exists, and f is not strong semi-balanced, then it can be computed with full security.*

Remark 1. Although only stated and proved for deterministic functionalities, Theorem 4 can be easily generalized to randomized functionalities by defining $\mathbf{M}_f(x,y) = \Pr\left[f(x,y) = 1\right]$ for all $x \in \mathcal{X}$ and $y \in \mathcal{Y}$.

The proof of Theorem 4 follows from the following three lemmata. The first lemma states the impossibility of computing strong semi-balanced. The second lemma, is a combination of the result of Halevi et al. [20] stating that any two-party functionality that can be computed fairly, can also be computed as a solitary output three-party functionality, and the result of sharov et al. [5] which identifies the non-semi-balanced as the only functionalities that can be computed fairly. Finally, the third lemma states that the remaining set of functionalities can be computed securely.

Lemma 1. *Let* $f : \mathcal{X} \times \mathcal{Y} \times \{\lambda\} \rightarrow \{0,1\}$ *be a strong semi-balanced solitary output three-party functionality. Then f cannot be computed with full security.*

Lemma 2 ([20, Theorem 4.1] and [5]). *Let* $f : \mathcal{X} \times \mathcal{Y} \times \{\lambda\} \rightarrow \{0,1\}$ *be a solitary output three-party non-semi-balanced functionality. Then, if a secure protocol for OT exists, f can be computed with full security.*

Lemma 3. *Let* $f : \mathcal{X} \times \mathcal{Y} \times \{\lambda\} \rightarrow \{0,1\}$ *be a solitary output three-party Boolean functionality. Assume there exists a locking strategy* **p** *for* A *satisfying*

$$\mathbf{p}^T \cdot \mathbf{M}_f = \mathbf{1}^T \quad and \quad \mathbf{1}^T \cdot \mathbf{p} \geq 1,$$

or there exists a locking strategy **q** *for* B *satisfying*

$$\mathbf{M}_f \cdot \mathbf{q} = \mathbf{1} \quad and \quad \mathbf{1}^T \cdot \mathbf{q} \geq 1.$$

Then, if a secure protocol for OT exists, f can be computed with full security.

Proof of Theorem 4. The negative direction is immediately implied by Lemma 1. For the other direction, let us assume that f is not strong semi-balanced. By

Lemma 2, we may assume that f is semi-balanced as otherwise f can be computed with full security. Therefore, there exist locking strategies $\mathbf{p}$ and $\mathbf{q}$ for A and B, respectively, such that

$$\begin{cases} \mathbf{p}^T \cdot \mathbf{M}_f = \mathbf{1}^T, \\ \mathbf{1}^T \cdot \mathbf{p} \neq 1, \end{cases} \quad \text{and} \quad \begin{cases} \mathbf{M}_f \cdot \mathbf{q} = \mathbf{1}, \\ \mathbf{1}^T \cdot \mathbf{q} \neq 1. \end{cases}$$

As f is not strong semi-balanced, the sum of entries in one of the above vectors must be greater than 1. Thus, by Lemma 3, f can be computed with full security. □

We prove Lemmas 1 and 3 in Sects. 4 and 5, respectively. To illustrate Theorem 4, we use it to analyze the parameters for which the *disjointness* functionality can be computed with full security. For parameters $n, k \in \mathbb{N}$, where $1 \leq k < n/2$, we define the solitary output three-party functionality disj as disj $(\mathcal{S}, \mathcal{T}) = 1$ if $\mathcal{S} \cap \mathcal{T} = \emptyset$, and disj $(\mathcal{S}, \mathcal{T}) = 0$ otherwise, where the domain of both A and B is $\{\mathcal{S} \subseteq [n] : k \leq |\mathcal{S}| \leq n - k\}$. We use Theorem 4 to prove the following.

Theorem 5. *Assuming a secure protocol for OT exists,* disj *can be computed with full security if and only if n is even.*

The proof is given in Sect. 6.

3.1 An Equivalent Characterization

Similarly to the characterization of [5] for two-party fairness, we can provide the following equivalent condition. Roughly, it states that f can be computed securely if and only if $\mathbf{0}$ or $\mathbf{1}$ can be described using a specific linear combination of either the rows or columns.

Theorem 6 (Equivalent characterization). *Let $f : \mathcal{X} \times \mathcal{Y} \times \{\lambda\} \to \{0,1\}$ be a solitary output three-party functionality. Then, if a secure protocol for OT exists, f can be computed with full security if and only if f is not strong semi-balanced if and only if one of the following hold.*

1. *$\mathbf{0}^T$ is an affine combination of the rows of $\mathbf{M}_f$.*
2. *$\mathbf{1}$ is a linear combination of the columns of $\mathbf{M}_f$, where the sum of coefficients is at least 1.*
3. *$\mathbf{1}^T$ is a linear combination of the rows of $\mathbf{M}_f$, where the sum of coefficients is at least 1.*
4. *$\mathbf{0}$ is an affine combination of the columns of $\mathbf{M}_f$.*

Towards proving Theorem 6, we use the following proposition proved by [5].

Proposition 1 ([5, Proposition 2.1]). *For any matrix $\mathbf{M}$, it holds that $\mathbf{0}^T$ is an affine combination of the rows of $\mathbf{M}$ if and only if $\mathbf{1}$ is not a linear combination of the columns of $\mathbf{M}$.*

Proof of Theorem 6. We first show that if f is not strong semi-balanced then one of Items 1 to 4 hold. Assume without loss of generality there is no locking strategy $\mathbf{q}$ for B such that

$$\mathbf{M}_f \cdot \mathbf{q} = \mathbf{1} \quad \text{and} \quad \mathbf{1}^T \cdot \mathbf{q} < 1.$$

The case where there is no locking strategy $\mathbf{p}$ for A is analogous. We show that either Item 1 or Item 2 hold. Indeed, either $\mathbf{1}$ is not a linear combination of the columns of $\mathbf{M}_f$, or it is a linear combination with the sum coefficient being at least 1. By Proposition 1, the former case implies that $\mathbf{0}^T$ is an affine combination of the rows of $\mathbf{M}$, thus concluding this direction.

To conclude the proof, we show that if one of Items 1 to 4 hold, then f is not strong semi-balanced. We show the proof assuming either Item 1 or Items 2 hold, as the other two cases are analogous. First, if $\mathbf{0}^T$ is an affine combination of the rows of $\mathbf{M}_f$, then by Proposition 1, $\mathbf{1}$ is *not* a linear combination of the columns of $\mathbf{M}_f$. Thus, there is no locking strategy for B. Assume now that there exists $\mathbf{q}$ such that

$$\mathbf{M}_f \cdot \mathbf{q} = \mathbf{1} \quad \text{and} \quad \mathbf{1}^T \cdot \mathbf{q} \geq 1.$$

The fact that f is not strong semi-balanced is a direct application of Lemma 3 and Theorem 4.

We next present a different argument that does not rely on the existence of a secure protocol, which in itself assumes the existence of oblivious transfer. Assume towards contradiction that f is strong semi-balanced. Then there exists locking strategies $\mathbf{p}$ and $\mathbf{q}'$ for A and B, respectively, satisfying

$$\begin{cases} \mathbf{p}^T \cdot \mathbf{M}_f = \mathbf{1}^T, \\ \mathbf{1}^T \cdot \mathbf{p} < 1, \end{cases} \quad \text{and} \quad \begin{cases} \mathbf{M}_f \cdot \mathbf{q}' = \mathbf{1}, \\ \mathbf{1}^T \cdot \mathbf{q}' < 1. \end{cases}$$

By considering $\mathbf{p}^T \cdot \mathbf{M}_f \cdot \mathbf{q}'$, it follows that $\mathbf{p}^T \cdot \mathbf{1} = \mathbf{1}^T \cdot \mathbf{q}'$. Similarly, by considering $\mathbf{p}^T \cdot \mathbf{M}_f \cdot \mathbf{q}$, it follows that $\mathbf{p}^T \cdot \mathbf{1} = \mathbf{1}^T \cdot \mathbf{q}$. Therefore,

$$1 \leq \mathbf{1}^T \cdot \mathbf{q} = \mathbf{1}^T \cdot \mathbf{q}' < 1,$$

which is clearly a contradiction. □

4   Impossibility of Computing Strong Semi-Balanced Functionalities

In this section, we prove our impossibility results, showing that strong semi-balanced cannot be computed with full security.

Lemma 4 (Restatement of Lemma 1). *Let $f : \mathcal{X} \times \mathcal{Y} \times \{\lambda\} \to \{0,1\}$ be a strong semi-balanced solitary output three-party functionality. Then f cannot be computed with full security.*

Proof. The proof is done in two steps. In the first step, we show that for any protocol computing f, there exists an adversary that can "bias" a certain correlation between the honest party's input, and the backup value corresponding to C and the honest party. We then show how this "bias" allows the adversary to increase its chances of guessing a certain property of the honest party's input. In the second step, we show that no simulator can do better. We next formalize the above proof strategy.

Assume towards contradiction that there exists a secure r-round protocol π computing f. We show there exists an adversary that cannot be simulated. We assume that each round is composed of 3 broadcast messages, the first sent by A, the second sent by B, and the third by C (this is without loss of generality, as we allow the adversary to be rushing). Fix two normalized locking strategies $\mathbf{p} \in \mathbb{R}^{|\mathcal{X}|}$ and $\mathbf{q} \in \mathbb{R}^{|\mathcal{Y}|}$ for A and B, respectively, with respect to which f is strong semi-balanced. That is, it holds that

$$\begin{cases} \mathbf{p}^T \cdot \mathbf{M}_f = \delta_1 \cdot \mathbf{1}^T, \text{ where } \delta_1 > 0 \\ \mathbf{1}^T \cdot \mathbf{p} < \delta_1, \\ \sum_{x \in \mathcal{X}} |p_x| = 1, \end{cases} \quad \text{and} \quad \begin{cases} \mathbf{M}_f \cdot \mathbf{q} = \delta_2 \cdot \mathbf{1}, \text{ where } \delta_2 > 0 \\ \mathbf{1}^T \cdot \mathbf{q} < \delta_2, \\ \sum_{y \in \mathcal{Y}} |q_y| = 1. \end{cases}$$

Throughout the rest of the proof, we consider an execution of π where the inputs x and y of A and B, respectively, are sampled independently according to $|\mathbf{p}|$ and $|\mathbf{q}|$, respectively. That is, A holds input x with probability $|p_x|$ and B holds input y with probability $|q_y|$.

Let us first introduce some notations. Let $\mathsf{flip}(x)$ output 0 if $p_x \geq 0$ and output 1 otherwise, and let $\mathsf{flip}(y)$ output 0 if $q_y \geq 0$ and output 1 otherwise. Let $p^- = 1 - p^+ = \sum_{x \in \mathcal{X}: p_x < 0} |p_x|$ denote the probability that $\mathsf{flip}(x) = 1$ and let $q^- = 1 - q^+ = \sum_{y \in \mathcal{Y}: q_y < 0} |q_y|$ denote the probability that $\mathsf{flip}(y) = 1$. Next, recall that in Definition 2, for every $i \in \{0, \dots, r\}$ we let a_i denote the output of C if B aborts after A sent i messages (and both A and C behave honestly through the remainder of the protocol). Similarly, we let b_i be the output of C in case A aborts after B sent i messages.

Recall that the idea is to let the adversary "bias" a certain correlation between the backup value and the honest party's input. We define this correlation to be the backup values, that are possibly flipped, depending on the value of $\mathsf{flip}(\cdot)$. Formally, for every $i \in \{0, \dots, r\}$ we let $\tilde{a}_i = a_i \oplus \mathsf{flip}(x)$ and we let $\tilde{b}_i = b_i \oplus \mathsf{flip}(y)$.

The next two lemmata formalize the aforementioned two steps of the proof strategy. Formally, the first lemma states that there exists a real world adversary that can "bias" either $\tilde{a}_i$ or $\tilde{b}_i$, thus allowing it to slightly improve its probability of guessing $\mathsf{flip}(\cdot)$ applied to the honest party's input. The second lemma states that no ideal world simulator can guess this value as well as the real world adversary.

Lemma 5. *There exists a constant $\xi > 0$ (independent of the protocol) such that one of the following holds.*

- *There exists an adversary corrupting* A *and* C *that can guess* flip(y) *with probability at least* $\delta_2 + q^- + \xi/r$.
- *There exists an adversary corrupting* B *and* C *that can guess* flip(x) *with probability at least* $\delta_1 + p^- + \xi/r$.

Lemma 6. *For any (possibly randomized) algorithm* $S_A : \mathcal{X} \times \{0,1\} \to \{0,1\}$ *and every* $x \in \mathcal{X}$, *it holds that*

$$\Pr_{y \leftarrow |\mathbf{q}|} [S_A(x, f(x,y)) = \mathsf{flip}(y)] \leq \delta_2 + q^-.$$

Similarly, for any (possibly randomized) algorithm $S_B : \mathcal{Y} \times \{0,1\} \to \{0,1\}$ *and every* $y \in \mathcal{Y}$, *it holds that*

$$\Pr_{x \leftarrow |\mathbf{p}|} [S_B(y, f(x,y)) = \mathsf{flip}(x)] \leq \delta_1 + p^-.$$

Clearly, Lemma 4 is implied by the above two lemmata. It is left to prove them. For both lemmata, we will use the following properties, proved by [21], that any semi-balanced functionality satisfy.

Lemma 7. *Let* $f : \mathcal{X} \times \mathcal{Y} \times \{\lambda\} \to \{0,1\}$ *be a semi-balance solitary output three-party functionality, with normalized locking strategies* $\mathbf{p}$ *and* $\mathbf{q}$ *for* A *and* B, *respectively. Let* δ_1, δ_2, $\mathsf{flip}(\cdot)$, p^-, p^+, q^-, *and* q^+ *be as above. Then the following hold.*

1. *[21, Lemma 6.4]:* $(p^+ - p^-)\delta_2 = (q^+ - q^-)\delta_1$.
2. *[21, Lemma 6.5]: For all* $y \in \mathcal{Y}$ *it holds that* $\Pr_{x \leftarrow |\mathbf{p}|} [f(x,y) \oplus \mathsf{flip}(x) = 1] = \delta_1 + p^-$.
3. *[21, Lemma 6.5]: For all* $x \in \mathcal{X}$ *it holds that* $\Pr_{y \leftarrow |\mathbf{q}|} [f(x,y) \oplus \mathsf{flip}(y) = 1] = \delta_2 + q^-$.

We first prove Lemma 5.

Proof of. Lemma 5. We first use Items 2. and 3. of Lemma 7 to show that the distributions of every $\tilde{a}_i$ and every $\tilde{b}_i$ are fixed throughout the execution of π.

Claim 7. *For every* $i \in \{0,\ldots,r\}$ *it holds that*

$$\left| \Pr[\tilde{a}_i = 1] - (\delta_1 + p^-) \right| = \mathsf{neg}(\kappa) \quad and \quad \left| \Pr[\tilde{b}_i = 1] - (\delta_2 + q^-) \right| = \mathsf{neg}(\kappa).$$

Proof. Fix $i \in \{0,\ldots,r\}$. We show only the first assertion (the second is analogous). Consider an adversary $\mathcal{B}$ corrupting (only) B, that aborts after receiving i messages from A. Then the output of an honest C is a_i. Since π is assumed to be secure, there exists a simulator $\mathsf{Sim}_\mathcal{B}$ for $\mathcal{B}$. By Item 2. of Lemma 7, in the ideal world it holds that $\Pr\left[\mathrm{OUT}^{\mathsf{ideal}}(x,y) \oplus \mathsf{flip}(x)\right] = \delta_1 + p^-$, regardless of what $\mathsf{Sim}_\mathcal{B}$ sends to the trusted party. Therefore, up to a negligible difference, the same holds in the real world. $\square$

Observe that as $\delta_1 > \mathbf{1}^T \cdot \mathbf{p} = p^+ - p^-$ and $\delta_1 > 0$, it follows that $\delta_1 + p^- \geq -\delta_1 + p^+$ as well. Similarly, it holds that $\delta_2 + q^- \geq -\delta_2 + q^+$. The next claim asserts that at some round i, there is a "jump" in the distribution of the (possibly flipped) backup values.

Claim 8. *There exists a value $z \in \{0,1\}$ and a constant $\xi > 0$ (independent of the protocol), such that one of the following holds. Either there exists a round $i \in [r]$ such that*

$$\left| \Pr\left[\tilde{a}_i = z \wedge \tilde{b}_{i-1} = 1 \right] + \Pr\left[\tilde{a}_i \neq z \wedge \tilde{b}_i = 1 \right] - (\delta_2 + q^-) \right| \geq \xi/r,$$

or

$$\left| \Pr\left[\tilde{b}_{i-1} = z \wedge \tilde{a}_{i-1} = 1 \right] + \Pr\left[\tilde{b}_{i-1} \neq z \wedge \tilde{a}_i = 1 \right] - (\delta_1 + p^-) \right| \geq \xi/r.$$

Proof. By Claim 7, for every $i \in [r]$ and every $z \in \{0,1\}$ we have:

$$\Pr\left[\tilde{a}_i = z \wedge \tilde{b}_{i-1} = 1 \right] + \Pr\left[\tilde{a}_i \neq z \wedge \tilde{b}_i = 1 \right] - (\delta_2 + q^-)$$

$$\geq \Pr\left[\tilde{a}_i = z \wedge \tilde{b}_{i-1} = 1 \right] + \Pr\left[\tilde{a}_i \neq z \wedge \tilde{b}_i = 1 \right] - \Pr\left[\tilde{b}_i = 1 \right] - \mathrm{neg}(\kappa)$$

$$= \Pr\left[\tilde{a}_i = z \wedge \tilde{b}_{i-1} = 1 \right] - \Pr\left[\tilde{a}_i = z \wedge \tilde{b}_i = 1 \right] - \mathrm{neg}(\kappa)$$

Similarly, it holds that

$$\Pr\left[\tilde{b}_{i-1} = z \wedge \tilde{a}_{i-1} = 1 \right] + \Pr\left[\tilde{b}_{i-1} \neq z \wedge \tilde{a}_i = 1 \right] - (\delta_1 + p^-)$$

$$\geq \Pr\left[\tilde{b}_{i-1} = z \wedge \tilde{a}_{i-1} = 1 \right] - \Pr\left[\tilde{b}_{i-1} = z \wedge \tilde{a}_i = 1 \right] - \mathrm{neg}(\kappa).$$

Let Δ denote the average of the absolute values of the above quantity, taken over all i's and z's, i.e.,

$$\Delta := \frac{1}{4r} \sum_{i=1}^{r} \sum_{z=0}^{1} \left[\left| \Pr\left[\tilde{a}_i = z \wedge \tilde{b}_{i-1} = 1 \right] - \Pr\left[\tilde{a}_i = z \wedge \tilde{b}_i = 1 \right] - \mathrm{neg}(\kappa) \right| \right.$$

$$\left. + \left| \Pr\left[\tilde{b}_{i-1} = z \wedge \tilde{a}_{i-1} = 1 \right] - \Pr\left[\tilde{b}_{i-1} = z \wedge \tilde{a}_i = 1 \right] - \mathrm{neg}(\kappa) \right| \right].$$

Observe that

$$
\begin{aligned}
4r \cdot \Delta = \sum_{i=1}^{r} \Big[& \Big| \Pr\big[\tilde{a}_i = 0 \wedge \tilde{b}_{i-1} = 1\big] - \Pr\big[\tilde{a}_i = 0 \wedge \tilde{b}_i = 1\big] - \mathrm{neg}(\kappa)\Big| \\
& + \Big| \Pr\big[\tilde{b}_{i-1} = 0 \wedge \tilde{a}_{i-1} = 1\big] - \Pr\big[\tilde{b}_{i-1} = 0 \wedge \tilde{a}_i = 1\big] - \mathrm{neg}(\kappa)\Big| \\
& + \Big| \Pr\big[\tilde{a}_i = 1 \wedge \tilde{b}_{i-1} = 1\big] - \Pr\big[\tilde{a}_i = 1 \wedge \tilde{b}_i = 1\big] - \mathrm{neg}(\kappa)\Big| \\
& + \Big| \Pr\big[\tilde{b}_{i-1} = 1 \wedge \tilde{a}_{i-1} = 1\big] - \Pr\big[\tilde{b}_{i-1} = 1 \wedge \tilde{a}_i = 1\big] - \mathrm{neg}(\kappa)\Big| \Big] \\
= \sum_{i=1}^{r} \Big[& \Big| \Pr\big[\tilde{a}_i = 0 \wedge \tilde{b}_{i-1} = 0\big] - \Pr\big[\tilde{a}_i = 0 \wedge \tilde{b}_i = 0\big] + \mathrm{neg}(\kappa)\Big| \\
& + \Big| \Pr\big[\tilde{b}_{i-1} = 0 \wedge \tilde{a}_{i-1} = 0\big] - \Pr\big[\tilde{b}_{i-1} = 0 \wedge \tilde{a}_i = 0\big] + \mathrm{neg}(\kappa)\Big| \\
& + \Big| \Pr\big[\tilde{a}_i = 1 \wedge \tilde{b}_{i-1} = 1\big] - \Pr\big[\tilde{a}_i = 1 \wedge \tilde{b}_i = 1\big] + \mathrm{neg}(\kappa)\Big| \\
& + \Big| \Pr\big[\tilde{b}_{i-1} = 1 \wedge \tilde{a}_{i-1} = 1\big] - \Pr\big[\tilde{b}_{i-1} = 1 \wedge \tilde{a}_i = 1\big] + \mathrm{neg}(\kappa)\Big| \Big] \\
\geq \sum_{i=1}^{r} \Big[& \Big| \Pr\big[\tilde{a}_i = \tilde{b}_{i-1}\big] - \Pr\big[\tilde{a}_i = \tilde{b}_i\big] + 2\,\mathrm{neg}(\kappa)\Big| \\
& + \Big| \Pr\big[\tilde{b}_{i-1} = \tilde{a}_{i-1}\big] - \Pr\big[\tilde{b}_{i-1} = \tilde{a}_i\big] + 2\,\mathrm{neg}(\kappa)\Big| \Big] \\
\geq \Big| \Pr\big[& \tilde{a}_0 = \tilde{b}_0\big] - \Pr\big[\tilde{a}_r = \tilde{b}_r\big] \Big| - 2r \cdot \mathrm{neg}(\kappa).
\end{aligned}
$$

where the inequalities follow from the triangle inequality.

Now, since $\tilde{a}_0$ and $\tilde{b}_0$ are computed before any interaction is done, they are independent. Thus, by Claim 7 it follows that

$$
\Big| \Pr\big[\tilde{a}_0 = \tilde{b}_0\big] - \big((\delta_1 + p^-)(\delta_2 + q^-) + (-\delta_1 + p^+)(-\delta_2 + q^+)\big) \Big| = \mathrm{neg}(\kappa).
$$

Additionally, since $\tilde{a}_r$ and $\tilde{b}_r$ correspond to the (possibly flipped) output of the protocol, it follows that they are equal if and only $\mathsf{flip}(x) = \mathsf{flip}(y)$. Thus,

$$
\Big| \Pr\big[\tilde{a}_r = \tilde{b}_r\big] - (p^- q^- + p^+ q^+) \Big| = \mathrm{neg}(\kappa).
$$

Therefore,

$$
\Delta \geq \frac{1}{4r} \big| 2\delta_1 \delta_2 + (q^- - q^+)\delta_1 + (p^- - p^+)\delta_2 \big| - \mathrm{neg}(\kappa).
$$

By Item 1. of Lemma 7, it holds that $(q^- - q^+)\delta_1 = (p^- - p^+)\delta_2$, hence

$$
\Delta \geq \frac{\delta_1}{2r} \big| \delta_2 + q^- - q^+ \big| - \mathrm{neg}(\kappa) \geq \frac{\delta_1}{3r} \big| \delta_2 + q^- - q^+ \big|.
$$

Since $\delta_1 \neq 0$ and $\delta_2 \neq \mathbf{1}^T \cdot \mathbf{q} = q^+ - q^-$, it follows that for $\xi := \delta_1 \cdot |\delta_2 + q^- - q^+|/3 > 0$ it holds that

$$\Delta \geq \xi/r.$$

The claim now follows from an averaging argument. □

We are now ready to construct our adversary. Assume without loss of generality that there exists $i \in [r]$ such that

$$\Pr\left[\tilde{a}_i = 1 \wedge \tilde{b}_{i-1} = 1\right] + \Pr\left[\tilde{a}_i \neq 1 \wedge \tilde{b}_i = 1\right] - (\delta_2 + q^-) \geq \xi/r.$$

The case where the expression on the left-hand side is upper bounded by $-\xi/r$ is handled by first observing that

$$\Pr[\tilde{a}_i = z, \tilde{b}_{i-1} = 1] + \Pr[\tilde{a}_i \neq z, \tilde{b}_i = 1] - (\delta_2 + q^-)$$
$$= \Pr[\tilde{a}_i = z] - \Pr[\tilde{a}_i = z, \tilde{b}_{i-1} = 0] + \Pr[\tilde{a}_i \neq z] - \Pr[\tilde{a}_i \neq z, \tilde{b}_i = 1] - (\delta_2 + q^-)$$
$$= -(\Pr[\tilde{a}_i = z, \tilde{b}_{i-1} = 0] + \Pr[\tilde{a}_i \neq z, \tilde{b}_i = 0] - (1 - \delta_2 - q^-)),$$

and then applying an analogous argument. We define the adversary $\mathcal{A}$ as follows.

1. Corrupt A and C, and instruct them to act honestly until receiving i messages from B.
2. Compute the backup value a_i as an honest A and C would in case B aborts. If $a_i \oplus \mathsf{flip}(x) = 1$ then instruct A to abort.
3. Otherwise, instruct A to send the next message honestly and then abort.
4. In both cases, C acts honestly until the end of the protocol, where it obtains a backup value b.
5. Output $b \oplus 1$ as the guess for $\mathsf{flip}(y)$.

Observe that $\mathcal{A}$ guesses $\mathsf{flip}(y)$ with a probability that is significantly greater than $\delta_2 + q^-$. Indeed,

$$\Pr\left[b \oplus 1 = \mathsf{flip}(y)\right] = \Pr\left[\tilde{a}_i = 1 \wedge b_{i-1} \oplus 1 = \mathsf{flip}(y)\right] + \Pr\left[\tilde{a}_i = 0 \wedge b_i \oplus 1 = \mathsf{flip}(y)\right]$$
$$= \Pr\left[\tilde{a}_i = 1 \wedge \tilde{b}_{i-1} = 1\right] + \Pr\left[\tilde{a}_i = 0 \wedge \tilde{b}_i = 1\right]$$
$$\geq \delta_2 + q^- + \xi/r.$$

□

We now prove Lemma 6.

Proof of Lemma 6. We only prove the first assertion, as the second is analogous. In the following, for the sake of brevity, we write S instead of S_A, and we fix $x \in \mathcal{X}$ and remove it from S. Additionally, denote $z = f(x, y)$ and $\tilde{z} = z \oplus \mathsf{flip}(y)$. It holds that

$$\Pr\left[S(z) = \text{flip}(y)\right] = \Pr\left[S(z) \oplus z = \tilde{z}\right]$$
$$= \Pr\left[S(0) = 0, z = 0, \tilde{z} = 0\right] + \Pr\left[S(1) = 1, z = 1, \tilde{z} = 0\right]$$
$$+ \Pr\left[S(0) = 1, z = 0, \tilde{z} = 1\right] + \Pr\left[S(1) = 0, z = 1, \tilde{z} = 1\right]$$
$$= \Pr\left[S(0) = 0\right] \cdot \Pr\left[z = 0, \tilde{z} = 0\right] + \Pr\left[S(1) = 1\right] \cdot \Pr\left[z = 1, \tilde{z} = 0\right]$$
$$+ \Pr\left[S(0) = 1\right] \cdot \Pr\left[z = 0, \tilde{z} = 1\right] + \Pr\left[S(1) = 0\right] \cdot \Pr\left[z = 1, \tilde{z} = 1\right]$$
$$\leq \max\{\Pr\left[z = 0, \tilde{z} = 0\right], \Pr\left[z = 0, \tilde{z} = 1\right]\}$$
$$+ \max\{\Pr\left[z = 1, \tilde{z} = 0\right], \Pr\left[z = 1, \tilde{z} = 1\right]\}.$$

Depending on which quantities are larger, the above expression is upper-bounded by one of the following.

- $\Pr\left[\tilde{z} = z\right] = \Pr\left[\text{flip}(y) = 0\right] = q^+$,
- $\Pr\left[\tilde{z} \neq z\right] = \Pr\left[\text{flip}(y) = 1\right] = q^-$,
- $\Pr\left[\tilde{z} = 0\right] = -\delta_2 + q^+$,
- $\Pr\left[\tilde{z} = 1\right] = \delta_2 + q^-$,

where the last equality in the first two equations is by the definition of q^+ and q^-, and the equality in the last two equations follows from Item 3. of Lemma 7. Since $\delta_2 > 0$ and $\delta_2 \geq \mathbf{1}^T \cdot \mathbf{q} = q^+ - q^-$, it follows that the maximum is $\delta_2 + q^-$. $\qquad\square$

$\square$

5   A Positive Result for Solitary Output Computation

In this section, we prove our positive results, showing that certain functionalities that are not strong semi-balanced can be computed with full security. Formally, we prove the following.

Lemma 8 (Restatement of Lemma 3). *Let $f : \mathcal{X} \times \mathcal{Y} \times \{\lambda\} \rightarrow \{0,1\}$ be a solitary output three-party Boolean functionality. Assume there exists a locking strategy $\mathbf{p}$ for A satisfying*

$$\mathbf{p}^T \cdot \mathbf{M}_f = \mathbf{1}^T \quad \text{and} \quad \mathbf{1}^T \cdot \mathbf{p} \geq 1.$$

Then, if a secure protocol for OT exists, f can be computed with full security.

Proof. First, observe that we may assume that $\mathbf{p}$ contains a negative entry, as otherwise f is forced (see Definition 4) and can be computed by the results of [20]. We next present the protocol in the dealer model (see Sect. 2). We first introduce some notations. We let $r = \omega(\log(\kappa))$ be the number of rounds, let $p^* = \min_{x \in \mathcal{X}} \{p_x\} < 0$, and we fix two parameters $\beta = (\mathbf{1}^T \cdot \mathbf{p})^{-1}$ and

$$\alpha = \frac{\beta^{-1}}{\beta^{-1} - p^* \cdot |\mathcal{X}|}.$$

Observe that $0 < \beta \leq 1$ by assumption, and that $0 < \alpha < 1$ since $p^* < 0$.

We are now ready to present the protocol. For the sake of presentation, we will describe it assuming that C never aborts, and that A and B cannot both abort. To handle those cases, if C aborts during any part of the protocol, then A and B halt, and if A and B abort then C outputs $f(x_0, y_0)$, where $x_0 \in \mathcal{X}$ and $y_0 \in \mathcal{Y}$ are default values. Our protocol can be seen as a generalization of the two-party protocol by [5]. Roughly, their protocol follows the ideas of the GHKL protocol, however, at round $i^* - 1$ the backup value of B is a constant bit independent of the parties' inputs (though the bit depends on the function). In our three-party protocol, at round $i^* - 1$ the backup value of (B, C) is 1 with probability β.

Protocol 9.
Private inputs: Party A *holds input* $x \in \mathcal{X}$ *and party* B *holds* $y \in \mathcal{Y}$. *Party* C *has no private input.*
Common input: All parties hold the security parameter 1^κ.

1. A *and* B *send their inputs to the dealer.*
2. *The dealer sample* $i^* \leftarrow \mathsf{Geom}(\alpha)$.
3. *The dealer computes* $w = f(x, y)$ *and set* $\tilde{b} = 1$ *with probability* β.
4. *The dealer computes backup values as follows: For all* $i \in \{0, \ldots, r\}$ *let*

$$a_i = \begin{cases} f(x, \tilde{y}_i) & \text{if } i < i^* \\ w & \text{otherwise} \end{cases} \quad \text{and} \quad b_i = \begin{cases} f(\tilde{x}_i, y) & \text{if } i < i^* - 1 \\ \tilde{b} & \text{if } i = i^* - 1 \\ w & \text{otherwise} \end{cases}$$

where $\tilde{x}_i \leftarrow \mathcal{X}$, $\tilde{y}_i \leftarrow \mathcal{Y}$, *and* $\tilde{b} = 1$ *with probability* β, *are all independent.*
5. *The dealer sends* b_0 *to* B *and* C, *held shared in a 2-out-of-2 additive secret sharing scheme.*
6. *For* $i = 1$ *to* r *the dealer does the following:*
   (a) *Send* a_i *to* A *and* C, *held shared in a 2-out-of-2 additive secret sharing scheme. If* A *aborts, then* B *sends to* C *it share of* b_{i-1} *who then outputs it.*
   (b) *Send* b_i *to* B *and* C, *held shared in a 2-out-of-2 additive secret sharing scheme. If* B *aborts, then* A *sends to* C *it's share of* a_i *who then outputs it.*
7. A *sends its share of* a_r *to* C *who then outputs it.*

Observe that correctness holds since $i^* > r$ occurs with only a negligible probability. We next show that the protocol is fully secure. First, observe that corrupting C (and possibly another party) will not provide the adversary with any advantage. Intuitively, this is due to the fact the adversary can obtain at most one application of f, applied to the honest party's input. We defer the formal arguments to the full version.

One subtlety that we need to consider is the last case, where exactly one party among A and B is corrupted. This is due to the fact that, although the view

consists of random shares, a single corrupted party might affect the correctness
of the output of C. Note that a corrupt B can be handled easily, since the
backup value of (A, C) at every round is of the form $f(x, y')$, for $y' \in \mathcal{Y}$ that is
either uniformly random, or equal to the real input y sent to the dealer. Thus,
a simulator can send according to the correct distribution by checking whether
the adversary aborts before or after round i^*.

We now consider the case where A is corrupted. Unlike the previous case,
the output of C in round $i^* - 1$ is not of the form $f(x', y)$ for any (even possibly
random) $x' \in \mathcal{X}$. Thus, the naive simulation from before does not work. Nevertheless, we next show that there exists a distribution over $\mathcal{X}$, such that the
output of C in the ideal world is identical to the output of C in the real world.
We defer the formal description of the simulator to the full version. We next
analyze the distribution of the output OUT of C in the real world and compare
it to an ideal execution.

In the following, all probabilities are conditioned on the adversary aborting
at round i and on $i^* \leq r$. Let $\mathbf{e}_x \in \mathbb{R}^{|\mathcal{X}|}$ denote the xth standard basis vector.
Observe that in the real world, it holds that

$$
\begin{aligned}
\Pr\left[\text{OUT} = 1\right] &= \Pr\left[i < i^*\right] \cdot \Pr\left[f(\tilde{x}_i, y) = 1\right] + \Pr\left[i = i^*\right] \cdot \beta + \Pr\left[i > i^*\right] \cdot f(x, y) \\
&= (1 - \alpha)^i \cdot \mathbf{u}_{\mathcal{X}} \cdot \mathbf{M}_f(\cdot, y) + (1 - \alpha)^{i-1} \cdot \alpha\beta \\
&\quad + \left(1 - (1 - \alpha)^{i-1}\right) \cdot \mathbf{e}_x \cdot \mathbf{M}_f(\cdot, y),
\end{aligned} \tag{1}
$$

where $\mathbf{u}_{\mathcal{X}}$ is the uniform probability (row) vector over $\mathcal{X}$. On the other hand,
in the ideal world, the simulator sends a value according to a distribution that
depends only on the input x and the round i in which the adversary aborted. We
denote this distribution by the row vector $\mathbf{x}_{x,i}$. As the ideal world is identically
distributed to the real world, it follows that for all $y \in \mathcal{Y}$ it holds that

$$
\begin{aligned}
\mathbf{x}_{x,i} \cdot \mathbf{M}_f(\cdot, y) &= (1 - \alpha)^i \cdot \mathbf{u}_{\mathcal{X}} \cdot \mathbf{M}_f(\cdot, y) + (1 - \alpha)^{i-1} \cdot \alpha\beta \\
&\quad + \left(1 - (1 - \alpha)^{i-1}\right) \cdot \mathbf{e}_x^T \cdot \mathbf{M}_f(\cdot, y).
\end{aligned}
$$

Since this must hold for all $y \in \mathcal{Y}$, we may write

$$
\begin{aligned}
\mathbf{x}_{x,i} \cdot \mathbf{M}_f &= (1 - \alpha)^i \cdot \mathbf{u}_{\mathcal{X}} \cdot \mathbf{M}_f + (1 - \alpha)^{i-1} \cdot \alpha\beta \cdot \mathbf{1}^T \\
&\quad + \left(1 - (1 - \alpha)^{i-1}\right) \cdot \mathbf{e}_x^T \cdot \mathbf{M}_f.
\end{aligned} \tag{2}
$$

We now show that Eq. (2) admits a solution $\mathbf{x}_{x,i}$ that is also a probability vector.
Since $\mathbf{1}^T = \mathbf{p}^T \cdot \mathbf{M}_f$, we may write the right-hand side as

$$
\left((1 - \alpha)^i \cdot \mathbf{u}_{\mathcal{X}} + (1 - \alpha)^{i-1} \cdot \alpha\beta \cdot \mathbf{p}^T + \left(1 - (1 - \alpha)^{i-1}\right) \cdot \mathbf{e}_x^T\right) \cdot \mathbf{M}_f.
$$

Thus, the row vector $\mathbf{v} := (1-\alpha)^i \cdot \mathbf{u}_{\mathcal{X}} + (1-\alpha)^{i-1} \cdot \alpha\beta \cdot \mathbf{p}^T + \left(1 - (1 - \alpha)^{i-1}\right) \cdot \mathbf{e}_x^T$
solves Eq. (2). To conclude the proof, we next show that $\mathbf{v}$ is a probability vector,
i.e., its entries are non-negative and sum to 1. First, observe that

$$\mathbf{v} \cdot \mathbf{1} = (1-\alpha)^i + (1-\alpha)^{i-1} \cdot \alpha\beta \cdot (\mathbf{p}^T \cdot \mathbf{1}) + 1 - (1-\alpha)^{i-1}$$
$$= (1-\alpha)^i + (1-\alpha)^{i-1} \cdot \alpha + 1 - (1-\alpha)^{i-1}$$
$$= 1.$$

Second, for every $x' \in \mathcal{X}$, it holds that

$$v(x') \geq (1-\alpha)^i \cdot \frac{1}{|\mathcal{X}|} + (1-\alpha)^{i-1} \cdot \alpha\beta \cdot p_{x'}$$
$$= (1-\alpha)^{i-1} \cdot \left(\frac{1-\alpha}{|\mathcal{X}|} + \alpha\beta \cdot p_{x'} \right)$$
$$= (1-\alpha)^{i-1} \cdot \frac{1 - \alpha\,(1 - \beta \cdot p_{x'} \cdot |\mathcal{X}|)}{|\mathcal{X}|}$$

Recall that $\alpha = \frac{\beta^{-1}}{\beta^{-1} - p^* \cdot |\mathcal{X}|}$, where $p^* \leq p_{x'}$ for all $x' \in \mathcal{X}$. Therefore,

$$v(x') \geq (1-\alpha)^{i-1} \cdot \frac{1 - \frac{\beta^{-1}}{\beta^{-1} - p^* \cdot |\mathcal{X}|}\,(1 - \beta \cdot p_{x'} \cdot |\mathcal{X}|)}{|\mathcal{X}|}$$
$$= (1-\alpha)^{i-1} \cdot \frac{p_{x'} - p^*}{\beta^{-1} - p^* \cdot |\mathcal{X}|}$$
$$\geq 0.$$

Thus, $\mathbf{v}$ is a probability vector as required.   □

6   Application: Analysis of the Disjointness Functionality

In this section, we use Theorem 4 to analyze the parameters for which the disjointness functionality can be computed with full security. Throughout the section, for natural numbers $k, m, n \in \mathbb{N}$ satisfying $k \leq m \leq n$, we denote

$$\binom{[n]}{k,m} = \{\mathcal{S} \subseteq [n] : k \leq |\mathcal{S}| \leq m\}.$$

We prove the following.

Theorem 10 (Restatement of Theorem 5). *Let $n, k \in \mathbb{N}$, where $1 \leq k < n/2$. Define the solitary output three-party Boolean functionality* disj $: \binom{[n]}{k,n-k}^2 \times \{\lambda\} \to \{0,1\}$ *as*

$$\mathsf{disj}\,(\mathcal{S}, \mathcal{T}) = \begin{cases} 1 & \text{if } \mathcal{S} \cap \mathcal{T} = \emptyset \\ 0 & \text{otherwise} \end{cases}$$

Then, if a secure protocol for OT exists, disj *can be computed with full security if and only if n is even.*

We will make use of the following two lemmas.

Lemma 9. *Let $n \in \mathbb{N}$ and let $k \in [n]$. Then*

$$\sum_{m=k}^{n} (-1)^{m+k} \cdot \binom{n}{m}\binom{m-1}{k-1} = 1.$$

Lemma 10. *Let $n, k \in \mathbb{N}$ be such that $1 \leq k < n/2$. Then*

$$\sum_{m=k}^{n-k} (-1)^{m+k} \cdot \binom{n}{m}\binom{m-1}{k-1} < 1$$

if n is odd, and

$$\sum_{m=k}^{n-k} (-1)^{m+k} \cdot \binom{n}{m}\binom{m-1}{k-1} > 1$$

if n is even.

We prove Lemma 9 below. Due to space limitations, the proof of Lemma 10 is deferred to the full version. We next show that the two lemmas imply Theorem 10.

Proof of Theorem 10. Throughout the proof, all summations over sets are restricted to summations over $\binom{[n]}{k,n-k}$.

We first show that A and B have locking strategies, regardless of the parity of n. We define the vector $\mathbf{p}$ over $\binom{[n]}{k,n-k}$ as $p_{\mathcal{S}} = (-1)^{|\mathcal{S}|+k} \cdot \binom{|\mathcal{S}|-1}{k-1}$. Then for any subset $\mathcal{T} \in \binom{[n]}{k,n-k}$ it holds that

$$
\begin{aligned}
\mathbf{p}^{T} \cdot \mathbf{M}_{\mathsf{disj}}(\cdot, \mathcal{T}) &= \sum_{\mathcal{S}: \mathcal{S} \cap \mathcal{T} = \emptyset} p_{\mathcal{S}} \\
&= \sum_{\mathcal{S}: \mathcal{S} \cap \mathcal{T} = \emptyset} (-1)^{|\mathcal{S}|+k} \cdot \binom{|\mathcal{S}|-1}{k-1} \\
&= \sum_{m=k}^{n-|\mathcal{T}|} \sum_{\substack{\mathcal{S}: |\mathcal{S}|=m \\ \mathcal{S} \cap \mathcal{T} = \emptyset}} (-1)^{m+k} \cdot \binom{m-1}{k-1} \\
&= \sum_{m=k}^{n-|\mathcal{T}|} (-1)^{m+k} \cdot \binom{m-1}{k-1}\binom{n-|\mathcal{T}|}{m} \\
&= 1,
\end{aligned}
$$

where the last equality follows from Lemma 9. Since disj is symmetric with respect to the input (i.e., $\mathsf{disj}(\mathcal{S}, \mathcal{T}) = \mathsf{disj}(\mathcal{T}, \mathcal{S})$), we define the locking strategy $\mathbf{q}$ for B exactly the same. Then by Theorem 4, disj can be computed with full security if and only if $\mathbf{1}^{T} \cdot \mathbf{p} \geq 1$. By Lemma 10, this occurs if and only if n is even. $\square$

It is left to prove Lemma 9. We will use the following well-known combinatorial identity.

Proposition 2. *For all $k, m, n \in \mathbb{N}$ where $k \leq m \leq n$ it holds that*

$$\binom{n}{m}\binom{m}{k} = \binom{n}{k}\binom{n-m}{m-k}.$$

Proof of Lemma 9. For every $k \in [n]$ let

$$s(k) = \sum_{m=k}^{n} (-1)^{m+k} \cdot \binom{n}{m}\binom{m-1}{k-1}.$$

Then by Pascal's identity, it holds that

$$s(k) - s(k+1) = \binom{n}{k} + \sum_{m=k+1}^{n} (-1)^{m+k} \cdot \binom{n}{m} \cdot \left[\binom{m-1}{k-1} + \binom{m-1}{k}\right]$$

$$= \binom{n}{k} + \sum_{m=k+1}^{n} (-1)^{m+k} \cdot \binom{n}{m}\binom{m}{k}$$

By Proposition 2 we obtain

$$s(k) - s(k+1) = \binom{n}{k} + \sum_{m=k+1}^{n} (-1)^{m+k} \cdot \binom{n}{k}\binom{n-k}{m-k}$$

$$= \binom{n}{k} \cdot \left[1 + \sum_{m=k+1}^{n} (-1)^{m+k} \cdot \binom{n-k}{m-k}\right]$$

$$= \binom{n}{k} \cdot \left[1 + \sum_{m=1}^{n-k} (-1)^{m} \cdot \binom{n-k}{m}\right]$$

$$= \binom{n}{k} \cdot \sum_{m=0}^{n-k} (-1)^{m} \cdot \binom{n-k}{m}$$

$$= 0,$$

where the last equality is due to the fact that the alternating sum of all binomial coefficients is 0. The proof now follows from the observation that $s(n) = 1$. ☐

Acknowledgements. The first author is supported by Israel Science Foundation grant 391/21. The work of the second author was supported in part by grants from the Israel Science Foundation (no.152/17), by the Ariel Cyber Innovation Center in conjunction with the Israel National Cyber directorate in the Prime Minister's Office, and by the Robert L. McDevitt, K.S.G., K.C.H.S. and Catherine H. McDevitt L.C.H.S. endowment at Georgetown University. Part of this work was done when the second author was hosted by Georgetown University. The third author was supported by a JPMorgan Chase Faculty Research Award, Technology, and Humanity Fund from the McCourt School of Public Policy at Georgetown University, and a Google Research Award.

References

1. Agarwal, N., Anand, S., Prabhakaran, M.: Uncovering algebraic structures in the MPC landscape. In: Ishai, Y., Rijmen, V. (eds.) EUROCRYPT 2019. LNCS, vol. 11477, pp. 381–406. Springer, Cham (2019). https://doi.org/10.1007/978-3-030-17656-3_14

2. Agrawal, S., Prabhakaran, M.: On fair exchange, fair coins and fair sampling. In: Canetti, R., Garay, J.A. (eds.) CRYPTO 2013. LNCS, vol. 8042, pp. 259–276. Springer, Heidelberg (2013). https://doi.org/10.1007/978-3-642-40041-4_15

3. Alon, B., Naor, M., Omri, E., Stemmer, U.: Mpc for tech giants (GMPC): enabling Gulliver and the lilliputians to cooperate amicably. arXiv preprint arXiv:2207.05047 (2022)

4. Asharov, G.: Towards characterizing complete fairness in secure two-party computation. In: Lindell, Y. (ed.) TCC 2014. LNCS, vol. 8349, pp. 291–316. Springer, Heidelberg (2014). https://doi.org/10.1007/978-3-642-54242-8_13

5. Asharov, G., Beimel, A., Makriyannis, N., Omri, E.: Complete characterization of fairness in secure two-party computation of boolean functions. In: Dodis, Y., Nielsen, J.B. (eds.) TCC 2015, Part I. LNCS, vol. 9014, pp. 199–228. Springer, Heidelberg (2015). https://doi.org/10.1007/978-3-662-46494-6_10

6. Beimel, A., Gabizon, A., Ishai, Y., Kushilevitz, E., Meldgaard, S., Paskin-Cherniavsky, A.: Non-interactive secure multiparty computation. In: Garay, J.A., Gennaro, R. (eds.) CRYPTO 2014. LNCS, vol. 8617, pp. 387–404. Springer, Heidelberg (2014). https://doi.org/10.1007/978-3-662-44381-1_22

7. Bell, J.H., Bonawitz, K.A., Gascón, A., Lepoint, T., Raykova, M.: Secure single-server aggregation with (poly) logarithmic overhead. In: Proceedings of the 2020 ACM SIGSAC Conference on Computer and Communications Security, pp. 1253–1269 (2020)

8. Ben-Or, M., Goldwasser, S., Wigderson, A.: Completeness theorems for noncryptographic fault-tolerant distributed computations. In: Proceedings of the 20th Annual ACM Symposium on Theory of Computing (STOC), pp. 1–10 (1988)

9. Bonawitz, K., et al.: Practical secure aggregation for privacy-preserving machine learning. In: proceedings of the 2017 ACM SIGSAC Conference on Computer and Communications Security, pp. 1175–1191 (2017)

10. Burkhalter, L., Lycklama, H., Viand, A., Küchler, N., Hithnawi, A.: Rofl: attestable robustness for secure federated learning. arXiv preprint arXiv:2107.03311 (2021)

11. Chaum, D., Crépeau, C., Damgard, I.: Multiparty unconditionally secure protocols. In: Proceedings of the Twentieth Annual ACM Symposium on Theory of Computing, pp. 11–19 (1988). https://doi.org/10.1145/62212.62214

12. Cleve, R.: Limits on the security of coin flips when half the processors are faulty (extended abstract). In: Proceedings of the 18th Annual ACM STOC (1986)

13. Dachman-Soled, D.: Revisiting fairness in MPC: polynomial number of parties and general adversarial structures. In: Pass, R., Pietrzak, K. (eds.) TCC 2020, Part II. LNCS, vol. 12551, pp. 595–620. Springer, Cham (2020). https://doi.org/10.1007/978-3-030-64378-2_21

14. Daza, V., Makriyannis, N.: Designing fully secure protocols for secure two-party computation of constant-domain functions. In: Kalai, Y., Reyzin, L. (eds.) TCC 2017, Part I. LNCS, vol. 10677, pp. 581–611. Springer, Cham (2017). https://doi.org/10.1007/978-3-319-70500-2_20

15. Feige, U., Killian, J., Naor, M.: A minimal model for secure computation. In: Proceedings of the Twenty-Sixth Annual ACM Symposium on Theory of Computing, pp. 554–563 (1994)

16. Goldreich, O., Micali, S., Wigderson, A.: How to play any mental game or a completeness theorem for protocols with honest majority. In: Proceedings of the 51st Annual ACM STOC, pp. 218–229 (1987)
17. Goldwasser, S., Levin, L.: Fair computation of general functions in presence of immoral majority. In: Menezes, A.J., Vanstone, S.A. (eds.) CRYPTO 1990. LNCS, vol. 537, pp. 77–93. Springer, Heidelberg (1991). https://doi.org/10.1007/3-540-38424-3_6
18. Gordon, S.D., Katz, J.: Complete fairness in multi-party computation without an honest majority. In: Reingold, O. (ed.) TCC 2009. LNCS, vol. 5444, pp. 19–35. Springer, Heidelberg (2009). https://doi.org/10.1007/978-3-642-00457-5_2
19. Gordon, S.D., Hazay, C., Katz, J., Lindell, Y.: Complete fairness in secure two-party computation. In: Proceedings of the 40th Annual ACM Symposium on Theory of Computing (STOC), pp. 413–422 (2008)
20. Halevi, S., Ishai, Y., Kushilevitz, E., Makriyannis, N., Rabin, T.: On fully secure MPC with solitary output. In: Hofheinz, D., Rosen, A. (eds.) TCC 2019, Part I. LNCS, vol. 11891, pp. 312–340. Springer, Cham (2019). https://doi.org/10.1007/978-3-030-36030-6_13
21. Makriyannis, N.: On the classification of finite Boolean functions up to fairness. In: Proceedings of the 9th Conference on Security and Cryptography for Networks (SCN), pp. 135–154 (2014)
22. Makriyannis, N., et al.: Fairness in two-party computation: characterizing fair functions. Ph.D. thesis, Universitat Pompeu Fabra (2016)
23. Rabin, T., Ben-Or, M.: Verifiable secret sharing and multiparty protocols with honest majority (extended abstract). In: Proceedings of the 30th Annual Symposium on Foundations of Computer Science (FOCS), pp. 73–85 (1989)
24. Yao, A.C.: Protocols for secure computations (extended abstract). In: Proceedings of the 23rd Annual Symposium on Foundations of Computer Science (FOCS), pp. 160–164 (1982)

SPRINT: High-Throughput Robust Distributed Schnorr Signatures

Fabrice Benhamouda[1]([✉]) [iD], Shai Halevi[1] [iD], Hugo Krawczyk[1] [iD], Yiping Ma[2] [iD], and Tal Rabin[1,2] [iD]

[1] AWS, New York, NY, USA
fabrice.benhamouda@gmail.com, shai.halevi@gmail.com, hugokraw@gmail.com
[2] University of Pennsylvania, Philadelphia, PA, USA
{yipingma,talr}@seas.upenn.edu

Abstract. We describe robust high-throughput threshold protocols for generating Schnorr signatures in an asynchronous setting with potentially hundreds of parties. The protocols run a single message-independent interactive ephemeral randomness generation procedure (i.e., DKG) followed by *non-interactive* signature generation for multiple messages, at a communication cost similar to one execution of a synchronous non-robust protocol in prior work (e.g., Gennaro et al.) and with a large number of parties (ranging from few tens to hundreds and more). Our protocols extend seamlessly to the dynamic/proactive setting where each run of the protocol uses a new committee with refreshed shares of the secret key; in particular, they support large committees periodically sampled from among the overall population of parties and the required secret state is transferred to the selected parties. The protocols work over a broadcast channel and are robust (provide guaranteed output delivery) even over asynchronous networks.

The combination of these features makes our protocols a good match for implementing a signature service over a public blockchain with many validators, where guaranteed output delivery is an absolute must. In that setting, there is a system-wide public key, where the corresponding secret signature key is distributed among the validators. Clients can submit messages (under suitable controls, e.g., smart contracts), and authorized messages are signed relative to the global public key.

Asymptotically, when running with committees of n parties, our protocols can generate $\Omega(n^2)$ signatures per run, while providing resilience against $\Omega(n)$ corrupted nodes and broadcasting only $O(n^2)$ group elements and scalars (hence $O(1)$ elements per signature).

We prove the security of our protocols via a reduction to the hardness of the discrete logarithm problem in the random oracle model.

F. Benhamouda, S. Halevi, H. Krawczyk and T. Rabin—Work done prior to joining Amazon, partially while at the Algorand Foundation.

M. Joye and G. Leander (Eds.): EUROCRYPT 2024, LNCS 14655, pp. 62–91, 2024.
https://doi.org/10.1007/978-3-031-58740-5_3

1   Introduction

In this work, we describe a suite of protocols that we call[1], aimed at generating many Schnorr signatures at a low amortized cost. SPRINT consists of a single interactive distributed key generation (DKG) for generating message-independent ephemeral randomness, followed by a *non-interactive and robust* signature generation for many messages. Here, *robustness* means that with a sufficient number of honest parties, the protocol is guaranteed to output the requested signatures.

Threshold Schnorr signature schemes have seen a revival due to applications in the blockchain space. However, the bulk of existing work focuses on the case of a small number of signers, targeting applications such as key custody and multi-signatures. For those cases, one can afford a non-robust scheme where a single misbehaving party can cause the protocol to abort: If the misbehaving party can be identified, then it can be removed before re-running the protocol. This is indeed the approach most recent schemes embrace (e.g., [8,15,27,28]). However, the remove-and-restart approach does not scale well with the number of signers, since the protocol may need to be restarted as many times as the number of misbehaving parties. Also, this approach cannot be used in a fully asynchronous setting, where there is no distinction between a malicious party that refuses to participate and an honest party that is just slow. Here, we study *robust* threshold Schnorr signatures in scenarios with many messages and many signers (possibly hundreds of them), in an asynchronous setting.

One of the motivating scenarios for considering a large set of signers signing many messages is provided by blockchain settings, where the validator nodes should generate signatures on behalf of the blockchain (see more below). That use case precludes non-robust protocols, as it requires an asynchronous protocol that remains feasible for many signers. At the same time, public blockchains provide tools such as a broadcast channel and PKI, which can simplify the design of the signature protocol. Moreover, the large number of parties makes it reasonable to assume a large honest majority, a significant advantage when building robust protocols.

Let us recall Schnorr-type signatures. They work over a group of prime order p with a generator G; a signature on a message M relative to secret key $s \in \mathbb{Z}_p$ and public key $S = s \cdot G$, has the form $(R, r + e \cdot s)$, where $r \in \mathbb{Z}_p$ is an ephemeral random secret, $R = r \cdot G$ is ephemeral randomness, and $e = \mathsf{Hash}(S, R, M) \in \mathbb{Z}_p$. A standard way to compute *robust* threshold Schnorr signatures among n parties who secret-share a long-term secret key s is to run a *distributed key generation (DKG)*[2] procedure [16] that produces a message-independent ephemeral randomness $R = r \cdot G$ where r is a fresh random value secret-shared among the parties. This phase is often called preprocessing or just DKG, and the message-

---

[1] SPRINT is a permuted acronym for "Robust Threshold Schnorr with Super-INvertible Packing".

[2] Throughout the paper, we use a DKG protocol for different purposes, including ephemeral Schnorr randomness generation, long-term key generation, and proactive refreshment.

independent ephemeral randomness is often called presignatures. Then, the parties use their shares of s and r to produce signature shares that can be combined into a single standard Schnorr signature. The bulk of the cost for signature generation is the DKG procedure that has $O(n^2)$ cost both in terms of bandwidth and computation.

Robust threshold Schnorr schemes have been known for over 20 years [16,37], but they are less efficient than their non-robust counterparts. These robust protocols include at least 2–3 rounds to generate message-independent ephemeral randomness, and at least one additional round for signature generation. Moreover, the randomness-generation rounds are expensive, using a bandwidth of at least $\Omega(n^2)$ broadcasted group elements. Non-robust schemes can reduce the randomness generation part to a single round, performed before knowing the message to be signed, and a single non-interactive message-dependent round (where parties just output signature shares).

Our robust signature protocol features a two-round message-independent distributed ephemeral randomness generation, followed by a single non-interactive signature generation round. However, the latter non-interactive round can produce signatures for *many messages*, hence amortizing the cost of the randomness generation protocol over many signatures. The protocols we present can produce thousands of signatures in each run, at a communication cost similar to one execution of a synchronous non-robust protocol in prior work [16].

Our protocols are flexible: they are useful in the fixed-committee setting where the same set of parties is used repeatedly, but extends seamlessly to the dynamic/proactive setting where each run of the protocol is done by a different committee with refreshed shares of the secret key. They naturally support large systems, where committees are periodically sub-sampled from among the overall population of parties and the required shared secret state is transferred to the selected parties. The protocols are also *modular*: we present a high-level protocol based on a generic agreement protocol (for the parties to agree on a set of correctly dealt shares) instantiated on an asynchronous broadcast channel. Without tying the high-level signature protocol to the details of the agreement or the communication model, we are able to take advantage of systems (such as blockchain) that natively provide agreement and communication primitives.

This agreement protocol is instrumental in achieving one of our significant design goals, namely, to perform well in the optimistic case of normal network conditions, but also to avoid degrading performance unnecessarily when network delays (possibly adversarially induced) are significant. Crucial for ensuring this property is to achieve agreement as soon as possible among a sufficient number of parties. This calls for forgoing techniques such as complete secret sharing [32] where all honest parties must receive shares of the secret, hence adding longer delays (and latency) to the protocol completion.

We next describe techniques used to achieve the above functional and performance properties of our solution, starting with two main components: (a) an early agreement protocol allowing non-complete sharing and (b) "extreme packing" that combines packed secret sharing [13] with super-invertible matrices [24] to extend the number of signatures we get from a single ephemeral-randomness creation stage.

A Simple Early-agreement Protocol. Many threshold systems require *complete secret sharing*, i.e., all honest parties must receive shares of the secret. This means that honest parties cannot terminate until they ensure that all other honest parties will eventually learn their shares. The completeness requirement often adds significant complexity to the protocol and an opportunity for the adversary to create high-latency executions in the asynchronous setting. In our protocols we forgo completeness and its adverse effects by only requiring that a sufficiently large subset of honest parties learn their shares so that they can generate signatures; there is no need to ensure that *all* honest parties get shares.

Weakening the completeness requirement of secret sharing allows us to use a very simple agreement protocol over the underlying asynchronous broadcast channel. Furthermore, the use of a broadcast channel enables *verifiable complaints* by shareholders, namely proofs that a dealer sent bad shares. Our use of these complaints is markedly different than in prior works. In protocols that aim at complete sharing (such as [19]), a party uses the complaints to inform other parties that it is missing its share, triggering a complex protocol by which the other honest shareholders help them get their missing shares. In contrast, we use the complaint to disqualify the bad dealer, there is no need to help the complaining shareholder get any more shares. This technique simplifies the agreement protocol and saves rounds of broadcast[3] (see Sects. 2.2 and 4 and our full version [4, Appendix E] for details). We believe that this simple agreement protocol could find other uses beyond DKG and threshold signatures.

Extreme Packing. To maximize efficiency, we introduce an efficiency parameter a, such that each run of the protocol produces $a(n - 2t)$ signatures where t is the maximal number of corrupted parties supported by the protocol. In more detail, we use super-invertible matrices [24] to get a sharing of at least $n - 2t$ random polynomials for every run of the ephemeral randomness generation, and use packed secret sharing [13] to put a random values in each of these polynomials (see Sects. 2.4 and 2.5).[4]

We pay for this extreme packing with a slight reduction in resilience: To withstand t corrupted parties, the number of nodes that we need is $n \geq 3t + 2a - 1$, compared to $n \geq 3t + 1$ for a naive protocol that generates a single signature.[5] The result is a bandwidth-optimal protocol, up to some not-too-large constants: With n parties, it provides resilience against $\Omega(n)$ corrupted parties, using broadcast bandwidth of only $O(1)$ group-elements/scalars per signature, in *both the optimistic and the pessimistic cases* (where the number of faulty parties is small or large, respectively). We stress that the odds of everybody participating

---

[3] Our use of an underlying broadcast channel also obviates the need to find a biclique of dealers and shareholders, which is sometimes needed when giving up completeness, and which can be computationally hard (cf. [2]).

[4] We also describe some optimizations related to faster multiplication by super-invertible matrices in our full version [4, Appendix B].

[5] Since our techniques apply in the asynchronous setting, they inherently require $n \geq 3t + 1$; see our full version [4, Appendix H].

honestly diminishes as the number of parties grows, so in the large-committee setting it becomes more important to have an efficient pessimistic path. In our protocol, the pessimistic case features additional complaints, but those add at most $O(t/a)$ group-elements/scalars per signature.

For a few examples in the static-committee setting (and assuming no complaints), setting the efficiency parameter at $a = n/5$, they withstand $t = n/5$ corrupted parties and consume broadcast bandwidth of roughly 17.33 scalars/group-elements per signature. To support $t = n/4$ we must reduce the efficiency parameter to $a = n/8$, resulting in a per-signature bandwidth of about 34 scalars/group-elements. This $O(1)$ complexity is to be contrasted with the $O(n^2)$ complexity of the standard threshold Schnorr scheme [16]. See our full version [4, Appendix C] for details.

1.1   Other Techniques

Achieving high efficiency requires the use of many ideas and techniques, beyond the two main ones that we described above. Below is a list of these techniques, in no particular order. See Sect. 2 for a detailed overview of the entire protocol and the roles that these techniques play.

Local SIMD Computation. Working with packed secret sharing increases the number of secrets shared, but current MPC solutions for using packed secret sharing entail non-trivial protocols, even for simple functions [18]. For Schnorr signatures we need to compute $s \cdot (e_1, \ldots, e_a) + (r_1, \ldots, r_a)$ where s and the r_v's are secret and the e_v's are public. While simple, an MPC protocol for computing that function still seems to require interaction, since it includes a product. Furthermore, when using simple Shamir sharing for s, some joint processing is needed to create multiple signatures.

To enable a more efficient protocol with full advantage of packing and to avoid interaction, we introduce the following technique. We share the long-term secret key in a packed vector $(s, \ldots, s)$ instead of just the single scalar s. This enables SIMD generation of the partial signature, with each party using only a local multiplication (without degree reduction), with randomization done locally as well. Using this technique, signature generation becomes non-interactive: The only communication required is for the party to broadcast their partial signature, after which anyone can assemble the signatures themselves. The cost is a reduction in the resilience to $t < (n - 2a + 2)/3$. See Sect. 2.6 for details.

Refreshing Packed Secrets. In the dynamic/proactive setting, we need to refresh the sharing of the packed vector $(s, \ldots, s)$. This requires a generalization to the GRR protocol [17], see Sect. 2.7 and our full version [4, Appendix I]. We remark that in the current version of the writeup we only prove security of the static protocol. The proof for the dynamic/proactive protocol should be a fairly straightforward extension, using the same techniques. See a brief discussion in our full version [4, Appendix G.7].

Security of Distributed Parallel Schnorr Signatures. The starting point for our protocol is similar (though not quite identical) to the GJKR distributed Schnorr signature protocol from [16], which we extend and optimize to sign many messages. However, GJKR-like protocols [16] are known to fail in the concurrent setting where the protocol is run in parallel for multiple messages; specifically, such protocols are open to ROS-type attacks [5,11]. Our work focuses on signing a given set of messages (a batch) in parallel. To enable this parallelism and avoid ROS-type attacks, we use a mitigation technique similar to prior work (e.g., [20,27]). As far as we know, prior to our work this specific technique was only analyzed in the generic group model for ECDSA signatures [20]. In our case, we show it is sufficient for proving the security of our protocols (for signing a single batch of messages) via reduction to the hardness of the discrete logarithm problem in the programmable random-oracle model. See Sect. 2.3 and our full version [4, Appendix G]. These techniques do not guarantee concurrent security for signing multiple batches in parallel. For this, Shoup [36] shows that technique from FROST can be combined with our protocols to obtain full concurrent security (see detailed discussion on this in Sect. 1.3).

Robust Threshold Signatures. Our protocols provide robustness in a strong sense. They terminate with signatures for all $a(n - 2t)$ input messages as soon as $t + 2a - 2$ honest parties output their shares. Invalid shares can be identified based on public information and discarded. This holds in both synchronous and asynchronous networks. In the former case, after two rounds of broadcast for generating ephemeral randomness, parties generate *non-interactively* the shares from which all signatures are recovered.

Smaller Sub-sampled Committees Using a Beacon. To use our protocols in massive systems with a huge number of nodes, one needs some mechanism to sub-sample the committees from among all the nodes in the system. One natural approach is to use self-selection via verifiable random functions (VRFs), as done, e.g., in [7]. However, this results in somewhat loose tail bounds and thus somewhat-too-big committees.

Instead, we note that we can get smaller committees by using a randomness beacon to implement the sub-sampling, resulting in better bounds and smaller committees. Thus, when acting in this large dynamic committee settings, we augment the signature protocol to implement this beacon, which turns out to be almost for free in our case. See Sect. 2.8 for more details. See also our full version [4, Appendix A] for an additional optimization in this setting: using smaller optimistic parameters by default with a safe fallback mechanism to pessimistic parameters.

1.2   Prior Work

Recent years saw a lot of activity trying to improve the efficiency of threshold signature schemes, including underlying techniques such as verifiable secret sharing (VSS) and distributed key generation (DKG), much of which focused on asynchronous protocols and some emphasizing robustness (guaranteed output delivery). Below we focus on some of the more recent works on these subjects.

Threshold Signatures. Komlo and Goldberg described FROST [27], a non-robust threshold Schnorr signature protocol that requires a single-round signing protocol after a single-round preprocessing phase. The improved round complexity comes at the expense of robustness, as it uses additive sharings and requires correct participation of all prescribed signers. In our case, we use two rounds of interaction in a message-independent phase but can then generate multiple signatures non-interactively and with guaranteed output delivery. Our schemes are designed to work in an asynchronous regime hence requiring a super-majority of honest parties (see details in our full version [4, Appendix H]).

ROAST [35] presents a wrapper technique that can transform concurrently secure non-robust threshold signature schemes with a single signing round and identifiable abort into a protocol with the same properties but also robust in the asynchronous model. In particular, this applies to the FROST protocol resulting in a scheme with concurrent security for any threshold $t < n$ and optimal robustness for up to $n - t$ parties. The price for this strengthening is significant: it involves $O(tn^2 + tn\lambda)$ per-signature transmitted bits (λ is a security parameter) assuming a trusted coordinator and $O(tn^3 + tn^2\lambda)$ without the coordinator; whereas we only require $O(\lambda)$ broadcasted bits (strictly better even when considering a quadratic overhead of the underlying broadcast).

Garillot et al. [15] implement a threshold Schnorr signature based on deterministic signing, e.g., EdDSA, in order to avoid the potential risks of randomness reuse. They present a dishonest-majority non-robust scheme using zero-knowledge proof and garbling techniques that, while optimized for this specific application, is much more expensive than protocols that do not offer deterministic signing (like FROST and our SPRINT protocols).

Lindell [28] presents a threshold Schnorr signature scheme proven under standard assumptions in the UC model. The focus of that work was conceptual simplicity and UC security rather than optimal efficiency. As in FROST, it utilizes additive sharing, hence necessitating the choice of a new set of signers when a chosen set fails to generate a signature.

For ECDSA signatures, Groth and Shoup [19] recently described a rather efficient ECDSA signing protocol, with emphasis on guaranteed output delivery over asynchronous channels. (The underlying VSS in their work achieves completeness, which is not needed in our case.) They use verifiable complaints in order to notify other parties that they do not have a share. These complaints trigger a complex protocol, by which honest shareholders help each other to get all their missing shares.

Joshi et al. [25] address the lack of concurrent security in the basic threshold Schnorr scheme from [16] by running two DKG executions per signature and using a mitigation technique similar to the one we use here to bind a batch of messages to be signed. However, while our solution generates multiple signatures with a single DKG run, theirs requires two such runs per single signed message.

Distributed Randomness Generation (DKG). [6] As we said, a key distinction between our work and previous DKG protocols in the signature setting [1,30,38], is that we *do not require complete sharing* (where all honest parties must receive their shares). While completeness may be desired in traditional MPC applications, eschewing this requirement is not a weakness but a feature in our case, as it enables more efficient signature protocols.

Neji et al. [30] design a DKG intended to avoid the need to reveal the shares of inactive (or slow) shareholders for disqualification as required in the GJKR [16] solution. However, they do so by requiring additional rounds of interaction and significant extra computational cost, namely the party who gets complained does $O(n)$ group additions and each other party does $O(t)$ scalar multiplications where t is the corruption threshold (these costs are merely for handling complaints beyond the verification). We achieve higher performance by using publicly verifiable complaints: in our protocols, each party can verify that a complaint is valid by doing a constant number of group operations and without any additional interaction.

Yurek et al. [38] described a randomness generation protocol over asynchronous communication channels, in the context of the offline phase of generic secure MPC. They provide completeness for secret sharing needed for their MPC applications. As in a recent work by Groth and Shoup [19], they use verifiable complaints, yet unlike our work, they do not disqualify dealers upon a verifiable complaint—they instead complete the set of shares. Their asynchronous VSS has an amortized network bandwidth $O(n \log n)$ in the optimistic case and $O(n^2 \log n)$ in the pessimistic case.

Abraham et al. describe Bingo [1], a packed method for asynchronous secret sharing that allows a dealer to generate many sharings at an amortized communication cost of $O(\lambda n)$ per secret. This solution requires KZG-style polynomial commitments [26] to get completeness (and thus relies on pairing-friendly groups). Specifically, the dealer performs a KZG commitment to a polynomial of degree $2t$ (where $n = 3t + 1$), which concretely is slightly more expensive than our protocol. Also, our agreement sub-protocol makes a more direct usage of the underlying broadcast channel than the agreement in Bingo, and is more efficient.

Various other papers (e.g., [9,10]) deal with the question of asynchronous DKG. However, they do not directly relate to our paper as the main thrust of their work is reaching an agreement in the asynchronous setting. In contrast, we assume an underlying broadcast channel, simplifying the agreement significantly.

---

[6] Recall we use DKG to refer to distributed key generation for long-term keys, for generating ephemeral randomness as needed in Schnorr signatures, and also for proactive refreshment.

1.3 Subsequent Work

There have been several papers published after our paper was first made public.

Shoup's Many Faces of Schnorr. In [36], Shoup presents a unifying framework for obtaining robust concurrently-secure threshold Schnorr signatures combining techniques from our work and FROST [29]. This framework applies to two-phase protocols, like ours, consisting of an offline phase for generating "presignatures" (a.k.a., ephemeral randomness), and then an online phase for generating signatures from those presignatures. The concurrent-security aspect of these protocols means that many copies of the online phase can be run concurrently, as long as sufficiently many unused presignatures are available. Shoup shows that concurrent security can be added to any protocol within this framework (including ours) in one of two ways: either using two fresh DKG-generated secret sharing of ephemeral randomness à-la-FROST (thus doubling the cost), or using a randomness beacon (which adds rounds of communication).

Groth-Shoup Asynchronous Robust DKG. In [21], Groth and Shoup present an asynchronous robust DKG protocol which can be used as a basis for a threshold signature protocol, that require a total of $O(n\lambda)$ bits of point-to-point communication per signature over the optimistic path (roughly when all parties behave honestly), amortized over $O(n^2)$ signatures. The optimistic path communication complexity matches (asymptotically) our communication complexity of $O(\lambda)$ bits broadcast per signature.[7]

However, the Groth-Shoup protocol is a lot less efficient on the pessimistic path, when parties misbehave: Its communication complexity increases by a factor $O(t')$ where t' is the number of actual misbehaving parties. In contrast, the communication complexity of our protocol increases by at most a small constant factor, no matter how many parties misbehave (as long as there are at most t of them). On the other hand, the Groth-Shoup protocol can withstand up to $(n-1)/3$ misbehaving parties, compared to our $t \leq (n - 2a + 1)/3$. Our protocol is therefore a better choice in the large-committee setting, where consistent performance also on the pessimistic path is important, and where it is reasonable to assume a larger honest majority. The Groth-Shoup protocol may be better in the small-committee setting, where higher resilience is more important and assuming the optimistic path makes more sense.

The main difference between our protocol and Groth-Shoup stems from the fact that the latter requires complete secret sharing, where all the honest parties get their shares. In particular, if a dealer misbehaves and does not appropriately distribute shares to some honest parties, these honest parties need other honest parties to help them reconstruct their shares, whereas our protocol just disqualifies that dealer. On the other hand, the Groth-Shoup protocol uses complete secret sharing to eliminate the need for polynomial commitments in the

---

[7] Broadcasting messages of size $\ell \geq n\lambda$ bits, as done in our protocol, can be achieved using a total point-to-point communication of $O(\ell n)$ bits [14,29].

sharing phase. Instead, they use error correction to reconstruct signature shares at the end of the protocol without having to check validity against some public commitment.

Another difference is that [21] uses a construction based on Pascal triangle for super-invertible matrices, which is better than the small Vandermonde construction (see details in [4, Appendix B]). This way, they reduce the cost of evaluating the product by the super-invertible matrix from $\approx (b-1)n \log n / \log p$ scalar-element products in that solution to $\approx b(n-(b+1)/2)+1$ group additions (which correspond to about $(b(n-(b+1)/2)+1)/(1.5 \log p)$ scalar-element products). Our proposal to use the ECFFT-EXTEND algorithm (see Sect. 2.4) is more efficient asymptotically ($O(k \log k)$ scalar-element products, for $k = \max(b, n-b)$) but the Pascal solution would most likely perform better up to $n \approx 8000$.

1.4 Organization

The rest of this manuscript is organized as follows: In Sect. 2, we provide a high-level step-by-step overview of our protocols and the various components that are used in them. In Sect. 3, we describe in more detail our high-level protocol for the static (fixed-committee) and dynamic settings. In Sect. 4, we describe the basic agreement protocol that we use in the static-committee setting, the agreement in the dynamic setting can be found in our full version [4, Appendix E]. Security proofs and additional details are deferred to appendices. In particular, in the full version [4, Appendix D], we discuss how to use SPRINT in one of our motivating applications to implement a large-scale signature service over a public blockchain.

2 Technical Overview

We consider a static setting where the set of parties (a shareholder committee) is fixed and a dynamic one where shareholder committees change over time while keeping the system's signing key (in particular, its public verification key) unchanged. In the latter case, shares are refreshed and proactivized between committees. We begin by describing our protocols in the static committee setting, and discuss only towards the end the extra components for the dynamic/proactive settings. The basic protocols for these two settings are shown in Figs. 1 and 2.

In the static case, we have a committee that holds shares of the long-term secret key s, shared via a degree-d polynomial $\mathbf{F}(X)$ with party i holding $\sigma_i = \mathbf{F}(i)$ (for some degree d that we determine later) and where $s = \mathbf{F}(0)$. They first run a distributed key-generation (DKG) protocol to generate a sharing of ephemeral randomness, then use their shares of the long-term secret and ephemeral randomness to generate Schnorr-type signatures on messages. The DKG and signature protocols can be pipelined, where the committee uses the randomness that was received in the previous run to sign messages, and at the same time prepares the randomness for the next run.

While the static setting features just a single committee, we still often refer to parties as *dealers* when they share secrets to others, and as *shareholders* when they receive those shares. In the dynamic setting, these will indeed be different parties, but in the static case, they may be the same.

Notations. We use Greek letters (e.g., σ, ρ, π, ϕ) and lowercase English letters (e.g., e, r, s) to denote scalars in $\mathbb{Z}_p$, and also use some English lowercase letters to denote indexes (i, j, k, ℓ, u, v) and parameters (a, b, n, t). We denote the set of integers from x to y (inclusive) by $[x, y]$, and also denote $[x] = [1, x]$. We rely on a group of prime order p generated by G. We use the additive notation for this group. Group elements are denoted by uppercase English letters $(G, S, R, \text{etc.})$. Polynomials are denoted by bold Uppercase English letters $(\mathbf{F}, \mathbf{H}, \mathbf{I}, \mathbf{Y}, \mathbf{Z})$, and commitments to them are sometimes denoted with a hat $(\hat{\mathbf{F}}, \hat{\mathbf{H}})$.

2.1   Starting Point: The GJKR Protocol

Our starting point is the protocol of Gennaro et al. [16] for distributed key generation (DKG), and a variation on their use of that protocol for Schnorr signatures. In their DKG protocol, each dealer uses Verifiable Secret Sharing (VSS) to share a random value; parties then add all the shares from dealers that shared their values correctly (thus requiring an agreement protocol on which dealers fall in this set, denoted QUAL). Specifically, each dealer D_i shares a random ephemeral secret (which is later used to compute ephemeral randomness and partial signatures) using a degree-d' polynomial $\mathbf{H}_i$ (for some degree d' that we define later), and commits publicly to this polynomial. Concretely, D_i shares the random ephemeral secret $\mathbf{H}_i(0)$ by sending shares $\mathbf{H}_j(i)$ to each shareholder P_i.

The shareholders then agree on a set QUAL of "qualified dealers" whose values will be used, and a corresponding shareholder set HOLD that were able to receive valid shares. Shareholders in HOLD can compute shares for the ephemeral secrets from the shares that they received from these qualified dealers. Namely, each shareholder can add the shares (i.e., the Shamir shares of ephemeral secrets of dealers) that they received from dealers in QUAL, and the resulting ephemeral secret is shared via the polynomial $\mathbf{H} = \sum_{i \in \mathsf{QUAL}} \mathbf{H}_i$.

In our protocol, shareholders use their shares on polynomials $\mathbf{H}$ (the ephemeral secret) and $\mathbf{F}$ (the long-term secret) to compute Shamir shares of the signatures, and then reconstruct the signatures themselves. We note that this is somewhat different from the signature protocol in [16]: there, it is the dealers in QUAL that generate the signature (and HOLD is only used as a backup to reconstruct the input of misbehaving dealers), whereas we let the shareholders in HOLD generate the signature directly. Our variant could be more round-efficient in some cases, and is easier to deploy in a proactive setting where the long-term key is shared using Shamir sharing (as opposed to additive sharing as used in the GJKR protocol). But otherwise these protocols are very similar.

Pedersen vs. Feldman Commitments. It was pointed out by Gennaro et al. [16] that sharing randomness usually requires the dealers to commit to their sharing polynomials using statistically-hiding commitments such as Pedersen's

[33]. Using the less expensive Feldman secret sharing, where dealers commit to coefficients h_{ij} of their polynomials by broadcasting the group elements $h_{ij} \cdot G$, are susceptible to rushing attacks in the DKG setting. Luckily, Gennaro et al. prove in [16, Sec 5] that for the purpose of generating the ephemeral randomness for Schnorr signatures, it is safe to use Feldman secret-sharing, and their proof techniques extend to our signature protocol as well.

We note that for efficiency reasons, in our protocols we use commitments to the value of the polynomials at certain evaluation points rather than to the coefficients as done in [16] (see details in [4, Appendix A]).

2.2   The Agreement Protocol

We utilize the QUAL-agreement protocol in two different settings: for generation of ephemeral randomness (in both the static and dynamic setting), and for re-sharing of the long-term key (in the dynamic setting only). We observe that randomness generation is less demanding of the agreement protocol than key-refresh: For key-refresh we need the shareholders to have shares from at least $d + 1$ dealers (d is the degree of the sharing polynomials), whereas randomness generation can work even with a single honest dealer. Therefore, in the static setting we use a weaker (and more efficient) agreement protocol than in the dynamic setting. Both protocols use PKI, and both operate over a total-order (aka atomic) broadcast channel, providing eventual delivery of messages from honest parties, sender authentication, and prefix consistency (i.e., the views of any two honest parties are such that one is a prefix of the other).

We start with the more efficient (but weaker) protocol for the static setting. The protocol begins with the dealers distributing their shares, and then the shareholders engage in a protocol to agree on sets of "qualified" and "bad" dealers QUAL, BAD, and a set of shareholders HOLD. We want the following properties: (i) every shareholder in HOLD received valid shares from every dealer in QUAL, and (ii) BAD consists entirely of dishonest dealers. This protocol is parameterized by d_0, d_1 (to be defined later as a function of the number of corrupt parties and some additional parameters), and it ensures that $|\mathsf{HOLD}| \geq d_0$ and $|\mathsf{QUAL}| + |\mathsf{BAD}| \geq d_1$.

In more detail, each dealer D_i broadcasts all the shares that it deals, encrypted under the keys of their intended recipients, together with commitments to the sharing polynomial $\mathbf{H}_i$. As this information is visible to all, shareholders that receive shares that are inconsistent with the commitments can broadcast a *verifiable complaint* against a dealer, consisting of a proof that the dealer has sent them a bad share.

The shareholders initially set QUAL to the first d_1 dealers whose messages appeared on the broadcast channel. Then each shareholder broadcasts verifiable complaints if they have any, and otherwise they broadcast the empty set (signifying that they have all the shares from dealers in QUAL). Now, QUAL contracts by eliminating all the dealers who have a valid verifiable complaint against them on the broadcast channel, moving them to the set BAD. The set HOLD is fixed to the first d_0 shareholders who broadcast verifiable complaints (or the empty set) that were verified as valid complaints. By construction, we have $|\mathsf{HOLD}| \geq d_0$ and $|\mathsf{QUAL}| + |\mathsf{BAD}| \geq d_1$, and the set BAD contains only (verifiably) dishonest dealers. Also, since $\mathsf{QUAL}, \mathsf{BAD}$, and HOLD are determined by what is visible on the broadcast channel, then all honest shareholders that read up to some point in the channel will agree on these sets. This protocol's specification can be found in Fig. 3, and the proof is provided in Theorem 4.1.

In the dynamic setting (that includes also key-refresh), we need to ensure $|\mathsf{QUAL}| \geq d_1$ (as opposed to just $|\mathsf{QUAL}| + |\mathsf{BAD}| \geq d_1$). To that end, we run iterations of the basic protocol above. At the beginning of the $i+1$'st iteration, we add to QUAL as many new dealers as the number of dealers that were added to BAD in the i'th iteration. Once no more dealers are added to BAD, we have $|\mathsf{QUAL}| \geq d_1$, and we are done. A full specification is in our full version [4, Appendix E].

2.3   Signing Many Messages in Parallel

Our large-scale signature service needs to handle signing many messages in parallel, which brings up a security problem: The proof of security from [16, Sec 5] when using Feldman commitments for Schnorr signatures, requires that the reduction algorithm makes a guess about which random oracle query the adversary intends to use for the signature. When signing many messages in parallel, the reduction will need to guess one random-oracle query per message, leading to exponential security loss. Moreover, Benhamouda et al. demonstrated in [5] that this is not just a problem with the reduction, indeed this protocol is vulnerable to an actual forgery attack when many messages are signed in parallel. To fix this problem, we use a mitigation technique somewhat similar to [20,27], where the ephemeral secrets are all "shifted" by a public random value δ, which is only determined after all the messages and commitments are known.

As recalled in the introduction, a Schnorr signature on a message M^v relative to secret key s and public key $S = s \cdot G$, has the form $(R^v, r^v + e^v \cdot s)$, where r^v is an ephemeral random secret, $R^v = r^v \cdot G$, and $e^v = \mathsf{Hash}(S, R^v, M^v)$, where Hash maps arbitrary strings into $\mathbb{Z}_p$. (We are using a superscript v to indicate a plurality of messages and their respective signatures.) In our context, we first run DKG to generate all the required r^v's and corresponding R^v's, and get from the calling application all the messages M^v's to be signed. Then we compute $\delta = \mathsf{Hash}(S, (R^1, M^1), (R^2, M^2), \ldots)$ and $\Delta = \delta \cdot G$. The signature on M^v is then set as $(R^v + \Delta, r^v + \delta + e^v \cdot s)$, where $e^v = \mathsf{Hash}(S, R^v + \Delta, M^v)$.

With this mitigation technique, the reduction only needs to guess the random-oracle query in which δ is computed, recovering the argument from [16, Sec 5] and reducing security to the hardness of computing discrete logarithms in the random-oracle model. See our full version [4, Appendix G.3]. We note that our specific mitigation techniques provide security for *a single run of the protocol* on input a set of multiple messages to be signed, but it does not imply concurrent security for multiple parallel runs of the protocol on different sets of messages. Following [36], we can obtain concurrent security by either adopting the FROST mitigation (that requires doubling the DKG cost) or by relying on a beacon (which would add one broadcast round).

2.4 Using Super-Invertible Matrices

As described so far, we would need to run a separate copy of the DKG protocol to generate each ephemeral secret r^v, but we can do much better. For starters, assume that we can ensure many honest dealers in the set QUAL (say at least b of them). Then we can use a (public) super-invertible matrix [24] to generate b random ephemeral values in each run of the protocol.

Recall that the DKG protocol has each dealer D_i share a random polynomial $\mathbf{H}_i$, then the shareholders compute a single random polynomial $\mathbf{H}' = \sum_{i \in \text{QUAL}} \mathbf{H}_i$ and the ephemeral random secret is $\mathbf{H}'(0)$. Intuitively, the polynomial $\mathbf{H}'$ is random if even a single $\mathbf{H}_i$ is random, so a single honest dealer in QUAL is enough to get a random ephemeral value. But if we have many honest dealers in QUAL, then we can get many random polynomials. Specifically, suppose we have b honest dealers in QUAL and let $\Psi = [\psi_i^u]$ be a b-by-n super-invertible matrix, i.e., each b-by-b sub-matrix of Ψ is invertible. Then we still have each dealer D_i share just a single polynomial $\mathbf{H}_i$, but now the shareholders can construct b random polynomials $\mathbf{H}^1, \ldots, \mathbf{H}^b$, by setting $\mathbf{H}^u = \sum_{i \in \text{QUAL}} \psi_i^u \mathbf{H}_i$ for all $u \in [b]$. By the same reasoning as before, if we have b honest dealers in QUAL with random input polynomials $\mathbf{H}_i$, then the b output polynomials will also be random and independent since the b-by-b matrix corresponding to the rows of these b honest dealers is invertible.

The actual proof is more involved since we still use Feldman commitments in the protocol, which means that a rushing adversary can bias the output polynomials somewhat. But using essentially the same reduction as before, we can still reduce the security of the Schnorr signature protocol to the hardness of computing discrete logarithms in the random oracle model. One technical point is that the security proof in the asynchronous communication model requires that the set QUAL is included in the hash function query that determines δ. That is, we compute $\delta = \mathsf{Hash}(S, \text{QUAL}, (R^1, M^1), (R^2, M^2), \ldots)$. The reason is that in the asynchronous case, we cannot guarantee that all honest dealers will be included in QUAL. If we didn't include it in the hash query, then the simulator would have to guess the set QUAL, incurring at least an $\binom{n}{b}$ loss factor in security.

We note that to ensure b honest dealers in QUAL, it is enough to run the "weaker" agreement protocol (Fig. 3) with $d_1 = b + t$, where t is an upper bound on the number of dishonest dealers. Indeed, that protocol ensures that $|\text{QUAL}| + |\text{BAD}| \geq d_1 = b + t$, and BAD contains only dishonest dealers. Therefore, the number of dishonest dealers in QUAL is at most $t - |\text{BAD}|$, and the number of honest dealers is at least $|\text{QUAL}| - (t - |\text{BAD}|) = |\text{QUAL}| + |\text{BAD}| - t = d_1 - t = b$.

Faster Multiplication by a Super-Invertible Matrix. While the use of super-invertible matrices enables us to produce many more random shared secrets without increasing bandwidth, computing all these sharings requires that each shareholder multiply their sub-shares by that super-invertible matrix "in the exponent".[8] The super-invertible matrix multiplication is the most computa-

---

[8] We use additive notation for group operations, but sometimes use the traditional exponentiation terminology.

tionally intensive operation in the protocol. We thus should carefully implement the matrix multiplication to have good computational efficiency in practice.

We propose two solutions to make these operations more efficient. The first solution, pointed out to us by Victor Shoup, is to use a Vandermonde matrix Ψ corresponding to the powers of small scalars. We show in our full version [4, Appendix B.1], that a variant of the Horner's rule allows to evaluate the multiply-by-Ψ operation using $(b-1)n$ scalar-by-element products with $\log n$-bit scalars (instead of full-length scalars, that is $\log p$-bit scalars). This is equivalent to about $(b-1)n \log n / \log p$ full scalar-by-element product, that is a $\log n / \log p$ speed-up over the naive solution. In practice, p has at least 256 bits, while $n = b+t$ varies but is unlikely to be higher than 10 bits, so this is a more than 25× speed-up.

Our second solution is new and consists of selecting Ψ so that it corresponds to FFT-related operations. However, when implementing Schnorr signatures over the elliptic curve ED25519, the scalar field $\mathbb{Z}_p$ does not even have a 2^3-th root of unity.[9] Instead, we show that we can use the ECFFT-EXTEND algorithm from Ben-Sasson et al. [3], resulting in $O(k \log k)$ scalar-by-element products, where $k = \max(b,t)$ and $n = b+t$. This is asymptotically better than the first solution. Details are provided in the full version [4, Appendix B.2].

We implemented both solutions, benchmarked them, and report results in [4, Appendix B.3]. In short, for ED25519, when $b = t$ is a power of 2, the small Vandermonde matrix solution is better in practice for up to $b = t = 2^8 = 256$, after which the ECFFT solution is more efficient.[10] The benchmarking code is available from https://github.com/fabrice102/ecfft-group, under the MIT license. This code is based on the code [6] and adapts it to work with polynomials with coefficients in a group, instead of in the base field.

2.5   Using Packed Secret Sharing

Similarly to above, we can also assume many honest parties among the set HOLD of shareholders, and use packed secret sharing [13] to get even more ephemeral shared values: If HOLD contains at least $2t + a$ shareholders (for some $a \geq 1$), then we can let each shared polynomial pack a values rather than just one: Each shared polynomial $\mathbf{H}^u$ will have degree $d' \geq t + a - 1$ (rather than $d' = t$) and will encode the a values $\mathbf{H}^u(0), \mathbf{H}^u(-1), \ldots, \mathbf{H}^u(-a+1)$. (Below we denote these scalar values by $r^{u,v} = \mathbf{H}^u(1-v)$, with the corresponding group elements $R^{u,v} = r^{u,v} \cdot G$.)

Importantly, this amplifies the effect of using super-invertible matrices: We have each dealer D_i sharing a single random polynomial $\mathbf{H}_i$ of degree d', packing a values, and we derive b random degree-d' polynomials $\mathbf{H}^u$ from these sharings, which gives us $a \cdot b$ shared random scalars.

---

[9] $p = 2^{252} + 27742317777372353535851937790883648493$ and the factorization of $p-1$ is $2^2 \times 3 \times 11 \times 198211423230930754013084525763697 \times 276602624281642239937218\allowbreak 680557139826668747$.

[10] The ECFFT solution performs better for $b = t$ is a power of two. But we show in the full version [4, Appendix B.2] that it also works for general b and t, with a cost depending on the smallest power of 2 larger or equal to $\max(b,t)$.

2.6 More Efficient Signing

Once the ephemeral secrets are shared, we use them—together with the shared long-term secret key—to generate many signatures. Computing on the packed ephemeral secrets would generically require a full-blown secure-MPC protocol among the shareholders, but we observe that we can generate all the a signatures from each packed random polynomial with only a single share-reconstruction operation.

To see how, recall again that a Schnorr-type signature has the form $(R^v, r^v + e^v \cdot s)$.[11] Our shareholders hold Shamir sharings of the secret key s and the vector $(r^1, r^2, \ldots, r^a)$ of ephemeral secrets (where $r^v = \mathbf{H}(1 - v)$ for $v \in [a]$). Also, the public key S, the messages M^v's, and the group elements R^v's are publicly known, so everyone can compute all the scalars $e^v = \mathsf{Hash}(S, R^v, M^v)$. To improve efficiency, we also share the long-term key s in a packed form, namely the shareholders hold a Shamir sharing of the vector $(s, s, \ldots, s)$, via a polynomial $\mathbf{F}$ of degree $d = t + a - 1$ (i.e., $\mathbf{F}(1 - v) = s$ for $v \in [a]$). All they need to do, therefore, is compute the pointwise linear function $(r^1, r^2, \ldots, r^a) + (e^1, e^2, \ldots, e^a) \odot (s, s, \ldots, s)$.

While pointwise addition can be computed locally, computing the pointwise product $(e^1, e^2, \ldots, e^a) \odot (s, s, \ldots, s)$ seems like still requiring a nontrivial interactive protocol, even for a known vector of e^v's. But we can eliminate even this little interaction, by assuming a larger honest majority and using higher-degree polynomials for the ephemeral randomness. Specifically, we assume that HOLD contains at least $2t + 2a - 1$ shareholders (so at least $t + 2a - 1$ honest ones), and modify the DKG protocol so that the sharing of the ephemeral secrets is done with random polynomials of degree $d' = d + a - 1 = t + 2a - 2$ (rather than degree $t + a - 1$).

Since the e^v's are known, each shareholder can interpolate the unique degree-$(a - 1)$ polynomial that packs the vector $(e^1, \ldots, e^a)$. Denote this polynomial as $\mathbf{Z}$ (we have $\mathbf{Z}(1 - v) = e^v$ for $v \in [a]$). Then each shareholder j with a share $\sigma_j = \mathbf{F}(j)$ for the long-term secret, can *locally* compute $\sigma'_j = \mathbf{Z}(j) \cdot \sigma_j$. Note now that the σ'_j's lie on the polynomial $\mathbf{Z} \cdot \mathbf{F}$ of degree $d + a - 1$ that packs the vector $(e^1 \cdot s, \ldots, e^a \cdot s)$, since $(\mathbf{Z} \cdot \mathbf{F})(1 - v) = e^v \cdot s$ for $v \in [a]$.

Each shareholder j, with share ρ_j on an ephemeral-randomness polynomial, computes and broadcasts $\pi_j = \sigma'_j + \rho_j$, and we note that these π_j's lie on a polynomial of degree d' that packs all the values $(r^1 + e^1 s, \ldots, r^a + e^a s)$. Moreover, if the ephemeral secrets were shared via a *random* degree-d' polynomial, then the π_j's constitute *a random sharing* of that vector. After seeing $d' + 1 = t + 2a - 1$ valid shares of these broadcast values, everyone can reconstruct the polynomial and read out all the scalars $\phi^v = r^v + e^v \cdot s$ that are needed for these a signatures.

2.7 The Dynamic Setting

So far, we have described our protocols for the static (fixed committee) setting. Here we present the additional components that we need in the dynamic case,

---

[11] We suppress here the index u, which is irrelevant for this discussion.

where we have different committees for the dealers and shareholders. Importantly, in all the protocols above we never assumed that the dealers and shareholders are the same committee, so they all still work as-is also in the dynamic setting. What is missing is a share-refresh protocol where the dealers can pass to the shareholders a sharing of the long-term secret s. Here we essentially just use the GRR protocols of Gennaro et al. from [17], with a minor adaptation since we need to share it in a packed manner.[12]

Each dealer D_i begins with a share σ_i of the long-term secret key s, shared using a "packed" polynomial $\mathbf{F}(X)$ of degree $d = t+a-1$. Namely, $\sigma_i = \mathbf{F}(i)$, and $\mathbf{F}(0) = \mathbf{F}(-1) = \cdots = \mathbf{F}(1-a) = s$. In addition, everyone knows a commitment to $\mathbf{F}$. D_i reshares its share using a fresh random degree-d polynomial $\mathbf{F}_i$ with $\mathbf{F}_i(0) = \mathbf{F}_i(-1) = \cdots = \mathbf{F}_i(1-a) = \sigma_i$, and also commits publicly to $\mathbf{F}_i$.

This is done in parallel to the sharing of the random, degree-d', polynomial $\mathbf{H}_i$. The shareholders then engage in an agreement protocol (full protocol description can be found in [4, Appendix E]) to determine the sets HOLD of shareholders, $\text{QUAL}_1, \text{BAD}_1$ for the $\mathbf{H}$ dealers, and $\text{QUAL}_2, \text{BAD}_2$ for the $\mathbf{F}$ dealers, with $|\text{HOLD}| \geq n - t$, $|\text{QUAL}_1| \geq n - t$, and $|\text{QUAL}_2| \geq d + 1$.[13] Having received $\sigma_{ij} = \mathbf{F}_i(j)$ from each dealer $D_i \in \text{QUAL}_2$, P_j then computes their share of the long-term secret as $\sigma'_j = \sum_{i \in \text{QUAL}_2} \lambda_i \sigma_{ij}$. The λ_i's are the Lagrange coefficients for recovering $Q(0)$ from $\{Q(i) : i \in \text{QUAL}_2\}$ for degree-d polynomials Q. As usual, denoting $\mathbf{F}' = \sum_{i \in \text{QUAL}_2} \lambda_i \mathbf{F}_i$, the shares of shareholders in HOLD satisfy $\sigma'_j = \mathbf{F}'(j)$, and also

$$\mathbf{F}'(0) = \sum_{i \in \text{QUAL}_2} \lambda_i \mathbf{F}_i(0) = \sum_{i \in \text{QUAL}_2} \lambda_i \mathbf{F}(i) = \mathbf{F}(0).$$

Moreover, since all the $\mathbf{F}_i$'s satisfy $\mathbf{F}_i(0) = \mathbf{F}_i(-1) = \cdots = \mathbf{F}_i(1-a)$, then so does $\mathbf{F}'$.

2.8 Sub-sampling the Committees

One of the main use cases for our protocol is an open system (such as a public blockchain), which could be very large. In this use case, the committees in each epoch must be sub-sampled from the entire population, and be large enough to ensure a sufficiently large honest majority with overwhelming probability.

One way of implementing this sub-sampling would be to use verifiable random functions (VRFs), but this would result in rather loose tail bounds and large committees. We can get smaller committees by having the committees implement also a randomness beacon, outputting a (pseudo)random value that the adversary cannot influence at the end of each run of the protocol. At the

---

[12] As described here, the protocol only works for resharing a packed vector of the form $(s, s, \ldots, s)$. But it is not very hard to extend it to reshare arbitrary packed vectors (using somewhat higher-degree polynomials), see the full version [4, Appendix I].

[13] Recall that in the dynamic setting we use an agreement protocol that provides stronger guarantees about the size of QUAL, than in the static setting. Namely $|\text{QUAL}| \geq d_1$ instead of just $|\text{QUAL}| + |\text{BAD}| \geq d_1$. See Sect. 2.2.

beginning of the $T + 1$'st protocol, everyone therefore knows the value U_T that was produced by the beacon in the T'th run. Members of the $T + 1$'st committee determine the members of the $T + 2$'nd committee by applying a PRG on U_T.

To see why this helps, note that when the total population is very large, the number of honest parties in a committee chosen by VRFs is approximated by a Poisson random variable with parameter $\lambda = (1 - f)n$, where f is the fraction of faulty parties in the overall population (and n is the expected committee size). On the other hand, the number of honest parties in a committee when using the randomness beacon follows a Binomial distribution with parameters $n, p = 1 - f$. The Binomial turns out to be much more concentrated than the Poisson, hence the number of honest parties is much closer to $(1 - f)n$ with the beacon than with the VRF.

Implementing the randomness beacon for our protocol turns out to be very easy. Since the T'th committee held a sharing of the long-term secret scalar s, they could locally compute a "sharing in the exponent" of $s \cdot \mathsf{Hash}'(T)$ (with Hash' hashing into the group). Namely, everyone computes the group element $E = \mathsf{Hash}'(T)$, then each dealer D_i in the T'th committee with share σ_i can compute and broadcast $U_{T,i} = \sigma_i \cdot E$, together with a Fiat-Shamir zero-knowledge proof that $U_{T,i}$ is consistent with the (public) Feldman commitment of σ_i (which is a proof of equality of discrete logarithms).[14] Once the qualified set QUAL_2 is determined, everyone can interpolate "in the exponent" and compute $U_T = \sum_{i \in \mathsf{QUAL}'} \lambda_i \cdot U_{T,i} = s \cdot E$, where the λ_i's are the Lagrange interpolation coefficients. The group element U_T is the next output of the beacon. Note that the adversary has no influence over the U_T's, they are always set as $U_T = s \cdot \mathsf{Hash}'(T)$. On the other hand, before the shares $U_{T,i}$ are broadcast, the value U_T is unpredictable (indeed pseudorandom) from the adversary's point of view.

2.9   More Optimizations

While quite efficient as-is, in many settings there are additional optimizations that can significantly improve the performance of our protocols, such as committing to evaluation points (rather than coefficients) and using optimistic parameters with safe fallback when sub-sampling committees (See details in [4, Appendix A]). Also, in the full version [4, Appendix H] we discuss the dishonest majority case for a mixed malicious/semi-honest adversary model.

2.10   Parameters and Performance

Various parameters and performance analysis are provided in the full version [4, Appendix C], here we give a very brief overview.

To get enough honest parties in HOLD, we need to have $n \geq 3t + 2a - 1$, and we often assume that this holds with equality. Then we set $d_1 = |\mathsf{QUAL}| = n - t$

---

[14] More precisely, there is a public commitment $\hat{\mathbf{F}}$ of $\mathbf{F}$ from which anyone can derive a Feldman commitment $\sigma_i \cdot G$ of σ_i. See Sect. 2.1.

and get $b = n - 2t$, hence we can get as many as $ab = a(n - 2t)$ signatures for each run of the protocol. Some example numbers are $n = 10, t = 2, a = 2, b = 6$ (12 signatures per run), or $n = 64, t = 15, a = 10, b = 34$ (340 signatures per run). In the setting of a large open system where committees are sub-sampled, we can even sign more messages in each run without reducing resiliency: for example, assuming 80% honest parties, we can sub-sample a committee of size $n = 992$ with $t = 336, a = 40, b = 320$, and sign 12880 messages in each run.[15]

If we set $t = a = n/5$, we can sign $3n^2/25$ messages per run, with an amortized bandwidth of fewer than 35 scalars/group elements broadcasted per signature. For the sub-sampling parameters above with $n = 992$ (with a group of size $\approx 2^{256}$), the total broadcast bandwidth is only under 100MB.

Given parameters n, t, a, the parties broadcast less than $4n^2$ scalars and group elements (in total). If we set $t = a = n/5$, we can sign $3n^2/25$ messages per run, with an amortized bandwidth of fewer than 35 scalars/group elements broadcasted per signature. For the sub-sampling parameters above with $n = 992$ (with a group of size $\approx 2^{256}$), the total broadcast bandwidth is only under 100MB.

In terms of computation, the most expensive part is multiplying the super-invertible matrix in the exponent (which is needed to compute the public R's). This part takes at most $at(n - 2t)$ products (using a naive algorithm), which is t scalar-elements multiplications per signature. But as we explain in Sect. 2.4, we can use much more efficient matrix-multiplication to reduce it, or just use small scalars. With the small-scalar Vandermonde optimization from above, the computation is about 1 min.

Since the super-invertible matrix multiplication is the most expensive part of the protocol, we wrote code to benchmark actual performances for both our possible optimizations from Sect. 2.4. In the full version [4, Appendix B.3], we show the results for various values of b. For $b = t = 256$, our first solution provides a 29× speed up compared to the naive solution and only takes 682ms when $a = 1$ (on a single core of a 2.20GHZ AMD EPIC 7601 CPU). Even with $a = 64$, the total super-invertible matrix multiplication would take less than 1 min on a single-core. In addition, this operation is trivially parallelizable, computations for each of the a packed values are completely independent of each other and can be run on different threads.

For $b = t = 512$, our second solution becomes faster and provides a 28× speed up compared to the naive solution. It only takes 2.80 s to compute the super-invertible matrix multiplication in that setting for $a = 1$, on a single core.

---

[15] We need $n \geq 657$ to get (statistical) safety failure $< 2^{-80}$ (and liveness failure $< 2^{-11}$), without packing (i.e., $a = 1$). Setting $a = 40$ only requires $n \geq 992$ while multiplying the number of messages that can be signed by 40 and while providing the same safety guarantees. This is because we have less than $(n - 1)/3$ corrupted parties selected in each committee with overwhelming probability. See details in the full version [4, Appendix D.1].

3   The SPRINT Protocols

3.1   Static-Committee Setting

We begin with our base protocol shown in Fig. 1, namely, a robust threshold Schnorr signature scheme for the static-committee case where the set of parties is fixed. It follows the design and rationale presented in Sect. 2 (particularly, till Sect. 2.6), resulting in a two-round ephemeral randomness generation phase (dependent on the number of messages to be signed but not on the messages themselves) followed by a *non-interactive* signing procedure. It considers n parties of which at most t are corrupted, and is given a packing parameter a and an amplification (via a super-invertible matrix) parameter b. It assumes an asynchronous broadcast channel. The protocol consists of three parts. An initial setup stage where parties obtain shares σ_i of a long-term secret key s, and corresponding public key $S = s \cdot G$, and $S_i = \sigma_i \cdot G$ are made public. We assume that sharing the secret key uses packed secret sharing, namely, the parties' shares σ_i lie on a polynomial $\mathbf{F}$ of degree $d = t + a - 1$, such that $\mathbf{F}(0) = \mathbf{F}(-1) = \ldots = \mathbf{F}(-a + 1) = s$. This initial setup can be done via a distributed key generation (DKG) protocol or another secure procedure.

The second part is the *generation of ephemeral randomness for Schnorr signatures*. Following the DKG blueprint of [16,34], each party P_i shares a random polynomial $\mathbf{H}_i$ by transmitting the value $\mathbf{H}_i(j)$ to each other party P_j and committing to $\mathbf{H}_i(\cdot)$ over a public broadcast channel. Our application allows for the use of the more efficient Feldman secret sharing [12]. In our case, parties commit to their polynomials $\mathbf{H}$ by broadcasting values $\mathbf{H}(v) \cdot G$ for $d' + 1$ different evaluation points v where d' is the degree of $\mathbf{H}$ (specifically, in our case, this set is defined as the interval $[-a + 1, t + a - 1]$).

A central part of such a protocol is for the parties to agree on sets of dealers (denoted QUAL, BAD) that shared their polynomials correctly/badly, and a large enough set of parties (denoted HOLD) that received correct sharings from all parties in QUAL. In Sect. 4.1 we describe an implementation of such a protocol over an asynchronous atomic broadcast channel.

The source of efficiency for SPRINT is the use of packing to share a secrets at a little more cost than sharing just one and attaining further amplification, by a factor of b, using super-invertible matrices [24] (see Sect. 2.4). Here, b is the number of rows in the super-invertible matrix Ψ, e.g., a Vandermonde matrix, and is set to its largest possible value (as analysis shows), $b = |\mathsf{QUAL}| - (t - |\mathsf{BAD}|)$. (Smaller values of b can be used too, if fewer messages need to be signed.) Once the randomness generation procedure is completed, each party in HOLD generates (non-interactively) signature shares consisting of a point on a polynomial $\mathbf{Y}$ that when reconstructed (via interpolation of $d' + 1$ signature shares) can be evaluated on a points to achieve a signatures. Remarkably, using super-invertible matrices one can generate b different polynomials $\mathbf{Y}$, hence resulting in $a \cdot b$ signatures at the cost of a single execution of the (interactive) randomness generation procedure.

Parameters: Integers $n, t, a \geq 1$, $d = t + a - 1$, $d' = t + 2a - 2$.

Setup: (Parties: $P_1, \ldots, P_n$)

- Each P_i holds a share $\sigma_i = \mathbf{F}(i)$, where $\mathbf{F}$ is a random degree-d polynomial subject to $\mathbf{F}(0) = \mathbf{F}(-1) = \ldots = \mathbf{F}(-a+1)$. Denote $s = \mathbf{F}(0)$.
- Public keys $S = s \cdot G$ and $S_i = \sigma_i \cdot G$ are publicly known.

Ephemeral randomness generation

1. Each $P_i, i \in [n]$, chooses a random degree-d' polynomial $\mathbf{H}_i$; it broadcasts Feldman commitments to $\mathbf{H}_i$ of the form $\hat{\mathbf{H}}_i(v) = \mathbf{H}_i(v) \cdot G$ for $v \in [-a + 1, t + a - 1]$. Encrypt the share $\rho_{ij} = \mathbf{H}_i(j)$ under the public key of P_j for all $j \in [n]$, and boardcast all the resulting ciphertexts.
2. $P_1, \ldots, P_n$ run the protocol from Fig. 3 to agree on $\mathsf{QUAL}, \mathsf{BAD}, \mathsf{HOLD} \subseteq \{P_1, \ldots, P_n\}$ with $d_0 = |\mathsf{HOLD}| = n - t$, $d_1 = |\mathsf{QUAL}| + |\mathsf{BAD}| = n - t$, and every $P_j \in \mathsf{HOLD}$ holds valid shares from all the dealers in QUAL.
3. Set $b = |\mathsf{QUAL}| - (t - |\mathsf{BAD}|)$; $\Psi = [\psi_i^u] \in \mathbb{Z}_p^{b \times |\mathsf{QUAL}|}$ a super-invertible matrix. For $u \in [b]$, $v \in [a]$, define $\mathbf{H}^u(\cdot) = \sum_{i \in \mathsf{QUAL}} \psi_i^u \mathbf{H}_i(\cdot)$, $r^{u,v} = \mathbf{H}^u(1 - v)$, $R^{u,v} = r^{u,v} \cdot G$.[a]
   Each $P_j \in \mathsf{HOLD}$ sets $\rho_j^u = \mathbf{H}^u(j) = \sum_{i \in \mathsf{QUAL}} \psi_i^u \rho_{ij}$ for all $u \in [b]$.

Signature share generation On input messages $M^{u,v}, u \in [b], v \in [a]$:

Each $P_j \in \mathsf{HOLD}$ sets $\delta = \mathsf{Hash}\big(S, \mathsf{QUAL}, \{(R^{u,v}, M^{u,v}) : u \in [b], v \in [a]\}\big)$ and $\Delta = \delta \cdot G$.

Then, it runs the following procedure, in parallel, for each $u \in [b]$:

1. Computes $e^{u,v} = \mathsf{Hash}(S, \Delta + R^{u,v}, M^{u,v})$ for $v \in [a]$;
2. Computes the degree-$(a-1)$ polynomial $\mathbf{Z}^u$, with $\mathbf{Z}^u(1 - v) = e^{u,v}$ for $v \in [a]$.
3. Outputs *signature share*: $\pi_j^u = \mathbf{Z}^u(j) \cdot \sigma_j + \rho_j^u$.

   Note: $\pi_j^u = \mathbf{Y}^u(j)$ for the degree-d' polynomial $\mathbf{Y}^u = \mathbf{Z}^u \cdot \mathbf{F} + \mathbf{H}^u$

Schnorr signature assembly (from signature shares)

For each issued signature share π_j^u verify, using commitments to $\mathbf{H}_i, i \in \mathsf{QUAL}$, and public key $S_j = \mathbf{F}(j) \cdot G$, that $\pi_j^u \cdot G = \mathbf{Z}^u(j) \cdot S_j + \mathbf{H}^u(j) \cdot G$.

When collecting $d' + 1$ verified shares π_j^u, reconstruct the polynomial $\mathbf{Y}^u$ and for all $v \in [a]$ set $\phi^{u,v} = \mathbf{Y}^u(1 - v)$. (Note: $\phi^{u,v} = \mathbf{Y}^u(1-v) = \mathbf{Z}^u(1-v) \cdot \mathbf{F}(1-v) + \mathbf{H}^u(v) = e^{u,v} \cdot s + r^{u,v}$.)

For $v \in [a], u \in [b]$, output the Schnorr signatures $(\Delta + R^{u,v}, \delta + \phi^{u,v})$ on message $M^{u,v}$.

---

[a] The values $R^{u,v}$ can be computed from commitments to the polynomials $\mathbf{H}_i$, hence public information.

Fig. 1. SPRINT Scheme in the Static-Committee Setting

In all, we have that after the randomness generation procedure, parties generate their shares of the signatures without any further interaction. Each party P_j computes locally their signature shares $\pi_j^u, u \in [b]$ and publishes them. Reconstructing the signature for each batch of a messages $M^{u1}, \ldots M^{ua}$ can be done by interpolation from any $d' + 1$ correct signature shares π_j^u. Moreover, signature shares can be verified individually by a Schnorr-like validation $\pi_j^u \cdot G = \mathbf{Z}^u(j) \cdot S_j + \rho_j^u \cdot G$, where all the required information is public. Thus, invalid signature shares can be discarded.

An additional ingredient in the protocol is the use of the "mitigation value" $\delta = \mathsf{Hash}(S, \mathsf{QUAL}, \{(R^{u,v}, M^{u,v}) : u \in [b], v \in [a]\})$ needed to achieve security when running the $a \cdot b$ signatures in parallel, as explained in Sect. 2.3.

We prove the security of the SPRINT protocol in Fig. 1 in the full version [4, Appendix G].

3.2 The Dynamic/Proactive Setting

The adaptation of SPRINT to the dynamic setting is shown in Fig. 2. See also Sect. 2.7. It requires two types of sharings. One is ephemeral randomness generation as in the static setting, where dealers have no input, and they just share random polynomials. The other is a share refresh (i.e., proactive resharing), in which the dealers have shares of the long-term secret, and they refresh the sharing of that secret to the shareholders. These two sharings are enabled by (almost) the same DKG-like protocol, both using the agreement protocol (see details in [4]) with the same set HOLD and two QUAL sets for the two sharings. Note that the use of the same set HOLD for both sharings is crucial to guarantee that enough parties (those in HOLD) have *both* shares of the secret s and of the ephemeral randomness as needed for generating signatures. Proving security of this protocol is very similar to the static case; see more details in our full version [4, Appendix G.7].

A Note on the "Traditional" Proactive Setting. The proactive setting [22,23,31] was originally envisioned as a periodic operation, say every week, in order to heal the system from active and passive corruptions. When running SPRINT in such a scenario, one would not want to perform a share refresh with each run of the signature generation protocol (Fig. 1) but only at the end of a full proactive period. However, by decoupling the two sharings (refresh and randomness generation), we lose the ability to use the same set HOLD for both cases. This raises a liveness issue: If the share refresh ends with a set HOLD of size $n - t$ and a subsequent execution of SPRINT ends with a *different* set HOLD' of the same size, then it may be the case that the intersection of these two sets will have less than $t + 1$ uncorrupted parties, hence unable to create signatures.

However, the traditional proactive setting already assumes the share refresh to happen within a more controlled environment.[16] Thus, it makes sense to con-

---

[16] E.g., it assumes human intervention to replace or reboot servers, to export public keys from new servers or servers that choose new (encryption) keys, etc. (see [23]).

Parameters: Integers $n, t, a \geq 1, d = t + a - 1, d' = t + 2a - 2$.

Parties: Dealers $D_1, \ldots, D_n$, shareholders $P_1, \ldots, P_n$

Setup: (D_i's)

- Each D_i holds a share $\sigma_i = \mathbf{F}(i)$, where $\mathbf{F}$ is a random degree-d polynomial subject to $\mathbf{F}(0) = \mathbf{F}(-1) = \ldots = \mathbf{F}(-a + 1)$. Denote $s = \mathbf{F}(0)$.
- Public keys S and $S_i = \sigma_i \cdot G$ are publicly known.

Ephemeral randomness generation and Re-sharing (The D_i's and P_j's)

1. Each $D_i, i \in [n]$, with share $\sigma_i = \mathbf{F}(i)$ chooses:
   - A random degree-d' polynomial $\mathbf{H}_i$;
   - A degree-d polynomial $\mathbf{F}_i$, random subject to $\mathbf{F}_i(0) = \cdots = \mathbf{F}_i(1 - a) = \sigma_i$.
   D_i broadcasts Feldman commitments to $\mathbf{F}_i, \mathbf{H}_i$;
   D_i encrypts $\rho_{ij} = \mathbf{H}_i(j)$ and $\sigma_{ij} = \mathbf{F}_i(j)$ under P_j's key $\forall j \in [n]$, and broadcasts all these ciphertexts.
2. $P_1, \ldots, P_n$ run the agreement protocol ([4, Appendix E]) to agree on $\mathsf{HOLD} \subseteq \{P_1, \ldots, P_n\}$, $\mathsf{QUAL}_1, \mathsf{QUAL}_2 \subseteq \{D_1, \ldots, D_n\}$ with $d_0 = |\mathsf{HOLD}| = n - t$, $d_1 = |\mathsf{QUAL}_1| = n - t$, $d_2 = |\mathsf{QUAL}_2| = t + a$, where every $P_j \in \mathsf{HOLD}$ received valid shares ρ_{ij} from all the dealers in QUAL_1 and valid shares σ_{ij} from all the dealers in QUAL_2.[a]
3. Set $b = |\mathsf{QUAL}_1| - t$; $\Psi = [\psi_i^u] \in \mathbb{Z}_p^{b \times |\mathsf{QUAL}_1|}$ a super-invertible matrix.
   For $u \in [b]$, $v \in [a]$, define $\mathbf{H}^u(\cdot) = \sum_{i \in \mathsf{QUAL}_1} \psi_i^u \mathbf{H}_i(\cdot)$, $r^{u,v} = \mathbf{H}^u(1 - v)$, $R^{u,v} = r^{u,v} \cdot G$.
   Each $P_j \in \mathsf{HOLD}$ sets $\rho_j^u = \sum_{i \in \mathsf{QUAL}_1} \psi_i^u \rho_{ij}$ for all $u \in [b]$.
4. Each $P_j \in \mathsf{HOLD}$ sets $\sigma_j' = \sum_{i \in \mathsf{QUAL}_2} \lambda_i \mathbf{F}_i(j)$, λ_i's are the Lagrange coefficients.
   Let $\mathbf{F}' = \sum_{i \in \mathsf{QUAL}_2} \lambda_i \mathbf{F}_i$; a commitment to $\mathbf{F}'$ is obtained from those of the $\mathbf{F}_i'$s.

Signature generation and assembly Same as in the static case in Fig. 1 but using polynomial $\mathbf{F}'$ instead of $\mathbf{F}$ in that figure.

---

[a] Valid σ_{ij} mean in particular that $\mathbf{F}_i'$ indeed has the required format, with $\mathbf{F}_i(0) = \cdots = \mathbf{F}_i(1 - a) = \sigma_i = \mathbf{F}(i)$.

Fig. 2. SPRINT Scheme in the Dynamic-Committee Setting

sider a more synchronous setting (with monitored and resolved delays) during refresh in which case the share refresh operation can be assumed to be completed after a defined amount of time for non-adversarial servers. In this case, parties that did not make it to HOLD by that time will be disqualified from participating in signature generation until the next proactive execution and be counted towards the bound t on corrupted parties. This guarantees that all honest parties in sets HOLD created by runs of SPRINT until the next refresh period will have valid shares of the secret s.

4 The Agreement Protocol

For agreement, we observe that in the static setting we can have a more efficient agreement protocol than in the proactive/dynamic setting. As a result, we present two protocols of a very similar flavor for the task of reaching agreement. In this section we describe in detail the base agreement protocol, which achieves the best results for the static setting. Then we sketch the enhancements that we need for the dynamic/proactive setting in what we refer to as the full protocol, which is described in the full version [4, Appendix E].

This protocol is designed to work over an asynchronous total-order (aka atomic) broadcast channel. Recall that a total-order broadcast channel provides the following guarantees:

- *Eventual delivery.* A message broadcasted by an honest party will eventually be seen (unmodified) by all honest parties. However, the adversary can change the order in which messages are delivered to the broadcast channel.
- *Prefix consistency.* Considering the views of the broadcast channel at a given time by two different honest parties, the view of one is a prefix of the other.
- *Authenticity.* Messages that are received on behalf of honest parties were indeed sent by those honest parties.

We also assume a PKI, i.e., each party has an encryption public key that is known to all other parties. The protocol below uses only the broadcast channel for communication, private messages are sent by encrypting them and broadcasting the ciphertext.

Time and Steps. While a total-order broadcast channel is not synchronous, and thus it has no absolute notion of time, we are still ensured that the parties all see the same messages in the same order. We can therefore define a "step T" as the time when the T'th message is delivered. Even though different parties may see it at different times, they will all agree on the message that was delivered at step T. If we have a protocol action that is based only on the messages that appeared on the broadcast channel up to (and including) the T'th message, we are ensured that all the honest parties will take the same action, and they will all know that they did it at "step T".

In the description below we distinguish between dealers and shareholders. The protocol begins with the dealers broadcasting messages, then the shareholders engage in a protocol among themselves based on the dealer messages that they see on the channel. For every dealer message and every shareholder, the shareholder either accepts this message or complains about it.

An important technique in our protocol is the use of "verifiable complaints": This is a complaint by a shareholder about a dealer, that will be accepted by all other honest shareholders. (In our context, it will be implemented by proving that the message sent by that dealer is invalid.) We say that a dealer message is "locally bad" for shareholder P_j, if that shareholder is able to generate a verifiable complaint against it. Importantly, we assume that it is impossible to produce a verifiable complaint against messages sent by honest dealers.

We denote the number of dealers as n_1, at least d_1 of them are assumed to be honest. The protocol is run among a set of n_0 shareholders, at least d_0 of which are assumed to be honest. We require that this base protocol terminates,

---

Parameters: n_0, d_0, n_1, d_1 (should agree on $|\mathsf{HOLD}| \geq d_0$, $|\mathsf{QUAL}| + |\mathsf{BAD}| \geq d_1$).

Precondition: We have up to n_1 dealers, at least d_1 of which are honest. We also have n_0 shareholders, at least d_0 of them are honest.

Shareholder P_j:
Initialize $\mathsf{HOLD} = \mathsf{QUAL} = \mathsf{BAD} = \emptyset$

1. **Enlarge QUAL.** While $|\mathsf{QUAL}| < d_1$, when receiving the (first) broadcast message of the right format[a] from dealer D_i, set $\mathsf{QUAL} := \mathsf{QUAL} \cup \{D_i\}$.
2. **Broadcast Complaints.** Once $|\mathsf{QUAL}| \geq d_1$, broadcast all the verifiable complaints against dealers in QUAL whose message was locally bad, in a single broadcast message. If this set is empty, broadcast the empty set.
3. **Contract and fix $\mathsf{QUAL}, \mathsf{BAD}$.** Collect all the valid complaint-sets (i.e., the ones whose complaints can be verified, or the empty set). Once there are d_0 valid complaint-sets, set $\mathsf{QUAL} := \mathsf{QUAL} \setminus \{D_i\}$ and $\mathsf{BAD} := \mathsf{BAD} \cup \{D_i\}$ for each verifiable complaint against dealer D_i;
4. **Fix HOLD.** To the first d_0 shareholders who broadcasted a valid complaint-set.

---

[a] In our context, a message has the right format if it contains all the commitments and ciphertexts that it was supposed to have.

Fig. 3. Base protocol for agreeing on $\mathsf{QUAL}, \mathsf{BAD}, \mathsf{HOLD}$

and that all honest shareholders output the same sets $\mathsf{HOLD}, \mathsf{QUAL}, \mathsf{BAD}$, where HOLD is a subset of the shareholder set with $|\mathsf{HOLD}| \geq d_0$, and $\mathsf{QUAL}, \mathsf{BAD}$ are disjoint subsets of the dealer set with $|\mathsf{QUAL}| + |\mathsf{BAD}| \geq d_1$.

The base protocol is described in Fig. 3 and proven in Theorem 4.1 (details in [4, Appendix F]). Here each shareholder initially sets QUAL to the first d_1 dealers whose broadcast message they receive. Then each shareholder broadcasts a message specifying which of these d_1 dealers sent correct shares and complaining about the ones that did not. Thereafter, each shareholder continuously adds to HOLD the shareholders whose message appeared on the channel, and moves dealers from QUAL to BAD when they see a verifiable complaint against them on the channel. The protocol terminates once HOLD reaches size d_0.

Theorem 4.1. *Consider an execution of the base agreement protocol from Fig. 3 over a total-order broadcast channel, among a set of n_0 shareholders of which at least d_0 are honest. Assume that at most n_1 dealers broadcast messages, at least d_1 of these dealers are honest, and no verifiable complaint can be constructed against any honest dealer. Then all honest shareholders will eventually terminate, all outputting the same sets with $|\mathsf{HOLD}| \geq d_0$ and $|\mathsf{QUAL}| + |\mathsf{BAD}| \geq d_1$. Moreover:*

- *No shareholder in HOLD complained against any dealer in QUAL; and*
- *Every dealer in BAD has at least one shareholder in HOLD that lodged a verifiable complaint against them.*

Dealer D_i (sharing a degreed-d polynomial, $\mathbf{F}_i(X)$):

1. Compute $\hat{\mathbf{F}}_i = \{\mathbf{F}_i(k) \cdot G : k \in [-a+1, \ldots, d-a]\}$;
2. Let $\sigma ij = \mathbf{F}_i(j)$ and $E_{ij} = ENC_{PK_j}(\sigma ij)$ for all $j \in [n]$;
3. Broadcast $(\{E_{i1}, \ldots, E_{in}\}, \hat{\mathbf{F}}_i)$.

Shareholder P_j:

1. Decrypt $\sigma_{ij} = DEC_{SK_j}(E_{ij})$ and verify $\sigma_{ij} \cdot G \overset{?}{=} \sum_{k=1-a}^{d-a} \lambda_{i,j,k} \cdot (\mathbf{F}_i(k) \cdot G)$, with $\lambda_{i,j,k}$ the relevant Lagrange coefficients;
2. If verification failed, create a verifiable complaint against E_{ij}, consisting of the decrypted value σ_{ij} and a proof-of-correct-decryption of E_{ij} relative to PK_j.

Fig. 4. Dealer messages and shareholder complaints

4.1 Agreement in SPRINT, the Static Case

To instantiate the base agreement protocol in SPRINT, we need to set the parameters n_0, d_0, n_1, d_1 and specify how the dealer's messages and verifiable complaints are generated and verified.

In our protocols, a dealer's message is just a Shamir sharing of secrets via polynomials. In the static case, we have one pair of QUAL, BAD for the DKG polynomials. We assume a PKI, and the dealers encrypt and broadcast all the shares under the public keys of their intended recipient, and also broadcast Feldman commitments to the polynomials themselves.

There are checks that all shareholders can perform on public information that the dealers broadcast, i.e. verifying that the committed polynomials are of the right degree, and that the dealer's message includes all the ciphertexts that it is supposed to. However, each shareholder is the only one who can check if the share encrypted under their public key is consistent with the committed polynomial.

If the encrypted share is *not* consistent with the committed polynomial, the shareholder will create a verifiable complaint, using the fact that the dealer's message is visible to all. A verifiable complaint from shareholder P_j, denoted π_{ji}, consists of the decrypted value from the ciphertext that D_i sent to P_j, and a proof-of-correct-decryption relative to P_j's public key.[17] Once other parties see the decrypted value they can all verify that the share indeed is not consistent with the committed polynomial.

The dealer messages and shareholder complaints are described in Fig. 4.

Parameters in the Static-committee Setting. In the static-committee setting, each dealer shares a single random polynomial H_i of degree $d' = t + 2a - 2$. To ensure that the resulting random polynomials can be recovered we need at

---

[17] The proof-of-decryption can be very simple: a proof of equality of discrete logs if using ElGamal encryption for the shares, or showing an inverted RSA ciphertext if using RSA-based encryption.

least $d'+1$ honest parties in HOLD, so we have to set $d_0 \geq t+d'+1 = 2t+2a-1$. But we can set it even bigger, it can be as large as $n-t$ since we know that there are at least as many honest shareholders. (This implies that we need $n-t \geq 2t+2s-1$, namely $n \geq 3t+2a-1$.)

We note that for the DKG protocol, the size of QUAL is unrelated to the degree of the polynomials H_i. The only constraint on it is that to get b output random polynomials we need $|QUAL| + |BAD| = d_1 \geq b+t$. To get the best amortized cost, we want to make b as large as possible, which means using as large an initial set $QUAL \cup BAD$ as we can get. Every party can serve as a dealer for the DKG protocol, so we have at least $n-t$ honest dealers and can set $d_1 = n-t$ (and therefore $b = n-2t$).

Hence, we run the agreement protocol with parameters $d_0 = d_1 = n-t$. (If we have fewer messages to sign, we can do with a smaller b, which means smaller d_1, any value $d_1 > t$ would work.)

4.2 Agreement in the Dynamic/Proactive Setting

In this setting, dealers share two types of polynomials, random polynomials $\mathbf{H}_i$ of degree $d' = t+2a-2$ for the DKG, and packed re-sharing polynomials $\mathbf{F}_i$ of degree $d = t+a-1$.

Here we must rely on stronger agreement guarantees. For the static case, it was enough to ensure that in a setting with d_1 honest dealers, we will end up with $|QUAL| + |BAD| \geq d_1$, this was enough to ensure $d_1 - t$ honest dealers in QUAL (which is the best we can so in the worst case, and is what's needed for the DKG). Now, however, we need to ensure the stronger condition $|QUAL| \geq d_1$, since this is what's needed for re-sharing the secret.

We therefore augment the agreement by running multiple iterations of the base protocol. In every iteration, we enlarge QUAL until it reaches side d_1, then have one round of complaints and potentially move some more dealers from QUAL to BAD. This is repeated until no more dealers are added to BAD, at which point we have $|QUAL| \geq d_1$. (Note that at the beginning of each iteration, we always have enough honest dealers whose messages were not yet incorporated in the protocol to reach QUAL of size-d_1 in this iteration.)

Another enhancement to the protocol is that we now have two separate QUAL's (and corresponding two BAD's): one pair $QUAL_1, BAD_1$ for the H_i's, and another pair $QUAL_2, BAD_2$ for the F_i's. We however only have one shareholder set HOLD (since we need the same shareholders to get both a share of the key and a share of the ephemeral secrets). The protocol is in the full version [4, Appendix E].

Parameters in the Dynamic-committee Setting. Here we have parameters n_0, d_0 for HOLD and n_1, d_1 for QUAL, BAD as before (for the H_i's), but in addition also n_2, d_2 for $QUAL', BAD'$. For the $\mathbf{H}_i$'s we have the same parameters as above, $n_0 = n_1 = n$ and $d_0 = d_1 = n-t$. For the $\mathbf{F}_i$'s, we need $d+1 = t+a$ dealers in $QUAL'$ in order for shareholders in HOLD to be able to recover their shares, so we set $d_2 = t+a$.

All the dealers in $\mathsf{QUAL'}$ must have shares of the long-term secret, so they had to be in HOLD in the previous epoch. Hence, the pool of dealers could be as small as $n_2 = d_0 = n - t$, and t of them could be corrupted, so we cannot set d_2 any larger than $n - 2t$. This implies the constraint $d_2 = n - 2t \geq t + a$ or $n \geq 3t + a$. This constraint is weaker than the constraint $n \geq 3t + 2a - 1$ from above.

Acknowledgements. We thank Victor Shoup for mentioning to us the solution using a Vandermonde matrix for fast multiplication by a super-invertible matrix.

References

1. Abraham, I., Jovanovic, P., Maller, M., Meiklejohn, S., Stern, G.: Bingo: adaptivity and asynchrony in verifiable secret sharing and distributed key generation. In: Handschuh, H., Lysyanskaya, A. (eds.) CRYPTO (2023). https://doi.org/10.1007/978-3-031-38557-5_2
2. Ben-Or, M., Canetti, R., Goldreich, O.: Asynchronous secure computation. In: 25th ACM STOC, pp. 52–61. ACM Press (May 1993). https://doi.org/10.1145/167088.167109
3. Ben-Sasson, E., Carmon, D., Kopparty, S., Levit, D.: Elliptic curve fast Fourier transform (ECFFT) part I: low-degree extension in time $O(n \log n)$ over all finite fields. In: Bansal, N., Nagarajan, V. (eds.) SODA 2023, Florence, Italy, January 22–25, 2023, pp. 700–737. SIAM (2023). https://doi.org/10.1137/1.9781611977554.ch30
4. Benhamouda, F., Halevi, S., Krawczyk, H., Ma, Y., Rabin, T.: SPRINT: high-throughput robust distributed Schnorr signatures. Cryptology ePrint Archive (2023). https://eprint.iacr.org/2023/427
5. Benhamouda, F., Lepoint, T., Loss, J., Orrù, M., Raykova, M.: On the (in)security of ROS. J. Cryptol. **35**(4), 25 (2022). https://doi.org/10.1007/s00145-022-09436-0
6. Borgeaud, W.: ECFFT algorithms on the BN254 base field (2023). https://github.com/wborgeaud/ecfft-bn254
7. Chen, J., Micali, S.: Algorand: a secure and efficient distributed ledger. Theor. Comput. Sci. (2019). https://doi.org/10.1016/j.tcs.2019.02.001
8. Crites, E.C., Komlo, C., Maller, M.: How to prove Schnorr assuming schnorr: security of multi- and threshold signatures. Cryptology ePrint Archive (2021). https://eprint.iacr.org/2021/1375
9. Das, S., Xiang, Z., Kokoris-Kogias, L., Ren, L.: Practical asynchronous high-threshold distributed key generation and distributed polynomial sampling. USENIX Security (2023)
10. Das, S., Yurek, T., Xiang, Z., Miller, A.K., Kokoris-Kogias, L., Ren, L.: Practical asynchronous distributed key generation. In: 2022 IEEE Symposium on Security and Privacy, pp. 2518–2534. IEEE Computer Society Press (May 2022). https://doi.org/10.1109/SP46214.2022.9833584
11. Drijvers, M., Edalatnejad, K., Ford, B., Kiltz, E., Loss, J., Neven, G., Stepanovs, I.: On the security of two-round multi-signatures. In: 2019 IEEE Symposium on Security and Privacy (SP), pp. 1084–1101 (2019). https://doi.org/10.1109/SP.2019.00050

12. Feldman, P.: A practical scheme for non-interactive verifiable secret sharing. In: 28th FOCS, pp. 427–437. IEEE Computer Society Press (Oct 1987). https://doi.org/10.1109/SFCS.1987.4

13. Franklin, M.K., Yung, M.: Communication complexity of secure computation (extended abstract). In: 24th ACM STOC, pp. 699–710. ACM Press (May 1992). https://doi.org/10.1145/129712.129780

14. Ganesh, C., Patra, A.: Optimal extension protocols for byzantine broadcast and agreement. Distributed Comput. **34**(1), 59–77 (2021). https://doi.org/10.1007/s00446-020-00384-1

15. Garillot, F., Kondi, Y., Mohassel, P., Nikolaenko, V.: Threshold Schnorr with stateless deterministic signing from standard assumptions. In: Malkin, T., Peikert, C. (eds.) CRYPTO 2021. LNCS, vol. 12825, pp. 127–156. Springer, Cham (2021). https://doi.org/10.1007/978-3-030-84242-0_6

16. Gennaro, R., Jarecki, S., Krawczyk, H., Rabin, T.: Secure distributed key generation for discrete-log based cryptosystems. J. Cryptol. **20**(1), 51–83 (Jan 2007). https://doi.org/10.1007/s00145-006-0347-3

17. Gennaro, R., Rabin, M.O., Rabin, T.: Simplified VSS and fast-track multiparty computations with applications to threshold cryptography. In: Coan, B.A., Afek, Y. (eds.) 17th ACM PODC, pp. 101–111. ACM (Jun / Jul 1998). https://doi.org/10.1145/277697.277716

18. Goyal, V., Polychroniadou, A., Song, Y.: Sharing transformation and dishonest majority MPC with packed secret sharing. In: Dodis, Y., Shrimpton, T. (eds.) CRYPTO (2022). https://doi.org/10.1007/978-3-031-15985-5_1

19. Groth, J., Shoup, V.: Design and analysis of a distributed ECDSA signing service. Cryptology ePrint Archive, Report 2022/506 (2022). https://eprint.iacr.org/2022/506

20. Groth, J., Shoup, V.: On the security of ECDSA with additive key derivation and presignatures. In: Dunkelman, O., Dziembowski, S. (eds.) EUROCRYPT 2022, Part I. LNCS, vol. 13275, pp. 365–396. Springer, Heidelberg (May / Jun 2022). https://doi.org/10.1007/978-3-031-06944-4_13

21. Groth, J., Shoup, V.: Fast batched asynchronous distributed key generation. Cryptology ePrint Archive (2023). https://eprint.iacr.org/2023/1175

22. Herzberg, A., Jakobsson, M., Jarecki, S., Krawczyk, H., Yung, M.: Proactive public key and signature systems. In: Graveman, R., Janson, P.A., Neuman, C., Gong, L. (eds.) ACM CCS 97, pp. 100–110. ACM Press (Apr 1997). https://doi.org/10.1145/266420.266442

23. Herzberg, A., Jarecki, S., Krawczyk, H., Yung, M.: Proactive secret sharing or: how to cope with perpetual leakage. In: Coppersmith, D. (ed.) CRYPTO 1995. LNCS, vol. 963, pp. 339–352. Springer, Heidelberg (1995). https://doi.org/10.1007/3-540-44750-4_27

24. Hirt, M., Nielsen, J.B.: Robust multiparty computation with linear communication complexity. In: Dwork, C. (ed.) CRYPTO 2006. LNCS, vol. 4117, pp. 463–482. Springer, Heidelberg (2006). https://doi.org/10.1007/11818175_28

25. Joshi, S., Pandey, D., Srinathan, K.: Atssia: asynchronous truly-threshold schnorr signing for inconsistent availability. In: Park, J.H., Seo, S.H. (eds.) Information Security and Cryptology - ICISC 2021, pp. 71–91. Springer International Publishing, Cham (2022)

26. Kate, A., Zaverucha, G.M., Goldberg, I.: Constant-size commitments to polynomials and their applications. In: Abe, M. (ed.) ASIACRYPT 2010. LNCS, vol. 6477, pp. 177–194. Springer, Heidelberg (2010). https://doi.org/10.1007/978-3-642-17373-8_11

27. Komlo, C., Goldberg, I.: FROST: flexible round-optimized schnorr threshold signatures. In: Dunkelman, O., Jacobson, Jr., M.J., O'Flynn, C. (eds.) SAC 2020. LNCS, vol. 12804, pp. 34–65. Springer, Cham (2021). https://doi.org/10.1007/978-3-030-81652-0_2

28. Lindell, Y.: Simple three-round multiparty schnorr signing with full simulatability. Cryptology ePrint Archive, Report 2022/374 (2022). https://eprint.iacr.org/2022/374

29. Nayak, K., Ren, L., Shi, E., Vaidya, N.H., Xiang, Z.: Improved extension protocols for byzantine broadcast and agreement. In: Attiya, H. (ed.) 34th International Symposium on Distributed Computing, DISC 2020, October 12-16, 2020, Virtual Conference. LIPIcs, vol. 179, pp. 28:1–28:17. Schloss Dagstuhl - Leibniz-Zentrum für Informatik (2020). https://doi.org/10.4230/LIPIcs.DISC.2020.28

30. Neji, W., Blibech, K., Ben Rajeb, N.: Distributed key generation protocol with a new complaint management strategy. Security Commun. Netw. 9(17), 4585–4595 (2016). https://doi.org/10.1002/sec.1651

31. Ostrovsky, R., Yung, M.: How to withstand mobile virus attacks (extended abstract). In: Logrippo, L. (ed.) 10th ACM PODC., pp. 51–59. ACM (Aug 1991). https://doi.org/10.1145/112600.112605

32. Patra, A., Choudhary, A., Rangan, C.P.: Efficient statistical asynchronous verifiable secret sharing with optimal resilience. In: Kurosawa, K. (ed.) ICITS 09. LNCS, vol. 5973, pp. 74–92. Springer, Heidelberg (Dec 2010). https://doi.org/10.1007/978-3-642-14496-7_7

33. Pedersen, T.P.: A threshold cryptosystem without a trusted party. In: Davies, D.W. (ed.) EUROCRYPT 1991. LNCS, vol. 547, pp. 522–526. Springer, Heidelberg (1991). https://doi.org/10.1007/3-540-46416-6_47

34. Pedersen, T.P.: Non-interactive and information-theoretic secure verifiable secret sharing. In: Feigenbaum, J. (ed.) CRYPTO 1991. LNCS, vol. 576, pp. 129–140. Springer, Heidelberg (1992). https://doi.org/10.1007/3-540-46766-1_9

35. Ruffing, T., Ronge, V., Jin, E., Schneider-Bensch, J., Schröder, D.: ROAST: robust asynchronous schnorr threshold signatures. In: Yin, H., Stavrou, A., Cremers, C., Shi, E. (eds.) ACM CCS 2022, pp. 2551–2564. ACM Press (Nov 2022). https://doi.org/10.1145/3548606.3560583

36. Shoup, V.: The many faces of Schnorr. Cryptology ePrint Archive (2023). https://eprint.iacr.org/2023/1019

37. Stinson, D.R., Strobl, R.: Provably secure distributed Schnorr signatures and a (t, n) threshold scheme for implicit certificates. In: Varadharajan, V., Mu, Y. (eds.) ACISP 2001. LNCS, vol. 2119, pp. 417–434. Springer, Heidelberg (2001). https://doi.org/10.1007/3-540-47719-5_33

38. Yurek, T., Luo, L., Fairoze, J., Kate, A., Miller, A.K.: hbACSS: How to robustly share many secrets. In: 29th Annual Network and Distributed System Security Symposium, NDSS 2022, San Diego, California, USA, April 24-28, 2022 (2022)

Efficient and Generic Methods to Achieve Active Security in Private Information Retrieval and More Advanced Database Search

Reo Eriguchi[1(✉)], Kaoru Kurosawa[1,2], and Koji Nuida[1,3]

[1] National Institute of Advanced Industrial Science and Technology, Tokyo, Japan
eriguchi-reo@aist.go.jp
[2] Research and Development Initiative, Chuo University, Tokyo, Japan
kaoru.kurosawa.kk@vc.ibaraki.ac.jp
[3] Institute of Mathematics for Industry, Kyushu University, Fukuoka, Japan
nuida@imi.kyushu-u.ac.jp

Abstract. Motivated by secure database search, we present secure computation protocols for a function f in the client-servers setting, where a client can obtain $f(x)$ on a private input x by communicating with multiple servers each holding f. Specifically, we propose generic compilers from passively secure protocols, which only keep security against servers following the protocols, to actively secure protocols, which guarantee privacy and correctness even against malicious servers. Our compilers are applied to protocols computing any class of functions, and are efficient in that the overheads in communication and computational complexity are only polynomial in the number of servers, independent of the complexity of functions. We then apply our compilers to obtain concrete actively secure protocols for various functions including private information retrieval (PIR), bounded-degree multivariate polynomials and constant-depth circuits. For example, our actively secure PIR protocols achieve exponentially better computational complexity in the number of servers than the currently best-known protocols. Furthermore, our protocols for polynomials and constant-depth circuits reduce the required number of servers compared to the previous actively secure protocols. In particular, our protocol instantiated from the sparse Learning Parity with Noise (LPN) assumption is the first actively secure protocol for multivariate polynomials which has the minimum number of servers, without assuming fully homomorphic encryption.

1 Introduction

Client-server outsourcing is a central problem in secure computation. In particular, there are a wide variety of deployed systems which allow a client to search a database stored in one or more servers for desired contents. Since a client's query may contain sensitive information, it is important to realize *secure database search*, enabling a client to search a database without revealing his or

M. Joye and G. Leander (Eds.): EUROCRYPT 2024, LNCS 14655, pp. 92–121, 2024.
https://doi.org/10.1007/978-3-031-58740-5_4

her query to the servers. A trivial solution is downloading the whole database and searching it locally. However, since the database size is typically very large, we need to construct protocols whose communication and client-side computational complexity is sublinear in the database size.

Traditionally, the problem of secure database search has been considered in two types of setting. In the *single-server* setting, there is only one server storing a database who may be corrupted; In the *multi-server* setting, there are m servers storing copies of a database and any t of them are corrupted. In this work, we focus on the multi-server setting since it is known to be impossible to efficiently achieve information-theoretic security in the single-server setting [21] and even in computational settings, the bounded collusion of servers allows better efficiency and weaker cryptographic assumptions than single-server protocols [12,13,26].

Private Information Retrieval (PIR) is a fundamental cryptographic primitive to realize the most basic database search. The goal of PIR is to enable an honest client to retrieve a data item a_i from a database $\boldsymbol{a} = (a_1, \ldots, a_N)$ hiding the index i from the servers[1]. To allow more complex queries such as partial match search, Barkol and Ishai [5] considered a more general setting in which a client has a private input x and servers share a function f, and the goal of the client is to obtain $f(x)$ by communicating with the servers. A rich line of works proposed secure protocols computing various classes of functions f including PIR [8–10,14, 17,27,28], bounded-degree multivariate polynomials [6,24,36,43], and bounded-depth circuits [5,16,39,40]. Note that the communication complexity of these protocols is much smaller than the size of circuits computing f, which is the main advantages over usual multiparty computation protocols [15,23,34,35].

We note that the above-mentioned protocols are *passively secure*, i.e., the privacy and correctness are guaranteed only if servers follow the protocol specifications. On the other hand, it is desirable to achieve *active security* in real-world scenarios. Namely, protocols should not only protect the privacy of queries but also guarantee the correctness of results even if some servers deviate from the protocols arbitrarily. For example, servers may try to let a client accept an incorrect result, or compute responses from an out-of-date copy of a database. This paper concerns a fundamental problem of constructing an efficient compiler from passively secure protocols to actively secure protocols. Given such a compiler, existing passively secure protocols can be directly upgraded into actively secure protocols with small overheads. Prior to our work, however, the only known passive-to-active compilers are the inefficient ones applied to PIR [11,29], which incurs exponentially large computational overheads in the number of servers (see Sect. 1.2 for more related works on compilers in different settings including GMW-style compilers).

1.1 Our Results

In this paper, we study the problem of secure computation in the client-servers setting, where a client can obtain $f(x)$ on a private input x by communicating

---

[1] Throughout the paper, a client is assumed to be honest.

with multiple servers each holding f. We demonstrate theoretical feasibility of compilers that upgrade passively secure k-server protocols into actively secure m-server protocols with $m > k$. We present two such compilers: The first one upgrades a one-round passively secure protocol into a multi-round actively secure protocol. It increases the number of servers by a corruption threshold t, which seems the best possible (see Remark 1). The second one upgrades a one-round passively secure protocol into a one-round actively secure protocol while increasing the number of servers by a larger factor. More specifically,

- Our first compiler transforms a one-round passively secure k-server protocol into an $O(m^2)$-round actively secure m-server protocol such that $m = k + t$.
- Our second compiler transforms a one-round passively secure k-server protocol into a one-round actively secure m-server protocol such that $m = O(k \log k) + 2t$.

Our compilers are generic and efficient in the sense that they are applied to protocols computing any class of functions f and the overheads in communication and computational complexity are only polynomial in m, independent of the complexity of f. Furthermore, our compilers are unconditional, i.e., requires no additional assumptions, which allows us to obtain actively secure protocols from various assumptions or even information-theoretically as shown below.

Along the way, we introduce two novel notions, *conflict-finding protocols* and *locally surjective map families*. The former is an intermediate notion between passively secure and actively secure protocols, which is used in our first compiler. The latter is a variant of perfect hash families with a stronger property, which is used in our second compiler. A key observation behind our techniques is that if a pair of servers return different answers to the same query, then a client finds that at least one of them is malicious. A difficulty is that we have to carefully design such a strategy, since just disclosing a query for one server to another may reveal his private input. See Sect. 2 for details on our techniques.

Remark 1. Our first compiler increases the number of servers by t but this seems the best possible. Indeed, the existence of a generic compiler for an actively secure protocol with $m' < t + k$ servers implies a compiler from a k-server protocol to a k'-server protocol for $k' := m' - t < k$ since an actively secure m'-server protocol implies a passively secure $(m' - t)$-server protocol[2]. Thus, the increase in the number of servers is optimal unless there is a generic method to reduce the number of servers. Such a method has not been found up until now.

Instantiations. Based on our compilers, we show concrete actively secure protocols for PIR, bounded-degree multivariate polynomials and constant-depth circuits. Remarkably, our protocol instantiated from the sparse LPN assumption is the first actively secure protocol for multivariate polynomials which has the minimum number of servers, without assuming fully homomorphic encryption.

---

[2] The active security enables a client to obtain a correct result by interacting with $m' - t$ servers and computing the responses of the other t servers arbitrarily.

PIR. There are compilers from a passively secure k-server PIR protocol to an actively secure m-server protocol for $m = k + 2t$ [11] and $m = k + t$ [29]. However, these compilers incur exponentially large multiplicative overheads $m^{O(t)}$ in client-side computational complexity. On the other hand, our first compiler gives an actively secure m-server protocol such that $m = k+t$ with a polynomial computational overhead $m^{O(1)}$. The only cost is that it requires $O(m^2)$ rounds of interaction between a client and servers. Our second compiler gives a one-round actively secure protocol with a polynomial computational overhead at the cost of a larger number of servers $m = O(k \log k) + 2t$. A detailed comparison is shown in Table 1.

In the information-theoretic setting, the currently most communication-efficient passively secure PIR protocol for $t \geq 2$ is the 3^t-server protocol in [10], which has sub-polynomial communication and computational complexity $N^{o(1)} \cdot 3^{t+o(t)}$ in the database size N. (Although the original protocols in [10,14] assume non-colluding servers, i.e., $t = 1$, the corruption threshold t can be amplified by using the technique in [7] as pointed out in [32].) By applying our compilers, we obtain actively secure $3^{t+o(t)}$-server PIR protocols whose computational complexity is $N^{o(1)} \cdot 2^{O(t)}$. It exponentially (in t) improves the complexities $N^{o(1)} \cdot 3^{t+o(t)} \cdot m^{O(t)} = N^{o(1)} \cdot 2^{O(t^2)}$ of actively secure protocols that are obtained from the previous compilers [11,29]. In the computational setting, if we apply our compilers to the protocol assuming one-way functions [14], we can achieve logarithmic communication and computational complexity in N and reduce the number of servers. A detailed description is shown in Table 2.

Table 1. Comparison of passive-to-active compilers for PIR

Method	Multiplicative overhead to client-side computation	# servers	# rounds
[11]	$m^{O(t)}$	$k + 2t$	1
[29]	$m^{O(t)}\lambda$	$k + t$	1
Ours (Theorem 3)	$O(m^5\lambda)$	$k + t$	$O(m^2)$
Ours (Theorem 5)	$O(tm^2)$	$O(k \log k) + 2t$	1

k and m denote the numbers of servers in passively secure and actively secure protocols, respectively, t denotes a corruption threshold, and λ denotes a security parameter.

Bounded-Degree Multivariate Polynomials. In the information-theoretic setting, there is a passively secure protocol for polynomials in [43], which can be made actively secure by using the technique in [38]. In the computational setting, a passively secure protocol is given in [24], which can be made actively secure by the standard error correction algorithm [41]. Now, by applying our compilers, we can reduce the required number of servers of these protocols by t. Based on the passively secure protocol in [36], we can further reduce the number of servers

Table 2. Comparison of PIR protocols with sub-polynomial communication and computational complexity in the database size N for a corruption threshold $t \geq 2$

	Method	Client-side computation	# servers	# rounds	Assumption
Passive	[10] + [7]	$N^{o(1)} 2^{O(t)}$	3^t	1	IT
	[14] + [7]	$\log N \cdot 2^{O(t)} \lambda^{O(1)}$	2^t	1	OWF
Active	[11] + [7] + [10]	$N^{o(1)} \cdot 2^{O(t^2)}$	$3^t + 2t$	1	IT
	[11] + [7] + [14]	$\log N \cdot 2^{O(t^2)}$	$2^t + 2t$	1	OWF
	[29] + [7] + [10]	$N^{o(1)} \cdot 2^{O(t^2)} \lambda$	$3^t + t$	1	IT
	[29] + [7] + [14]	$\log N \cdot 2^{O(t^2)} \lambda^{O(1)}$	$2^t + t$	1	OWF
	Theorem 3 + [7] + [10]	$N^{o(1)} \cdot 2^{O(t)} \lambda$	$3^t + t$	$O(3^{2t})$	IT
	Theorem 3 + [7] + [14]	$\log N \cdot 2^{O(t)} \lambda^{O(1)}$	$2^t + t$	$O(2^{2t})$	OWF
	Theorem 5 + [7] + [10]	$N^{o(1)} \cdot 2^{O(t)}$	$O(t3^t)$	1	IT
	Theorem 5 + [7] + [14]	$\log N \cdot 2^{O(t)}$	$O(t2^t)$	1	OWF

λ denotes a security parameter. "IT" stands for "information-theoretic" (i.e., no cryptographic assumption is necessary) and "OWF" stands for "one-way functions."

by a factor of d assuming homomorphic encryption for degree-d polynomials. Notably, our protocol instantiated from [24] achieves the minimum number of servers $2t + 1$.[3] A detailed comparison is shown in Table 3.

Table 3. Comparison of actively secure protocols for multivariate polynomials

Method	# servers	# rounds	Assumption
[38] + [43]	$\left(\frac{D}{2} + 2\right) t + 1$	1	IT
Theorem 3 + [43]	$\left(\frac{D}{2} + 1\right) t + 1$	$O((Dt)^2)$	IT
Theorem 3 + [36]	$\left(\frac{D}{d+1} + 1\right) t + 1$	$O((Dt)^2)$	d-HE
[41] + [24]	$3t + 1$	1	sparse LPN
Theorem 3 + [24]	$2t + 1$	$O(t^2)$	sparse LPN

D denotes the degree of the polynomials and t denotes a corruption threshold. "IT" stands for "information-theoretic" and "d-HE" stands for homomorphic encryption for polynomials of degree d.

Constant-Depth Circuits. Barkol and Ishai [5] proposed a passively secure protocol for unbounded fan-in constant-depth circuits (i.e., the complexity class AC^0). It can be made actively secure by applying the error correction algorithm [41], and the resulting protocol needs at least $(\frac{1}{2}(\log M + O(1))^{D-1} + 2)t$ servers, where M and $D = O(1)$ are the size and depth of circuits, respectively. On the other hand, if we apply our first compiler, we need only $(\frac{1}{2}(\log M + O(1))^{D-1} + 1)t$

---

[3] The active security is impossible if the majority of servers are corrupted, i.e., $m \leq 2t$, since there is an attack for corrupted servers to replace their input f with another function f'.

servers, which decreases the number of servers of [5] by t. For example, for the partial match problem on an M-sized database (which can be captured by depth-2 circuits of size M), our protocol requires only $(\log M + 2.5)t$ servers while the protocol obtained from [5] requires $(\log M + 3.5)t$ servers.

A beneficial consequence is that our compilers can be directly applied to future developments in passively secure protocols in the client-servers scenario and may yield new efficient constructions of actively secure protocols.

1.2 Related Work

Passive-to-Active Compilers. Within the context of PIR, there are compilers from a passively secure k-server protocol to an actively secure m-server protocol for $m = k + 2t$ [11] and $m = k + t$ [29]. As said above, however, these compilers are not only less generic in that they are applied only to PIR, but also inefficient since they incur exponential overhead $\binom{m}{t} = m^{O(t)}$ in computational complexity. There are also passive-to-active compilers in a more general multi-client setting where a private input is arbitrarily distributed among multiple clients [15,23,34, 35]. However, in actively secure protocols resulting from these compilers, servers need to interactively evaluate a circuit gate by gate. Consequently, protocols require communication and computational complexity that is proportional to the size of a function, and do not work efficiently if the function encodes a large database.

PIR. There are direct constructions of m-server PIR protocols in a malicious setting [3,25,33,38,47]. However, the communication complexities of [3,25,33, 38] are all polynomial $N^{O(t/m)}$ in the database size N, while those of ours are $N^{o(1)}$, i.e., smaller than any polynomial function in N. The protocol in [47] does not guarantee privacy if malicious servers collude, and thus does not satisfy active t-security for $t > 1$ in our sense[4]. There are also constructions of PIR with a weaker security guarantee [19,22], which can only tell a client the existence of malicious servers. Actively secure PIR is also considered in a special setting where the length of each entry of a database is sufficiently large (e.g., [4,44] and references therein). The protocols in [4,44] assume that the length of each entry of a database is at least exponential in N and hence result in exponentially large communication complexity in N.

Protocols in the Single-Server Setting. Generally, if we have a passively secure single-server protocol, then we can obtain an actively secure protocol with the minimum number of servers $2t + 1$ since a client just runs the passively secure protocol with each server and computes the majority of $2t+1$ outputs. However, there is an impossibility result on efficient single-server protocols for PIR in the information-theoretic setting [21]. Even if we go for computational security, it seems to be impossible to construct single-server PIR protocols from the minimal assumption of one-way functions [26], and for a general function, we currently

---

[4] We mean by t-security that at most t servers are corrupted.

need to assume fully homomorphic encryption, which is only instantiated from a narrow class of assumptions [31,42].

Verifiable Computation. The problem of dealing with malicious servers has also been considered within the context of verifiable computation in the single-server setting [2,20,30] and in the multi-server setting [1,45,46]. However, these verifiable computation protocols only detect malicious behavior of servers and cannot achieve active security in our sense. The protocol in [18] uses a similar idea that a client compares answers from one server with those from another. However, it does not consider the setting where a client's input x should be private and also assumes that all parties agree on a function f in advance, while in our setting the client does not know f since it corresponds to an unknown database.

2   Technical Overview

In this section, we provide an overview of our compilers to construct an actively t-secure m-server protocol Π' from any one-round passively t-secure k-server protocol Π such that $k < m$. Let $V = \{S_1, \ldots, S_m\}$ be the set of m servers of Π'. A key observation behind our constructions is that if a pair of servers in V return different answers to the same query of Π, then at least one of them is malicious[5]. We call such two servers a *conflicting pair*. The client continues to remove conflicting pairs from V in an appropriate way. Finally, the client executes a protocol only with remaining honest servers and obtains a correct result. For ease of exposition, we first explain our non-interactive actively secure protocol and then explain our interactive protocol with fewer servers.

2.1   Non-interactive Actively Secure Protocols

As a first attempt, we consider the following basic construction.

1. A client C partitions $V = \{S_1, \ldots, S_m\}$ into k groups $V = G_1 \cup \ldots \cup G_k$ in such a way that each G_j contains at least one honest server.
2. C computes k queries of Π on his private input and sends the j-th query to all servers in the j-th group G_j.

If every group contains no conflicting pair (i.e., all servers in each G_j return the same answer), then C can compute the correct result from the k answers of the k groups. Otherwise, C removes a conflicting pair from V, and repeats the above process at most t times to remove all malicious servers. This method, however, requires a large number of servers $m = \Omega(kt)$ since the size of each group G_j needs to be larger than t.

   We reduce the number of servers to $m \approx 2t + k$ by introducing a novel notion of locally surjective map families. Technically, we consider a family $\mathcal{F}$ of maps from the set $V = \{S_1, \ldots, S_m\}$ of m servers to $[k] := \{1, 2, \ldots, k\}$. Each map

---

[5] Here, we assume that the server-side computation is deterministic.

$f \in \mathcal{F}$ defines a partition $V = G_{f,1} \cup \cdots \cup G_{f,k}$, where $G_{f,j} = \{S_i : f(S_i) = j\}$. For each map $f \in \mathcal{F}$, the client C computes k queries of Π on his private input and sends the j-th query to all servers in the j-th group $G_{f,j}$. Our strategy is that C proceeds in t steps to detect and remove at least one new malicious server per step. In each step,

- If for every (f, j), all the remaining servers in $G_{f,j}$ return the same answer $\mathsf{ans}_{f,j}$, then C computes an output x_f of Π from $(\mathsf{ans}_{f,1}, \ldots, \mathsf{ans}_{f,k})$ for each f and decides the final output by the majority vote over the x_f's;
- Otherwise, i.e., if two remaining servers in some $G_{f,j}$ give different answers, then C removes this conflicting pair and proceeds to the next step.

Observe that in the latter case, at least one of the two servers is malicious and hence at least one malicious server is always removed. The requirement for C to succeed is that in the former case, more than half of the x_f's are correct. A sufficient condition is that for more than half of the f's, there remains at least one honest server in each of $G_{f,1}, \ldots, G_{f,k}$. Indeed, for such f's, C receives the correct answer from servers in each of $G_{f,1}, \ldots, G_{f,k}$, or proceeds to the latter case and removes a conflicting pair. Since there remains at least $m - 2t$ honest servers at every step, the condition can be formulated as the family $\mathcal{F}$ of maps satisfying that for any subset $H \subseteq V$ of size $m - 2t$, there exist more than half of the f's such that $f(H) = [k]$. We name such a family as a *locally surjective map family*.

We can prove by a probabilistic argument the existence of a locally surjective map family $\mathcal{F}$ of size $O(m)$ if $k = O((m - 2t)/\log(m - 2t))$. Therefore, we can obtain an actively t-secure m-server protocol Π' from a passively t-secure k-server protocol Π if $m = O(k \log k) + 2t$. Since the client can run all instances of Π in parallel, the resulting protocol Π' is one-round and only incurs a $O(tm|\mathcal{F}|) = O(tm^2)$ multiplicative overhead to communication and computational complexity.

2.2   Interactive Actively Secure Protocols

We further reduce the number of servers from $m = O(k \log k) + 2t$ to $m = t + k$. In our first construction, if a client C finds a conflicting pair of servers, then he removes both servers from the set V. After eliminating all t malicious servers, the number of remaining servers is reduced to $m - 2t$ in the worst case. Therefore, as long as this approach is used, the number of servers must be $m \geq 2t + k$ since it should hold that $m - 2t \geq k$.

Our second construction reduces the required number of servers to $m = t + k$ by introducing a notion of *t-conflict-finding* protocols, which is an intermediate notion between passively t-secure protocols and actively t-secure ones. Intuitively, in a conflict-finding protocol, a client C obtains a correct result or a non-trivial partition (G_0, G_1) of the set V of servers such that all honest servers are included in G_0 or G_1 (and hence the other group consists of malicious servers only)[6]. A pair of servers crossing the partition (G_0, G_1) is supposed to be conflicting.

More concretely, we consider a graph $\mathcal{G}$ with m vertices each of which represents a server. Our protocol starts with $\mathcal{G}$ being a complete graph, and repeats the following steps:

1. The client C executes a conflict-finding protocol Π_{CF} with some subset $V' \subseteq V$ which forms a connected subgraph of size $k = m - t$ in $\mathcal{G}$ (which can be efficiently found).
2. If all servers in V' behave honestly, then C obtains the correct output.
3. Otherwise C can find a partition (G_0, G_1) of V' thanks to the conflict-finding property of Π_{CF}. Note that there is always an edge $e = (S_i, S_j)$ between G_0 and G_1 since $G_0 \cup G_1 = V'$ is connected. Furthermore, since all honest servers in V' are included in G_0 or G_1, at least one of S_i and S_j is malicious. Now, C removes the edge e from $\mathcal{G}$ instead of eliminating the two servers, and goes back to the first step.

Since all edges among honest servers remain unremoved (and hence the set of all honest servers remains connected), C can successfully find a set of $k = m - t$ honest servers within $O(m^2)$ rounds. Note that in the above construction, C chooses a set of servers with which he executes Π_{CF}, depending on the answers that are maliciously computed in the previous rounds. Thus servers may learn some information on the client input x by seeing which servers C removes. To address this problem, we impose an additional property that the distribution of the partition (G_0, G_1) is independent of x regardless of how malicious servers behave. Then, an edge removed in each round leaks no information on x and hence the privacy of x is preserved.

Two-Round Conflict-Finding Protocols. The remaining problem is how to construct conflict-finding protocols. We show a construction of a two-round t-conflict-finding k-server protocol Π_{CF} from a passively t-secure k-server one Π. For simplicity, let $V' = (S_1, \ldots, S_k)$. In the first round, a client computes real queries $(que_i)_{i \in [k]}$ on his private input x according to Π as usual. He also computes dummy queries $(que'_i)_{i \in [k]}$ on a default input x_{def} which is independent of x. He then sends a random permutation of (que_i, que'_i) to each server S_i. Note that the privacy of Π and the random permutation ensure that servers cannot distinguish which queries are computed on x or x_{def}. Each server S_i returns answers (ans_i, ans'_i) to the two queries as usual. In the second round, the client sends all the dummy queries $(que'_i)_{i \in [k]}$ on x_{def} to all servers in V', which does not affect privacy since x_{def} is independent of x. In response, each server S_j returns $v_j := (ans'_i(j))_{i \in [k]}$ to $(que'_i)_{i \in [k]}$, where $ans'_i(j)$ is the answer which S_i would compute to the dummy query que'_i.

For simplicity, suppose that S_1 is the only malicious server. If S_1 behaved honestly in the first round, it holds that $ans'_1 = ans'_1(2) = \cdots = ans'_1(k)$.

---

[6] We say that a partition (G_0, G_1) is non-trivial if neither of G_0 nor G_1 is empty.

If S_1 returned an incorrect answer to que'_1, it is different from any of $ans'_1(2), \ldots, ans'_1(k)$. From this observation, the client C trusts the answer ans_1 of S_1 to the main query que_1 in the first round if and only if $ans'_1 = ans'_1(2) = \cdots = ans'_1(k)$. Generalizing this, we let C compute an output based on $(ans_1, ans_2, \ldots, ans_k)$ if all the v_j's take the same value. Otherwise, he partitions the set of servers into equivalence classes by placing S_i and S_j into the same class if and only if $v_i = v_j$, and outputs a non-trivial partition (G_0, G_1) in some way. Note that any pair of honest servers S_i, S_j return the same answer in the second round, i.e., $v_i = v_j$, and hence they are placed in the same class. A malicious server successfully submits an incorrect answer without being detected only if it guesses correctly which query encodes the client's true input x. As we said above, it happens with probability $1/2$. More generally, if the client prepares $M - 1$ sets of dummy queries, the cheating probability of malicious servers can be reduced to $1/M$. This can be made even negligible by executing sufficiently many (say, κ) instances in parallel. If a conflict is found in some instance, C outputs a non-trivial partition (G_0, G_1) obtained in that instance. Otherwise, he outputs the majority of the κ outputs if it exists. To let this protocol fail, malicious servers need to let the client output valid but incorrect outputs in at least $\kappa/2$ instances. The cheating probability is thus $O(M^{-\kappa/2})$, which is negligible.

To see that the partition (G_0, G_1) leaks no information on the client's input x, observe that (G_0, G_1) is determined by answers $(v_j)_{j \in [k]}$. These answers are independent of x since they can be simulated from dummy queries and t queries for x that malicious servers see. The former is independent of x in the first place and the latter leaks no information on x due to the privacy of Π.

To summarize, we obtain an $O(m^2)$-round actively t-secure m-server protocol from a passively t-secure k-server protocol if $k \leq m - t$. The communication and computational overhead is a multiplicative polynomial factor in m.

3   Preliminaries

Notations. For $m \in \mathbb{N}$, define $[m] = \{1, 2, \ldots, m\}$. Let X, Y be sets. If $X \subseteq Y$, we define $Y \setminus X = \{y \in Y : y \notin X\}$ and simply denote it by $\overline{X}$ if Y is clear from the context. We write $u \leftarrow_\$ X$ if u is chosen uniformly at random from X. Define $\binom{X}{k}$ as the set of all subsets of X of size k. Define $\mathrm{Map}(X, Y)$ as the set of all maps from X to Y. If $X = [m]$ and $Y = [k]$, we simply denote it by $\mathrm{Map}(m, k)$. Let $\log x$ denote the base-2 logarithm of x and $\ln x$ denote the base-e logarithm of x, where e is the Napier's constant. We call a function $f : \mathbb{N} \ni \lambda \mapsto f(\lambda) \in \mathbb{R}$ *negligible* if for any $c > 0$, there exists $\lambda_0 \in \mathbb{N}$ such that $0 \leq f(\lambda) < \lambda^{-c}$ for any $\lambda > \lambda_0$. We call f *polynomial* there exists $c > 0$ such that $0 \leq f(\lambda) < \lambda^c$ for all λ. Throughout the paper, we use the following notations:

- m denotes the total number of servers, which is polynomial in a security parameter λ.
- t denotes the number of corrupted servers.
- C denotes a client and S_i denotes the i-th server.

The notation $\widetilde{O}(\cdot)$ hides a polylogarithmic factor in a security parameter λ.

3.1 Secure Computation in the Client-Servers Setting

We follow the client-servers model used in [5]. In this model, there is an honest client C who holds a private input x, and m servers $S_1, \ldots, S_m$ who all hold the same input p. The goal is:

Byzantine-Robustness. The client learns the value $F(p, x)$ for a publicly known function F even if t servers behave maliciously;

Privacy. The client keeps his input x hidden from any collusion of t servers.

We do not assume any interaction between servers. We call a message from a client to servers a *query* and a message from servers to the client an *answer*.

In the above setting, we assume that the function F takes a common input p from servers. Typically, the input p will be a description of a function f applied to the input x of a client (e.g., a description of a circuit or a polynomial) and F is the universal function defined by $F(p, x) = f(x)$.

If $m \geq 2t + 1$, there is a trivial 1-round protocol achieving the above goal: C downloads p from all servers, finds the correct p by the majority vote, and computes $F(p, x)$ by himself. However, this protocol results in large communication and client-side computational complexity that is linear in the description length of p. In applications to database search, p encodes a large database and its size is proportional to the database size. From this point of view, we say that a protocol is *efficient* if its communication and client-side computational complexity is sublinear in the description length of p and linear in that of x.

More formally, we define a secure computation protocol in the client-servers setting as an abstract primitive. First, we show the syntax and correctness.

Definition 1. *Let* $\mathcal{P} = (P_\lambda)_{\lambda \in \mathbb{N}}$, $\mathcal{X} = (X_\lambda)_{\lambda \in \mathbb{N}}$, *and* $\mathcal{Y} = (Y_\lambda)_{\lambda \in \mathbb{N}}$ *be sequences of sets with polynomial-size descriptions and* $\mathcal{F} = (F_\lambda : P_\lambda \times X_\lambda \to Y_\lambda)_{\lambda \in \mathbb{N}}$ *be sequences of functions with polynomial-size descriptions. An ℓ-round m-server protocol for* $\mathcal{F}$ *is a tuple of three polynomial-time algorithms* $\Pi = (\mathsf{Query}, \mathsf{Answer}, \mathsf{Output})$, *where:*

- $\mathsf{Query}(1^\lambda, x, \mathsf{st}^{(j-1)}, (\mathsf{ans}_i^{(j-1)})_{i \in [m]}) \to ((\mathsf{que}_i^{(j)})_{i \in [m]}, \mathsf{st}^{(j)})$: Query *is a possibly randomized algorithm that takes* $x \in X_\lambda$, *a state* $\mathsf{st}^{(j-1)}$ *and answers* $(\mathsf{ans}_i^{(j-1)})_{i \in [m]}$ *in round $j - 1$ as input, and outputs queries* $(\mathsf{que}_i^{(j)})_{i \in [m]}$ *and a state* $\mathsf{st}^{(j)}$ *in round j, where we define* $\mathsf{st}^{(0)}$, $\mathsf{ans}_i^{(0)}$ *as the empty string;*
- $\mathsf{Answer}(1^\lambda, p, \mathsf{que}_i^{(j)}) \to \mathsf{ans}_i^{(j)}$: Answer *is a deterministic algorithm that takes* $p \in P_\lambda$ *and a query* $\mathsf{que}_i^{(j)}$ *in round j as input, and outputs an answer* $\mathsf{ans}_i^{(j)}$ *in round j;*
- $\mathsf{Output}(1^\lambda, \mathsf{st}^{(\ell)}, (\mathsf{ans}_i^{(\ell)})_{i \in [m]}) \to y$: Output *is a possibly randomized algorithm that takes a state* $\mathsf{st}^{(\ell)}$ *and answers* $(\mathsf{ans}_i^{(\ell)})_{i \in [m]}$ *in round ℓ as input, and outputs* $y \in Y_\lambda$;

satisfying the following property:

Correctness. *There exists a negligible function* $\mathsf{negl}(\lambda)$ *such that for any* $\lambda \in \mathbb{N}$ *and any* $(p, x) \in P_\lambda \times X_\lambda$,

$$\Pr\left[\mathsf{Output}(1^\lambda, \mathsf{st}^{(\ell)}, (\mathsf{ans}_i^{(\ell)})_{i\in[m]})) = F_\lambda(p, x)\right] \geq 1 - \mathsf{negl}(\lambda),$$

where

$$((\mathsf{que}_i^{(j)})_{i\in[m]}, \mathsf{st}^{(j)}) \leftarrow \mathsf{Query}(1^\lambda, x, \mathsf{st}^{(j-1)}, (\mathsf{ans}_i^{(j-1)})_{i\in[m]}),$$
$$\mathsf{ans}_i^{(j)} \leftarrow \mathsf{Answer}(1^\lambda, p, \mathsf{que}_i^{(j)})$$

for all $j \in [\ell]$ *and* $i \in [m]$.

We note that an answer algorithm Answer is not always defined to be deterministic in the literature but all the instantiations considered in this paper actually have deterministic answer algorithms. We omit a security parameter 1^λ from inputs if it is clear from the context.

An abstract primitive $\Pi = (\mathsf{Query}, \mathsf{Answer}, \mathsf{Output})$ immediately implies an ℓ-round protocol in the above client-servers setting. Indeed, a client has a private input x and m servers have a common input p. In each round, the client runs Query, sends queries to servers and stores a state in his memory. In response, servers run Answer on the queries that they receive, and send answers back to the client. In the final round, the client runs Output on his state and servers' answers, and obtains $y = F_\lambda(p, x)$. Due to this correspondence, we will use the terminologies interchangeably for the sake of readability.

The above-mentioned trivial 1-round protocol corresponds to the scheme in which Query outputs nothing, Answer outputs p and then Output computes $y = F_\lambda(p, x)$. To rule out this, we define the efficiency measures of Π as follows. Let $\mathsf{que}_i^{(j)}$ and $\mathsf{ans}_i^{(j)}$ be queries and answers computed by Π and denote their bit-lengths by $|\mathsf{que}_i^{(j)}|$ and $|\mathsf{ans}_i^{(j)}|$, respectively. Define the *communication complexity* $\mathsf{Comm}_\lambda(\Pi)$ as

$$\mathsf{Comm}_\lambda(\Pi) = \sup_{(p,x)\in P_\lambda \times X_\lambda} \sum_{i\in[m], j\in[\ell]} (|\mathsf{que}_i^{(j)}| + |\mathsf{ans}_i^{(j)}|).$$

Define the *client-side computational complexity* $\mathsf{c\text{-}Comp}_\lambda(\Pi)$ as the sum of the running time of $\mathsf{Query}(1^\lambda, x, \cdot, \cdot)$ and $\mathsf{Output}(1^\lambda, \cdot, \cdot)$ with worst-case inputs $(p, x) \in P_\lambda \times X_\lambda$. Let $\mathsf{Comm}(\Pi) = (\mathsf{Comm}_\lambda(\Pi))_{\lambda\in\mathbb{N}}$ and $\mathsf{c\text{-}Comp}(\Pi) = (\mathsf{c\text{-}Comp}_\lambda(\Pi))_{\lambda\in\mathbb{N}}$. We say that Π is *efficient* if there exists a sublinear function $g(\ell) = o(\ell)$ such that

$$\max\{\mathsf{Comm}(\Pi), \mathsf{c\text{-}Comp}(\Pi)\} \in g(|p|) \cdot |x| \cdot \mathsf{poly}(m, \lambda), \tag{1}$$

where $|p|$ and $|x|$ are the description lengths of elements of P_λ and X_λ, respectively. One can also define the *server-side computational complexity* $\mathsf{s\text{-}Comp}_\lambda(\Pi)$ as the running time of $\mathsf{Answer}(1^\lambda, p, \cdot)$, and define $\mathsf{s\text{-}Comp}(\Pi) = (\mathsf{s\text{-}Comp}_\lambda(\Pi))_{\lambda\in\mathbb{N}}$. We see the communication and client-side complexity as a primary efficiency measure and the server-side computational complexity as a secondary measure.

Next, we show the security requirements.

Definition 2. *Let $\Pi = (\mathsf{Query}, \mathsf{Answer}, \mathsf{Output})$ be an ℓ-round m-server protocol for $\mathcal{F} = (F_\lambda : P_\lambda \times X_\lambda \to Y_\lambda)_{\lambda \in \mathbb{N}}$. We say that Π is actively t-secure if it satisfies the following requirements:*

Privacy. *There exists a negligible function $\mathsf{negl}(\lambda)$ such that for any stateful algorithm $\mathcal{A}$ and any $\lambda \in \mathbb{N}$,*

$$\mathsf{Adv}_{\Pi,\mathcal{A}}(\lambda) := \left| \Pr\left[\mathsf{Priv}^0_{\Pi,\mathcal{A}}(\lambda) = 0\right] - \Pr\left[\mathsf{Priv}^1_{\Pi,\mathcal{A}}(\lambda) = 0\right] \right| < \mathsf{negl}(\lambda),$$

where for $b \in \{0,1\}$, $\mathsf{Priv}^b_{\Pi,\mathcal{A}}(\lambda)$ is the output b' of $\mathcal{A}$ in the following experiment:
1. *$(x_0, x_1, p, T) \leftarrow \mathcal{A}(1^\lambda)$, where $x_0, x_1 \in X_\lambda$, $p \in P_\lambda$ and $T \subseteq [m]$ is of size at most t.*
2. *For each $j = 1, 2, \ldots, \ell$,*
   (a) *Let $((\mathsf{que}^{(j)}_i)_{i \in [m]}, \mathsf{st}^{(j)}) \leftarrow \mathsf{Query}(1^\lambda, x_b, \mathsf{st}^{(j-1)}, (\mathsf{ans}^{(j-1)}_i)_{i \in [m]})$ and give $(\mathsf{que}^{(j)}_i)_{i \in T}$ to $\mathcal{A}$.*
   (b) *If $j < \ell$, $\mathcal{A}$ outputs $(\mathsf{ans}^{(j)}_i)_{i \in T}$. If $j = \ell$, $\mathcal{A}$ outputs a bit $b' \in \{0,1\}$.*

Byzantine-robustness. *There exists a negligible function $\mathsf{negl}(\lambda)$ such that for any stateful algorithm $\mathcal{A}$ and any $\lambda \in \mathbb{N}$,*

$$\Pr\left[\mathsf{BR}_{\Pi,\mathcal{A}}(\lambda) = 1\right] < \mathsf{negl}(\lambda),$$

where $\mathsf{BR}_{\Pi,\mathcal{A}}(\lambda)$ is the output of the following experiment:
1. *$(x, p, T) \leftarrow \mathcal{A}(1^\lambda)$, where $x \in X_\lambda$, $p \in P_\lambda$ and $T \subseteq [m]$ is of size at most t.*
2. *For each $j = 1, 2, \ldots, \ell$,*
   (a) *Let $((\mathsf{que}^{(j)}_i)_{i \in [m]}, \mathsf{st}^{(j)}) \leftarrow \mathsf{Query}(1^\lambda, x_b, \mathsf{st}^{(j-1)}, (\mathsf{ans}^{(j-1)}_i)_{i \in [m]})$ and give $(\mathsf{que}^{(j)}_i)_{i \in T}$ to $\mathcal{A}$.*
   (b) *$\mathcal{A}$ outputs $(\mathsf{ans}^{(j)}_i)_{i \in T}$.*
3. *Return 1 if $\mathsf{Output}(1^\lambda, \mathsf{st}^{(\ell)}, (\mathsf{ans}^{(\ell)}_i)_{i \in [m]}) \neq F_\lambda(p, x)$, and otherwise return 0.*

We say that Π is *passively t-secure* if it satisfies the above requirements for *semi-honest* adversaries $\mathcal{A}$, i.e., those following the instructions of Π. Note that for semi-honest adversaries, the Byzantine-robustness of Π immediately follows from the correctness of Π. We say that Π is *computationally actively t-secure* (resp. *computationally passively t-secure*) if it satisfies the above requirements for probabilistic polynomial-time (PPT) adversaries $\mathcal{A}$ (resp. semi-honest PPT adversaries $\mathcal{A}$).

3.2   Existing Passively Secure Protocols

Private Information Retrieval. Let $N = N(\lambda)$ be a polynomial function. Define $\mathrm{INDEX}_N = (F_\lambda : \{0,1\}^N \times [N] \to \{0,1\})_{\lambda \in \mathbb{N}}$ as a sequence of functions such that for each $\lambda \in \mathbb{N}$,

$$F_\lambda((a_1, \ldots, a_N), x) = a_x, \quad \forall (a_1, \ldots, a_N) \in \{0,1\}^N, \forall x \in [N].$$

An m-server protocol for INDEX_N is called an m-server private information retrieval (PIR) protocol for N-sized databases. In the information-theoretic setting, the most communication-efficient passively secure 3-server PIR protocol was given by [10] and in the computational setting, the passively secure 2-server PIR protocol was given by [14] assuming the existence of one-way functions. Although the original protocols in [10,14] assume $t = 1$, the corruption threshold t can be amplified by using the technique in [7] as pointed out in [32]. More specifically, the following propositions hold.

Proposition 1. *There exists a passively t-secure 1-round 3^t-server protocol Π for INDEX_N such that*

- $\text{Comm}(\Pi) = \exp(O(\sqrt{\log N \log \log N})) \cdot t3^t = N^{o(1)} \cdot 2^{O(t)}$;
- $\text{c-Comp}(\Pi) = \exp(O(\sqrt{\log N \log \log N})) \cdot t3^t = N^{o(1)} \cdot 2^{O(t)}$;
- $\text{s-Comp}(\Pi) = N^2 \cdot \exp(O(\sqrt{\log N \log \log N})) \cdot 2^t = N^{2+o(1)} \cdot 2^t$.

Note that the above protocol satisfies the efficiency requirement (1) since $\text{Comm}(\Pi)$ and $\text{c-Comp}(\Pi)$ are sub-polynomial (i.e., less than any polynomial) in the description length N of elements of $P_\lambda = \{0,1\}^N$.

Proposition 2. *Assume a pseudorandom generator $G : \{0,1\}^\lambda \to \{0,1\}^{2(\lambda+1)}$. There exists a computationally passively t-secure 1-round 2^t-server protocol Π for INDEX_N such that*

- $\text{Comm}(\Pi) = O(\log N \cdot \lambda \cdot t2^t)$;
- $\text{c-Comp}(\Pi)$ *is* $O(\log N \cdot t2^t)$ *invocations of* G;
- $\text{s-Comp}(\Pi)$ *is* $O(N^2 \log N \cdot t)$ *invocations of* G.

Remark 2. Dvir and Gopi [27] devised a technique to optimize the 3-server protocol in [28] and obtained a 2-server PIR protocol with $N^{o(1)}$ communication. However, since the answer length is not constant, the passively t-secure protocol obtained by applying the amplification technique of [7] has larger communication complexity $\exp(O(t\sqrt{\log N \log \log N}))$ and does not satisfy the efficiency requirement (1).

Bounded-Degree Polynomials. Let $N = N(\lambda)$, $D = D(\lambda)$ and $M = M(\lambda)$ be polynomial functions. We define $\text{POLY}_{N,D,M}(R) = (F_\lambda)_{\lambda \in \mathbb{N}}$ as a sequence of functions such that $F_\lambda(p, \mathbf{x}) = p(\mathbf{x})$ for any N-variate polynomial p over a ring R with degree D and number of monomials M, and for any $\mathbf{x} \in R^N$. The following is implicit in [43].

Proposition 3. *Let $N, D, M \in \text{poly}(\lambda)$. Let R be a ring such that for any $a \in \{1, 2, \ldots, m-1\}$, an element $a \cdot 1_R$ has an inverse in R, where 1_R is the multiplicative identity of R. Suppose that $m > Dt/2$. Then, there exists a passively t-secure 1-round m-server protocol Π for $\text{POLY}_{N,D,M}(R)$ such that*

- $\text{Comm}(\Pi)$ *is* $O(Nm)$ *ring elements;*
- $\text{c-Comp}(\Pi)$ *is* $O(Ntm)$ *ring operations;*
- $\text{s-Comp}(\Pi)$ *is* $O(NMD)$ *ring operations.*

Since the description length of a polynomial with M monomials is $\widetilde{O}(MD \log |R|)$, the above protocol satisfies the efficiency requirement (1) if $MD = \omega(N)$.

Ishai, Lai and Malavolta [36] showed that assuming homomorphic encryption for degree-d polynomials, the number of servers in Proposition 3 can be decreased by a factor of d.

Proposition 4. *Let $d = O(1)$ and R be a ring such that for any $a \in \{1, 2, \ldots, \max\{d, m-1\}\}$, an element $a \cdot 1_R$ has an inverse in R, where 1_R is the multiplicative identity of R. Assume a homomorphic encryption scheme* HE *for degree-d polynomials over R. Let $M, N \in \mathsf{poly}(\lambda)$ and $D = O(1)$. Suppose that $m > Dt/(d+1)$. Then there exists a computationally passively t-secure 1-round m-server protocol Π for $\mathrm{POLY}_{N,D,M}(R)$ such that*

- $\mathrm{Comm}(\Pi) = O(Nm \cdot \ell_{\mathsf{ct}})$, *where ℓ_{ct} is the description length of ciphertexts of* HE;
- c-$\mathrm{Comp}(\Pi) = O((Nt \cdot \tau_{\mathsf{Enc}} + \tau_{\mathsf{Dec}})m)$, *where τ_{Enc} and τ_{Dec} are the running time of the encryption and decryption algorithms of* HE, *respectively;*
- s-$\mathrm{Comp}(\Pi) = O(MN \cdot \tau_{\mathsf{Eval}})$, *where τ_{Eval} is the running time of the evaluation algorithm of* HE *per operation.*

Note that we have $\max\{d, m-1\} = \mathsf{poly}(\lambda)$ since $d = O(1)$ and $m = \mathsf{poly}(\lambda)$. On the other hand, homomorphic encryption schemes mentioned in [36] assume that R is a prime field of size q or a ring of integers modulo $n = q_1 q_2$ for exponentially large primes q, q_1, q_2. In these cases, $a \cdot 1_R$ has an inverse in R if $a \in \{1, 2, \ldots, \max\{d, m-1\}\}$.

Under the sparse Learning Parity with Noise (LPN) assumption over a field $\mathbb{F}_q$, Dao et al. [24] proposed a passively t-secure $(t+1)$-server protocol for polynomials of degree $D = O(\log \lambda / \log \log \lambda)$. Although the original protocol does not have sublinear-size upload cost when evaluating a single polynomial, it can be seen that the upload cost is amortized if sufficiently many polynomials are evaluated on the same input. Specifically, let $N = N(\lambda)$, $D = D(\lambda)$, $M = M(\lambda)$, and $L = L(\lambda)$ be polynomial functions. We define $\mathrm{POLY}_{N,D,M}^L(R) = (F_\lambda)_{\lambda \in \mathbb{N}}$ as a sequence of functions such that $F_\lambda((p_1, \ldots, p_L), \mathbf{x}) = (p_1(\mathbf{x}), \ldots, p_L(\mathbf{x}))$ for any N-variate polynomials $p_1, \ldots, p_L$ over a ring R with degree D and number of monomials M, and for any $\mathbf{x} \in R^N$.

Proposition 5. *Assume that the (δ, q)-sLPN assumption holds for a constant $0 \leq \delta \leq 1$ and a sequence $q = (q(\lambda))_{\lambda \in \mathbb{N}}$ of prime powers that are computable in polynomial time in λ. Let $L, M, N \in \mathsf{poly}(\lambda)$ and $D = O(\log \lambda / \log \log \lambda)$. Then, there exists a computationally passively t-secure 1-round $(t+1)$-server protocol Π for $\mathrm{POLY}_{N,D,M}^L(\mathbb{F}_q)$ such that*

- $\mathrm{Comm}(\Pi) = \widetilde{O}((M^{2/\delta}N + L)(\log q)m\lambda)$;
- c-$\mathrm{Comp}(\Pi) = \widetilde{O}((M^{2/\delta}N + L)(\log q)m\lambda)$;
- s-$\mathrm{Comp}(\Pi) = \widetilde{O}(M^{1/\delta+1}L(\log q)\lambda)$.

Note that the description length of L polynomials each with M monomials is $\widetilde{O}(ML \log q)$ if the degree is $D = o(\log \lambda)$. Thus, if $L = \omega(M^{2/\delta-1})$, the above protocol satisfies the efficiency requirement (1). See [24] for the details including the definition of the sparse LPN assumption.

Constant-Depth Circuits. We consider Boolean circuits of constant depth with unbounded fan-in and fan-out. Formally, a Boolean circuit C is a labelled directed acyclic graph. The nodes with no incoming edges are labelled with input variables, their negations, or constants. The other nodes are called gates and are labelled with one of operators in $\{\mathsf{AND}, \mathsf{OR}, \mathsf{NOT}\}$. Nodes with no outgoing edges are called output nodes. We only consider a circuit with a single output node. The size of a circuit is the number of edges and its depth is the length of the longest path from an input node to the output node. We define the output of C on input x, which we denote by $C(x)$, as the value of the output node after input values proceed through a sequence of gates.

Let $N = N(\lambda)$, $D = D(\lambda)$ and $M = M(\lambda)$ be polynomial functions. We define $\mathrm{CIRC}_{N,D,M} = (F_\lambda)_{\lambda \in \mathbb{N}}$ as a sequence of functions such that $F_\lambda(C, x) = C(x)$ for any Boolean circuit C with N input variables, depth D and size M, and for any N-bit string x.

Proposition 6. *Let $N, M \in \mathsf{poly}(\lambda)$ and $D = O(1)$. Suppose that $m \geq (\log M + 3)^{D-1}t/2$. Then, there exists a passively t-secure 1-round m-server protocol Π for $\mathrm{CIRC}_{N,D,M}$ such that*

- $\mathrm{Comm}(\Pi) = O((\log M)^{D-1}N(\log N)\lambda m);$
- $\mathrm{c\text{-}Comp}(\Pi) = O((\log M)^{D-1}N(\log N)tm + (\log M)^2\lambda m);$
- $\mathrm{s\text{-}Comp}(\Pi) = O(M(\log M)N\lambda).$

The protocol is efficient since $\mathrm{Comm}(\Pi)$ and $\mathrm{c\text{-}Comp}(\Pi)$ are linear in N and polylogarithmic in the size M of circuits, omitting factors in λ and m.

4   Interactive Actively Secure Protocols

In this section, we show our compiler from one-round passively t-secure k-server protocols to $O(m^2)$-round actively t-secure m-server protocols such that $m \geq k + t$. To this end, we introduce a notion of *conflict-finding* protocols, which is an intermediate notion between passively secure and actively secure protocols. We show a generic compiler from conflict-finding to actively secure protocols in Sect. 4.3 and then show a generic compiler from passively secure to conflict-finding protocols.

4.1 Graph Theory

To begin with, we recall the standard terminology of graph theory (see [37, Chapter 2] for instance). A (simple and undirected) graph $\mathcal{G}$ is a pair (V, E), where V is a set of vertices and E is a set of edges $(i, j) \in V \times V$. Throughout the paper, we only consider the cases where V is either $[m]$ or a subset of $[m]$. Thus we may assume that V is a totally ordered set. The total order on V naturally induces a lexicographic order on E, which is also a total order on E. A graph $\mathcal{G}$ is called *connected* if there is a path between each pair of vertices. It is a standard result that there is a deterministic algorithm $\mathcal{D}$ which decomposes $\mathcal{G}$ into connected components in time $O(|V| + |E|)$ [37]. For $S \subseteq V$, we denote by $\mathcal{G}[S]$ the induced subgraph, i.e., the graph whose vertex set is S and whose edge set consists of the edges in E that have both endpoints in S.

We show a deterministic algorithm $\mathcal{C}'_k$ such that for any connected graph $\mathcal{G} = (V, E)$ with at least k vertices, $\mathcal{C}'_k(\mathcal{G})$ outputs a subset $S \subseteq V$ such that $|S| = k$ and $\mathcal{G}[S]$ is connected. First, $\mathcal{C}'_k$ chooses the minimum node s of V with respect to the total order on V. Secondly, $\mathcal{C}'_k$ runs the "textbook" depth-first search algorithm [37] starting at the vertex s, except that it stops searching if it visits k vertices. Finally, $\mathcal{C}'_k$ outputs the set S of all vertices it visited so far. By definition, S is of size k. Since any pair of vertices in S are connected via s, $\mathcal{G}[S]$ is connected. The running time of $\mathcal{C}'_k$ is $O(|V| + |E|)$.

Next, we show a deterministic algorithm $\mathcal{C}_k$ such that for any graph $\mathcal{G} = (V, E)$, if $\mathcal{G}$ contains a connected component of size at least k, $\mathcal{C}_k(\mathcal{G})$ outputs a subset $S \subseteq V$ of size k such that $\mathcal{G}[S]$ is connected, and otherwise, it outputs the empty set $\emptyset$. First, $\mathcal{C}_k$ lists all the connected components of $\mathcal{G}$, $(\mathcal{G}_1, \dots, \mathcal{G}_q) \leftarrow \mathcal{D}(\mathcal{G})$. Secondly, $\mathcal{C}_k$ lets $q_{\min}$ be the minimum index q such that $\mathcal{G}_q$ has at least k vertices. If no component has k vertices, $\mathcal{C}_k$ outputs $\emptyset$. Otherwise, $\mathcal{C}_k$ outputs $S \leftarrow \mathcal{C}'_k(\mathcal{G}_{q_{\min}})$. The correctness of $\mathcal{C}_k$ immediately follows from those of $\mathcal{D}$ and $\mathcal{C}'_k$. The running time of $\mathcal{C}_k$ is $O(|V| + |E|)$.

Finally, we show a trivial but frequently-used algorithm $\mathcal{E}$, which takes as input a graph $\mathcal{G} = (V, E)$ and a pair of disjoint non-empty subsets $G_0, G_1 \subseteq V$, and outputs the minimum edge $e = (i, j) \in E$ (with respect to the total order on E) such that $i \in G_0$ and $j \in G_1$, or $j \in G_0$ and $i \in G_1$. The running time of $\mathcal{E}$ is $O(|E|)$.

4.2 Formalization of Conflict-Finding Protocols

Roughly speaking, in a conflict-finding protocol, a client obtains (y, z), where y is the main output (supposed to be $F(p, x)$) and z is an auxiliary string. The string z is either output, failure, or a non-trivial partition (G_0, G_1) of the set of servers[7]. The security requirements are:

Soundness. The probability that $z = $ output and $y \neq F(p, x)$ is negligible, and the probability that the protocol outputs $z = $ failure is also negligible;

---

[7] We say that a partition (G_0, G_1) is *non-trivial* if $G_0 \neq \emptyset$ and $G_1 \neq \emptyset$.

Conflict-Finding. If z is a non-trivial partition (G_0, G_1) of the set of servers, then one of G_0 or G_1 contains all honest servers (and hence the other group consists of malicious servers only);

Privacy. An adversary should not learn a client's input x even if she knows z.

Intuitively, the conflict-finding property ensures that a client learns a subset of malicious servers only, which allows him to find a pair of servers such that at least one of them is malicious. We require the privacy should hold even if z is leaked, in order for an adversary not to learn additional information from a set of servers the client removes. Below, we show formal definitions.

Definition 3. *We say that* $\Pi = $ (Query, Answer, Output) *is an ℓ-round t-conflict-finding m-server protocol for* $\mathcal{F} = (F_\lambda : P_\lambda \times X_\lambda \to Y_\lambda)_{\lambda \in \mathbb{N}}$ *if it satisfies the following properties:*

Syntax. *The syntax of* Query *and* Answer *is the same as that of* Π *as an ℓ-round m-server protocol for* $\mathcal{F}$ *(Definition 1). The algorithm* Output *takes a state* $\mathsf{st}^{(\ell)}$ *and answer* $(\mathsf{ans}_i^{(\ell)})_{i \in [m]}$ *in round ℓ as input, and outputs (y, z) such that (1) $y \in Y_\lambda$ and $z = $ output, (2) $y = \bot$ and $z = (G_0, G_1)$, which is a non-trivial partition of $[m]$, or (3) $y = \bot$ and $z = $ failure. We call the first (resp. second) component of the output of* Output *the y-output (resp. z-output).*

Correctness. *There exists a negligible function* $\mathsf{negl}(\lambda)$ *such that for any $\lambda \in \mathbb{N}$ and any $(p, x) \in P_\lambda \times X_\lambda$, it holds that*

$$\Pr\left[(y, z) \leftarrow \mathsf{Output}(1^\lambda, \mathsf{st}^{(\ell)}, (\mathsf{ans}_i^{(\ell)})_{i \in [m]})) : y = F_\lambda(p, x)\right] \geq 1 - \mathsf{negl}(\lambda),$$

where

$$((\mathsf{que}_i^{(j)})_{i \in [m]}, \mathsf{st}^{(j)}) \leftarrow \mathsf{Query}(1^\lambda, x, \mathsf{st}^{(j-1)}, (\mathsf{ans}_i^{(j-1)})_{i \in [m]}),$$
$$\mathsf{ans}_i^{(j)} \leftarrow \mathsf{Answer}(1^\lambda, p, \mathsf{que}_i^{(j)})$$

for all $j \in [\ell]$ and $i \in [m]$.

Soundness. *There exists a negligible function* $\mathsf{negl}(\lambda)$ *such that for any stateful algorithm $\mathcal{A}$ and any $\lambda \in \mathbb{N}$,*

$$\Pr\left[\mathsf{Sound}_{\Pi, \mathcal{A}}(\lambda) = 1\right] < \mathsf{negl}(\lambda), \tag{2}$$

where $\mathsf{Sound}_{\Pi, \mathcal{A}}(\lambda)$ *is the output of the following experiment:*

1. $(x, p, T) \leftarrow \mathcal{A}(1^\lambda)$, *where $x \in X_\lambda$, $p \in P_\lambda$ and $T \subseteq [m]$ is of size at most t.*
2. *For each $j = 1, 2, \dots, \ell$,*
   (a) *Let* $((\mathsf{que}_i^{(j)})_{i \in [m]}, \mathsf{st}^{(j)}) \leftarrow \mathsf{Query}(1^\lambda, x, \mathsf{st}^{(j-1)}, (\mathsf{ans}_i^{(j-1)})_{i \in [m]})$ *and give* $(\mathsf{que}_i^{(j)})_{i \in T}$ *to $\mathcal{A}$.*
   (b) *$\mathcal{A}$ outputs* $(\mathsf{ans}_i^{(j)})_{i \in T}$.
3. *Let* $(y, z) \leftarrow \mathsf{Output}(1^\lambda, \mathsf{st}^{(\ell)}, (\mathsf{ans}_i^{(\ell)})_{i \in [m]})$.
4. *Return 1 if $y \in Y_\lambda \setminus \{F_\lambda(p, x)\}$ and $z = $ output, or $y = \bot$ and $z = $ failure. Otherwise return 0.*

Conflict-Finding. *For any stateful algorithm $\mathcal{A}$ and any $\lambda \in \mathbb{N}$,*

$$\Pr\left[\mathsf{CF}_{\Pi,\mathcal{A}}(\lambda) = 1\right] = 0,$$

where $\mathsf{CF}_{\Pi,\mathcal{A}}(\lambda)$ is the output of the following experiment:
1. $(x, p, T) \leftarrow \mathcal{A}(1^\lambda)$, *where $x \in X_\lambda$, $p \in P_\lambda$ and $T \subseteq [m]$ is of size at most t.*
2. *For each $j = 1, 2, \ldots, \ell$,*
   (a) *Let $((\mathsf{que}_i^{(j)})_{i\in[m]}, \mathsf{st}^{(j)}) \leftarrow \mathsf{Query}(1^\lambda, x, \mathsf{st}^{(j-1)}, (\mathsf{ans}_i^{(j-1)})_{i\in[m]})$ and give $(\mathsf{que}_i^{(j)})_{i\in T}$ to $\mathcal{A}$.*
   (b) *$\mathcal{A}$ outputs $(\mathsf{ans}_i^{(j)})_{i\in T}$.*
3. *Let $(y, z) \leftarrow \mathsf{Output}(1^\lambda, \mathsf{st}^{(\ell)}, (\mathsf{ans}_i^{(\ell)})_{i\in[m]})$.*
4. *Return 1 if $z = (G_0, G_1)$, $G_0 \not\subseteq T$ and $G_1 \not\subseteq T$. Otherwise return 0.*

Privacy. *There exists a negligible function $\mathsf{negl}(\lambda)$ such that for any stateful algorithm $\mathcal{A}$ and any $\lambda \in \mathbb{N}$,*

$$\mathsf{Adv}_{\Pi,\mathcal{A}}^{\mathsf{CF}}(\lambda) := \left|\Pr\left[\mathsf{Priv}_{\Pi,\mathcal{A}}^{\mathsf{CF},0}(\lambda) = 0\right] - \Pr\left[\mathsf{Priv}_{\Pi,\mathcal{A}}^{\mathsf{CF},1}(\lambda) = 0\right]\right| < \mathsf{negl}(\lambda),$$

where for $b \in \{0,1\}$, $\mathsf{Priv}_{\Pi,\mathcal{A}}^{\mathsf{CF},b}(\lambda)$ is the output b' of $\mathcal{A}$ in the following experiment:
1. $(x_0, x_1, p, T) \leftarrow \mathcal{A}(1^\lambda)$, *where $x_0, x_1 \in X_\lambda$, $p \in P_\lambda$ and $T \subseteq [m]$ is of size at most t.*
2. *For each $j = 1, 2, \ldots, \ell$,*
   (a) *Let $((\mathsf{que}_i^{(j)})_{i\in[m]}, \mathsf{st}^{(j)}) \leftarrow \mathsf{Query}(1^\lambda, x_b, \mathsf{st}^{(j-1)}, (\mathsf{ans}_i^{(j-1)})_{i\in[m]})$ and give $(\mathsf{que}_i^{(j)})_{i\in T}$ to $\mathcal{A}$.*
   (b) *$\mathcal{A}$ outputs $(\mathsf{ans}_i^{(j)})_{i\in T}$.*
3. *Let $(y, z) \leftarrow \mathsf{Output}(1^\lambda, \mathsf{st}^{(\ell)}, (\mathsf{ans}_i^{(\ell)})_{i\in[m]})$ and give z to $\mathcal{A}$.*
4. *$\mathcal{A}$ outputs a bit $b' \in \{0,1\}$.*

For a (possibly non-negligible) function $\epsilon(\lambda)$, we define a weaker notion of a ϵ-*sound* t-conflict-finding protocol Π as the one satisfying the requirements in Definition 3 except that the condition (2) is replaced with

$$\Pr\left[\mathsf{Sound}_{\Pi,\mathcal{A}}(\lambda) = 1\right] < \epsilon.$$

We say that Π is *computationally t-conflict-finding* if it satisfies the above requirements for PPT adversaries $\mathcal{A}$.

4.3   Compiler from Conflict-Finding to Actively Secure Protocols

We construct an actively t-secure m-server protocol from a t-conflict-finding $(m-t)$-server protocol. We give a sketch here and defer the formal proof to the full version.

Theorem 1. *Suppose that there exists an ℓ-round (resp. computationally) t-conflict-finding k-server protocol Π_{CF} for $\mathcal{F} = (F_\lambda : P_\lambda \times X_\lambda \to Y_\lambda)_{\lambda \in \mathbb{N}}$. If $m \geq t + k$, there exists an $O(\ell m^2)$-round (resp. computationally) actively t-secure m-server protocol Π for $\mathcal{F}$ such that*

- *Comm$(\Pi) = O(m^2 \cdot \mathrm{Comm}(\Pi_{\mathrm{CF}}))$;*
- *c-Comp$(\Pi) = O(m^2 \cdot \mathrm{c\text{-}Comp}(\Pi_{\mathrm{CF}}) + m^4)$;*
- *s-Comp$(\Pi) = O(m^2 \cdot \mathrm{s\text{-}Comp}(\Pi_{\mathrm{CF}}))$.*

Proof (sketch). Define $N := \binom{m}{2} - \binom{m-t}{2} + 1 = O(m^2)$. Let V be the set of all m servers and $\mathcal{G}^{(1)}$ be the complete graph on V. Consider the following protocol Π: For each $j = 1, 2, \ldots, N$,

1. The client C finds a k-sized subset $S^{(j)}$ of V such that $\mathcal{G}^{(j)}[S^{(j)}]$ is connected, based on the algorithm $\mathcal{C}_k$ in Sect. 4.1.
2. C executes the conflict-finding protocol Π_{CF} with k servers in $S^{(j)}$, and obtain an output $(y^{(j)}, z^{(j)})$.
3. If $z^{(j)} = \mathsf{output}$, then C outputs the y-output $y^{(j)}$.
4. If $z^{(j)} = \mathsf{failure}$, then C outputs any default value y_0.
5. If $z^{(j)}$ is a non-trivial partition $(G_0^{(j)}, G_1^{(j)})$ of $S^{(j)}$, then C does the following:
   (a) Find an edge $e^{(j)}$ of $\mathcal{G}^{(j)}$ crossing the partition $(G_0^{(j)}, G_1^{(j)})$ based on the algorithm $\mathcal{E}$ in Sect. 4.1. Such an edge exists since $\mathcal{G}^{(j)}[S^{(j)}]$ is connected.
   (b) Let $\mathcal{G}^{(j+1)}$ be a graph obtained by removing $e^{(j)}$ from $\mathcal{G}^{(j)}$.
   (c) Go back to Step 1.

Privacy. An adversary corrupting a set T of at most t servers cannot learn a client's input from interaction at Step 2 due to the fact that $|T \cap S^{(j)}| \leq |T| \leq t$ and the privacy of Π_{CF}. The adversary can also see a sequence of graphs $\mathcal{G}^{(1)}, \mathcal{G}^{(2)}, \ldots, \mathcal{G}^{(N)}$ but as shown at Step 5, the sequence is determined only by a sequence of z-outputs $z^{(1)}, z^{(2)}, \ldots, z^{(N)}$. Since Π_{CF} guarantees privacy even if z-outputs are leaked, she learns no additional information.

Byzantine-Robustness. The client C outputs an incorrect result only if one of the following events occurs: (1) $z^{(j)} = \mathsf{output}$ and $y^{(j)}$ is an incorrect result for some $j \in [N]$, (2) $z^{(j)} = \mathsf{failure}$ for some $j \in [N]$, or (3) $z^{(j)}$ is a non-trivial partition for all $j \in [N]$. It follows from the soundness of Π_{CF} that the first and second cases occur only with negligible probability.

We argue that the third case never occurs. Assume otherwise, then for all j, the z-output $z^{(j)}$ of the j-th iteration is a non-trivial partition $(G_0^{(j)}, G_1^{(j)})$ of $S^{(j)}$. Since the conflict-finding property of Π_{CF} ensures that either $G_0^{(j)}$ or $G_1^{(j)}$ includes the set of honest servers $H := [m] \setminus T$, the removed edge $e^{(j)} = (i_1, i_2)$ satisfies $i_1 \in T$ or $i_2 \in T$ and hence the subgraph $\mathcal{G}^{(j)}[H]$ is a complete graph for all j. Since N is larger than the total number $N' = \binom{m}{2} - \binom{m-|T|}{2}$ of unordered pairs (i_1, i_2) such that $i_1 \in T$ or $i_2 \in T$, $\mathcal{G}^{(N')}$ has no edge $e = (i_1, i_2)$ such that $i_1 \in T$ or $i_2 \in T$. Therefore, a set of servers $S^{(N')}$ involved in the N'-th iteration is a subset of H since $k \leq m - t \leq |H|$. We have assumed that $z^{(N')}$ is a non-trivial partition $(G_0^{(N')}, G_1^{(N')})$ of $S^{(N')}$ but the conflict-finding property ensures that $H \subseteq G_0^{(N')}$ or $H \subseteq G_1^{(N')}$, which is contradiction. $\qquad\square$

4.4 Compiler from Passively Secure to Conflict-Finding Protocols

First, we show a basic construction of ϵ-sound conflict-finding protocols for non-negligible ϵ. We give a sketch here and defer the formal proof to the full version.

Proposition 7. *Let Π be a 1-round (resp. computationally) passively t-secure m-server protocol for $\mathcal{F} = (F_\lambda : P_\lambda \times X_\lambda \to Y_\lambda)_{\lambda \in \mathbb{N}}$. Let $M = \mathsf{poly}(\lambda)$. Then, there exists a 2-round (resp. computationally) ϵ-sound t-conflict-finding m-server protocol Π' for $\mathcal{F}$ such that*

- $\mathrm{Comm}(\Pi') = O(mM \cdot \mathrm{Comm}(\Pi))$;
- $\mathrm{c\text{-}Comp}(\Pi') = O(m^2 M \cdot \mathrm{c\text{-}Comp}(\Pi))$;
- $\mathrm{s\text{-}Comp}(\Pi') = O(mM \cdot \mathrm{s\text{-}Comp}(\Pi))$;

where $\epsilon = m/M + \mathsf{negl}(\lambda)$ for some negligible function $\mathsf{negl}(\lambda)$.

Proof (sketch). Consider the following protocol Π':

First Round
1. The client C chooses μ_* uniformly at random from $[M]$.
2. For all $\mu \in [M]$, C computes queries $(\mathsf{que}_1^{\langle \mu \rangle}, \ldots, \mathsf{que}_m^{\langle \mu \rangle})$ of Π on his true input x if $\mu = \mu_*$, and on a default input x_{def} otherwise.
3. C sends the queries $(\mathsf{que}_i^{\langle \mu \rangle})_{\mu \in [M]}$ to each server S_i as usual, who returns answers $(\mathsf{ans}_i^{\langle \mu \rangle})_{\mu \in [M]}$ to them.

Second Round
1. C sends all the queries $(\mathsf{que}_k^{\langle \mu \rangle})_{k \in [m], \mu \neq \mu_*}$ for the default input x_{def} to all servers.
2. For all $k \in [m]$ and $\mu \in [M] \setminus \{\mu_*\}$, each server S_i returns an answer $\mathsf{ans}_k^{\langle \mu \rangle}(i)$ as S_k would answer to $\mathsf{que}_k^{\langle \mu \rangle}$.

To obtain an output, C defines $v_i = (\mathsf{ans}_k^{\langle \mu \rangle}(i))_{k \in [m], \mu \neq \mu_*}$ for all $i \in [m]$. For simplicity, we here assume that $\mathsf{ans}_i^{\langle \mu \rangle}(i) = \mathsf{ans}_i^{\langle \mu \rangle}$ for all $i \in [m]$. This is because otherwise, it means that a server S_i returns different answers in the first and second rounds and hence S_i is immediately found malicious. The client C partitions the set of servers into equivalence classes $G'_0, \ldots, G'_\ell$ under the equivalence relation defined as: $i \sim j \overset{\mathrm{def}}{\iff} v_i = v_j$. If $\ell = 0$ (i.e., all servers belong to the same equivalence class), then he runs the output algorithm of Π on the answers $(\mathsf{ans}_1^{\langle \mu_* \rangle}, \ldots, \mathsf{ans}_m^{\langle \mu_* \rangle})$ to the queries for his true input. He then outputs the result y along with $z = \mathsf{output}$. If $\ell \geq 1$, then he outputs $y = \bot$ and $z = (G_0, G_1)$, where $G_0 = G'_0$ and $G_1 = G'_1 \cup \cdots \cup G'_\ell$.

Conflict-Finding. Let T be a set of corrupted servers. Since honest servers $i, j \notin T$ always return the same answer to the same query, we have that $\mathsf{ans}_k^{\langle \mu \rangle}(i) = \mathsf{ans}_k^{\langle \mu \rangle}(j)$ for all $k \in [m]$ and $\mu \in [M] \setminus \{\mu_*\}$, and hence $v_i = v_j$. Therefore, the set of honest servers is contained in an equivalence class and it holds that $\overline{T} \subseteq G_0 = \overline{G_1}$ or $\overline{T} \subseteq G_1 = \overline{G_0}$.

Soundness. In the first place, the protocol Π' never outputs $z = \mathsf{failure}$. Assume that Π' outputs $z = \mathsf{output}$. Then, all servers belong to the same equivalence class, which implies that $v_i = v_j$ for any $i, j \in [m]$. To let the client accept an incorrect result, an adversary needs to let at least one corrupted server S_i submit an incorrect answer exactly to the query $\mathsf{que}_i^{\langle \mu_* \rangle}$ for the client's true input. (This is because if a corrupted server submits incorrect $\mathsf{ans}_i^{\langle \mu \rangle}$ for some $\mu \neq \mu_*$, then it is detected when compared with an answer $\mathsf{ans}_i^{\langle \mu \rangle}(j)$ from an honest server $j \notin T$.) However, the adversary cannot learn which query encodes the client's true input due to the privacy of Π. Therefore, her best possible strategy is to guess μ_* uniformly at random, which succeeds only with probability $1/M$. The union bound implies that the error probability is at most m/M.

Privacy. Since M queries are generated independently, an adversary learns no information on the client's input x in the first round. The queries revealed in the second round are the ones for a default input x_{def}, which is independent of x, and hence the adversary learns no additional information. The privacy holds even if the z-output z is leaked, since z is determined only by $(v_i)_{i \in [m]}$, which can be simulated from information that the adversary learns up to the second round.   □

Next, we show that the error probability of the basic construction can be made negligible by parallel execution. The proof is deferred to the full version.

Theorem 2. *Let Π be a 1-round (resp. computationally) passively t-secure m-server protocol for $\mathcal{F} = (F_\lambda : P_\lambda \times X_\lambda \to Y_\lambda)_{\lambda \in \mathbb{N}}$. Then there exists a 2-round (resp. computationally) t-conflict-finding m-server protocol Π_{CF} for $\mathcal{F}$ such that*

- $\mathrm{Comm}(\Pi_{\mathrm{CF}}) = O(m^2 \lambda \cdot \mathrm{Comm}(\Pi))$;
- $\mathrm{c\text{-}Comp}(\Pi_{\mathrm{CF}}) = O(m^3 \lambda \cdot \mathrm{c\text{-}Comp}(\Pi))$;
- $\mathrm{s\text{-}Comp}(\Pi_{\mathrm{CF}}) = O(m^2 \lambda \cdot \mathrm{s\text{-}Comp}(\Pi))$.

Finally, by combining Theorems 1 and 2, we obtain our generic construction of an $O(m^2)$-round actively t-secure m-server protocol from any 1-round passively t-secure k-server protocol for $k \leq m - t$.

Theorem 3. *Suppose that $m > 2t$. Let $k \leq m - t$ and Π be a 1-round (resp. computationally) passively t-secure k-server protocol for $\mathcal{F}$. Then there exists an $O(m^2)$-round (resp. computationally) actively t-secure m-server protocol Π' for $\mathcal{F}$ such that*

- $\mathrm{Comm}(\Pi') = O(m^4 \lambda \cdot \mathrm{Comm}(\Pi))$;
- $\mathrm{c\text{-}Comp}(\Pi') = O(m^5 \lambda \cdot \mathrm{c\text{-}Comp}(\Pi))$;
- $\mathrm{s\text{-}Comp}(\Pi') = O(m^4 \lambda \cdot \mathrm{s\text{-}Comp}(\Pi))$.

4.5   Instantiations

By applying our compiler in Theorem 3 to the passively secure protocols in Propositions 1 and 2, we obtain actively secure protocols for INDEX_N.

Corollary 1. *Suppose that $m \geq 3^t + t$. Let $N \in \mathsf{poly}(\lambda)$. Then, there exists an actively t-secure $O(m^2)$-round m-server protocol Π for* INDEX_N *such that*

- $\mathrm{Comm}(\Pi) = \exp(O(\sqrt{\log N \log \log N})) \cdot t3^t m^4 \lambda;$
- $\text{c-Comp}(\Pi) = \exp(O(\sqrt{\log N \log \log N})) \cdot t3^t m^5 \lambda;$
- $\text{s-Comp}(\Pi) = N^2 \cdot \exp(O(\sqrt{\log N \log \log N})) \cdot 2^t m^4 \lambda.$

In particular, $\max\{\mathrm{Comm}(\Pi), \text{c-Comp}(\Pi)\} = N^{o(1)} \cdot 2^{O(t)} \lambda.$

Corollary 2. *Assume a pseudorandom generator* $G : \{0,1\}^\lambda \to \{0,1\}^{2(\lambda+1)}$. *Suppose that $m \geq 2^t + t$. Let $N \in \mathsf{poly}(\lambda)$. Then, there exists a computationally actively t-secure 1-round m-server protocol Π for* INDEX_N *such that*

- $\mathrm{Comm}(\Pi) = O(\log N \cdot \lambda^2 \cdot t2^t m^4);$
- $\text{c-Comp}(\Pi)$ *is* $O(\log N \cdot t2^t m^5)$ *invocations of* $G;$
- $\text{s-Comp}(\Pi)$ *is* $O(N^2 \log N \cdot tm^4)$ *invocations of* $G.$

In particular, $\max\{\mathrm{Comm}(\Pi), \text{c-Comp}(\Pi)\} = \log N \cdot 2^{O(t)} \cdot \mathsf{poly}(\lambda).$

By applying Theorem 3 to Proposition 3, we obtain an actively secure protocol for multivariate polynomials.

Corollary 3. *Let $N, D, M \in \mathsf{poly}(\lambda)$. Let R be a ring such that for any $a \in \{1, 2, \ldots, m-1\}$, an element $a \cdot 1_R$ has an inverse in R. Suppose that*

$$m > \left(\frac{D}{2} + 1\right) t.$$

Then, there exists an actively t-secure 1-round m-server protocol Π for $\mathrm{POLY}_{N,D,M}(R)$ *such that*

- $\mathrm{Comm}(\Pi) = O(Nm^4\lambda)$ *ring elements;*
- $\text{c-Comp}(\Pi) = O(Ntm^6\lambda)$ *ring operations;*
- $\text{s-Comp}(\Pi) = O(NMDm^4\lambda)$ *ring operations.*

In particular, $\max\{\mathrm{Comm}(\Pi), \text{c-Comp}(\Pi)\} = N \cdot \mathsf{poly}(m, \lambda).$

By applying Theorem 3 to Proposition 4, we can reduce the required number of servers by a factor of d assuming homomorphic encryption for degree-d polynomials.

Corollary 4. *Let $d = O(1)$ and R be a ring such that for any $a \in \{1, 2, \ldots, \max\{d, m-1\}\}$, an element $a \cdot 1_R$ has an inverse in R, where 1_R is the multiplicative identity of R. Assume a homomorphic encryption scheme* HE *for degree-d polynomials over R. Suppose that*

$$m > \left(\frac{D}{d+1} + 1\right) t$$

Let $M, N \in \mathsf{poly}(\lambda)$ and $D = O(1)$. Then there exists a computationally actively t-secure $O(m^2)$-round m-server protocol Π for $\mathrm{POLY}_{N,D,M}(R)$ *such that*

- $\text{Comm}(\Pi) = O(Nm^5\lambda \cdot \ell_{\text{ct}})$, where ℓ_{ct} is the description length of ciphertexts of HE;
- $\text{c-Comp}(\Pi) = O((Nt \cdot \tau_{\text{Enc}} + \tau_{\text{Dec}})m^6\lambda)$, where τ_{Dec} and τ_{Enc} are the running time of the decryption and encryption algorithms of HE, respectively;
- $\text{s-Comp}(\Pi) = O(M \cdot m^4\lambda\tau_{\text{Eval}})$, where τ_{Eval} is the running time per operation of the evaluation algorithm of HE.

In particular, $\max\{\text{Comm}(\Pi), \text{c-Comp}(\Pi)\} = N \cdot \text{poly}(m,\lambda)$.

By applying Theorem 3 to Proposition 5, we obtain an actively t-secure protocol for polynomials achieving the minimum number of servers $2t + 1$.

Corollary 5. *Suppose that $m = 2t+1$. Assume that the (δ, q)-sLPN assumption holds for a constant $0 \le \delta \le 1$ and a sequence $q = (q(\lambda))_{\lambda \in \mathbb{N}}$ of prime powers that are computable in polynomial time in λ. Let $L, M, N \in \text{poly}(\lambda)$ and $D = O(\log \lambda / \log \log \lambda)$. Then, there exists a computationally actively t-secure $O(m^2)$-round m-server protocol Π for $\text{POLY}^L_{N,D,M}(\mathbb{F}_q)$ such that*

- $\text{Comm}(\Pi) = \widetilde{O}((M^{2/\delta}N + L)(\log q)m^5\lambda^2)$;
- $\text{c-Comp}(\Pi) = \widetilde{O}((M^{2/\delta}N + L)(\log q)m^6\lambda^2)$;
- $\text{s-Comp}(\Pi) = \widetilde{O}(M^{1/\delta+1}L(\log q)m^4\lambda^2)$.

In particular, $\max\{\text{Comm}(\Pi), \text{c-Comp}(\Pi)\} = (M^{2/\delta}N + L)\log q \cdot \text{poly}(m,\lambda)$.

Finally, by applying Theorem 3 to Proposition 6, we obtain an actively secure protocol for constant-depth circuits.

Corollary 6. *Let $N, M \in \text{poly}(\lambda)$ and $D = O(1)$. Suppose that*

$$m \ge \left(\frac{(\log M + 3)^{D-1}}{2} + 1\right)t.$$

Then, there exists an actively t-secure $O(m^2)$-round m-server protocol Π for $\text{CIRC}_{N,D,M}$ such that

- $\text{Comm}(\Pi) = O((\log M)^{D-1}N(\log N)\lambda^2 m^5)$;
- $\text{c-Comp}(\Pi) = O((\log M)^{D-1}N(\log N)\lambda t m^6 + (\log M)^2\lambda^2 m^6)$;
- $\text{s-Comp}(\Pi) = O(M(\log M)Nm^4\lambda^2)$.

In particular, $\max\{\text{Comm}(\Pi), \text{c-Comp}(\Pi)\} = N \cdot \text{poly}(m,\lambda)$.

5 Non-interactive Actively Secure Protocols

In this section, we show our compiler from one-round passively t-secure k-server protocols to one-round actively t-secure m-server protocols such that $m = O(k \log k) + 2t$. To this end, we introduce a novel combinatorial object of *locally surjective map families*, which is a variant of perfect hash families with a stronger property. We show a probabilistic construction of such families in Sect. 5.1 and then show a generic compiler from passively secure to actively secure protocols in Sect. 5.2.

5.1   Locally Surjective Map Family

We show the formal definition of locally surjective map families.

Definition 4. *Let $m, h, k \in \mathbb{N}$ and $\mathcal{L}$ be a family of maps from $[m]$ to $[k]$. We call $\mathcal{L}$ an (m, h, k)-locally surjective map family if $|A_H| > |\mathcal{L}|/2$ for any $H \in \binom{[m]}{h}$, where $A_H = \{f \in \mathcal{L} : f(H) = [k]\}$.*

A locally surjective map family satisfies a stronger property than a nearly perfect hash family $\mathcal{L}'$ introduced in [11], which assumes that for any $H \in \binom{[m]}{h}$, there exists *at least one* map $f \in \mathcal{L}'$ such that $f(H) = [k]$.

We show a probabilistic construction of an (m, h, k)-locally surjective map family of size $O(m)$ for $k = O(h/\log h)$. The formal proof is deferred to the full version.

Proposition 8. *Let $m, h, k \in \mathbb{N}$ be such that $h \geq 15$, $m \geq 15$ and $k \leq h/(\gamma \ln h)$, where $\gamma := 1 + (\ln 3 - \ln \ln 15)/(\ln 15) < 1.04$. Then, there exists an (m, h, k)-locally surjective map family $\mathcal{L}$ such that $w := |\mathcal{L}| = 14m$.*

5.2   Compiler from Passively Secure to Actively Secure Protocols

Based on locally surjective map families, we show our construction of one-round actively secure protocols from any one-round passively secure protocol. We give a sketch here and defer the formal proof to the full version.

Theorem 4. *Suppose that there exists a 1-round (resp. computationally) passively t-secure k-server protocol $\Pi = (\mathsf{Query}, \mathsf{Answer}, \mathsf{Output})$ for $\mathcal{F} = (F_\lambda : P_\lambda \times X_\lambda \to Y_\lambda)_{\lambda \in \mathbb{N}}$. If there exists an $(m, m-2t, k)$-locally surjective map family $\mathcal{L}$ of size $w = \mathsf{poly}(\lambda)$, there exists a 1-round (resp. computationally) actively t-secure m-server protocol $\Pi' = (\mathsf{Query}', \mathsf{Answer}', \mathsf{Output}')$ for $\mathcal{F}$ such that*

- $\mathrm{Comm}(\Pi') = O(twm \cdot \mathrm{Comm}(\Pi))$;
- $\mathrm{c\text{-}Comp}(\Pi') = O(twm \cdot \mathrm{c\text{-}Comp}(\Pi))$;
- $\mathrm{s\text{-}Comp}(\Pi') = O(tw \cdot \mathrm{s\text{-}Comp}(\Pi))$.

Proof (sketch). Let $\mathcal{L} = \{f_1, \ldots, f_w\}$ be an (m, h, k)-locally surjective map family, where $h = m - 2t$. For $u \in [w]$ and $j \in [k]$, define $G_{u,j} = f_u^{-1}(j) = \{i \in [m] : f_u(i) = j\}$. Consider the following protocol Π': For all $u \in [w]$ and $\ell \in [t+1]$ (in parallel),

1. The client C computes k queries $(\mathsf{que}_1^{(u,\ell)}, \ldots, \mathsf{que}_k^{(u,\ell)})$ of Π.
2. C sends $\mathsf{que}_{f_u(i)}^{(u,\ell)}$ to each server S_i.
3. Each S_i returns an answer $\mathsf{ans}_i^{(u,\ell)}$ as the $f_u(i)$-th server would answer to $\mathsf{que}_{f_u(i)}^{(u,\ell)}$ in Π.

To obtain an output, C sets $S \leftarrow [m]$ and $L \leftarrow 1$, and does the following:

1. Check whether for all $u \in [w]$ and $j \in [k]$, the answers $\mathsf{ans}_i^{(u,L)}$ returned by servers S_i in $G_{u,j}$ are identical with each other.
2. If so, let $\alpha_{u,j}$ be the unique answer by servers in $G_{u,j}$ and run the output algorithm of Π on $(\alpha_{u,1}, \ldots, \alpha_{u,k})$ to obtain y_u. Then, output the majority of $y_1, \ldots, y_w$.
3. Otherwise, find a pair (i_1, i_2) of servers who are mapped to the same group $G_{u,j}$ but returned different answers. That is, $f_u(i_1) = f_u(i_2)$ and $\mathsf{ans}_{i_1}^{(u,L)} \neq \mathsf{ans}_{i_2}^{(u,L)}$ for some $u \in [w]$. Note that at least one of them are malicious. Then, update $S \leftarrow S \setminus \{i_1, i_2\}$ and $L \leftarrow L + 1$, and go back to Step 1.

Privacy. An adversary corrupting a set T of at most t servers can only learn queries received by a set $f_u(T)$ of servers in Π. Since $|f_u(T)| \leq |T| \leq t$, the privacy of Π' follows from that of Π.

Byzantine-Robustness. An adversary succeeds in letting the client accept an incorrect result only if at least $w/2$ out of $y_1, \ldots, y_w$ are incorrect in some iteration (say, L) in the output phase of C. This implies that for at least $w/2$ u's, there exists a remaining corrupted server $i \in T \cap S$ who submits an incorrect answer $\widetilde{\mathsf{ans}}_i^{(u,L)} \neq \mathsf{ans}_i^{(u,L)}$. On the other hand, since at most one honest server is eliminated from S in each iteration, it holds that $|H \cap S| \geq (m - t) - t = m - 2t$, where H is the set of all honest servers. Therefore, the property of locally surjective map families ensures that $f_u(H \cap S) = [k]$ holds for at least one of the above $w/2$ u's. In other words, there exists a remaining honest server $i' \in H \cap S$ such that $f_u(i') = f_u(i)$, and the answer $\widetilde{\mathsf{ans}}_i^{(u,L)}$ is compared with the correct answer $\mathsf{ans}_{i'}^{(u,L)}$ from the honest server i'. Thus, the client can detect the malicious behavior of the corrupted server i. Therefore, the client can successfully eliminate at least one malicious server in each iteration and obtain the correct result after at most t iterations. □

To obtain a concrete compiler from Theorem 4, we plug in the (m, h, k)-locally surjective map family in Proposition 8 with $h = m - 2t$.

Theorem 5. *Suppose that there exists a 1-round (resp. computationally) passively t-secure k-server protocol Π for $\mathcal{F}$. If*

$$ m \geq 2t + 15 \text{ and } \frac{m - 2t}{\gamma \ln(m - 2t)} \geq k, $$

where $1 < \gamma < 1.04$ is the constant in Proposition 8, then there exists a 1-round (resp. computationally) actively t-secure m-server protocol Π' for $\mathcal{F}$ such that

- Comm$(\Pi') = O(tm^2 \cdot \text{Comm}(\Pi))$;
- c-Comp$(\Pi') = O(tm^2 \cdot \text{c-Comp}(\Pi))$;
- s-Comp$(\Pi') = O(tm \cdot \text{s-Comp}(\Pi))$.

Remark 3. The computational complexity of the construction in Theorem 5 does not take into account that of finding a locally surjective map family $\mathcal{L}$. We note that the choice of $\mathcal{L}$ does not affect the security of a protocol. Hence we can construct it before the protocol starts and the family is reusable any number of times.

5.3 Instantiations

By applying our compiler in Theorem 5 to the protocols in Propositions 1 and 2, we obtain the following corollaries. The formal proof appears in the full version.

Corollary 7. *Suppose that $m \geq \max\{2t3^t + 2t, 2t + 15\}$. Let $N \in \mathsf{poly}(\lambda)$. Then, there exists a computationally actively t-secure 1-round m-server protocol Π for* INDEX$_N$ *such that*

- $\mathrm{Comm}(\Pi) = \exp(O(\sqrt{\log N \log \log N})) \cdot t^2 3^t m^2;$
- $\mathrm{c\text{-}Comp}(\Pi) = \exp(O(\sqrt{\log N \log \log N})) \cdot t^2 3^t m^2;$
- $\mathrm{s\text{-}Comp}(\Pi) = N^2 \cdot \exp(O(\sqrt{\log N \log \log N})) \cdot t2^t m.$

In particular, $\max\{\mathrm{Comm}(\Pi), \mathrm{c\text{-}Comp}(\Pi)\} = N^{o(1)} \cdot 2^{O(t)}.$

Corollary 8. *Assume a pseudorandom function $G : \{0,1\}^\lambda \to \{0,1\}^{2(\lambda+1)}$. Suppose that $m \geq \max\{t2^{t+1} + 2t, 2t + 15\}$. Let $N \in \mathsf{poly}(\lambda)$. Then, there exists an actively t-secure 1-round m-server protocol Π for* INDEX$_N$ *such that*

- $\mathrm{Comm}(\Pi) = O(\log N \cdot \lambda \cdot t^2 2^t m^2);$
- $\mathrm{c\text{-}Comp}(\Pi)$ *is* $O(\log N \cdot t^2 2^t m^2)$ *invocations of G;*
- $\mathrm{s\text{-}Comp}(\Pi)$ *is* $O(N^2 \log N \cdot t2^t m)$ *invocations of G.*

In particular, $\max\{\mathrm{Comm}(\Pi), \mathrm{c\text{-}Comp}(\Pi)\} = \log N \cdot 2^{O(t)} \cdot \mathsf{poly}(\lambda).$

Note that it is possible to apply the compiler in Theorem 5 to the passively secure k-server protocols in Propositions 3, 4, 5, and 6. Since $k > t$, the number of servers of the resulting protocols is $\Omega(k \log k) + 2t = \Omega(t \log t)$. On the other hand, these protocols can also be made actively secure by using the standard error correction algorithm [41] or the technique of [38], and one can then obtain actively secure protocols that has a smaller number of servers $O(t)$. We thus do not show instantiations based on these protocols.

Acknowledgements. This research was partially supported by JSPS KAKENHI Grant Numbers JP20J20797 and JP19H01109, Japan, JST CREST Grant Numbers JPMJCR2113 and JPMJCR22M1, Japan, and JST AIP Acceleration Research JPMJCR22U5, Japan.

References

1. Ananth, P., Chandran, N., Goyal, V., Kanukurthi, B., Ostrovsky, R.: Achieving privacy in verifiable computation with multiple servers – without FHE and without pre-processing. In: Krawczyk, H. (ed.) PKC 2014. LNCS, vol. 8383, pp. 149–166. Springer, Heidelberg (2014). https://doi.org/10.1007/978-3-642-54631-0_9
2. Applebaum, B., Ishai, Y., Kushilevitz, E.: From secrecy to soundness: efficient verification via secure computation. In: Abramsky, S., Gavoille, C., Kirchner, C., Meyer auf der Heide, F., Spirakis, P.G. (eds.) ICALP 2010. LNCS, vol. 6198, pp. 152–163. Springer, Heidelberg (2010). https://doi.org/10.1007/978-3-642-14165-2_14

3. Augot, D., Levy-dit-Vehel, F., Shikfa, A.: A storage-efficient and robust private information retrieval scheme allowing few servers. In: Gritzalis, D., Kiayias, A., Askoxylakis, I. (eds.) CANS 2014. LNCS, vol. 8813, pp. 222–239. Springer, Cham (2014). https://doi.org/10.1007/978-3-319-12280-9_15

4. Banawan, K., Ulukus, S.: The capacity of private information retrieval from Byzantine and colluding databases. IEEE Trans. Inf. Theory 65(2), 1206–1219 (2019)

5. Barkol, O., Ishai, Y.: Secure computation of constant-depth circuits with applications to database search problems. In: Shoup, V. (ed.) CRYPTO 2005. LNCS, vol. 3621, pp. 395–411. Springer, Heidelberg (2005). https://doi.org/10.1007/11535218_24

6. Barkol, O., Ishai, Y., Weinreb, E.: On d-multiplicative secret sharing. J. Cryptol. 23(4), 580–593 (2010)

7. Barkol, O., Ishai, Y., Weinreb, E.: On locally decodable codes, self-correctable codes, and t-private PIR. Algorithmica 58(4), 831–859 (2010)

8. Beimel, A., Ishai, Y., Kushilevitz, E., Raymond, J.F.: Breaking the o(n/sup 1/(2k-1)/) barrier for information-theoretic private information retrieval. In: The 43rd Annual IEEE Symposium on Foundations of Computer Science, 2002. Proceedings, pp. 261–270 (2002)

9. Beimel, A., Ishai, Y.: Information-theoretic private information retrieval: a unified construction. In: Automata, Languages and Programming, pp. 912–926 (2001)

10. Beimel, A., Ishai, Y., Kushilevitz, E., Orlov, I.: Share conversion and private information retrieval. In: 2012 IEEE 27th Conference on Computational Complexity, pp. 258–268 (2012)

11. Beimel, A., Stahl, Y.: Robust information-theoretic private information retrieval. J. Cryptol. 20(3), 295–321 (2007)

12. Boyle, E., Gilboa, N., Ishai, Y.: Function secret sharing. In: Oswald, E., Fischlin, M. (eds.) EUROCRYPT 2015. LNCS, vol. 9057, pp. 337–367. Springer, Heidelberg (2015). https://doi.org/10.1007/978-3-662-46803-6_12

13. Boyle, E., Gilboa, N., Ishai, Y.: Breaking the circuit size barrier for secure computation under DDH. In: Robshaw, M., Katz, J. (eds.) CRYPTO 2016, Part I. LNCS, vol. 9814, pp. 509–539. Springer, Heidelberg (2016). https://doi.org/10.1007/978-3-662-53018-4_19

14. Boyle, E., Gilboa, N., Ishai, Y.: Function secret sharing: improvements and extensions. In: Proceedings of the 2016 ACM SIGSAC Conference on Computer and Communications Security, pp. 1292–1303, CCS 2016 (2016)

15. Boyle, E., Gilboa, N., Ishai, Y., Nof, A.: Sublinear GMW-style compiler for MPC with preprocessing. In: Malkin, T., Peikert, C. (eds.) CRYPTO 2021. LNCS, vol. 12826, pp. 457–485. Springer, Cham (2021). https://doi.org/10.1007/978-3-030-84245-1_16

16. Boyle, E., Kohl, L., Scholl, P.: Homomorphic secret sharing from lattices without FHE. In: Ishai, Y., Rijmen, V. (eds.) EUROCRYPT 2019, Part II. LNCS, vol. 11477, pp. 3–33. Springer, Cham (2019). https://doi.org/10.1007/978-3-030-17656-3_1

17. Bunn, P., Kushilevitz, E., Ostrovsky, R.: CNF-FSS and its applications. In: Hanaoka, G., Shikata, J., Watanabe, Y. (eds.) Public-Key Cryptography – PKC 2022, vol. 13177, pp. 283–314. Springer, Cham (2022). https://doi.org/10.1007/978-3-030-97121-2_11

18. Canetti, R., Riva, B., Rothblum, G.N.: Refereed delegation of computation. Inf. Comput. 226, 16–36 (2013)

19. de Castro, L., Lee, K.: VeriSimplePIR: verifiability in simplePIR at no online cost for honest servers. In: 33rd USENIX Security Symposium (USENIX Security 2024) (2024, to appear). https://www.usenix.org/conference/usenixsecurity24/presentation/de-castro

20. Choi, S.G., Katz, J., Kumaresan, R., Cid, C.: Multi-client non-interactive verifiable computation. In: Sahai, A. (ed.) TCC 2013. LNCS, vol. 7785, pp. 499–518. Springer, Heidelberg (2013). https://doi.org/10.1007/978-3-642-36594-2_28

21. Chor, B., Goldreich, O., Kushilevitz, E., Sudan, M.: Private information retrieval. J. ACM **45**(6), 965–982 (1998)

22. Colombo, S., Nikitin, K., Corrigan-Gibbs, H., Wu, D.J., Ford, B.: Authenticated private information retrieval. In: 32nd USENIX Security Symposium (USENIX Security 2023), pp. 3835–3851 (2023)

23. Damgård, I., Orlandi, C., Simkin, M.: Yet another compiler for active security or: efficient MPC over arbitrary rings. In: Shacham, H., Boldyreva, A. (eds.) CRYPTO 2018. LNCS, vol. 10992, pp. 799–829. Springer, Cham (2018). https://doi.org/10.1007/978-3-319-96881-0_27

24. Dao, Q., Ishai, Y., Jain, A., Lin, H.: Multi-party homomorphic secret sharing and sublinear MPC from sparse LPN. In: Handschuh, H., Lysyanskaya, A. (eds.) Advances in Cryptology – CRYPTO 2023. LNCS, vol. 14082, pp. 315–348. Springer, Cham (2023). https://doi.org/10.1007/978-3-031-38545-2_11

25. Devet, C., Goldberg, I., Heninger, N.: Optimally robust private information retrieval. In: 21st USENIX Security Symposium (USENIX Security 2012), pp. 269–283 (2012)

26. Di Crescenzo, G., Malkin, T., Ostrovsky, R.: Single database private information retrieval implies oblivious transfer. In: Preneel, B. (eds.) Advances in Cryptology – EUROCRYPT 2000. LNCS, vol. 1807, pp. 122–138. Springer, Cham (2000). https://doi.org/10.1007/3-540-45539-6_10

27. Dvir, Z., Gopi, S.: 2-server PIR with subpolynomial communication. J. ACM **63**(4), 1–15 (2016)

28. Efremenko, K.: 3-query locally decodable codes of subexponential length. SIAM J. Comput. **41**(6), 1694–1703 (2012)

29. Eriguchi, R., Kurosawa, K., Nuida, K.: On the optimal communication complexity of error-correcting multi-server PIR. In: Kiltz, E., Vaikuntanathan, V. (eds.) Theory of Cryptography, TCC 2022. LNCS, vol. 13749, pp. 60–88. Springer, Cham (2022). https://doi.org/10.1007/978-3-031-22368-6_3

30. Gennaro, R., Gentry, C., Parno, B.: Non-interactive verifiable computing: outsourcing computation to untrusted workers. In: Rabin, T. (ed.) CRYPTO 2010. LNCS, vol. 6223, pp. 465–482. Springer, Heidelberg (2010). https://doi.org/10.1007/978-3-642-14623-7_25

31. Gentry, C.: Fully homomorphic encryption using ideal lattices. In: Proceedings of the Forty-First Annual ACM Symposium on Theory of Computing, STOC 2009, pp. 169–178 (2009)

32. Gilboa, N., Ishai, Y.: Distributed point functions and their applications. In: Nguyen, P.Q., Oswald, E. (eds.) EUROCRYPT 2014. LNCS, vol. 8441, pp. 640–658. Springer, Heidelberg (2014). https://doi.org/10.1007/978-3-642-55220-5_35

33. Goldberg, I.: Improving the robustness of private information retrieval. In: 2007 IEEE Symposium on Security and Privacy (SP'07). pp. 131–148 (2007)

34. Hazay, C., Ishai, Y., Marcedone, A., Venkitasubramaniam, M.: LevioSA: lightweight secure arithmetic computation. In: Proceedings of the 2019 ACM SIGSAC Conference on Computer and Communications Security, pp. 327–344, CCS 2019 (2019)

35. Hazay, C., Venkitasubramaniam, M., Weiss, M.: The price of active security in cryptographic protocols. In: Canteaut, A., Ishai, Y. (eds.) EUROCRYPT 2020. LNCS, vol. 12106, pp. 184–215. Springer, Cham (2020). https://doi.org/10.1007/978-3-030-45724-2_7

36. Ishai, Y., Lai, R.W.F., Malavolta, G.: A geometric approach to homomorphic secret sharing. In: Garay, J.A. (ed.) PKC 2021. LNCS, vol. 12711, pp. 92–119. Springer, Cham (2021). https://doi.org/10.1007/978-3-030-75248-4_4

37. Korte, B.H., Vygen, J.: Combinatorial Optimization, vol. 1. Springer, Cham (2011). https://doi.org/10.1007/978-3-642-77489-8

38. Kurosawa, K.: How to correct errors in multi-server PIR. In: Galbraith, S.D., Moriai, S. (eds.) ASIACRYPT 2019. LNCS, vol. 11922, pp. 564–574. Springer, Cham (2019). https://doi.org/10.1007/978-3-030-34621-8_20

39. Orlandi, C., Scholl, P., Yakoubov, S.: The Rise of Paillier: homomorphic secret sharing and public-key silent OT. In: Canteaut, A., Standaert, F.-X. (eds.) EURO-CRYPT 2021. LNCS, vol. 12696, pp. 678–708. Springer, Cham (2021). https://doi.org/10.1007/978-3-030-77870-5_24

40. Roy, L., Singh, J.: Large message homomorphic secret sharing from DCR and applications. In: Malkin, T., Peikert, C. (eds.) CRYPTO 2021. LNCS, vol. 12827, pp. 687–717. Springer, Cham (2021). https://doi.org/10.1007/978-3-030-84252-9_23

41. Rudra, A.: Lecture 27: Berlekamp-Welch algorithm. https://cse.buffalo.edu/faculty/atri/courses/coding-theory/lectures/lect27.pdf

42. van Dijk, M., Gentry, C., Halevi, S., Vaikuntanathan, V.: Fully homomorphic encryption over the integers. In: Gilbert, H. (ed.) EUROCRYPT 2010. LNCS, vol. 6110, pp. 24–43. Springer, Heidelberg (2010). https://doi.org/10.1007/978-3-642-13190-5_2

43. Woodruff, D., Yekhanin, S.: A geometric approach to information-theoretic private information retrieval. SIAM J. Comput. **37**(4), 1046–1056 (2007)

44. Yao, X., Liu, N., Kang, W.: The capacity of multi-round private information retrieval from Byzantine databases. In: 2019 IEEE International Symposium on Information Theory (ISIT), pp. 2124–2128 (2019)

45. Yoshida, M., Obana, S.: Verifiably multiplicative secret sharing. IEEE Trans. Inf. Theory **65**(5), 3233–3245 (2019)

46. Zhang, L.F., Wang, H.: Multi-server verifiable computation of low-degree polynomials. In: 2022 IEEE Symposium on Security and Privacy (SP), pp. 596–613 (2022)

47. Zhang, L.F., Wang, H., Wang, L.P.: Byzantine-robust private information retrieval with low communication and efficient decoding. In: Proceedings of the 2022 ACM on Asia Conference on Computer and Communications Security, pp. 1079–1085, ASIA CCS 2022 (2022)

Constant-Round Simulation-Secure Coin Tossing Extension with Guaranteed Output

Damiano Abram[1]([✉]) [ID], Jack Doerner[2,3,4], Yuval Ishai[2] [ID],
and Varun Narayanan[5] [ID]

[1] Aarhus University, Aarhus, Denmark
damiano.abram@cs.au.dk
[2] Technion, Haifa, Israel
[3] Reichman University, Herzliya, Israel
[4] Brown University, Providence, USA
[5] University of California, Los Angeles, USA

Abstract. Common randomness is an essential resource in many applications. However, Cleve (STOC 86) rules out the possibility of tossing a fair coin from scratch in the presence of a dishonest majority. A second-best alternative is a *Coin Tossing Extension* (CTE) protocol, which uses an "online" oracle that produces a few common random bits to generate many common random-looking bits. We initiate the systematic study of *fully-secure* CTE, which guarantees output even in the presence of malicious behavior. A fully-secure two-party statistical CTE protocol with black-box simulation was implicit in Hofheinz et al. (Eurocrypt 06), but its round complexity is nearly linear in its output length. The problem of constant-round CTE with superlogarithmic stretch remained open.

We prove that *statistical* CTE with full black-box security and super-logarithmic stretch must have superconstant rounds. In the *computational* setting we prove that with $N \geq 2$ parties and polynomial stretch:

- *One round* suffices for CTE under subexponential LWE, even with Universally Composable security against adaptive corruptions.
- One-round CTE is implied by DDH or the hidden subgroup assumption in class groups, with a short, reusable Uniform Random String, and by DCR and QR, with a reusable *Structured* Reference String.
- One-way functions imply CTE with $O(N)$ rounds, and thus constant-round CTE for any constant number of parties.

Such results were not previously known even in the two-party setting with standalone, static security. We also extend one-round CTE to sample from *any* efficient distribution, via strong assumptions including IO.

Our one-round CTE protocols can be interpreted as *explainable* variants of classical randomness extractors, wherein a (short) seed and a source instance can be efficiently reverse-sampled given a random output. Such explainable extractors may be of independent interest.

The full version of this work is available via https://eprint.iacr.org/.

© International Association for Cryptologic Research 2024
M. Joye and G. Leander (Eds.): EUROCRYPT 2024, LNCS 14655, pp. 122–154, 2024.
https://doi.org/10.1007/978-3-031-58740-5_5

1   Introduction

Common randomness is a crucial resource in many applications, yet after 40 years of research, it remains difficult and sometimes even impossible to generate in many settings. The problem of flipping common coins was first posed and solved by Blum [12] in the two-party context, but his protocol did not ensure that both parties received an output in the case that one of them deviated from the protocol instructions. Shortly thereafter, Cleve [17] proved that this "fairness" problem is inherent and unconditional: *any* r-round coin-tossing protocol that is guaranteed to output a common bit must suffer an inverse-polynomial bias of $\Omega(1/r)$ if a majority of the participants may be corrupted. In any round of interaction, corrupted parties may *rush* to see the messages of the honest parties before they transmit their own, and condition their responses (or choose not to respond) on the honest parties' contributions.

Cleve's bound has left a dichotomy in the plain model: in the face of a dishonest majority, either one must accept biased coins, or one must accept that the adversary can block the sampling of common coins entirely. Follow-up works have followed both pathways; for example, Buchbinder et al. [13] finally achieved guaranteed output with optimal bias for any constant number of parties, while Lindell [27] showed that polynomially-many coins can be tossed in constant rounds without guaranteed output, under the minimal assumption of one-way functions in the plain model. The impossibility of reliable unbiased coin tossing remains barrier to constructing a wide swath of essential primitives with guarantees against adversarial denial-of-service in the plain model, such as broadcast and consensus protocols, election protocols, lotteries, *Common Random String* (CRS) setup for cryptographic protocols, and many others.

The only means to evade Cleve's bound is to assume the impossibility away. Suppose there exists an oracle that outputs a small number n of common random coins when invoked (n can be thought of as a security parameter). This oracle might be implemented, for example, by a natural process or by an expensive honest-majority protocol. From such an ideal object, a protocol to flip at least one unbiased coin is trivial. We call this oracle $\mathcal{F}^n_{\text{Coin}}$.

Even in settings where unbiased common coins can be found, it is prudent to assume that they are few or expensive to access. If an ideal n-coin oracle allows one to evade Cleve for the flipping of one coin, can it do so for $n + 1$ coins, or more? In other words, can the oracle's output serve as a seed? A multiparty protocol that uses an n-coin seed oracle to sample m apparently-uniform common coins for $m > n$ is known as a *Coin Tossing Extension* (CTE) protocol; if it invokes the seed oracle t times, we say that it has a *stretch* of $m - t \cdot n$. Bellare et al. [11] originally introduced the notion of CTE, motivated primarily by concrete efficiency and *without* any guarantee that output will be produced in the presence of malicious behavior. CTE protocols can be thought of as the distributed analogue of classical randomness extractors, and like classical extractors they require that the uniform seed be independent of the entropy source. This can be ensured by revealing the seed at the *end* of the protocol, after the corrupt parties (who exert partial control over the source) are committed to their contributions, which necessitates an "online" seed oracle, rather than a seed established ahead of time.

Game-Based Security is not Enough. If we insist only that a coin tossing extension protocol produce a common output that is indistinguishable from a uniform bit string, then optimal CTE protocols with guaranteed output and unconditional security are easy to construct. If one way functions exist, then so does a trivial protocol: the parties simply use the n-bit output of $\mathcal{F}^n_{\text{Coin}}$ to seed a *Pseudorandom Generator* (PRG), which can produce a string of $m(n)$ bits for any polynomial m that is indistinguishable from uniform to all adversaries whose runtimes are also bounded polynomially in n. Notice that this protocol does not involve any communication at all, apart from invoking the oracle! If one way functions do not exist or the adversary is unbounded, then the solution need not be much more complicated. Consider the following simple protocol for N parties:

Protocol 1.1. Game-based Statistical Coin Tossing Extension

1. The parties exchange ℓ-bit uniformly-sampled strings over a broadcast channel; if any party fails to send a string then its string is taken to be all zeroes.
2. The parties query $\mathcal{F}^n_{\text{Coin}}$, receiving $u \in \{0,1\}^n$ in response.
3. They concatenate their strings to form $x \in \{0,1\}^{\ell \cdot N}$.
4. The parties individually apply a classical randomness extractor: $s \leftarrow$ Extract(x, u), and output s.

This protocol produces an output ε-close to uniform if there exists an (ℓ, ε)-extractor Extract : $\{0,1\}^{\ell \cdot N} \times \{0,1\}^n \to \{0,1\}^m$ [29]. For $\varepsilon \in \text{negl}(n)$ and $\ell \in O(m+n)$, there is a construction of such extractors from universal hashing [24].

The simplicity of these protocols comes with a shortcoming: though they may produce outputs indistinguishable from uniform, their outputs *cannot* be used to replace a truly uniform string in any given context. This can be seen by means of a simple example: suppose that the adversary is challenged to produce an n-bit representation of m uniformly sampled bits, for $n < m$. If these m bits are sampled by $\mathcal{F}^m_{\text{Coin}}$ directly, then the adversary will fail with probability overwhelming in $m - n$. On the other hand, if the bits are produced by the simple computational CTE protocol we have just described, then the n-bit intermediate output of the seed oracle $\mathcal{F}^n_{\text{Coin}}$ is *exactly* such a representation, and thus the protocol cannot be used in place of the oracle, even though their outputs are indistinguishable from one another. This is a simple and specific example of the general separation between *game*-based security and *simulation*-based security.[1]

Simulation-Secure CTE. Simulation-based security—otherwise known as security in the real/ideal-paradigm [14,21]—insists that there exist an efficient simulator algorithm to produce a protocol transcript given any protocol output,

---

[1] Hofheinz et al. [23] proved that Protocol 1.1 can in fact be simulated for some parameterizations, but not all.

and that the simulated transcript must be indistinguishable from a transcript of the real protocol. If the oracle $\mathcal{F}_{\mathsf{Coin}}^m$ in the *ideal* world is replaced by some simulation-secure protocol in the *real* world, then the simulator ensures that for any attack on the protocol, an equivalent attack can be mounted against $\mathcal{F}_{\mathsf{Coin}}^m$: thus, the protocol can be used in any context $\mathcal{F}_{\mathsf{Coin}}^m$ can be. A protocol is said to *black-box* simulation-secure if the simulator does not need to inspect the code of the protocol's adversary, but only to run the adversary as a subroutine. It is said to be *Universally Composable* (UC) [15] if the simulation property is guaranteed to hold in an arbitrary protocol context defined by an adversarial environment,[2] and it is said to have *standalone* security if simulatability is only guaranteed to hold for one instance at a time. We refer to any protocol that has both guaranteed output and black-box standalone-simulatable (or universally composable) security against a malicious adversary corrupting a dishonest majority of participants as *fully secure.*

Hofheinz et al. [23] gave a thorough treatment of simulation-secure CTE *without* guaranteed output (i.e. permitting the adversary to force the protocol to abort), with a specific focus on the *feasibility* of CTE for two parties in a set of six contexts comprising each combination of perfect, statistical, or computational security, and either black-box standalone security or universally composable security. They proved that perfectly secure CTE and statistically universally composable CTE are both impossible even for *one bit* of stretch. On the other hand, they proved that it is possible to achieve *polynomial* stretch in the computational universally composable case via a constant-round construction based on commitments; their protocol explicitly allows aborts to occur. They also proved that it is possible to achieve polynomial stretch in the statistical standalone case via a protocol with a round count linear in the number of output bits. Although they make no explicit claim about guaranteed output, this protocol does not in fact contain an abort: to our knowledge this makes it the *first* fully-secure CTE protocol, and the first to evade Cleve's bound.

Evading Cleve with Fully-Secure CTE. In this work, we initiate the systematic study of fully-secure coin tossing extension, and pose the question:

How many rounds does fully-secure coin tossing extension require?

It is clear that there must be at least one invocation of an "online" oracle, or else Cleve's bound would apply and we would be forced to sacrifice either guaranteed output or unbiased output. It is also clear that there must be at least one round of communication among the parties, or else there could be no additional entropy with which to extend the coins that the oracle produces. We begin our study by proving that any interaction after the coin-tossing oracle $\mathcal{F}_{\mathsf{Coin}}^n$ is invoked is useless. This implies that if the adversary is given the (standard) power to rush, then the communication of the parties must occur *before* the invocation of $\mathcal{F}_{\mathsf{Coin}}^n$ and thus the minimal interaction for *any* fully-secure CTE protocol is one round, followed by one oracle invocation. This result is proven in the full version of our work [2, Section 4.1].

---

[2] Other models exist that achieve a similar goal. UC security is always black-box.

In the black-box standalone statistical setting, we prove much more interaction than this is required: specifically, we prove that a protocol with r rounds of interaction before the oracle's invocation cannot output more than $O(r \cdot \log \lambda)$ bits, where λ is a security parameter. This implies that the protocol of Hofheinz et al. is *nearly* optimal with linear stretch, and with a simple adjustment optimality can easily be achieved. Since Hofheinz et al. have already proved that statistically universally composable CTE is impossible, even without guaranteed output or polynomial stretch, this effectively closes the question of the round complexity of statistical CTE with black-box simulation. This result is proven in the full version of our work [2, Section 8].

To evade the bound we have just proved, we turn to computational security and cryptographic assumptions. Under the subexponential *Learning with Errors* (LWE) Assumption [34], we construct an N-party protocol that achieves polynomial stretch with the optimal interaction pattern: *one* round, followed by an invocation of $\mathcal{F}^n_{\mathsf{Coin}}$. Furthermore, this protocol is universally composable and secure against malicious adversaries *adaptively* corrupting up to $N-1$ parties. Due to its basis in a lattice assumption it is also plausibly post-quantum secure. Indeed, we do not know of a stronger bounded adversary than the one implied by this combination of attributes. This result is proven in Sect. 3.

By allowing a trusted setup and settling for weaker notions of security, we expand the set of assumptions we can rely on: using a general *hidden subgroup* framework, we devise a one-round fully-secure and universally composable N-party CTE protocol in the Common Reference String (CRS) model. Unlike our previous construction, this one is proven only to have security against the *static* corruption of $N-1$ participants. We show how to instantiate our framework from the *Decisional Diffie-Hellman* (DDH) assumption [18] and the *Hard Subgroup Membership* (HSM) assumption[3] on class groups [16]: both of these assumptions yield short, reusable, *uniform* CRSes that can be sampled via one extra call the very same coin oracle $\mathcal{F}^n_{\mathsf{Coin}}$ that the protocol extends. We also give an instantiation of the framework using Paillier encryption [30] (and thus under both the *Decisional Composite Residuosity* (DCR) and *Quadratic Residuosity* (QR) assumptions); this instantiation requires a reusable *structured* CRS that cannot be so trivially sampled. These results are proven in the full version of our work [2, Section 6].

We find a result in even the weakest of computational assumptions: *One-Way Functions* (OWFs). A close inspection of the OWF-based constant-round N-party coin tossing protocol of Goyal et al. [22] reveals that it can achieve *Identifiable Abort* (IA) [25], though the authors did not claim this. This type of security does not guarantee an output, but does ensure that if no output is produced, then the honest parties can agree upon the identity of at least one malicious party. Simple iteration of this protocol to eliminate cheating parties one-by-one can ensure that an output is produced in $O(N)$ rounds, even if $N-1$ parties are corrupt, but cannot prevent the adversary from biasing that output. We describe a simple way to eliminate this bias using a sample from $\mathcal{F}^n_{\mathsf{Coin}}$,

---

[3] Also known as the Hidden Subgroup Assumption.

yielding a constant-round fully-secure coin tossing protocol for any constant number of parties. This result is proven in the full version [2, Section 7].

Fully-Secure Distributed Sampling. Abram et al. [4,5] recently introduced the notion of *Distributed Sampling*, which can be thought of as a generalization of coin tossing to any (efficiently-samplable) distribution, and they proved the existence of one-round distributed samplers in the malicious, dishonest-majority setting under a set of strong assumptions, including *Indistinguishability Obfuscation* (iO) [10]. They could not, however, construct one-round unbiased distributed samplers with guaranteed output without running afoul of Cleve [17], and settled instead for a notion they referred to as *indistinguishability-preservingness*. In this work, we augment their techniques with a single call to the coin tossing oracle $\mathcal{F}_{\mathsf{Coin}}^{n}$ to achieve what they could not. This result is proven in the full version of our work [2, Section 9].

Explainable Randomness Extractors. At the beginning of this section, we explained coin tossing extension as the multiparty analogue of a randomness extractor. This analogy is not an accident: when the parties in a coin tossing extension protocol perform a final local computation to recover the protocol's output from the coin oracle's output and the transcript of the protocol before the oracle was invoked, they are *precisely* invoking a randomness extractor with the pre-oracle transcript as the source and the oracle's output as the seed. For one-round protocols as several of ours are, the source is simply the concatenation of the parties' single messages. The black-box simulatability of our protocols suggests a heretofore-unidentified property of certain extractors: it is efficient to find a seed and source that yield a chosen output under the extractor, such that the distribution of seeds is independent of the output, and the sources belong to some well-defined distribution that is tolerated by the extractor. We refer to this property as *explainability*, and formally prove the correspondence; as corollaries our other results imply explainable *computational* extractors for various source distributions under various assumptions. Correspondingly, the statistical CTE protocol of Hofheinz et al. [23] implies an explainable *statistical* extractor for a particular source distribution. This result is proven in the full version of our work [2, Section 4.2].

Open Questions. This work leaves an interesting question open:

> *Do there exist constant-round and statistically simulation-secure coin tossing extension protocols with $\omega(\log \lambda)$ stretch?*

This paper shows that if we relax this question by considering computational security, the answer is *yes* (under standard cryptographic assumptions). On the other hand, for the more stringent variant of the question that requires *black-box simulation*, the answer is unconditionally *no*. Thus, an affirmative answer to our question would separate black-box and non-black-box simulation in the statistical security setting. We are not aware of such a separation in the literature.

2 Technical Overview

Notation. Let λ be the security parameter. For any $n \in \mathbb{N}$, we use $[n]$ to denote the set $\{1, \ldots, n\}$. We use $\lfloor x \rfloor$ to denote the integral part of the number x. We use bold font to denote vectors and capital letters for matrices. We use $\|\cdot\|_\infty$ to denote the ℓ_∞-norm (i.e. the maximum magnitude of the entries of the vector). We use $=$ to denote equality, $:=$ to denote equality by definition of the left hand side by the right hand side, $\equiv$ to denote congruence, and $\leftarrow$ to denote deterministic assignment. We use $\overset{\$}{\leftarrow}$ in an overloaded fashion to denote sampling from a distribution, assignment using a randomized algorithm, or, if the right hand side is a domain, uniform sampling from that domain. We use $\sim$ to denote that two scalars approximate each other, or in some contexts that they are negligibly close in the security parameter, and we use $\approx_s$ and $\approx_c$ to denote that distributions are statistically or computationally indistinguishable, respectively.

A *Coin Tossing Extension* (CTE) protocol consists of an N-party protocol that produces m unbiased random bits given a source of $n < m$ unbiased random coins. Formally, our security definition is based on black-box simulation: we insist that a CTE protocol *realizes* the functionality $\mathcal{F}_{\mathsf{Coin}}^m$ that provides all parties with a random string $s \overset{\$}{\leftarrow} \{0,1\}^m$ in the presence of a malicious PPT adversary corrupting up to $N-1$ parties, in the *hybrid model* of the functionality $\mathcal{F}_{\mathsf{Coin}}^n$ (otherwise known as the *seed oracle*) that supplies a random string $u \overset{\$}{\leftarrow} \{0,1\}^n$. $\mathcal{F}_{\mathsf{Coin}}^n$ and $\mathcal{F}_{\mathsf{Coin}}^m$ are identical, apart from their parametrization.

Functionality 2.1. $\mathcal{F}_{\mathsf{Coin}}^n$. The Coin Tossing Functionality

Initialisation: On `init` from all parties, the functionality activates.

Coins: On receiving (`flip`, sid) from all parties, the functionality samples $s \overset{\$}{\leftarrow} \{0,1\}^{n(\lambda)}$ and sends (`coins`, sid, s) to all parties.

We highlight that $\mathcal{F}_{\mathsf{Coin}}^m$ has *guaranteed output*, and thus our CTE protocols achieve *full security*: even if the corrupted parties deviate from the protocol, the honest parties will always agree on an unbiased random output. In general, both n and m may be polynomials in the security parameter λ, but we often leave this implicit. We define the round complexity of the protocol to be the number of rounds of interaction between the parties before the final invocation of $\mathcal{F}_{\mathsf{Coin}}^n$, the sampling complexity t to be the number of times $\mathcal{F}_{\mathsf{Coin}}^n$ is invoked, the additive stretch to be $m - t \cdot n$, and the multiplicative stretch to be $m/(t \cdot n)$.

Throughout this paper, we consider different flavours of security: most of our constructions achieve computational security in the UC model, and one is only standalone-secure. One construction achieves security against adaptive corruptions. Our lower bound applies to the information-theoretic case with black-box simulation. We always assume that the parties are connected by authenticated, private, point-to-point channels, and by an authenticated broadcast medium.

2.1   The Round Structure of CTE Protocols

In a coin tossing extension protocol, the seed oracle behaves very differently from a typical *trusted setup*: in order to evade Cleve's impossibility [17], the random coins must be delivered throughout the execution of the protocol and not at the beginning. We begin by proving that any round of interaction after the last call to the seed oracle is essentially useless. Immediately after the last call, the parties must already agree on an unbiased random string of the right length. This fact holds even for CTE protocols that rely on non-black-box simulators.

Theorem 2.2 (Informal Version of [2, Theorem 4.3]). *Let Π be a CTE protocol producing m random bits. Let Π' be the protocol in which the parties behave exactly as in Π until the last call to the seed oracle, after which they stop interacting. Π' is a secure coin tossing extension protocol producing m random bits.*

Proving the above theorem begins with the simple observation that the output of any honest party P_i in Π' is the value it would return if it were executing Π and all other parties ceased interacting (as they might, if they are corrupt) after last call to the entropy source. This implies that P_i's output in Π' cannot be noticeably biased by the adversary. It is more challenging to prove that the outputs of the honest parties in Π' all coincide. We show this by following the blueprint of Cleve's impossibility result [17] and applying a similar argument in the N-party setting. Let α be the index of one (arbitrary) bit of the output, and let P_i and P_j be two honest parties. Let the random variables $b_{i,r}$ and $b_{j,r}$ be the αth bit that P_i and P_j would output in Π if all other parties ceased interacting in the rth round *after* the last call to the seed oracle. By the security of Π, the bits $b_{i,r}$ and $b_{j,r}$ must be equal for sufficiently large r, because, at the end of the protocol, P_i and P_j are guaranteed to agree. Our goal is to prove that, whatever the value of α and the behaviour of the adversary $\mathcal{A}$, the bits $b_{i,0}$ and $b_{j,0}$ are equal. For every adversary $\mathcal{A}$, every round r, and $b \in \{0,1\}$, we define two modified adversaries, $\mathcal{A}_{r,0}^b$ and $\mathcal{A}_{r,1}^b$. The adversary $\mathcal{A}_{r,0}^b$ corrupts all parties except P_i. Any parties that $\mathcal{A}$ would corrupt behave when corrupted by $\mathcal{A}_{r,0}^b$ as they would when corrupted by $\mathcal{A}$; for all other parties, $\mathcal{A}_{r,0}^b$ follows the protocol. At the rth round after the last call to the seed oracle, $\mathcal{A}_{r,0}^b$ simulates the execution of the round in its head using P_i's message ($\mathcal{A}_{r,0}^b$ is a rushing adversary, and thus has this message before the round completes). If it predicts that $b_{j,r+1} = b$, then $\mathcal{A}_{r,0}^b$ sends no further messages; otherwise, it sends the messages of the execution it simulated in its head and ceases communication thereafter. The adversary $\mathcal{A}_{r,1}^b$ is slightly simpler: it corrupts all parties except P_j and determines their behavior just like $\mathcal{A}_{r,0}^b$ did. At the rth round after the last call to the seed oracle, $\mathcal{A}_{r,1}^b$ checks whether $b_{i,r} = b$, and sends no further messages if so; otherwise, it ceases communication at the end of the following round. Using Cleve's argument [17], we can prove that unless $b_{i,0} = b_{j,0}$, at least one of the adversaries $(\mathcal{A}_{r,0}^b, \mathcal{A}_{r,1}^b)_{r,b}$ must bias the αth bit of the output of Π by a non-negligible amount, with overwhelming probability.

This result is formalized in the full version of our work [2, Section 4.1].

2.2   Coin Tossing Extension and Explainable Extractors

A randomness extractor is a primitive that converts samples from a high-entropy source into true randomness, with the aid of an auxiliary source of truly random bits, referred to as a *seed*. The samples provided by the high-entropy source should be independent of the seed, and the seed is typically required to be much shorter than the output. Formally, we require that for every source of sufficiently high entropy S, the following distribution is indistinguishable from the uniform distribution:

$$\left\{ \mathsf{Extract}(\boldsymbol{x}, \boldsymbol{u}) \,\middle|\, \boldsymbol{x} \xleftarrow{\$} S, \boldsymbol{u} \xleftarrow{\$} \{0,1\}^n \right\}$$

In the full version of our work [2, Section 4.2], we introduce the notion of an *explainable extractor*: a randomness extractor that satisfies a stronger, simulation-based security definition relative to some class of entropy sources $\mathcal{S}$. Specifically, for every source $S \in \mathcal{S}$, there must exist a PPT simulator $\mathsf{Explain}_S$ such that the following distributions are indistinguishable:

$$\left\{ \mathsf{aux}, \boldsymbol{x}, \boldsymbol{u}, \boldsymbol{s} \,\middle|\, \begin{array}{l} (\boldsymbol{x}, \mathsf{aux}) \xleftarrow{\$} S \\ \boldsymbol{u} \xleftarrow{\$} \{0,1\}^n \\ \boldsymbol{s} \leftarrow \mathsf{Extract}(\boldsymbol{x}, \boldsymbol{u}) \end{array} \right\} \quad \left\{ \mathsf{aux}, \boldsymbol{x}, \boldsymbol{u}, \boldsymbol{s} \,\middle|\, \begin{array}{l} \boldsymbol{s} \xleftarrow{\$} \{0,1\}^m \\ (\mathsf{aux}, \boldsymbol{x}, \boldsymbol{u}) \xleftarrow{\$} \mathsf{Explain}_S(\boldsymbol{s}) \end{array} \right\}$$

We prove that fully-secure CTE protocols imply explainable extractors. In particular, any CTE protocol can be viewed as an explainable extractor for the class of entropy sources that is generated by running the CTE protocol with an adversary corrupting at most $N-1$ parties, and then outputting the transcript $\boldsymbol{x}$ and the view of the adversary aux just before the last call to the seed oracle. The extractor $\mathsf{Extract}(\boldsymbol{x}, \boldsymbol{u})$ simply emits an honest party's (truly random) output using the transcript, simulating the seed oracle via $\boldsymbol{u}$, and performing any final computations via the honest party's code. The algorithm $\mathsf{Explain}_S$ can easily be derived from the simulator of the CTE protocol.

In Sect. 3, we use this fact to prove the existence of an explainable extractor for the class of entropy sources that produce N blocks of $\mathsf{poly}(\lambda)$ bits $\boldsymbol{x}_1, \ldots, \boldsymbol{x}_N$, such that one block (say $\boldsymbol{x}_i$) is truly random, and the other blocks and aux are produced by any PPT algorithm receiving $\boldsymbol{x}_i$ as input. See Corollary 3.7.

2.3   Computational Coin Tossing Extension with Long Stretch

We now describe our CTE constructions starting from the simplest to the most sophisticated. All of our schemes achieve security against adversaries corrupting up to $N-1$ parties and require a single call to the seed oracle.

On UC-Security and Arbitrary Polynomial Stretch at No Round Cost. If a UC-secure coin tossing extension protocol generates $m > n$ random bits using a single call to the seed oracle, then we immediately obtain a UC-secure coin tossing extension protocol with the same round complexity, a single call to the seed oracle, and arbitrary polynomial stretch: all we must do is run the original CTE protocol many times in parallel. We use the coins produced by the seed oracle in the first execution, and then use n bits of the resulting output as the seed for the second execution, reserving at least one bit for the final output, and so on. We obtain at least one additional bit per instance.

From One-Way Functions via Coin Tossing with Identifiable Abort. We start from the simplest construction: we consider a secondary coin tossing functionality with identifiable abort and *not* guaranteed output. We refer to this functionality as $\mathcal{F}_{\mathsf{Coin+IA}}^m$; it can be realized by the protocol of Goyal et al. [22] in the standalone setting assuming one-way functions exist. We might naïvely hope to build a fully-secure CTE protocol via player elimination. The parties invoke $\mathcal{F}_{\mathsf{Coin+IA}}^m$, and if the invocation succeeds, then they output the random string produced by it; otherwise, they repeat the invocation of $\mathcal{F}_{\mathsf{Coin+IA}}^m$ *without* the party that cause the abort. After at most $N-1$ attempts, the honest parties are guaranteed to agree on a random string. Unfortunately, this construction allows the adversary to bias the output. Remember, we have not relied on the seed oracle, so Cleve's impossibility [17] must apply. During each invocation of $\mathcal{F}_{\mathsf{Coin+IA}}^m$, the adversary learns the candidate output before the honest parties, and can choose to abort or accept the result; conditioning this choice on the candidate output allows bias to be injected. For example, if the adversary desires the initial bit of the output to be 0, then it can abort the invocation of $\mathcal{F}_{\mathsf{Coin+IA}}^m$ only when the candidate output starts with a 1.

We prevent this bias attack by "encrypting" the output of the CTE protocol using a PRG. Specifically, after $\mathcal{F}_{\mathsf{Coin+IA}}^m$ produces an output, the parties invoke the seed oracle $\mathcal{F}_{\mathsf{Coin}}^\lambda$ to obtain a λ-bit seed, where λ denotes the security parameter. They expand this seed with a PRG, and output the XOR of the expansion and the output of $\mathcal{F}_{\mathsf{Coin+IA}}^m$.

We highlight that even with this modification, the adversary still has the ability to cause an abort and force the honest parties to invoke $\mathcal{F}_{\mathsf{Coin+IA}}^m$ repeatedly. Compared to the naïve protocol, the adversary must now face the choice of whether to abort blindly: even given the candidate output of $\mathcal{F}_{\mathsf{Coin+IA}}^m$, the adversary cannot predict the output of the CTE protocol. At the time the adversary must make the decision, the privacy of the final output is guaranteed by the security of the PRG, because the λ-bit seed chosen by the seed oracle is not yet revealed. This result is expounded in the full version of our work [2, Section 7]. Ultimately, we prove:

Corollary 2.3. *If one-way functions exist, then for any constant number of parties there is a constant-round fully-secure CTE protocol in the plain model, with standalone black-box simulatability against a malicious PPT adversary statically corrupting all parties but one. This construction is black-box in the OWF.*

An Algebraic Framework for Coin-Tossing Extension. After discovering a fully-secure CTE protocol from coin tossing with identifiable abort, we wondered whether it is possible to guarantee output without restarting in response to malicious behavior. We answer this question affirmatively, and moreover demonstrate that only a *single* round of interaction followed by a single call to the seed oracle is required in the CRS model. Our construction is an *algebraic framework* for coin tossing extension that can be instantiated using DDH groups, class groups, or Paillier Encryption.

One-Round CTE Against Rushing Adversaries. One of the main challenges in designing a one-round CTE protocol is dealing with rushing behaviour. For the moment, imagine that our goal is to construct a protocol with black-box simulation and *no* CRS. In the ideal world, the corresponding functionality provides the simulator with the output of the protocol, and then the simulator must generate fake but consistent messages for the honest parties. The simulator must do this without knowing the messages of the corrupted players, since the honest party is assumed to speak first. In principle, the adversary might be able to inject so much randomness in the protocol that the Shannon entropy of the output s conditioned on the messages generated by the simulator U_H is greater than $n + \omega(\log \lambda)$; specifically

$$\mathsf{H}(s|U_H) \geq n + \omega(\log \lambda). \tag{1}$$

Indeed, what happens if the adversary is the simulator itself, using a random string in place of the functionality's output? Without a CRS, this is a possibility! If (1) holds, the simulator is doomed to fail: the only power it has is to rewind, or generate a random-looking n-bit response u on behalf of the seed oracle. The latter will not help because the entropy of u is bounded by n; it is too low to fully correct the bias induced by the adversary. Rewinding will not help, since it is equivalent to restarting: each execution is overwhelmingly likely to fail.

Relying on a CRS: the Hidden Subgroup Framework. Now that we have understood what the main challenges are, we relax our requirements to permit a CRS. We hope that by relying on the common reference string, we can restrict the influence of the adversary while allowing full freedom to the simulator. We demonstrate that this is possible using an algebraic framework inspired by the work of Abram et al. [1], which we refer to as the *the hidden subgroup framework.*

Theorem 2.4 (Informal Version of [2, Theorem 6.4]). *Given any instantiation of the hidden subgroup framework, there exists a one-round N-party fully-secure protocol in the $\mathcal{F}_{\mathsf{Coin}}^n$-hybrid CRS model that UC-realizes $\mathcal{F}_{\mathsf{Coin}}^m$ in the presence of a malicious PPT adversary statically corrupting up to $N-1$ parties.*

Consider a multiplicative group G with a smaller subgroup H. Suppose that we can efficiently sample uniformly random elements from both groups, but the two distributions are computationally indistinguishable. Our CRS consists of a description of G and H along with the CRS for a simulation-extractable NIZK. Each party P_i broadcasts a random sample $h_i \in H$, along with a NIZK proving that the sample belongs to H. If any NIZK does not verify, the party that generated it is excluded from the execution of the protocol (without restarting).

Next, the seed oracle provides the parties with the description of another random element $h \in H$. The parties output the product $h \cdot \prod_i h_i$, ignoring every h_j for which the corresponding NIZK does not verify.

We argue that from the adversary's perspective, the output is indistinguishable from a random element in G. Indeed, a simulator that receives $g \overset{\$}{\leftarrow} G$ from the functionality can generate a trapdoored CRS for the NIZK and send $g \cdot h_\iota$ instead of h_ι on behalf of an arbitrary honest party P_ι. The corresponding NIZK is simulated using the trapdoor, and the simulator sends a correcting term $h \leftarrow \prod_i h_i^{-1}$ on behalf of the seed oracle (where, again, the product ignores all indices corresponding to non-verifying NIZKs). Notice that h is a random element in H due to h_ι. The output of this protocol execution is g, and the transcript is indistinguishable from a real protocol transcript due to the security of the NIZK and the indistinguishability of uniform elements in G and H.

The Representation of the Group Elements. There is a problem yet to be solved in the blueprint we have just given: a CTE protocol must produce more random bits than those provided by the seed oracle. The entropy of a random element in G is higher than the entropy of random elements in H, but since the two distributions are indistinguishable, it would seem that the representations of elements in G and H require strings of the same length. In other words, it seems that in the foregoing construction, the seed oracle provides as many bits as are produced by the protocol. This is not the case, however: the stretch depends on how we represent the response of the seed oracle. This representation can be compressed because it is known to *always* be in H. If H is a cyclic group of order q and h_0 is a generator, then the seed oracle can represent any $h = h_0^r$ as $r \bmod q$. This representation is optimal as it requires roughly $\log q = \log|H| < \log|G|$ bits, and it yields a protocol with positive stretch.

Using such a representation introduces another issue, though: how can the simulator obtain a succinct representation of $\prod_i h_i^{-1}$? Doing so implies computing a discrete logarithm. This is the purpose of the simulation-extractable NIZKs: the simulator samples the discrete logarithms of the elements chosen by the honest parties (including h_ι), and extracts the discrete logarithms of the elements of the corrupted parties using their NIZKs.

We require three additional properties from our framework:

– There should exist a succinct representation for the elements of H. For any $h_i \in H$, we denote the representation by ρ_i. This representation may not be unique.
– Given elements $h_1, \ldots, h_\ell \in H$ and corresponding succinct representations $\rho_1, \ldots, \rho_\ell$, we must be able to obtain a succinct representation of $\prod_{i \in [\ell]} h_i^{-1}$
– There must be a way to sample h_1 and a corresponding succinct representation ρ_1 such that, for every $h_2, \ldots, h_\ell \in H$ and corresponding $\rho_2, \ldots, \rho_\ell$, the succinct representation of $\prod_{i \in [\ell]} h_i^{-1}$ derived from $\rho_1, \rho_2 \ldots, \rho_\ell$ is indistinguishable from the succinct representation of a uniform element in H.

One Last Property: Converting the Output into Bits. A CTE protocol is supposed to produce random bits. The protocol we described above outputs a random group element $g \in G$ instead. How do we convert this into a random string? This can be surprisingly challenging! We cannot simply apply an arbitrary hash function f; the procedure must be explainable. There must be a way for the simulator to convert the random string s obtained from the functionality into a random group element g such that $f(g) = s$. In other words, our framework also requires the existence of an efficiently invertible deterministic function f such that the following distributions are indistinguishable.[4]

$$\left\{ g, f(g) \,\middle|\, g \xleftarrow{\$} G \right\} \qquad \left\{ f^{-1}(s), s \,\middle|\, s \xleftarrow{\$} \{0,1\}^m \right\}$$

Instantiations of the Framework. We present three instantiations of the hidden subgroup framework: one based on DDH over cyclic groups, one based on Paillier Encryption [30], and one based on class groups of imaginary quadratic fields [16].

- Let $\widehat{G}$ be a cyclic group of prime order p wherein DDH is hard. Inspired by Peikert et al. [32], we choose G to be the product $\widehat{G} \times \widehat{G}$. The subgroup H consists of all pairs $(g_1, g_2) \in G$ such that $g_2 = g_1^\alpha$ for a randomly sampled, secret $\alpha \xleftarrow{\$} \mathbb{Z}_p$. It is easy to see that H is a proper subgroup of G. Furthermore, it is hard to distinguish between the uniform distributions over G and H under the DDH assumption. Since H is cyclic with order p, we can also succinctly represent any element in H as the usual discrete logarithm of (g_1, g_2) with respect to some generator (g_0, g_0^α). This succinct representation satisfies the properties required by the framework. Finally, the matter of conversion from G into random bits depends greatly on the choice of $\widehat{G}$. If the latter is a cyclic subgroup of $\mathbb{F}_q^*$ for some power of a prime q or of an elliptic curve, conversion is usually easy as long as the cofactor is small.
- Consider the Paillier group $G := \mathbb{Z}_{N^2}^*$ where N is the product of two large, random, safe primes $p = 2p' + 1$ and $q = 2q' + 1$. The subgroup H will consist of all $2N^{\text{th}}$ powers of G. H is a subgroup of order $p' \cdot q'$, and since $p' \neq q'$ are primes, all abelian groups of this order are cyclic. Under the QR assumption and the DCR assumption, no PPT adversary can distinguish between a random element in G and a random $2N^{\text{th}}$ power. As before, we can succinctly represent any element in H via the discrete logarithm with respect to a fixed generator h_0 (h_0 can be a random $2N^{\text{th}}$ power). This instantiation differs from the previous one only in that the order of H is unknown: to sample a random element in H with a known succinct representation, we must sample $\rho \xleftarrow{\$} [N]$ and set $h \leftarrow h_0^\rho$. We use flooding to ensure the third property of succinct representations.
- Consider a class group $\widehat{G}$ and let F denote the cyclic subgroup of prime order q where the discrete logarithm problem is easy. Let h_0 be a random element in $\widehat{G}$ of order coprime with q. Let ℓ be 2^λ times greater than an upper-bound on the order of h_0. The subgroup H is generated by h_0 and G is $F \times H$. Under the hidden subgroup membership assumption, the uniform distributions over

---

[4] f^{-1} may be non-deterministic.

H and G are indistinguishable. Once again, we can succinctly represent the elements of H through their discrete logarithm with respect to h_0, and as in the Paillier case, the order of H is unknown, so we generate random elements with a known succinct representation by sampling $\rho \xleftarrow{\$} [\ell]$ and computing $h \leftarrow h_0^\rho$. Also as in the Paillier case, we use flooding to ensure the third property of succinct representations. While our class group instantiation has an advantage over our Paillier instantiation in that we can generate the parameters of the group transparently, there is also an important disadvantage: as far as we know, there exists no explainable procedure that converts random elements in G into random strings of bits. In other words, we do not know how to ensure the last property of our framework.

These results are formalized in the full version of our work [2, Section 6], with the three instantiations of our framework being presented in Subsects. 6.1, 6.2 and 6.3 respectively.

One-Round Setup-Free Adaptively-Secure Coin Tossing Extension. We return to the question of whether it is possible to built one-round CTE protocols *without* a CRS. As we explained in the context of our construction from the hidden subgroup framework, the goal of using a CRS is to limit adversarial influence on the output, while giving the simulator freedom. With no CRS, the simulator can only restrict the influence of the adversary through the responses of the seed oracle. This creates a new challenge: because the responses of the seed oracle are revealed only at the end, we cannot use well-studied primitives, such as NIZKs. We have eliminated the most common non-interactive MPC tool for preventing malicious behavior. We must therefore develop new techniques.

Lattice-Based Lossy Trapdoor Functions. Our solution comes from lattice-based cryptography. In our protocol, each party P_i will broadcast L vectors $\boldsymbol{x}_{i,1}, \dots, \boldsymbol{x}_{i,L} \in \mathbb{Z}_q^M$ sampled from a discrete Gaussian distribution. The seed oracle will provide matrices $A_1, \dots, A_N \in \mathbb{Z}_q^{K \times M}$ and $B_1, \dots, B_N \in \mathbb{Z}_q^{V \times M}$. For every index $i \in [N]$, we define the function

$$f_i : \mathbb{Z}_q^M \longrightarrow \mathbb{Z}_q^{K+V} \qquad \text{such that} \qquad f_i : \boldsymbol{x} \longmapsto (A_i \cdot \boldsymbol{x}, B_i \cdot \boldsymbol{x})$$

For the moment, assume that the parties output $\sum_{i \in [N]} f_i(\boldsymbol{x}_{i,\ell})$ for every $\ell \in [L]$, where L is a free parameter that controls the protocol's stretch.[5] We will adjust this provisional protocol several times as we explore its properties in order to achieve the properties we desire.

Each f_i can be viewed as a lossy trapdoor function [33] under the hardness of LWE. In particular, if M is sufficiently large compared to K, V and $\log q$, then there is a way to sample the matrices (A_i, B_i) along with a trapdoor T

---

[5] Note that in this provisional version, the output length is linear in L but the seed length is independent of L; the analysis of the *final* protocol's stretch will be more complex.

so that, for every $v_1 \in \mathbb{Z}_q^K$, $v_2 \in \mathbb{Z}_q^V$, the trapdoor T can be used to sample a low-norm vector $x \in \mathbb{Z}_q^M$ such that $A_i \cdot x = v_1$ and $B_i \cdot x = v_2$. Furthermore, this sampling method yields A_i and B_i that are statistically close to uniform and x is indistinguishable from a discrete Gaussian sample [7,8,19,28]. When the matrices are sampled in this way, f_i is in *injective* mode.

To use f_i in *lossy* mode, suppose that we generate B_i as $S \cdot A_i + E_i$, where $A_i \in \mathbb{Z}_q^{K \times M}$ and $S \in \mathbb{Z}_q^{V \times K}$ are sampled uniformly and $E_i \in \mathbb{Z}_q^{V \times M}$ comes from a discrete Gaussian distribution. Under LWE, the matrix B_i is indistinguishable from uniform, but every time we apply f_i on a small norm vector, we obtain a pair $(v_1, v_2) \in \mathbb{Z}_q^K \times \mathbb{Z}_q^V$ such that v_2 is close in norm to $S \cdot v_1$.

Limiting the Influence of the Adversary Using Lossy Trapdoor Functions. Let us consider the ideal world execution of the protocol we described above. The simulator starts by picking an arbitrary honest party P_ι. It generates the matrices $(A_i, B_i)_{i \in [N]}$ so that f_ι is in injective mode (let T_ι be the trapdoor), while all the other functions are in lossy mode. In particular, for every $i \neq \iota$, the simulator ensures that $B_i = S \cdot A_i + E_i$, where $S \xleftarrow{\$} \mathbb{Z}_q^{V \times K}$, $A_i \xleftarrow{\$} \mathbb{Z}_q^{K \times M}$ and E_i comes from a discrete Gaussian distribution over $\mathbb{Z}^{V \times M}$.

If all of the parties are honest, then the simulator has full control of the output of the protocol: if we desire the output to be the vectors $u_1, \dots, u_L \in \mathbb{Z}_q^{K+V}$, the simulator must simply generate messages $x_{i,1}, \dots, x_{i,L}$ following the protocol for every $i \neq \iota$. Then, using the trapdoor T_ι, it generates $x_{\iota,1}, \dots, x_{\iota,L}$ such that $f_\iota(x_{\iota,\ell}) = u_\ell - \sum_{i \neq \iota} f_i(x_{i,\ell})$ for every $\ell \in [L]$. That ensures that the output is exactly as desired.

If some parties are corrupted, however, the adversary has the ability to bias the output in an unpredictable but limited way by using its ability to rush. If the adversary waits until after the honest parties (including P_ι) are committed to their inputs before transmitting those of the corrupted parties, then it can contribute an additive term of $(v_{1,\ell}, v_{2,\ell}) := \sum_{j \in \mathcal{C}} f_j(x_{j,\ell})$ to ℓ-th vector produced the protocol, and the simulator cannot compensate using the mechanism we have just described. Since all f_j for $j \in \mathcal{C}$ are in lossy mode with respect to the same matrix S, and they are all linear, it follows that $v_{2,\ell} = S \cdot v_{1,\ell} + e_\ell'$ where e_ℓ' is a vector of small norm. In other words, the entropy that the adversary can introduce is limited in this construction because the lossy trapdoor functions corresponding to the parties it corrupts are in lossy mode. We must add an additional mechanism to the protocol to correct for this adversarially-induced shift.

Adding a Correction Term. In order to allow the simulator to correct the offset induced by a rushing adversary, we augment the response of the seed oracle with two new matrices $C \in \mathbb{Z}_q^{K \times W}$ and $D \in \mathbb{Z}_q^{V \times W}$ that are indistinguishable from uniform, and a list of discrete Gaussian samples $(e_\ell)_{\ell \in [L]}$ over $\mathbb{Z}_q^W$.[6] The output of our *new* protocol is the list of all vectors

$$(s_{1,\ell}, s_{2,\ell}) := \sum_{i \in [N]} f_i(x_{i,\ell}) + (C \cdot e_\ell, D \cdot e_\ell) \quad \text{for every } \ell \in [L].$$

The simulator samples (C, D) such that they constitute a lossy-mode lossy trapdoor function. In other words, the matrix D is computed as $D \leftarrow S \cdot C + F$ where F is sampled according to a discrete Gaussian distribution over $\mathbb{Z}_q^{V \times W}$. Under the LWE assumption, D is indistinguishable from uniform, from the adversary's perspective. However, C is not sampled uniformly, as A_i for $i \neq \iota$ were. Instead, C is sampled together with a trapdoor T, much like A_ι and T_ι. The trapdoor T allows the simulator to sample preimages with respect to C that are indistinguishable from discrete Gaussian samples.

Suppose that we would like the output to be the random vectors $(u_{1,1}, u_{2,1}), \ldots, (u_{1,L}, u_{2,L}) \in \mathbb{Z}_q^K \times \mathbb{Z}_q^V$. The simulator generates the messages of all honest parties except for P_ι by following the protocol, then it samples $w_1, \ldots, w_L \xleftarrow{\$} \mathbb{Z}_q^K$ and, using the trapdoor T_ι, it generates the messages $x_{\iota,1}, \ldots, x_{\iota,L}$ of P_ι such that

$$f_\iota(x_{\iota,\ell}) = (u_{1,\ell} + w_\ell, u_{2,\ell} + S \cdot w_\ell).$$

Now, for every $\ell \in [L]$, let

$$(v_{1,\ell}, v_{2,\ell}) := \sum_{i \in [N]} f_i(x_{i,\ell})$$

where $v_{1,\ell} \in \mathbb{Z}_q^K$ and $v_{2,\ell} \in \mathbb{Z}_q^V$. Since all of the functions $(f_i)_{i \neq \iota}$ are in lossy mode with respect to the same matrix S, we have that for every $\ell \in [L]$,

$$v_{2,\ell} = u_{2,\ell} + S \cdot (v_{1,\ell} - u_{1,\ell}) + e_\ell''$$

where e_ℓ'' is a small-norm error vector. Therefore, if the simulator uses the trapdoor T to generate the discrete Gaussian samples $(e_\ell)_{\ell \in [L]}$ such that $C \cdot e_\ell = u_{1,\ell} - v_{1,\ell}$, then we have

$$(s_{1,\ell}, s_{2,\ell}) = (u_{1,\ell}, u_{2,\ell}') \qquad \text{such that} \qquad u_{2,\ell}' = u_{2,\ell} + e_\ell'' + F \cdot e_\ell$$

for every $\ell \in [L]$. The term $e_\ell'' + F \cdot e_\ell$ has low norm, and thus $u_{2,\ell}'$ is close in norm to $u_{2,\ell}$. We will require one further adjustment to our protocol to make them equal. Notice first that if our output vector $u_{1,\ell}$ is uniform, then $u_{1,\ell} - v_{1,\ell}$ is uniform and consequently the simulated vector e_ℓ is indistinguishable from a discrete Gaussian sample. Furthermore, notice that $x_{\iota,\ell}$ leaks nothing about $u_{1,\ell}$, because w_ℓ acts as a mask.

---

[6] For convenience, we say that the seed oracle outputs discrete Gaussian samples directly, but in order to meet the definition of a seed oracle it must actually output uniform coins from which such samples can be calculated. We highlight that discrete Gaussians are explainable distributions [6]. In other words, given a Gaussian sample e, we are able to efficiently produce coins that produce the sample e when provided as randomness for the distribution, and the distribution of these coins is uniform, as required.

Final Adjustments. If two (distributions of) vectors have a low-norm difference, then their high-order bits are likely the same. Our protocol as currently written admits a simulator that can force the output to be close in norm to any desired value, so taking *only* the high-order bits to be the protocol's output will allow the very same simulation strategy to produce an exact match. Specifically, we will modify the protocol to pick a second modulus $p \ll q$ and round down each entry of $s_{2,\ell}$ to the closest multiple of q/p.

In this next iteration of the protocol, the parties first compute

$$(s_{1,\ell}, s_{2,\ell}) \leftarrow \sum_{i \in [N]} f_i(x_{i,\ell}) + (C \cdot e_\ell, D \cdot e_\ell)$$

such that $s_{2,\ell} \in \mathbb{Z}_q^V$ for every $\ell \in [L]$, and then compute the vector $s'_{2,\ell} \in \mathbb{Z}_p^V$ that minimizes $\|s_{2,\ell} - q/p \cdot s'_{2,\ell}\|_\infty$ (we write $s'_{2,\ell} \leftarrow \lceil s_{2,\ell} \rfloor_p$). The output of the protocol is $(s_{1,1}, s'_{2,1}), \ldots, (s_{1,L}, s'_{2,L})$. If we would like the output to be the vectors $(u_{1,1}, u_{2,1}), \ldots, (u_{1,L}, u_{2,L}) \in \mathbb{Z}_q^K \times \mathbb{Z}_p^V$, then the simulator samples $u''_{2,\ell} \in \mathbb{Z}_q^V$ for $\ell \in [L]$ uniformly subject to $\lceil u''_{2,\ell} + z \rfloor_p = u_{2,\ell}$ for every bounded-norm noise vector z, uses the trapdoor T_ι to generate the messages $x_{\iota,1}, \ldots, x_{\iota,L}$ of P_ι such that

$$f_\iota(x_{\iota,\ell}) = (u_{1,\ell} + w_\ell, u''_{2,\ell} + S \cdot w_\ell)$$

and continues the simulation as before.

To guarantee negligible simulation error while using this technique, we must take q to be larger than p by a *superpolynomial* factor. Moreover, we must set the magnitude of the LWE noise to $\alpha \cdot q$ for a negligible function $\alpha(\lambda)$. In other words, we must assume the hardness of LWE with superpolynomial modulus-to-noise ratio. This completes the first version of our construction.

Adaptive Security. Our protocol is secure against adaptive corruption as a consequence of the non-interactive nature of the construction and the explainability of discrete Gaussian distributions [6]. Given a discrete Gaussian sample x, it is possible to efficiently produce random coins that, when provided as randomness for the distribution, produce the sample x. We rely on this procedure every time that the adversary decides to corrupt a party after the end of the only round of interaction; recall that the messages of the parties are simply discrete Gaussian samples.

The Stretch of our First Construction. The number of random bits produced by the first version of our construction is $L \cdot (K \cdot \log q + V \cdot \log p)$, whereas the seed oracle provides

$$(K + V) \cdot (M \cdot N + W) \cdot \log q \tag{2}$$

bits for the matrices $(A_1, \ldots, A_N, B_1, \ldots B_N, C, D)$, and $L \cdot W \cdot \mathsf{poly}(\lambda) = L \cdot K \cdot \log q \cdot \mathsf{poly}(\lambda)$ bits for the discrete Gaussian samples $(e_\ell)_{\ell \in [L]}$. We observe that (2) is independent of L, so, if we pick L to be sufficiently large, then $L \cdot (K \cdot \log q + V \cdot \log p)$ becomes arbitrarily greater than (2). Similarly, the number of bits necessary for the discrete Gaussian samples is independent of V, so we can pick V sufficiently large to make $L \cdot (K \cdot \log q + V \cdot \log p)$ arbitrarily greater than $L \cdot W \cdot \mathsf{poly}(\lambda)$. This proves that our construction achieves an arbitrary polynomial stretch. However, notice that Eq. 2 depends linearly on N: this means that the number of bits supplied by the seed oracle grows with the number of *parties*, which is undesirable. In order to fix this, we will need to make the slightly stronger assumption that LWE is hard with a *subexponential* (rather than superpolynomial) modulus-to-noise ratio. We present only this *second* construction in full in Sect. 3, but remark that the first construction that we have just sketched remains interesting, due to the slightly weaker assumption that it requires.

Improving the Complexity in the Number of Parties. Our first construction requires a number of random bits from the seed oracle that scales linearly in the number of parties. Is this necessary? We prove that it is not by devising a mechanism to deal matrices $(A_i, B_i)_{i \in [N]}$ that satisfy the properties necessary for the security of the protocol using just $O(\log N) \cdot \mathsf{poly}(\lambda)$ uniformly random bits from the seed oracle. We leverage the *fully homomorphic encryption* (FHE) scheme Gentry et al. [20], hereafter called *GSW*.

In the GSW FHE scheme, the public key is a uniform-looking matrix $U \in \mathbb{Z}_q^{\Delta \times M}$ for some $\Delta \in \mathbb{N}$. An encryption of a bit b under U consists of

$$U \cdot R + b \cdot G$$

where $R \xleftarrow{\$} \mathbb{Z}_2^{M \times \Delta \cdot \log q}$ is a random binary matrix and $G \in \mathbb{Z}_q^{\Delta \times \Delta \log q}$ is the gadget matrix, i.e. a matrix for which there exists an efficient deterministic algorithm G^{-1} that produces a binary matrix $X' \in \mathbb{Z}_2^{\Delta \cdot \log q \times M'}$ such that $G \cdot X' = Y'$ for any input $Y' \in \mathbb{Z}_q^{\Delta \times M'}$ and some $M' \in \mathbb{N}$. Under the hardness of LWE, all ciphertexts look like random matrices over $\mathbb{Z}_q^{\Delta \times \Delta \cdot \log q}$. Furthermore, due to the homomorphic properties of this scheme, there exists an efficient algorithm Eval that takes as input the encryptions of bits $b_1, \ldots, b_t$ under a public key U and the description of a function $f : \{0,1\}^t \to \{0,1\}$, and produces a ciphertext $Z_f = U \cdot R_f + f(b_1, \ldots, b_t) \cdot G$ where R_f is a small norm matrix.

We modify the seed oracle so that it provides $\log N + 1$ random matrices

$$X_1, \ldots, X_{\log N} \in \mathbb{Z}_q^{(K+V) \times (K+V) \log q} \qquad \text{and} \qquad Y \in \mathbb{Z}_q^{(K+V) \times M}.$$

The parties regard $X_1, \ldots, X_{\log N}$ as GSW ciphertexts with $\Delta = K + V$,[7] and each party P_j obtains its matrices (A_j, B_j) by computing

$$(A_j^\mathsf{T} \| B_j^\mathsf{T})^\mathsf{T} = Z_j \leftarrow \mathsf{Eval}(\delta_j, X_1, \ldots, X_{\log N}) \cdot G^{-1}(Y).$$

where δ_j denotes the Kronecker delta function centered on j. We assume that δ_j takes as input $\log N$ bits and regards them as the description of an integer in $[N]$. Note that A_j comprises the first K rows of Z_j and B_j the last V rows.

---

[7] Note that in the real world, these "ciphertexts" are uniformly random and there is *no* public key corresponding to them.

In the ideal world, the simulator determines the GSW public key U by sampling the first K rows uniformly over $\mathbb{Z}_q^{K \times M}$ (we denote these rows by U_1) and setting the last V rows to be $U_2 \leftarrow S \cdot U_1 + E$, where E is a discrete Gaussian sample over $\mathbb{Z}^{V \times M}$. Under LWE, U is indistinguishable from a uniformly sampled public key. Next, the simulator generates $X_1, \ldots, X_{\log N}$ by encrypting the bits of ι under U; recall that ι is the index of the honest party chosen by the simulator. It also samples the matrix Y together with a trapdoor T' that allows the simulator to compute preimages with respect to Y that are indistinguishable from discrete Gaussian samples.

The correctness of FHE evaluation implies that for any $j \neq \iota$,

$$B_j = U_2 \cdot R_{\delta_j} \cdot G^{-1}(Y) = S \cdot (U_1 \cdot R_{\delta_j} \cdot G^{-1}(Y)) + E \cdot R_{\delta_j} \cdot G^{-1}(Y) \sim S \cdot A_j.$$

In other words, the trapdoor function f_j is in lossy mode with respect to S. On the other hand, if we denote the first K rows of G and Y by G_1 and Y_1 respectively, and the last V rows by G_2 and Y_2, we have

$$A_\iota - Y_1 = U_1 \cdot R_{\delta_\iota} \cdot G^{-1}(Y) + G_1 \cdot G^{-1}(Y) - Y_1 = U_1 \cdot R_{\delta_\iota} \cdot G^{-1}(Y),$$
$$B_\iota - Y_2 = U_2 \cdot R_{\delta_\iota} \cdot G^{-1}(Y) + G_2 \cdot G^{-1}(Y) - Y_2$$
$$= S \cdot (U_1 \cdot R_{\delta_\iota} \cdot G^{-1}(Y)) + E \cdot R_{\delta_\iota} \cdot G^{-1}(Y) \sim S \cdot (A_\iota - Y_1).$$

In other words, f_ι is the sum of two trapdoor functions, one in injective mode (described by the matrix Y) and one in lossy mode with respect to S, and the simulator's trapdoor for f_ι is now T' rather than T_ι. The lossy-mode component of f_ι clearly introduces some error terms into the output, but we can correct them together with the bias introduced by the adversary via $(e_\ell)_{\ell \in [L]}$.

The Stretch of our Second Construction. Like our first construction, this construction produces $L \cdot (K \cdot \log q + V \cdot \log p)$ random bits, but the number of bits provided by the seed oracle has been reduced to

$$\log N \cdot (K + V)^2 \cdot \log q + (K + V) \cdot M \cdot \log q + (K + V) \cdot W \cdot \log q \qquad (3)$$

for the matrices $(X_1, \ldots, X_{\log N}, Y, C, D)$, and $L \cdot W \cdot \mathsf{poly}(\lambda) = L \cdot K \cdot \log q \cdot \mathsf{poly}(\lambda)$ for the discrete Gaussian samples $(e_\ell)_{\ell \in [L]}$. As before, (3) is independent of L and the number of bits necessary for the discrete Gaussian samples is independent of V; we can again pick L and V to be sufficiently large so that $L \cdot (K \cdot \log q + V \cdot \log p)$ becomes arbitrarily greater than (3) and $L \cdot (K \cdot \log q + V \cdot \log p)$ becomes arbitrarily greater than $L \cdot W \cdot \mathsf{poly}(\lambda)$. This proves that our construction achieves an arbitrary polynomial stretch.

Final Remarks. Due to the noise growth induced by homomorphically evaluating the Kronecker delta function, it no longer suffices to assume the hardness of LWE with a superpolynomial modulus-to-noise ratio. The Kronecker delta function over the domain $[N]$ has a multiplicative depth of $O(\log N)$. If we assume that $N \in \mathsf{poly}(\lambda)$ then the depth is $O(\log \lambda)$ and in the simulation, the size of the noise in the GSW ciphertexts $Z_1, \ldots, Z_N$ increases by a factor $O(\log \lambda)$ relative to our first construction. Since the magnitude of the noise is now quasipolynomial, we must select a modulus-to-noise ratio that is greater than quasipolynomial in order to guarantee the correctness of the simulation with overwhelming probability. We will formalize our second construction in Sect. 3 and show in that section that the hardness of LWE with a *subexponential* modulus-to-noise ratio is sufficient.

Theorem 2.5 (Informal Version of Theorem 3.3). *If the subexponential LWE assumption holds, then there exists a fully-secure N-party protocol in the $\mathcal{F}^n_{\mathsf{Coin}}$-hybrid model that UC-realizes $\mathcal{F}^m_{\mathsf{Coin}}$ in the presence of a malicious PPT adversary adaptively corrupting $N - 1$ parties.*

2.4   A Lower Bound for Statistical Coin Tossing Extension

We now focus our attention on information-theoretic CTE. Hofheinz et al. [23] proved that perfectly secure CTE is impossible in any model and that statistically secure CTE is impossible in the UC model, and constructed one-round statistically secure CTE with $O(\log \lambda)$ additive stretch and black-box standalone simulation. We ask whether one-round statistically secure CTE with $\omega(\log \lambda)$ additive stretch is possible, and prove that if we insist upon black-box simulation, then it is not.

Theorem 2.6. *Every r-round CTE protocol with one call to the seed oracle and black-box standalone statistical simulation security against semi-malicious adversaries who corrupt a majority of parties must have additive stretch in $O(r \cdot \log \lambda)$.*

Tools and Notation. Consider any r-round statistically secure CTE protocol with black-box simulation and a single call to the seed oracle. Due to Theorem 2.2, we can assume without loss of generality that the parties stop interacting after the call to the seed oracle. Let s denote the output of the protocol, let u be the random coins provided by the seed oracle. For every $i \in [r]$, let U^i_H and U^i_C denote all the messages sent by the honest parties and the corrupted parties respectively, up to and including the ith round. We consider a very specific and rather unusual adversary (at least, in the context of lower bounds): the adversary that simply follows the protocol as if it was honest, but at the same time uses rushing; i.e., it reveals the messages of the corrupted players only after seeing the messages of the honest parties. Considering this extremely weak type of adversary makes our lower bound stronger. Our argument focuses on the *information diagram* [35] of the protocol, and it is reminiscent of a technique used by Abram et al. [3].[8] We will make use of a handful of basic tools and lemmas from information theory, including Shannon entropy (denoted H), and mutual information (denoted I); these are reviewed in the full version of our work [2, Section 3.2].

---

[8] Our setting is simpler since we consider only statistical security, but on the other hand Abram et al. focused on the one-round setting, whereas our argument applies to protocols with multiple rounds.

Output Entropy and Round Count. We start by observing that s is uniquely determined by U_H^r, U_C^r, and u. Translating this into entropy, we have $H(s|U_H^r, U_C^r, u) = 0$ in the real world. In the ideal-world execution, this quantity could be negligibly-far from 0 due to simulation error; we write $H(s|U_H^r, U_C^r, u) \sim 0$ to indicate this. We can bound m as follows:

$$
\begin{aligned}
m \sim H(s) &= I(s; (u, U_C^r, U_H^r)) + H(s|U_H^r, U_C^r, u) \\
&\sim I(s; u|U_C^r, U_H^r) + I(s; (U_C^r, U_H^r)) \\
&\leq n + \sum_{i=1}^{r}(I(U_H^i; s|U_H^{i-1}, U_C^{i-1}) + I(U_C^i; s|U_H^i, U_C^{i-1})). \quad (4)
\end{aligned}
$$

In the second and last inequality, we used the chain rule of mutual information; in the last inequality we also used the fact that $I(s; u|U_C^r, U_H^r) \leq H(u) = n$.

Rewinding-Induced Correlation in the Ideal World. Consider a straight-line ideal-world experiment involving a statistically secure CTE protocol. In round i, the adversary (who essentially behaves honestly), receives the honest parties' messages U_H^i, and then produces the message of corrupt parties U_C^i for round i according to its view, which contains U_H^{i-1} and U_C^{i-1}. This necessarily implies that U_C^i is independent of U_H^i and s, conditioned on U_H^{i-1} and U_C^{i-1}. However, the simulator might not be straight-line. We allow it the power to *rewind* the adversary, which means that it can accept or reject U_C^i based on its knowledge of s and U_H^i. This introduces some correlation between the variables.

Each time the experiment is rewound, the adversary samples a fresh U_C^i that is independent of U_H^i, s, and all of the messages it produced in the previous rewindings, conditioned on U_H^{i-1} and U_C^{i-1}. Because of this independence and the fact that the number of rewindings is upper bounded by the running time Q of the simulator, the simulator can induce at most $\log Q$ bits of correlation between U_C^i and (U_H^i, s), conditioned on U_H^{i-1} and U_C^{i-1}. That is, when $Q = \text{poly}(\lambda)$, $I(U_C^i; (U_H^i, s)|U_H^{i-1}, U_C^{i-1}) \leq O(\log \lambda)$. By the chain rule of mutual information, this implies

$$
I(U_C^i; s|U_H^i, U_C^{i-1}) \leq I(U_C^i; (U_H^i, s)|U_H^{i-1}, U_C^{i-1}) \leq O(\log \lambda).
$$

Since we are considering an honestly-behaving adversary in the dishonest-majority setting, our entropy diagram must be symmetric: we can switch the roles of honest and corrupted parties. This leads us to conclude that $I(U_H^i; s|U_H^{i-1}, U_C^{i-1}) \leq I(U_H^i; (U_C^i, s)|U_H^{i-1}, U_C^{i-1}) \leq O(\log \lambda)$.

Putting It All Together. In the ideal world, we can now use the bounds $I(U_C^i; s|U_H^i, U_C^{i-1}) \leq O(\log \lambda)$ and $I(U_H^i; s|U_H^{i-1}, U_C^{i-1}) \leq O(\log \lambda)$ for all $i \in [r]$ in Eq. 4, to get the required bound $m \leq n + r \cdot O(\log(\lambda))$. This result is formalized in the full version of our work [2, Section 8].

2.5   One-Round Unbiased Sampling from Any Distribution

Our results so far have shown that in the dishonest majority setting, it is possible to simulatably sample m-bit random strings with guaranteed output delivery and no adversarial bias, assuming the existence of a seed oracle that produces $n \ll m$ unbiased random coins. Moreover, this can be done with a single round of interaction followed by one call to the seed oracle. We ask a final question: is there anything special about the uniform distribution, or can we actually sample values from any distribution with the same security guarantees, in the same setting? Specifically, given any efficient distribution $\mathcal{D}$, is it possible for N parties to agree on a random sample from $\mathcal{D}$ with the help of a uniform seed oracle, while leaking no additional information and allowing no bias, and denying the adversary the power to abort, even if it corrupts all of the parties but one? Can we achieve this using a single round of interaction? We prove that under strong cryptographic assumptions, this is indeed possible!

Theorem 2.7 (Informal Version of [2, Theorem 9.5]). *Let $\mathcal{D}$ be an efficient distribution. Assuming the existence of indistinguishability obfuscation, injective length-doubling PRGs, and indistinguishability-preserving distributed samplers [5], there exists a one-round N-party protocol in the $\mathcal{F}_{\mathsf{Coin}}^n$-hybrid CRS model that UC-realizes the functionality $\mathcal{F}_{\mathcal{D}}$ that provides all parties with a sample from $\mathcal{D}$ in the presence of a malicious PPT adversary statically corrupting up to $N - 1$ parties.*

Indistinguishability-Preserving Distributed Samplers. Distributed samplers [3–5] are one-round protocols that securely sample a common output from some distribution $\mathcal{D}$. Though several security definitions have been proposed for this primitive, our final protocol relies specifically upon *indistinguishability-preserving* distributed samplers [5], which are known to exist in the CRS model under a combination of subexponentially secure indistinguishability obfuscation, multi-key FHE, extremely lossy functions [36], and other, weaker tools. Unlike other flavors of distributed sampler, indistinguishability-preserving ones *do not* require idealized models such as the random oracle. Suppose that Π is an r-round protocol relying on a CRS sampled from $\mathcal{D}$, and that Π realizes some functionality $\mathcal{F}$. If Π satisfies some particular properties, indistinguishability-preserving distributed samplers permit us to compile Π into an $r + 1$-round protocol realizing the same functionality $\mathcal{F}$. This new protocol will rely on a simpler CRS that is reusable, unstructured (i.e. uniformly distributed), and of length independent of $\mathcal{D}$ and Π. In our setting, we can generate this simpler CRS for the compiled protocol by a making once-and-for-all call to the seed oracle.

The Protocol We Will Compile. The protocol Π that we will compile has *zero* rounds of communication. The CRS consists of an obfuscated program that hides a puncturable PRF key. When provided with a λ-bit string s as input, this program evaluates the puncturable PRF on s and uses the result to compute a sample from $\mathcal{D}$, which is the program's output. In our zero-round protocol, the parties generate s by calling the seed oracle, feed s into the obfuscated program that is encoded in the CRS, and output the result.

It is easy to see that forgoing protocol realizes the functionality $\mathcal{F}_{\mathcal{D}}$. The simulator must simply sample a random $\hat{s}$ and modify the obfuscated program so that it outputs the sample chosen by the functionality on input $\hat{s}$. Then, when the parties call the seed oracle, the simulator provides $\hat{s}$. Since our protocol is zero rounds before compilation, it will have one round after compilation, with calls to the seed oracle at the beginning and end.

In the full version of our work [2, Section 9], we formalize the above intuition and prove that the zero-round protocol satisfies the conditions required by indistinguishability-preserving distributed samplers. This is why we construct such an unusual zero-round protocol, rather than the trivial protocol that simply provides a sample from $\mathcal{D}$ as a CRS for the parties to output: the latter trivial protocol clearly implements $\mathcal{F}_{\mathcal{D}}$, but it cannot be compiled by an indistinguishability-preserving distributed sampler, because if $\mathcal{D}$ outputs random strings of bits, then the result would be a fully-secure coin tossing protocol that contradicts Cleve's impossibility [17].

3 One-Round, One-Sample Adaptive Coin Tossing Extension from LWE

In this section, we present our construction for one-round one-query CRS-free CTE with universally composable security against adaptive adversaries, from subexponential LWE. We previously overviewed this construction in Sect. 2.3, and invite the reader to review the basic definitions and common tools we use in the full version of our work [2, Section 3.1, 3.3]. We begin with our protocol, then prove it secure and show by corollary the class of explainable extractors that it implies.

Protocol 3.1. One-Round, One-Query CTE from LWE

Let $K, M, V, W, L, s_0, s_1 : \mathbb{N} \to \mathbb{N}$ be polynomial functions in the security parameter. Assume that $K = \Omega(\lambda)$. Define $p := 2$ and $q := 2^t$ where $t = \Theta(\lambda)$.[a] Let χ_0 be $\mathcal{D}_{\mathbb{Z}, s_0}$, let χ_1 be $\mathcal{D}_{\mathbb{Z}, s_1}$. Suppose that $W \geq \beta \cdot K \cdot \log q$ and $M \geq \beta \cdot (K + V) \cdot \log q$, where β is the constant defined in [2, Theorem 3.5]. Assume also that $s_0 = \sqrt{(K+V)\log q} \cdot \omega(\sqrt{\log(K+V)})$ and $s_1 = \sqrt{K \log q} \cdot \omega(\sqrt{\log K})$. Let G be a $(K+V) \times (K+V) \cdot t$ gadget matrix, and let G^{-1} be the deterministic algorithm that, on input a matrix $Y' \in \mathbb{Z}_q^{(K+V) \times M'}$ for some $M' \in \mathbb{N}$, outputs a matrix X' such that $G \cdot X' = Y'$ and $\|Q\|_\infty = 1$ (see Gentry et al. [20]). For every $j \in [N]$, let δ_j denote the Kronecker delta function centered on j.

Protocol. Each party P_i performs the following operations.
1. $\forall \ell \in [L] : \quad \boldsymbol{x}_{i,\ell} \xleftarrow{\$} \chi_0^M$
2. Broadcast $(\boldsymbol{x}_{i,1}, \ldots, \boldsymbol{x}_{i,L})$
3. For any $j \in [N]$ and $\ell \in [L]$ such that $\|\boldsymbol{x}_{j,\ell}\|_\infty > \sqrt{K} \cdot s_0$, set $\boldsymbol{x}_{j,\ell} \leftarrow \boldsymbol{0}$.
4. Call $\mathcal{F}_{\mathsf{Coin}}^n$ and interpret the response as values $(X_i)_{i \in [\lceil \log N \rceil]}, Y, C, D$ and $(\boldsymbol{e}_\ell)_{\ell \in [L]}$ where
    - $\forall i \in [\lceil \log N \rceil] : X_i \in \mathbb{Z}_q^{(K+V) \times M}$
    - $Y \in \mathbb{Z}_q^{(K+V) \times M}$

    – $C \in \mathbb{Z}_q^{K \times W}$
    – $D \in \mathbb{Z}_q^{V \times W}$
    – e_ℓ is a sample from $\chi_1{}^W$

5. $\forall j \in [N] : Z_j \leftarrow \mathsf{Eval}(\delta_j, X_1, \ldots, X_{\lceil \log N \rceil}) \cdot G^{-1}(Y)$ (see Algorithm 3.2)[b]
6. For every $j \in [N]$, let $A_j \in \mathbb{Z}_q^{K \times M}$ consist of the first K rows of Z_j. Let $B_j \in \mathbb{Z}_q^{V \times M}$ consist of the last V rows of Z_j.
7. $\forall \ell \in [L] : u_\ell \leftarrow \sum_{j \in [N]} A_j \cdot x_{j,\ell} - C \cdot e_\ell$
8. $\forall \ell \in [L] : v_\ell \leftarrow \lceil \sum_{j \in [N]} B_j \cdot x_{j,\ell} - D \cdot e_\ell) \rfloor_p$
9. Output $(u_1, \ldots, u_L, v_1, \ldots, v_L)$

---

[a] The protocol can be generalised to any p, q such that $p \cdot 2^{\log^2 \lambda} \cdot \alpha$ and p/q are negligible.
[b] We can compute $\delta_j(x)$ where $x \in \{0,1\}^{\lceil \log N \rceil}$ by first flipping x_h for every h such that the h-th bit of j is 1. Then, we multiply all $\lceil \log N \rceil$ bits obtained in this way and we flip the result.

Algorithm 3.2. $\mathsf{Eval}(f, X_1, \ldots, X_m)$ [20]

Represent $f : \mathbb{Z}_q^m \to \mathbb{Z}_q$ as an arithmetic circuit over $\mathbb{Z}_q$. Then, perform the following operations:

1. Associate X_i to the i-th input wire for every $i \in [m]$.
2. For every gate, perform the following operations:
    – If the gate is an addition gate and the input wires are associated with the matrices Z_1, Z_2, associate the output wire with $Z_1 + Z_2$.
    – If the gate adds a constant $k \in \mathbb{Z}_q$ to a wire associated with the matrix Z_1, associate the output wire with $Z_1 + k \cdot G$.
    – If the gate switches the sign of a wire associated with the matrix Z_1, associate the output wire with $-Z_1$.
    – If the gate is a multiplication gate and the input wires are associated with the matrices Z_1, Z_2, associate the output wire with $Z_1 \cdot G^{-1}(Z_2)$.
    – If the gate multiplies a wire associated with the matrix Z_1 by a constant $k \in \mathbb{Z}_q$, associate the output wire with $Z_1 \cdot G^{-1}(k \cdot G)$.
3. Output the matrix associated with the output wire of the circuit.

The following theorem essentially formalizes Theorem 2.5.

Theorem 3.3. *Assuming the hardness of the Learning with Errors (LWE) problem with a subexponential modulus-to-noise ratio (see [2, Definition 3.3]), Protocol 3.1 UC-realizes $\mathcal{F}_{\mathsf{Coin}}^m$ among N parties in the $\mathcal{F}_{\mathsf{Coin}}^n$-hybrid model, with security against a malicious PPT adversary adaptively corrupting up to $N - 1$ parties. For any function $\eta = \mathsf{poly}(\lambda)$, if we set $s_1 = \sqrt{K \cdot \log q} \cdot \log K$, $M = \beta \cdot (K + V) \cdot \log q$, $W = \beta \cdot K \cdot \log q$, $V = (\eta \cdot \lambda^2 - 1) \cdot K \cdot t$, and $L = \eta^2 \cdot t^3 \cdot \lambda^2 \cdot \log N \cdot K$, then the* multiplicative *stretch of the construction is $m/(t \cdot n) = \Omega(\eta)$.*

Proof. We start by proving security. Let ι be the index of a party that is honest in the first round of the protocol. Define $\alpha := 2^{-\omega(\log^2 \lambda)}$ and set $s_2 \leftarrow \alpha \cdot q$. Let

χ_2 be $\mathcal{D}_{\mathbb{Z},s_2}$. We proceed to prove security using a sequence of indistinguishable hybrids starting from the real world and arriving at the ideal world.

Hybrid $\mathcal{H}_0$. This hybrid corresponds to the real execution of the protocol.

Hybrid $\mathcal{H}_1$. In this hybrid, whenever a party P_i is corrupted after sending $(x_{i,\ell})_{\ell \in [L]}$, instead of providing the randomness used to produce these values, we provide the adversary with $\mathsf{Explain}_{\chi_0^M}(1^\lambda, x_{i,\ell})$ for every $\ell \in [L]$ ($\mathsf{Explain}_{\chi_0^M}(1^\lambda, x_{i,\ell})$ is an algorithm that produces random-looking coins that, when input in χ_0^M, produce $x_{i,\ell}$). This hybrid is indistinguishable from $\mathcal{H}_0$ due to the explainability of discrete Gaussians [6,19].

Hybrid $\mathcal{H}_2$. In this hybrid, instead of providing the adversary with the randomness that produces $(e_\ell)_{\ell \in [L]}$, we provide it with $\mathsf{Explain}_{\chi_1^W}(1^\lambda, e_\ell)$ for every $\ell \in [L]$. This hybrid is indistinguishable from $\mathcal{H}_1$ due to the explainability of discrete Gaussians [6,19] (see [2, Theorem 3.7]).

Hybrid $\mathcal{H}_3$. In this hybrid, we change the distribution of $X_1, \ldots, X_{\lceil \log N \rceil}$. In particular, we sample $U \xleftarrow{\$} \mathbb{Z}_q^{(K+V) \times M}$ and $R_1, \ldots, R_{\lceil \log N \rceil} \xleftarrow{\$} \mathbb{Z}_2^{M \times (K+V) \cdot t}$. We then set $X_j \leftarrow U \cdot R_j + \iota_j \cdot G$ for every $j \in [[\lceil \log N \rceil]]$ where ι_j denote the j-th bit of ι. $\mathcal{H}_3$ is statistically indistinguishable from $\mathcal{H}_2$ thanks to the leftover hash lemma (see [2, Lemma 3.4], we are using the fact that $M \geq \beta \cdot (K + V) \cdot \log q$, $\beta > 1$ and $K = \Omega(\lambda)$).

Hybrid $\mathcal{H}_4$. In this hybrid, we change the distribution of U and D. In particular, we sample $U_1 \xleftarrow{\$} \mathbb{Z}_q^{K \times M}$, $S \xleftarrow{\$} \mathbb{Z}_q^{V \times K}$, $E_1 \xleftarrow{\$} \chi_2^{V \times M}$ and $E_2 \xleftarrow{\$} \chi_2^{V \times W}$. We then set $U_2 \leftarrow S \cdot U_1 + E_1$, $U^\intercal \leftarrow (U_1^\intercal \| U_2^\intercal)$ and $D \leftarrow S \cdot C + E_2$. $\mathcal{H}_4$ is indistinguishable from $\mathcal{H}_3$ thanks to the security of LWE with subexponential modulus-to-noise ratio (see [2, Definition 3.3]).

Hybrid $\mathcal{H}_5$. In this hybrid, we change the distribution of C. In particular, we sample it along with a lattice trapdoor, i.e., $(C, T) \xleftarrow{\$} \mathsf{TrapGen}(1^K, 1^W, q)$. This hybrid is statistically indistinguishable from $\mathcal{H}_4$ (see [7,8,19,28] and [2, Theorem 3.5], we are using the fact that $W \geq \beta \cdot K \cdot \log q$ and $K = \Omega(\lambda)$).

Hybrid $\mathcal{H}_6$. In this hybrid, we change the distribution of Y. In particular, we sample it along with a lattice trapdoor, i.e., $(Y, T') \xleftarrow{\$} \mathsf{TrapGen}(1^{K+V}, 1^M, q)$. This hybrid is statistically indistinguishable from $\mathcal{H}_5$ (see [7,8,19,28] and [2, Theorem 3.5], we are using the fact that $M \geq \beta \cdot (K + V) \cdot \log q$ and $K = \Omega(\lambda)$).

Hybrid $\mathcal{H}_7$. In this hybrid, we change the distribution of $(x_{\iota,\ell})_{\ell \in [L]}$. In particular, for every $\ell \in [L]$, we sample $u_\ell \xleftarrow{\$} \mathbb{Z}_q^K$ $u_\ell'' \xleftarrow{\$} \mathbb{Z}_q^K$ and $v_\ell' \xleftarrow{\$} \mathbb{Z}_q^V$. For every $\ell \in [L]$, we set $v_\ell'' \leftarrow S \cdot u_\ell''$ and sample a preimage $x_{\iota,\ell} \xleftarrow{\$} \mathsf{PreSample}(T', w_\ell, s_0)$ where w_ℓ is the vector obtained by concatenating $u_\ell + u_\ell''$ and $v_\ell' + v_\ell''$ (in other words, $x_{\iota,\ell}$ looks like a discrete Gaussian sample such that $Y \cdot x_{\iota,\ell} = w_\ell$). This hybrid is statistically indistinguishable from $\mathcal{H}_6$ (see [7,8,19,28] and [2, Theorem 3.5, Lemma 3.4, Lemma 3.6], we are using the fact that $s_0 = \sqrt{(K+V)\log q} \cdot \omega(\sqrt{\log(K+V)})$, $M \geq \beta \cdot (K+V) \cdot \log q$, $\beta > 1$ and $K = \Omega(\lambda)$). We observe that the probability that $\|x_{\iota,\ell}\|_\infty > \sqrt{K} \cdot s_0$ is negligible in λ (see [2, Lemma 3.6], we are using the fact that $K = \Omega(\lambda)$).

Hybrid $\mathcal{H}_8$. In this hybrid, we change the distribution of $(e_\ell)_{\ell\in[L]}$. In particular, for every $\ell \in [L]$, we compute $\tilde{u}_\ell \leftarrow u_\ell'' + \sum_{i\neq\iota} A_i \cdot x_{i,\ell} + U_1 \cdot F_\iota \cdot G^{-1}(Y) \cdot x_{\iota,\ell}$ where $R_\iota \leftarrow \mathsf{FullEval}(\delta_\iota, X_1, \ldots, X_{\lceil\log N\rceil}, R_1, \ldots, R_{\lceil\log N\rceil}, \iota)$ (see Algorithm 3.4). Then, we sample a preimage $e_\ell \xleftarrow{\$} \mathsf{PreSample}(T, \tilde{u}_\ell, s_1)$ (in other words, e_ℓ looks like a discrete Gaussian sample such that $C \cdot e_\ell = \tilde{u}_\ell$). This hybrid is statistically indistinguishable from $\mathcal{H}_7$ (see [7,8,19,28] and [2, Theorem 3.5, Lemma 3.4, Lemma 3.6], we are using the fact that $s_1 = \sqrt{K\log q} \cdot \omega(\sqrt{\log K})$, $W \geq \beta \cdot K \cdot \log q$, $\beta > 1$ and $K = \Omega(\lambda)$). Observe that $x_{\iota,\ell}$ leaks nothing about u_ℓ'' as u_ℓ and v_ℓ' mask all the information.

Algorithm 3.4. $\mathsf{FullEval}(f, X_1, \ldots, X_m, R_1, \ldots, R_m, x)$ [20]

Represent $f : Z_q^m \rightarrow \mathbb{Z}_q$ as an arithmetic circuit over $\mathbb{Z}_q$. Then, perform the following operations:

1. Associate (X_i, R_i, x_i) to the i-th input wire for every $i \in [m]$.
2. For every gate, perform the following operations:
   - If the gate is an addition gate and the input wires are associated with the triples $(Z_1, S_1, z_1), (Z_2, S_2, z_2)$, associate the output wire with $(Z_1 + Z_2, S_1 + S_2, z_1 + z_2)$.
   - If the gate adds a constant $k \in \mathbb{Z}_q$ to a wire associated with the triple (Z_1, S_1, z_1), associate the output wire with $(Z_1 + k \cdot G, S_1, z_1 + k)$.
   - If the gate switches the sign of a wire associated with the triple (Z_1, S_1, z_1), associate the output wire with $(-Z_1, -S_1, -z_1)$.
   - If the gate is a multiplication gate and the input wires are associated with the triples $(Z_1, S_1, z_1), (Z_2, S_2, z_2)$, associate the output wire with $(Z_1 \cdot G^{-1}(Z_2), S_1 \cdot G^{-1}(Z_2) + z_1 \cdot S_2, z_1 \cdot z_2)$.
   - If the gate multiplies a wire associated with the triple (Z_1, S_1, z_1) by a constant $k \in \mathbb{Z}_q$, associate the output wire with $(Z_1 \cdot G^{-1}(k \cdot G), S_1 \cdot G^{-1}(k \cdot G), k \cdot z_1)$.
3. Output the second element of the triple associated with the output wire of the circuit.

Claim 3.5 ([20]). *Let $X_i = U \cdot R_i + x_i \cdot G$ where $R_i \in \mathbb{Z}_2^{M\times(K+V)\cdot t}$ for every $i \in [m]$. Let $f : Z_q^m \rightarrow \mathbb{Z}_q$ be a function. Then, $\mathsf{Eval}(f, X_1, \ldots, X_m) = U \cdot R_f + f(x) \cdot G$, where $R_f \leftarrow \mathsf{FullEval}(f, X_1, \ldots, X_m, R_1, \ldots, R_m, x)$.*

Proof. For every wire w, let X_w be the matrix associated with w during the execution of $\mathsf{Eval}(f, X)$. Let R_w be the second element in the pair associated with w during the execution of $\mathsf{FullEval}(f, X, R)$. Let x_w be the value associated with w during the evaluation of $f(x)$. We show that for any wire w, we have $X_w = U \cdot R_w + x_w \cdot G$. This true for the input wires, and we show that it holds for every other wire w by induction. Consider the gate that outputs wire w:

– If the gate is an addition gate with input wires u, v, then

$$\begin{aligned} X_w = X_u + X_v &= U \cdot R_u + x_u \cdot G + U \cdot R_v + x_v \cdot G \\ &= U \cdot (R_u + R_v) + (x_u + x_v) \cdot G = U \cdot R_w + x_w \cdot G. \end{aligned}$$

– If the gate adds a constant $k \in \mathbb{Z}_q$ to a wire u, then

$$\begin{aligned} X_w = X_u + k \cdot G &= U \cdot R_u + x_u \cdot G + k \cdot G \\ &= U \cdot R_u + (x_u + k) \cdot G = U \cdot R_w + x_w \cdot G. \end{aligned}$$

– If the gate switches the sign of a wire u, then

$$\begin{aligned} X_w = -X_u &= -U \cdot R_u - x_u \cdot G \\ &= U \cdot (-R_u) + (-x_u) \cdot G = U \cdot R_w + x_w \cdot G. \end{aligned}$$

– If the gate is a multiplication with input wires u, v, then

$$\begin{aligned} X_w = X_u \cdot G^{-1}(X_v) &= U \cdot R_u \cdot G^{-1}(X_v) + x_u \cdot G \cdot G^{-1}(X_v) \\ &= U \cdot R_u \cdot G^{-1}(X_v) + x_u \cdot X_v \\ &= U \cdot R_u \cdot G^{-1}(X_v) + x_u \cdot (U \cdot R_v + x_v \cdot G) \\ &= U \cdot (R_u \cdot G^{-1}(X_v) + x_u \cdot R_v) + (x_u \cdot x_v) \cdot G = U \cdot R_w + x_w \cdot G. \end{aligned}$$

– If the gate multiplies a wire u by a constant $k \in \mathbb{Z}_q$, then

$$\begin{aligned} X_w = X_u \cdot G^{-1}(k \cdot G) &= U \cdot R_u \cdot G^{-1}(k \cdot G) + x_u \cdot G \cdot G^{-1}(k \cdot G) \\ &= U \cdot (R_u \cdot G^{-1}(k \cdot G)) + (k \cdot x_u) \cdot G = U \cdot R_w + x_w \cdot G. \end{aligned}$$

This ends the proof of the claim. $\square$

Let G_1 denote the matrix consisting of the first K rows of G. Let G_2 be the matrix consisting of the last V rows of G. Let Y_1 be the matrix consisting of the first K rows of Y. Let Y_2 be the matrix consisting of the last V rows of Y. Observe that, for every $\ell \in [L]$, we have

$$\sum_{i \in [N]} A_i \cdot \boldsymbol{x}_{i,\ell} - C \cdot \boldsymbol{e}_\ell = A_\iota \cdot \boldsymbol{x}_{\iota,\ell} - C \cdot \boldsymbol{e}_\ell + \sum_{i \neq \iota} A_i \cdot \boldsymbol{x}_{i,\ell}$$

$$= U_1 \cdot F_\iota \cdot G^{-1}(Y) \cdot \boldsymbol{x}_{\iota,\ell} + \delta_\iota(\iota) \cdot G_1 \cdot G^{-1}(Y) \cdot \boldsymbol{x}_{\iota,\ell} - \tilde{\boldsymbol{u}}_\ell + \sum_{i \neq \iota} A_i \cdot \boldsymbol{x}_{i,\ell}$$

$$= Y \cdot \boldsymbol{x}_{\iota,\ell} - \boldsymbol{u}''_\ell = \boldsymbol{u}_\ell.$$

$$\sum_{i \in [N]} B_i \cdot \boldsymbol{x}_{i,\ell} - D \cdot \boldsymbol{e}_\ell = B_\iota \cdot \boldsymbol{x}_{\iota,\ell} - D \cdot \boldsymbol{e}_\ell + \sum_{i \neq \iota} B_i \cdot \boldsymbol{x}_{i,\ell}$$

$$= \sum_{i \in [N]} \left(U_2 \cdot F_i \cdot G^{-1}(Y) \cdot \boldsymbol{x}_{i,\ell} + \delta_i(\iota) \cdot G_2 \cdot G^{-1}(Y) \cdot \boldsymbol{x}_{i,\ell} \right) - (S \cdot C + E_2) \cdot \boldsymbol{e}_\ell$$

$$= \sum_{i \in [N]} (S \cdot U_1 + E_1) \cdot F_i \cdot G^{-1}(Y) \cdot \boldsymbol{x}_{i,\ell} + Y_2 \cdot \boldsymbol{x}_{\iota,\ell} - (S \cdot C + E_2) \cdot \boldsymbol{e}_\ell$$

$$= \boldsymbol{v}'_\ell + \boldsymbol{v}''_\ell + S \cdot \left(\sum_{i \in [N]} U_1 \cdot F_i \cdot G^{-1}(Y) \cdot \boldsymbol{x}_{i,\ell} - C \cdot \boldsymbol{e}_\ell \right)$$

$$+ \sum_{i \in [N]} E_1 \cdot F_i \cdot G^{-1}(Y) \cdot \boldsymbol{x}_{i,\ell} - E_2 \cdot \boldsymbol{e}_\ell$$

$$= \boldsymbol{v}'_\ell + S \cdot \boldsymbol{u}''_\ell + S \cdot \left(U_1 \cdot F_\iota \cdot G^{-1}(Y) \cdot \boldsymbol{x}_{\iota,\ell} + \sum_{i \neq \iota} A_i \cdot \boldsymbol{x}_{i,\ell} - \tilde{\boldsymbol{u}}_\ell \right)$$

$$+ \sum_{i \in [N]} E_1 \cdot F_i \cdot G^{-1}(Y) \cdot \boldsymbol{x}_{i,\ell} - E_2 \cdot \boldsymbol{e}_\ell$$

$$= \boldsymbol{v}'_\ell + \sum_{i \in [N]} E_1 \cdot F_i \cdot G^{-1}(Y) \cdot \boldsymbol{x}_{i,\ell} - E_2 \cdot \boldsymbol{e}_\ell.$$

If Γ is an upper-bound on $\|F_i\|_\infty$ for every $j \in [N]$, the bound on discrete Gaussians [9,31] summarised in [2, Lemma 3.6] implies a polynomial $c(\lambda)$ such that for every $\ell \in [L]$, with overwhelming probability,

$$\left\| \sum_{i \in [N]} E_1 \cdot F_i \cdot G^{-1}(Y) \cdot \boldsymbol{x}_{i,\ell} - E_2 \cdot \boldsymbol{e}_\ell \right\|_\infty$$
$$\leq M^{\frac{5}{2}} \sqrt{M + W}(K + V)t \cdot s_0 \cdot \Gamma \cdot \alpha q + W^{\frac{3}{2}} \sqrt{M + W} s_1 \cdot \alpha q$$
$$\leq c \cdot \Gamma \cdot \alpha q.$$

If we compute δ_i as in Protocol 3.1, then for every $i \in [N]$,

$$\|F_i\|_\infty \leq ((K + V) \cdot t)^{\lceil \log N \rceil}$$

Since N, K, V and t are polynomial quantities in λ, we have $\|F_i\|_\infty \leq 2^{O(\log^2 \lambda)}$.

Hybrid $\mathcal{H}_9$. In this hybrid, we changed the distribution of $(\boldsymbol{v}'_\ell)_{\ell \in [L]}$. Specifically, for every $\ell \in [L]$, first, we sample $\boldsymbol{v}_\ell \xleftarrow{\$} \mathbb{Z}_p^V$ and then, we set $\boldsymbol{v}'_\ell$ to be a random element in $\mathbb{Z}_q^V$ such that $\lceil v'_\ell + z \rfloor_p = v_\ell$ for every $z \in \mathbb{Z}^V$ having $\|z\|_\infty \leq c \cdot \Gamma \cdot \alpha \cdot q$. This hybrid is statistically indistinguishable from $\mathcal{H}_8$. Indeed, since $\alpha(\lambda), 1/q(\lambda) \leq \mathsf{negl}(\lambda)$, the statistical distance between the distribution of v'_ℓ in this hybrid and in the previous one is upper-bounded by

$$V \cdot p \cdot \frac{2c \cdot \alpha \cdot q + 1}{q} \leq \mathsf{negl}(\lambda).$$

This is because each entry of v'_ℓ is now uniformly distributed over a set with $q - p \cdot (2c \cdot \alpha \cdot q + 1)$ (i.e. all the elements in $\mathbb{Z}_q$ except those that have distance smaller than $c \cdot \alpha \cdot q$ from $q/4$ and $(3/4)q$). $\mathcal{H}_9$ corresponds to the ideal execution of the protocol. The simulation strategy is sketched in simulator 3.6.

Simulator 3.6. One-Round One-Query CTE from LWE

1. Receive the output from the functionality and interpret it as a vector $(u_1, \ldots, u_L, v_1, \ldots, v_L)$ where, for every $\ell \in [L]$, $u_\ell \in \mathbb{Z}_q^K$ and $v_\ell \in \mathbb{Z}_p^V$.
2. $\forall \ell \in [L]$, sample a random $v'_\ell \in \mathbb{Z}_q^V$ such that $\lceil v'_\ell + z \rfloor_p = v_\ell$ for every $z \in \mathbb{Z}^V$ having $\|z\|_\infty \leq c \cdot \Gamma \cdot \alpha \cdot q$.
3. $S \xleftarrow{\$} \mathbb{Z}_q^{V \times K}$
4. $\forall \ell \in [L]$, $u''_\ell \xleftarrow{\$} \mathbb{Z}_q^K$
5. $\forall \ell \in [L]$, $v''_\ell \leftarrow S \cdot u''_\ell$
6. $\forall \ell \in [L]$, $w_\ell \leftarrow (u_\ell + u''_\ell \| v'_\ell + v''_\ell)$
7. $(Y, T') \xleftarrow{\$} \mathsf{TrapGen}(\mathbb{1}^{K+V}, \mathbb{1}^M, q)$
8. $\forall \ell \in [L]$, $x_\ell \xleftarrow{\$} \mathsf{PreSample}(T', w_\ell, s_0)$
9. Take the first honest party P_ι activated by the adversary and send $(x_\ell)_{\ell \in [L]}$ on its behalf.
10. For any other honest party P_i, send $x_{i,\ell} \xleftarrow{\$} \chi_0^M$ for every $\ell \in [L]$
11. When any honest party P_i is corrupted, provide the adversary with $\mathsf{Explain}_{\chi_0^M}(\mathbb{1}^\lambda, x_{i,\ell})$ for every $\ell \in [L]$.
12. After all parties have sent their messages, for any $i \in [N]$ and $\ell \in [L]$ such that $\|x_{i,\ell}\|_\infty > \sqrt{K} \cdot s_0$, set $x_{i,\ell} \leftarrow 0$.
13. $U_1 \xleftarrow{\$} \mathbb{Z}_q^{K \times M}$
14. $(C, T) \xleftarrow{\$} \mathsf{TrapGen}(\mathbb{1}^K, \mathbb{1}^W, q)$
15. $E_1 \xleftarrow{\$} \chi_2^{V \times M}$
16. $E_2 \xleftarrow{\$} \chi_2^{V \times W}$
17. $U_2 \leftarrow S \cdot U_1 + E_1$
18. $D \leftarrow S \cdot C + E_2$
19. $U \leftarrow (U_1^\mathsf{T} \| U_2^\mathsf{T})$
20. $\forall j \in [\lceil \log N \rceil] : F_j \xleftarrow{\$} \mathbb{Z}_2^{M \times (K+V) \cdot t}$
21. $\forall j \in [\lceil \log N \rceil] : X_j \leftarrow U \cdot R_j + \iota_j \cdot G$
22. $\forall i \in [N] : Z_i \leftarrow \mathsf{Eval}(\delta_i, X_1, \ldots, X_{\lceil \log N \rceil}) \cdot G^{-1}(Y)$
23. For every $i \in [N]$, let $A_i \in \mathbb{Z}_q^{K \times M}$ consist of the first K rows of Z_i. Let $B_i \in \mathbb{Z}_q^{V \times M}$ consist of the last V rows of Z_i.
24. $F_\iota \leftarrow \mathsf{FullEval}(\delta_\iota, X_1, \ldots, X_{\lceil \log N \rceil}, R_1, \ldots, R_{\lceil \log N \rceil}, \iota)$

25. $\forall \ell \in [L]$, $\tilde{u}_\ell \leftarrow u''_\ell + \sum_{i \neq \ell} A_i \cdot x_{i,\ell} + U_1 \cdot F_\iota \cdot G^{-1}(Y) \cdot x_{\iota,\ell}$
26. $\forall \ell \in [L]$, $e_\ell \xleftarrow{\$} \mathsf{PreSample}(T, \tilde{u}_\ell, s_1)$
27. Send $(X_j)_{j \in [\lceil \log N \rceil]}$, Y C, D and $(\mathsf{Explain}_{\chi_1^W}(\mathbb{1}^\lambda, e_\ell))_{\ell \in [L]}$ on behalf of $\mathcal{F}^n_{\mathsf{Coin}}$.

We now analyse our protocol's stretch. The number of seed bits is

$$n = O\Big(\log N \cdot (K + V) \cdot M \cdot t + (K + V) \cdot W \cdot t + L \cdot W \cdot \lambda^2 + L \cdot W \cdot \lambda \cdot \log s_1\Big).$$

If $s_1 = \sqrt{K \cdot \log q} \cdot \log K$, $M = \beta \cdot (K + V) \cdot \log q$ and $W = \beta \cdot K \cdot \log q$, then

$$n = O\Big(\log N \cdot (K + V)^2 \cdot t^2 + L \cdot K \cdot t \cdot (\lambda^2 + \lambda \cdot \log K + \lambda \cdot \log t))\Big).$$

Now, t, K are polynomial quantities in λ, so $\log t, \log K \in O(\log \lambda)$, and thus

$$n = O\Big(\log N \cdot (K + V)^2 \cdot t^2 + L \cdot K \cdot t \cdot \lambda^2\Big).$$

The number of coins produced by the protocol is $L \cdot (K \cdot t + V)$, which implies that if we pick $V = (\eta \cdot \lambda^2 - 1) \cdot K \cdot t$ and $L = \eta^2 \cdot t^3 \cdot \lambda^2 \cdot \log N \cdot K$, then the multiplicative stretch of our construction becomes $\Omega(\eta)$. $\qquad \square$

Corollary 3.7. *Under the hardness of LWE with a subexponential modulus-to-noise ratio, for any polynomial function $N(\lambda)$, there exists a polynomial $L(\lambda)$ and a computational explainable extractor for the class of entropy sources $\mathcal{S}$, such that for every $S \in \mathcal{S}$, there exist $i \in [N]$ and a PPT algorithm $\mathcal{M}$ such that the source S can be sampled as follows:*

1. $x_i \xleftarrow{\$} \{0,1\}^{L(\lambda)}$
2. $((x_j)_{j \neq i}, \mathsf{aux}) \xleftarrow{\$} \mathcal{M}(\mathbb{1}^\lambda, x_i)$
3. *Output* $(x_1, \ldots, x_N), \mathsf{aux}$.

Acknowledgements. Damiano Abram was supported by a GSNS travel grant from Aarhus University, by the Aarhus University Research Foundation (AUFF) and by the Independent Research Fund Denmark (DFF) under project number 0165-00107B (C3PO). Jack Doerner was supported by the ERC projects NTSC (742754) and HSS (852952), ISF grant 2774/20, the Azrieli Foundation, and the Brown University Data Science Institute. Yuval Ishai was supported by ERC grant NTSC (742754), BSF grant 2022370, ISF grant 2774/20, and ISF-NSFC grant 3127/23. Varun Narayanan was supported by NSF grants CNS-2246355, CCF-2220450, and CNS-2001096.

References

1. Abram, D., Damgård, I., Orlandi, C., Scholl, P.: An algebraic framework for silent preprocessing with trustless setup and active security. In: Dodis, Y., Shrimpton, T. (eds.) CRYPTO 2022, Part IV. LNCS, vol. 13510, pp. 421–452. Springer, Heidelberg (2022). https://doi.org/10.1007/978-3-031-15985-5_15

2. Abram, D., Doerner, J., Ishai, Y., Narayanan, V.: Constant-Round Simulation-Secure Coin Tossing Extension with Guaranteed Output. Cryptology ePrint Archive, 2024 (2024)

3. Abram, D., Obremski, M., Scholl, P.: On the (Im)possibility of Distributed Samplers: Lower Bounds and Party-Dynamic Constructions. Cryptology ePrint Archive, Paper 2023/863 (2023)

4. Abram, D., Scholl, P., Yakoubov, S.: Distributed (correlation) samplers: how to remove a trusted dealer in one round. In: Dunkelman, O., Dziembowski, S. (eds.) EUROCRYPT 2022, Part I. LNCS, vol. 13275, pp. 790–820. Springer, Heidelberg (2022). https://doi.org/10.1007/978-3-031-06944-4_27

5. Abram, D., Waters, B., Zhandry, M.: Security-preserving distributed samplers: how to generate any CRS in one round without random oracles. In: Handschuh, H., Lysyanskaya, A. (eds.) CRYPTO 2023. LNCS, vol. 14081, pp. 489–514. Springer, Cham (2023). https://doi.org/10.1007/978-3-031-38557-5_16

6. Agrawal, S., Wichs, D., Yamada, S.: Optimal broadcast encryption from LWE and pairings in the standard model. In: Pass, R., Pietrzak, K. (eds.) TCC 2020. LNCS, vol. 12550, pp. 149–178. Springer, Cham (2020). https://doi.org/10.1007/978-3-030-64375-1_6

7. Ajtai, M.: Generating hard instances of the short basis problem. In: Wiedermann, J., van Emde Boas, P., Nielsen, M. (eds.) ICALP 1999. LNCS, vol. 1644, pp. 1–9. Springer, Heidelberg (1999). https://doi.org/10.1007/3-540-48523-6_1

8. Alwen, J., Peikert, C.: Generating shorter bases for hard random lattices. In: STACS (2009)

9. Banaszczyk, W.: New bounds in some transference theorems in the geometry of numbers. Mathematische Annalen (1993)

10. Barak, B., et al.: On the (Im)possibility of obfuscating programs. In: Kilian, J. (ed.) CRYPTO 2001. LNCS, vol. 2139, pp. 1–18. Springer, Heidelberg (2001). https://doi.org/10.1007/3-540-44647-8_1

11. Bellare, M., Garay, J.A., Rabin, T.: Distributed pseudo-random bit generators - a new way to speed-up shared coin tossing. In: Burns, J.E., Moses, Y. (eds.) 15th ACM PODC, pp. 191–200. ACM, August 1996. https://doi.org/10.1145/248052.248090

12. Blum, M.: Coin flipping by telephone. In: Proceedings IEEE Spring COMPCOM, pp. 133–137 (1982)

13. Buchbinder, N., Haitner, I., Levi, N., Tsfadia, E.: Fair coin flipping: tighter analysis and the many-party case. In: Klein, P.N. (ed.) 28th SODA, pp. 2580–2600. ACM-SIAM, January 2017. https://doi.org/10.1137/1.9781611974782.170

14. Canetti, R.: Security and composition of multiparty cryptographic protocols. J. Cryptol. **13**(1), 143–202 (2000). https://doi.org/10.1007/s001459910006

15. Canetti, R.: Universally composable security: a new paradigm for cryptographic protocols. In: 42nd FOCS, pp. 136–145. IEEE Computer Society Press, October 2001. https://doi.org/10.1109/SFCS.2001.959888

16. Castagnos, G., Laguillaumie, F.: Linearly homomorphic encryption from DDH. In: Nyberg, K. (ed.) CT-RSA 2015. LNCS, vol. 9048, pp. 487–505. Springer, Cham (2015). https://doi.org/10.1007/978-3-319-16715-2_26

17. Cleve, R.: Limits on the security of coin flips when half the processors are faulty (extended abstract). In: 18th ACM STOC, pp. 364–369. ACM Press, May 1986. https://doi.org/10.1145/12130.12168
18. Diffie, W., Hellman, M.E.: New directions in cryptography. IEEE Trans. Inf. Theory **22**(6), 644–654 (1976)
19. Gentry, C., Peikert, C., Vaikuntanathan, V.: Trapdoors for hard lattices and new cryptographic constructions. In: Ladner, R.E., Dwork, C. (eds.) 40th ACM STOC, pp. 197–206. ACM Press (2008). https://doi.org/10.1145/1374376.1374407
20. Gentry, C., Sahai, A., Waters, B.: Homomorphic encryption from learning with errors: conceptually-simpler, asymptotically-faster, attribute-based. In: Canetti, R., Garay, J.A. (eds.) CRYPTO 2013. LNCS, vol. 8042, pp. 75–92. Springer, Heidelberg (2013). https://doi.org/10.1007/978-3-642-40041-4_5
21. Goldreich, O.: Foundations of Cryptography: Basic Applications, vol. 2. Cambridge University Press, Cambridge, UK (2004)
22. Goyal, V., Lee, C.K., Ostrovsky, R., Visconti, I.: Constructing non-malleable commitments: a black-box approach. In: 53rd FOCS, pp. 51–60. IEEE Computer Society Press, October 2012. https://doi.org/10.1109/FOCS.2012.47
23. Hofheinz, D., Müller-Quade, J., Unruh, D.: On the (Im-)possibility of extending coin toss. In: Vaudenay, S. (ed.) EUROCRYPT 2006. LNCS, vol. 4004, pp. 504–521. Springer, Heidelberg (2006). https://doi.org/10.1007/11761679_30
24. Impagliazzo, R., Levin, L.A., Luby, M.: Pseudo-random generation from one-way functions (extended abstracts). In: 21st ACM STOC, pp. 12–24. ACM Press, May 1989. https://doi.org/10.1145/73007.73009
25. Ishai, Y., Ostrovsky, R., Zikas, V.: Secure multi-party computation with identifiable abort. In: Garay, J.A., Gennaro, R. (eds.) CRYPTO 2014. LNCS, vol. 8617, pp. 369–386. Springer, Heidelberg (2014). https://doi.org/10.1007/978-3-662-44381-1_21
26. Ladner, R.E., Dwork, C. (eds.): 40th ACM STOC. ACM Press, May 2008
27. Lindell, Y.: Parallel coin-tossing and constant-round secure two-party computation. J. Cryptol. **16**(3), 143–184 (2003). https://doi.org/10.1007/s00145-002-0143-7
28. Micciancio, D., Peikert, C.: Trapdoors for lattices: simpler, tighter, faster, smaller. In: Pointcheval, D., Johansson, T. (eds.) EUROCRYPT 2012. LNCS, vol. 7237, pp. 700–718. Springer, Heidelberg (2012). https://doi.org/10.1007/978-3-642-29011-4_41
29. Nisan, N., Zuckerman, D.: Randomness is linear in space. J. Comput. Syst. Sci. **52**(1), 43–52 (1996). https://doi.org/10.1006/jcss.1996.0004
30. Paillier, P.: Public-key cryptosystems based on composite degree residuosity classes. In: Stern, J. (ed.) EUROCRYPT 1999. LNCS, vol. 1592, pp. 223–238. Springer, Heidelberg (1999). https://doi.org/10.1007/3-540-48910-X_16
31. Peikert, C., Rosen, A.: Efficient collision-resistant hashing from worst-case assumptions on cyclic lattices. In: Halevi, S., Rabin, T. (eds.) TCC 2006. LNCS, vol. 3876, pp. 145–166. Springer, Heidelberg (2006). https://doi.org/10.1007/11681878_8
32. Peikert, C., Vaikuntanathan, V., Waters, B.: A framework for efficient and composable oblivious transfer. In: Wagner, D. (ed.) CRYPTO 2008. LNCS, vol. 5157, pp. 554–571. Springer, Heidelberg (2008). https://doi.org/10.1007/978-3-540-85174-5_31
33. Peikert, C., Waters, B.: Lossy trapdoor functions and their applications. In: Ladner, R.E., Dwork, C. (eds.) 40th ACM STOC, pp. 187–196. ACM Press, May 2008. https://doi.org/10.1145/1374376.1374406

34. Regev, O.: On lattices, learning with errors, random linear codes, and cryptography. In: Gabow, H.N., Fagin, R. (eds.) 37th ACM STOC, pp. 84–93. ACM Press, May 2005. https://doi.org/10.1145/1060590.1060603

35. Yeung, R.: A new outlook on Shannon's information measures. IEEE Trans. Inf. Theory **37**(3), 466–474 (1991). https://doi.org/10.1109/18.79902

36. Zhandry, M.: The magic of ELFs. In: Robshaw, M., Katz, J. (eds.) CRYPTO 2016. LNCS, vol. 9814, pp. 479–508. Springer, Heidelberg (2016). https://doi.org/10.1007/978-3-662-53018-4_18

Witness Semantic Security

Paul Lou[1]([✉]), Nathan Manohar[2], and Amit Sahai[1]

[1] UCLA, Los Angeles, CA, USA
paul96lou@gmail.com
[2] IBM T.J. Watson Research Center, Yorktown Heights, NY, USA

Abstract. To date, the strongest notions of security achievable for two-round *publicly-verifiable* cryptographic proofs for NP are witness indistinguishability (Dwork-Naor 2000, Groth-Ostrovsky-Sahai 2006), witness hiding (Bitansky-Khurana-Paneth 2019, Kuykendall-Zhandry 2020), and super-polynomial simulation (Pass 2003, Khurana-Sahai 2017). On the other hand, zero-knowledge and even weak zero-knowledge (Dwork-Naor-Reingold-Stockmeyer 1999) are impossible in the two-round publicly-verifiable setting (Goldreich-Oren 1994). This leaves an enormous gap in our theoretical understanding of known achievable security and the impossibility results for two-round publicly-verifiable cryptographic proofs for NP.

Towards filling this gap, we propose a new and natural notion of security, called *witness semantic security*, that captures the natural and strong notion that an adversary should not be able to learn any partial information about the prover's witness beyond what it could learn given only the statement x. Not only does our notion of witness semantic security subsume both witness indistinguishability and witness hiding, but it also has an easily appreciable interpretation.

Moreover, we show that assuming the subexponential hardness of LWE, there exists a two-round public-coin publicly-verifiable witness semantic secure argument. To our knowledge, this is the strongest form of security known for this setting.

As a key application of our work, we show that non-interactive zero-knowledge (NIZK) arguments in the common reference string (CRS) model can additionally maintain witness semantic security even when the CRS is maliciously generated. Our work gives the first construction from (subexponential) standard assumptions that achieves a notion stronger than witness-indistinguishability against a malicious CRS authority.

In order to achieve our results, we give the first construction of a ZAP from subexponential LWE that is adaptively sound. Additionally, we propose a notion of simulation using non-uniform advice about a malicious CRS, which we also believe will be of independent interest.

1 Introduction

Cryptographic proofs for languages in NP, first studied by Goldwasser et al. [24], are fundamental and powerful primitives. The strongest security guarantee, zero-knowledge (ZK), allows a prover to convince a verifier that a statement is true

© International Association for Cryptologic Research 2024
M. Joye and G. Leander (Eds.): EUROCRYPT 2024, LNCS 14655, pp. 155–184, 2024.
https://doi.org/10.1007/978-3-031-58740-5_6

without revealing anything beyond its validity. This seemingly magical capability, however, has a price. In the plain model, a ZK protocol for any language outside of BPP requires at least three rounds of communication between the prover and the verifier as shown by Goldreich and Oren [21]. In fact, as observed by Bitansky et al. [9], this impossibility result rules out even publicly-verifiable, weak ZK [17] in two rounds.

This barrier is rather unfortunate as two-round public-coin publicly-verifiable protocols are enormously useful because publicly-verifiable, or better yet public-coin, protocols allow for a single back-and-forth between parties, and typically allow the first round message to be re-used[1].

Our collective understanding of what qualitative level of security is achievable in the two-round publicly-verifiable setting for NP is quite limited. To our knowledge, witness indistinguishability (WI) [16,28], witness hiding (WH) [9,18,33], and super-polynomial simulation (SPS) [32,36] are the only known achievable notions in this setting[2]. Worse yet, with all these notions, it's not clear in general how to intuitively interpret a limit on the information leaked by the proof. This leaves an enormous gap in our qualitative understanding of what level of security is possible for this setting.

What Do We Want from a Two-Round Publicly-Verifiable Cryptographic Proof?
Suppose that Alice is an auditor, and a prover would like to send to Alice an encrypted signed financial document and a proof that attests the underlying signed financial document would pass an audit. What level of security is sufficient to preserve the privacy of this financial document? If the encryption scheme has perfect decryption, then there is a unique witness given by a unique message and unique encryption randomness, so WI gives no meaningful security at all as there is a unique witness. Witness hiding only prevents Alice from recovering the entire signed document and randomness of the prover; WH does not prevent Alice from extracting out critical partial information, such as a bank account number or a partial transaction history. This state of affairs begs the question,

Can we achieve a qualitatively stronger security notion than witness indistinguishability and witness hiding for two-round publicly-verifiable proofs?

Our Contribution: Witness Semantic Security. In this work, we propose a naturally motivated notion of security, *witness semantic security* (WSS). Informally speaking, witness semantic security guarantees that any partial information about the witness[3] that an adversary can learn from seeing the proof, the

---

[1] All our protocols will have this reusability property!.

[2] A work of Khurana [31] achieves a different kind of cryptographc proof, but one that does not allow the prover to prove a fixed NP statement of its choosing. This is done via a new security notion termed non-interactive distributional indistinguishability (NIDI). In NIDI protocols, the statement is sampled from a distribution simultaneously with the proof.

[3] This partial information is modeled as a predicate (or indeed more generally, a function) of the witness, exactly as partial information is modeled in the definition of semantic security for encryption schemes [23].

adversary could have also learned from seeing only the statement being proven! This definition subsumes both WI and WH. Furthermore, *witness semantic security gives a qualitative security guarantee that is easy to understand*, and nevertheless, we show how to construct a two-round public-coin publicly-verifiable protocol achieving witness semantic security from the subexponential hardness of learning with errors. Our construction effectively addresses a significant gap in our understanding of what qualitative security guarantees are theoretically possible in the two-round publicly-verifiable setting.

1.1 Application: Malicious-CRS Security for Non-interactive Zero-Knowledge

As a key application of our ideas, we also construct a non-interactive zero-knowledge (NIZK) argument for NP in the CRS model that additionally achieves a new simulation-based definition of security even when the CRS is maliciously generated. We show that any NIZK protocol in the CRS model that satisfies this notion, which we term malicious CRS non-uniform zero-knowledge (malicious CRS NUZK), immediately translates into a plain model two-round publicly-verifiable protocol achieving witness semantic security. Our construction of this NIZK argument, in of itself, advances our collective knowledge of the qualitative security guarantees attainable in what has been called the subverted CRS setting [6]. We now motivate this setting and explain the significance of this contribution.

Non-interactive Zero-Knowledge. Non-interactive zero-knowledge (NIZK) protocols involve only a single message to the verifier. It is well-known that non-interactive zero-knowledge protocols for all of NP cannot be constructed in the plain model [11]. However, they can be constructed in the common reference/random string (CRS) model, where a trusted party (the CRS authority) publishes a (possibly uniformly random) public string that is used during the protocol execution. While the CRS authority is modeled as a completely trusted entity, in the real world, unconditionally trusted parties do not exist. Indeed, misplaced trust in an entity has led to real world consequences: It is widely believed that the Dual EC deterministic random bit generators had intentional backdoors built in by the NSA [13]. Returning our attention to NIZKs, the standard definition of NIZKs does not—indeed, it cannot!—guarantee zero-knowledge when a CRS authority behaves maliciously. In fact, the malicious CRS authority may be capable of recovering the prover's entire witness! This naturally leads to the following fundamental question, which is also *highly motivated* by recent and ongoing examples of central authority misbehavior and subversion by authorities and governments.

What privacy guarantees for the prover's witness can be achieved for NIZKs in the CRS model if the CRS is generated maliciously?

There have been several previous approaches to tackling this issue, which we summarize next. However, as we describe below, these previous works have all suffered from various drawbacks. In our work, we will address these drawbacks through our concept of witness semantic security.

Prior Work: Subversion in the CRS Model. The study of NIZKs with a malicious CRS was initiated by Bellare et al. [6], who study various notions of security for NIZKs under a subverted CRS, showing both impossibility and feasibility results. For example, they show that a natural extension of soundness to the subverted CRS setting (subversion soundness) is incompatible with zero-knowledge even when zero knowledge is only required with an honestly generated CRS. Since we demand zero-knowledge to hold under an honestly generated CRS, we therefore cannot hope to achieve subversion soundness; thus our focus will be to achieve the strongest form of security for the witness possible under a malicious CRS.

Bellare et al. [6] also propose a notion of zero-knowledge against a maliciously generated CRS, which they term subversion zero-knowledge. However, this definition of subversion zero-knowledge has two drawbacks: Firstly, it inherently only addresses security with respect to uniform adversaries and is (trivially) unachievable against non-uniform adversaries, which are the standard model for adversaries in cryptography. Moreover, all known constructions of NIZKs achieving the notion of subversion zero-knowledge rely on knowledge-extraction assumptions that are neither falsifiable nor standard assumptions.

In particular, [6] show that under the Diffie-Hellman knowledge-of-exponent assumption (DH-KEA), there exists a NIZK protocol that also satisfies subversion zero-knowledge. In general, these knowledge extraction assumptions require the existence of a type of extractor that is related to the notion of extractable one-way functions whose existence is incompatible with the existence of indistinguishability obfuscation [8], a primitive we now have from well-founded assumptions [30]. While the DH-KEA assumption is not known to be false as stated in [6], in this work, we show that it is false in a world with uniform auxiliary input. Indeed, we show that if there were a world where some external party instantiates a selectively secure one-time universal sampler [29], then the DH-KEA assumption is false. Such selectively secure one-time universal samplers exist assuming indistinguishability obfuscation and one-way functions. The DH-KEA assumption is also quantum broken. Other constructions of proof systems with subversion ZK [1,5,19] rely either on similar knowledge-extraction assumptions or even stronger Generic/Algebraic Group Models.

To the best of our knowledge, without using a knowledge-of-exponent assumption, the strongest form of subversion zero-knowledge that we know how to obtain for a NIZK in the standard CRS model is subversion witness indistinguishability [6]. Unfortunately, witness indistinguishability (WI) provides no security guarantees when a statement has a unique witness (resp. structured witness) and could reveal the entire witness (resp. structured part of the witness[4]).

---

[4] For example, suppose for a particular instance x, all witnesses are of the form $w \circ w'$, for a fixed string w, but where w' can be any string. Then a WI protocol can reveal all of w.

Prior Work: Accountability in the CRS Model. Recently, Ananth et al. [2] began a line of work on notions of accountability in the CRS model. A malicious authority may use a maliciously generated CRS to create proofs of false statements that pass the verifier's validity check. Indeed, for any NIZK system, such power to prove false statements is inevitable (as argued by [6]). However, a malicious authority can be "caught red-handed" if it is convinced/bribed to produce a proof for a statement that is known to be false (e.g. a statement in coNP with a witness of falsity). Our systems will retain this basic form of accountability for authorities that misbehave to prove false statements. We will not address accountability for soundness further, however, as our focus is on privacy.

Ananth et al. propose a method to hold the CRS authority accountable in such instances. Informally, they construct a NIZK proof from SXDH that satisfies a notion of accountability: if a malicious CRS authority sells an *entire witness* from a proof to a buyer who then turns this over to an investigator, then there is an extractor that can produce a piece of evidence τ that convinces an algorithm Judge that the CRS authority has misbehaved.

Unfortunately, the construction of [2] comes with two drawbacks: (1) Accountability against a malicious CRS authority is only possible if the CRS authority can learn the prover's *entire* witness. In particular, their construction provides no guarantees against a malicious CRS authority that only learns partial information about the prover's witness (see the beginning of the introduction, and below, for an example). (2) Their construction relies on the quantum-broken assumption of SXDH.

Our Contributions to Malicious CRS NIZKs. As our main application of witness semantic security, we achieve two crucial objectives simultaneously:

- Security from a **standard assumption**. Ideally, this assumption should also be post-quantum secure.
- A security notion that **hides partial information** about the prover's witness.

The Importance of Hiding Partial Information About Witnesses. We have already discussed why it is crucial to hide partial information earlier in this introduction. As another example, consider a scenario in which a naïve prover has a document digitally signed by a credit score company that contains not only the prover's credit score but also other personal data (e.g. date of birth, home address, social security number, etc.). The prover can use this document as a witness for the statement, "The prover's credit score is greater than 750." If the prover produces a NIZK argument/proof π using a maliciously generated CRS and sends π to the verifier—a crooked loanshark—then the verifier can ask the malicious CRS authority to extract only part of the witness, such as the prover's social security number, from the proof π. Such a situation is clearly undesirable for the prover, yet the notion of accountability proposed in [2] does not protect against this. Observe that this part of the witness (the prover's social security number) is otherwise hard to predict from only knowing whether the prover's credit score is greater than 750. Therefore, our notion of witness semantic security will provide strong protection in this setting!

1.2   Our Results

In this work, we introduce a new notion that we call *witness semantic security* for cryptographic proofs.

Witness Semantic Security. Witness semantic security generalizes witness hiding to hiding even partial information about the witness. We use the terminology "semantic security" in the original sense proposed by Goldwasser and Micali [22] for probabilistic encryption (not to be confused with the notion of ciphertext indistinguishability [23], which was shown to be equivalent in the context of encryption). That is, our definitions capture the guarantee that any hard-to-compute function of the witness, when given only the statement, remains hard to compute when also given a proof of the statement. Witness hiding, first defined in the seminal work of Feige and Shamir [18], can be seen as a (much) weaker version of our definition, which only guarantees that the entire witness cannot be extracted from the proof. Yet, to our knowledge, surprisingly this natural extension of hiding partial information has not been explored other than through the standard definition of zero-knowledge or weak zero-knowledge. However, as we show in this work, it is possible to achieve witness semantic security by a two-round publicly-verifiable plain model argument system and by NIZK arguments in the CRS model where witness semantic security additionally holds even with a malicious CRS.

For the definition of witness semantic security to be meaningful, it is defined with respect to some distribution over instances, witnesses, auxiliary information, and a family of deterministic functions.' This is necessary because there are certainly easy-to-learn deterministic functions f of a witness w for which the adversary has non-negligible advantage of obtaining $f(w)$ when given only x and f (for example, the constant function f that is always 0), so witness semantic security is defined with respect to sensible distributions where $f(w)$ is hard to learn given only x and f.

Informally, witness semantic security states that (with respect to a suitable distribution), an adversary $\mathcal{A}$, on input a statement x, a function f, auxiliary input Aux, and a proof π generated using a witness w, is unable to output $f(w)$ with non-negligible advantage.

Extending Witness Semantic Security. Our definition above is most meaningful in the case where, for each input x, there is a unique witness for x. This setting immediately separates the notion of WSS from WI. It is also meaningful if all valid witnesses for x share a very long common substring – this is indeed very common in cryptography, where for example the witness includes the entire plaintext for some ciphertext that is part of the statement x. Nevertheless, a natural question is whether witness semantic security can be meaningfully extended to setting of multiple witnesses. We define (and achieve) what we believe to be important progress towards this, for functions f with long verifiable outputs.

More precisely, we define an extension of witness semantic security where we additionally require that there exist a polynomial-time verification algorithm V_f, associated with the function f, such that $V_f(x, y) = 1$ if and only if there exists some witness w' for x such that $y = f(w')$. We then require, roughly speaking, that all such verifiable functions that are hard to predict given only x, are still hard to predict when given the proof as well. We term this extension of witness semantic security as verifiable witness semantic security (VWSS).

We observe that verifiable witness semantic security implies witness hiding for NP languages. This follows by setting f as the identity function and letting V_f be the NP verification algorithm. More broadly, verifiable witness semantic security generalizes witness hiding to hiding any verifiable function of any valid witness. In fact, the notion of VWSS is easily separated from WH by considering the language $L_{\mathsf{AND}} = \{(x, x') : x, x' \in \mathsf{SAT}\}$ and the function f that on witnesses of the form (w, w') outputs w, the witness for x. Since SAT is in NP, there exists an NP verifier V_f that serves as the verification function in the definition of VWSS. Observe that a proof system that produces proofs (w, π'), where π' is a WH proof for x', is WH for L_{AND}, yet this proof system is not VWSS since one can trivially recover $w = f((w, w'))$.

Whether our notion of verifiable witness semantic security can be meaningfully strengthened even further is an important open question. We give some evidence that this is a nontrivial question in the full version.

Reusable Witness Semantic Security. The notion of witness semantic security only deals with hiding partial information about a single witness w used to generate a proof π for a single statement x. We additionally define a strengthening of witness semantic security, called *reusable* witness semantic security, that captures the notion that an adversary should be unable to recover partial information $f(w_1, \ldots, w_n)$ about many witnesses $\{w_i\}$ used to generate proofs $\{\pi_i\}$ for statements $\{x_i\}$ even against an adversary that is allowed to adaptively query statements x_i and receive proofs π_i. Our constructions achieve this stronger definition, without needing to make any additional assumptions beyond subexponential security of LWE.

Achieving Witness Semantic Security. Assuming subexponentially secure LWE, we construct both (1) two-round public-coin publicly verifiable (reusable) WSS and VWSS cryptographic proofs, and (2) NIZKs that additionally satisfies (reusable) WSS and VWSS even in the presence of a malicious CRS.

Witness Hiding Trivially Implies Accountability. We observe that the accountability and defamation-free notions in [2] are trivially satisfiable if it is possible to prevent the malicious CRS authority from ever extracting a witness from a proof, regardless of whether or not the CRS was honestly generated (e.g. if the NIZK is witness-hiding [18] even in the presence of a maliciously generated CRS). In such a situation, the algorithm Judge would simply never accept any evidence τ, and the accountability notion is vacuous since a malicious CRS authority is never capable of obtaining the witness from a proof. We observe that witness-hiding [18] is a stronger form of accountability since instead of proving to a judge that the CRS authority was capable of learning a prover's witness, we simply prevent the CRS authority from learning the prover's witness in the first place! Our notion of verifiable witness semantic security implies witness hiding, and, therefore, our NIZK construction achieves a much stronger security guarantee than accountability if the CRS authority is malicious.

Additional Contributions. In order to construct our NIZK from subexponential LWE satisfying witness semantic security with a malicious CRS, we construct a ZAP from subexponential LWE that is adaptively sound. Previous constructions of ZAPs from LWE [3] were not adaptively sound. Along the way to our construction, we construct what we call *super-dense public-key encryption* from LWE, where super-dense refers to the property that *every* possible public key string has a working decryption key. We believe this tool may prove to be useful in other contexts.

Additionally, we show that the Diffie-Hellman knowledge-of-exponent assumption [6] is false in a world with uniform auxiliary input, giving further evidence that knowledge-of-exponent assumptions are significantly shakier than standard assumptions.

Finally, we propose the notion of simulation using *non-uniform advice about a malicious CRS* – which we also believe will be of independent interest.

1.3   Other Related Works

Besides the aforementioned results about the round complexity of the interactive cryptographic proofs and the results for the single CRS model, there are other models which address the issue of trusting a CRS authority such as the multi-string model [4,7,12,27] and the updatable CRS model [26].

1. **The multi-string model**: This model generates a single CRS from multiple CRS's generated by multiple parties with the guarantee that the overall CRS is secure as long as at least one party in the fixed set of participants behaves honestly. Thus, trust is distributed across multiple parties instead of relying on a single trusted authority. This trust model, however, raises the issue of how this fixed set of participants is chosen.

2. **The updatable CRS model**: This model addresses the above concern of a fixed set of parties by allowing the CRS to be updated by an arbitrary party. Once an honest party updates the CRS, soundness is preserved for subsequent computations based on the updated CRS even after subsequent (possibly malicious) updates. This feature allows an honest verifier to update the CRS, thereby circumventing the impossibility result of [6]. We emphasize that all known constructions in this line of work use either knowledge extraction assumptions [26,35] or the use of idealized models like the Random Oracle Model or Algebraic Group Model to prove security [14,15].

2   Technical Overview

2.1   Defining Witness Semantic Security

We desire a notion of witness hiding that stipulates that an adversary cannot learn any hard-to-learn function of the witness used by the honest prover. Intuitively, this notion captures the idea that for some instance-witness pair $(x, w) \in R_L$ for an NP relation R_L, if it is hard to learn $f(w)$ for some function f given only x, then it should also be hard to learn $f(w)$ when interacting with the honest prover. In the malicious CRS setting, it should be that for any adversary who maliciously chooses a CRS, if it is hard to learn $f(w)$ for some function f given only x, then it should also be hard to learn $f(w)$ given a proof π that $x \in L$ with respect to a maliciously chosen CRS. This leads to the following two definitions.

Definition 1 (Witness Semantic Security).   *An interactive argument system* $(\mathcal{P}, \mathcal{V})$ *for a language* $L \in$ NP *is witness semantic secure if for all polynomially-bounded efficiently samplable probability ensembles* D *over* $\{(x, w, \mathsf{Aux}, f, y) \mid y = f(w), (x, w) \in R_L, \mathsf{Aux} \in \{0,1\}^*, f \in \mathscr{F}\}$, *where* $\mathscr{F}$ *is a set of deterministic functions, for all polynomial sized* $\mathcal{A}_1$ *and polynomial sized* $\mathcal{A}_2$ *which additionally takes as input a state* τ *generated by* $\mathcal{A}_1$, *there exists a polynomial sized* $\mathcal{B}$ *and there exists a negligible function* $\mu(\cdot)$ *such that for all* $\lambda \in \mathbb{N}$

$$\Pr_{(x,w,\mathsf{Aux},f,y)\leftarrow D(\lambda)} \left[\mathcal{A}_2 \left(1^\lambda, \tau, \langle \mathcal{P}(1^\lambda, x, w), \mathcal{A}_1(1^\lambda) \rangle, x, \mathsf{Aux}, f \right) = y \right]$$

$$\leq \Pr_{(x,w,\mathsf{Aux},f,y)\leftarrow D(\lambda)} \left[\mathcal{B}(1^\lambda, x, \mathsf{Aux}, f) = y \right] + \mu(\lambda).$$

Remark 1. In this work, all interactive protocols we consider are two rounds. Note that in the definition above, the verifier does not see any outputs of D when generating its first message. The typical situation we consider is one where the verifier's first message is sent much earlier than the generation of any statement or proof. Our construction satisfies the property that the verifier's first message can be reused across multiple proofs.

Definition 2 (Malicious CRS Witness Semantic Security).   *A non-interactive argument system* (GenCRS, Prove, Verify) *for a language* $L \in$ NP *is malicious CRS witness semantic security if for all polynomially-bounded efficiently samplable probability ensembles* D *over* $\{(x, w, \mathsf{Aux}, f, y) \mid y = f(w), (x, w) \in R_L, \mathsf{Aux} \in \{0,1\}^*, f \in \mathscr{F}\}$ *where* $\mathscr{F}$ *is a set of deterministic functions, for all unbounded* $\mathcal{A}_1$ *and polynomial-sized* $\mathcal{A}_2$, *there exists a polynomial sized* $\mathcal{B}$ *and a negligible function* $\mu(\cdot)$ *such that for all* $\lambda \in \mathbb{N}$

$$\Pr_{(x,w,\mathsf{Aux},f,y)\leftarrow D(\lambda)} \begin{bmatrix} (\mathsf{CRS}^*,\tau)\leftarrow \mathcal{A}_1(1^\lambda) \\ \pi \leftarrow \mathsf{Prove}(\mathsf{CRS}^*,x,w) \\ y \leftarrow \mathcal{A}_2(1^\lambda,\tau,x,\pi,\mathsf{Aux},f) \end{bmatrix}$$

$$\leq \Pr_{(x,w,\mathsf{Aux},f,y)\leftarrow D(\lambda)} \left[\mathcal{B}(1^\lambda,x,\mathsf{Aux},f)=y \right] + \mu(\lambda).$$

At this point, we make two quick observations. The first is that WSS implies WI and the second is that any NIZK argument for $L \in$ NP that satisfies malicious CRS WSS can be immediately converted to a two-round publicly-verifiable WSS argument in the plain model, allowing us to focus only on constructing a NIZK satisfying malicious CRS WSS.

Verifiable Witness Semantic Security. The above definition of witness semantic security only addresses preventing an adversary from learning $f(w)$, where w is the witness used in constructing a proof π. It, however, does not provide any guarantee about the adversary learning $f(w')$ for a different witness w' that was not used in generating π. As discussed previously, we can define an extension of witness semantic security, called verifiable witness semantic security, that states that the adversary should not be able to learn $f(w')$ for any valid witness w' if it is possible to efficiently verify that an output y is indeed $f(w')$ for some w'.

Definition 3 (Verifiable Witness Semantic Security). *An interactive argument system $(\mathcal{P},\mathcal{V})$ for a language $L \in$ NP is verifiable witness semantic secure (VWSS) if for all polynomially-bounded efficiently samplable probability ensembles D over $\{(x,w,\mathsf{Aux},f) \mid (x,w) \in R_L, \mathsf{Aux} \in \{0,1\}^*, f \in \mathscr{F}\}$ where $\mathscr{F}$ is a set of deterministic functions such that for all $f \in \mathscr{F}$, there exists a polynomial-time verification algorithm V_f such that $V_f(x,y)=1$ if and only if $y=f(w')$ for some w' such that $(x,w') \in R_L$, for all polynomial sized $\mathcal{A}_1$ and polynomial sized $\mathcal{A}_2$ which additionally takes as input a state τ generated by $\mathcal{A}_1$, there exists a polynomial sized $\mathcal{B}$ and there exists a negligible function $\mu(\cdot)$ such that*

$$\Pr_{(x,w,\mathsf{Aux},f)\leftarrow D(\lambda)} \begin{bmatrix} y \leftarrow \mathcal{A}_2\left(1^\lambda,\tau,\langle\mathcal{P}(1^\lambda,x,w),\mathcal{A}_1(1^\lambda)\rangle,x,\mathsf{Aux},f\right) \\ s.t.\ \exists w', y=f(w') \wedge (x,w') \in R_L \end{bmatrix}$$

$$\leq \Pr_{(x,w,\mathsf{Aux},f)\leftarrow D(\lambda)} \left[y \leftarrow \mathcal{B}(1^\lambda,x,\mathsf{Aux},f): \exists w', y=f(w') \wedge (x,w') \in R_L \right] + \mu(\lambda),$$

where WLOG Aux contains a description of V_f.

Definition 4 (Malicious CRS Verifiable Witness Semantic Security). *A non-interactive argument system $(\mathsf{GenCRS},\mathsf{Prove},\mathsf{Verify})$ for a language $L \in$ NP is malicious CRS verifiable witness semantic security if for all polynomially-bounded efficiently samplable probability ensembles D over $\{(x,w,\mathsf{Aux},f) \mid (x,w) \in R_L, \mathsf{Aux} \in \{0,1\}^*, f \in \mathscr{F}\}$ where $\mathscr{F}$ is a set of deterministic functions such that for all $f \in \mathscr{F}$, there exists a polynomial-time verification algorithm V_f such that $V_f(x,y)=1$ if and only if $y=f(w')$ for some w' such that*

$(x, w') \in R_L$, *if for all unbounded* $\mathcal{A}_1$ *and polynomial-sized* $\mathcal{A}_2$, *there exists a polynomial-sized* $\mathcal{B}$ *and a negligible function* $\mu(\cdot)$ *such that*

$$\Pr_{(x,w,\mathsf{Aux},f)\leftarrow D(\lambda)} \begin{bmatrix} (\mathsf{CRS}^*, \tau) \leftarrow \mathcal{A}_1(1^\lambda) \\ \pi \leftarrow \mathsf{Prove}(\mathsf{CRS}^*, x, w) \\ y \leftarrow \mathcal{A}_2(1^\lambda, \tau, x, \pi, \mathsf{Aux}, f) \\ y = f(w') \wedge (x, w') \in R_L \end{bmatrix}$$
$$\leq \Pr_{(x,w,\mathsf{Aux},f)\leftarrow D(\lambda)} \left[y \leftarrow \mathcal{B}(1^\lambda, x, \mathsf{Aux}, f) : \exists w', y = f(w') \wedge (x, w') \in R_L \right] + \mu(\lambda).$$

Without loss of generality, assume that V_f *is given in the auxiliary input* Aux.

We now make several observations regarding verifiable witness semantic security.

1. Any NIZK protocol satisfying malicious CRS VWSS immediately gives a two-round publicly-verifiable VWSS protocol.
2. Witness hiding is a special case of verifiable witness semantic security. This is seen by considering a singleton set $\mathscr{F}$ that contains only the identity function. Conceptually, this is because NP relations are efficiently verifiable, therefore an adversary cannot extract any witness for x unless it was already easy to do so from just the statement x alone. Thus, malicious CRS verifiable witness semantic security is a stronger security notion than malicious CRS witness hiding.
3. Malicious CRS witness hiding trivially implies accountability [2] and makes the defamation-free guarantee meaningless by rendering the Judge algorithm useless. Therefore, any protocol that satisfies malicious CRS verifiable witness semantic security trivially satisfies accountability in that a malicious CRS authority *cannot* extract a witness except with negligible probability. This is formally shown in Sect. 4.
4. Observe that WSS (Definition 1) is incomparable to VWSS (Definition 3). Definition 1 does not impose a condition on efficient verifiability and applies to functions whose output is only a single bit but only prevents the adversary from recovering the $f(w)$ for the *specific* witness w used in a proof π. On the other hand, Definition 3 captures a more general security property, but only for a smaller family of functions with long outputs for which the verifiability property holds and the function is hard-to-learn on any witness.

Barriers to Strengthening Verifiable Witness Semantic Security. One can consider a natural strengthening of Definition 3 where we remove the requirement of the existence of a verification algorithm V. In the full version, we give a reasonable conjecture (one provable in the Random Oracle Model) and an interactive protocol that under the conjecture satisfies distributional zero-knowledge yet does not satisfy this strengthening of verifiable witness semantic security. We leave further investigation of this strengthening to future work.

Reusable Witness Semantic Security. We also define a strengthening of Definition 2 called malicious reusable CRS witness semantic security that captures the notion that an adversary should be unable to recover partial information $f(w_1, \ldots, w_n)$ about many witnesses $\{w_i\}$ used to generate proofs $\{\pi_i\}$ for statements $\{x_i\}$ even against an adversary that is allowed to adaptively query statements x_i and receive proofs π_i. This is formally defined in Sect. 4.5.

2.2 NIZK Satisfying Witness Semantic Security with a Malicious CRS

Our main result is the following informal theorem and its informal corllary:

Theorem 1 (Informal Main Result). *Assuming the subexponential hardness of* LWE*, there exists a NIZK argument system that also satisfies malicious CRS witness semantic security, malicious CRS verifiable witness semantic security, and malicious reusable CRS witness semantic security.*

Corollary 1 (Informal Main Corollary). *Assuming the subexponential hardness of* LWE*, there exists a two-round public-coin publicly-verifiable argument system that satisfies witness semantic security, and verifiable witness semantic security, where the first message is reusable.*

We note that our NIZK argument has a CRS generator that, when behaving honestly, generates *uniformly* random CRS's. To achieve such a construction, we introduce and build what we call super-dense public-key encryption.

Super-Dense PKE. A critical building block towards building our NIZK arguments with the desired properties is a "super-dense" PKE scheme, which was not known from the hardness of LWE prior to this work[5]. Denseness refers to the public-key space and dense PKE schemes in the existing literature have the property that with an overwhelming probability, a randomly chosen public key has a decryption key for which correctness holds. This property is not good enough for our purposes, and we need "super dense" PKE schemes in which *every* possible string of the appropriate length has a corresponding decryption key. Our starting point is the dual Regev encryption scheme [20].

Dual Regev Encryption Scheme [20]:

Let $n = n(\lambda), m = m(\lambda), q = q(\lambda)$ be polynomials in λ where $m > 2n \log q$. Let χ denote the LWE error distribution.

- Keygen(1^λ): Sample uniform randomly $\mathbf{A} \leftarrow \mathbb{Z}_q^{m \times n}$ and $\mathbf{s} \in \{-1, 0, 1\}^m$. Let $\mathsf{pk} = \mathbf{A}' = \begin{bmatrix} \mathbf{A} \\ \mathbf{s}^\top \mathbf{A} \end{bmatrix}$ and $\mathsf{sk} = (\mathbf{s}^\top, -1)$. Output $(\mathsf{pk}, \mathsf{sk})$.

- Enc($1^\lambda, \mathsf{pk}, b \in \{0, 1\}$): Parse pk as $\mathbf{A}'$. Sample a random error vector $\mathbf{e}'$ from χ^{m+1}. Sample a random vector $\mathbf{u} \leftarrow \mathbb{Z}_q^n$. Let $\mathbf{b} \in \mathbb{Z}_q^{m+1}$ be

---

[5] In fact, the work of Badrinarayanan et al. [3] writes that such a scheme is "unfortunately not known to exist based on LWE".

a vector with $b \cdot \lfloor q/2 \rfloor$ in $(m+1)$th index and 0 elsewhere. Output $\mathsf{ct} = \mathbf{A}'\mathbf{u} + \mathbf{e} + \mathbf{b}$.
- $\mathsf{Dec}(1^\lambda, \mathsf{sk}, \mathsf{ct})$: Parse sk as $\mathbf{s}'^\top = (\mathbf{s}^\top, -1) \in \mathbb{Z}_q^{m+1}$. Parse ct as $\mathbf{a}'' \in \mathbb{Z}_q^{m+1}$. Compute $r \leftarrow \mathbf{s}'^\top \cdot \mathbf{a}'' \in \mathbb{Z}_q$ and round r to closer of 0 and $\lfloor q/2 \rfloor$. If r rounds to 0, then output 0. Otherwise output 1.

Observe that the dual Regev encryption scheme is dense but not super dense. Ideally, the totality of the SIS problem, which guarantees a short solution for every matrix $\mathbf{A} \in \mathbb{Z}_q^{(m+1)\times n}$ for $m > 2n\log q$, gives us a corresponding decryption key given by this short solution. A quick observation is that any short solution with a zero in the last coordinate would fail to be a good decryption key because the decryption algorithm simply computes the inner product between the decryption key and the ciphertext, in which case the message bit would be multiplied by 0 and the message bit is lost. Unfortunately, there are many matrices $\mathbf{A}$ for which the only short solutions must have a 0 in the last entry, as evidenced by the all zeroes matrix whose last column's entries are all $\lfloor q/2 \rfloor$.

To prevent this correctness violation and achieve a super dense PKE scheme, we introduce a "super dense" dual Regev encryption scheme, in which the encryption algorithm outputs $n + 1$ many dual Regev encryptions where the ith encryption of the bit b places the message bit in the ith entry instead of the last entry. By doing so, any non-zero short solution to any matrix $\mathbf{A}$ is a valid decryption key, thus achieving the super dense property. Moreover, the security remains due to the hardness of the decisional LWE problem with polynomially many samples. A formal description and proof is given in the full version. This super dense PKE scheme allows us to give the first construction of a ZAP from subexponential LWE with adaptive soundness. This ZAP will play a critical role in our construction of the NIZK as we now explain.

Adapting Pass' Two-Round Witness Hiding Protocol. As a simpler goal, we will first construct a NIZK that satisfies witness hiding even with a malicious CRS. While it remains an open problem to construct non-interactive witness hiding in the plain model, there exist two-round witness hiding schemes. Such schemes involve the verifier first sending a message and then the prover responding to the verifier's message with a proof. Moreover, there exist constructions where the proof is publicly verifiable given the protocol transcript.

Since we are focused on non-interactive protocols, we must compress the verifier's message. In the CRS model for NIZKs, we can move the first round message of the two-round witness hiding protocols into the CRS. Since the two-round witness hiding protocol is publicly verifiable, it remains verifiable even if the verifier's first round message is instead viewed as the CRS. Our construction of the NIZK, therefore, is based on compressing the Pass construction [33,36] for two-round witness hiding in the plain model into the CRS model.

We review the two-round witness hiding Pass construction: Let x be a statement for language $L \in \mathsf{NP}$ and let w be a witness for x. Let R_L denote the NP relation for L. Let $f : \{0,1\}^n \to \{0,1\}^k$ be any surjective one-way function, let Com be a perfectly binding commitment scheme, and let Π_{NIWI} be a non-interactive witness indistinguishable argument system for the language of statements $\{S_{b,c_w,c_r}\}$ where S_{b,c_w,c_r} is defined over arbitrary strings b, c_w, c_r as

$$S_{b,c_w,c_r} \triangleq (\exists w', R' \text{ such that } c_w = \mathsf{Com}(w'; R') \wedge ((x, w') \in R_L))$$
$$\vee (\exists r', R' \text{ such that } c_r = \mathsf{Com}(r'; R') \wedge (b = f(r')))$$

in the two-round Pass construction:

Two-round witness hiding Pass construction:

1. The Verifier samples a random $r \leftarrow \{0,1\}^k$ from the codomain of f.
2. Let $c_w = \mathsf{Com}(w; R)$, $c_r = \mathsf{Com}(0; R')$ for randomness R, R'. The Prover outputs (c_w, c_r, π) where π is a NIWI proof for S_{b,c_w,c_r} where the witness the Prover uses is (w, R).
3. The Verifier runs the NIWI verification process on (c_w, c_r, π).

Using Surjectivity Against Malicious CRS Authorities. Suppose, as discussed above, that the verifier's message was moved into the CRS. Our main observation is that if a (possibly maliciously chosen) CRS is from the codomain of a surjective one-way function, then no matter the choice of randomness r' used in the commitment c, there exists a preimage of r' under f. This fact guarantees a second witness for a fixed NIWI proof therefore enabling a hybrid argument using the witness-indistinguishability property to argue witness hiding. In fact, we obtain zero-knowledge in the case of an honestly generated CRS by observing the fact that for every CRS, the simulator can use the second witness to produce a proof. The surjectivity of the one-way function guarantees witness hiding even if the CRS is maliciously chosen. However, surjectivity certainly removes the possibility of obtaining a *proof* (statistical soundness) and arguing computational soundness must be carefully done.

Instantiating the Cryptographic Primitives. A few objectives naturally arise from attempting to compress the two-round Pass construction into a NIZK in the CRS model where we insist that the one-way function f is surjective:

1. To instantiate the surjective one-way function, we observe that the short integer solution (SIS) problem gives a suitable instantiation for the surjective one-way function. The SIS problem takes a uniform random matrix $\mathbf{A} \in \mathbb{Z}_q^{n \times m}$ where $m = \Omega(n \log q)$ and asks whether it is difficult to find a nonzero vector $\mathbf{x} \in \mathbb{Z}^m$ with ℓ_2-norm bounded by some real number β such that $\mathbf{A}\mathbf{x} \equiv \mathbf{0} \bmod q$. Straightforward counting shows that any matrix $\mathbf{A} \in \mathbb{Z}_q^{n \times m}$ for $m = 2n \log q$ has a short vector solution whose ℓ_2-norm is bounded by $\sqrt{m}$. This fact guarantees a second witness for a suitable statement chosen with respect to $\mathbf{A}$, analogously to how the statements in Pass' construction are defined with respect to f. Then we proceed by a careful complexity leveraging argument with respect to the SIS problem to obtain computational soundness of our NIZK.
2. We'd like to replace the NIWI protocol with a primitive based on well-founded post-quantum secure assumptions. Currently, NIWIs are only known from bilinear pairing assumptions [28] and indistinguishability obfuscation [10].

However, we can relax the non-interactive requirement on the NIWIs to a two-round protocol and place the first round message of the two-round protocol in the CRS. Two-round public coin witness indistinguishable protocols, known as ZAPs [16], are known from LWE [3,25]. These constructions, however, have only non-adaptive soundness while we need adaptively sound witness-indistinguishable argument systems. This requirement is because the suitable statement we define is chosen in response to the matrix $\mathbf{A}$ placed in the CRS. At the cost of downgrading from public-coin to public-verifiability, [34] obtains computational adaptive soundness in a construction from subexponential LWE. We observe, however, that a simple construction along the ideas proposed in the introduction of [3], and similar to that of [34], achieves both public-coin and computational adaptive soundness. This construction idea requires the existence of super dense PKE from LWE, which was not known to exist. In the full version, we give the first such construction and use it to construct a computational adaptively sound ZAP.

3. So far, we have only discussed how to achieve witness hiding in the presence of a malicious CRS. However, we would like to strengthen this and achieve the notions of security discussed previously, malicious CRS witness semantic security and malicious CRS verifiable witness semantic security. It turns out that our NIZK protocol satisfies a notion of simulation, where the simulator is allowed to non-uniformly depend on the malicious CRS, that implies malicious CRS witness semantic security, malicious CRS verifiable witness semantic security, and malicious reusable CRS witness semantic security. Essentially, the CRS consists of a string s in the codomain of a surjective one-way function f, and the non-uniform advice dependent on the CRS that the simulator requires is a preimage of s under f.

3   Preliminaries

We use λ to denote the security parameter, $\mathsf{negl}(\lambda)$ to denote any function asymptotically smaller than $\frac{1}{p(\lambda)}$ for any polynomial $p(\cdot)$. If S is a set, then $x \xleftarrow{\$} S$ denotes sampling element x from S uniformly at random. If D is a distribution, then $x \leftarrow D$ denotes sampling element x according to D.

For a language $L \in \mathsf{NP}$, let V be a verifier for L, then define the relation R_L as the corresponding set of instance-witnesses, $R_L \triangleq \{(x,w) : V(x,w) = 1\}$. Define $R_L(x) \triangleq \{w : V(x,w) = 1\}$ to be the set of all witnesses for instance x.

Let $\langle P(x,w), V(x) \rangle$ denote an execution, or transcript, of a protocol with instance x and witness w. Let $\mathsf{Output}_V(\langle P(x,w), V(x) \rangle)$ denote the verifier's final output.

In the case of a two-message interactive proof/argument, we use α to denote the first message (verifier to prover) and π to denote the second message (prover to verifier).

All other preliminaries can be found in the full version.

4   Witness Semantic Security

Recall that, informally, we would like to hide partial information about the prover's witness from an adversarial verifier interacting with the prover. We capture this intuition by formally defining *witness semantic security*, which states that interacting with an honest prover only gives negligibly more advantage in extracting out a function of the witness than attempting to extract out a function of the witness from the statement alone. This is captured by Definition 1 as stated in the technical overview.

Remark 2. Observe that this definition captures the case where $\mathcal{F}$ consists of a single function.

Lemma 1 (WSS implies Witness Indistinguishability). *If an interactive argument system $(\mathcal{P}, \mathcal{V})$ for a language $L \in$ NP is witness semantic secure (WSS), then it is witness indistinguishable (WI).*

Proof. We prove the contrapositive. Consider any language $L \in$ NP and a corresponding relation R_L on statements and witnesses. Suppose that $(\mathcal{P}, \mathcal{V})$ is not witness indistinguishable. Then, there exists a sequence of statements and witnesses $\left(x_\lambda, w_\lambda^{(1)}, w_\lambda^{(2)}\right)_{\lambda \in \mathbb{N}}$ where $w_\lambda^{(1)}, w_\lambda^{(2)} \in R_L(x_\lambda)$, and $w_\lambda^{(1)} \neq w_\lambda^{(2)}$ (such a second witness can always exist WLOG by two different paddings), and a polynomial sized $\mathcal{A}, \mathcal{V}^*$ such that $\mathcal{V}^*$ distinguishes with non-negligible advantage between the probability ensembles $\{\langle \mathcal{P}(x_\lambda, w_\lambda^{(1)}), \mathcal{V}^*(x_\lambda)\rangle\}$ and $\{\langle \mathcal{P}(x_\lambda, w_\lambda^{(2)}), \mathcal{V}^*(x_\lambda)\rangle\}$. Then we construct a specific probability ensemble D for which WSS is violated. Let i_λ to be the smallest index on which the string $w_\lambda^{(1)}$ differs from the string $w_\lambda^{(2)}$. Then, let f_λ be a function that on input w outputs the i_λ-th bit. Now consider the distribution $D(\lambda)$ that samples $(x_\lambda, w_\lambda^{(1)}, \mathsf{Aux} = (w_\lambda^{(1)}, w_\lambda^{(2)}), f_\lambda, f_\lambda(w_\lambda^{(1)}))$ with probability $1/2$ and $(x_\lambda, w_\lambda^{(2)}, \mathsf{Aux} = (w_\lambda^{(1)}, w_\lambda^{(2)}), f_\lambda, f_\lambda(w_\lambda^{(2)}))$ otherwise. Observe that *any* algorithm given $(1^\lambda, x_\lambda, \mathsf{Aux} = (w_\lambda^{(1)}, w_\lambda^{(2)}), f_\lambda)$ has at best $1/2$ probability of guessing $f_\lambda(w_\lambda^{(b)})$ sampled from $D(\lambda)$. Yet, an algorithm additionally given the transcript $\langle \mathcal{P}(x_\lambda, w_\lambda^{(2)}), \mathcal{V}^*(x_\lambda)\rangle$ can run $\mathcal{A}$ to recover $f_\lambda(w_\lambda^{(b)})$ with non-negligible advantage over $1/2$.   □

Having defined witness semantic security, we now define malicious CRS witness semantic security. This definition captures the intuition that the adversary, in the CRS model and in the non-interactive setting, should not be capable of learning a function of the witness even given a proof with respect to a malicious CRS that the adversary has knowledge about. This is captured by Definition 2 as stated in the technical overview.

In the following Lemma, we make the simple observation that any interactive proof (argument) that satisfies malicious CRS witness semantic security implies a two-round publicly-verifiable, witness semantic secure proof (argument) in the plain model. Note that the converse is not true as the definition of malicious CRS witness semantic security considers unbounded adversaries $\mathcal{A}_1$ that generate a CRS. This observation justifies our focus on the malicious CRS setting for the main construction in the paper.

Lemma 2 (Malicious CRS WSS implies Two-Round WSS). *If there exists a NIZK proof (argument)* $\Pi = (\mathsf{GenCRS}, \mathsf{Prove}, \mathsf{Verify})$ *for a language* $L \in \mathsf{NP}$ *that satisfies malicious CRS witness semantic security (Definition 2), then there exists a two-round publicly-verifiable witness semantic secure proof (argument) (Definition 1) for* L *in the plain model. If the CRS generation in the NIZK proof is additionally uniformly random, then the two-round protocol is also public coin.*

Proof. Define V_1 as a polynomial-time algorithm that on input 1^λ outputs $\mathsf{msg}_1 \leftarrow \Pi.\mathsf{GenCRS}(1^\lambda)$. Define P as a polynomial-time algorithm that takes as input $(1^\lambda, x, w, \mathsf{msg}_1)$ and outputs $\pi \leftarrow \Pi.\mathsf{Prove}(1^\lambda, \mathsf{msg}_1, x, w)$. Define V_2 as a polynomial-time algorithm that on input $(1^\lambda, x, \mathsf{msg}_1, \pi)$ outputs $\Pi.\mathsf{Verify}(1^\lambda, \mathsf{msg}_1, x, \pi)$. The claim is that $(P, V = (V_1, V_2))$ is a two-round publicly-verifiable witness semantic secure proof (argument). Completeness, adaptive soundness, and witness semantic security follow immediately from the definitions. Public verifiability also immediately follows since $\Pi.\mathsf{Verify}$ has only public inputs given by the first and second round messages since no state information was passed from V_1 to V_2. With regards to being public coin, if the CRS is uniformly random, then the first round message is uniformly random. □

As previously stated, our construction will focus on the malicious CRS setting because all security results in the malicious CRS setting translate via Lemma 2 to the two-round setting.

4.1 Verifiable Witness Semantic Security

To motivate the following definitions, recall that the standard notion of witness hiding with respect to some distribution D over statements asks that any adversary is unable to use the proof to produce *any* new witness it could not have produced by only seeing the statement. Therefore, witness hiding is *not* immediately implied by witness semantic security (Definition 1) because Definition 1 only prevents an adversary from learning information about a *specific* witness. A desirable objective is then to define a notion of witness semantic security that captures witness hiding.

Preventing an adversary from producing *any* witness, or even a fixed function f of *any* witness, via zero-knowledge implicitly requires an efficient verification procedure. For example, consider the task of proving that zero-knowledge implies witness hiding. Assuming we have an efficient algorithm that breaks witness hiding by extracting some non-trivial witness for a statement from an honestly generated proof, we can construct an efficient reduction that breaks zero-knowledge by distinguishing between an honest prover's output and a simulator's output. Crucially, this distinguisher needs to efficiently verify the validity of the witness, a task that is efficient because the language L is in NP.

Now consider the following issue: suppose we define a variant of witness semantic security to prevent an adversary, with some statement x, from learning any value y such that $y = f(w')$ for any witness w' for x. Then, the reduction that shows zero-knowledge implies this variant may be inefficient if verifying that y is $f(w')$ for some witness w' for x is inefficient. In fact, in the full version we show that without imposing an efficient verifiability property, such a privacy guarantee is unlikely to be provided by even distributional zero-knowledge. Therefore, we introduce the following notion of verifiable witness semantic security in a manner similar to the definitions introduced for witness semantic security (Definition 1). Note that we focus on functions f with long outputs instead of predicates since a predicate f would be trivially easy-to-learn if there ever existed distinct witnesses w and w' where $f(w) = 0$ and $f(w') = 1$. We now refer to the definition of verifiable witness semantic security as given in the technical overview in Definition 3.

Lemma 3 (VWSS Implies Witness Hiding). *If an interactive argument system $(\mathcal{P}, \mathcal{V})$ for a language $L \in$ NP is verifiable witness semantic secure (VWSS), then it is witness hiding.*

Proof. The proof follows by viewing the definition of witness hiding as a special case of verifiable witness semantic security (Definition 3). The specific case is immediately seen by considering all distributions D where the distribution has support with syntax as given in Definition 3, in which $\mathcal{F}$ contains only the identity function.   □

The malicious CRS verifiable witness semantic security definition was given in the technical overview as Definition 4

Lemma 4 (Malicious CRS VWSS implies Two Round VWSS). *If there exists a NIZK proof (argument) $\Pi = (\mathsf{GenCRS}, \mathsf{Prove}, \mathsf{Verify})$ that satisfies malicious CRS VWSS (Definition 4), then there exists a two-round publicly-verifiable witness semantic secure proof (argument) (Definition 3) in the plain model. If the CRS generation in the NIZK proof is additionally uniformly random, then the two-round protocol is also public coin.*

Proof. The proof is identical to that of Lemma 2.   □

Malicious CRS Verifiable Witness Semantic Security Implies Accountability. We observe that the definition of malicious CRS verifiable witness semantic security (Definition 4) implies accountability [2]. More specifically, the conditional statement in the definition of accountability is rendered vacuously true: No adversary participating in the experiment $\mathsf{Acc.Real}_{\Pi,\mathcal{A},q}(\lambda)$ succeeds with non-negligible probability. Since no adversary can cheat with more than negligible probability, the concept of a Judge algorithm can be removed and the defamation-free property becomes meaningless.

Lemma 5 (Malicious CRS Verifiable Witness Semantic Security Implies Accountability). *Let D be an efficiently samplable distribution defined over instance-witness pairs for an NP language L such that for $(x, w) \leftarrow D$ any polynomially-sized adversary given x has negligible probability of finding a witness w' such that $(x, w') \in R_L$. If $\Pi = (\mathsf{GenCRS}, \mathsf{Prove}, \mathsf{Verify})$ is a NIZK argument/proof that satisfies malicious CRS verifiable witness semantic security (Definition 4), then Π also satisfies accountability with respect to D.*

Proof. Here, the function f is implicitly the identity function. Observe that malicious CRS verifiable witness semantic security implies that for any polynomial-sized adversary $\mathcal{A}$, the probability that the real experiment in the accountability security game, $\mathsf{Acc.Real}_{\Pi, \mathcal{A}, q}(\lambda) = 1$, must be negligible. Therefore, accountability holds as the conditional statement is vacuously true. □

4.2 Malicious CRS Non-uniform Zero-Knowledge with Auxiliary Information

In order to show that our NIZK construction satisfies Definition 2 and Definition 4, we will actually show that our NIZK construction satisfies a stronger simulation-based definition, given below, that we term *malicious CRS non-uniform zero-knowledge with auxiliary information*. This definition implies the two forms of witness semantic security above (Definition 2 and Definition 4). The term non-uniform refers to the fact that the simulator is a polynomial-sized circuit that *non-uniformly* depends on the CRS.

Definition 5 (Malicious CRS Non-uniform Zero-Knowledge with Auxiliary Information (NUZK)). *A NIZK protocol for language $L \in \mathsf{NP}$ is malicious CRS non-uniform zero-knowledge with auxiliary information if for all constants $c_1, c_2, c_3, c_4, c_5 > 0$, there exists $\lambda^* \in \mathbb{N}$ such that for all $\lambda > \lambda^*$, for all common reference strings $\mathsf{CRS} \in \{0, 1\}^{\lambda^{c_1}}$, there exists a circuit $\mathsf{Sim}_{\mathsf{CRS}}$ of size λ^{c_2}, such that for all (x, w, Aux) such that $|x| \leq \lambda^{c_3}$, $|w| \leq \lambda^{c_4}$, and $|\mathsf{Aux}| \leq \lambda^{c_5}$ and $(x, w) \in R_L$, the following holds:*

$$(x, \mathsf{CRS}, \mathsf{Prove}(\mathsf{CRS}, x, w), \mathsf{Aux}) \approx_c (x, \mathsf{CRS}, \mathsf{Sim}_{\mathsf{CRS}}(x), \mathsf{Aux}).$$

Observe that in Definition 5, the CRS is fixed and not output by the simulator; this is in contrast to the traditional definition of non-interactive zero-knowledge. The simulator $\mathsf{Sim}_{\mathsf{CRS}}$ crucially non-uniformly depends on this CRS, and there is not one simulator that works for every CRS. In the rest of this section, we show that a NIZK that satisfies Definition 5 satisfies both Definition 2 and Definition 4. We begin by defining an intermediate notion that we will use in the proof.

Definition 6 (Malicious CRS Non-uniform *Distributional* Zero-Knowledge with Auxiliary Information (NUDZK)). *A NIZK protocol for language $L \in \mathsf{NP}$ is malicious CRS non-uniform distributional zero-knowledge with auxiliary information if for all constants $c_1, c_2, c_3 > 0$, there exists λ^* such that* *for all* $\lambda > \lambda^*$, *for all common reference strings* CRS, *there exists a polynomial sized* $\mathsf{Sim}_{\mathsf{CRS}}$ *such that for all probability ensembles* D *in which the distribution* $D(\lambda)$ *outputs* (x, w, Aux) *such that* $|x| \leq \lambda^{c_1}$, $|w| \leq \lambda^{c_2}$, *and* $|\mathsf{Aux}| \leq \lambda^{c_3}$ *and* $(x, w) \in R_L$ *the following holds for all polynomial-sized* $\mathcal{A}$:

$$\left| \Pr_{(x,w,\mathsf{Aux}) \leftarrow D(\lambda)} \left[\mathcal{A}(1^\lambda, x, \mathsf{CRS}, \mathsf{Prove}(\mathsf{CRS}, x, w), \mathsf{Aux}) = 1 \right] \right.$$
$$\left. - \Pr_{(x,w,\mathsf{Aux}) \leftarrow D(\lambda)} \left[\mathcal{A}(1^\lambda, x, \mathsf{CRS}, \mathsf{Sim}_{\mathsf{CRS}}(x), \mathsf{Aux}) = 1 \right] \right| = \mathsf{negl}(\lambda).$$

We next give the following lemma, showing that Definition 5 implies Definition 6

Lemma 6 (Malicious CRS NUZK Implies Malicious CRS NUDZK). *If a NIZK protocol* $\Pi = (\mathsf{GenCRS}, \mathsf{Prove}, \mathsf{Verify})$ *for a language* $L \in \mathsf{NP}$ *is malicious CRS non-uniform zero-knowledge with auxiliary information, then* Π *is malicious CRS non-uniform distributional zero-knowledge with auxiliary information.*

Proof. We show the contrapositive. Suppose that NIZK Π is not malicious CRS non-uniform distributional zero-knowledge with auxiliary information. Then for infinitely many values of $\lambda \in \mathbb{N}$, there exists CRS_λ of length bounded by a polynomial in λ such that for all polynomial sized $\mathsf{Sim}_{\mathsf{CRS}_\lambda}$ there exists a probability ensemble D such that the distribution $D(\lambda)$ outputs (x, w, Aux) where x, w, Aux have length bounded by a polynomial in λ such that the distinguishing advantage

$$\left| \Pr_{(x,w,\mathsf{Aux}) \leftarrow D(\lambda)} \left[\mathcal{A}(x, \mathsf{CRS}, \mathsf{Prove}(\mathsf{CRS}, x, w), \mathsf{Aux}) = 1 \right] \right.$$
$$\left. - \Pr_{(x,w,\mathsf{Aux}) \leftarrow D(\lambda)} \left[\mathcal{A}(x, \mathsf{CRS}, \mathsf{Sim}_{\mathsf{CRS}}(x), \mathsf{Aux}) = 1 \right] \right|$$

is non-negligible. By an averaging argument, there exists (x, w, Aux) from the support of $D(\lambda)$ on which $\mathcal{A}$'s distinguishing advantage is non-negligible. The existence of such (x, w, Aux) immediately implies that Π is not Malicious CRS NUZK. □

4.3 Malicious CRS NUZK Implies Malicious CRS Witness Semantic Security

We now show that malicious CRS NUZK (Definition 6) implies malicious CRS witness semantic security (Definition 2).

Lemma 7. *If a NIZK protocol* $\Pi = (\mathsf{GenCRS}, \mathsf{Prove}, \mathsf{Verify})$ *for a language* $L \in \mathsf{NP}$ *is malicious CRS non-uniform distributional zero-knowledge with auxiliary information, then* Π *is malicious CRS witness semantic security.*

Proof. For syntax type checking between the distributions in the two definitions, first observe that we can equivalently express the support of distribution D as $\{(x, w, \mathsf{Aux}')\}$ where $\mathsf{Aux}' = (\mathsf{Aux}, f, y)$. Then by the definition of malicious CRS NUDZK, for every CRS and for all $\lambda \in \mathbb{N}$ sufficiently large, there exists a polynomial sized $\mathsf{Sim}_{\mathsf{CRS}}$ such that for all polynomial-sized $\mathcal{B}$:

$$
\left| \Pr_{(x,w,\mathsf{Aux}')\leftarrow D(\lambda)} \left[\mathcal{B}(1^\lambda, x, \mathsf{CRS}, \mathsf{Prove}(\mathsf{CRS}, x, w), \mathsf{Aux}') = 1 \right] \right.
$$

$$
\left. - \Pr_{(x,w,\mathsf{Aux}')\leftarrow D(\lambda)} \left[\mathcal{B}(1^\lambda, x, \mathsf{CRS}, \mathsf{Sim}_{\mathsf{CRS}}(x), \mathsf{Aux}') = 1 \right] \right| = \mathsf{negl}(\lambda). \quad (1)
$$

We will show that if we assume that Π is not malicious CRS witness semantically secure, then there exists a CRS for which we can construct a distinguisher between the distributions on $(x, \mathsf{CRS}, \mathsf{Prove}(\mathsf{CRS}, x, w), \mathsf{Aux}')$ and $(x, \mathsf{CRS}, \mathsf{Sim}_{\mathsf{CRS}}(x), \mathsf{Aux}')$, contradicting malicious CRS NUDZK. If Π is not malicious CRS witness semantically secure, then there exists an adversary $\mathcal{A} = (\mathcal{A}_1, \mathcal{A}_2)$ where $\mathcal{A}_1$ is computationally unbounded and $\mathcal{A}_2$ is polynomial sized and such that for each polynomial sized $\mathcal{B}$ there exists a polynomial $p(\lambda)$ such that for every $N \in \mathbb{N}$ there exists a $\lambda > N$ such that

$$
\Pr_{(x,w,\mathsf{Aux},f,y)\leftarrow D(\lambda)} \left[\begin{array}{l} (\mathsf{CRS}^*, \tau) \leftarrow \mathcal{A}_1(1^\lambda) \\ \pi \leftarrow \mathsf{Prove}(\mathsf{CRS}^*, x, w) \\ y \leftarrow \mathcal{A}_2(1^\lambda, \tau, x, \pi, \mathsf{Aux}, f) \end{array} \right]
$$

$$
\geq \Pr_{(x,w,\mathsf{Aux},f,y)\leftarrow D(\lambda)} \left[\mathcal{B}(1^\lambda, x, \mathsf{Aux}, f) = y \right] + \frac{1}{p(\lambda)}. \quad (2)
$$

Fix the CRS considered to be the CRS^* produced by $\mathcal{A}_1(1^\lambda)$. Then observe that the polynomial-sized $\mathcal{A}_2$ is exactly our desired distinguisher for this fixed value of CRS^*. More formally, we construct a polynomial sized distinguisher $\mathcal{B}_\tau$ where for each $\lambda \in \mathbb{N}$, it has an advice string given by τ_λ, where τ_λ is a polynomial-length state produced by $\mathcal{A}_1$ on input 1^λ that can contain the corresponding CRS^* and any possible trapdoors without loss of generality, such that the existence of $\mathcal{B}_\tau$ contradicts Eq. 1.

$\mathcal{B}_\tau(1^\lambda, x, \mathsf{CRS}, \pi, (\mathsf{Aux}, f, y))$

1. If the output of $\mathcal{A}_2(1^\lambda, \tau, x, \pi, (\mathsf{Aux}, f))$ is equal to y, then output 0, where 0 represents a guess that π is an honest proof. Otherwise output 1, where 1 represents a guess that π is the simulated proof.

Observe that when π is produced by the simulator $\mathsf{Sim}_{\mathsf{CRS}^*}(x)$, running $\mathcal{A}_2(1^\lambda, \tau, x, \pi, (\mathsf{Aux}, f))$ is running a circuit of the form $\mathcal{B}(1^\lambda, x, \mathsf{Aux}, f)$, corresponding to the right hand side of Eq. 2. On the other hand, when π is produced by the honest prover, running $\mathcal{A}_2(1^\lambda, \tau, x, \pi, (\mathsf{Aux}, f))$ corresponds exactly to the left hand side of Eq. 2. Therefore, the statement on Eq. 2 implies there exists a polynomial $p(\lambda)$ such that for every $N \in \mathbb{N}$ there exists a $\lambda > N$ such that

$$\left| \Pr_{(x,w,\mathsf{Aux}') \leftarrow D(\lambda)} \left[\mathcal{B}_\tau(1^\lambda, x, \mathsf{CRS}^*, \mathsf{Prove}(\mathsf{CRS}^*, x, w), \mathsf{Aux}') = 1 \right] \right.$$

$$\left. - \Pr_{(x,w,\mathsf{Aux}') \leftarrow D(\lambda)} \left[\mathcal{B}_\tau(1^\lambda, x, \mathsf{CRS}, \mathsf{Sim}_{\mathsf{CRS}^*}(x), \mathsf{Aux}') = 1 \right] \right| \geq \frac{1}{p(\lambda)}$$

Hence, we obtain our desired contradiction with Eq. 1 and we conclude that Π must be malicious CRS witness semantically secure. $\qquad \square$

Corollary 2 (Malicious CRS NUZK Implies Malicious CRS Witness Semantic Security). *If a NIZK protocol $\Pi = (\mathsf{GenCRS}, \mathsf{Prove}, \mathsf{Verify})$ for a language $L \in \mathsf{NP}$ is malicious CRS non-uniform zero-knowledge with auxiliary information, then Π satisfies malicious CRS witness semantic security.*

Proof. The statement follows directly from Lemma 6 and Lemma 7. $\qquad \square$

4.4 Malicious CRS NUZK Implies Malicious CRS Verifiable Witness Semantic Security

Any NIZK protocol Π that satisfies malicious CRS NUZK also satisfies malicious CRS verifiable witness semantic security.

Lemma 8 (Malicious CRS NUDZK Implies Malicious CRS Verifiable Witness Semantic Security). *If $\Pi = (\mathsf{GenCRS}, \mathsf{Prove}, \mathsf{Verify})$ is a NIZK for a language $L \in \mathsf{NP}$ that satisfies malicious CRS NUDZK, then Π also satisfies malicious CRS verifiable witness semantic security.*

Proof. The proof is completely analogous to the proof of Lemma 7 and remains nearly identical. More details are given in the full proof. $\qquad \square$

Corollary 3 (Malicious CRS NUZK Implies Malicious CRS Verifiable Witness Semantic Security). *If $\Pi = (\mathsf{GenCRS}, \mathsf{Prove}, \mathsf{Verify})$ is a NIZK protocol for a language $L \in \mathsf{NP}$ that satisfies malicious CRS NUZK, then Π also satisfies malicious CRS verifiable witness semantic security.*

Proof. Lemma 6 implies the protocol Π is malicious CRS NUDZK, and Lemma 8 implies that Π is malicious CRS VWSS. $\qquad \square$

4.5 Malicious Reusable CRS Witness Semantic Security

To address sequential and concurrent composition, we introduce the notion of malicious *reusable* CRS witness semantic security. That is, we extend the above security definition—which guarantees the inability of a malicious authority to recover partial information $f(w)$, for a single sampled $(x, w) \in R_L$ from a distribution—to the setting in which a malicious authority has the ability to adaptively query statements x_i and receive proofs π_i in order to learn $f'(w_1, \ldots, w_n)$ for an arbitrary deterministic function of interest f'. The witnesses $w_1, \ldots, w_n$ can even be correlated. Our security notion captures the hardness of guessing even a single bit of information on the joint distribution of the witnesses.

We will consider the following two experiments where $\mathcal{A}_1$ is computationally unbounded, $\mathcal{A}_2$ is a stateful PPT algorithm, and $\mathcal{B}$ is polynomial sized. The first experiment is as follows.

$\mathsf{ReWSS.NoProofs}_{\mathcal{A}_1, \mathcal{A}_2, \mathcal{B}}(1^\lambda)$

1. $\mathsf{CRS}^*, \mathsf{Aux}_1 \leftarrow \mathcal{A}_1(1^\lambda)$.
2. $(x_1, w_1, \mathsf{st}_1) \leftarrow \mathcal{A}_2(1^\lambda, \mathsf{Aux}_1)$.
3. $\pi_1 \leftarrow \mathsf{Prove}(1^\lambda, \mathsf{CRS}^*, x_1, w_1)$.
4. Query phase which repeats for $i \in [n-1]$ where n depends on $\mathcal{A}_2$:
   (a) $(x_{i+1}, w_{i+1}, \mathsf{st}_{i+1}) \leftarrow \mathcal{A}_2(1^\lambda, \mathsf{st}_i, \pi_i)$.
   (b) $\pi_{i+1} \leftarrow \mathsf{Prove}(1^\lambda, \mathsf{CRS}^*, x_{i+1}, w_{i+1})$.
5. $(\mathsf{Aux}_2, f) \leftarrow \mathcal{A}_2(1^\lambda, \mathsf{st}_n)$ where n is the number of queries made.
6. $y \leftarrow \mathcal{B}(1^\lambda, \mathsf{Aux}_1, \{x_i\}, \mathsf{Aux}_2, f)$.
7. If $y = f(w_1, \ldots, w_n)$, then the value of this experiment is 1. Otherwise, the value is 0.

The second experiment differs from the first only in that $\mathcal{B}$ also receives the generated proofs as input. This difference is marked in red below.

$\mathsf{ReWSS.WithProofs}_{\mathcal{A}_1, \mathcal{A}_2, \mathcal{B}}(1^\lambda)$

1. $\mathsf{CRS}^*, \mathsf{Aux}_1 \leftarrow \mathcal{A}_1(1^\lambda)$.
2. $(x_1, w_1, \mathsf{st}_1) \leftarrow \mathcal{A}_2(1^\lambda, \mathsf{Aux}_1)$.
3. $\pi_1 \leftarrow \mathsf{Prove}(1^\lambda, \mathsf{CRS}^*, x_1, w_1)$.
4. Query phase which repeats for $i \in [n-1]$ where n depends on $\mathcal{A}_2$:
   (a) $(x_{i+1}, w_{i+1}, \mathsf{st}_{i+1}) \leftarrow \mathcal{A}_2(1^\lambda, \mathsf{st}_i, \pi_i)$.
   (b) $\pi_{i+1} \leftarrow \mathsf{Prove}(1^\lambda, \mathsf{CRS}^*, x_{i+1}, w_{i+1})$.
5. $(\mathsf{Aux}_2, f) \leftarrow \mathcal{A}_2(1^\lambda, \mathsf{st}_n)$ where n is the number of queries made.
6. $y \leftarrow \mathcal{B}(1^\lambda, \mathsf{Aux}_1, \{x_i\}, \{\pi_i\}, \mathsf{Aux}_2, f)$.
7. If $y = f(w_1, \ldots, w_n)$, then the value of this experiment is 1. Otherwise, the value is 0.

Intuitively, the first scenario captures the hardness of learning $f(w_1, \ldots, w_n)$ given only the statements $\{x_i\}$. The second scenario captures the hardness of learning $f(w_1, \ldots, w_n)$ when given the proofs $\{\pi_i\}$ that were generated with CRS^*. Naturally, we desire that seeing the proofs $\{\pi_i\}$ only makes guessing $f(w_1, \ldots, w_n)$ negligibly easier.

Remark 3. To be absolutely clear, in both scenarios, the circuit $\mathcal{B}$ aims to recover $f(w_1, \ldots, w_n)$ and is not attempting to distinguish between the two experiments. The circuits $\mathcal{B}$ in the two games have different input domains, and are parameterized by different circuits $\mathcal{B}$ (with possibly the same functionality). Another trivial observation is that one can consider an adversary $\mathcal{A}_2$ that places all the witnesses in the auxiliary input Aux_2. In this case, the same such adversary $\mathcal{A}_2$ would behave identically in both games, trivially satisfying Definition 7.

Definition 7 (Malicious Reusable CRS WSS). *A NIZK protocol* $\Pi =$ *(GenCRS, Prove, Verify) satisfies malicious reusable CRS witness semantic security if for all unbounded* $\mathcal{A}_1$, *all stateful polynomial sized* $\mathcal{A}_2$, *for all polynomial sized* $\mathcal{B}$, *there exists an unbounded* $\mathcal{A}'_1$, *a stateful polynomial sized* $\mathcal{A}'_2$, *a polynomial sized* $\mathcal{B}'$ *and a negligible function* $\mu : \mathbb{N} \to \mathbb{N}$ *such that*

$$\Pr \left[\mathsf{ReWSS.WithProofs}_{\mathcal{A}_1, \mathcal{A}_2, \mathcal{B}}(1^\lambda) = 1 \right]$$
$$\leq \Pr \left[\mathsf{ReWSS.NoProofs}_{\mathcal{A}'_1, \mathcal{A}'_2, \mathcal{B}'}(1^\lambda) = 1 \right] + \mu(\lambda).$$

As before, in order to show that our NIZK construction satisfies Definition 7, we will define notion of non-uniform simulation in which the simulator can depend on the CRS. We consider the following game-based definition for which we first define two experiments in which $\mathcal{A}_1$ is computationally unbounded and $\mathcal{A}_2$ is stateful and polynomial sized.

$\mathsf{ReNUZK.Real}_{\mathcal{A}_1, \mathcal{A}_2}(1^\lambda)$

1. $\mathsf{CRS}^*, \mathsf{Aux}_1 \leftarrow \mathcal{A}_1(1^\lambda)$.
2. $(x_1, w_1, \mathsf{st}_1) \leftarrow \mathcal{A}_2(1^\lambda, \mathsf{Aux}_1)$.
3. $\pi_1 \leftarrow \mathsf{Prove}(1^\lambda, \mathsf{CRS}^*, x_1, w_1)$.
4. Query phase which repeats for $i \in [n-1]$ where n is the number of queries $\mathcal{A}_2$ makes:
    (a) $(x_{i+1}, w_{i+1}, \mathsf{st}_{i+1}) \leftarrow \mathcal{A}_2(1^\lambda, \mathsf{st}_i, \pi_i)$.
    (b) $\pi_{i+1} \leftarrow \mathsf{Prove}(1^\lambda, \mathsf{CRS}^*, x_{i+1}, w_{i+1})$.
5. $\mathsf{Aux}_2 \leftarrow \mathcal{A}_2(1^\lambda, \mathsf{st}_n)$ where n is the number of queries made.
6. Output $(\mathsf{CRS}^*, \{x_i\}_{i \in [n]}, \{\pi_i\}_{i \in [n]}, \mathsf{Aux}_2)$.

The above experiment captures the real execution of the NIZK protocol in which an adversary can adaptively choose statements to obtain proofs for. The next experiment captures an ideal world in which all proofs are produced by a polynomial sized simulator Sim who depends on the CRS (this dependence is modeled by providing Sim with a trapdoor for the CRS computed by a computationally unbounded entity) and is given only the statements.

$\mathsf{ReNUZK.Ideal}_{\mathcal{A}_1, \mathcal{A}_2, \mathsf{Sim}, \mathsf{Ext}}(1^\lambda)$

1. $\mathsf{CRS}^*, \mathsf{Aux}_1 \leftarrow \mathcal{A}_1(1^\lambda)$.
2. $\tau \leftarrow \mathsf{Ext}(\mathsf{CRS}^*)$.
3. $(x_1, w_1, \mathsf{st}_1) \leftarrow \mathcal{A}_2(1^\lambda, \mathsf{Aux}_1)$.
4. $\tilde{\pi}_1 \leftarrow \mathsf{Sim}(1^\lambda, \tau, x_1)$.
5. Query phase which repeats for $i \in [n-1]$ where n depends on $\mathcal{A}_2$:
    (a) $(x_{i+1}, w_{i+1}, \mathsf{st}_{i+1}) \leftarrow \mathcal{A}_2(1^\lambda, \mathsf{st}_i, \tilde{\pi}_i)$.
    (b) $\tilde{\pi}_{i+1} \leftarrow \mathsf{Sim}(1^\lambda, \tau, x_{i+1})$.

6. $\mathsf{Aux}_2 \leftarrow \mathcal{A}_2(1^\lambda, \mathsf{st}_n)$ where n is the number of queries made.
7. Output $(\mathsf{CRS}^*, \{x_i\}_{i\in[n]}, \{\tilde{\pi}_i\}_{i\in[n]}, \mathsf{Aux}_2)$.

Definition 8 (Malicious Reusable CRS NUZK). *A NIZK protocol $\Pi =$ (GenCRS, Prove, Verify) satisfies malicious reusable CRS non-uniform zero-knowledge with auxiliary information if there exists a computationally unbounded extractor* Ext *and there exists a polynomial sized* Sim *such that for all computationally unbounded $\mathcal{A}_1$ and for all stateful polynomial sized $\mathcal{A}_2$, the following holds:*

$$\mathsf{ReNUZK.Real}_{\mathcal{A}_1,\mathcal{A}_2}(1^\lambda) \approx_c \mathsf{ReNUZK.Ideal}_{\mathcal{A}_1,\mathcal{A}_2,\mathsf{Sim},\mathsf{Ext}}(1^\lambda).$$

Lemma 9 (Malicious CRS NUZK Implies Malicious Reusable CRS NUZK). *If a NIZK protocol $\Pi =$ (GenCRS, Prove, Verify) satisfies malicious CRS non-uniform zero-knowledge with auxiliary information (Definition 5), then Π satisfies malicious reusable CRS non-uniform zero-knowledge with auxiliary information (Definition 8).*

Proof The proof is a conceptually straightforward hybrid argument and can be found in the full version. □

Lemma 10 (Malicious Reusable CRS NUZK Implies Malicious Reusable CRS WSS). *If a NIZK protocol $\Pi =$ (GenCRS, Prove, Verify) satisfies malicious reusable CRS non-uniform zero-knowledge with auxiliary information (Definition 8), then Π satisfies malicious reusable CRS witness semantic security (Definition 7).*

Proof. The intuition for the proof is straightforward and is entirely analogous to the proof of Lemma 7. A formal proof can be found in the full version. □

Malicious Reusable CRS Verifiable Witness Semantic Security. One can also consider an analogous extension of Definition 3 where we allow the adversary to adaptively query statements x_i and receive proofs π_i in order to learn y such that $y = f(w_1,\ldots,w_n)$ for some valid witnesses $w_1,\ldots,w_n$. As in Definition 3, we require the existence of a verification algorithm $V_f(x_1,\ldots,x_n,y)$ that outputs 1 if and only if $y = f(w_1,\ldots,w_n)$ for some valid witnesses $w_1,\ldots,w_n$. Our NIZK will also satisfy malicious reusable CRS verifiable witness semantic security, since it can be shown that malicious reusable CRS NUZK implies malicious reusable CRS verifiable witness semantic security via an analogous proof to Lemma 10.

5 NIZK with Malicious CRS Witness Semantic Security from LWE

In this section, we construct a NIZK that additionally satisfies malicious CRS witness semantic security, malicious CRS verifiable witness semantic security, and malicious reusable CRS witness semantic security, assuming the subexponential hardness of LWE. We show the following main theorem and its immediate corollary.

Theorem 2 (NIZK with Malicious CRS NUZK from LWE). *Assuming the subexponential hardness of LWE, there exists a NIZK argument $\Pi = (\mathsf{GenCRS}, \mathsf{Prove}, \mathsf{Verify})$ such that Π additionally satisfies malicious CRS nonuniform zero knowledge with auxiliary information (malicious CRS NUZK).*

Corollary 4. *Assuming the subexponential hardness of LWE, there exists a NIZK argument $\Pi = (\mathsf{GenCRS}, \mathsf{Prove}, \mathsf{Verify})$ such that Π additionally satisfies malicious CRS witness semantic security, malicious CRS verifiable witness semantic security, and malicious reusable CRS witness semantic security.*

Proof. This immediately follows from Theorem 2, Corollary 2, Corollary 3, and Lemma 10. □

Corollary 5. *Assuming the subexponential hardness of LWE, there exists two-round public-coin publicly-verifiable argument (P, V) in the plain model that satisfies witness semantic security and verifiable witness semantic security. Moreover, the first round message is reusable in that it preserves witness semantic security.*

Proof. This follows from Corollary 4, Lemma 2 and Lemma 4. □

5.1 Building Blocks

We require the following building blocks and assumptions for our construction:

1. Let $\lambda \in \mathbb{N}$ be a security parameter. For appropriate parameters n, m, q, β, we assume the subexponential hardness of the $\mathsf{SIS}_{n,m,q,\beta}$-problem against nonuniform adversaries of size $2^{\lambda^{\epsilon}}$ for some constant $\epsilon \in (0,1)$ and we assume that $\mathsf{SIS}_{n,m,q,\beta}$ is broken against 2^{λ}-sized adversaries.
2. Let Com be a perfectly binding non-interactive commitment scheme parameterized by a security parameter $\tilde{\lambda} \in \mathbb{N}$. We assume that Com is hiding against $2^{\tilde{\lambda}^{\epsilon}}$-sized adversaries and broken against $2^{\tilde{\lambda}}$-sized adversaries. This type of commitment can be obtained from LWE-based PKEs.
3. Let $(\mathsf{ZAP}_1, \mathsf{ZAP}_2, \mathsf{ZAP}_V)$ be an adaptively computationally sound ZAP satisfying computational witness indistinguishability against all polynomial sized adversaries. This is obtained from subexponential LWE in the full version.

Definition 9 (SIS Parameter Generator). *We define a parameter generator algorithm $\mathsf{ParamGen}(1^{\lambda})$ for $\lambda \in \mathbb{N}$ that outputs $n = n(\lambda), m = m(\lambda), q = q(\lambda), \beta = \beta(\lambda)$ such that (1) $n > 2m \log q$, $\beta > \sqrt{m}$ (2) the $\mathsf{SIS}_{n,m,q,\beta}$-problem is secure against $2^{\lambda^{\epsilon}}$ time adversaries for some constant $\epsilon \in (0,1)$, and (3) broken against 2^{λ} time adversaries.*

Remark 4. (Complexity Leveraging Summary) Suppose we generate $n, m, q, \beta \leftarrow$ ParamGen(1^λ) where the subexponential hardness involves some constant $\epsilon \in (0,1)$. Then we have that $\mathsf{SIS}_{n,m,q,\beta}$ problem is secure against $T_{\mathsf{SIS}}(\lambda) \triangleq 2^{\lambda^\epsilon}$ sized adversaries and broken against 2^λ sized adversaries. Let $\tilde{\lambda} = \lambda^{\epsilon'}$ for some constant $\epsilon' = \epsilon/2$. Instantiating the commitment scheme with security parameter $\tilde{\lambda}$, we see that the commitment scheme is secure against adversaries of size $T_{\mathsf{Com}}(\lambda) \triangleq 2^{\tilde{\lambda}^\epsilon} = 2^{\lambda^{\epsilon \cdot (\epsilon/2)}}$ and broken against adversaries of size $T_{\mathsf{Extract}}(\lambda) \triangleq 2^{\tilde{\lambda}} = 2^{\lambda^{\epsilon/2}}$. Therefore, we have

$$T_{\mathsf{Com}} \ll T_{\mathsf{Extract}} \ll T_{\mathsf{SIS}}$$

Notation. Throughout the construction, the notation $\mathsf{Com}(x; r)$ implicitly denotes a commitment instantiated with security parameter $\tilde{\lambda} \in \mathbb{N}$: $\mathsf{Com}(1^{\tilde{\lambda}}, x; r)$. As mentioned in a previous remark, the commitment to a string is performed bit-by-bit.

5.2   The Construction

Protocol 1 (NIZK with Malicious CRS (V)WSS)

Parameters: Let L be a language in NP. Generate $n, m, q, \beta \leftarrow$ ParamGen(1^λ) for constant $\epsilon \in (0,1)$. Set $\tilde{\lambda} = \lambda^{\epsilon'}$ for constant $\epsilon' = \epsilon/2$. Instantiate the commitment with security parameter $\tilde{\lambda}$. Then we have the following:

GenCRS(1^λ):

1. $z \leftarrow \mathsf{ZAP}_1(1^\lambda)$.
2. Choose a uniformly random matrix $\mathbf{A} \in \mathbb{Z}_q^{n \times m}$.
3. Output $\mathsf{CRS} = (\mathsf{CRS}_0, \mathsf{CRS}_1)$ where $\mathsf{CRS}_0 := \mathbf{A}$ and $\mathsf{CRS}_1 := z$.

Prove(CRS, x, w):

1. Parse CRS as $(\mathsf{CRS}_0, \mathsf{CRS}_1)$. Let $\mathbf{A} := \mathsf{CRS}_0$.
2. $c \leftarrow \mathsf{Com}(\mathbf{0}; R)$ for uniformly chosen randomness R.
3. Define statement $S_{\mathsf{CRS}_0, x, c}$ as $\exists \mathbf{r}, R, w'$ such that (a) OR (b) holds where
   (a) $c = \mathsf{Com}(\mathbf{r}; R)$
       $\wedge\ \mathbf{r} \in \{-1, 0, 1\}^m$
       $\wedge\ \mathbf{r} \neq \mathbf{0}$
       $\wedge\ \mathbf{A}\mathbf{r} \equiv \mathbf{0} \mod q$
   (b) $(x, w') \in R_L$.
   Observe that a witness is a triple of the form $(\mathbf{r}, R, w')$. The set of statements that have a witness define a language L'.
4. $\pi_z \leftarrow \mathsf{ZAP}_2(\mathsf{CRS}_1, S_{\mathsf{CRS}_0, x, c}, (\bot, \bot, w))$
5. Output $\pi \leftarrow (c, \pi_z)$.

Verify(CRS, x, π):

---

1. *Parse* CRS *as* $(\mathsf{CRS}_0, \mathsf{CRS}_1)$ *and parse* π *as* (c, π_z).
2. *Output* $\mathsf{ZAP}_V(\mathsf{CRS}_1, S_{\mathsf{CRS}_0, x, c}, \pi_z)$.

Remark 5. Perfectly binding commitments are required in the above construction to ensure that the statements for the new language constructed are not trivially true.

The proofs that this protocol satisfies completeness, soundness, zero-knowledge, malicious CRS NUZK can be found in the full version.

Acknowledgements. We thank the anonymous Eurocrypt reviewers for their helpful feedback regarding this work. We also thank Aayush Jain and Rex Fernando for elucidating discussions regarding ZAPs and Abhishek Jain for a helpful discussion about the two-round public-coin setting.

This research was supported in part from a Simons Investigator Award, DARPA SIEVE award, NTT Research, BSF grant 2018393, a Xerox Faculty Research Award, a Google Faculty Research Award, and an Okawa Foundation Research Grant. This material is based upon work supported by the Defense Advanced Research Projects Agency through Award HR00112020024.

References

1. Abdolmaleki, B., Baghery, K., Lipmaa, H., Zajac, M.: A subversion-resistant SNARK. In: Takagi, T., Peyrin, T. (eds.) ASIACRYPT 2017, Part III. LNCS, vol. 10626, pp. 3–33. Springer, Heidelberg (2017). https://doi.org/10.1007/978-3-319-70700-6_1
2. Ananth, P., Asharov, G., Dahari, H., Goyal, V.: Towards accountability in CRS generation. In: Canteaut, A., Standaert, F.X. (eds.) EUROCRYPT 2021, Part III. LNCS, vol. 12698, pp. 278–308. Springer, Heidelberg (2021). https://doi.org/10.1007/978-3-030-77883-5_10
3. Badrinarayanan, S., Fernando, R., Jain, A., Khurana, D., Sahai, A.: Statistical ZAP arguments. In: Canteaut, A., Ishai, Y. (eds.) EUROCRYPT 2020, Part III. LNCS, vol. 12107, pp. 642–667. Springer, Heidelberg (2020). https://doi.org/10.1007/978-3-030-45727-3_22
4. Badrinarayanan, S., Jain, A., Manohar, N., Sahai, A.: Secure MPC: laziness leads to GOD. In: Moriai, S., Wang, H. (eds.) ASIACRYPT 2020, Part III. LNCS, vol. 12493, pp. 120–150. Springer, Heidelberg (2020). https://doi.org/10.1007/978-3-030-64840-4_5
5. Baghery, K.: Subversion-resistant simulation (knowledge) sound NIZKs. In: Albrecht, M. (ed.)Cryptography and Coding. IMACC 2019. LNCS, vol. 11929, pp. 42–63. Springer, Cham (2019). https://doi.org/10.1007/978-3-030-35199-1_3
6. Bellare, M., Fuchsbauer, G., Scafuro, A.: NIZKs with an untrusted CRS: Security in the face of parameter subversion. In: Cheon, J.H., Takagi, T. (eds.) ASIACRYPT 2016, Part II. LNCS, vol. 10032, pp. 777–804. Springer, Heidelberg (2016). https://doi.org/10.1007/978-3-662-53890-6_26
7. Ben-Sasson, E., Chiesa, A., Green, M., Tromer, E., Virza, M.: Secure sampling of public parameters for succinct zero knowledge proofs. In: 2015 IEEE Symposium on Security and Privacy, SP 2015, San Jose, 17–21 May 2015, pp. 287–304. IEEE Computer Society (2015). https://doi.org/10.1109/SP.2015.25

8. Bitansky, N., Canetti, R., Paneth, O., Rosen, A.: On the existence of extractable one-way functions. In: Shmoys, D.B. (ed.) 46th ACM STOC, pp. 505–514. ACM Press (2014)

9. Bitansky, N., Khurana, D., Paneth, O.: Weak zero-knowledge beyond the black-box barrier. In: Charikar, M., Cohen, E. (eds.) 51st ACM STOC, pp. 1091–1102. ACM Press (2019)

10. Bitansky, N., Paneth, O.: ZAPs and non-interactive witness indistinguishability from indistinguishability obfuscation. In: Dodis, Y., Nielsen, J.B. (eds.) TCC 2015, Part II. LNCS, vol. 9015, pp. 401–427. Springer, Heidelberg (2015). https://doi.org/10.1007/978-3-662-46497-7_16

11. Blum, M., Feldman, P., Micali, S.: Non-interactive zero-knowledge and its applications (extended abstract). In: 20th ACM STOC, pp. 103–112. ACM Press (1988)

12. Bowe, S., Gabizon, A., Green, M.D.: A multi-party protocol for constructing the public parameters of the pinocchio zk-snark. In: Zohar, A., et al. (eds.) Financial Cryptography and Data Security. FC 2018. LNCS, vol. 10958, pp. 64–77. Springer, Heidelberg (2018). https://doi.org/10.1007/978-3-662-58820-8_5

13. Checkoway, S., et al.: On the practical exploitability of dual EC in TLS implementations. In: Proceedings of the 23rd USENIX Conference on Security Symposium (SEC 2014), pp. 319–335 (2014)

14. Chiesa, A., Hu, Y., Maller, M., Mishra, P., Vesely, N., Ward, N.P.: Marlin: preprocessing zkSNARKs with universal and updatable SRS. In: Canteaut, A., Ishai, Y. (eds.) EUROCRYPT 2020, Part I. LNCS, vol. 12105, pp. 738–768. Springer, Heidelberg (2020). https://doi.org/10.1007/978-3-030-45721-1_26

15. Daza, V., Ràfols, C., Zacharakis, A.: Updateable inner product argument with logarithmic verifier and applications. In: Kiayias, A., Kohlweiss, M., Wallden, P., Zikas, V. (eds.) PKC 2020, Part I. LNCS, vol. 12110, pp. 527–557. Springer, Heidelberg (2020). https://doi.org/10.1007/978-3-030-45374-9_18

16. Dwork, C., Naor, M.: Zaps and their applications. In: 41st FOCS, pp. 283–293. IEEE Computer Society Press (2000)

17. Dwork, C., Naor, M., Reingold, O., Stockmeyer, L.J.: Magic functions. In: 40th FOCS, pp. 523–534. IEEE Computer Society Press (1999)

18. Feige, U., Shamir, A.: Witness indistinguishable and witness hiding protocols. In: 22nd ACM STOC, pp. 416–426. ACM Press (1990)

19. Fuchsbauer, G.: Subversion-zero-knowledge SNARKs. In: Abdalla, M., Dahab, R. (eds.) PKC 2018, Part I. LNCS, vol. 10769, pp. 315–347. Springer, Heidelberg (2018). https://doi.org/10.1007/978-3-319-76578-5_11

20. Gentry, C., Peikert, C., Vaikuntanathan, V.: Trapdoors for hard lattices and new cryptographic constructions. In: Ladner, R.E., Dwork, C. (eds.) 40th ACM STOC, pp. 197–206. ACM Press (2008)

21. Goldreich, O., Oren, Y.: Definitions and properties of zero-knowledge proof systems. J. Cryptol. 7(1), 1–32 (1994). https://doi.org/10.1007/BF00195207

22. Goldwasser, S., Micali, S.: Probabilistic encryption and how to play mental poker keeping secret all partial information. In: 14th ACM STOC, pp. 365–377. ACM Press (1982)

23. Goldwasser, S., Micali, S.: Probabilistic encryption. J. Comput. Syst. Sci. 28(2), 270–299 (1984). https://www.sciencedirect.com/science/article/pii/0022000084900709

24. Goldwasser, S., Micali, S., Rackoff, C.: The knowledge complexity of interactive proof-systems (extended abstract). In: 17th ACM STOC, pp. 291–304. ACM Press (1985)

25. Goyal, V., Jain, A., Jin, Z., Malavolta, G.: Statistical zaps and new oblivious transfer protocols. In: Canteaut, A., Ishai, Y. (eds.) EUROCRYPT 2020, Part III. LNCS, vol. 12107, pp. 668–699. Springer, Heidelberg (2020). https://doi.org/10.1007/978-3-030-45727-3_23

26. Groth, J., Kohlweiss, M., Maller, M., Meiklejohn, S., Miers, I.: Updatable and universal common reference strings with applications to zk-SNARKs. In: Shacham, H., Boldyreva, A. (eds.) CRYPTO 2018, Part III. LNCS, vol. 10993, pp. 698–728. Springer, Heidelberg (2018). https://doi.org/10.1007/978-3-319-96878-0_24

27. Groth, J., Ostrovsky, R.: Cryptography in the multi-string model. In: Menezes, A. (ed.) CRYPTO 2007. LNCS, vol. 4622, pp. 323–341. Springer, Heidelberg (2007). https://doi.org/10.1007/978-3-540-74143-5_18

28. Groth, J., Ostrovsky, R., Sahai, A.: Non-interactive zaps and new techniques for NIZK. In: Dwork, C. (ed.) CRYPTO 2006. LNCS, vol. 4117, pp. 97–111. Springer, Heidelberg (2006). https://doi.org/10.1007/11818175_6

29. Hofheinz, D., Jager, T., Khurana, D., Sahai, A., Waters, B., Zhandry, M.: How to generate and use universal samplers. In: Cheon, J.H., Takagi, T. (eds.) ASIACRYPT 2016, Part II. LNCS, vol. 10032, pp. 715–744. Springer, Heidelberg (2016). https://doi.org/10.1007/978-3-662-53890-6_24

30. Jain, A., Lin, H., Sahai, A.: Indistinguishability obfuscation from well-founded assumptions. In: Proceedings of the 53rd Annual ACM SIGACT Symposium on Theory of Computing (STOC 2021), pp. 60–73. Association for Computing Machinery, New York (2021). https://doi.org/10.1145/3406325.3451093

31. Khurana, D.: Non-interactive distributional indistinguishability (NIDI) and non-malleable commitments. In: Canteaut, A., Standaert, F.X. (eds.) EUROCRYPT 2021, Part III. LNCS, vol. 12698, pp. 186–215. Springer, Heidelberg (2021). https://doi.org/10.1007/978-3-030-77883-5_7

32. Khurana, D., Sahai, A.: How to achieve non-malleability in one or two rounds. In: Umans, C. (ed.) 58th FOCS, pp. 564–575. IEEE Computer Society Press (2017)

33. Kuykendall, B., Zhandry, M.: Towards non-interactive witness hiding. In: Pass, R., Pietrzak, K. (eds.) TCC 2020, Part I. LNCS, vol. 12550, pp. 627–656. Springer, Heidelberg (2020). https://doi.org/10.1007/978-3-030-64375-1_22

34. Lombardi, A., Vaikuntanathan, V., Wichs, D.: 2-message publicly verifiable WI from (subexponential) LWE. Cryptology ePrint Archive, Report 2019/808 (2019). https://eprint.iacr.org/2019/808

35. Maller, M., Bowe, S., Kohlweiss, M., Meiklejohn, S.: Sonic: zero-knowledge SNARKs from linear-size universal and updatable structured reference strings. In: Cavallaro, L., Kinder, J., Wang, X., Katz, J. (eds.) ACM CCS 2019, pp. 2111–2128. ACM Press (2019)

36. Pass, R.: On deniability in the common reference string and random oracle model. In: Boneh, D. (ed.) CRYPTO 2003. LNCS, vol. 2729, pp. 316–337. Springer, Heidelberg (2003). https://doi.org/10.1007/978-3-540-45146-4_19

Garbled Circuit Lookup Tables
with Logarithmic Number of Ciphertexts

David Heath[1]($\boxtimes$), Vladimir Kolesnikov[2], and Lucien K. L. Ng[2]

[1] University of Illinois Urbana-Champaign, Champaign, USA
daheath@illinois.edu
[2] Georgia Institute of Technology, Atlanta, USA
{kolesnikov,kng68}@gatech.edu

Abstract. Garbled Circuit (GC) is a basic technique for practical secure computation. GC handles Boolean circuits; it consumes significant network bandwidth to transmit encoded gate truth tables, each of which scales with the computational security parameter κ. GC optimizations that reduce bandwidth consumption are valuable.

It is natural to consider a generalization of Boolean two-input one-output gates (represented by 4-row one-column lookup tables, LUTs) to arbitrary N-row m-column LUTs. Known techniques for this do not scale, with naïve size-$O(Nm\kappa)$ garbled LUT being the most practical approach in many scenarios.

Our novel garbling scheme – logrow – implements GC LUTs while sending only a *logarithmic* in N number of ciphertexts! Specifically, let $n = \lceil \log_2 N \rceil$. We allow the GC parties to evaluate a LUT for $(n-1)\kappa + nm\kappa + Nm$ bits of communication. logrow is compatible with modern GC advances, e.g. half gates and free XOR.

Our work improves state-of-the-art GC handling of several interesting applications, such as privacy-preserving machine learning, floating-point arithmetic, and DFA evaluation.

Keywords: Multiparty Computation · Garbled Circuits · Lookup Tables

1 Introduction

Garbled Circuit (GC) allows two parties to jointly evaluate circuits without leaking anything that cannot be inferred from the output of the computation. In contrast with other secure computation (MPC) techniques, *e.g.* GMW, GC requires only a constant number of communication rounds, independent of the circuit's size and depth.

In GC, the garbler G steps through the circuit gate by gate. At each gate, G constructs and sends to the evaluator E an encryption (garbling) of the gate's truth table. Altogether, these messages consume significant communication. Indeed, communication is the bottleneck of GC performance, so reducing communication is a central goal of GC research.

© International Association for Cryptologic Research 2024
M. Joye and G. Leander (Eds.): EUROCRYPT 2024, LNCS 14655, pp. 185–215, 2024.
https://doi.org/10.1007/978-3-031-58740-5_7

Most prior GC communication improvements have come in the form of new methods for handling fan-in two gates. While Yao's original construction [43] required four ciphertexts per gate, subsequent works improved cost to zero ciphertexts per XOR gate and 1.5 ciphertexts per AND gate [24,25,31,35,40,44]. Despite intense interest, progress has slowed and lower bounds began to emerge [44]. [40]'s intricate technique improves over the previous best [44] by less than 25%.

Seeking significant GC cost improvement, we look at a broader problem: efficient evaluation of general-purpose multi-input/multi-output gates. No such garbled gates were proposed (but see discussion of related techniques in Sect. 2). In contrast, in the non-constant-round GMW setting, multi-input/multi-output gates are known, e.g. [7,21].

We bring multi-input/multi-output gates to GC, generalizing from fan-in-two Boolean gates to arbitrary N-row m-column *lookup tables* (LUTs).

LUT Applications. LUTs are useful in many settings, such as privacy-preserving machine learning (PPML) [33]. SiRnn [38] uses LUTs to accelerate and better approximate non-linear functions needed for PPML, *e.g.*, sigmoid, tanh, and $1/\sqrt{x}$. It uses size-1020 LUTs as part of its implementation of inverse square root. LUTs can also simplify floating point arithmetic [36,37]. [37] uses size-128 LUTs in their implementation of tan and size-256 LUTs to convert integers to floating points. [36] uses size-2^{12} LUTs for sigmoid and tanh over 16-bit floating points. [39] uses LUTs to accelerate fixed-point comparison, an essential operation in PPML [32,33]. It is also possible to, for instance, use LUTs to implement state transition tables for Deterministic Finite Automata (DFAs), which is useful in a variety of problems, such as substring matching and DNA pattern search [41].

More generally, LUTs open opportunities for more efficient secure computation, similar to how LUTs enable more efficient plaintext computation in Field Programmable Gate Arrays (FPGA). Yet, the above applications are now only implemented with (GMW-style) interactive primitives [7,21,23], meaning that performance is highly susceptible to network latency.

Until Our Work the most concretely efficient non-interactive and composable technique for natural LUT applications (e.g. above) was the straightforward transmission of a full encrypted truth table. This consumes $\Theta(Nm\kappa)$ bits of communication, linear in the size of the table. The recent one-hot garbling technique [13] enables highly efficient GC LUTs that consume only $O(\log N \cdot \kappa)$ bits, but *only* in a setting where the evaluator E is allowed to learn which row is looked up from each table. While [13] used these *privacy-free* GC LUTs in securely computing highly structured functions with convenient algebraic properties, their technique does not apply in the less structured settings we consider.

1.1   Contribution

We realize N-row m-column GC LUTs while sending only a *logarithmic* in N number of ciphertexts per LUT! Namely, our approach securely executes

Table 1. Comparison of various GC techniques for computing $[\![a]\!] \mapsto [\![f(a)]\!]$ inside GC where $f : \{0,1\}^n \to \{0,1\}^m$ is a table with $N = 2^n$ rows. Each ✗ symbol indicates a weakness of the respective approach. $\tilde{O}$ includes polylog(N) factors; $O^!$ includes polylog(n) factors. All schemes other than linear scan and GRAM require that G knows f. We emphasize the low constants in our communication.

Approach	Communication (bits)	Computation (bit ops.)	E knows f	E knows x	Amortized
Ours	$(n-1)\kappa + nm\kappa + Nm$	$O((N(1 + \frac{m}{\kappa}) + nm)c_\kappa + Nm\kappa)$			
Linear Scan	$O(Nm\kappa)$	$O(Nmc_\kappa)$			
One-Hot	$(n-1)\kappa$	$O(Nm\kappa + Nc_\kappa)$	✗	✗	
SGC	$O(n^2\kappa + nm\kappa)$	$O(N^{2.389}mc_\kappa)$	✗		
GPIR	$\tilde{O}(\sqrt{N}m\kappa)$	$\tilde{O}(Nmc_\kappa)$	✗		
GRAM	$O^!(nm\kappa + n^3\kappa)$	$O^!(nmc_\kappa + n^3c_\kappa)$			✗

programs that arbitrarily compose any number of LUTs, each potentially computing a different function, all in constant rounds.

Our construction is lean: for computational security parameter κ and for $n = \lceil\log_2 N\rceil$ our garbled LUT gate uses precisely $(n-1)\kappa + nm\kappa + Nm$ bits of communication. Our computational cost is $O((N(1 + \frac{m}{\kappa}) + nm)c_\kappa + Nm\kappa)$, requiring $O(N(1 + \frac{m}{\kappa}) + nm)$ evaluations of a hash function (c_κ denotes the computational cost of evaluating the hash function; see Sect. 3.1 for the hash function definition). Notably, this is a concrete and asymptotic computation improvement over linear scan of the LUT (i.e., including each of the N rows in a garbled table).

At a very high level, our protocol uses the recent One-Hot Garbling (OHG) technique [13] to evaluate a *masked* LUT on a masked index. The masks are then efficiently taken off inside GC. Efficient masking and unmasking are achieved by our new core technique, which allows the parties to efficiently evaluate a *random function* inside GC. Our technique hides the random function from the GC evaluator and only requires that the garbler send a logarithmic number of ciphertexts.

We formalize our construction as a garbling scheme [3] and prove security. Our scheme is compatible with Free XOR [25] and with Free-XOR based GC improvements, e.g. [13,15,40,44]. As a garbling scheme, our construction immediately implies 2PC protocols in semi-honest, malicious, covert, and publicly verifiable covert models.

Our garbling scheme is compatible with the Stacked Garbling technique [14]; it can be used in the context of conditional branches that are "stacked".

2   Related Work

We propose a technique for securely evaluating functions inside GC. Given a function $f : \{0,1\}^n \to \{0,1\}^m$ and garbled input $[\![a]\!]$, we compute the garbled value $[\![f(a)]\!]$ (see Sect. 3 for detail of this notation). We evaluate f described *only* by its $N = 2^n$ row lookup table. Thus, our technique is suited to settings where f is *arbitrarily complex*.

In this review of related work, we focus on other GC approaches that can also be used to evaluate functions via their truth tables. We summarize our comparison in Table 1, and we give detailed discussion below.

Basic Boolean Gates and Linear Scans. Classic GC allows to securely compute Boolean circuits with fan-in two gates. The most recent gate-by-gate construction requires $\approx 1.5\kappa$ bits of communication per AND gate [40]; XOR gates are communication-free [25].

Boolean gates can implement lookup tables via *linear scans*. To implement a function $f : \{0,1\}^n \to \{0,1\}^m$, the parties compute gates that touch each entry of the function's truth table. The truth table is a string of length $2^n m = Nm$, so in total $O(Nm\kappa)$ bits of communication are needed.

While expensive, simply enumerating the truth table remained the best approach to LUTs for many values N, due to the excellent constants involved in this basic technique.

Our technique asymptotically improves over basic linear scans by factor κ and is concretely superior for all values of $N \geq 4$ (see Sect. 6).

One-Hot Garbling (OHG) [13] enables communication-efficient *privacy-free* LUTs. The technique allows the parties to compute $[\![f(x)]\!]$ while using only $(n-1)\kappa$ bits of communication (and is reduced to $(n-1)\kappa$ bits recently [11]), but only when E knows both f and x. [13] demonstrates that this building block can be used to implement privacy-preserving computations, but only for certain functions with friendly algebraic properties, such as linearity. The technique improves highly structured functions, including binary vector outer products, integer multiplication, and more. OHG is poorly suited to *general* functions f, since arbitrary functions do not have exploitable algebraic properties.

We build on top of OHG to implement $[\![f(x)]\!]$ for arbitrary f. We require additional communication, but remove the requirement that E knows f and x.

Stacked Garbling (or Stacked GC, SGC) [12,14,22] is a GC improvement that allows for efficient handling of programs with conditional branching. The technique allows the garbler to send a GC proportional only to one program execution path, not to the full computation.

SGC can implement a function f by representing f as a conditional:

$$f(x) = \begin{cases} f(0) & \text{if } x = 0 \\ \dots \\ f(N-1) & \text{if } x = N-1 \end{cases}$$

This requires care. SGC uses extra gadgets to enter/exit conditionals, and these gadgets require communication. For a conditional with n input wires, m output wires, and b branches, the parties consume $O(b^2(n+m)\kappa)$ bits of communication. Thus, using SGC to implement a switch statement over the $b = N$ branches of f leads to cost $O(Nm\kappa)$, no better than a linear scan. Indeed, evaluating a large number of very small branches is not SGC's intended application [12].

A more effective approach is to use SGC *recursively*, encoding the function as a binary tree of nested IF statements. Indeed, if G and E agree on f, they can securely compute $[\![f(x)]\!]$ this way while using only $O(n^2\kappa + nm\kappa)$ bits of communication. Each recursive call to SGC requires encoding/decoding gadgets of size (only) $O((n+m)\kappa)$. This is because we only need to "pass through" $O(n)$ choice bits to the lower levels of recursion. In total, n SGC gadgets are executed, resulting in overall quadratic in n complexity. This communication performance is surprisingly good for an unintended application of SGC.

The problem is computation. SGC achieves communication improvement at the cost of computation, and in this case the increase is significant. Nested execution of SGC over N branches consumes unacceptably high computation, scaling with $O(N^{2.389}m\kappa)$ [10]. We emphasize the limits of scaling using this technique. Consider a size $N = 2^{16}$ LUT, a case suitable for 16-bit operations and easily handled by our approach. Here, SGC will require a clearly unacceptable $> 2^{38}$ CCRH evaluations for $m = 1$ (approximately a day of computation on a modern laptop). This is less attractive than a simple $O(Nm\kappa)$ linear scan.

Our technique evaluates arbitrary LUT gates, while matching computation scaling of linear scans. As a bonus, our approach allows us to hide f from E.

Garbled Private Information Retrieval. [9] recently proposed a GC extension called *Garbled Private Information Retrieval* (GPIR). In GPIR, G and E agree on a public database. Then, the GC may privately and non-interactively query one index of the database and pass the result as input to subsequent GC gates. The technique is similar to PIR in the sense that G and E jointly play a server and the GC plays a client. [9] implements GPIR for a database with N entries each of size m while using only $\tilde{O}(\sqrt{N}m\kappa)$ bits of communication ($\tilde{O}$ includes concretely significant polylog(N) factors). We note that [9] does not include concrete evaluation or estimates of their cost.

In GPIR, G and E must agree on the database. [9] point out that this require-ment can be relaxed by instead agreeing on an *encrypted* database and requiring the GC to decrypt the query result. While this works, it requires non-black-box evaluation of cryptographic primitives, which is extremely expensive.

Our approach allows G to secretly choose the LUT. More importantly, for many sizes of database N, our approach has superior communication. We achieve low concrete constants and avoid the need for extra polylog(N) factors.

Garbled RAM. Garbled RAM (GRAM) [29] is a powerful GC extension that enables garbling of RAM programs. The technique allows G and E to repeatedly, securely, and non-interactively access an array, and it is possible to use GRAM to implement a function LUT. Recent works [15,34] dramatically improved GRAM. For an array of $N = 2^n$ elements each of size m, GRAM now requires only $O^!(nm\kappa + n^3\kappa)$ communication and computation per access, where $O^!$ includes polylog(n) factors.

Our approach is better suited to evaluating LUTs than GRAM in three ways.

First, GRAM's cost is *amortized* over $O(N)$ accesses. Hence, if a function f is needed $o(N)$ times in the execution of a program, then GRAM is the wrong approach. The first time a function table is used, the parties must immediately consume $\tilde{O}(Nm\kappa)$ communication (where $\tilde{O}$ includes polylog(N) factors), *significantly* worse than even a linear scan. This required amortization means that GRAM is particularly poorly applicable when using a variety of *different* LUTs f_i in a program – players would have to initialize a separate GRAM for each f_i.

Second, GRAM's constants remain relatively high. [15]'s technique is the best GRAM for small sizes, and for $m = 128$ it only begins to outperform trivial linear-scan-based GRAM at around $N = 512$. For smaller m, GRAM will perform far worse.

Third, known (non-trivial) GRAMs are *incompatible* with Stacked Garbling, and hence so is a GRAM-based LUT implementation. Resolving GRAM-SGC incompatibility requires hiding from the GC evaluator ORAM access patterns, likely requiring a costly solution.

Our technique has lean constants and can flexibly implement an arbitrary number of different functions in a single program. At $m = 8$ and $N = 512$, our approach outperforms linear scan communication by more than 30×. Finally, our garbled LUT is compatible with Stacked Garbling (SGC) in the sense that it can appear safely in an SGC conditional branch; formally, our garbling scheme is *strongly stackable* (see our full version).

Of course, GRAM is a powerful technology – it simply is not well suited to the LUT setting. We view GRAM and our approach as complimentary technologies.

Non-GC-Based LUTs. Lookup-table-based MPC has been considered outside of GC [5,7,21,30] in the multi-round setting. Our work brings efficient lookup tables to the important constant-round GC-based MPC.

We stress that solutions in our compositional non-interactive setting are inherently different, and harder to achieve. Indeed, in the non-interactive setting, one party's (garbler's) actions inherently cannot depend in any way on intermediate values (even on the masked intermediate values!) of the computation.

To practically motivate our interest in GC (vs interactive) LUT, we highlight the high cost of latency. Unless the program is highly parallelizable (e.g. matrix multiplication and other operations), multiplicative depth of the program circuit would incur significant costs due to latency. For example, recent experiments reported in [42] show $\approx 1600\times$ improvement by switching from a GMW-based multi-round solution to a constant-round GC-based protocol, with the primary factor behind the speed up being network latency. Of course, this is just an example, and the costs depend on network properties and the program itself.

Interestingly, the interactive techniques of [7,21] are similar to ours in that their cost comprises two components, one proportional to κ (a 1-out-of-N random OT) and one proportional to the size of a truth table. While costs are similar, the constructions themselves are completely different from ours, which is in the *much* harder setting.

[5] is the latest work addressing interactive lookup-tabled-based 2PC. Their total communication cost (in bits) is as follows: $(MT + 4)(2^n - n - 1) + 2m$, where MT denotes the cost of preprocessing a multiplication triple. In terms of computation, the technique executes $O(2^n)$ OTs in the preprocessing phase.

Using communication-efficient OT [4], the total cost is $O(2^n + m)$ bits, which does not scale with the total truth table size $2^n m$. Our communication scales with the full truth table, but our technique is non-interactive.

Private simultaneous messaging (PSM) is an MPC special case that considers several senders, each with private input, and a single referee who receives a function f of these inputs [2,8,18,19]. The original PSM construction [8] showed how to evaluate arbitrary LUTs in this setting. In their construction, which works for two senders and the referee, the senders randomize (mask) the LUT and shuffle its rows. One sender then sends to the referee a message proportional to the LUT size; the other sends a pointer to a row in the LUT and a mask. This allows the referee to decrypt (only) the single selected row, obliviously yielding the function output. [2] extends this technique to generalize to multiple senders: each sender applies a random mask to the LUT and then reveals a portion of its mask, depending on its plaintext input. This similarly allows the referee to learn (only) the right LUT row.

We have a related step in our construction: We mask the LUT and then unmask portions of it based on each (encrypted) bit of the LUT's input. We approach and solve the problem in a much more complex non-interactive composable (GC) setting. [2] works with plaintext input and output, complicating composition. Further, *each* [2]'s party communicates proportionally to LUT size. It is unclear how to port the [8] and [2] approach to the non-interactive GC setting without incurring factor-κ blow-up, resulting in performance similar to classical Yao (Linear Scan in Table 1).

[44]'s Lower Bound. [44] proved a lower bound on the communication needed per GC AND gate. They define *linear* garbling schemes and show that any linear scheme *must* use at least 2κ bits per AND gate. While [40] recently circumvented this lower bound by working outside the linear definition and achieved $\approx 1.5\kappa$ bits per AND gate, the [44] lower bound still seems to imply intense difficulty in substantially improving GC gates.

Our work circumvents the [44] lower bound in two ways. First, we work with larger gates, not just two-input one-output AND gates. Second, we leverage the ability of G to send to E a cleartext truth table; this sending of a truth table is outside [44]'s definition of linearity. We believe that our work demonstrates that while basic GC Boolean gates are hard to improve, opportunities may remain to significantly improve GC overall.

3 Preliminaries

3.1 Notation and Assumptions

- κ denotes the computational security parameter (*e.g.*, 128).
- G is the GC garbler. We refer to G by he/him.
- E is the GC evaluator. We refer to E by she/her.
- We denote by $\langle\langle x, y \rangle\rangle$ a pair of values where G holds x and E holds y.
- We work with extensively with bit vectors interpreted as arrays:

- If $a \in \{0,1\}^n$ is a vector, we denote the ith entry of a by $a[i]$.
- We use zero-based indexing. An array $a \in \{0,1\}^n$ is the sequence of elements $(a[0], ..., a[n-1])$.
- $a[i : j]$ denotes the sub-array of elements $(a[i], ..., a[j-1])$.
- For an array $a \in \{0,1\}^n$, $a[0]$ is the least significant bit and $a[n-1]$ is the most significant bit.

- $[x]$ (without any prefix) denotes the set $\{0, 1, ..., x-1\}$.
- N is the number of rows in the lookup table.
- n is the number of bits needed to index a LUT, i.e., $n = \lceil \log_2 N \rceil$.
- m is the number of the LUT's columns, equal to the number of output bits.
- $\mathcal{H}(a)$ is the one-hot vector encoding of a (cf. Definition 4).
- $\mathcal{T}(f)$ is the truth table of a function f (cf. Definition 5).
- H is a circular correlation robust hash function (CCRH, Definition 1).
- v denotes a nonce, usually an argument to H. G and E publicly agree on the value of each nonce.
- c_κ denotes the computational cost of evaluating H.

We assume a circular correlation robust hash function H [6]. We use the following definition, given by [44]:

Definition 1 (Circular Correlation Robustness). *Let H be a function. We define two oracles:*

- $circ_\Delta(i, x, b) \triangleq H(x \oplus \Delta, i) \oplus b\Delta$ *where* $\Delta \in 1\{0,1\}^{\kappa-1}$.
- $\mathcal{R}(i, x, b)$ *is a random function with κ-bit output.*

A sequence of oracle queries (i, x, b) is legal *when the same value (x, i) is never queried with different values of b. H is circular correlation robust if for all polytime adversaries $\mathcal{A}$:*

$$\left| \Pr_\Delta \left[\mathcal{A}^{circ_\Delta}(1^\kappa) = 1 \right] - \Pr_\mathcal{R} \left[\mathcal{A}^\mathcal{R}(1^\kappa) = 1 \right] \right| \text{ is negligible.}$$

3.2   Garbled Sharing

We build on Free XOR garbling [25]. For each bit that appears on a GC wire, we arrange that G and E hold a kind of sharing called a *garbled sharing*, a notation introduced in [13]. G's share contains a pair of length-κ labels. One label corresponds to a logical zero, the other to a logical one. Meanwhile, E's share contains a specific label from G's pair. Thus, the two shares together specify the value on the wire. More precisely:

Definition 2 (Garbled Sharing [13]). *Let $a \in \{0,1\}$ be a bit. Let $A \in \{0,1\}^\kappa$ be a bitstring. We say that the pair $\langle\langle A, A \oplus a\Delta \rangle\rangle$ is a garbled sharing of a over (usually implicit) $\Delta \in 1\{0,1\}^{\kappa-1}$. I.e., Δ is uniform except that its least significant bit is 1. We denote a garbled sharing of a by writing $[\![a]\!]$:*

$$[\![a]\!] \triangleq \langle\langle A, A \oplus a\Delta \rangle\rangle$$

Note that in our definition, the zero label is the bitstring A, whereas the one label is the bitstring $A \oplus \Delta$ where Δ is global to the circuit. As defined and used in this work, garbled sharing $[\![a]\!]$ is Free XOR-specific.

Garbled Arrays. We generalize from sharings of bits to sharings of arrays. Let $a \in \{0,1\}^n$ be an array. We use $[\![a]\!]$ to denote the bit-by-bit encoding of a:

$$[\![a]\!] \triangleq ([\![a[0]\!]\!], ..., [\![a[n-1]\!]\!])$$

Free XOR. Garbled sharings are XOR-homomorphic [25]:

$$[\![a]\!] \oplus [\![b]\!] = [\![a \oplus b]\!] \qquad \text{Definition 2}$$

Injecting G's Secrets. Garbled sharings allow G to easily inject bits into the circuit. Namely, let $a \in \{0,1\}$ be a bit chosen by G. To inject his input, the parties simply use the following pair:

$$\langle\!\langle a\Delta, 0 \rangle\!\rangle = [\![a]\!] \qquad \text{Definition 2}$$

This capability is used not only for G's top-level input, but also to provide auxiliary bits needed for our construction.

Revealing Bits to E. At times, it is useful for the GC to reveal particular wire values to E (while taking care to preserve input privacy). It is easy to decrypt a particular wire value to E. Note that Definition 2 enforces that the least significant bit of Δ is a one. To reveal the cleartext value of a sharing $[\![a]\!] = \langle\!\langle A, A \oplus a\Delta \rangle\!\rangle$, G can send to E the least significant bit of his garbled share $\mathsf{lsb}(A)$. Then, E computes:

$$\mathsf{lsb}(A) \oplus \mathsf{lsb}(A \oplus a\Delta) = \mathsf{lsb}(A) \oplus \mathsf{lsb}(A) \oplus a \cdot \mathsf{lsb}(\Delta) = a$$

Revealing a bit to E requires only one bit of communication.

3.3   Garbling Schemes

We formalize our approach as a *garbling scheme* [3].

Definition 3 (Garbling Scheme [3]). *A garbling scheme is a tuple of algorithms (Gb, Ev, En, De) that specify how to garble/evaluate a circuit:*

- $Gb(1^\kappa, \mathcal{C}) \to (\mathcal{M}, e, d)$ *garbles circuits. It takes as input the security parameter κ and a circuit description $\mathcal{C}$. The procedure outputs garbled circuit material $\mathcal{M}$ as well as two strings e and d that respectively contain information needed to encode inputs and decode outputs.*
- $En(e, x) \to X$ *encodes the party inputs. It takes as input the encoding string e and a cleartext input $x \in \{0,1\}^n$ and outputs E's input wire labels X.*
- $Ev(\mathcal{M}, X) \to Y$ *evaluates GCs. It takes as input material $\mathcal{M}$ and wire labels X and outputs wire labels Y.*
- $De(d, Y) \to y$ *decodes circuit outputs. It takes as input the output decoding string d and E's output wire labels Y. The procedure outputs cleartext $y \in \{0,1\}^m$. The procedure may also output $\perp$ to indicate failure.*

A garbling scheme factors circuit evaluation $\mathcal{C}(x)$ into multiple steps. Namely, for all $\mathcal{C}$ and x, [3] insist that the following correctness condition holds:

$$De(d, Ev(\mathcal{M}, En(e, x))) = \mathcal{C}(x) \qquad \text{where } (\mathcal{M}, e, d) \leftarrow Gb(1^\kappa, \mathcal{C})$$

The crucial [3] security property is *obliviousness*, which states that the pair of material and input labels $(\mathcal{M}, X)$ can be simulated. Obliviousness is the basis[1] for GC-based protocols, because it implies that an evaluator who views the GC cannot deduce anything about the garbler's input.

We formalize our garbling scheme in Sect. 5. We provide definitions for garbling scheme properties and prove that our scheme satisfies them in Sect. 7.

Projectivity. [3]'s framework allows for a variety of schemes that support non-Boolean encoded values, but our scheme only handles Boolean wires. Formally, our scheme is *projective* [3], which means that each circuit wire is associated with two labels that respectively encode logical 0/logical 1. Projective schemes have standard and simple definitions for En and De.

From Schemes to Protocols. Garbling schemes have been used as the basis for protocols in the semi-honest, malicious, covert, and PVC models [3,16,17,26,28]. Hence, our construction implies 2PC protocols in these models.

3.4   One-Hot Garbling

One-Hot Garbling [13] is a recent GC improvement that goes beyond Boolean gate evaluation. The technique allows *privacy-free* (i.e. with E learning the accessed index) GC LUTs where communication is logarithmic in the number of LUT rows N. The technique reduces communication consumption via so-called *garbled one-hot encodings*. We build on top of one-hot garbling to achieve efficient *privacy-preserving* GC LUT.

[13] *Review.* It is useful to construct *one-hot* encodings inside the GC:

Definition 4 (One-Hot Encoding). *Let $x \in \{0,1\}^n$ be a bitstring. The one-hot encoding of x is a length-2^n bitstring denoted $\mathcal{H}(x)$ that is zero everywhere, except at index x, where it is one:*

$$\mathcal{H}(x)[i] \triangleq \begin{cases} 1 & \text{if } i = x \\ 0 & \text{otherwise} \end{cases}$$

Consider the case where the parties hold an n-bit share $[\![x]\!]$ and where E knows x in the clear. [13]'s construction allows E to efficiently compute a length-2^n garbled vector $[\![\mathcal{H}(x)]\!]$. We list the interface to [13]'s procedure in Fig. 1.

---

[1] [3] also defines *privacy* and *authenticity*. While these security properties are technically incomparable with obliviousness, for most GC schemes (including ours) they follow easily from obliviousness. We prove that our scheme satisfies all three properties in Sect. 7.

- PARAMETERS: Parties agree on input size n
- INPUT:
  - Parties input a sharing $[\![x]\!]$ where $x \in \{0,1\}^n$.
  - E inputs x.
- OUTPUT:
  - Parties output a sharing $\langle\!\langle X_G, X_E \rangle\!\rangle = [\![\mathcal{H}(x)]\!]$ such that for each index i:

$$X_E[i] = \begin{cases} X_G[i] & \text{if } i \neq x \\ X_G[i] \oplus \Delta & \text{otherwise} \end{cases}$$

- COMMUNICATION: G sends to E $(2n-1)\kappa$ bits.
- COMPUTATION: Each party uses $O(2^n c_\kappa)$ computation.

Fig. 1. The interface to the key One-Hot Garbling [13] operation. The operation enables the parties to efficiently compute $[\![x]\!] \mapsto [\![\mathcal{H}(x)]\!]$. Note that E must know x in the clear. Our construction builds on this operation.

[13] leverage their new procedure in conjunction with the fact that one-hot encodings are, in a sense, fully homomorphic. Given a one-hot encoding $\mathcal{H}(x)$, we can compute $f(x)$ via *a sequence of XORs alone*. More precisely, we can multiply the one-hot vector with f's truth table:

Definition 5 (Truth Table). *Let $f : \{0,1\}^n \to \{0,1\}^m$ be an arbitrary function. The* truth table *for f, denoted $\mathcal{T}(f)$, is a $2^n \times m$ matrix where:*

$$\mathcal{T}(f)[i][j] = f(i)[j]$$

[13] exploits the following simple but crucial fact:

Lemma 1. *Let $f : \{0,1\}^n \to \{0,1\}^m$ be an arbitrary function and let $x \in \{0,1\}^n$ be a bitstring:*

$$\mathcal{T}(f)^\mathsf{T} \cdot \mathcal{H}(x) = f(x)$$

Proof. Intuitively, the one-hot encoding $\mathcal{H}(x)$ "selects" row x of the truth table. More precisely, consider the i-th bit of $\mathcal{T}(f)^\mathsf{T} \cdot \mathcal{H}(x)$:

$$\begin{aligned}
&(\mathcal{T}(f)^\mathsf{T} \cdot \mathcal{H}(x))[i] && \\
&= \bigoplus\nolimits_j \mathcal{T}(f)^\mathsf{T}[i][j] \cdot \mathcal{H}(x)[j] && \text{Definition Matrix Mult.} \\
&= \bigoplus\nolimits_j \mathcal{T}(f)[j][i] \cdot \mathcal{H}(x)[j] && \text{Definition Matrix Transpose} \\
&= \mathcal{T}(f)[x][i] && \text{Definition 4} \\
&= f(x)[i] && \text{Definition 5}
\end{aligned}$$

Since this holds for each output bit i, we have $\mathcal{T}(f)^\mathsf{T} \cdot \mathcal{H}(x) = f(x)$ $\qquad\square$

The upshot of Lemma 1 is that if the parties hold $[\![x]\!]$ and if E knows x, then the parties can compute $[\![\mathcal{H}(x)]\!]$ via Fig. 1, then compute:

$$\mathcal{T}(f)^\mathsf{T} \cdot [\![\mathcal{H}(x)]\!] = [\![f(x)]\!]$$

This matrix multiplication is well-defined thanks to Free XOR (see Sect. 3.2). In other words, if the parties can afford to write out the long encoding $[\![\mathcal{H}(x)]\!]$, then they can efficiently compute $[\![f(x)]\!]$ for *any* function f and without using any additional communication. However, the technique only works if E knows the one-hot active location x.

We build on top of basic one-hot garbling to evaluate arbitrary functions f even when E does not know the function's argument and even when she does not know f.

One Bit Output Special Case. In Sect. 4, we introduce our technique at a high level. There, we for simplicity specialize to functions with only one bit of output. This allows us to consider the following corollary of Lemma 1:

Corollary 1. *Let* $f : \{0,1\}^n \to \{0,1\}$ *be an arbitrary function and* $x \in \{0,1\}^n$ *be a bitstring:*

$$\langle \mathcal{T}(f) \cdot \mathcal{H}(x) \rangle = f(x)$$

Above, $\langle x \cdot y \rangle$ denotes the inner product of vectors x and y. By Corollary 1 and Free XOR, the following holds for any $f : \{0,1\}^n \to \{0,1\}$:

$$\langle \mathcal{T}(f) \cdot [\![\mathcal{H}(x)]\!] \rangle = [\![f(x)]\!]$$

In our formal construction (see Sect. 5), we consider the general case of functions with m bits of output.

4 Technical Overview

In this section, we present a detailed overview of our construction. We proceed in two steps. First, Sect. 4.1 demonstrates a reduction from securely computing an arbitrary function f to computing a *random* function r. Evaluating random functions often helps with evaluation of general functions (e.g., [1,8,20] and many more). Second, Sect. 4.2 introduces our **main contribution** – an efficient procedure for evaluating a random function inside GC.

For simplicity, in this section we introduce our construction for a function $f : \{0,1\}^n \to \{0,1\}$ with only one bit of output. Our formal construction (see Sect. 5) generalizes to LUTs with m bits of output.

4.1 Reducing Lookup Tables to Random Function Evaluation

Our starting point is the one-hot garbling technique [13] (see Sect. 3.4). Recall that if the parties hold $[\![a]\!]$ and if E knows a, then Fig. 1 can be leveraged to evaluate an arbitrary function f:

$$\langle \mathcal{T}(f) \cdot [\![\mathcal{H}(a)]\!] \rangle = [\![f(a)]\!]$$

Thus, one-hot garbling directly enables *privacy-free LUTs*. Our scheme builds on top of these privacy-free LUTs to implement *privacy-preserving* garbled

LUTs. Namely, the looked up index remains hidden from E and, as a bonus, the content of the table can be chosen by G and hidden from E. To achieve this, we carefully introduce a mask on the index and a mask on the table itself. The mask on the table is generated from seeds in a way that uses low communication.

Masking a. Privacy-free LUTs leak the evaluation point a to E. As a starting point, we add a uniform mask α to a. (In fact, we use the least significant bit of G's share of $[\![a]\!]$ as α; this allows us to cleanly introduce a mask without sending extra bits). Rather than computing $\mathcal{H}(a)$, we instead compute $\mathcal{H}(a \oplus \alpha)$ where α is a uniform mask. However, there remains a problem in the *usage* of this vector. We cannot directly multiply $\mathcal{H}(a \oplus \alpha)$ by a truth table, because our evaluation point a is no longer the distinguished location of the one-hot vector. As a first attempt, the parties could try agreeing on the following function:

$$\mathrm{bad}(x) \triangleq f(x \oplus \alpha)$$

Then, the parties could compute:

$$\langle \mathcal{T}(\mathrm{bad}) \cdot [\![\mathcal{H}(a \oplus \alpha)]\!]\rangle = [\![\mathrm{bad}(a \oplus \alpha)]\!] = [\![f(a)]\!]$$

While correct, this is insecure. To compute her share, E must *know* bad, and this leaks α, and thus a.

Masking the LUT. Suppose we can efficiently compute inside the GC a *uniformly random* function $r : \{0,1\}^n \to \{0,1\}$ whose value is known to G but unknown to E; we will show how to do this shortly. We define a new function f':

$$f'(x) \triangleq f(x \oplus \alpha) \oplus r(x)$$

Now, G can safely send $\mathcal{T}(f')$ to E: this table leaks nothing about f because the table is masked by r. Note, this transmission scales linearly with $N = 2^n$, but is *independent* of the computational security parameter κ: G sends E the full *cleartext* truth table.

The GC now conveys to E the cleartext value $x \triangleq a \oplus \alpha$. Again, suppose for now that the parties can somehow compute $[\![r(x)]\!]$; we discuss this core contribution in Sect. 4.2. The parties compute:

$$
\begin{aligned}
&\langle \mathcal{T}(f') \cdot [\![\mathcal{H}(x)]\!]\rangle \oplus [\![r(x)]\!] \\
={}& \langle \mathcal{T}(f') \cdot [\![\mathcal{H}(a \oplus \alpha)]\!]\rangle \oplus [\![r(a \oplus \alpha)]\!] && \text{Definition } x \\
={}& [\![f'(a \oplus \alpha)]\!] \oplus [\![r(a \oplus \alpha)]\!] && \text{Corollary 1} \\
={}& [\![f((a \oplus \alpha) \oplus \alpha) \oplus r(a \oplus \alpha)]\!] \oplus [\![r(a \oplus \alpha)]\!] && \text{Definition } f' \\
={}& [\![f(a)]\!]
\end{aligned}
$$

This computation hides a. E observes the point $a \oplus \alpha$, but α masks a. Moreover, the function r masks the truth table for f and ensures that E cannot use the truth table to deduce a.

Thus, if we can securely evaluate $[\![r(x)]\!]$, then we can securely evaluate $[\![f(a)]\!]$.

4.2 Evaluating a Uniformly Random Function $[\![r(x)]\!]$

Suppose that the parties hold both $[\![x]\!]$ and $[\![\mathcal{H}(x)]\!]$; the computation of one-hot encoding $[\![\mathcal{H}(x)]\!]$ was already discussed in Sect. 4.1. Our goal is to build a procedure that cheaply implements the following:

$$[\![x]\!], [\![\mathcal{H}(x)]\!] \mapsto [\![r(x)]\!]$$

where $r : \{0,1\}^n \to \{0,1\}$ is uniformly random and hidden from E.

As we will see, we will construct r from a (logarithmic in N) number of "half-hidden" uniform functions.

Half-Hidden Uniform Functions. Our crucial insight is that it is possible to efficiently evaluate a uniformly random function $[\![r_0(x)]\!]$ where $r_0 : \{0,1\}^n \to \{0,1\}$ such that E learns only *half* of the truth table for r_0. We later show how to use multiple such functions to account for the leaked half.

Before starting, we establish useful notation. Let $\langle\!\langle X_G, X_E \rangle\!\rangle = [\![\mathcal{H}(x)]\!]$ be G and E's shares of the garbled one-hot vector. Define r_0's truth table $R_0 \triangleq \mathcal{T}(r_0)$. We will be working extensively with the left and right halves of vectors, so for convenience, we set the following (recall, $A[i : j] = (A[i], ..., A[j-1])$):

$$R_0^\ell \triangleq R_0[0 : N/2] \qquad R_0^r \triangleq R_0[N/2 : N]$$
$$X_G^\ell \triangleq X_G[0 : N/2] \qquad X_G^r \triangleq X_G[N/2 : N]$$
$$X_E^\ell \triangleq X_E[0 : N/2] \qquad X_E^r \triangleq X_E[N/2 : N]$$
$$\mathcal{H}(x)^\ell \triangleq \mathcal{H}(x)[0 : N/2] \qquad \mathcal{H}(x)^r \triangleq \mathcal{H}(x)[N/2 : N]$$

Now, consider $[\![x[n-1]]\!]$, the most significant bit of $[\![x]\!]$, and recall that E's share of this bit is one of two possible labels: Y or $Y \oplus \Delta$, where Y is G's share of the bit. G *defines* the function r_0 by applying a hash function H to each of these labels (appropriately setting length of H's output):

$$R_0^\ell \triangleq H(v_R, Y) \qquad R_0^r \triangleq H(v_R, Y \oplus \Delta)$$

Here, v_R is a fresh nonce. If $x[n-1] = 0$, then E holds Y, so she can locally compute the left half of the truth table $H(v_R, Y) = R_0^\ell$; else she can compute the right half R_0^r. For sake of example, suppose that $x[n-1]$ is zero, so E learns the left half of the table; the one case is symmetric.

Recall that if E knew the *entire* truth table for r_0, then since the parties hold $[\![\mathcal{H}(x)]\!]$, they could compute:

$$\langle R_0 \cdot [\![\mathcal{H}(x)]\!] \rangle = \langle \mathcal{T}(r_0) \cdot [\![\mathcal{H}(x)]\!] \rangle = [\![r_0(x)]\!]$$

However, as E only knows the first half of the table, she can only compute (her share of the garbling of) *half* of the summands in the above inner-product:

$$\langle R_0^\ell \cdot X_E^\ell \rangle$$

E cannot directly compute the second "half" $\langle R_0^r \cdot X_E^r \rangle$, but notice that the corresponding indices of the one-hot encoding $\mathcal{H}(x)^r$ all hold zeros; this is guaranteed by the fact that the single one-hot active position is in the range 0 to $N/2$ when $x[n-1] = 0$. Thus in our example, $X_G^r = X_E^r$.

G does not know which half of the table E is missing, but he *does* know the encoding of zero for each index of the one-hot vector, so he can precompute both possible sums that E could be missing. He encrypts these halves such that E can decrypt only her missing half:

$$H(v_{\text{row}}, Y \oplus \Delta) \oplus \langle R_0^\ell \cdot X_G^\ell \rangle \oplus Z \qquad H(v_{\text{row}}, Y) \oplus \langle R_0^r \cdot X_G^r \rangle \oplus Z$$

Above, v_{row} is a fresh nonce and $Z \in \{0,1\}^\kappa$ is a uniform string. G sends these two ciphertexts to E. (In fact, we can remove one of these two ciphertexts via the classic garbled row reduction technique [31].) In our example, E decrypts the second row and adds the result to the sum she already computed:

$$\begin{aligned} &\langle R_0^\ell \cdot X_E^\ell \rangle \oplus \langle R_0^r \cdot X_G^r \rangle \oplus Z \\ =\ &\langle R_0^\ell \cdot X_E^\ell \rangle \oplus \langle R_0^r \cdot X_E^r \rangle \oplus Z \qquad x[n-1] = 0 \implies X_G^r = X_E^r \\ =\ &\langle R_0 \cdot X_E \rangle \oplus Z \\ =\ &\langle \mathcal{T}(r_0) \cdot X_E \rangle \oplus Z \qquad\qquad\qquad\qquad \text{Definition } R_0 \end{aligned}$$

Meanwhile, G locally computes $\langle \mathcal{T}(r_0) \cdot X_G \rangle \oplus Z$, matching E's share. Thus, the parties hold:

$$\begin{aligned} &\langle\!\langle\!\langle \mathcal{T}(r_0) \cdot X_G \rangle \oplus Z, \langle \mathcal{T}(r_0) \cdot X_E \rangle \oplus Z \rangle\!\rangle \\ =\ &[\![\langle \mathcal{T}(r_0) \cdot \mathcal{H}(x) \rangle]\!] \qquad\qquad\qquad\qquad \langle\!\langle X_G, X_E \rangle\!\rangle = [\![\mathcal{H}(x)]\!] \\ =\ &[\![r_0(x)]\!] \qquad\qquad\qquad\qquad\qquad\qquad\quad \text{Corollary 1} \end{aligned}$$

Therefore, G and E can compute $[\![r_0(x)]\!]$ while leaking only half of r_0's function table to E and while consuming only κ bits of communication. The key idea was to reveal to E one half of the truth table, allowing her to apply that half via a linear map, and G accounts for the second hidden half by sending a ciphertext.

Masking the Opened Half via Recursion. We showed how to compute $[\![r_0(x)]\!]$ where E knows the half of r_0's truth table containing index x. Recall our goal is to evaluate $[\![r(x)]\!]$ where r is *fully* hidden from E. Observe that we can construct and evaluate a new hidden uniform function $r' : \{0,1\}^{n-1} \to \{0,1\}$ and define

$$r(x) \triangleq r_0(x) \oplus r'(x[0 : n-1])$$

If r' is hidden from E, then so is r: we leaked $N/2$ bits of r_0's truth table, and the $N/2$ bits in $\mathcal{T}(r')$ (literally) cover those revealed bits. Indeed, each index of r is masked either by (1) the hidden parts of r_0 or (2) the function r'. Thus, our new task is to evaluate a secret uniform function $[\![r'(x[0 : n-1])]\!]$, which would accomplish our goal.

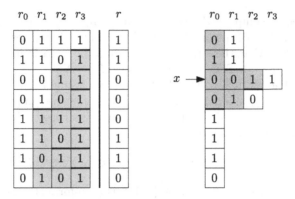

Fig. 2. G recursively composes the uniform function $r : \{0,1\}^n \rightarrow \{0,1\}$ from the XOR of $n+1$ uniform functions $r_i : \{0,1\}^{n-i} \rightarrow \{0,1\}$ (see left). We depict an example where $n = 3/N = 8$. Suppose that the evaluation point x is 2. Our construction reveals to E the half of each function $r_{i<n}$ that holds index x (see right; E learns the entries depicted in green and not the entries depicted in white). r_n is a function of zero bits and so G represents the function by injecting a secret uniform bit. Ultimately, E learns nothing about r because in each row there is at least one uniform bit that is XORed in and that she does not know. (Color figure online)

But this task is just a smaller version of the same problem we are already trying to solve! Indeed, we are designing a procedure to map $[\![x]\!], [\![\mathcal{H}(x)]\!] \rightarrow [\![r(x)]\!]$, and hence we can solve the problem by simply recursively computing:

$$[\![x[0 : n-1]]\!], [\![\mathcal{H}(x[0 : n-1])]\!] \mapsto [\![r'(x[0 : n-1])]\!]$$

We terminate the recursion when the parties need evaluate a uniform function with 0 bits of input; in this base case, G simply injects a uniform bit.

The needed one-hot encoding $[\![\mathcal{H}(x[0 : n-1])]\!]$ can be computed from $[\![\mathcal{H}(x)]\!]$ via simple linear operations alone. Namely, for each index of the output vector, the parties simply XOR two corresponding indices from the input vector:

$$[\![\mathcal{H}(x[0 : n-1])]\!] = [\![\mathcal{H}(x)]\!][0 : N/2] \oplus [\![\mathcal{H}(x)]\!][N/2 : N]$$

Thus, we can indeed efficiently apply our procedure recursively.

Unwinding the Recursion. It is instructive to consider the direct, non-recursive definition of r. Unwinding the recursion, we see:

$$r(x) \triangleq \bigoplus_{i=0}^{n} r_i(x[0 : n-i])$$

Each function r_i is a uniform function chosen by the hash function H, and E views half of the truth table of each $r_{i<n}$. At the base case, the function r_n takes no bits of input; as output, G injects a uniform bit which is trivially hidden from E. Together, the functions r_i hide r from E; see Fig. 2 for an example.

- PARAMETERS: Parties agree on input size n and output size m.
- INPUT:
    - G inputs a function $f : \{0,1\}^n \to \{0,1\}^m$.
    - Parties input a shared function input $[\![a]\!]$ where $a \in \{0,1\}^n$.
- OUTPUT: Parties output a sharing $[\![f(a)]\!]$.
- COMMUNICATION : G sends to E $(2n-1)\kappa + nm\kappa + 2^n m$ bits.
- COMPUTATION: Parties use $O(2^n c_\kappa + 2^n m\kappa + nmc_\kappa + 2^n mc_\kappa/\kappa)$ computation.
- PROCEDURE:
    - Let $\langle\!\langle A, A \oplus a\Delta \rangle\!\rangle = [\![a]\!]$.
    - G computes $\alpha \triangleq \mathsf{lsb}(A)$. Let $x = a \oplus \alpha$. E computes:

$$\mathsf{lsb}(A \oplus a\Delta) = \mathsf{lsb}(A) \oplus a \cdot \mathsf{lsb}(\Delta) = \alpha \oplus a = x$$

    - G injects $\langle\!\langle \alpha\Delta, 0 \rangle\!\rangle = [\![\alpha]\!]$ as input. Parties compute $[\![x]\!] = [\![a]\!] \oplus [\![\alpha]\!]$.
    - Parties use one-hot garbling (Figure 1) to compute $[\![\mathcal{H}(x)]\!]$.
    - Parties use Figure 5 to compute $[\![r(x)]\!]$ where $r : \{0,1\}^n \to \{0,1\}^m$ is a uniformly random function. As a side-effect, G now holds r.
    - Let f' be a function that computes the following:

$$f'(x) \triangleq f(x \oplus \alpha) \oplus r(x)$$

    - G computes the truth table $\mathcal{T}(f')$ for f' and sends $\mathcal{T}(f')$ to E.
    - Parties compute and output:

$$
\begin{aligned}
&(\mathcal{T}(f')^{\mathsf{T}} \cdot [\![\mathcal{H}(x)]\!]) \oplus [\![r(x)]\!] && \\
&= [\![f'(x)]\!] \oplus [\![r(x)]\!] && \text{Lemma 1} \\
&= [\![f'(a \oplus \alpha)]\!] \oplus [\![r(a \oplus \alpha)]\!] && \text{Definition } x \\
&= [\![f((a \oplus \alpha) \oplus \alpha) \oplus r(a \oplus \alpha)]\!] \oplus [\![r(a \oplus \alpha)]\!] && \text{Definition } f' \\
&= [\![f(a)]\!] &&
\end{aligned}
$$

Fig. 3. Garbled LUT Evaluation. We reduce the evaluation $[\![f(a)]\!]$ for arbitrary f to the evaluation $[\![r(a \oplus \alpha)]\!]$ for random r (see Fig. 4).

In sum, our approach allows G and E to efficiently compute a uniform function r from a sequence of half-hidden uniform functions r_i. We use r to hide the function f, which in turn allows the parties to securely compute $[\![f(a)]\!]$.

5 Approach

In this section, we formalize our approach as a *garbling scheme* (Definition 3).

On the Function Output Length m. For readability, we presented our technical overview for function output length $m = 1$. There are efficiency gains from batching over m bits of output rather than applying m separate LUTs. Specifically, we amortize costs associated with constructing one-hot encodings across the m output bits. Our formal construction is presented for general m. Consequently, one notable change in this section as compared to Sect. 4 is that we use matrix

- PARAMETERS: Parties agree on input size n and output size m.
- INPUT:
  - Parties input a sharing $[\![x]\!]$ where $x \in \{0,1\}^n$.
  - Parties input a shared one-hot vector $[\![\mathcal{H}(x)]\!]$.
  - E inputs x.
- OUTPUT:
  - G outputs a function $r : \{0,1\}^n \to \{0,1\}^m$ that has a uniform truth table.
  - Parties output a sharing $[\![r(x)]\!]$.
- COMMUNICATION: G sends to E $nm\kappa$ bits.
- COMPUTATION: Each party uses $O(2^n m\kappa + nmc_\kappa + 2^n mc_\kappa/\kappa)$ computation.
- PROCEDURE:
  - If $n = 0$:
    * G samples uniform $s \in_\$ \{0,1\}^m$ as the output of $r : \emptyset \to \{0,1\}^m$.
    * Parties output $[\![r(x)]\!] = \langle\!\langle s\Delta, 0 \rangle\!\rangle$ and halt.
  - Parties evaluate a half-hidden uniform function $[\![\hat{r}(x)]\!]$ (Figure 5), where $\hat{r} \in \{0,1\}^n \to \{0,1\}^m$. G learns $\hat{r}$ during evaluation. As a side effect, E learns "half" of $\hat{r}$.
  - Parties evaluate another uniform function $[\![r'(x[0 : n-1])]\!]$ by recursively invoking this procedure, where $r' \in \{0,1\}^{n-1} \to \{0,1\}^m$, with the following specification:
    * Parties agree on input size $n-1$ and output size m.
    * Parties input $[\![x[0 : n-1]]\!]$.
    * Parties input $[\![\mathcal{H}(x[0 : n-1])]\!] = [\![\mathcal{H}(x)]\!][0:2^{n-1}] \oplus [\![\mathcal{H}(x)]\!][2^{n-1}:2^n]$.
    * E inputs $x[0 : n-1]$.
    * Parties receive $[\![r'(x[0 : n-1])]\!]$, and G learns r'.
  - G computes and outputs:

$$\mathcal{T}(r) \triangleq \mathcal{T}(\hat{r}) \oplus (\mathcal{T}(r')\|\mathcal{T}(r'))$$

    The concatenation $\mathcal{T}(r')\|\mathcal{T}(r')$ is along the rows.
  - Parties compute and output:

$$[\![r(x)]\!] \triangleq [\![\hat{r}(x)]\!] \oplus [\![r'(x[0 : n-1])]\!]$$

Fig. 4. The core of our approach allows G and E to efficiently evaluate a uniformly random function r such that E does not know r. We compose r from n "half-hidden" uniform functions $\hat{r}$ (see Fig. 5). For each function $\hat{r}$, E learns half of the corresponding truth table, but these tables are XORed together in such a way that E learns nothing about r.

products (Lemma 1) rather than inner products (Corollary 1) to apply truth tables to one-hot encodings.

On Garbled Sharing Notation. We present our construction using the language of garbled sharing (Definition 2), as was first done by [13]. We find this notation simple and clear, as it allows to simultaneously formally discuss garbling, evaluation, and wire value encoding/sharing. Formally, each of our figures presents *two* procedures, one executed by G and one executed by E. Our figures *never* specify that E sends a message to G. When we write that G sends a message to

- INPUT:
  - Parties input a shared one-hot vector $[\![\mathcal{H}(x)]\!]$ and a sharing $[\![x]\!]$, where $x \in \{0,1\}^n$.
  - E inputs x.
- OUTPUT:
  - G outputs function $\hat{r} : \{0,1\}^n \to \{0,1\}^m$ with uniform truth table $\mathcal{T}(\hat{r})$.
  - E outputs $\mathcal{T}(\hat{r})[0 : 2^{n-1}]$ if $x[n-1]$ is 1; else $\mathcal{T}(\hat{r})[2^{n-1} : 2^n]$.
  - Parties output a sharing $[\![\hat{r}(x)]\!]$.
- COMMUNICATION: G sends to E $m\kappa$ bits.
- COMPUTATION: Each party uses $O(2^n m\kappa + mc_\kappa + 2^n mc_\kappa/\kappa)$ computation.
- PROCEDURE:
  - Let $\langle\!\langle Y, Y \oplus x[n-1]\Delta \rangle\!\rangle = [\![x[n-1]]\!]$.
  - Let $\langle\!\langle X_G, X_E \rangle\!\rangle = [\![\mathcal{H}(x)]\!]$.
  - $\hat{r} : \{0,1\}^n \to \{0,1\}^m$ is a (not-yet-defined) uniform function and $\hat{R} \triangleq \mathcal{T}(\hat{r})$.
  - We define the left and right halves of vectors:

$$\hat{R}^\ell \triangleq \hat{R}[0 : 2^{n-1}] \qquad \hat{R}^r \triangleq \hat{R}[2^{n-1} : 2^n]$$
$$X_G^\ell \triangleq X_G[0 : 2^{n-1}] \qquad X_G^r \triangleq X_G[2^{n-1} : 2^n]$$
$$X_E^\ell \triangleq X_E[0 : 2^{n-1}] \qquad X_E^r \triangleq X_E[2^{n-1} : 2^n]$$
$$\mathcal{H}(x)^\ell \triangleq \mathcal{H}(x)[0 : 2^{n-1}] \qquad \mathcal{H}(x)^r \triangleq \mathcal{H}(x)[2^{n-1} : 2^n]$$

  - G defines $\hat{r}$ by hashing labels Y and $Y \oplus \Delta$:

$$\hat{R}^\ell \triangleq H(v_{\hat{r}}, Y) \qquad\qquad \hat{R}^r \triangleq H(v_{\hat{r}}, Y \oplus \Delta)$$

  - G defines the following two length-$m\kappa$ strings (row reduction):

$$Z \triangleq H(v_{\mathsf{row}}, Y) \oplus ((\hat{R}^r)^\intercal \cdot X_G^r) \qquad \mathsf{row} \triangleq H(v_{\mathsf{row}}, Y \oplus \Delta) \oplus ((\hat{R}^\ell)^\intercal \cdot X_G^\ell) \oplus Z$$

  - G sends row to E and sets his output share $(\mathcal{T}(\hat{r}))^\intercal \cdot X_G \oplus Z$.
  - E computes:

$$
\begin{cases}
(H(v_{\hat{r}}, Y)^\intercal \cdot X_E^\ell) \oplus H(v_{\mathsf{row}}, Y) & \text{if } x[n-1] = 0 \\
(H(v_{\hat{r}}, Y \oplus \Delta)^\intercal \cdot X_E^\ell) \oplus H(v_{\mathsf{row}}, Y \oplus \Delta) \oplus \mathsf{row} & \text{otherwise}
\end{cases}
$$

$$
=
\begin{cases}
((\hat{R}^\ell)^\intercal \cdot X_E^\ell) \oplus (((\hat{R}^r)^\intercal \cdot X_G^r) \oplus Z) & \text{if } x[n-1] = 0 \\
((\hat{R}^r)^\intercal \cdot X_E^\ell) \oplus (((\hat{R}^\ell)^\intercal \cdot X_G^\ell) \oplus Z) & \text{otherwise}
\end{cases}
$$

$$
=
\begin{cases}
((\hat{R}^\ell)^\intercal \cdot X_E^\ell) \oplus (\hat{R}^r)^\intercal \cdot X_G^r) \oplus Z & \text{if } x[n-1] = 0 \\
((\hat{R}^r)^\intercal \cdot X_E^r) \oplus (\hat{R}^\ell)^\intercal \cdot X_E^\ell) \oplus Z & \text{otherwise}
\end{cases}
$$

$$= (\hat{R}^\intercal \cdot X_E) \oplus Z = (\mathcal{T}(\hat{r})^\intercal \cdot X_E) \oplus Z$$

  - Parties output:

$$\langle\!\langle (\mathcal{T}(\hat{r})^\intercal \cdot X_G) \oplus Z, (\mathcal{T}(\hat{r})^\intercal \cdot X_E) \oplus Z \rangle\!\rangle = [\![(\mathcal{T}(\hat{r})^\intercal \cdot \mathcal{H}(x))]\!] = [\![\hat{r}(x)]\!]$$

Fig. 5. Our low-level primitive allows "half-hidden uniform function evaluation". The parties output $[\![\hat{r}(x)]\!]$ for input x; G outputs uniform function $\hat{r} \in \{0,1\}^n \to \{0,1\}^m$ and E outputs "half" of $\hat{r}$.

E, this formally means that G's procedure appends the message to the garbled circuit material and that E reads the message from the material.

Our Construction. We now formalize our garbling scheme. The most important part of our construction is specified in Fig. 3 by reference to Figs. 1, 4 and 5. These figures formalize G's and E's handling of LUT gates.

Aside from these figures, our formalism is relatively standard. The following construction plugs LUT gate handling into a garbling scheme that we later (in Sect. 7) prove satisfies [3]'s considered security notions.

Construction 1. logrow *is a garbling scheme (Definition 3) that supports circuits with three gate types:*

- *Standard two-input, one-output XOR gates and AND gates.*
- *LUT gates. A LUT gate is parameterized over function $f : \{0,1\}^n \mapsto \{0,1\}^m$ with LUT $T(f)$. It takes as input a bitstring $a \in \{0,1\}^n$ and outputs $f(a)$.*

The garbling procedure are defined as follows:

- $Gb(1^\kappa, \mathcal{C})$ *proceeds in several steps:*
  - *Uniformly sample $\Delta \in_\$ 1\{0,1\}^{\kappa-1}$.*
  - *For each circuit input $x[i]$, sample uniform zero label $X[i] \in_\$ \{0,1\}^\kappa$.*
  - *Assemble the input encoding string e as a vector of pairs of labels:*

$$e[i] = (X[i], X[i] \oplus \Delta)$$

  This choice of e is consistent with projectivity.
  - *Step through the circuit gate by gate. For each XOR gate, XOR the gate's input zero labels and place the result on the output wire [25]. For each AND gate, run the AND gate garbling procedure formalized by [44]. For each LUT gate, run G's procedure described in Fig. 3. Let $\mathcal{M}$ be the string of material concatenated from all "messages sent to E".*
  - *For each output wire $y[i]$, let $Y[i]$ be the output zero label. Assemble the output decoding string d as a vector of pairs, where for each index i the pair is specified as:*

$$d[i] = (H(\nu, Y[i]) \parallel \mathsf{lsb}(Y[i]), H(\nu, Y[i] \oplus \Delta) \parallel \mathsf{lsb}(Y[i] \oplus \Delta))$$

  Here, ν is a fresh nonce. This choice of d ensures that E will be able to compute only one entry of each pair. (We include the least significant bit of each label to ensure perfect correctness.)
  - *Output $(\mathcal{M}, e, d)$.*
- $En(e, x)$ *is a standard projective procedure. For each input bit $x[i]$, En outputs a label appropriate for evaluation:*

$$e[i][x[i]] = X[i] \oplus x[i]\Delta$$

- $Ev(\mathcal{M}, X)$ steps through the circuit gate by gate, using $\mathcal{M}$ to map gate input labels to gate output labels. Namely, the procedure proceeds as follows: For each XOR gate, XOR the input labels together [25]. For each AND gate, run the AND gate evaluation procedure formalized by [44]. For each LUT gate, run E's procedure described in Fig. 3. The procedure collects each output wire label $Y[i]$ and outputs Y.
- $De(d, Y)$ is a standard projective procedure. For each of E's output labels $Y[i]$, the procedure computes:

$$y[i] = \begin{cases} 0 & \text{if } (H(\nu, Y[i]) \,\|\, \mathsf{lsb}(Y[i])) = d[i][0] \\ 1 & \text{if } (H(\nu, Y[i]) \,\|\, \mathsf{lsb}(Y[i])) = d[i][1] \\ \bot & \text{otherwise} \end{cases}$$

If any label $Y[i]$ fails to decode (i.e., above computes $\bot$), then the procedure simply outputs $\bot$. Otherwise, the procedure outputs the decoded string y. Inclusion of lsbs in the output decoding string ensures perfect correctness. (Namely, $\bot$ will never arise, unless malicious E tries to forge an output.)

Compatibility with Other Garbling Techniques. Construction 1 provides the essential interfaces and functionalities for traditional two-input one-output Boolean gates as well as arbitrary n-input m-output lookup tables.

logrow is compatible with many modern techniques in GC, including state-of-the-art Boolean gates [40], GRAM, one-hot accelerated operations, and SGC. Amongst these, compatibility with SGC is by far the most complex, since it requires proving an additional security property. *Strong Stackability* enforces that the garbling of a circuit "look uniform", which allows SGC to safely stack these garblings together [14]. In our full version, we prove our scheme is strongly stackable.

Hiding LUTs from E. Formally, [3] require the definition of a *side-information function* Φ. Given a particular circuit $\mathcal{C}$, this function specifies what information about $\mathcal{C}$ is made available to E. In typical GC constructions, this side-information function is *trivial* in the sense that E is allowed to see the entire circuit, so the side-information function is often omitted from formal discussion.

In our construction, however, we can be stricter and hide from E the specification of each LUT gate function. Thus we give an explicit definition for Φ:

Definition 6. *For a circuit $\mathcal{C}$ with XOR gates, AND gates, and LUT gates, we define the* side-information function $\Phi(\mathcal{C})$ *to be the circuit topology and the type of each gate. $\Phi(\mathcal{C})$ explicitly does not include the function f of each LUT gate.*

6 Performance

We argue Construction 1 achieves our claimed performance. Namely, each LUT gate transmits roughly $nm\kappa + Nm$ bits and requires $O(2^n c_\kappa + 2^n m\kappa + nmc_\kappa +$

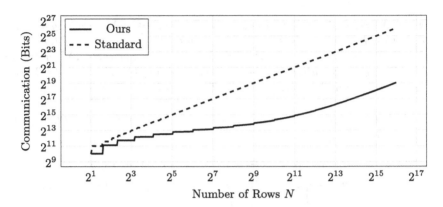

Fig. 6. logrow's communication cost for a single LUT gate. We assume $m = 8$ column in the LUT and $\kappa = 128$. Our approach consistently outperforms the (standard) Yao's encrypted truth table approach by orders of magnitude. For $N > 97$, our communication is more than $10\times$ lower than that of the standard approach. For $N > 2^{13}$, our communication is more than $100\times$ lower.

$2^n mc_\kappa/\kappa)$ computation from each party. Figure 6 plots our communication consumption as compared to a basic H-row encrypted truth table.

Theorem 1. *In* logrow, *consider a LUT gate with function* $f : \{0,1\}^n \rightarrow \{0,1\}^m$. *Each such gate incurs the following cost:*

- $2^n m + (n-1)\kappa + nm\kappa$ *bits of communication.*
- $O(2^n c_\kappa + 2^n m\kappa + nmc_\kappa + 2^n mc_\kappa/\kappa)$ *computation.*

Proof. By inspection of Figs. 1 and 3 to 5.

Communication Cost. Recall that we compute $[\![a]\!] \mapsto [\![f(a)]\!]$. There are three steps in our construction where G must transmit information to E:

- G sends the truth table for $f'(x) \triangleq f(x \oplus \alpha) \oplus r(x)$. **Cost:** Nm bits.
- G and E compute $[\![\mathcal{H}(x)]\!]$. **Cost:** $(n-1)\kappa$ bits [13].
- G sends n strings each of length $m\kappa$ to implement n half-hidden uniform functions (Sect. 4.2). **Cost:** $nm\kappa$ bits.

In total, G must send $Nm + (n-1)\kappa + nm\kappa$ bits. Figure 6 demonstrates that our protocol significantly outperforms a standard encrypted truth table.

Computation Cost. Below, we count the computation cost of each component of our construction.

- The parties first compute $[\![\mathcal{H}(x)]\!]$. **Cost:** $O(2^n c_\kappa)$ computation [13].
- The parties compute a random function $[\![r(x)]\!] = \bigoplus_{i \in [n+1]} [\![r_i(x)]\!]$. Each half hidden random function $[\![r_i(x)]\!]$ incurs the following computation cost:

- Derive the (2^{n-i-1})-bit strings R_i^ℓ / R_i^r by hashing. **Cost:** $O(2^{n-i}mc_\kappa/\kappa)$ computation.
- Compute $[\![\mathcal{H}(x[0:n-i])]\!]$ via linear map. **Cost:** $O(2^{n-i}\kappa)$ computation.
- Construct (resp. decrypt) a garbled row:

$$Z \triangleq H(v_{\mathsf{row}}, Y) \oplus ((\hat{R}^r)^{\mathsf{T}} \cdot X_G^r)$$
$$\mathsf{row} \triangleq H(v_{\mathsf{row}}, Y \oplus \Delta) \oplus ((\hat{R}^\ell)^{\mathsf{T}} \cdot X_G^\ell) \oplus Z$$

  Cost: $O(mc_\kappa)$.
- Compute the following sum:

$$[\![r_i(x)]\!] = ((R_i^\ell)^{\mathsf{T}} \cdot [\![\mathcal{H}(x[0:n-i])^\ell]\!]) \oplus ((R_i^r)^{\mathsf{T}} \cdot [\![\mathcal{H}(x[0:n-i])^r]\!]) \oplus Z$$

  Cost: $O(2^{n-i}m\kappa)$ computation.
  It takes $O(2^{n-i}mc_\kappa/\kappa + mc_\kappa + 2^{n-i}m\kappa)$ computation to compute $[\![r_i(x)]\!]$. Altogether, the n half hidden random functions **cost:** $O(2^n mc_\kappa/\kappa + nmc_\kappa + 2^n m\kappa)$.

- The parties compute $[\![f'(x)]\!] = \mathcal{T}(f')^{\mathsf{T}} \cdot [\![\mathcal{H}(x)]\!]$. Both parties use $O(2^n m\kappa)$ bit XORs to compute the matrix product. In addition, G must compute $\mathcal{T}(f')$ from $\mathcal{T}(f)$ and $\mathcal{T}(r_i)$. This uses only $O(2^n m)$ computation. **Cost:** $O(2^n m\kappa)$ computation.
- Finally, the parties compute $[\![f(x)]\!] = [\![f'(x)]\!] \oplus [\![r(x)]\!]$. **Cost:** $O(m\kappa)$.

In total, both G and E use $O(2^n c_\kappa + 2^n m\kappa + nmc_\kappa + 2^n mc_\kappa/\kappa)$ computation. $\square$

7   Security Theorems and Proofs

In this section, we formally state and prove our security claim. Following [3]'s framework for GC, we prove the *correctness*, *obliviousness*, *privacy*, and *authenticity* of logrow. These properties ensure that logrow can instantiate GC-based protocols. logrow is also compatible with Stacked Garbling, which is shown by proving logrow satisfies *strong stackability*.

We note that amongst our proofs, *correctness* and *obliviousness* are the most crucial. For many typical schemes, including ours, *privacy* and *authenticity* follow from obliviousness without much extra effort. Indeed, these proofs are mostly boilerplate, and are similar to proofs given in prior work, e.g. [15]. *Strong stackability* is also relatively straightforward. The most important requirement of strong stackability is that the garbling of a circuit (together with active input labels) be simulatable by an appropriately-sized uniform string. Our obliviousness proof directly shows that this is the case, so our proof of strong stackability is mostly an appeal to our proof of obliviousness. See our full version for security proofs.

Definition 7 (Correctness). *A garbling scheme is* correct *if for any circuit* $\mathcal{C}$ *and all inputs* x:

$$De(d, Ev(\mathcal{M}, En(e, x))) = \mathcal{C}(x) \qquad where\ (\mathcal{M}, e, d) \leftarrow Gb(1^\kappa, \mathcal{C})$$

Theorem 2. logrow *is correct.*

Proof. By the correctness of individual gates.

Technically, the correctness of each gate proceeds by case analysis. XOR and AND gates are handled using known techniques [25,44], and so they are correct. Thus, we need only show that our new LUT gates are correct. For the most part, correctness of each LUT gate is argued inline in Figs. 3 to 5. In the following, we focus the non-trivial aspects of correctness.

Figure 3 shows that LUT gates are correct, given that Fig. 4 indeed (1) delivers random function r to G and (2) delivers shares $[\![r(x)]\!]$ to G and E.

Correctness of Uniform Function Evaluation (Fig. 4). Now, we argue that the recursive uniform function evaluation is correct; namely, the output share $[\![r(x)]\!]$ is indeed a share of $r(x)$, and G's r agrees on $[\![r(x)]\!]$. Because Fig. 4 proceeds recursively, our proof proceeds by induction on n.

In the base case $n = 0$, G learns $r(\bot) = s$, and the parties output $\langle\!\langle s\Delta, 0 \rangle\!\rangle$, which is a correct sharing by construction.

In the inductive case $n > 0$, we can assume that the recursive evaluation is correct: the parties indeed hold shares $[\![r'(x)]\!]$ that agree with G's function $r' : \{0,1\}^{n-1} \to \{0,1\}^m$. Additionally, Fig. 5 indeed correctly computes a half-hidden uniform function $\hat{r}$; correctness is argued inline.

To complete the inductive step, we closely examine how G defines r. Recall that he defines the truth table $T(r)$ as follows:

$$T(r) \triangleq T(r') \oplus (T(\hat{r})\|T(\hat{r}))$$

Converting this to a function definition, we know that for any $a \in \{0,1\}^n$

$$
\begin{aligned}
r(a) &= T(r)^\mathsf{T} \cdot \mathcal{H}(a) \\
&= (T(\hat{r}) \oplus (T(r')\|T(r'))^\mathsf{T} \cdot \mathcal{H}(a)) \\
&= (T(\hat{r})^\mathsf{T} \cdot \mathcal{H}(a)) \oplus (T(r')^\mathsf{T} \cdot \mathcal{H}(a)[0 : 2^{n-1}]) \oplus (T(r')^\mathsf{T} \cdot \mathcal{H}(a)[2^{n-1} : 2^n]) \\
&= (T(\hat{r})^\mathsf{T} \cdot \mathcal{H}(a)) \oplus (T(r')^\mathsf{T} \cdot (\mathcal{H}(a)[0 : 2^{n-1}] \oplus \mathcal{H}(a)[2^{n-1} : 2^n])) \\
&= (T(\hat{r})^\mathsf{T} \cdot \mathcal{H}(a)) \oplus (T(r')^\mathsf{T} \cdot \mathcal{H}(a[0 : n-1])) \\
&= \hat{r}(a) \oplus r'(a[0 : n-1])
\end{aligned}
$$

This matches the parties computed shares $[\![r(x)]\!] = [\![\hat{r}(x)]\!] \oplus [\![r'(x[0 : n-1])]\!]$, so we can conclude that G's function r agrees with $[\![r(x)]\!]$. By induction, the recursive uniform function evaluation is correct, and so LUT gates are correct.

Since each gate type is correct, logrow is correct.   □

Definition 8 (Obliviousness). *A garbling scheme is oblivious if for any circuit $\mathcal{C}$ and for all inputs x there exists a simulator $\mathcal{S}_{\mathsf{obv}}$ such that the following computational indistinguishability holds:*

$$(\mathcal{M}, X) \overset{c}{\approx} \mathcal{S}_{\mathsf{obv}}(1^\kappa, \Phi(\mathcal{C})) \quad \text{where } (\mathcal{M}, e, d) \leftarrow Gb(1^\kappa, \mathcal{C}) \text{ and } X \leftarrow En(e, x)$$

Theorem 3. logrow *is oblivious.*

Proof. By construction of a simulator $\mathcal{S}_{\mathsf{obv}}$.

Obliviousness is arguably the most important GC security notion, as it ensures that the GC alone conveys no information to the evaluator.

At a high level, $\mathcal{S}_{\mathsf{obv}}$ proceeds gate-by-gate through the circuit, at each gate simulating appropriate GC material. To handle AND/XOR gates, our simulator simply calls out to gate simulators defined by prior work [44].

The non-standard part of the simulation – and our focus in this proof – is the handling of a single LUT gate. At a high level, this simulation is straightforward. E receives only three kinds of messages from G:

- A truth table $\mathcal{T}(f')$ (see Fig. 3). $\mathcal{T}(f')$ is masked by a random function r, and so can by simulated by a uniform matrix of appropriate dimension.
- $n - 1$ garbled rows needed to construct the one-hot encoding $[\![\mathcal{H}(x)]\!]$. [13] demonstrated that each of these length-κ rows can be simulated by uniform strings of length κ.
- n garbled rows each of length $m\kappa$. Each of these rows is encrypted by H, and the definition of circular correlation robustness (Definition 1) is sufficient to ensure that these can also be simulated by uniform bits.

In short, each LUT gate is simulated by a uniform string of appropriate length.

In more detail, $\mathcal{S}_{\mathsf{obv}}$ proceeds as follows. First, we simulate the label for each input bit $x[i]$ with a uniform string $\hat{X}[i]$. This is indistinguishable because the real label $X[i]$ (or $X[i] \oplus \Delta$) is also sampled uniformly.

$\mathcal{S}_{\mathsf{obv}}$ then proceeds gate-by-gate through $\mathcal{C}$. Note, the topology of $\mathcal{C}$ is explicitly contained in $\Phi(\mathcal{C})$ (Definition 6). At each gate, we use the simulated gate input labels to simulate appropriate material and gate output labels. After simulating each gate, $\mathcal{S}_{\mathsf{obv}}$ returns $(\hat{\mathcal{M}}, \hat{Y})$ where $\hat{\mathcal{M}}$ is the collection of gate material and $\hat{Y}$ is the collection of simulated labels on circuit output wires. The core task of $\mathcal{S}_{\mathsf{obv}}$ is to proceed by case analysis on each gate.

XOR Gates are 'free,' since no material is required. To simulate the gate, $\mathcal{S}_{\mathsf{obv}}$ simply XORs the simulated input labels, places the result on the output wire, and then continues to the next gate.

AND Gates are implemented by the half-gate technique [44]. [44, p.13] provides an explicit simulator procedure for AND gates which we call which we call $\mathcal{S}_{\mathsf{AND}}$. For each AND gate, $\mathcal{S}_{\mathsf{obv}}$ feeds the input labels to $\mathcal{S}_{\mathsf{AND}}$, obtains the output label, and appends the two ciphertexts (for the half gates) to $\hat{\mathcal{M}}$.

LUT Gates require G to deliver three kinds of material to E (see high level summary above). We argue that $\mathcal{S}_{\mathsf{obv}}$ can simulate all of this material with uniform bits.

- G sends to E the material for $[\![\mathcal{H}(x)]\!]$. [13, p.15] provides an explicit simulator for simulating the one-hot garbling procedure listed in Fig. 1. We call this simulator $\mathcal{S}_{\mathcal{H}}$. $\mathcal{S}_{\text{obv}}$ invokes $\mathcal{S}_{\mathcal{H}}$ on simulated input labels, resulting in simulated material and simulated output labels. It appends the resultant material to $\hat{\mathcal{M}}$.

- G sends one length $m\kappa$ string to E for each of n half-hidden uniform function evaluations (Fig. 5). To simulate each of these strings, $\mathcal{S}_{\text{obv}}$ samples a $m\kappa$-bit uniform string $\hat{Z}$ and appends it to $\hat{\mathcal{M}}$. We argue that each of these m bits is indistinguishable. Recall that G sends the following to E:

$$H(v_{\text{row}}, Y \oplus \Delta) \oplus ((\hat{R}^\ell)^\mathsf{T} \cdot X_G^\ell) \oplus H(v_{\text{row}}, Y) \oplus ((\hat{R}^r)^\mathsf{T} \cdot X_G^r)$$

(Here, we have inlined the definition of Z listed in Fig. 5.) Let $\hat{Y}$ be the simulated input label for Y and let $\hat{X}$ be the simulated garbling of the one-hot vector $[\![\mathcal{H}(x)]\!]$. WLOG, suppose the simulated value $x[n-1]$ is 0; the indistinguishability argument for $x[n-1] = 1$ is symmetric. We also define the following:

$$L \triangleq ((\hat{R}^\ell)^\mathsf{T} \cdot X_G^\ell) \qquad R \triangleq ((\hat{R}^r)^\mathsf{T} \cdot X_G^r)$$

Note the following indistinguishability (which holds even in the context of appropriate input labels):

$$\hat{Y} \overset{c}{\approx} \hat{Y} \oplus L \oplus H(v_{\text{row}}, Y) \oplus R \qquad\qquad \hat{Y} \text{ is a one-time pad}$$
$$\overset{c}{\approx} \mathcal{R}(v_{\text{row}}, Y, 0) \oplus L \oplus H(v_{\text{row}}, Y) \oplus R \qquad \mathcal{R} \text{ is a random function}$$
$$\overset{c}{\approx} circ_\Delta(v_{\text{row}}, Y, 0) \oplus L \oplus H(v_{\text{row}}, Y) \oplus R \qquad\qquad \text{Definition 1}$$
$$\overset{c}{\approx} H(v_{\text{row}}, Y \oplus \Delta) \oplus L \oplus H(v_{\text{row}}, Y) \oplus R \qquad\qquad\qquad \text{Real}$$

In short, the inclusion of the call to H on one label that E does not know ensures that the row appears uniform.

- G sends to E the truth table for $f'(x) \triangleq f(x \oplus \alpha) \oplus r(x)$. $\mathcal{S}_{\text{obv}}$ simulates this truth table by appending to $\hat{\mathcal{M}}$ an appropriately sized ($2^n m$-bits) uniform string. Since $\mathcal{T}(f') = \mathcal{T}(f) \oplus \mathcal{T}(r)$, as long as we can show the uniformity of $\mathcal{T}(r)$, $\mathcal{T}(f')$ is also uniform.

One tricky issue is that $r(x) \triangleq \bigoplus_{i=0}^{n} r_i(x[0 : n-i])$, and the adversary knows half of each $r_{i<n}$. Still, we can show that for any $a \in \{0,1\}^n$, $r(a)$ is uniformly distributed regardless of the adversary's knowledge of $r_{i<n}$.

We prove this by showing that for any a, $r(a)$ is masked by a uniform value $r_i(a)$ that is *not* known to the adversary. Importantly, this value is not "reused" to mask any other $r(\cdot)$, so the distribution of the full string r is uniform. We show this by induction.

In the base case $n = 0$, $r(\bot) = s$ is a uniform value only known to G, and hence unavailable to the adversary. I.e., $\mathcal{S}_{\text{obv}}$ can simulate s by a uniform string. **In the inductive case** $n' < n$, $\mathcal{S}_{\text{obv}}$ can simulate r' by a uniform string. Now we show that a uniform string can also simulate $r(x) \triangleq \hat{r}(x) \oplus r'(x)$. For $a \in \{0,1\}^n$, there are two possible cases:

- $a[n-1] = x[n-1]$. By the uniformity of r', $r'(a[0 : n-1])$ is uniform. Thus, $r(a) = \hat{r}(a) \oplus r'(a[0 : n-1])$ is uniform.

- $a[n-1] = x[n-1] \oplus 1$. Since the adversary does not have the label for $[\![x[n-1] \oplus 1]\!]$, and $r(a)$ is generated by hashing the label of $[\![x[n-1] \oplus 1]\!]$ that the adversary does not have, $r(a)$ is uniform.

Notice that for each a, $r(a)$ can be independently simulated by a uniform string. Hence, $\mathcal{T}(r)$, defined as the concatenation of these strings, is uniform.

Thus, the full LUT gate can be simulated simply by drawing uniform strings of appropriate length.

From here, the proof of indistinguishability follows a basic hybrid argument, similar to the standard proof of GC security given by [27].

logrow is oblivious. $\square$

Definition 9 (Privacy). *A garbling scheme is* private *if for any circuit $\mathcal{C}$ and for all inputs x there exists a simulator $\mathcal{S}_{\mathsf{prv}}$ such that the following computational indistinguishability holds*

$$(\mathcal{M}, X, d) \stackrel{c}{\approx} \mathcal{S}_{\mathsf{prv}}(1^\kappa, y, \varPhi(\mathcal{C}))$$

where $(\mathcal{M}, e, d) \leftarrow Gb(1^\kappa, \mathcal{C})$, $X \leftarrow En(e, x)$, $y \leftarrow \mathcal{C}(x)$.

Theorem 4. logrow *is private.*

We refer readers to our full version for the proof.

Definition 10 (Authenticity). *A garbling scheme is* authentic *if for all circuits $\mathcal{C}$, all inputs x, and all probabilistic polynomial time (PPT) adversaries $\mathcal{A}$, the following probability is negligible in κ:*

$$\Pr[Ev(\mathcal{M}, x) \neq y' \wedge De(d, y') \neq \perp]$$

where $(\mathcal{M}, e, d) \leftarrow Gb(1^\kappa, c)$, $x \leftarrow En(e, x)$, and $y' \leftarrow \mathcal{A}(\mathcal{C}, \mathcal{M}, x)$.

Authenticity ensures that even a malicious evaluator $\mathcal{A}$ cannot compute output labels that successfully decode, except by running the GC as intended.

Notably, $\mathcal{A}$ is given the full circuit description $\mathcal{C}$, not just the side-information function $\phi(\mathcal{C})$. Thus, $\mathcal{A}$ has access to the function of each LUT gate. This captures scenarios where the evaluator may have side information about each LUT.

Theorem 5. logrow *is authentic.*

We refer readers to our full version for the proof.

Acknowledgements. This research was developed with funding from a Visa research award, a Cisco research award, a USDA APHIS research award (under opportunity number USDA-APHIS-10025-VSSP0000-23-0003), and NSF awards CNS-2246353, CNS-2246354, and CCF-2217070.

References

1. Beaver, D.: Efficient multiparty protocols using circuit randomization. In: Feigenbaum, J. (ed.) CRYPTO 1991. LNCS, vol. 576, pp. 420–432. Springer, Heidelberg (1992). https://doi.org/10.1007/3-540-46766-1_34
2. Beimel, A., Kushilevitz, E., Nissim, P.: The complexity of multiparty PSM protocols and related models. In: Nielsen, J.B., Rijmen, V. (eds.) EUROCRYPT 2018, Part II. LNCS, vol. 10821, pp. 287–318. Springer, Cham (2018). https://doi.org/10.1007/978-3-319-78375-8_10
3. Bellare, M., Hoang, V.T., Rogaway, P.: Foundations of garbled circuits. In: Yu, T., Danezis, G., Gligor, V.D. (eds.) ACM CCS 2012, pp. 784–796. ACM Press, October 2012. https://doi.org/10.1145/2382196.2382279
4. Boyle, E., Couteau, G., Gilboa, N., Ishai, Y., Kohl, L., Scholl, P.: Efficient pseudorandom correlation generators: silent OT extension and more. In: Boldyreva, A., Micciancio, D. (eds.) CRYPTO 2019, Part III. LNCS, vol. 11694, pp. 489–518. Springer, Cham (2019). https://doi.org/10.1007/978-3-030-26954-8_16
5. Bruggemann, A., Hundt, R., Schneider, T., Suresh, A., Yalame, H.: Flute: fast and secure lookup table evaluations. In: 2023 IEEE Symposium on Security and Privacy (SP), pp. 515–533. IEEE Computer Society, Los Alamitos, CA, USA, May 2023. https://doi.org/10.1109/SP46215.2023.10179345
6. Choi, S.G., Katz, J., Kumaresan, R., Zhou, H.-S.: On the security of the "free-XOR" technique. In: Cramer, R. (ed.) TCC 2012. LNCS, vol. 7194, pp. 39–53. Springer, Heidelberg (2012). https://doi.org/10.1007/978-3-642-28914-9_3
7. Dessouky, G., Koushanfar, F., Sadeghi, A.R., Schneider, T., Zeitouni, S., Zohner, M.: Pushing the communication barrier in secure computation using lookup tables. In: NDSS 2017. The Internet Society, February/March 2017
8. Feige, U., Kilian, J., Naor, M.: A minimal model for secure computation (extended abstract). In: 26th ACM STOC, pp. 554–563. ACM Press, May 1994. https://doi.org/10.1145/195058.195408
9. Haque, A., Heath, D., Kolesnikov, V., Lu, S., Ostrovsky, R., Shah, A.: Garbled circuits with sublinear evaluator. In: Dunkelman, O., Dziembowski, S. (eds.) EUROCRYPT 2022, Part I. LNCS, vol. 13275, pp. 37–64. Springer, Heidelberg (2022). https://doi.org/10.1007/978-3-031-06944-4_2
10. Heath, D.: New directions in garbled circuits. Ph.D. thesis, Georgia Institute of Technology, Atlanta, GA, USA (2022). http://hdl.handle.net/1853/66604
11. Heath, D.: Efficient arithmetic in garbled circuits. Cryptology ePrint Archive, Paper 2024/139 (2024). https://eprint.iacr.org/2024/139
12. Heath, D., Kolesnikov, V.: Stacked Garbling - garbled circuit proportional to longest execution path. In: Micciancio, D., Ristenpart, T. (eds.) CRYPTO 2020, Part II. LNCS, vol. 12171, pp. 763–792. Springer, Cham (2020). https://doi.org/10.1007/978-3-030-56880-1_27
13. Heath, D., Kolesnikov, V.: One hot garbling. In: Vigna, G., Shi, E. (eds.) ACM CCS 2021, pp. 574–593. ACM Press, November 2021. https://doi.org/10.1145/3460120.3484764
14. Heath, D., Kolesnikov, V.: LogStack: stacked garbling with $O(b \log b)$ computation. In: Canteaut, A., Standaert, F.-X. (eds.) EUROCRYPT 2021, Part III. LNCS, vol. 12698, pp. 3–32. Springer, Cham (2021). https://doi.org/10.1007/978-3-030-77883-5_1

15. Heath, D., Kolesnikov, V., Ostrovsky, R.: EpiGRAM: practical garbled RAM. In: Dunkelman, O., Dziembowski, S. (eds.) EUROCRYPT 2022, Part I. LNCS, vol. 13275, pp. 3–33. Springer, Heidelberg (2022). https://doi.org/10.1007/978-3-031-06944-4_1
16. Hong, C., Katz, J., Kolesnikov, V., Lu, W., Wang, X.: Covert security with public verifiability: faster, leaner, and simpler. In: Ishai, Y., Rijmen, V. (eds.) EURO-CRYPT 2019, Part III. LNCS, vol. 11478, pp. 97–121. Springer, Cham (2019). https://doi.org/10.1007/978-3-030-17659-4_4
17. Huang, Y., Katz, J., Kolesnikov, V., Kumaresan, R., Malozemoff, A.J.: Amortizing garbled circuits. In: Garay, J.A., Gennaro, R. (eds.) CRYPTO 2014, Part II. LNCS, vol. 8617, pp. 458–475. Springer, Heidelberg (2014). https://doi.org/10.1007/978-3-662-44381-1_26
18. Ishai, Y., Kushilevitz, E.: Private simultaneous messages protocols with applications. In: Proceedings of the Fifth Israeli Symposium on Theory of Computing and Systems, pp. 174–183 (1997). https://doi.org/10.1109/ISTCS.1997.595170
19. Ishai, Y., Kushilevitz, E.: Randomizing polynomials: a new representation with applications to round-efficient secure computation. In: 41st FOCS. pp. 294–304. IEEE Computer Society Press, November 2000. https://doi.org/10.1109/SFCS.2000.892118
20. Ishai, Y., Kushilevitz, E., Meldgaard, S., Orlandi, C., Paskin-Cherniavsky, A.: On the power of correlated randomness in secure computation. In: Sahai, A. (ed.) TCC 2013. LNCS, vol. 7785, pp. 600–620. Springer, Heidelberg (2013). https://doi.org/10.1007/978-3-642-36594-2_34
21. Kennedy, W.S., Kolesnikov, V., Wilfong, G.: Overlaying conditional circuit clauses for secure computation. In: Takagi, T., Peyrin, T. (eds.) ASIACRYPT 2017, Part II. LNCS, vol. 10625, pp. 499–528. Springer, Cham (2017). https://doi.org/10.1007/978-3-319-70697-9_18
22. Kolesnikov, V.: FreeIF: how to omit inactive branches and implement S-universal garbled circuit (almost) for free. In: Peyrin, T., Galbraith, S. (eds.) ASIACRYPT 2018, Part III. LNCS, vol. 11274, pp. 34–58. Springer, Cham (2018). https://doi.org/10.1007/978-3-030-03332-3_2
23. Kolesnikov, V., Kumaresan, R.: Improved OT extension for transferring short secrets. In: Canetti, R., Garay, J.A. (eds.) CRYPTO 2013, Part II. LNCS, vol. 8043, pp. 54–70. Springer, Heidelberg (2013). https://doi.org/10.1007/978-3-642-40084-1_4
24. Kolesnikov, V., Mohassel, P., Rosulek, M.: FleXOR: flexible garbling for XOR gates that beats free-XOR. In: Garay, J.A., Gennaro, R. (eds.) CRYPTO 2014, Part II. LNCS, vol. 8617, pp. 440–457. Springer, Heidelberg (2014). https://doi.org/10.1007/978-3-662-44381-1_25
25. Kolesnikov, V., Schneider, T.: Improved garbled circuit: free XOR gates and applications. In: Aceto, L., Damgård, I., Goldberg, L.A., Halldórsson, M.M., Ingólfsdóttir, A., Walukiewicz, I. (eds.) ICALP 2008, Part II. LNCS, vol. 5126, pp. 486–498. Springer, Heidelberg (2008). https://doi.org/10.1007/978-3-540-70583-3_40
26. Lindell, Y., Pinkas, B.: An efficient protocol for secure two-party computation in the presence of malicious adversaries. In: Naor, M. (ed.) EUROCRYPT 2007. LNCS, vol. 4515, pp. 52–78. Springer, Heidelberg (2007). https://doi.org/10.1007/978-3-540-72540-4_4
27. Lindell, Y., Pinkas, B.: A proof of security of Yao's protocol for two-party computation. J. Cryptol. 22(2), 161–188 (2009). https://doi.org/10.1007/s00145-008-9036-8

28. Lindell, Y., Riva, B.: Cut-and-choose YAO-based secure computation in the online/offline and batch settings. In: Garay, J.A., Gennaro, R. (eds.) CRYPTO 2014, Part II. LNCS, vol. 8617, pp. 476–494. Springer, Heidelberg (2014). https://doi.org/10.1007/978-3-662-44381-1_27

29. Lu, S., Ostrovsky, R.: How to garble RAM programs? In: Johansson, T., Nguyen, P.Q. (eds.) EUROCRYPT 2013. LNCS, vol. 7881, pp. 719–734. Springer, Heidelberg (2013). https://doi.org/10.1007/978-3-642-38348-9_42

30. Naor, M., Nissim, K.: Communication preserving protocols for secure function evaluation. In: 33rd ACM STOC, pp. 590–599. ACM Press, July 2001. https://doi.org/10.1145/380752.380855

31. Naor, M., Pinkas, B., Sumner, R.: Privacy preserving auctions and mechanism design. In: Proceedings of the 1st ACM Conference on Electronic Commerce, pp. 129–139. ACM (1999)

32. Ng, L.K.L., Chow, S.S.M.: GForce: GPU-friendly oblivious and rapid neural network inference. In: Bailey, M., Greenstadt, R. (eds.) USENIX Security 2021, pp. 2147–2164. USENIX Association, August 2021

33. Ng, L.K., Chow, S.S.: SoK: cryptographic neural-network computation. In: 2023 IEEE Symposium on Security and Privacy (SP), pp. 497–514 (2023)

34. Park, A., Lin, W.K., Shi, E.: NanoGRAM: garbled RAM with $\widetilde{O}(\log N)$ overhead. Cryptology ePrint Archive, Report 2022/191 (2022). https://eprint.iacr.org/2022/191

35. Pinkas, B., Schneider, T., Smart, N.P., Williams, S.C.: Secure two-party computation is practical. In: Matsui, M. (ed.) ASIACRYPT 2009. LNCS, vol. 5912, pp. 250–267. Springer, Heidelberg (2009). https://doi.org/10.1007/978-3-642-10366-7_15

36. Rathee, D., Bhattacharya, A., Gupta, D., Sharma, R., Song, D.: Secure floating-point training. Cryptology ePrint Archive (2023)

37. Rathee, D., Bhattacharya, A., Sharma, R., Gupta, D., Chandran, N., Rastogi, A.: SecFloat: accurate floating-point meets secure 2-party computation. In: 2022 IEEE Symposium on Security and Privacy, pp. 576–595. IEEE Computer Society Press, May 2022. https://doi.org/10.1109/SP46214.2022.9833697

38. Rathee, D., et al.: SiRnn: a math library for secure RNN inference. In: 2021 IEEE Symposium on Security and Privacy, pp. 1003–1020. IEEE Computer Society Press, May 2021. https://doi.org/10.1109/SP40001.2021.00086

39. Rathee, D., et al.: CrypTFlow2: practical 2-party secure inference. In: Ligatti, J., Ou, X., Katz, J., Vigna, G. (eds.) ACM CCS 2020, pp. 325–342. ACM Press, November 2020. https://doi.org/10.1145/3372297.3417274

40. Rosulek, M., Roy, L.: Three halves make a whole? Beating the half-gates lower bound for garbled circuits. In: Malkin, T., Peikert, C. (eds.) CRYPTO 2021, Part I. LNCS, vol. 12825, pp. 94–124. Springer, Cham (2021). https://doi.org/10.1007/978-3-030-84242-0_5

41. Troncoso-Pastoriza, J.R., Katzenbeisser, S., Celik, M.: Privacy preserving error resilient DNA searching through oblivious automata. In: Ning, P., De Capitani di Vimercati, S., Syverson, P.F. (eds.) ACM CCS 2007, pp. 519–528. ACM Press, October 2007. https://doi.org/10.1145/1315245.1315309

42. Yang, Y., Peceny, S., Heath, D., Kolesnikov, V.: Towards generic MPC compilers via variable instruction set architectures (visas). IACR Cryptol. ePrint Arch., p. 953 (2023). https://eprint.iacr.org/2023/953

43. Yao, A.C.C.: How to generate and exchange secrets (extended abstract). In: 27th FOCS, pp. 162–167. IEEE Computer Society Press, October 1986
44. Zahur, S., Rosulek, M., Evans, D.: Two halves make a whole. In: Oswald, E., Fischlin, M. (eds.) EUROCRYPT 2015, Part II. LNCS, vol. 9057, pp. 220–250. Springer, Heidelberg (2015). https://doi.org/10.1007/978-3-662-46803-6_8

Publicly Verifiable Secret Sharing Over Class Groups and Applications to DKG and YOSO

Ignacio Cascudo[1]([✉]) and Bernardo David[2]

[1] IMDEA Software Institute, Madrid, Spain
ignacio.cascudo@imdea.org
[2] IT University of Copenhagen, Copenhagen, Denmark
bernardo@bmdavid.com

Abstract. Publicly Verifiable Secret Sharing (PVSS) allows a dealer to publish encrypted shares of a secret so that parties holding the corresponding decryption keys may later reconstruct it. Both dealing and reconstruction are non-interactive and any verifier can check their validity. PVSS finds applications in randomness beacons, distributed key generation (DKG) and in YOSO MPC (Gentry *et al.* CRYPTO'21), when endowed with suitable publicly verifiable re-sharing as in YOLO YOSO (Cascudo *et al.* ASIACRYPT'22).

We introduce a PVSS scheme over class groups that achieves similar efficiency to state-of-the art schemes that only allow for reconstructing *a function* of the secret, while our scheme allows the reconstruction of the original secret. Our construction generalizes the DDH-based scheme of YOLO YOSO to operate over class groups, which poses technical challenges in adapting the necessary NIZKs in face of the unknown group order and the fact that efficient NIZKs of knowledge are not as simple to construct in this setting.

Building on our PVSS scheme's ability to recover the original secret, we propose two DKG protocols for discrete logarithm key pairs: a biasable 1-round protocol, which improves on the concrete communication/computational complexities of previous works; and a 2-round unbiasable protocol, which improves on the round complexity of previous works. We also add publicly verifiable resharing towards anonymous committees to our PVSS, so that it can be used to efficiently transfer state

Ignacio Cascudo was partially supported by the Spanish Government under the project SecuRing (ref. PID2019-110873RJ-I00) and the PRODIGY Project (TED2021-132464B-I00), both funded by MCIN/AEI/10.13039/501100011033/. PRODIGY is also funded by the European Union NextGenerationEU/PRTR. He was also partially supported by the European Union under GA 101096435 (CONFIDENTIAL-6G). Views and opinions expressed are however those of the author(s) only and do not necessarily reflect those of the European Union or the European Commission. Neither the European Union nor the European Commission can be held responsible for them. Bernardo David was supported by the Independent Research Fund Denmark (IRFD) grant number 0165-00079B.

M. Joye and G. Leander (Eds.): EUROCRYPT 2024, LNCS 14655, pp. 216–248, 2024.
https://doi.org/10.1007/978-3-031-58740-5_8

among committees in the YOSO setting. Together with a recent construction of MPC in the YOSO model based on class groups (Braun *et al.* CRYPTO'23), this results in the most efficient full realization (*i.e.* without assuming receiver anonymous channels) of YOSO MPC based on the CDN framework with transparent setup.

1 Introduction

Publicly Verifiable Secret Sharing [38] (PVSS) allows for a dealer to publish encrypted secret shares in such a way that any verifier can check their validity. Moreover, after the parties holding the corresponding decryption keys reconstruct the secret, any verifier can also check the secret's validity with respect to the encrypted shares (typically by checking the consistency between the encrypted and plaintext shares used for reconstruction). Many PVSS schemes are known [4, 8, 9, 24, 27, 31, 36, 37], but the state-of-the-art constructions [11] based on number theoretic assumptions only allow for reconstructing g^s, where $g \in \mathbb{G}$ is the generator of a cyclic group $\mathbb{G}$ and $s \in \mathbb{Z}_p$ is the secret. This limitation can be circumvented [12] by sharing a random secret s' with the PVSS and publishing a one-time pad of the actual secret s with a key derived (e.g. via a random oracle) from the reconstructable secret $g^{s'}$. However, this solution limits the efficiency of a number of PVSS applications. In particular, the secret sharing scheme derived in this way is no longer linear.

Distributed Key Generation (DKG). Besides randomness beacons (*e.g.* [8, 9]), one of the main applications of PVSS schemes is in constructing Distributed Key Generation (DKG) protocols. Such protocols [23, 25, 29, 30, 33, 34] allow for parties to obtain Shamir shares sk_i of a secret key $\mathsf{sk} \in \mathbb{Z}_p$ and the corresponding public key g^{sk} while revealing nothing else. The recent unbiasable DKG protocol of [12] builds on the PVSS scheme of [9] to achieve higher efficiency than previous protocols in terms of round/computational complexities (and in many cases [23, 25, 29] also better communication complexity). However, even though it requires only 2 rounds in case there is no cheating, it still falls short of round optimality [33] in case a malicious party triggers a dispute phase that requires 2 extra rounds. This issue stems from the fact that, in order to allow the parties to retrieve s_i, the DKG of [12] must publish a separate encryption of shares s_i apart from the original PVSS [9] encrypted shares, since those can only be reconstructed to g^{s_i}. In case the PVSS encrypted shares are not consistent with the extra encryption, the dispute phase must be triggered to avoid bias.

The YOSO Model. The recent introduction of the You Only Speak Once (YOSO) model for multiparty computation (MPC) protocols [26] and related models [1, 18, 20] has sparked a renewed interest in PVSS schemes with added properties. In the YOSO model, each round of the protocol is executed by a fresh randomly selected committee of parties who remain anonymous until they send their first message, after which they no longer participate in the execution. This is interesting as it improves scalability because small committees are sufficient to execute each round, as well as resulting in protocols resistant to

218 I. Cascudo and B. David

adaptive corruptions, given that the adversary does not know who to corrupt. However, due to the ephemeral nature of these committees, each of them must transfer their secret state to the next, which is hard given their anonymity. In the YOSO model, it is assumed that all parties have access to ideal receiver anonymous communication channels (RACC), which allow for sending messages to an anonymous party to be randomnly chosen at a later point. Hence, protocols in the YOSO model assume RACCs as setup but aim at minimizing their use. In particular, it was observed in [26] that the Cramer-Damgård-Nielsen (CDN) [19] approach to MPC via threshold encryption is particularly well suited to this setting, as secret key shares are the only secret state maintained by parties. Only very recently, Braun *et al.* proposed a YOSO MPC protocol [6] following the CDN approach without assuming pre-distribution of secret key shares as trusted setup. This protocol assumes access to ideal RACCs in order to realize a threshold encryption scheme over class groups with a matching DKG and a protocol for re-sharing the secret key at every round.

PVSS in the YOSO Model. A number of tools [3,7,28] have been proposed to implement RACCs but only recently an efficient publicly verifiable (re-)sharing scheme compatible with such techniques was proposed in YOLO YOSO [11]. The YOLO YOSO scheme allows for parties to share secrets by publishing publicly verifiable encrypted shares and then re-share those secrets into a fresh set of shares for the next anonymous committee without assuming access to an ideal RACC, thus providing a way to realize the communication infrastructure of the YOSO model using only a random oracle and a Public Key Infrastructure (PKI) as setup (*i.e.* a transparent setup). However, besides suffering from the issue that only g^s can be reconstructed from encrypted shares of s, YOLO YOSO is based on DDH and not directly compatible with class groups. Hence, if YOLO YOSO was used to realize the RACC setup required in the protocol of [6] one would need to rely on freakishly large groups where DDH is hard and be prepared to rely both on DDH and on hardness assumptions over class groups.

1.1 Our Contributions

We introduce an efficient PVSS scheme based on class groups that allows for reconstructing the original secret, enabling applications to DKG and YOSO MPC. Our main results are summarized as follows:

PVSS over class groups: We construct a PVSS scheme over class groups [16] that allows for reconstructing the original secret achieving similar efficiency[1] as previous works [9,11] that only allowed for recovering functions of the secret. Moreover, our scheme achieves a stronger security guarantee. In addition to this, privacy is based solely on the DDH-f assumption [17], known to be implied by both DDH and hard subgroup membership on class groups.

---

[1] Up to a constant due to the time for group operations and size for group elements in class groups being higher than those for DDH-hard groups based on elliptic curves.

Efficient NIZKs of encrypted share validity: Our design differs from the schemes of [9,11], overcoming the hurdles of avoiding extracting witnesses and adapting the SCRAPE [8] share validity test to the class group setting.

DKG protocols for Discrete Logarithm key pairs: We show how our PVSS can be used to construct a 1-round biasable DKG protocol that outperforms the state-of-the-art [29]. We also construct a 2-round unbiasable protocol which is round-optimal [33], improving on the state-of-the-art [12].

Full realization of Efficient YOSO MPC with transparent setup:
Our PVSS can be endowed with publicly verifiable re-sharing towards anonymous committees, lifted from YOLO YOSO [11] via our new NIZKs of share validity. Using this efficient realization of the RACC setup needed by the communication-efficient protocol of [6] yields the most efficient full realization (*i.e.* without assuming ideal RACCs) of YOSO MPC with transparent setup based solely on class groups.

When constructing our PVSS scheme, we face the main technical hurdle of constructing an efficient NIZK of share validity over class groups. Similarly to [9,11], we start from Shamir's secret sharing, encrypt the shares (using encryption over class groups) and want to apply the SCRAPE [8] test to verify share validity. However, we cannot apply the SCRAPE test directly, since the security analysis of this technique crucially relies on the group order, which is unknown for class groups. Moreover, current techniques [6,13,14] for zero knowledge proof systems over class groups do not allow for efficient proofs of knowledge for complex relations such as that of share validity via the SCRAPE test. In order to overcome both of these difficulties we make the following main technical contributions: 1. a new analysis of the SCRAPE test for encrypted shares over groups of unknown order (*i.e.* class groups); 2. a new efficient NIZK proof of share validity (but *not of knowledge*) based on the SCRAPE test for Shamir shares encrypted over class groups; 3. a new proof strategy for our PVSS scheme based on a NIZK that does not allow for extracting adversarial shares.

We construct our 2-round unbiasable DKG protocol as a direct application of our new PVSS protocol. First, all parties publish encrypted shares of random secrets along with proofs of share validity, which are checked so that invalid share vectors and their creators are ignored. Next, honest parties decrypt the shares they received and combine them to generate their share of the secret key and a partial public key, which is published along with a correctness proof so that all parties may compute the final public key. While a similar approach was taken in Mt. Random [12], that DKG requires two extra rounds in case of cheating. The ALBATROSS [9] PVSS used in [12] only allows parties to share g^{s_i}, not the original share s_i, requiring an extra ciphertext containing s_i to be published. When the share in the separate ciphertext differs from the PVSS encrypted share, a dispute phase consisting of 2 extra rounds is executed. We eliminate the dispute phase and achieve a round-optimal [33] protocol by relying on the fact that we can recover the original s_i in our new PVSS scheme's encrypted shares.

Our 1-round DKG protocol publishes the information needed for computing public key shares and the final public key along with the encrypted shared of our PVSS scheme. Doing so avoids the need for the second round where this information is revealed but allows for an adversary to bias the public key by observing the shares published by the honest parties before publishing its own shares. While this bias is unavoidable in 1-round DKG protocols [33], it does not pose a problem when DKG is used in many applications (see e.g. [30]). Our approach cannot be implemented by a simple modification of our 2-round protocol, since it is necessary to prove consistency between encrypted shares used to derive the secret key and public shares used to derive the public key. In order to do so, we design an efficient NIZK proving this relation for our PVSS scheme. Our 1-round protocol requires computing less group operations and communicating less group elements than the work of Kate et al. [32], which in turn is shown to be more efficient than the Groth [29] DKG. Hence, our 1-round DKG improves on the concrete efficiency of [29,32].

Another application of our new PVSS scheme is in efficiently realizing publicly verifiable (re-)sharing towards anonymous committees selected at random, which is crucial in the YOSO model. We adapt our techniques for proving encrypted share validity over class groups to obtain an efficient NIZK of encrypted re-sharing data validity. We remark that efficiently and non-interactively proving re-sharing validity is the main hurdle when constructing secret sharing schemes for the YOSO model, where all parties must do re-sharing at every round. This extended PVSS with re-sharing can be combined with the shuffle-based encryption to the future scheme from YOLO YOSO [11], which only requires a publicly verifiable mixnet, known to be realizable with proofs of shuffle correctness [2] for linearly homomorphic encryption schemes (e.g. based on class groups [16]). The resulting publicly verifiable secret (re-)sharing scheme towards anonymous committees implements the communication infrastructure needed for the efficient YOSO MPC protocol proposed in [6], which follows the CDN [19] approach to reduce the size of secret state transferred among anonymous committees to a minimum and is based on class groups to achieve transparent setup. However, our solution does not require assuming ideal receiver anonymous communication channels (RACC) as in [6], while improving on the efficiency of the proof of resharing, which in [6] requires executing two instances of an inefficient PVSS-like protocol. Hence, combining our results with the protocol of [6] yields the most efficient full realization of YOSO MPC with transparent setup.

1.2   Related Works

Cryptography Over Class Groups: The Castagnos-Laguillaumie (CL) framework for encryption based on class groups was introduced in [16] and later refined in [6,13–15,17,39]. This framework creates a finite group of unknown order where the discrete logarithm is assumed hard to compute, together with a cyclic subgroup where the discrete logarithm is actually easy. This allows for constructing additively homomorphic ElGamal-style encryption, where it is possible to encode plaintexts into the group where the discrete logarithm is easy, compute linear operations on multiple ciphertexts and obtain the result m instead of g^m.

Publicly Verifiable Secret Sharing: Many PVSS schemes based on different techniques for proving share validity are known [4,24,31,36–38]. SCRAPE [8] was the first scheme to achieve $O(n)$ complexity for share validity verification, allowing for executions with tens of thousands of parties. ALBATROSS [9] built on the SCRAPE techniques to construct a compact NIZK for share validity and also achieved sharing of large batches of secrets. This NIZK was generalized and further improved in YOLO YOSO [11], where support for re-sharing and anonymous committees was also efficiently achieved for the first time. Recently, Mt. Random [12] extended ALBATROSS, showing how to slowly release sub-batches of secrets. While these previous works build on number theoretical assumptions, an efficient PVSS scheme from lattice-based assumptions is constructed in [27].

Distributed Key Generation: Most DKG protocols use secret sharing in a similar way as ours, the key difference being how parties prove the correctness of their shares and public information. The classic DKG by Pedersen [34], employs Feldman's VSS, resulting in a protocol with 1 round in case of no disputes, and 2 extra rounds if there are disputes. Fouque and Stern [23] proposed a one-round DKG based on the Paillier cryptosystem that still allows the adversary to bias public keys. Groth [29] proposed a 1-round protocol based on pairings. Recently, Katz [33] showed that all 1-round protocols are biasable and proposed round-optimal protocols. Gennaro *et al.* [25] were the first to observe that Pedersen's DKG is biased and made it unbiasable by introducing a new round of interaction and a new round of dispute resolution. Gurkan *et al.* [30] introduces a pairing-based DKG based on the notion of aggregation via gossip. Cascudo *et al.* [12] introduce the Mt. Random DKG, which follows a similar approach as our constructions but is based on the ALBATROSS [9] PVSS, requiring 2 extra conflict resolution rounds to avoid bias. Recently, Kate *et al.* introduced a DKG based on class groups improving on the performance of Groth [29].

YOSO MPC: The original YOSO MPC model and the first constructions were introduced in [26], while similar models with less stringent restrictions on interaction and matching protocols were introduced in Fluid MPC [18] and in SCALES [1]. A similar model without anonymity but stricter interaction restrictions and matching protocols were introduced in [20]. Further protocols for the Fluid MPC and YOSO MPC models were proposed in [6,35], respectively. Suitable receiver anonymous communication channels for original YOSO model (where parties remain anonymous until they act) were first constructed in [3,28], respectively suffering from a low corruption threshold (less than 1/4 of parties) and from high complexity. Towards solving this issue, the notion of Encryption to the Future (EtF) was introduced in [7] and efficient DDH-based EtF schemes with matching PVSS (and re-sharing) were introduced in [11].

Independent Work: Several 2-round (*i.e.* round optimal) unbiasable DKG protocols based on generic secret sharing, encryption and NIZK schemes are proposed in [33]. However, the core technical issue of obtaining efficient concrete instantiations is not addressed. In [32], the authors propose 1-round (biasable) and 2-round (unbisable) DKG protocols based on "leaky" non-interactive VSS

(NI-VSS) protocol. This NI-VSS achieves a weaker security notion than our PVSS as it leaks information about the secret, which is shown to be sufficient for their DKG constructions but is clearly insufficient for general use (*e.g.* our YOSO MPC application). Moreover, the NIZK of share validity of [32] is based on a NIZK of exponent knowledge and requires more communication/computation than our NIZKs, which circumvent the need for extracting witnesses.

2   Preliminaries

For $m, n \in \mathbb{Z}$, we denote $[m, n] := \{m, m + 1, \ldots, n\}$. Moreover, we write $[n] = [1, n] = \{1, \ldots, n\}$. For a finite set S, we denote by $x \leftarrow_\$ S$ the selection of a uniformly random element in S. If we are sampling from a non-necessarily uniform distribution $\mathcal{D}$, then we write $x \leftarrow \mathcal{D}$. In this paper q will always denote a prime number and then $\mathbb{Z}_q := \mathbb{Z}/q\mathbb{Z}$ is the field of integers modulo q. $\mathbb{Z}_q[X]_{\leq t}$ denotes the set of polynomials in $\mathbb{Z}_q[X]$ of degree at most t. Let $S \subseteq \mathbb{N}$ a finite set and $A = \{\alpha_i : i \in S\}$ be a set of pairwise distinct points contained in a field $\mathbb{F}$. For $i \in S$, we define the Lagrange interpolation polynomial $\mathrm{Lag}_{i,S,A}(X) := \prod_{j \in S \setminus \{i\}} \frac{X - \alpha_j}{\alpha_i - \alpha_j}$. Recall that $L(X) = \sum_{i \in S} y_i \cdot \mathrm{Lag}_{i,S,A}(X)$ is the unique polynomial in $\mathbb{F}[X]$ of degree at most $|S| - 1$ with $L(\alpha_i) = y_i$ for all $i \in S$.

Relations are written as $\mathcal{R} = \{(x; w) : R(x, w) = 1\}$ where x is the statement, w is the witness and R is some predicate. We write $\mathtt{NIZK}(\mathcal{R})$ (respectively $\mathtt{NIZKPoK}(\mathcal{R})$) to denote a generic non-interactive zero knowledge proof (respectively proof of knowledge) for relation $\mathcal{R}$, without instantiating it at that point.

2.1   Publicly Verifiable Secret Sharing(PVSS)

We first present our definitions of a publicly verifiable secret sharing scheme and security properties, where we mainly adopt the definitions from [11]. After that, we recall the SCRAPE test [8] which has been of great utility in several works on publicly verifiable secret sharing and applications [8,9,11,30].

Model. A PVSS scheme consists of the following algorithms.

- *Setup*
  - $\mathsf{Setup}(1^\lambda, \mathsf{ip}) \to \mathsf{pp}$ outputs public parameters pp. The initial parameters ip contain information about number of parties, privacy and reconstruction thresholds and spaces of secrets and shares. The public parameters include a description of spaces of private and public keys SK and PK and the relation $\mathcal{R}_{\mathsf{Key}} \subseteq \mathsf{PK} \times \mathsf{SK}$ describing valid key pairs.
  - $\mathsf{KeyGen}(\mathsf{pp}, id) \to (\mathsf{sk}, \mathsf{pk}, \mathsf{Pf}_{\mathsf{pk}})$, where $(\mathsf{pk}; \mathsf{sk}) \in \mathcal{R}_{\mathsf{Key}}$ and $\mathsf{Pf}_{\mathsf{pk}}$ is a proof meant to assert that pk is a valid public key.
  - $\mathsf{VerifyKey}(\mathsf{pp}, id, \mathsf{pk}, \mathsf{Pf}_{\mathsf{pk}}) \to 0/1$ (as a verdict on whether pk is valid).

– *Distribution*
  • $\mathsf{Dist}(\mathsf{pp}, (\mathsf{pk}_i)_{i \in [n]}, \mathbf{s}) \to ((C_i)_{i \in [n]}, \mathsf{Pf}_{\mathsf{Sh}})$ where $\mathbf{s} \in \mathcal{S}$ is a secret, outputs "encrypted shares" C_i and a proof $\mathsf{Pf}_{\mathsf{Sh}}$ of sharing correctness.
– *Distribution Verification*
  • $\mathsf{VerifySharing}(\mathsf{pp}, (\mathsf{pk}_i, C_i)_{i \in [n]}, \mathsf{Pf}_{\mathsf{Sh}}) \to 0/1$ (as a verdict on whether the sharing is valid).
– *Reconstruction*
  • $\mathsf{DecShare}(\mathsf{pp}, \mathsf{pk}_i, \mathsf{sk}_i, C_i) \to (A_i, \mathsf{Pf}_{\mathsf{Dec}_i})$, outputs a decrypted share A_i and a proof $\mathsf{Pf}_{\mathsf{Dec}_i}$ of correct decryption.
  • $\mathsf{Rec}(\mathsf{pp}, \{A_i : i \in \mathcal{T}\})$ for some $\mathcal{T} \subseteq [n]$ outputs an element of the secret space $\mathbf{s}' \in \mathcal{S}$ or an error symbol $\bot$.
– *Reconstruction Verification*
  • $\mathsf{VerifyDec}(\mathsf{pp}, \mathsf{pk}_i, C_i, A_i, \mathsf{Pf}_{\mathsf{Dec}_i}) \to 0/1$ (as a verdict on whether A_i is a valid decryption of C_i).

Security Properties. The formal security definitions for a PVSS scheme are presented in the full version [10], but we sum them up here. *Correctness* with r-reconstruction means that, if every party acts honestly, any subset of r parties can jointly reconstruct the secret correctly. *Verifiability* means that parties cannot cheat in key generation, share distribution (including encrypting inconsistent shares) and share decryption without being caught with high probability. *Privacy* is captured via the notion of t-*indistinguishability*, which means that no set of t corrupted parties can distinguish between sharings of two secrets, given their secret keys and public information. While some previous PVSS such as [8,9] can only achieve IND1-privacy, where the two secrets are chosen randomly by a challenger, in this paper we use the stronger IND2 property that ensures indistinguishability holds even if the adversary has chosen the two secrets.

The SCRAPE Test. We recall the SCRAPE test from [8]. Given fixed evaluation points $\alpha_1, \ldots, \alpha_n$ in a finite field $\mathbb{F}$, the SCRAPE test allows to check whether a vector $\mathbf{y} = (y_1, ..., y_n) \in \mathbb{F}^n$ is of the form $(p(\alpha_1), \ldots, p(\alpha_n))$ for some $p(X) \in \mathbb{F}[X]_{\leq d}$, by computing the inner product of $\mathbf{y}$ with a vector sampled uniformly at random from a certain set.[2] This is summed up in Theorem 1.

Theorem 1 (SCRAPE test, [8]). *Let $\mathbb{F}$ be a finite field, $\alpha_1, \ldots, \alpha_n$ pairwise distinct elements of $\mathbb{F}$, $y_1, \ldots, y_n$ arbitrary elements of $\mathbb{F}$, $0 \leq d \leq n - 2$ an integer. Let $v_i = \prod_{j \in [n] \setminus \{i\}} (\alpha_i - \alpha_j)^{-1}$. Let $m^*(X) := m_0 + m_1 X + \cdots + m_{n-d-2} X^{n-d-2} \leftarrow_\$ \mathbb{F}[X]_{\leq n-d-2}$ and*

$$T := \sum_{i=1}^{n} v_i m^*(\alpha_i) y_i$$

---

[2] In coding-theoretic this set is the dual code to the Reed-Solomon code formed by the evaluations of polynomials of degree $\leq d$.

1. *If there exists a polynomial $p \in \mathbb{F}[X]$ of degree $\leq d$ such that $y_i = p(\alpha_i)$ for all $i \in [n]$, then $\Pr[T = 0] = 1$.*
2. *Otherwise, $\Pr[T = 0] = 1/|\mathbb{F}|$.*

where the probability is over the uniform choice of $m^*(X)$.

For completion, we provide a proof of this theorem in the full version [10].

2.2 Background on Class Groups

The CL Framework [16]. We first provide some background on the CL framework for encryption based on class groups. First, there is a probabilistic algorithm CLGen which is given security parameter λ, and some prime $q > 2^\lambda$, and outputs $\mathsf{pp}_{\mathsf{CL}} = (q, \bar{s}, \hat{G}, F, f, g_q, \rho) \leftarrow \mathsf{CLGen}(1^\lambda, q; \rho)$. Here $\rho \in \{0,1\}^\lambda$ is the randomness used by CLGen and it is included in the output to signify that it can be publicly known. We will omit it from the argument of CLGen when it is not important. The (non-necessarily cyclic) group $\hat{G}$ has odd cardinality $q \cdot \hat{s}$ where $\gcd(q, \hat{s}) = 1$, and where $\hat{s}$ is unknown but we know an upper bound $\bar{s}$, i.e. $\hat{s} \leq \bar{s}$. For technical reasons, we also assume without loss of generality $\gcd(q, \bar{s}) = 1$.

Having $F = \langle f \rangle$ denote the subgroup of cardinality q, $\hat{G}$ is a direct product $\hat{G} = \hat{G}^q \times F$, where $\hat{G}^q$ is the group of containing the q-th powers of elements in $\hat{G}$, and is of order $\hat{s}$. $\hat{G}$ is not necessarily cyclic, but there is a cyclic subgroup $G \subseteq \hat{G}$ of order $q \cdot s$ (again s is unknown) that factors as $G = G^q \times F$ where $G^q = \langle g_q \rangle$ again contains the q-th powers of elements in G. Note then that $G = \langle g \rangle$ with $g = f \cdot g_q$. Given some element in $\hat{G}$ it is not known how to determine if it is in G efficiently.

A key feature of this framework is that for subgroup $F \leq G$ there is an efficient deterministic discrete logarithm algorithm CLSolve that given $f' \in F$ computes the unique $x \leftarrow \mathsf{CLSolve}(\mathsf{pp}_{CL}, f')$, with $x \in [0, q-1]$ such that $f^x = f'$.

We will need distributions $\mathcal{D}, \mathcal{D}_q$, over the integers such that $\{g^x : x \leftarrow \mathcal{D}\}$ and $\{g_q^x : x \leftarrow \mathcal{D}_q\}$ are statistically close to the uniform distributions in G and G^q, respectively. $\mathcal{D}, \mathcal{D}_q$ can be instantiated by either uniform or discrete Gaussian distributions [15,16,39]: in particular, choosing $\mathcal{D}$ (resp. $\mathcal{D}_q$) to be the uniform distribution in $[q\bar{s}2^{\kappa-2}]$ (resp. $[\bar{s}2^{\kappa-2}]$) leads to distributions whose statistical distances to the uniform distributions in the respective groups are at most $2^{-\kappa}$. Note also that the distribution $\{g_q^{x'} \cdot f^a : x' \leftarrow \mathcal{D}_q, a \leftarrow_\$ \mathbb{Z}_q\}$ is almost uniform in G, as a consequence of the factorization $G = G^q \times F$.

Based on this framework, Castagnos and Laguillaumie construct a linearly homomorphic encryption scheme for messages in $\mathbb{Z}_q$ in [16]. Later, variations of this encryption scheme were presented in [17]. In particular, the share distribution in our PVSS is closely related to one of the schemes presented in [17]: concretely the scheme where $\mathsf{sk} \leftarrow \mathcal{D}_q$, $\mathsf{pk} = g_q^{\mathsf{sk}}$ and the encryption of $m \in \mathbb{Z}_q$ under pk and randomness $r \leftarrow \mathcal{D}_q$ is the pair $(c_1, c_2) = (g_q^r, \mathsf{pk}^r f^m) \in G^q \times G$. The message can then be decrypted as $m = \mathsf{CLSolve}(c_2 \cdot c_1^{-\mathsf{sk}})$. The scheme was proved IND-CPA secure under the hard subset membership (HSM) assumption, described below. We describe first the assumptions we will need directly for our proofs.

First there is the DDH-f assumption from [17]

Definition 1 (*DDH-f* assumption, [17]). For a PPT $\mathcal{A}$, let $\mathsf{Adv}_{\mathcal{A}}^{\text{DDH-f}}(\lambda)$ be

$$\left| \Pr\left[b^* = b \mid \mathsf{pp}_{CL} \leftarrow \mathsf{CLGen}(1^\lambda, q),\ x, y \leftarrow_\$ \mathcal{D},\ u \leftarrow_\$ \mathbb{Z}_q,\ X = g^x,\ Y = g^y, \right.\right.$$
$$\left.\left. b \leftarrow_\$ \{0,1\},\ Z_0 = g^{xy},\ Z_1 = g^{xy}f^u, b^* \leftarrow \mathcal{A}(\mathsf{pp}_{CL}, X, Y, Z_b) \right] - 1/2 \right|.$$

DDH-f is hard for CLGen if for all PPT $\mathcal{A}$, $Adv_{\mathcal{A}}^{\text{DDH-f}}(\lambda)$ is negligible in λ.

Second, the more recent rough order assumption from [6].

Definition 2 (Rough Order assumption, [6]). *For a natural number $C \in \mathbb{N}$ and security parameter λ, consider $\mathcal{D}_C^{rough}$ the uniform distribution in the set $\{\rho \in \{0,1\}^\lambda : \mathsf{pp}_{CL} \leftarrow \mathsf{CLGen}(1^\lambda, q; \rho) \land \forall \text{ prime } p < C,\ p \nmid \mathrm{ord}(\hat{G})\}$. Let*

$$\mathsf{Adv}_{\mathcal{A}}^{RO_C}(\lambda) = \left| \Pr\left[b = b^* \middle| \rho_0 \leftarrow_\$ \{0,1\}^\lambda, \rho_1 \leftarrow \mathcal{D}_C^{rough}, b \leftarrow_\$ \{0,1\}, b^* \leftarrow \mathcal{A}(1^\lambda, \rho_b) \right] - 1/2 \right|$$

RO_C is hard for CLGen if for all PPT $\mathcal{A}$, the $\mathsf{Adv}_{\mathcal{A}}^{RO_C}(\lambda)$ is negligible in λ.

We refer to [6] for the discussion of why this assumption is plausible. Moreover, we remark, as was also done in [6], that the assumption involves an inefficient challenger (as we do not know how to sample from $\mathcal{D}_C^{rough}$ efficiently). However, also as [6] does, we will only use the assumption inside a security proof, namely that of Theorem 7,[3] to argue that if an adversary successfully attacks a protocol, it would be able to determine that that given class group has a low order element, contradicting the assumption.

Other Hardness Assumptions on Class Groups. The standard Decisional Diffie-Hellman (DDH) assumption on G states that distinguishing tuples (g^x, g^y, g^{xy}) from tuples (g^x, g^y, g^z) where x, y, z are sampled independently from $\mathcal{D}$ is hard. More precisely:

Definition 3 (*DDH*-assumption on G). *For a PPT $\mathcal{A}$, let $\mathsf{Adv}_{\mathcal{A}}^{DDH}(\lambda)$ be*

$$\left| \Pr\left[b^* = b \mid \mathsf{pp}_{CL} \leftarrow \mathsf{CLGen}(1^\lambda, q),\ x, y, z \leftarrow_\$ \mathcal{D},\ X = g^x,\ Y = g^y, \right.\right.$$
$$\left.\left. b \leftarrow_\$ \{0,1\},\ Z_0 = g^{xy},\ Z_1 = g^z, b^* \leftarrow \mathcal{A}(\mathsf{pp}_{CL}, X, Y, Z_b) \right] - 1/2 \right|$$

We say that the DDH problem is hard for CLGen if for all PPT $\mathcal{A}$, $Adv_{\mathcal{A}}^{DDH}(\lambda)$ is negligible in λ.

The HSM assumption states that it is hard to distinguish elements sampled from G from elements sampled from G^q (using $\mathcal{D}$ and $\mathcal{D}_q$ respectively).

---

[3] As well as for using the ZK proof protocol from [6] which we show in next section.

Definition 4 (Hard Subgroup Membership (*HSM*) assumption, [17]). For a PPT $\mathcal{A}$, let $\mathsf{Adv}_{\mathcal{A}}^{\mathsf{HSM}}(\lambda)$ be

$$\left| \Pr \left[b = b^* \mid \mathsf{pp}_{CL} \leftarrow \mathsf{CLGen}(1^\lambda, q), x \leftarrow \mathcal{D}, y \leftarrow \mathcal{D}_q, \right. \right.$$
$$\left. \left. b \leftarrow_\$ \{0,1\}, Z_0 = g^x, Z_1 = g_q^y, b^* \leftarrow \mathcal{A}(\mathsf{pp}_{\mathsf{CL}}) \right] - 1/2 \right|$$

We say that the HSM problem is hard for CLGen if for all PPT $\mathcal{A}$, $Adv_{\mathcal{A}}^{\mathsf{HSM}}(\lambda)$ is negligible in λ.

2.3   Zero Knowledge Proofs for Class Groups

In this section, we recall some proofs for statements involving discrete logarithms in class groups from recent works. In this paper we will need both proofs of knowledge of discrete logarithm and proofs of discrete logarithm equality. However, in the second case we will not need the proofs to be proofs of knowledge.

Proofs of Knowledge of Discrete Logarithm. We consider two proofs of knowledge of discrete logarithm, introduced respectively in [13,14].[4]. Let $\mathcal{R}_{\mathsf{DL}} = \{((h,x);w) \in (G \times G) \times \mathbb{Z} : h^w = x\}$. For these and all the proofs below to be statistically honest-verifier zero knowledge, we will require the witness w to be in an interval $[-S, S]$ for some public bound S (the proofs require to set parameters which depend on S). We remark that the soundness does not guarantee that the witness is in that interval. There is a tradeoff between both proofs in terms of complexity and security assumptions: the first proof is less efficient but does not require any assumption; the second one is more efficient but is based on the hardness assumptions (i.e. it is an argument of knowledge) LO_C and SR; perhaps more importantly, it requires h to be uniformly random, and in particular not decided by the adversary. We give a brief description of these proof systems and refer the readers to [13,14] for more details. The proof (Fig. 1) is parameterized by natural numbers A and ℓ. We will refer to its non-interactive version via Fiat-Shamir with the name Π_{DL1}.

Theorem 2 (Adapted from [13]). The interactive proof in Fig. 1 is a Proof of Knowledge for $\mathcal{R}_{\mathsf{DL}}$ with knowledge soundness $2^{-\ell}$, and it is statistically zero-knowledge as long as $w \in [-S, S]$, ℓ is polynomial and $\ell S/A$ is negligible. By the Fiat-Shamir heuristic, the non-interactive version has the same properties in the random oracle model.

Theorem 3 (Adapted from [14]). Under the LO_C and SR assumption, and assuming h is uniformly random in a large enough subset in G^q, the protocol in Fig. 2 is a computationally sound proof of knowledge for $\mathcal{R}'_{\mathsf{DL}}$ with knowledge soundness error $4/C$, complete if $w \in [-S, S]$, and statistically special honest-verifier zero knowledge as long as $w \in [-S, S]$ and SC/A is negligible. By the Fiat-Shamir heuristic, the non-interactive version has the same properties in the random oracle model.

---

[4] The proofs were in fact introduced for slightly more involved relations, but for simplicity we adapt them for just proving knowledge of discrete logarithm.

Proof of knowledge of discrete logarithm from [13]

Proof of knowledge for $\mathcal{R}_{\mathsf{DL}} = \{((h,x);w) \in (G \times G) \times \mathbb{Z} : h^w = x\}$

Interactive version:
Repeat ℓ times in parallel:
- The prover chooses $r \leftarrow_\$ [0, A]$ and sends $t = h^r$ to the verifier
- The verifier chooses $b \leftarrow_\$ \{0, 1\}$
- The prover answers with $u = r + bw$
- The verifier accepts if $u \in [-S, A + S]$ and $h^u = t \cdot x^b$

Non-interactive (Fiat-Shamir) version:
Let $\mathcal{H} : \{0,1\}^* \to \{0,1\}^\ell$ be a random oracle.
$\Pi_{\mathsf{DL1}}.\mathsf{Prove}((h,x);w)$:
- The prover chooses $\mathbf{r} := (r_1, \ldots, r_\ell) \leftarrow_\$ [A]^\ell$, constructs $t_1 = h^{r_1}, \ldots, t_\ell = h^{r_\ell}$ and computes $\mathbf{b} := (b_1, \ldots, b_\ell) = \mathcal{H}(h, x, t_1, \ldots, t_\ell)$ and $\mathbf{u} = \mathbf{r} + w\mathbf{b}$ with the sum and scalar product operating componentwise.
- Output $\mathsf{Pf} = (\mathbf{b}, \mathbf{u})$.
$\Pi_{\mathsf{DL1}}.\mathsf{Verify}((h,x), \mathsf{Pf})$:
Check $\mathbf{u} \in [A + S]^\ell$, compute $t'_j = x^{-b_j} \cdot h^{u_j}$ for $j \in [\ell]$, check that $\mathbf{b} = \mathcal{H}(h, x, t'_1, \ldots, t'_\ell)$ and accept the proof if all checks accept.

Fig. 1. Proof of knowledge of discrete logarithm from [13]

Sound Proofs of Discrete Logarithm Equality and Linear Relations. The proofs of knowledge above are either somewhat inefficient, in the first case, or require that the basis is not controlled by the adversary, in the second. In several cases we will need proofs of discrete logarithm equality where we can settle for proofs with soundness, instead of proofs of knowledge. We can instantiate these from the proofs for linear relations in a class group introduced in [6]. In this case, soundness requires the rough-order assumption also introduced in [6].

Consider the following relation $\mathcal{R}_{\mathsf{LinCL}}$ given by[5]

$$\{((X_{i,j})_{i \in [n], j \in [m]}, (Y_i)_{i \in [n]}; (w_j)_{j \in [m]}) \in (G)^{nm+n} \times \mathbb{Z}^m : Y_i = \prod_{j=1}^{m} X_{i,j}^{w_j} \ \forall i \in [n]\}$$

For $m = 1$, this is in fact the discrete logarithm equality relation

$$\mathcal{R}_{\mathsf{DLEQ}} = \{((X_i)_{i \in [n]}, (Y_i)_{i \in [n]}; w) \in (G)^{2n} \times \mathbb{Z} : Y_i = X_i^w \ \forall i \in [n]\}$$

A Σ-protocol for $\mathcal{R}_{\mathsf{LinCL}}$, parametrized by $A, C \in \mathbb{N}$, is given in Fig. 3. We denote $\mathbf{X} = (X_{i,j})_{i \in [n], j \in [m]}$, $\mathbf{Y} = (Y_i)_{i \in [n]}$, $\mathbf{w} = (w_j)_{j \in [m]}$.

Lemma 1 ([6]). *The interactive proof in Fig. 3 is complete, computationally sound with soundness error $1/C + \mathsf{negl}$ under the RO_C assumption and statistically*

---

[5] Notation: To avoid confusion with the group G^q of q-th powers of elements from G, we denote the direct product of m copies of G, for $m \in \mathbb{N}$, as $(G)^m$.

Proof of knowledge of discrete logarithm from [14]

Proof of knowledge for $\mathcal{R}'_{DL} = \{((h,x);(w_0,w_1)) \in (G^q \times \hat{G}) \times \mathbb{Z}^2 : h^{2^{-w_0}w_1} = x\}$
where a honest prover uses integer $w = 2^{-w_0}w_1 \in \mathbb{Z}$.
The proof is parametrized by integers A and C and presented in Figure 2
Interactive version:
  - The prover chooses $r \leftarrow_\$ [A]$ and sends $t = h^r$ to the verifier.
  - The verifier chooses $c \leftarrow_\$ [C]$
  - The prover answers with $u = r + cw$.
  - The verifier accepts if $u \in [-SC, SC + A]$ and $h^u = t \cdot x^c$.

Non-Interactive version:
Let $\mathcal{H} : \{0,1\}^* \to [C]$ be a random oracle.
$\Pi_{DL2}.\text{Prove}((h,x);w)$:
  - Choose $r \leftarrow_\$ [A]$, construct $t = h^r$ and compute $c = \mathcal{H}(h,x,t)$ and $u = r + cw$.
  - Output $Pf = (u,c)$.
$\Pi_{DL2}.\text{Verify}((h,x),Pf)$:
Checks that $u \in [-SC, SC + A]$, compute $t' = x^{-c}h^u$, check that $c = \mathcal{H}(h,x,t')$
and accept the proof if both checks accept.

Fig. 2. Proof of knowledge of discrete logarithm from [14]

special honest-verifier zero knowledge if SC/A is negligible. By the Fiat-Shamir heuristic, the non-interactive version has the same properties in the random oracle model.

Remark 1. By the result of [22], the non-interactive version of the proof in Fig. 3 obtained via the Fiat-Shamir transform in the random oracle model is simulation sound.

3   PVSS over Class Groups

3.1   The PVSS Scheme

Our PVSS is similar to the DHPVSS scheme in YOLO YOSO [11], which we recall in the full version [10] for comparison. In particular we replace the El Gamal encryption used there by the Castagnos-Laguillaumie-Tucker encryption from [17]. The benefit we obtain over DHPVSS is that in our scheme parties can reconstruct the share "field" secret $s \in \mathbb{Z}_q$, where in DHPVSS they can only reconstruct g^s (with g being a generator of the DDH-hard group $\mathbb{G}$). This is fine for applications of PVSS such as distributed randomness beacons [8] and can also be turned into a PVSS for $\mathbb{Z}_q$ by defining the secret to be $s' = H(g^s) + a$, for some efficiently computable $H : \mathbb{G} \to \mathbb{Z}_q$ and an element a published by the dealer. But then the PVSS is no longer linear, which makes it harder to be used for MPC-related applications and DKG.

In exchange, there arise some technical challenges with respect to [11]. First, several steps of the construction need ZK proofs, and ZK proofs of knowledge

---

Proof of linear class group relations from [6]

Proof for $\mathcal{R}_{\mathsf{LinCL}} = \left\{ (\mathbf{X}, \mathbf{Y}; \mathbf{w}) \in G^{nm+n} \times \mathbb{Z}^m : Y_i = \prod_{j=1}^{m} X_{i,j}^{w_j} \ \forall i \in [n] \right\}$

Interactive version:
1. The prover chooses $(r_1, \ldots, r_m) \leftarrow_\$ [A]^m$, constructs $T_i = \prod_{j=1}^{m} X_{i,j}^{r_j}$ for $i \in [n]$ and sends $(T_1, \ldots, T_n)$.
2. The verifier chooses $c \leftarrow_\$ [C]$ and sends it to the prover.
3. The prover computes $u_j = r_j + c w_j$ for $j \in [m]$ and sends them to the verifier.
4. The verifier checks $u_j \in [-SC, SC + A]$ for all $j \in [m]$, and also $T_i \cdot Y_i^c = \prod_{j=1}^{m} X_{i,j}^{u_j}$ and accepts if all checks pass.

Non-interactive version:
Let $\mathcal{H} : \{0,1\}^* \to [C]$
$\Pi_{\mathsf{LinCL}}.\mathsf{Prove}(\mathbf{X}, \mathbf{Y}; \mathbf{w})$:
- Choose $\mathbf{r} = (r_1, \ldots, r_m) \leftarrow_\$ [0, A]^m$, construct $T_i = \prod_{j=1}^{m} X_{i,j}^{r_j}$ for $i \in [n]$, compute $c = \mathcal{H}(\mathbf{X}, \mathbf{Y}, \mathbf{T})$, and $\mathbf{u} = \mathbf{r} + c\mathbf{w}$ (coordinatewise)
- Output $\mathsf{Pf} = (\mathbf{u}, c)$
$\Pi_{\mathsf{LinCL}}.\mathsf{Verify}((\mathbf{X}, \mathbf{Y}), \mathsf{Pf})$:
Check $\mathbf{u} \in [-SC, SC + A]^m$, compute $T_i = Y_i^{-c} \cdot \prod_{j=1}^{m} X_{i,j}^{u_j}$ for $i \in [n]$, check $c = \mathcal{H}(\mathbf{X}, \mathbf{Y}, \mathbf{T})$, accept if both checks accept.

Fig. 3. Proof of linear class group relations from [6]

are somewhat inefficient or only applicable under certain conditions (see remarks above and Sect. 2.3). Fortunately, we show that we only really need proofs of knowledge in the key generation algorithm. This means that using less efficient PoKs (Π_{DL1} in Sect. 2.3) may not be so problematic as key generation can be carried out long before the PVSS takes place; but also one can use the more efficient proof Π_{DL2} from [14] (Section 2.3) by randomizing the generator g_q. The second issue will be the construction of an efficient (constant in the number of parties n) proof of correct sharing, but we defer this discussion to Sect. 3.2.

We present our scheme for a general case where the space of secrets is $\mathbb{Z}_q^k$. For applications in this paper we only need $k = 1$, but the general case is not much harder to present an in addition PVSS with larger secrets have been considered for some applications e.g. in [9].

PVSS Scheme qCLPVSS. Let λ be the security parameter and $q > 2^\lambda$ prime. Let k (size of the secret), t (privacy threshold) and n (number of parties) be natural numbers, with $k, t, n = \mathsf{poly}(\lambda)$ (and hence we can assume $n + k \leq q$) and $k + t \leq n$. Our scheme qCLPVSS consists of the tuple of algorithms (Setup, KeyGen, VerifyKey, Dist, VerifySharing, DecShare, Rec, VerifyDec) below:

- qCLPVSS.Setup($1^\lambda, q, k, t, n$):
  1. Specify a set of pairwise distinct points $\{\beta_1, \ldots, \beta_k, \alpha_1, \ldots, \alpha_n\} \subset \mathbb{Z}_q$. Let $\mathsf{pp}_{\mathsf{Sh}} = (q, k, t, n, (\beta_j)_{j \in [k]}, (\alpha_i)_{i \in [n]})$
  2. Run $\mathsf{pp}_{\mathsf{CL}} := (q, \bar{s}, f, g_q, \hat{G}, F, \rho) \leftarrow \mathsf{CLGen}(1^\lambda, q)$.

3. The output is then pp = (pp_{Sh}, pp_{CL}).
- qCLPVSS.KeyGen(pp, i):
  1. Sample $sk_i \leftarrow \mathcal{D}_q$ and compute $pk_i = g_q^{sk_i}$.
  2. Create proof $Pf_{pk_i} = \text{NIZKPoK}_{DL}.\text{Prove}(\{(g_q, pk_i); sk_i : pk_i = g_q^{sk_i}\})$
  3. Output(sk_i, pk_i, Pf_{pk_i}).
- qCLPVSS.VerifyKey(pp, i, pk_i, Pf_{pk_i}):

  Run $\text{NIZKPoK}_{DL}.\text{Verify}$ on Pf_{pk_i} with respect to statement (g_q, pk_i) and output its result.

- qCLPVSS.Dist(pp, $(pk_i)_{i\in[n]}$, **s**), where **s** $= (s_1, \ldots, s_k) \in \mathbb{Z}_q^k$:
  1. Create a Shamir sharing of **s**: sample a polynomial $p(X) \in \mathbb{Z}_q[X]_{\leq t+k-1}$ with $p(\beta_j) = s_j$ for $j \in [k]$ and set $\sigma_i = p(\alpha_i)$ for $i \in [n]$.
  2. Sample $r \leftarrow \mathcal{D}_q$ and compute $R = g_q^r$.
  3. Create $B_i = pk_i^r \cdot f^{\sigma_i}$.
  4. Create the sharing proof (not necessarily of knowledge)

  $$Pf_{Sh} = \text{NIZK}_{Sh}.\text{Prove}(\{(f, g_q, (pk_i)_{i=1}^n, R, (B_i)_{i=1}^n); (p(X), r) :$$

  $$\deg p(X) \leq t + k - 1, \ R = g_q^r, \ B_i = pk_i^r \cdot f^{p(\alpha_i)} \ \forall i \in [n]\})$$

  We show how to instantiate NIZK_{Sh} in Sect. 3.2.
  5. Output $(R, B_1, \ldots, B_n, Pf_{Sh})$. To make it syntactically consistent with our definition in Sect. 2.1, we define $C_i := (R, B_i)$ for all $i \in [n]$, and notice that $(R, B_1, \ldots, B_n, Pf_{Sh})$ contains the same information as $(C_1, \ldots, C_n, Pf_{Sh})$.
- qCLPVSS.VerifySharing(pp, $(pk_i)_{i\in[n]}$, $(C_1, \ldots, C_n, Pf_{Sh})$), where $C_i = (R, B_i)$:

  Run $\text{NIZK}_{Sh}.\text{Verify}$ on Pf_{Sh} with respect to statement $(f, g_q, (pk_i)_{i=1}^n, R, (B_i)_{i=1}^n)$ and output its result.
- qCLPVSS.DecShare(pp, pk_i, sk_i, C_i), where $C_i = (R, B_i)$:
  1. Compute $f_i = B_i \cdot R^{-sk_i}$, $A_i = \text{CLSolve}(f_i)$ and $M_i = f_i^{-1} \cdot B_i$.
  2. Compute $Pf_{Dec_i} = \text{NIZK}_{DLEQ}.\text{Prove}(\{(g_q, R, pk_i, M_i); sk_i : g_q^{sk_i} = pk_i, R^{sk_i} = M_i\})$. Again this does not need to be a proof of knowledge.
  3. Output (A_i, Pf_{Dec_i}).
- qCLPVSS.Rec(pp, $\{A_i : i \in T\}$):
  1. If $|T| < t + k$, output $\bot$.
  2. Otherwise select $T' \subseteq T$, with $|T'| = t + k$ (e.g. the first $t + k$ indices in T).
  3. For each $j \in [k]$, define $s'_j = \sum_{i\in T'} A_i \cdot L_i(\beta_j)$ where $L_i(X) = \text{Lag}_{i,T'}$, $\{\alpha_i : i \in T'\}$.[6]
  4. Output **s**$' = (s'_1, \ldots, s'_k)$.

---

[6] Recall, that by definition of Lag, $L_i(X) = \prod_{j\in T'\setminus\{i\}} \frac{X-\alpha_j}{\alpha_i - \alpha_j}$.

- qCLPVSS.VerifyDec($\mathsf{pp}, C_i, A_i, \mathsf{Pf}_{\mathsf{Dec}_i}$) where $C_i = (R, B_i)$:

  Compute $M_i = f^{-A_i} \cdot B_i$ and run NIZK$_{\mathsf{DLEQ}}$.Verify on $\mathsf{Pf}_{\mathsf{Dec}_i}$ with respect to statement $(g_q, R, \mathsf{pk}_i, M_i)$, and output the result of the verification.

We now show that the PVSS above guarantees the security properties from Sect. 2.1. In particular there is $t + k$-reconstruction and t-IND2-privacy.

Theorem 4. qCLPVSS *is a correct PVSS with* $t + k$-*reconstruction*

Proof. The proof is quite immediate, we give a detailed proof in the full version [10].

Theorem 5. – *If* NIZKPoK$_{DL}$ *is a proof of knowledge with knowledge error negligible in* λ *then* qCLPVSS *has verifiability of key generation.*
- *If* NIZK$_{Sh}$ *is a proof with soundness error negligible in* λ *then* qCLPVSS *has verifiability of sharing distribution.*
- *If* NIZK$_{DLEQ}$ *with soundness error negligible in* λ *then* qCLPVSS *has verifiability of share decryption.*

Proof. Trivial as the statements proved by the NIZK proofs exactly guarantee correct key generation, sharing distribution and share decryption, respectively.

In order to prove t-IND2-secrecy, we need to introduce a modified hardness assumption, and show it is implied by DDH-f. The new assumption, DDH-qf is very similar to DDH-f but the generator of G is replaced by the generator of G^q.

Definition 5 (*DDH-qf hardness assumption*). *For a PPT* $\mathcal{A}$ *let*

$$\mathsf{Adv}_{\mathcal{A}}^{DDH\text{-}qf}(\lambda) := \Big| Pr[b^* = b | \mathsf{pp}_{CL} \leftarrow \mathsf{CLGen}(1^\lambda, q), x, y \leftarrow \mathcal{D}_q, u \leftarrow_{\$} \mathbb{Z}_q, X = g_q^x,$$

$$Y = g_q^y, b \leftarrow_{\$} \{0, 1\}, Z_0 = g_q^{xy}, Z_1 = g_q^{xy} f^u, b^* \leftarrow \mathcal{A}(\mathsf{pp}_{CL}, X, Y, Z_b)] - 1/2 \Big|$$

DDH-qf is hard for CLGen *if* $\forall$ *PPT* $\mathcal{A}$, $Adv_{\mathcal{A}}^{DDH\text{-}qf}(\lambda)$ *is negligible in* λ.

Lemma 2. *If* DDH-f *is hard for* CLGen, *then* DDH-qf *is hard for* CLGen.

Proof. We show the proof in the full version [10].

Theorem 6. qCLPVSS *is* t-*IND2-secret under* DDH-f, *assuming* NIZK$_{Sh}$, NIZK$_{DLEQ}$ *are zero-knowledge proofs and* NIZKPoK$_{DL}$ *is a zero-knowledge proof of knowledge.*

Proof. The proof is presented in the full version [10].

3.2   Instantiating the Proofs

Sharing Proof. We discuss how to instantiate the sharing proof $\mathsf{Pf_{Sh}}$, which we consider the main technical challenge of the PVSS construction. Recall this is a zero knowledge proof for the language

$$\{(f, g_q, (\mathsf{pk}_i)_{i=1}^n, R, (B_i)_{i=1}^n); (p(X), r) : \deg p(X) \leq t, R = g_q^r, B_i = \mathsf{pk}_i^r f^{p(\alpha_i)} \; \forall i \in [n]\}.$$

As we have mentioned before, we use the overall idea from YOLO YOSO [11], which in turn consists in using the SCRAPE check from Theorem 1 in an efficient way which yields a constant size (in n) proof, but we will need to do adjustments to this strategy.

The idea from [11], translated to our class group framework, is as follows: if we sample a random polynomial $m^* \in \mathbb{Z}_q[X]_{\leq n-t-k+1}$ then for any correct sharing $(\sigma_i = p(\alpha_i)$ with $\deg p(X) \leq t)$ we must have $\sum_{i=1}^n \sigma_i \cdot v_i \cdot m^*(\alpha_i) = 0$ in $\mathbb{Z}_q$ for the v_i's defined in Theorem 1.

We embed $w_i = v_i \cdot m^*(\alpha_i) \in \mathbb{Z}_q$ as integers in $[q-1]$, and compute the products $U = \prod_{i=1}^n \mathsf{pk}_i^{w_i}$ and $V = \prod_{i=1}^n B_i^{w_i}$. If the B_i's are correct then $V = \prod_{i=1}^n \mathsf{pk}_i^{rw_i} f^{\sigma_i w_i}$ but the second term cancels out because $\sum_{i=1}^n \sigma_i w_i = 0 \mod q$ (recall f is of order q). So then $V = U^r$ which can be proved using a proof of discrete logarithm equality with $R = g_q^r$. If the σ_i's are not valid, with large probability $\sum_{i=1}^n \sigma_i w_i \neq 0 \mod q$ (by Theorem 1), the F-part of the product does not cancel out, and the proof will not pass.

However, there is a problem that did not appear in the setting of [11]: it may be that a malicious prover sets $B_i = (H_i \mathsf{pk}_i^r) \cdot f^{\sigma_i}$, with correct shares σ_i but where $H_i \neq 1$ are elements in $\hat{G}^q$ such that, when computing V the product $\prod H_i^{w_i}$ cancels out and this is not caught by the proof.

We solve this problem as follows: we randomize further the values w_i by replacing them with $w_i' = w_i + c_i q$ for some random $c_i \in [C]$. This does not affect the F-part of the equation, as we are adding a multiple of q, but as we will see the prover can only pass this test with high probability by either setting all $H_i = 1$ (and then the shares are correct) or by breaking the rough order assumption from [6]. In addition, this modification does not affect the communication complexity, while the computation only increases slightly by computing n products and sums of integers. The proof Π_{Sh} of correct sharing is presented in Fig. 4.

To prove the soundness of Π_{Sh} we first need the following lemma.

Lemma 3. *Let $H_i \in \hat{G}^q$ be elements in $\hat{G}^q$ such that there is at least one element $H_j \neq 1$. Let $w_i \in \mathbb{Z}$. Sample $(c_1, \ldots, c_n) \leftarrow_\$ [C]^n$ for some integer $C > 1$. Then if H_j has order $\geq C$, the probability that $\prod_{i=1}^n H_i^{w_i + c_i q} = 1$ is at most $1/C$.*

Proof. Without loss of generality, we assume $j = 1$, i.e. the order of H_1 is at least C. Then fix any $(c_2, \ldots, c_n) \in [C]^{n-1}$ and consider the quantities $M_c = H_1^{w_1 + cq} \prod_{i=2}^n H_i^{w_i + c_i q}$. Clearly if $M_c = M_{c'}$ for $c \neq c'$ then $1 = M_c \cdot M_{c'}^{-1} = H_1^{(c-c')q}$. But since the order of $\hat{G}^q$ is coprime to q, then $H_1^{(c-c')} = 1$, a contradiction with the order of H_1 (since $|c - c'| \leq C - 1$). Therefore at most one M_c can equal 1. Since this is for any $(c_2, \ldots, c_{n-1}) \in [C]^{n-1}$ we obtain the lemma.

Proof Π_{Sh} of correct sharing:

Proof for the relation

$$\mathcal{R}_{\mathsf{Sh}} = \{(f, g_q, (\mathsf{pk}_i)_{i=1}^n, R, (B_i)_{i=1}^n); (p(X), r) : p(X) \in \mathbb{Z}_q[X]_{\leq t+k-1},$$

$$r \in \mathbb{Z}, R = g_q^r, B_i = \mathsf{pk}_i^r f^{p(\alpha_i)} \; \forall i \in [n]\}.$$

The proof is parametrized by $C \in \mathbb{Z}$. We assume a random oracle $\mathcal{H} : \{0,1\}^* \to \mathbb{Z}_q[X]_{\leq n-t-k-1} \times [C]^n$ and a NIZK proof $\mathsf{NIZK}_{\mathsf{DLEQ}}$ for discrete logarithm equality in class groups, given by algorithms $\mathsf{NIZK}_{\mathsf{DLEQ}}.\mathsf{Prove}$, $\mathsf{NIZK}_{\mathsf{DLEQ}}.\mathsf{Verify}$.

$\Pi_{\mathsf{Sh}}.\mathsf{Prove}((f, g_q, (\mathsf{pk}_i)_{i=1}^n, R, (B_i)_{i=1}^n); (p(X), r))$:
1. Compute $(m^*(X), c_1, \ldots, c_n) = \mathcal{H}(\mathsf{pk}_1, \ldots, \mathsf{pk}_n, R, B_1, \ldots, B_n)$. Note $m^*(X) \in \mathbb{Z}_q[X]_{\leq n-t-k-1}$ and $c_i \in [C]$ for each $i \in [n]$.
   Let $v_i = \prod_{j \in [n] \setminus \{i\}} (\alpha_i - \alpha_j)^{-1} \in \mathbb{Z}_q$.
2. Define $w_i = m^*(\alpha_i) \cdot v_i$ where the evaluation and product is in $\mathbb{Z}_q$. From now on see w_i as integers (in $[q-1]$).
3. Compute $w_i' = w_i + c_i q$ over the integers.
4. Compute $U = \prod_{i=1}^n \mathsf{pk}_i^{w_i'}$ and $V = \prod_{i=1}^n B_i^{w_i'}$.
5. Compute $\mathsf{NIZK}_{\mathsf{DLEQ}}((g_q, U, R, V); r) : g_q^r = R \wedge U^r = V)$. We write $\mathsf{Pf}_{\mathsf{Sh}} = \mathsf{NIZK}_{\mathsf{DLEQ}}.\mathsf{Prove}((g_q, U, R, V); r)$.
6. Output $\mathsf{Pf}_{\mathsf{Sh}}$.

$\Pi_{\mathsf{Sh}}.\mathsf{Verify}((f, g_q, (\mathsf{pk}_i)_{i=1}^n, R, (B_i)_{i=1}^n), \mathsf{Pf}_{\mathsf{Sh}})$:
1. Compute $(m^*(X), c_1, \ldots, c_n) = \mathcal{H}(\mathsf{pk}_1, \ldots, \mathsf{pk}_n, R, B_1, \ldots, B_n)$.
2. Compute w_i' from $m^*(X)$ and the public information as the dealer does.
3. Compute $U = \prod_{i=1}^n \mathsf{pk}_i^{w_i'}$ and $V = \prod_{i=1}^n B_i^{w_i'}$.
4. Output $\mathsf{NIZK}_{\mathsf{DLEQ}}.\mathsf{Verify}((g_q, U, R, V), \mathsf{Pf}_{\mathsf{Sh}})$.

Fig. 4. Proof for correct PVSS sharing

Theorem 7. *In the random oracle model, and assuming RO_C is hard for CLGen, Π_{Sh} in Fig. 4 is a proof for the relation $\mathcal{R}_{\mathsf{Sh}}$ with soundness error $\epsilon_{\mathsf{DLEQ}} + 1/C + 1/q + \mathsf{negl}(\lambda)$, where ϵ_{DLEQ} is the soundness error of $\mathsf{NIZK}_{\mathsf{DLEQ}}$. It is zero knowledge assuming $\mathsf{NIZK}_{\mathsf{DLEQ}}$ is.*

Proof. The proof is shown in the full version [10].

Remark 2. By [22], Π_{Sh} is simulation sound in the random oracle model.

Discrete Logarithm Knowledge and Discrete Logarithm Equality. We have seen that $\mathsf{NIZK}_{\mathsf{Sh}}$, and hence the sharing distribution algorithm $\mathsf{qCLPVSS.Share}$, can be instantiated by Π_{Sh} as long as we have a proof $\mathsf{NIZK}_{\mathsf{DLEQ}}$ of discrete logarithm equality. Moreover, we also need $\mathsf{NIZK}_{\mathsf{DLEQ}}$ for the sharing decryption $\mathsf{DecShare}$. In both cases, we do not need a proof of knowledge of the exponent, so we can use Π_{LinCL} in Fig. 3. This proof requires the RO_C assumption, but we already need this assumption for Π_{Sh} anyway.

Finally, we do need a proof of knowledge $\mathtt{NIZKPoK_{DL}}$ of discrete logarithm in the key generation algorithm $\mathtt{qCLPVSS.KeyGen}$. We have listed two options in Sect. 2.3: either we use Π_{DL1}, which has a higher complexity but which does not require hardness assumptions and can be applied regardless of how g_q is chosen; or we use Π_{DL2} which relies on the LO_C and SR assumptions and where we need to slightly modify the setup to replace g_q by a randomized $g_q' = g_q^{\rho}$ for a random ρ which the adversary cannot control. We remark that, although Π_{DL2} only guarantees witness extraction for the slightly different relation $\mathcal{R}'_{DL}$ where only knowledge of integers ρ_0 and ρ_1 with $g_q^{2^{-\rho_0}\rho_1} = \mathsf{pk}_i$ is guaranteed, this is not really a big problem for us: the one place where we need extraction of the exponent is in the proof of Theorem 6, and there we can replace the extracted sk_i by $2^{-\rho_{i,0}}\rho_{i,1}$ and use the fact that square roots in G^q are computed efficiently.

3.3   Complexity

We focus on the communication complexity of $\mathtt{qCLPVSS}$, since this is usually the main bottleneck in PVSS applications. Let κ be a statistical security parameter for soundness, zero knowledge (so both soundness error and statistical distance in the zero knowledge simulation are bounded by $2^{-\kappa}$), and also so that we instantiate $\mathcal{D}_q$ by sampling uniformly in $[2^{\kappa}\bar{s}]$ (see Sect. 2.2).[7]

- $\mathtt{qCLPVSS.KeyGen}$: 1 element in G and $\sim \kappa^2 + \kappa \log \kappa$ bits (using Π_{DL1}) or $\sim 3\kappa + \log(\bar{s})$ (using Π_{DL2}) bits per party.
- $\mathtt{qCLPVSS.Dist}$: $n + 1$ elements in G and $\sim 3\kappa + \log(\bar{s})$ bits
- $\mathtt{qCLPVSS.DecShare}$: $\sim 3\kappa + \log(\bar{s}) + \log q$ bits (per party)

Moreover, the encrypted shares are n CL-HSM ciphertexts (where we only send R once) and may benefit from compression techniques [5].

Although we do not estimate the computational complexity in details, the main point of our construction is that it maintains the linear complexity in terms of group operations that was achieved in previous works [8,9,11]. While group operations on class groups have higher complexity than over groups defined on elliptic curves, the concrete times estimated in [5] show that the overhead in computation time is of about an order of magnitude.

Comparison with YOLO YOSO [11]. The PVSS scheme in YOLO YOSO requires essentially the same amount of group operations computation and group elements communication. Since our scheme operates over class groups, it clearly has an overhead in relation to elliptic curve implementations of YOLO YOSO as estimated in [5]. However, we achieve more flexibility in being able to retrieve the original shared secret s (or the result s' of linear operations on multiple secrets), whereas YOLO YOSO only allows for obtaining g^s (or the result s' of linear operations on multiple secrets). Moreover, we prove the IND-2-security notion from [31], whereas YOLO YOSO only shows the weaker IND-1-security also from [31], although we think it can also be proved IND-2-secure. In contrast, previous

---

[7] In practice we consider $\kappa = 40$ is reasonable.

(and less efficient) PVSS using similar techniques [8,9]are only IND-1. This is because these are based on a OW-CPA secure encryption scheme that allows for the necessary linear operations used in the NIZKs of sharing correctness.

Comparison with [32]. The work [32] constructs a PVSS scheme from class groups, motivated by distributed key generation. The shares are encrypted in the same way as ours (namely the dealer sends $(R, (B_i)_{i=1}^n)$. However, our scheme presents several advantages: the remaining communication of the sharing phase (the size of the proof $\mathsf{Pf_{Sh}}$) is independent of n and t, while they require to send commitments to the t coefficients of the polynomial, as well as somewhat larger proofs. Moreover, our PVSS achieves the strong IND-2-security property, while their construction does not satisfy the notion of indistinguishability of secrets, but a weaker notion of privacy that allows leakage. This leakage is fine for their DKG application, but it may not be adequate in other applications.

4 Application: Distributed Key Generation

We extend qCLPVSS to construct a distributed key generation protocol for a given cyclic group $\mathbb{H}$ of prime order q where DDH is assumed to be hard (e.g. an elliptic curve group). We assume a static adversary that can corrupt at most $t \leq \frac{n-1}{2}$ parties. Our goal is for parties to generate partial public keys $\mathsf{tpk}_i = h^{p(\alpha_i)}$ and a global public key $\mathsf{tpk} = h^{p(\beta)}$, where each party i privately knows $\mathsf{tsk}_i = p(\alpha_i)$. The global secret key is implicitly defined as $\mathsf{tsk} = p(\beta)$.

We will present two constructions of discrete key generation: the first one has two rounds of communication but has the property that the public key can not be biased by the adversary. The second is a non-interactive protocol (only one round of communication) but a rushing adversary can bias the public key. Note this is unavoidable for one-round distributed key generation (see [33]).

4.1 Two-Round DKG with Unbiasable Public Key

In this section we will implement the functionality $\mathcal{F}_{\mathsf{DKG}}$ in Fig. 5. Note that when interacting with this functionality, the adversary can decide on the threshold partial secret keys tsk_i of the corrupted parties. But the global secret key tsk is chosen by the functionality uniformly at random and independently of these tsk_i, and hence the adversary has no control on the threshold public key tpk.

The strategy follows the general template by Katz [33], using our PVSS. Every party PVSSs a contribution s_j to the secret key. This determines a set $\mathcal{Q}$ of parties whose sharing proofs pass the check. Parties define their tsk_i summing the shares received from parties in $\mathcal{Q}$. In the second round, parties publish $\mathsf{tpk}_i = h^{\mathsf{tsk}_i}$ and prove this is consistent with the encrypted shares received before.

Theorem 8. *Under the DDH-f (for privacy of* qCLPVSS*) and ROC (for verifiability of* qCLPVSS *and simulation soundness of* Π_{Sh} *and* Π_{LinCL}*) assumptions the protocol* Π_{DKG} *in Fig. 6 realizes* $\mathcal{F}_{\mathsf{DKG}}$ *securely in the random model in the presence of a malicious static adversary corrupting* $t \leq \frac{n-1}{2}$ *parties.*

Proof. The proof is shown in the full version [10].

Functionality $\mathcal{F}_{\mathsf{DKG}}$

$\mathcal{F}_{\mathsf{DKG}}$ is parameterized by a DDH-hard cyclic group $\mathbb{H}$ of prime order q, with generator h. Let n and $1 \leq t \leq (n-1)/2$ be integers. Let $\beta, \alpha_1, \ldots, \alpha_n$ be pairwise distinct elements in $\mathbb{Z}_q$. $\mathcal{F}_{\mathsf{DKG}}$ interacts with parties $ID_1, \ldots, ID_n$ and an adversary $\mathcal{S}$ that corrupts at most t parties. $\mathcal{F}_{\mathsf{DKG}}$ works as follows:

- Upon receiving $(\mathrm{GEN}, sid, ID_i)$ from a party ID_i:
  1. If ID_i is honest, forward $(\mathrm{GEN}, sid, ID_i)$ to $\mathcal{S}$.
  2. If ID_i is corrupted, wait for $\mathcal{S}$ to send $(\mathrm{SETSHARE}, sid, ID_i, \mathsf{tsk}_i)$ where $\mathsf{tsk}_i \in \mathbb{Z}_q$ and set $\mathsf{tpk}_i = g^{\mathsf{tsk}_i}$.
- Let J be the set of all parties ID_j who sent $(\mathrm{GEN}, sid, ID_j)$. If all honest parties are in J, proceed as follows:
  1. Sample a random polynomial p of degree at most t with $p(\alpha_i) = \mathsf{tsk}_i$ for all tsk_i sent by $\mathcal{S}$ in the previous step^a For every party ID_ℓ for which no tsk_i has been received, set $\mathsf{tsk}_\ell = p(\alpha_\ell)$ and $\mathsf{tpk}_\ell = h^{\mathsf{tsk}_\ell}$.
  2. Set $\mathsf{tpk} = h^{p(\beta)}$. ^{b}
  3. For all corrupted $ID_c \in J$, send $(\mathrm{KEYS}, sid, \mathsf{tsk}_c, \{\mathsf{tpk}_j\}_{j \in J}, \mathsf{tpk})$ to $\mathcal{S}$.
  4. Wait for $\mathcal{S}$ to send (ABORT, sid, C) where C is a set of corrupted parties.
  5. Send $(\mathrm{KEYS}, sid, \mathsf{tsk}_j, \{\mathsf{tpk}_k\}_{k \in J \setminus C}, \mathsf{tpk})$ to each honest party ID_j.

---

^{a} At least one such polynomial exists because there are at most t corrupted parties.
^{b} Note that $p(\beta)$ is uniformly random in $\mathbb{Z}_q$ independently of the tsk_i sent in the previous step, and hence tpk is uniform in $\mathbb{H}$ conditioned on those tsk_i.

Fig. 5. Distributed Key Generation Functionality $\mathcal{F}_{\mathsf{DKG}}$

4.2 One-Round Biasable Public-Key Version

We now show a protocol that implements the functionality in Fig. 7 in one round of communication. In this case, the functionality allows the adversary to bias the public key: the functionality sends some "temporary" public keys tpk, $\{\mathsf{tpk}_i\}_{i \in [n]}$ as well as temporary secret keys tsk_i for the corrupted parties, and then the adversary can choose to update the secret sharing polynomial by adding a contribution $p'(X)$. This reflects the fact that in a one-round real protocol an adversary can wait until all honest parties have spoken, see all information it is allowed to, and in that moment then make one or more corrupted parties execute the PVSS honestly with sharing polynomials adding to some chosen $p'(X)$.

As in the two-round protocol, every party j shares a secret s_j with the PVSS, sending $R_j = g_q^{r_j}$ $B_{j,i} = \mathsf{pk}_i^{r_j} f^{\sigma_{j,i}}$ where $\sigma_{j,i} = p_j(\alpha_i)$ are Shamir shares of $p_j(\beta) = s_j$. But now, they also publish the values $D_{j,i} := h^{\sigma_{j,i}} \in \mathbb{H}$. This allows every party to eventually compute the i-th threshold public key as $\mathsf{tpk}_i = \prod_{j \in \mathcal{Q}} h^{\sigma_{j,i}}$ where $\mathcal{Q}$ is again the set of parties that created the sharing honestly.

To be included in $\mathcal{Q}$, party j needs to prove not only that $(R_j, B_{j,i})$ form a correct PVSS sharing but also that $B_{j,i}$ and $D_{j,i}$ are consistent. In other words, we will need a NIZK proof $\mathsf{Pf}_{\mathsf{ExtSh}}$ for the relation

$$\mathcal{R}_{\mathsf{ExtSh}} = \{(f, g_q, h, R, (\mathsf{pk}_i)_{i \in [n]}, (B_i)_{i \in [n]}, (D_i)_{i \in [n]}; (r, p(X)) :$$

Two-round DKG protocol Π_{DKG} with Unbiasable Public Key

Let q be a prime and $0 \le t < n \le q$ be positive integers. Let $\mathbb{H}$ be a cyclic group of order q generated by h.

Setup:

1. Parties run $\mathsf{pp} \leftarrow \mathsf{qCLPVSS.Setup}(1^\lambda, q, 1, t, n)$
2. Each party i runs $(\mathsf{sk}_i, \mathsf{pk}_i, \mathsf{Pf}_{\mathsf{pk}_i}) \leftarrow \mathsf{qCLPVSS.KeyGen}(\mathsf{pp}, i)$

Only parties who have produced $(\mathsf{sk}_i, \mathsf{pk}_i, \mathsf{Pf}_{\mathsf{pk}_i})$ that pass the verification $\mathsf{qCLPVSS.VerifyKey}$ are accepted to participate in the protocol.

Protocol:

1. Each party $j \in [n]$:
   (a) Samples uniformly random $s_j \in \mathcal{F}_q$
   (b) Runs $(R_j, (B_{j,i})_{i \in [n]}, \mathsf{Pf}_{\mathsf{Sh}j}) \leftarrow \mathsf{qCLPVSS.Share}(\mathsf{pp}, (\mathsf{pk}_i)_{i \in [n]}, s_j)$.
   (c) Publishes $(R_j, (B_{j,i})_{i \in [n]}, \mathsf{Pf}_{\mathsf{Sh}j})$
2. Let $\mathcal{Q}$ be the set of j for which

$$\mathsf{qCLPVSS.VerifySharing}(\mathsf{pp}, (\mathsf{pk}_i)_{i \in [n]}, R_j, (B_{j,i})_{i \in [n]}, \mathsf{Pf}_{\mathsf{Sh}j})) = 1.$$

Parties compute $R_{\mathcal{Q}} = \prod_{j \in \mathcal{Q}} R_j$, $B_{\mathcal{Q},i} = \prod_{j \in \mathcal{Q}} B_{j,i}$ for all $i \in \mathcal{Q}$.
Each party $i \in \mathcal{Q}$:
   (a) Computes $f_i = B_{\mathcal{Q},i} \cdot R_{\mathcal{Q}}^{-\mathsf{sk}_i}$, $\mathsf{tsk}_i = \mathsf{CLSolve}(f_i)$ and $\mathsf{tpk}_i = h^{\mathsf{tsk}_i}$.
   (b) Creates a proof $\mathsf{Pf}_{\mathsf{tpk}_i} = \Pi_{\mathsf{LinCL}}.\mathsf{Prove}(\{(f, R_{\mathcal{Q}}, B_{\mathcal{Q},i}, h, \mathsf{tpk}_i, \mathsf{pk}_i); (\mathsf{tsk}_i, \mathsf{sk}_i):$
   $f^{\mathsf{tsk}_i} R_{\mathcal{Q}}^{\mathsf{sk}_i} = B_{\mathcal{Q},i}, \ h^{\mathsf{tsk}_i} = \mathsf{tpk}_i, \ g_q^{\mathsf{sk}_i} = \mathsf{pk}_i\})$. (Section 2.3)
   (c) Publishes $(\mathsf{tpk}_i, \mathsf{Pf}_{\mathsf{tpk}_i})$
3. Let I be the set of parties i for which the (public, deterministic) verification of the proof $\mathsf{Pf}_{\mathsf{tpk}_i}$ accepts, and let $\mathcal{T}$ any set of $t + 1$ parties in I (e.g. the first $t + 1$ with respect to some pre-agreed indexing). The global public key tpk is $\mathsf{tpk} = \prod_{i \in \mathcal{T}} \mathsf{tpk}_i^{\lambda_i}$ where $\lambda_i = \prod_{k \in \mathcal{T} \setminus \{i\}} \frac{\beta - \alpha_j}{\alpha_i - \alpha_j}$

Fig. 6. Two-round DKG protocol Π_{DKG} with Unbiasable Public Key

---

Functionality $\mathcal{F}_{\mathsf{BDKG}}$

$\mathcal{F}_{\mathsf{BDKG}}$ is parameterized by a DDH-hard cyclic group $\mathbb{H}$ of prime order q, with generator h. Let n and $1 \le t \le (n-1)/2$ be integers. Let $\beta, \alpha_1, \ldots, \alpha_n$ be pairwise distinct elements in $\mathbb{Z}_q$. $\mathcal{F}_{\mathsf{BDKG}}$ interacts with parties $ID_1, \ldots, ID_n$ and an adversary $\mathcal{S}$ that corrupts at most t parties. $\mathcal{F}_{\mathsf{BDKG}}$ works as follows:

1. Upon receiving $(\mathsf{GEN}, sid, ID_i)$ from a honest party ID_i, forward $(\mathsf{GEN}, sid, ID_i)$ to $\mathcal{S}$. When all honest parties have done this, continue.
2. Sample a random polynomial p of degree at most t. For every party $ID_j \in [n]$, set $\mathsf{tsk}_j = p(\alpha_j)$ and $\mathsf{tpk}_j = h^{\mathsf{tsk}_j}$, $\mathsf{tpk} = h^{p(\beta)}$.
3. Send $(\mathsf{KEYS}, sid, \{\mathsf{tpk}_j\}_{j \in [n]}, \mathsf{tpk}, \{\mathsf{tsk}_j\}_{j \in \mathsf{Corr}})$ to $\mathcal{S}$.
4. Upon receiving (BIAS, sid, p') from $\mathcal{S}$, where p' is a polynomial of degree at most t then update $\mathsf{tpk}' = \mathsf{tpk} \cdot h^{p'(\beta)}$, $\mathsf{tpk}'_j = \mathsf{tpk}_j \cdot h^{p'(\alpha_j)}$ and $\mathsf{tsk}'_j = \mathsf{tsk}_j + p'(\alpha_j)$ for all $j \in [n]$.
5. For all parties ID_i, send $(\mathsf{KEYS}, sid, \mathsf{tsk}'_i, \{\mathsf{tpk}'_j\}_{j \in [n]}, \mathsf{tpk}')$ to ID_i.

Fig. 7. Biasable Distributed Key Generation Functionality $\mathcal{F}_{\mathsf{BDKG}}$

$$\deg p \le t, R = g_q^r, \text{ and } \forall\, i \in [n],\ B_i = \mathsf{pk}_i^r f^{p(\alpha_i)}, D_i = h^{p(\alpha_i)}\}$$

We show how to accomplish this with a *constant-size proof* next.

As in qCLPVSS, we can reduce testing whether B_i are of the correct form with respect to R (i.e. $B_i = \mathsf{pk}_i^r f^{p(\alpha_i)}$ for $p(X) \in \mathbb{Z}_q[X]_{\le t}$ and where $r \in \mathbb{Z}$ is such that g_q^r) to a DLEQ proof $g_q^r = R$, $U^r = V$. Moreover, thanks to the SCRAPE test, verifiers can locally check if $D_i = h^{\hat{p}(\alpha_i)}$ for some $\hat{p} \in \mathbb{Z}_q[X]_{\le t}$.

We still need to guarantee that $p(X) = \hat{p}(X)$, i.e. the shares hidden by B_i and D_i are the same. It is enough to prove that $p(\alpha_i) = \hat{p}(\alpha_i)$ for all $i \in [t+1]$. We can do this by testing $\sum_{i=1}^{t+1} e_i p(\alpha_i) =^? \sum_{i=1}^{t+1} e_i \hat{p}(\alpha_i)$ for random $e_1, \ldots, e_{t+1} \in \mathbb{Z}_q$ sampled via the random oracle. This would guarantee the property with probability $1 - 1/q$ over the random choice of the e_i.

To test this we define $D = \prod_{i=1}^{t+1} D_i^{e_i}$ and $B = \prod_{i=1}^{t+1} B_i^{e_i}$, $M = \prod_{i=1}^{t+1} \mathsf{pk}_i^{e_i}$ (all of which can be computed publicly) and $d = \sum_{i=1}^{t} e_i p(\alpha_i)$ (computed privately by the prover). If the prover has been honest then $M^r f^d = B$. This suggests we can reduce the problem to proving existence of r in $\mathbb{Z}$ and d in $\mathbb{Z}_q$ with $g_q^r = R$, $U^r = V$, $M^r f^d = B$, $h^d = D$. We will indeed prove this is sound. Finally, this last statement can then be addressed with a proof similar to the Π_{LinCL} in Sect. 2.3, with the only difference that h, D are in a different group and d is in $\mathbb{Z}_q$. We remark this type of "mixed" statements have already been addressed in similar ways in papers such as [6,13,14].

We start by presenting this last proof, which we call Π_{MDLEQ} in Fig. 8. Again, as in other similar protocols, the proof is paramtetrized by $C, A \in \mathbb{N}$ and to guarantee zero knowledge, we need that the witness is in an interval $[-S, S]$ and CS/A is negligible.

Theorem 9. *The interactive proof in Fig. 8 has soundness error $1/C + \mathsf{negl}(\lambda)$ if the $R0_C$ assumption holds. It is statistically zero-knowledge if the witness r is in $[-S, S]$ and CS/A is negligible. By the Fiat-Shamir heuristic, the non-interactive version has the same properties in the random oracle model.*

We use Π_{MDLEQ} as a building block for the proof Π_{ExtSh}, Fig. 9.

Theorem 10. *In the random oracle model, and assuming $R0_C$ is hard for CLGen, Π_{ExtSh} (Fig. 9) is a simulation sound proof for the relation $\mathcal{R}_{\mathsf{ExtSh}}$ with soundness error $\epsilon_{\mathsf{MDLEQ}} + 1/C + 3/q + \mathsf{negl}(\lambda)$, where $\epsilon_{\mathsf{MDLEQ}}$ is the soundness error of Π_{MDLEQ}. If we use the same C in Π_{MDLEQ} as in this proof, the soundness error is $2/C + 3/q + \mathsf{negl}(\lambda)$. Moreover, it is zero-knowledge assuming Π_{MDLEQ} is.*

Finally, we present our one-round DKG protocol in Fig. 10.

Theorem 11. *Under the DDH-f (for privacy of qCLPVSS) and $R0_C$ (for verifiability of qCLPVSS and simulation soundness of Π_{LinCL}) assumptions the protocol Π_{BDKG} in Fig. 10 realizes $\mathcal{F}_{\mathsf{BDKG}}$ securely in the random model in the presence of a malicious static adversary corrupting $t \le \frac{n-1}{2}$ parties.*

The proofs of Theorems 9, 10 and 11 are presented in the full version [10].

Zero-Knowledge Proof for "Mixed" Discrete Logarithm Equality

Zero Knowledge Proof for relation

$$\mathcal{R}_{\mathsf{MDLEQ}} = \{(g_q, U, M, f, h, R, V, B, D; r, d) : g_q^r = R, U^r = V, M^r f^d = B, h^d = D\}$$

Interactive version:
- Prover samples $r_* \leftarrow_\$ [0, A]$, $d_* \leftarrow_\$ \mathbb{Z}_q$, computes $R_* = g_q^{r_*}$, $V_* = U^{r_*}$, $B_* = M^{r_*} f^{d_*} = B$, $D_* = h^{d_*}$, sends R_*, V_*, B_*, D_* to verifier.
- Verifier samples $c \in [C]$.
- Prover computes and sends $u_r = r_* + cr$ (in $\mathbb{Z}$), $u_d = d_* + cd \mod q$.
- Verifier checks $g_q^{u_r} = R_* R^c$, $U^{u_r} = V_* \cdot V^c$, $M^{u_r} f^{u_d} = B_* \cdot B^c$, $h^{u_d} = D_* \cdot D^c$ and accepts if all checks pass.

Non-Interactive version:
Requires Random Oracle $\mathcal{H} : \{0,1\}^* \to [C]$:
$\Pi_{\mathsf{MDLEQ}}.\mathsf{Prove}(\mathbf{X}, \mathbf{w})$ (where $\mathbf{X} = (g_q, U, M, f, h, R, V, B, D)$, $\mathbf{w} = (r, d)$)
- Sample $r_* \leftarrow_\$ [0, A]$, $d_* \leftarrow_\$ \mathbb{Z}_q$, computes $R_* = g_q^{r_*}$, $V_* = U^{r_*}$, $B_* = M^{r_*} f^{d_*} = B$, $D_* = h^{d_*}$, $c = \mathcal{H}(\mathbf{X}, \mathbf{Y})$, where $\mathbf{Y} = (R_*, V_*, B_*, D_*)$, and $u_d = d_* + cd \mod q$, $u_r = r_* + cr$ (in $\mathbb{Z}$).
- Output $\mathsf{Pf}_{\mathsf{MDLEQ}} = (c, u_d, u_r)$

$\Pi_{\mathsf{MDLEQ}}.\mathsf{Verify}(\mathbf{X}, \mathsf{Pf}_{\mathsf{MDLEQ}})$
Compute $R_* = R^{-c} g_q^{u_r}$, $V_* = V^{-c} U^{u_r}$, $B_* = B^{-c} M^{u_r} f^{u_d}$, $D_* = D^{-c} h^{u_d}$. Define $\mathbf{Y} = (R_*, V_*, B_*, D_*)$). Check $c = \mathcal{H}(\mathbf{X}, \mathbf{Y})$. Accept if that is the case.

Fig. 8. Zero-Knowledge Proof for "Mixed" Discrete Logarithm Equality

Communication Complexity and Comparison. In Table 1 we list the communication complexities of our two protocols, and compare them to the currently best round-efficient distributed key generation protocols for the cases of biasable and unbiasable public keys, which are both based on Paillier encryption. For the one-round, biasable public key case, we use the Fouque-Stern [23] protocol. For the two-round case, we use the suggested instantiation with Paillier from [33], where we instantiate the NIZKs as in Fouque-Stern. We observe that the communication is dominated by the first summand and that therefore for a moderately large amount of parties, our DKG protocol will communicate less information as long as $k_{\hat{G}}$ is somewhat smaller than $3k_N$. Current security estimations ([5,21]) indicate this is the case for reasonable security parameters, e.g. 128-bit security. In fact, note that the dominating factor in our protocol consists of the n^2 share encryptions (n per party), which are in fact roughly $\frac{1}{2}n^2$ CL-HSM ciphertexts (since R_j is common to all encryptions by party j), the Paillier based constructions communicate $3n^2 k_N$ bits ($\sim \frac{3}{2}n^2$ Paillier ciphertexts) and [5] estimates each CL-ciphertext to be 1.5 to 2.3 shorter than a Paillier ciphertext depending on the security parameter and for q of 224 bits. Hence, our communication is around 4.5 to 7 times smaller than [23,33].

Zero Knowledge Proof for correct "extended" sharing

Non-interactive Proof for the relation

$$\mathcal{R}_{\mathsf{ExtSh}} = \{(f, g_q, h, (\mathsf{pk}_i)_{i=1}^n, R, (B_i)_{i=1}^n), (D_i)_{i=1}^n); (p(X), r) : r \in \mathbb{Z},$$

$$p(X) \in \mathbb{Z}_q[X]_{\leq t}, R = g_q^r, B_i = \mathsf{pk}_i^r f^{p(\alpha_i)} \wedge D_i = h^{p(\alpha_i)} \; \forall i \in [n]\}.$$

The proof is parametrized by $C \in \mathbb{Z}$.
We assume a random oracle $\mathcal{H} : \{0, 1\}^* \to \mathbb{Z}_q[X]_{\leq n-t-2} \times [C]^n \times \mathbb{Z}_q^{t+1}$.
Let $\mathsf{X} := (f, g_q, h, (\mathsf{pk}_i)_{i=1}^n, R, (B_i)_{i=1}^n, (D_i)_{i=1}^n)$, $\mathsf{wit} := (p(X), r)$

$\Pi_{\mathsf{ExtSh}}.\mathsf{Prove}(\mathsf{X}; \mathsf{wit})$:
1. Compute $(m^*(X), c_1, \ldots, c_n, e_1, \ldots, e_{t+1}) = \mathcal{H}(\mathsf{X})$.
   Let $v_i = \prod_{j \in [n] \setminus \{i\}} (\alpha_i - \alpha_j)^{-1} \in \mathbb{Z}_q$.
2. Define $w_i = m^*(\alpha_i) \cdot v_i$ for each $i \in [n]$ where the evaluation and product is in $\mathbb{Z}_q$. From now on see w_i as integers (in $[0, q-1]$).
3. Compute $w_i' = w_i + c_i q$ over the integers for $i \in [n]$.
4. Compute $U = \prod_{i=1}^n \mathsf{pk}_i^{w_i'}$ and $V = \prod_{i=1}^n B_i^{w_i'}$.
5. Compute $d = \sum_{i=1}^{t+1} e_i p(\alpha_i)$, $B = \prod_{i=1}^{t+1} B_i^{e_i}$, $D = \prod_{i=1}^{t+1} D_i^{e_i}$, $M = \prod_{i=1}^{t+1} \mathsf{pk}_i^{e_i}$
6. Output $\mathsf{Pf}_{\mathsf{ExtSh}} = \Pi_{\mathsf{MDLEQ}}.\mathsf{Prove}(g_q, U, M, f, h, R, V, B, D; r, d)$ as in Figure 8.
   Recall this is a proof for the relations $g_q^r = R, U^r = V, M^r \cdot f^d = B, h^d = D$.

$\Pi_{\mathsf{Ext-Sh}}.\mathsf{Verify}(\mathsf{X}, \mathsf{Pf}_{\mathsf{Sh}})$:
1. Compute $(m^*(X), c_1, \ldots, c_n, e_1, \ldots, e_{t+1}) = \mathcal{H}(\mathsf{X})$.
2. Compute w_i and w_i' from $m^*(X)$ and the public information as the prover does.
3. Check $\prod_{i=1}^n D_i^{w_i} = 1_{\mathbb{H}}$. If not, output reject. Otherwise, continue.
4. Compute U, V, B, D, M from w_i', e_i and public information as the prover does.
5. Output $\Pi_{\mathsf{MDLEQ}}.\mathsf{Verify}((g_q, U, M, f, h, R, V, B, D, \mathsf{Pf}_{\mathsf{ExtSh}})$.

Fig. 9. Zero Knowledge Proof for correct "extended" sharing

5 Application: YOSO MPC

In the YOSO model, parties can only speak once, *i.e.* after each party sends a message it can no longer participate in the execution. Moreover, the next committee of parties that take over the execution is selected at random and remains anonymous until they act. This requires a mechanism for transferring the secret state kept by each party in the comittee responsible for the current round to the committee responsible to the next round. As observed in [26], starting from the protocol [19] is a promising approach for keeping this state to a minimum. In the CDN protocol, the only secret state that parties must hold throughout the execution consists of shares of a secret key for a linearly homomorphic threshold encryption scheme, instead of requiring parties to hold shares of each intermediate gate output. In a recent work [6], linearly homomorphic threshold encryption based on the CL-framework was leveraged to realize this approach with a transparent setup by constructing a suitable DKG and a re-sharing protocol that

---

One-round Distributed Key Generation Π_{BDKG}

Let q be a prime and $0 \le t < n \le q$ be positive integers. Let $\mathbb{H}$ be a cyclic group of order q generated by h.

Setup:
1. Parties run $\mathsf{pp} \leftarrow \mathsf{qCLPVSS.Setup}(1^\lambda, q, 1, t, n)$
2. Each party i runs $(\mathsf{sk}_i, \mathsf{pk}_i, \mathsf{Pf}_{\mathsf{pk}_i}) \leftarrow \mathsf{qCLPVSS.KeyGen}(\mathsf{pp}, i)$

Only parties who have produced $(\mathsf{sk}_i, \mathsf{pk}_i, \mathsf{Pf}_{\mathsf{pk}_i})$ that pass the verification $\mathsf{qCLPVSS.VerifyKey}$ are accepted to participate in the protocol.

Protocol:
In the only communication round, each party $j \in [n]$:
1. Samples uniformly random $s_j \leftarrow_\$ \mathbb{Z}_q$
2. Runs $(R_j, (B_{j,i})_{i \in [n]}, \cdot) \leftarrow \mathsf{qCLPVSS.Share}(\mathsf{pp}, (\mathsf{pk}_i)_{i \in [n]}, s_j)$. By this notation we mean we omit the proof of correct sharing, as we replace it by the one below. Let $p_j(X)$ the sharing polynomial, $\sigma_{j,i} = p_j(\alpha_i)$ the share for party i, obtained as part of the PVSS.
3. Computes $D_{i,j} = h^{\sigma_{j,i}}$ for all $i \in [n]$
4. Use $\Pi_{\mathsf{ExtSh}}.\mathsf{Prove}$ to compute a proof $\mathsf{Pf}_{\mathsf{ExtSh}_j}$ for the statement $\exists r_j \in \mathbb{Z}, p_j(X) \in \mathbb{Z}_q[X]_{\le t}$, such that $R = g_q^{r_j}$, $B_{j,i} = \mathsf{pk}_i^{r_j} \cdot f_j^{p_j(\alpha_i)}$ $\forall i \in [n]$, and $D_{j,i} = h^{p_j(\alpha_i)}$ $\forall i \in [n]$.
5. Publishes $(R_j, (B_{j,i})_{i \in [n]}, (D_{j,i})_{i \in [n]}, \mathsf{Pf}_{\mathsf{ExtSh}_j})$

Global output:
Let $\mathcal{Q}$ be the set of j for which the (deterministic, public) verification $\Pi_{\mathsf{ExtSh}}.\mathsf{Verify}$ accepts $\mathsf{Pf}_{\mathsf{ExtSh}_j}$. Then:
- For every $i \in [n]$, tpk_i is defined as $\mathsf{tpk}_i = \prod_{j \in \mathcal{Q}} D_{j,i}$.
- Let $\mathcal{T} = [t+1]$. The global public key tpk is $\mathsf{tpk} = \prod_{i \in \mathcal{T}} \mathsf{tpk}_i^{\lambda_i}$ where λ_i is the Lagrange interpolation coefficient $\lambda_i = \prod_{k \in \mathcal{T} \setminus \{i\}} \frac{\beta - \alpha_k}{\alpha_i - \alpha_k}$.

Private output:
Each party $i \in [n]$:
1. Computes $B_{\mathcal{Q},i} = \prod_{j \in \mathcal{Q}} B_{j,i}$, $R_{\mathcal{Q}} = \prod_{j \in \mathcal{Q}} R_j$
2. Computes $f_i = B_{\mathcal{Q},i} \cdot R_{\mathcal{Q}}^{-\mathsf{sk}_i}$ and outputs $\mathsf{tsk}_i = \mathsf{CLSolve}(f_i)$.

Fig. 10. One-round Distributed Key Generation (with biasable public key)

Table 1. Comparison of DKG schemes for a DDH-hard group $\mathbb{H}$ where n is the total number of parties, t is the number of corrupted parties, $k_{\mathbb{H}}$ is the number of bits of an element of $\mathbb{H}$ which to simplify we set to $\log q$, k_N is the number of bits of the Paillier cryptosystem modulus N, $k_{\hat{G}}$ is the number of bits of a representation of an element in $\hat{G}$, $\bar{s}$ is the upper bound for the order of $\hat{G}^q$.

Scheme	Comm. (bits)	Rounds	Bias Resist.	Assump.
Katz [33], using Paillier	$3n^2 k_N + 2n^2 \kappa + (n^2 + tn + n)k_{\mathbb{H}}$	2	Yes	DCR
Π_{DKG}	$(n^2 + n)k_{\hat{G}} + 3n \log(\bar{s}) + 9n\kappa + nk_{\mathbb{H}}$	2	Yes	DDH-f, RO_C
Fouque-Stern [23]	$3n^2 k_N + 2n^2 \kappa + (2n^2 + tn + n)k_{\mathbb{H}}$	1	No	DCR
Π_{BDKG}	$(n^2 + n)k_{\hat{G}} + n \log(\bar{s}) + 3n\kappa + n^2 k_{\mathbb{H}}$	1	No	DDH-f, RO_C

allows for transferring secret key shares among committees (assuming receiver anonymous communication channels).

As a first step, we endow our PVSS scheme qCLPVSS with a publicly verifiable re-sharing scheme in order to construct an efficient mechanism for transferring secret state among committees in the YOSO model. This re-sharing mechanism already improves on the efficiency of the one proposed in [6]. We only need to publish a set of encrypted shares and a NIZK of re-sharing validity as many elements of $\mathbb{Z}_q$ as encrypted shares, whereas the protocol of [6] has each committee execute one VSS instance towards the next committee and one towards the second next committee. Later on, we show how the efficient encryption to the future scheme of YOLO YOSO can be combined with this approach to realize the full communication infrastructure needed to transfer state among committees.

5.1 Resharing

We consider how a set of parties who have a correct PVSS sharing of a secret with qCLPVSS can reshare this to a new set of parties. In the following we assume the case $k = 1$ (one secret in $\mathbb{Z}_q$) and we consider a starting set of n_0 parties, with privacy threshold t_0 and we denote their evaluation points $\overline{\alpha_1}, \ldots, \overline{\alpha_{n_0}}$ for the shares and $\overline{\beta}$ for the secret. Moreover, let $\overline{\mathsf{pk}_i}, \overline{\mathsf{sk}_i}$ their keys. Meanwhile for the next set of parties we have respectively $\alpha_1, \ldots, \alpha_{n_1}, \beta$ and $\mathsf{pk}_i, \mathsf{sk}_i$ respectively. Now given a secret s shared with degree-t_0 Shamir secret sharing, with shares $\overline{\sigma_i}$ for $i \in [n_0]$ we know that, for any set $\mathcal{T}$ of size $t_0 + 1$, $s = \sum_{i \in \mathcal{T}} \overline{\lambda_i} \overline{\sigma_i}$ where $\overline{\lambda_i} = L_i(\beta)$ for $L_i = \mathrm{Lag}_{i, \mathcal{T}, (\overline{\alpha_i})}$, i.e. $\overline{\lambda_i} = \prod_{j \in \mathcal{T} \setminus \{i\}} (\overline{\beta} - \overline{\alpha_j})(\overline{\alpha_i} - \overline{\alpha_j})^{-1}$. Since Shamir secret sharing is linear, it is enough that such a set $\mathcal{T}$ correctly reshare their shares to the new committee of parties: party i, having received $\sigma_{j,i}$ as a share of $\overline{\sigma_j}$ for each $j \in \mathcal{T}$, can then compute $\sum_{i \in \mathcal{T}} \overline{\lambda_i} \sigma_{j,i}$ and by linearity this will form a new sharing of s.

Note that in PVSS, we have the advantage that there is no need for dispute resolution: everyone can compute $\mathcal{T}$ by themselves, provided that there is a proof of correct sharing. This enables its use in the YOSO model, as share receivers do not need to speak at that point. We do need that there are at least $t_0 + 1$ honest parties in the first set, i.e. $2t_0 + 1 \le n$.

The crux of the protocol is proving a correct resharing. If $(\overline{R}, (\overline{B}_j)_{j \in [n_0]})$ is the original sharing, party j will create a polynomial with $p_j(\beta) = \overline{\sigma_j}$, use qCLPVSS for creating a sharing $(R_j, B_{j,i})$ where the $B_{j,i}$ encrypt $p_j(\alpha_i)$ and show not only correctness of this sharing, but also that $(\overline{R}, \overline{B}_j)$ decrypts to $p_j(\beta)$.

We show the resharing protocol in Fig. 11 and later we explain the proof of resharing in more detail below. As for security, note that the IND2 security property of the PVSS directly guarantees that a set containing at most t_0 parties of the first committee and t_1 parties of the second can still not distinguish between sharings of two secrets. The soundness of the proofs will guarantee that a party is included in $\mathcal{Q}$ if they have reshared their share correctly. From $\mathcal{Q}$ parties can then determine $\mathcal{T}$.

Protocol for PVSS Resharing to a new committee

Input: A PVSS $(\overline{R}, (\overline{B}_i)_{i \in [n_0]}$ of a secret $s \in \mathbb{Z}_q$

Output: A PVSS $(R, (B_i)_{i \in [n_1]}$ of the same secret $s \in \mathbb{Z}_q$

We assume at most t_0 corrupted parties in the first set and t_1 corrupted parties in the second. Moreover $2t_0 + 1 \leq n_0$ (to guarantee at least $t_0 + 1$ honest parties)

1. Every party $j \in [n_0]$:
   (a) Retrieves $\overline{\sigma}_j \leftarrow \mathsf{qCLPVSS.DecShare}(\mathsf{pp}, \overline{\mathsf{sk}}_j, \overline{R}, \overline{B}_j)$
   (b) Chooses $p_j \in \mathbb{Z}_q[X]_{\leq t_1}$ uniformly at random such that $p_j(\beta) = \overline{\sigma}_j$
   (c) Chooses $r_j \leftarrow \mathcal{D}_q$ and computes $R_j = g_q^{r_j}$, $B_{j,i} = \mathsf{pk}_i^{r_j} f^{p_j(\alpha_i)}$. Let
   $\mathbf{X}_j := (g_q, h, f, (\mathsf{pk}_i)_{i \in [n_1]}, \overline{\mathsf{pk}}_j, \overline{R}, \overline{B}_j, R_j, (B_{j,i})_{i \in [n_1]})$, $\mathbf{w}_j := (\overline{\mathsf{sk}}_j, r_j, p_j)$.
   (d) Using Π_{Resh} in Figure 12 below compute a proof $\mathsf{Pf}_{\mathsf{Resh}\,j} = \Pi_{\mathsf{Resh}}.\mathsf{Prove}(\mathbf{X}_j; \mathbf{w}_j)$ for the relation given by $\deg p_j \leq t_1, g_q^{\overline{\mathsf{sk}}_j} = \overline{\mathsf{pk}}_j, \overline{B}_j = \overline{R}^{\overline{\mathsf{sk}}_j} \cdot f^{p_j(\beta)}, R_j = g_q^{r_j}$, and $B_{j,i} = \mathsf{pk}_i^{r_j} \cdot f^{p_j(\alpha_i)} \; \forall i \in [n_1]$.
   (e) Output $(R_j, (B_{j,i})_{i \in [n_1]}, \mathsf{Pf}_{\mathsf{Resh}\,j})$.

2. Let $\mathcal{Q}$ the set of parties j in $[n_0]$ for which $\mathsf{Pf}_{\mathsf{Resh}\,j}$ passes. Let $\mathcal{T} \subseteq \mathcal{Q}$ be a subset of $t_0 + 1$ parties. Then define $R = \sum_{j \in \mathcal{T}} R_j^{\overline{\lambda}_j}$, and $B_i = \sum_{j \in \mathcal{T}} B_{j,i}^{\overline{\lambda}_j}$ for $i \in [n_1]$, where $\overline{\lambda}_j = \sum_{k \in \mathcal{T} \setminus \{j\}} (\beta - \overline{\alpha}_k)(\overline{\alpha}_j - \overline{\alpha}_k)^{-1}$ computed over $\mathbb{Z}_q$ and then considered as an integer in $[0, q-1]$.

3. Output $(R, (B_i)_{i \in [n_1]})$.

Fig. 11. Protocol for resharing to a new committee

We now detail the proof of resharing Π_{Resh} (Figure 12). Consider

$$\mathcal{R}_{\mathsf{Resh}} = \{(g_q, h, f, (\mathsf{pk}_i)_{i \in [n_1]}, \overline{\mathsf{pk}}, \overline{R}, \overline{B}, R, (B_i)_{i \in [n_1]}); (\overline{\mathsf{sk}}, r, p(X)) : p \in \mathbb{Z}_q[X]_{\leq t},$$
$$r \in \mathbb{Z}, \; g_q^{\overline{\mathsf{sk}}} = \overline{\mathsf{pk}}, \; \overline{B} = \overline{R}^{\overline{\mathsf{sk}}} \cdot f^{p(\beta)}, \; R = g_q^r, \; B_i = \mathsf{pk}_i^r f^{p(\alpha_i)} \; \forall i \in [n_1]\}.$$

This is the usual $\mathcal{R}_{\mathsf{Sh}}$ augmented with the fact that the secret $p(\beta)$ is the value committed by $(\overline{\mathsf{pk}}, \overline{B}) = (g_q^{\overline{\mathsf{sk}}}, \overline{R}^{\overline{\mathsf{sk}}} \cdot f^{p(\beta)})$. We will use the SCRAPE test, now applied to the $n + 1$ evaluation points $\beta, \alpha_1, \ldots, \alpha_n$. We rename $\alpha_0 := \beta$ for simplicity. Then we need to sample m^* of degree $n - t - 1$ (rather than $n - t - 2$ as before), and define v_i, now for all $i \in [0, n]$ and including α_0. Given $w_i = m^*(\alpha_i) \cdot v_i$, the SCRAPE test implies $\sum_{i=0}^{n} p(\alpha_i) w_i = 0$ for any p of $\deg p \leq t$.

Now if we compute $U = \prod_{i=1}^{n} \mathsf{pk}_i$ and $V = \prod_{i=1}^{n} B_i^{w_i}$ as in previous proofs, we can eventually reduce the task to showing existence of $r, \overline{\mathsf{sk}}$ with $g_q^r = R$, $g_q^{\overline{\mathsf{sk}}} = \overline{\mathsf{pk}}$ and $U^r \cdot (\overline{R}^{w_0})^{\mathsf{sk}} = V \cdot \overline{B}^{w_0}$ which can be addressed with the proof Π_{LinCL} (Fig. 3, Sect. 2.3). However, there is the same problem with soundness as in Sect. 3.2, caused by the fact that the adversary could have concocted $B_i = \mathsf{pk}_i^r \cdot f^{p(\alpha_i)} \cdot H_i$ (and now also $\overline{B} = \overline{R}^{\overline{\mathsf{sk}}} \cdot f^{p(\beta)} \cdot H_0$) so that $\prod_{i=0}^{n} H_i^{w_i}$ cancels out. This is solved

---

Zero Knowledge Proof for correct resharing

Non-interactive Proof for the relation

$$\mathcal{R}_{\mathsf{Resh}} = \{((g_q, h, f, (\mathsf{pk}_i)_{i \in [n_1]}, \overline{\mathsf{pk}}, \overline{R}, \overline{B}, R, (B_i)_{i \in [n_1]}); (\overline{\mathsf{sk}}, r, p(X)) : r \in \mathbb{Z},$$

$$p(X) \in \mathbb{Z}_q[X]_{\le t}, \; g_q^{\overline{\mathsf{sk}}} = \overline{\mathsf{pk}}, \; \overline{B} = \overline{R}^{\overline{\mathsf{sk}}} \cdot f^{p(\beta)}, \; R = g_q^r, \; B_i = \mathsf{pk}_i^r f^{p(\alpha_i)} \; \forall i \in [n_1]\}.$$

The proof is parametrized by $C \in \mathbb{Z}$.
We assume a random oracle $\mathcal{H} : \{0,1\}^* \to \mathbb{Z}_q[X]_{\le n-t-1} \times [C]^{n+1}$.
Let $\mathsf{X} := (g_q, h, f, (\mathsf{pk}_i)_{i \in [n_1]}, \overline{\mathsf{pk}}, \overline{R}, \overline{B}, R, (B_i)_{i \in [n_1]})$, $\mathsf{wit} := (\overline{\mathsf{sk}}, r, p(X))$. For ease of notation let $\alpha_0 = \beta$.

$\Pi_{\mathsf{Resh}}.\mathsf{Prove}(\mathsf{X}; \mathsf{wit})$:
1. Compute $(m^*(X), c_0, c_1, \ldots, c_n) = \mathcal{H}(\mathsf{X})$. For $i \in [0, n]$ let $v_i = \prod_{j \in [0,n] \setminus \{i\}} (\alpha_i - \alpha_j)^{-1} \in \mathbb{Z}_q$.
2. Define $w_i = m^*(\alpha_i) \cdot v_i$ for each $i \in [0, n]$ where the evaluation and product is in $\mathbb{Z}_q$. From now on see w_i as integers (in $[0, q-1]$).
3. Compute $w_i' = w_i + c_i q$ over the integers for $i \in [n]$.
4. Compute $U = \prod_{i=1}^n \mathsf{pk}_i^{w_i'}$ and $V = \prod_{i=1}^n B_i^{w_i'}$. Also let $\overline{R_0} = \overline{R}^{w_0'}$ and $\overline{B_0} = \overline{B}^{w_0'}$
5. Compute a proof, using Π_{LinCL} (Figure 3, Section 2.3) of the following relation

$$\{((U, \overline{R_0}, V, g_q, \overline{\mathsf{pk}}, R); (r, \overline{\mathsf{sk}}) : U^r \cdot (R_0)^{\overline{\mathsf{sk}}} = V \cdot B_0, \; g_q^{\overline{\mathsf{sk}}} = \overline{\mathsf{pk}}, \; g_q^r = R\}$$

6. Output this proof as $\mathsf{Pf}_{\mathsf{Resh}}$.

$\Pi_{\mathsf{Ext-Sh}}.\mathsf{Verify}(\mathsf{X}, \mathsf{Pf}_{\mathsf{Resh}})$:
1. Compute $(m^*(X), c_0, c_1, \ldots, c_n) = \mathcal{H}(\mathsf{X})$.
2. Compute w_i, w_i', U, V, $\overline{R_0}$, $\overline{B_0}$ from $m^*(X)$ and the public information as the prover does.
3. Verify $\mathsf{Pf}_{\mathsf{Resh}}$ is a valid proof for the relation above.

Fig. 12. Zero Knowledge Proof for correct resharing

exactly in the same way as in Sect. 3.2 by randomizing $w_i' = w_i + c_i q$ and using the rough order assumption.

Theorem 12. *In the random oracle model, and assuming RO_C is hard for CLGen, Π_{Resh} in Fig. 12 is a proof for the relation $\mathcal{R}_{\mathsf{Resh}}$ with soundness error $\epsilon_{\mathsf{LinCL}} + 1/C + 1/q + \mathsf{negl}(\lambda)$, where $\epsilon_{\mathsf{LinCL}}$ is the soundness error of $NIZK_{\mathsf{LinCL}}$. It is zero knowledge assuming $NIZK_{\mathsf{LinCL}}$ is.*

Proof. The proof follows analogously to Theorem 7, with the changes above.

5.2 Realizing Efficient YOSO MPC

Building upon our qCLPVSS PVSS scheme and the associated resharing scheme in Fig. 11, we realize an efficient YOSO MPC protocol by combining the DKG and preprocessing/online phases from [6] with our PVSS. The protocol of [6] first generates a shard key for a linearly homomorphic threshold encryption scheme based on the CL-framework, which is then used to generate encrypted Beaver triples. In an online phase, parties use distributed decryption to obtain the necessary information for evaluating private multiplications using the preprocessed encrypted Beaver triples. However, at every round, the current committee of parties must reshare the secret key towards the next committee. We aim at replacing the resharing scheme of [6] with our scheme from Fig. 11.

At first, we assume we have public keys for the next committee despite it being anonymous, and later argue about how to remove this assumption. Each party in the first committee to obtain shares of the secret key via the DKG of [6] converts them into shares of our qCLPVSS scheme. This can be done using standard tricks for share conversion or simply by a single execution of an inefficient YOSO MPC that publishes qCLPVSS shares given shares in a different format. Once a committee has qCLPVSS shares of the secret key, it can use our resharing scheme from Fig. 11 to efficiently transfer those to the next committee at every round of the MPC protocol of [6].

This simple application of our resharing scheme still requires each committee to know public keys for the next random anonymous committee. While this could be done by means of Random-index RPIR [28] or ideal receiver anonymous communication channels (RACC), we would like to perform the necessary encryption towards the next anonymous committee in a more efficient way. In order to do so, one can use the YOLO YOSO [11] encryption to the future scheme based on mixnets with publicly verifiable proofs of shuffle correctness (and the associated scheme for authententication from the past). These schemes allows for encrypting a message under a public key associated to a randomly chosen party without learning their identity, later allowing the recipient to sign messages by proving that they indeed received the ciphertext. Since the YOLO YOSO construction can be realized from proof of correctness shuffle, it can be implemented in our setting by using a proof system [2] that works over linearly homomorphic encryption schemes, such as those in the CL-framework. Hence, we can obtain a more efficient realization of YOSO MPC based on the protocol of [6] and our PVSS scheme with resharing qCLPVSS that only uses transparent setup and does not require ideal RACCs.

References

1. Acharya, A., Hazay, C., Kolesnikov, V., Prabhakaran, M.: SCALES - MPC with small clients and larger ephemeral servers. In: Kiltz, E., Vaikuntanathan, V. (eds.) TCC 2022. LNCS, vol. 13748, pp. 502–531. Springer, Heidelberg (2022). https://doi.org/10.1007/978-3-031-22365-5_18
2. Bayer, S., Groth, J.: Efficient zero-knowledge argument for correctness of a shuffle. In: Pointcheval, D., Johansson, T. (eds.) EUROCRYPT 2012. LNCS, vol. 7237, pp. 263–280. Springer, Heidelberg (2012). https://doi.org/10.1007/978-3-642-29011-4_17
3. Benhamouda, F., et al.: Can a public blockchain keep a secret? In: Pass, R., Pietrzak, K. (eds.) TCC 2020. LNCS, vol. 12550, pp. 260–290. Springer, Heidelberg (2020). https://doi.org/10.1007/978-3-030-64375-1_10

4. Boudot, F., Traoré, J.: Efficient publicly verifiable secret sharing schemes with fast or delayed recovery. In: Varadharajan, V., Yi, M. (eds.) ICICS 1999. LNCS, vol. 1726, pp. 87–102. Springer, Heidelberg (1999). https://doi.org/10.1007/978-3-540-47942-0_8

5. Bouvier, C., Castagnos, G., Imbert, L., Laguillaumie, F.: I want to ride my BICYCL?: BICYCL implements cryptography in class groups. J. Cryptol. **36**(3), 17 (2023)

6. Braun, L., Damgård, I., Orlandi, C.: Secure multiparty computation from threshold encryption based on class groups. In: Handschuh, H., Lysyanskaya, A., (eds.) Advances in Cryptology - CRYPTO 2023 - 43rd Annual International Cryptology Conference, CRYPTO 2023, Santa Barbara, CA, USA, August 20-24, 2023, Proceedings, Part I, vol. 14081. LNCS, pp. 613–645. Springer, Cham (2023). https://doi.org/10.1007/978-3-031-38557-5_20

7. Campanelli, M., David, B., Khoshakhlagh, H., Konring, A., Nielsen, J.B.: Encryption to the future - a paradigm for sending secret messages to future (anonymous) committees. In: Agrawal, S., Lin, D. (eds.) ASIACRYPT 2022. LNCS, vol. 13793, pp. 151–180. Springer, Heidelberg (2022). https://doi.org/10.1007/978-3-031-22969-5_6

8. Cascudo, I., David, B.: SCRAPE: scalable randomness attested by public entities. In: Gollmann, D., Miyaji, A., Kikuchi, H. (eds.) ACNS 17. LNCS, vol. 10355, pp. 537–556. Springer, Heidelberg (2017). https://doi.org/10.1007/978-3-319-61204-1_27

9. Cascudo, I., David, B.: ALBATROSS: publicly attestable batched randomness based on secret sharing. In: Moriai, S., Wang, H. (eds.) ASIACRYPT 2020. LNCS, vol. 12493, pp. 311–341. Springer, Heidelberg (2020). https://doi.org/10.1007/978-3-030-64840-4_11

10. Cascudo, I., David, B.: Publicly verifiable secret sharing over class groups and applications to DKG and YOSO. Cryptology ePrint Archive, Paper 2023/1651 (2023). https://eprint.iacr.org/2023/1651

11. Cascudo, I., David, B., Garms, L., Konring, A.: YOLO YOSO: fast and simple encryption and secret sharing in the YOSO model. In: Agrawal, S., Lin, D. (eds.) ASIACRYPT 2022. LNCS, vol. 13791, pp. 651–680. Springer, Heidelberg (2022)

12. Cascudo, I., David, B., Shlomovits, O., Varlakov, D.: Mt. random: multi-tiered randomness beacons. In: Tibouchi, M., Wang, X., (eds.) Applied Cryptography and Network Security - 21st International Conference, ACNS 2023, Kyoto, Japan, June 19-22, 2023, Proceedings, Part II, vol. 13906, LNCS, pages 645–674. Springer, Cham (2023.) https://doi.org/10.1007/978-3-031-33491-7_24

13. Castagnos, G., Catalano, D., Laguillaumie, F., Savasta, F., Tucker, I.: Two-party ECDSA from hash proof systems and efficient instantiations. In: Boldyreva, A., Micciancio, D. (eds.) CRYPTO 2019. LNCS, vol. 11694, pp. 191–221. Springer, Heidelberg (2019). https://doi.org/10.1007/978-3-030-26954-8_7

14. Castagnos, G., Catalano, D., Laguillaumie, F., Savasta, F., Tucker, I.: Bandwidth-efficient threshold EC-DSA. In: Kiayias, A., Kohlweiss, M., Wallden, P., Zikas, V. (eds.) PKC 2020. LNCS, vol. 12111, pp. 266–296. Springer, Heidelberg (2020). https://doi.org/10.1007/978-3-030-45388-6_10

15. Castagnos, G., Imbert, L., Laguillaumie, F.: Encryption switching protocols revisited: Switching modulo p. In: Katz, J., Shacham, H. (eds.) CRYPTO 2017. LNCS, vol. 10401, pp. 255–287. Springer, Heidelberg (2017). https://doi.org/10.1007/978-3-319-63688-7_9

16. Castagnos, G., Laguillaumie, F.: Linearly homomorphic encryption from DDH. In: Nyberg, K., (ed.) Topics in Cryptology - CT-RSA 2015, The Cryptographer's Track at the RSA Conference 2015, San Francisco, CA, USA, April 20-24, 2015. Proceedings, vol. 9048, LNCS, pp. 487–505. Springer, Cham (2015). https://doi.org/10.1007/978-3-319-16715-2_26

17. Castagnos, G., Laguillaumie, F., Tucker, I.: Practical fully secure unrestricted inner product functional encryption modulo p. In: Peyrin, T., Galbraith, S. (eds.) ASIACRYPT 2018. LNCS, vol. 11273, pp. 733–764. Springer, Heidelberg (2018). https://doi.org/10.1007/978-3-030-03329-3_25

18. Choudhuri, A.R., Goel, A., Green, M., Jain, A., Kaptchuk, G.: Fluid MPC: secure multiparty computation with dynamic participants. In: Malkin, T., Peikert, C. (eds.) CRYPTO 2021. LNCS, vol. 12826, pp. 94–123. Springer, Cham (2021). https://doi.org/10.1007/978-3-030-84245-1_4

19. Cramer, R., Damgård, I., Nielsen, J.B.: Multiparty computation from threshold homomorphic encryption. In: Pfitzmann, B. (ed.) EUROCRYPT 2001. LNCS, vol. 2045, pp. 280–299. Springer, Heidelberg (2001)

20. David, B., et al.: Perfect MPC over layered graphs. In: Handschuh, H., Lysyanskaya, A., (eds.), Advances in Cryptology - CRYPTO 2023 - 43rd Annual International Cryptology Conference, CRYPTO 2023, Santa Barbara, CA, USA, August 20-24, 2023, Proceedings, Part I, vol. 14081, LNCS, pp. 360–392. Springer, Cham (2023). https://doi.org/10.1007/978-3-031-38557-5_12

21. Dobson, S., Galbraith, S.D., Smith, B.: Trustless unknown-order groups. Math. Cryptol. 1(2), 25–39 (2022)

22. Faust, S., Kohlweiss, M., Marson, G.A., Venturi, D.: On the non-malleability of the Fiat-Shamir transform. In: Galbraith, S.D., Nandi, M. (eds.) INDOCRYPT 2012. LNCS, vol. 7668, pp. 60–79. Springer, Heidelberg (2012). https://doi.org/10.1007/978-3-642-34931-7_5

23. Fouque, P.-A., Stern, J.: One round threshold discrete-log key generation without private channels. In: Kim, K. (ed.) PKC 2001. LNCS, vol. 1992, pp. 300–316. Springer, Heidelberg (2001). https://doi.org/10.1007/3-540-44586-2_22

24. Fujisaki, E., Okamoto, T.: A practical and provably secure scheme for publicly verifiable secret sharing and its applications. In: Nyberg, K. (ed.), EUROCRYPT 1998, vol. 1403, LNCS, pp. 32–46. Springer, Heidelberg (1998). https://doi.org/10.1007/BFb0054115

25. Gennaro, R., Jarecki, S., Krawczyk, H., Rabin, T.: Secure distributed key generation for discrete-log based cryptosystems. In: Stern, J. (ed.) EUROCRYPT 1999. LNCS, vol. 1592, pp. 295–310. Springer, Heidelberg (1999)

26. Gentry, C., et al.: YOSO: you only speak once - secure MPC with stateless ephemeral roles. In: Malkin, T., Peikert, C., (eds.) CRYPTO 2021, Part II, vol. 12826, LNCS, pp. 64–93. Springer, Heidelberg (2021)

27. Gentry, C., Halevi, S., Lyubashevsky, V.: Practical non-interactive publicly verifiable secret sharing with thousands of parties. In: Dunkelman, O., Dziembowski, S. (eds.) EUROCRYPT 2022, Part I, vol. 13275, LNCS, pp. 458–487. Springer, Heidelberg (2022). https://doi.org/10.1007/978-3-031-06944-4_16

28. Gentry, C., Halevi, S., Magri, B., Nielsen, J.B., Yakoubov, S.: Random-index PIR and applications. In: Nissim, K., Waters, B. (eds.) TCC 2021. LNCS, vol. 13044, pp. 32–61. Springer, Heidelberg (2021). https://doi.org/10.1007/978-3-030-90456-2_2

29. Groth, J.: Non-interactive distributed key generation and key resharing. Cryptology ePrint Archive, Paper 2021/339 (2021). https://eprint.iacr.org/2021/339

30. Gurkan, K., Jovanovic, P., Maller, M., Meiklejohn, S., Stern, G., Tomescu, A.: Aggregatable distributed key generation. In: Canteaut, A., Standaert, F.-X. (eds.) EUROCRYPT 2021. LNCS, vol. 12696, pp. 147–176. Springer, Heidelberg (2021). https://doi.org/10.1007/978-3-030-77870-5_6

31. Heidarvand, S., Villar, J.L.: Public verifiability from pairings in secret sharing schemes. In: Avanzi, R.M., Keliher, L., Sica, F., (eds.) SAC 2008, vol. 5381, LNCS, pp. 294–308. Springer, Heidelberg (2009). https://doi.org/10.1007/978-3-642-04159-4_19

32. Kate, A., Mangipudi, E.V., Mukherjee, P., Saleem, H., Aravinda, S., Thyagarajan, K.: Non-interactive VSS using class groups and application to DKG. Cryptology ePrint Archive, Paper 2023/451 (2023). https://eprint.iacr.org/2023/451

33. Katz, J.: Round optimal robust distributed key generation. Cryptology ePrint Archive, Paper 2023/1094 (2023). https://eprint.iacr.org/2023/1094

34. Pedersen, P.T.: A threshold cryptosystem without a trusted party (extended abstract) (rump session). In: Davies, D.W. (ed.) EUROCRYPT 1991. LNCS, vol. 547, pp. 522–526. Springer, Heidelberg (1991). https://doi.org/10.1007/3-540-46416-6_47

35. Rachuri, R., Scholl, P.: Le Mans: dynamic and fluid MPC for dishonest majority. In: Dodis, Y., Shrimpton, T. (eds.) CRYPTO 2022. LNCS, vol. 13507, pp. 719–749. Springer, Heidelberg (2022). https://doi.org/10.1007/978-3-031-15802-5_25

36. Ruiz, A., Villar, J.L.: Publicly verifiable secret sharing from Paillier's cryptosystem. In: WEWoRC 2005–Western European Workshop on Research in Cryptology (2005)

37. Schoenmakers, B.: A simple publicly verifiable secret sharing scheme and its application to electronic. In: Wiener, M.J. (ed.) CRYPTO 1999. LNCS, vol. 1666, pp. 148–164. Springer, Heidelberg (1999). https://doi.org/10.1007/3-540-48405-1_10

38. Stadler, M.: Publicly verifiable secret sharing. In: Maurer, U.M. (ed.) EUROCRYPT 1996. LNCS, vol. 1070, pp. 190–199. Springer, Heidelberg (1996). https://doi.org/10.1007/3-540-68339-9_17

39. Tucker, I.: Functional encryption and distributed signatures based on projective hash functions, the benefit of class groups. (Chiffrement fonctionnel et signatures distribuées fondés sur des fonctions de hachage à projection, l'apport des groupes de classe). Ph.D. thesis, University of Lyon, France (2020)

Bulletproofs++: Next Generation Confidential Transactions via Reciprocal Set Membership Arguments

Liam Eagen, Sanket Kanjalkar, Tim Ruffing🆔, and Jonas Nick[(✉)]

Blockstream Research, Victoria, Canada
jonas@n-ck.net

Abstract. Zero-knowledge proofs are a cryptographic cornerstone of privacy-preserving technologies such as "Confidential Transactions" (CT), which aims at hiding monetary amounts in cryptocurrency transactions. Due to its asymptotically logarithmic proof size and transparent setup, most state-of-the-art CT protocols use the Bulletproofs (BP) [8] zero-knowledge proof system for set membership proofs such as range proofs. However, even taking into account recent efficiency improvements, BP comes with a serious overhead in terms of concrete proof size as well as verifier running time and thus puts a large burden on practical deployments of CT and its extensions.

In this work, we introduce Bulletproofs++ (BP++), a drop-in replacement for BP that improves its concrete efficiency and compactness significantly. As for BP, the security of BP++ relies only on the hardness of the discrete logarithm problem in the random oracle model, and BP++ retains all features of Bulletproofs including transparent setup and support for proof aggregation, multi-party proving and batch verification. Asymptotically, BP++ range proofs require only $O(n/\log n)$ group scalar multiplications compared to $O(n)$ for BP and BP+.

At the heart of our construction are novel techniques for permutation and set membership, enabling highly efficient proofs of statements encoded as arithmetic circuits. Concretely, a single BP++ range proof to establish that a committed value is in a 64-bit range (as commonly required by CT) is just 416 bytes over a 256-bit elliptic curve, 38% smaller than an equivalent BP and 27% smaller than BP+. When instantiated on the secp256k1 curve as used in Bitcoin, our benchmarks show that proving is about 5 times faster than BP and verification is about 3 times faster than BP+. When aggregating 32 range proofs, proving and verification are about 9.5 times and 5.5 times faster, respectively.

1 Introduction

Cryptocurrencies like Bitcoin [40] enable decentralized, peer-to-peer payments by maintaining a distributed public ledger called the blockchain. While this innovation has permitted an unprecedented degree of financial autonomy on the Internet, the fact that every transaction leaves a permanent record in the

© International Association for Cryptologic Research 2024
M. Joye and G. Leander (Eds.): EUROCRYPT 2024, LNCS 14655, pp. 249–279, 2024.
https://doi.org/10.1007/978-3-031-58740-5_9

blockchain poses a substantial threat to the financial privacy of users. Even though cryptocurrency transactions are not typically associated with real-world identities, a surprisingly large amount of information can be extracted from the information in the blockchain [24,38,48].

Among the most glaring pieces of data that an observer can extract are the amounts of funds that transactions move from sender to recipient. These monetary amounts are stored as plain integers in many popular cryptocurrencies, including Bitcoin, which makes it easy for blockchain nodes to verify that a transaction is balanced, i.e., that the sum of all its input amounts equals the sum of all its output amounts (except for a small fee given to the miners).

Confidential Transactions. A common countermeasure to this leak of information, e.g., as suggested first in the "Confidential Transactions" proposal [26, 37] (CT), is to hide the monetary amounts in homomorphic commitments such as Pedersen commitments. The additive homomorphism ensures that blockchain nodes can verify the amounts in a confidential transaction without learning the plain amounts, by performing the necessary additions for checking the balance equation on the homomorphic commitments instead of the plain amounts. However, this approach is only sound if the amounts do not overflow during the homomorphic addition, because this would allow an attacker to violate balance and thus create money out of thin air. To exclude overflow, transactions are required to carry a non-interactive zero-knowledge (NIZK) *range proof* that demonstrates that committed amounts are in a range $[0, 2^b)$ of non-negative integers much smaller than the message space of the commitment space.

Bulletproofs. Motivated by this application, the seminal Bulletproofs (BP) by Bünz et al. [8] was the first to achieve range proofs with an asymptotic size logarithmic in the number of bits in the range as well as concrete sizes less than 1 kB. Moreover, BP supports aggregate proving, i.e., a single range proof can cover multiple commitments at once, and this proof is significantly more compact than proving each commitment separately. This efficiency makes it feasible to use BP in cryptocurrencies, and BP range proofs have been successfully deployed in Grin [27] and Monero [39] in conjunction with other privacy-preserving features.

However, even though Monero has subsequently upgraded [47] to Chung et al. [15]'s recent improvement Bulletproofs+ (BP+), which reduces the size of a single 64-bit range proof to 576 bytes, range proofs still account for 29% to 42% of the size of a typical Monero transaction.[1] These concrete storage costs as well as the concrete verification efficiency still leave much to be desired, considering that all nodes in a cryptocurrency are required to download and verify the entirety of all range proofs created within the system.

---

[1] A transaction with one input and two outputs has a size of about 1530 bytes, and a transaction with two inputs and two outputs has a size of about 2220 bytes after the v15 hardfork [47]. In either case, the aggregated range proof covering the two output amounts has a size of 640 bytes on a 256-bit elliptic curve (see also Table 1).

Multi-asset Confidential Transactions (MACT). While the initial CT proposal [37] supports only a single asset (e.g., only Bitcoin), the protocol by Poelstra *et al.* [43] (as deployed for instance in the Liquid sidechain [41]) extends the idea to *multi-asset confidential transactions* (MACT), i.e., a single transaction can transfer multiple assets simultaneously, and no observer can learn the transacted amounts or the involved assets. Moreover, the range proof construction used in this protocol supports multi-party proving for transactions created by multiple senders. This is a prerequisite to using coin mixing protocols [36] on top of MACT, which further enhance privacy.

However, it is thus far unclear how to fully leverage the potential of BP in MACT protocols. While it is possible to implement the range proofs in MACT using BP, the protocol by Poelstra *et al.* [43] requires additional zero-knowledge *surjection proofs* to show that the assets on the output side of the transaction are a permutation of the assets on the input side of the transactions. These additional proofs are large and since they are constructed using techniques different from BP, it is not possible to aggregate them together with BP range proofs. The approach taken by the Cloak [50] MACT protocol overcomes this problem by using BP to encode a permutation argument as an arithmetic circuit. This avoids surjection proofs, but the way the circuit is constructed makes it incompatible with known multi-party proving techniques for BP. In summary, there is currently no solution to MACT that is practical and compatible with BP.

1.1 Contributions

The main contribution of this work is Bulletproofs++ (BP++), a zero-knowledge argument of knowledge for arithmetic circuits in the discrete logarithm setting.

Reciprocal Argument. At the core of BP++ is the *reciprocal argument*, a novel interactive argument protocol that generalizes permutation arguments and set membership arguments. This approach builds on the work by Bayer, Groth [3], who encode a multiset as the roots of a polynomial, and whose basic technique has been extended to show richer permutation arguments in plookup [21] and plays a critical role in protocols based on Plonk [22]. These protocols use a "grand product", i.e., the product of numerous committed values, to show that a particular permutation, which encodes the structure of an arithmetic circuit, was applied correctly. The reciprocal argument of BP++ is essentially the logarithmic derivative of the polynomials used by Bayer-Groth permutation arguments. The logarithmic derivative transforms a product of linear factors into a sum, thereby linearizing the representation of the multiset.

Since the initial publication of a preprint of our work, the reciprocal argument has already been used in several other works: Haböck [31] modifies the "grand product" of Hyperplonk [13] to use a variant of the reciprocal argument, which he rederives via the logarithmic derivative. Eagen, Fiore, Gabizon [18] develop a more asymptotically and concretely performant lookup argument, improving

Table 1. Range proof sizes compared to previous work. The range column of the table $(m \times n)$ indicates the number of aggregated proofs (m) and bits of range proven (n) by each proof. We express the resulting proof size in terms of the number of group elements g and scalars s. Values denoted by dash (—) are not provided in the Flashproofs paper [51].

Range	BP++	BP+	BP	SwiftRange	Flashproofs
1×64	$10g + 3s$	$15g + 3s$	$16g + 5s$	$16g + 9s$	$17g + 10s$
2×64	$10g + 5s$	$17g + 3s$	$18g + 5s$	$20g + 9s$	$27g + 17s$
8×64	$14g + 5s$	$21g + 3s$	$22g + 5s$	$28g + 9s$	$65g + 28s$
16×64	$15g + 4s$	$23g + 3s$	$24g + 5s$	$32g + 9s$	$103g + 48s$
64×64	$19g + 4s$	$27g + 3s$	$28g + 5s$	$40g + 9s$	—

upon the sequence of works beginning with Caulk [45,54].[2] As evident from these works, the reciprocal argument is clearly of independent interest.

Compactness and Efficiency. BP++'s novel techniques improve the compactness and efficiency of BP(+) significantly. Table 1 compares the size of BP++ range proofs with SwiftRange [52], Flashproofs [51], BP [8] and BP+ [15] range proofs. As demonstrated by the table, BP++ has a clear advantage in terms of proof size compared to the alternatives.

The time needed for proving and verification is dominated in practice by multiplications of group elements with scalars. In BP and BP+ range proofs, the count of these multiplications scales linearly with n. However, BP++ offers an asymptotic improvement, reducing the count to $O(n/\log n)$. The benchmarks in Sect. 7 demonstrate that BP++'s improvements do in fact translate to actual implementations. A 64-bit range proof takes roughly 4 ms for proving and 0.9 ms for verifying, making it 5× quicker than BP in proving and 3× quicker in verification.

Modularity Without Sacrificing Performance. Since BP++ is capable of proving arbitrary statements encoded in arithmetic circuits, it is possible to construct range proofs and MACT simply by an arithmetic circuit that encodes the relation. As opposed to BP(+), we adopted this methodology because our techniques allow for the creation of a range proof that is nearly as efficient as a direct construction of such a proof. Our approach simplifies the security analysis of range proofs and MACT, as they inherit the security properties of the arithmetic circuit protocol, providing the circuit accurately encodes the relation.

---

[2] After a per-table setup procedure, these arguments allow the prover to construct an argument for correctness of table look ups in time independent of the table size. This case is particularly interesting, as it is not currently known how to construct an analogous product check that depends only on the number of non-identity values being multiplied.

This demonstrates the potential of reusing the BP++ arithmetic circuit protocol with the reciprocal argument in other applications.

MACT. On the MACT side, we introduce a BP++ MACT protocol (again by specifying an arithmetic circuit) that relies on the same asset representation as Cloak but uses an instance of the reciprocal argument, substantially simplifying the permutation argument. The marginal cost of a BP++ MACT over an aggregated range proof is negligible in prover and verifier time, and proof size.

Compatibility with BP. Since BP++ maintains the same interface and security assumptions established by BP(+), BP++ is a drop-in replacement for existing uses of BP(+). For example, BP range proofs in existing protocols like Grin [27], Monero [39], and Liquid [41] can be replaced without any change in security assumptions and with only minimal modification to existing protocols. This is also true for statements encoded as general arithmetic circuits. Moreover, the MACT protocol uses the same asset representation as Cloak, and so can be directly substituted for Cloak for smaller proof sizes and faster prover and verifier. These replacements retain all benefits of BP:

Aggregate proving. A prover who would like to prove multiple statements simultaneously can create a single aggregated proof, which is more compact than simply giving multiple independent proofs. For example, in the common case that a cryptocurrency transaction creates $m \geq 1$ commitments, an aggregate range proof can prove that m committed values are in range in just $O(\log n + \log m)$ bits, instead of $m \cdot O(\log n)$ bits in the case of m separate range proofs.

Multi-party aggregate proving. For the case that multiple provers want to create a single aggregated proof, BP++ offers a natural MPC protocol. Multi-party proving yields large space savings when CT is combined with coin mixing protocols [46].

Batch verification. Multiple (possibly aggregated) proofs can be verified in a batch computation, improving efficiency further.

Conservative cryptographic assumptions. BP++ is provably secure assuming only the hardness of the discrete logarithm problem and can be made non-interactive in the random oracle model, thus ensuring compatibility with assumptions widely accepted by engineers and users in the cryptocurrency ecosystem. Concretely, BP++ neither requires pairings nor cycles of curves and can be instantiated on the secp256k1 elliptic curve which used in Bitcoin, for which a wide range of implementations exist.

Transparent setup. Since the public setup parameters only consist of random group elements, the setup is trustless assuming a common random string or the random oracle model.

1.2   Related Work

Range Proofs. An alternative to digit decomposition range proofs are those based on Lagrange's four square theorem. This theorem states that any positive integer can be written as a sum of four squares, as originally proposed by Lipmaa [35]. In practice, this is often transformed to an instance of the three square theorem as was originally observed by Groth [28]. To show that a value $v < B$ one can find a four, or three, square decomposition of the value $B - v$, which is positive only if the initial condition is met. These protocols require integer commitments, which require either RSA groups, and hence a trusted setup, or ideal class groups.

More recently, Couteau *et al.* [16] developed a bounded integer commitment protocol that requires only the discrete logarithm assumption in a group of known order. This allows them to construct three-square range proofs using elliptic curves, which are highly performant and smaller than BP and BP+ range proofs. However, BP++ range proofs remain smaller as compared to their approach. Moreover, since their bounded integer commitment scheme requires the committed values to remain in a bounded interval, their approach requires a curve with order somewhat larger than 256 bits at the 128-bit security level. This lower bound on the group size or, equivalently, on the security of their approach is inherent and applies even if one ignores the non-tightness of the security analysis when setting parameters, as often done in practice. This limits their applicability to existing blockchains.

MACT. As explained above, the original Confidential Assets protocol [43] uses surjection proofs to hide the asset type of each output from a set of possible assets. In general, the size of this set is equal to the number m of inputs to the transaction. Thus, for n outputs, the prover will do $O(n \cdot m)$ work as compared to only $O(n + m)$ for BP++. Since it is not known how to aggregate surjection proofs, the proof size is in $O(n \cdot m)$.

Cloak [50] uses a more complex construction to encode a permutation over the assets into a BP circuit. This approach is a large constant factor more expensive than BP++ in terms of prover work.

Generalizations of BP. There are a number of other works building on BP, including BP+ [15] which uses a weighted inner product argument to reduce proving time and uses several other improvements to reduce proof size, and Flashproofs [51] which combine the BP inner product argument with Groth polynomial commitments [29] to reduce verifier complexity and attempt to minimize Ethereum gas costs. There has also been work to unify BP with the large, existing body of work on Sigma protocols [1], and to further generalize this to other related contexts like groups of unknown order [10] to support homomorphic commitments of arbitrary order. BP have also been generalized to inner product arguments in other contexts, including by Lee [33], who propose a general purpose SNARK protocol over a pairing friendly curve that uses an inner product to avoid trusted setup requirements. BP are also core to the structure of Halo [6] and Halo2 [49], which are now implemented in Zcash [7] and have inspired the development of accumulation schemes [9]. These allow a prover to efficiently aggregate multiple proofs in such a way that verification time depends only on the time to verify a single proof.

2 Preliminaries

Notation. Hereafter, we denote the set of *polynomially-bounded* functions in the security parameter λ by $poly = \{f : \exists a \in \mathbb{N}, \ f(\lambda) \in O(\lambda^a)\}$, the set of *negligible* functions in the security parameter λ by $negl = \{f : f(\lambda)^{-1} \notin poly\}$. A function f is *overwhelming* if $1 - f$ is negligible.

A probabilistic interactive Turing machine $\mathcal{A}$ is *probabilistic polynomial-time (PPT)* if its runtime is in *poly*; it is *probabilistic expected polynomial-time (expected-PPT)* if its expected runtime is in *poly*; it is *deterministic polynomial-time (DPT)* if it is PPT and does not read from its randomness tape.

We denote by $\mathbb{G}$ a cyclic group of prime order p written additively, which is in practice typically a subgroup of an elliptic curve. We write group elements in $\mathbb{G}$ with capital letters and scalars in $\mathbb{F} := \mathbb{F}_p$ with lower case letters. We write $\mathbb{F}[X]$ for the ring of polynomials over $\mathbb{F}$ in indeterminate X; when we treat it a vector space, then as vector space over the field $\mathbb{F}$.

Vectors. Vectors are written with bold letters, and matrices with capital letters. These can be distinguished from $\mathbb{G}$ elements from context. We write the diagonal matrix of powers of μ starting with μ^0 as $\mathrm{diag}(\mu)$. Vectors are zero indexed and implicitly padded with zeros on the right as necessary for various operations to be well-defined, i.e. addition and inner products. We denote the vector of all zeros by $\mathbf{0}$ and the vector of all ones by $\mathbf{1}$. We use $|v|$ to denote the length of v. We use "slice" notation $v_{i:j}$ to denote the subvector of v consisting of components i to $j - 1$; we may omit i if $i = 0$, and j if $j = |v| - 1$. To access a component of a slice, we write $(v_{i:})_k = v_{i+k}$.

We write the inner product of two vectors using angle brackets and an optional subscript to denote weighting by powers of the subscript. If the subscript is not present, it is implicitly 1. Inner products are defined for any vectors of quantities that can be multiplied, i.e. scalars and scalars or scalars and group elements. The norm of a vector refers to its self inner product and uses the same subscripting convention for weights. For example, the weighted inner product of x and G and the weighted norm of x are written

$$\langle \boldsymbol{x}, \boldsymbol{G} \rangle_\mu = \sum\nolimits_{i=0} x_i G_i \mu^{i+1} \quad \text{and} \quad |\boldsymbol{x}|_\mu^2 = \langle \boldsymbol{x}, \boldsymbol{x} \rangle_\mu .$$

We write concatenation of vectors using $||$, the component-wise product of vectors (Hadamard product) using $\circ$ and tensor product of vectors using $\otimes$. An iterated tensor product is evaluated from left to right and obeys the convention

$$\bigotimes\nolimits_{i=0}^{n} (1, x_i) = \left(1, x_0, x_1, x_0 x_1, x_2, \ldots, \prod\nolimits_{i=0}^{n} x_i \right) .$$

This is convenient for describing, e.g., the vector of challenges used by the verifier for the norm linear argument.

We denote the vector of powers from μ^0 to μ^{n-1} by $\mathbf{e}_n(\mu)$. It obeys the tensor product equation

$$\mathbf{e}_{ab}(\mu) = \mathbf{e}_a(\mu) \otimes \mathbf{e}_b(\mu^a) = (1, \mu, \ldots, \mu^{ab-1}).$$

We decompose vectors into subvectors of even (indices 0, 2, ...) and odd (indices 1, 3, ...) components, instead of left and right halves as in BP, written as written as $[a]_0$ and $[a]_1$ respectively. This transformation simplifies certain parts of the protocol, and may help with locality in implementations. BP and BP+ can easily be modified to use even and odd halves, as can BP++ to use left and right halves.

Discrete Logarithm Relation Problem. BP++ is provably secure assuming the expected-PPT hardness of the *discrete logarithm relation (DLR) problem*, which is well-known to be tightly equivalent to the standard discrete logarithm problem [32, Lemma 3].

Definition 1 (Discrete Logarithm Relation (DLR) Problem). *The discrete logarithm relation (DLR) problem in $\mathbb{G}$ is hard if for all $n \geq 1$ and for all expected-PPT adversaries $\mathcal{A}$,*

$$\Pr[\langle a, G\rangle = 0_{\mathbb{G}} \wedge a \neq 0 \mid \mathbb{G} \leftarrow \mathsf{Setup}(1^\lambda); G \leftarrow_\$ \mathbb{G}^n; a \leftarrow \mathcal{A}(G)] \leq negl(\lambda).$$

2.1 Zero-Knowledge Arguments of Knowledge

A zero-knowledge argument of knowledge consists of a non-interactive PPT Turing machine $\mathcal{K}$ which outputs a *common random string* σ, and two interactive PPT Turing machines $\mathcal{P}$ (prover) and $\mathcal{V}$ (verifier). Critically, the randomness used by $\mathcal{K}$ is public and σ can be reproduced transparently (no trusted setup). The prover and verifier interacting will produce a transcript π and output a bit b indicating whether the verifier accepts, which we write $\pi \leftarrow \langle \mathcal{P}(\sigma, u, w), \mathcal{V}(\sigma, u)\rangle = b$. Here, for any σ, a value w is a *witness* for a *statement* u if it satisfies the polynomial time relation $(\sigma, u, w) \in \mathcal{R}$.

A zero-knowledge argument of knowledge must satisfy completeness, soundness, and zero-knowledge.

Definition 2 (Completeness). *The protocol $(\mathcal{K}, \mathcal{P}, \mathcal{V})$ satisfies perfect completeness if for all PPT $\mathcal{A}$,*

$$\Pr\left[\begin{array}{c}\langle \mathcal{P}(\sigma, u, w), \mathcal{V}(\sigma, u)\rangle = 1 \\ \vee (\sigma, u, w) \notin \mathcal{R}\end{array} \middle| \begin{array}{c}\sigma \leftarrow \mathcal{K}(1^\lambda); \\ (u, w) \leftarrow \mathcal{A}(\sigma)\end{array}\right] = 1.$$

The soundness notion we consider in this work is computational witness-extended emulation [30,34].

Definition 3 (Computational Witness-Extended Emulation). *The protocol $(\mathcal{K}, \mathcal{P}, \mathcal{V})$ has witness-extended emulation (WEE) if for all DPT provers $\mathcal{P}^*$, there exists an expected-PPT emulator $\mathcal{E}^O$ with access to rewinding oracle $O = \langle \mathcal{P}^*(\sigma, u, s), \mathcal{V}(\sigma, u)\rangle$ such that for all pairs of adversaries $(\mathcal{A}_1, \mathcal{A}_2)$,*

$$\left| \begin{array}{c}\Pr\left[\mathcal{A}_2(\sigma, \pi) = 1 \mid \sigma \leftarrow \mathcal{K}(1^\lambda); (u, s) \leftarrow \mathcal{A}_1(\sigma); \pi \leftarrow O\right] \\ -\Pr\left[\begin{array}{c}(\pi \text{ is accepting} \Rightarrow \\ (\sigma, u, w) \in \mathcal{R}) \\ \wedge \mathcal{A}_2(\sigma, \pi) = 1\end{array} \middle| \begin{array}{c}\sigma \leftarrow \mathcal{K}(1^\lambda); \\ (u, s) \leftarrow \mathcal{A}_1(\sigma); \\ (\pi, w) \leftarrow \mathcal{E}^O(\sigma, u)\end{array}\right]\end{array} \right| \leq negl(\lambda).$$

The protocol has computational witness-extended emulation (CWEE) *when adversaries A_1 and A_2 are restricted to non-uniform polynomial time.*

In the zero-knowledge notion used in this work, the simulator has access to randomness used by the verifier; this is commonly called "special" zero-knowledge in the literature and requires the protocol to be public coin.

Definition 4 (Public Coin). *The protocol $(\mathcal{K}, \mathcal{P}, \mathcal{V})$ is public coin if the i-th message sent by $\mathcal{V}(\sigma, u; \rho)$ is the i-th component of its randomness argument ρ.*

Definition 5 (Perfect Special Honest Verifier Zero-Knowledge). *The protocol $(\mathcal{K}, \mathcal{P}, \mathcal{V})$ has perfect* Special Honest Verifier Zero-Knowledge (SHVZK) *if there exists a PPT simulator $\mathcal{S}$ such that for all pairs of adversaries $(\mathcal{A}_1, \mathcal{A}_2)$,*

$$\Pr\left[\begin{array}{l} (\sigma, u, w) \in \mathcal{R} \\ \wedge\ \mathcal{A}_2(\sigma, \pi) = 1 \end{array}\middle|\ \begin{array}{l} \sigma \leftarrow \mathcal{K}(1^\lambda); (u, w, \rho) \leftarrow \mathcal{A}_1(\sigma); \\ \pi \leftarrow \langle \mathcal{P}(\sigma, u, w), \mathcal{V}(\sigma, u; \rho)\rangle \end{array}\right]$$

$$= \Pr\left[\begin{array}{l} (\sigma, u, w) \in \mathcal{R} \\ \wedge\ \mathcal{A}_2(\sigma, \pi) = 1 \end{array}\middle|\ \begin{array}{c} \sigma \leftarrow \mathcal{K}(1^\lambda); (u, w, \rho) \leftarrow \mathcal{A}_1(\sigma); \\ \pi \leftarrow \mathcal{S}(u, \rho) \end{array}\right].$$

General Forking Lemma. To show CWEE, we will use the generalized forking lemma by Bootle *et al.* [5]. It allows handling extractors for multi-round zero-knowledge argument of knowledge generically.

Trustless Common Setup. As a convention, all zero-knowledge arguments in this work use the same setup algorithm $\mathcal{K}$, which outputs $\sigma = (G, \boldsymbol{H}, \boldsymbol{G})$, where G and the components of the two vectors $\boldsymbol{H}, \boldsymbol{G}$ (of sufficient size, which will be clear from the context) are random generators in $\mathbb{G}$. Since $\mathcal{K}$ is transparent, it is possible to use make the setup trustless in the random oracle model.

Non-interactive Proofs from Fiat-Shamir. All zero-knowledge arguments presented in this paper are public coin, interactive protocols between a prover and honest verifier. This means that they can be made non-interactive via the Fiat-Shamir transform [4], and honest-verifier zero-knowledge of the interactive protocols immediately implies that the Fiat-Shamir transformed variants are non-interactive zero-knowledge in the random oracle model. Recent work has shown that also soundness is retained, even for multi-round protocols [2,25,53]. Concretely, we establish that our protocols achieve special soundness, which implies that their Fiat-Shamir version achieves knowledge soundness as shown by Attema, Fehr, Klooß [2, Theorem 4] and further elaborated on by Ganesh *et al.* [23, Section 2.8].

Commitments as Inputs. Our zero-knowledge arguments accept witness inputs in Pedersen vector commitments. For convenience later, given generators $\sigma = (G, \boldsymbol{H}, \dots)$ from the zero-knowledge setup, we define a commitment to message $\boldsymbol{v}$ with randomness s to be $\mathsf{Com}(\boldsymbol{v}; s) = v_0 G + s H_0 + \langle \boldsymbol{v}_{1:}, \boldsymbol{H}_{8:}\rangle$. Generators $\boldsymbol{H}_{1:8} = (H_1, \dots, H_7)$ are intentionally not used for commitments; this will simplify the notation in later sections.

Pedersen commitments are homomorphic, perfectly hiding, and computationally binding up to the hardness of the discrete logarithm relation problem. We omit a formal treatment of these properties because the security analysis of our protocols uses the underlying group directly and does not invoke these abstract properties.

3   Technical Overview

BP++ consists of four primary improvements over earlier, transparent discrete logarithm-based range proof protocols. First, we substitute the BP+ inner product argument by a norm argument, which reduces verifier time by approximately half in many common cases. Second, we introduce a novel set membership and permutation argumentcalled the reciprocal argument, which has already found significant applications beyond BP++. Third, we modify the BP arithmetic circuit protocol to accomplish "blinding" in one round of communication of a single group element, which can be easily adapted to other similarly constructed protocols. These modified circuits are extended to support first order use of the reciprocal argument, similarly to integration of plookup [21] into Halo2 [49]. Finally, we use these techniques to construct the shortest, and most verifier performant transparent range proof and MACT protocols.

3.1   Recap: Bulletproofs and Bulletproofs+

BP, at its core, uses a recursive argument to show the inner product relation

$$\mathcal{R}_{ip} = \left\{ \begin{pmatrix} \boldsymbol{G}, \boldsymbol{H} \in \mathbb{G}^n, G \in \mathbb{G}; \\ C \in \mathbb{G}; \boldsymbol{x}, \boldsymbol{y} \in \mathbb{Z}_p^n \end{pmatrix} : C = \langle \boldsymbol{x}, \boldsymbol{y} \rangle \, G + \langle \boldsymbol{x}, \boldsymbol{G} \rangle + \langle \boldsymbol{y}, \boldsymbol{H} \rangle \right\}. \quad (1)$$

The recursive structure of the argument is itself derived from the recursive structure in Bootle $et\ al.$ [5]. In each round, a commitment to a scalar v and vectors $\boldsymbol{x}$ and $\boldsymbol{y}$ of length n is reduced to a commitment to vectors $\boldsymbol{x}'$ and $\boldsymbol{y}'$ of length $n/2$. If this commitment satisfies the relation, then the original commitment satisfies the relation with overwhelming probability.

In our notation, given a commitment C, the prover sends the verifier commitments (L, R), and the verifier chooses a challenge γ. The reduced commitment is defined as

$$C' = C + \gamma^{-2}L + \gamma^2 R = v'G + \langle \boldsymbol{x}', \boldsymbol{G}' \rangle + \langle \boldsymbol{y}', \boldsymbol{H}' \rangle. \quad (2)$$

Each round of the protocol forms essentially a vector valued polynomial commitment. The key to ensuring that the reduced vectors are of length $n/2$ comes from the folding relation. The reduced vectors are defined, in terms of the challenge

$$\boldsymbol{x}' = \gamma[\boldsymbol{x}]_0 + \gamma^{-1}[\boldsymbol{x}]_1 \qquad \boldsymbol{y}' = \gamma^{-1}[\boldsymbol{y}]_0 + \gamma[\boldsymbol{y}]_1. \quad (3)$$

Computing the inner product of these vectors as polynomials in γ, we find that the original inner product $\langle \boldsymbol{x}, \boldsymbol{y} \rangle$ from the inner product relation occurs as the γ^0 term

$$\langle \boldsymbol{x}', \boldsymbol{y}' \rangle = \langle \boldsymbol{x}, \boldsymbol{y} \rangle + \gamma^2 \langle [\boldsymbol{x}]_0, [\boldsymbol{y}]_1 \rangle + \gamma^{-2} \langle [\boldsymbol{x}]_1, [\boldsymbol{y}]_0 \rangle. \quad (4)$$

BP applies this same relation to the inner products between the basis points $\boldsymbol{G}$ and $\boldsymbol{H}$ and the witness vectors. That is, the reduced basis points are defined in terms of γ to be

$$\boldsymbol{G}' = \gamma^{-1}[\boldsymbol{G}]_0 + \gamma[\boldsymbol{G}]_1 \qquad \boldsymbol{H}' = \gamma[\boldsymbol{H}]_0 + \gamma^{-1}[\boldsymbol{H}]_1. \tag{5}$$

This means when the inner products $\langle \boldsymbol{x}', \boldsymbol{G}' \rangle$ and $\langle \boldsymbol{y}', \boldsymbol{H}' \rangle$ are evaluated, the original inner products will appear on the γ^0 term. The γ^{-2} coefficients from all three reduced inner products are then collected into L and likewise the γ^2 coefficients into R. This reduction is applied until the reduced vectors are of length 2, at which point the reduced vectors are sent to the verifier.

BP+ uses a very similar recursive structure that also incorporates weights to show a weighted inner product relation, with the inner product replaced by a weighted inner product.

3.2   Reciprocal Argument

The primary technique that makes BP++ range proofs and MACT possible is a simple interactive protocol called the *reciprocal argument*. It operates on *collections* that are finite sets A of pairs (m, s) consisting of symbols $s \in \mathbb{F}$ with associated multiplicities $m \in \mathbb{F}$. In more details, the reciprocal argument lets a prover convince a verifier that the total multiplicity $\hat{m}_s = \sum_{(m',s')\in A\,:\,s'=s} m'$ of each symbol $s \in \mathbb{F}$ *vanishes* (i.e., equals zero). In that case, we also say that A itself vanishes. (For example, $A = \{(-3, 42), (5, 17), (7, 42), (-4, 42), (-5, 17), (0, 1)\}$ vanishes.) In the protocols we will construct, some or all of the m and s may be private to the prover and thus appear only in committed form.

Vanishing is powerful enough to express many relations commonly used to construct zero-knowledge arguments: For example, assuming that no wraparound occurs when summing up multiplicities, which is guaranteed if $|A| \ll |\mathbb{F}|$, some (committed) sequence U is a permutation of another (committed) sequence T if and only if $A = \{(-1, u) : u \in U\} \cup \{(1, t) : t \in T\}$ vanishes. As a second example, consider a "lookup argument": the components of U form a subset of a some public set T (called "table") if, for each $t \in T$, there exists a multiplicity m_t (only known to the prover) such that $A = \{(-1, u) : u \in U\} \cup \{(m_t, t) : t \in T\}$ vanishes.

The underlying idea of the protocol is that we can associate to A a rational function $f_A(X)$ defined as a sum of reciprocals such that for all $(m, s) \in A$, $f_A(X)$ has a pole $-s$ of multiplicity m:

$$f_A(X) = \sum_{(m,s)\in A} \frac{m}{X + s}. \tag{6}$$

Function f_A vanishes (i.e., is zero everywhere) if and only if the total multiplicity $\hat{m}_s$ for each symbol s vanishes. To show that this function vanishes, it suffices to evaluate it at a uniformly random input X. In the reciprocal argument protocol, this input is a challenge chosen by verifier after the prover has committed to A. We note that the function f_A has the structure of a logarithmic derivative, see the full version [20] for more background.

Application to Range Proofs. Consider the problem of constructing a range proof. We want to prove that some (committed) integer value v is in a range $[0, b^k)$ A natural solution is to consider the k base-b digits d_i of v and use a lookup argument (as described above) that shows that all digits d_i occur in the "table" $T = \{0, \ldots, b-1\}$. In that case, the rational function $f_A(X)$ is

$$f_A(X) = \sum_i \frac{-1}{X + d_i} + \sum_{j=0}^{b-1} \frac{m_j}{X + j}. \tag{7}$$

In contrast, both BP and BP+ construct a range proof by proving the validity of each digit *individually*, then showing that the linear combination of these digits equals the committed value. Binary digits (i.e., $b = 2$) are used since their validity can be checked with just one multiplication per digit: $d \in \{0, 1\}$ if and only if $d(d-1) = 0$.

However, Camenisch, Chaabouni, shelat [11] suggest to select b such that $b^b \approx B - A$. This base uses only $O(n/\log n)$ digits, where $n = \lceil \log_2(B - A) \rceil$, which is optimal in the sense that the witness length is a function of the base b and the number n of digits and is minimized when they are equal. Unfortunately, the natural generalization of the binary digit check $d_i(d_i - 1)$ to bases $b > 2$ does not result in a more efficient proof in BP. In the binary case, each digit requires a single multiplication, but the number of multiplications increases linearly in the size of the base.

In BP++, we sidestep this performance trade-off via the reciprocal argument, which we use as an efficient lookup argument. Rather than checking each digit is the root of some polynomial separately as in BP, we can use Eq. (7) to check membership of each digit in the set of valid digits. This enables us to construct range proofs with "optimal" bases $b > 2$ while retaining efficiency.

Application to MACT. For MACT, we face a related problem when proving multi-asset conservation of money. In this case, we have two collections of amounts and types of tokens I and O corresponding to the inputs and outputs of a transaction. We want to show that the total amount of each token in I is equal to the total amount of each token in O and that each amount in I and O is a positive integer. The latter claim can be shown using a range proof and the former using a new invocation of the reciprocal argument. Let $A = \{(v, t) : (v, t) \in I\} \cup \{(-v, t) : (v, t) \in O\}$. If A vanishes then the sum of all the amounts in I equals the sum of all the amounts in O for each token t. If the amounts are all positive integers much smaller than p, it follows that no tokens were created or destroyed in the transaction. In this case $f_A(X)$ is

$$f_A(X) = \sum_{(v,t) \in I} \frac{v}{X + t} - \sum_{(v,t) \in O} \frac{v}{X + t}. \tag{8}$$

3.3 Norm Linear Argument

As described in Sect. 3.1, BP and BP+ show a (weighted) inner product relation involving two vectors $\boldsymbol{x}$ and $\boldsymbol{y}$ by letting the prover send commitments to both

x and y. This introduces undesirable redundancy in some cases. Consider the example of a binary range proof: A prover wants to show $d_i(d_i - 1) = 0$ for each digit d_i in the vector d that encodes the binary representation of some value v. In a BP range proof, this requires committing to both $x = d$ and $y = -(1 - d)$, even though y is entirely determined by x up to the addition of a constant.

To avoid this redundancy in BP++, we can rewrite $d_i(d_i - 1) = 0$ into the equivalent constraint $(2d_i - 1)^2 = 1$. This allows us to substitute the inner product relation by a BP++ *norm relation*, which is a relation involving the inner product of a *single* vector with itself, and thus requires only a commitment to that single vector. As a result, we not only save data to be committed and hence communication, but also roughly half the prover and verifier cost.

However, while this motivating example provides an intuition for why a norm relation can be preferable over an inner product relation, it turns out that in practice, it is almost always more efficient to use a BP++ reciprocal range proof instead of a BP++ binary range proof. As a consequence, we defer the details of BP++ binary range proofs to the full version [20], and now turn our attention towards arithmetic circuits instead.

In the case of arithmetic circuits, similarly as for binary range proofs, using a norm argument allows reducing the verifier time by half, provided we can commit to only a single vector per commitment instead of two. Unfortunately, the inner product relation of BP and the weighted inner product relation of BP+ cannot work for this purpose, since even if the initial $x = y$ the reduction is asymmetric so $x' \neq y'$. To show a norm relation, we need a new reduction technique that is symmetric in the way it reduces x and y. Unlike BP, the reduced vectors are now defined to be

$$x' = [x]_0 + \gamma[x]_1 \qquad y' = [y]_0 + \gamma[y]_1. \tag{9}$$

The reduction can be derived by computing the coefficients of the three polynomials $1, \gamma, \gamma^2 - 1 \in \mathbb{F}[\gamma]$ where in BP we computed the coefficients of the polynomials $\gamma^{-2}, 1, \gamma^2 \in \mathbb{F}[\gamma]$. Since these polynomials are linearly independent in $\mathbb{F}[\gamma]$, the reduction is sound. Setting $x = y = n$ we can show a norm relation, and with some modifications can show a weighted norm relation.

A norm by itself is not sufficient; we want to be able to show that the witness satisfies linear constraints without introducing extraneous terms. We can apply this reduction relation to an inner product of an additional vector l and a public constraint vector c. This will be especially relevant when handling the blinding procedure for arithmetic circuits and also helps in the MPC proving setting. Thus, BP++ will show the weighted norm linear relation for a witness (v, l, n) and public (μ, c) satisfy $v = \langle c, l \rangle + |n|_\mu^2$.

3.4   Arithmetic Circuits

In BP and BP+, arithmetic circuits are given as a separate protocol from range proofs. The circuit is encoded as four matrices and a vector (W_L, W_R, W_O, W_V, c). A witness (w_L, w_R, w_O, v) satisfies the circuit if

$$W_L w_L + W_R w_R + W_O w_O = W_V v + c \qquad w_L \circ w_R = w_O. \qquad (10)$$

While one could use an arithmetic circuit to prove a range proof in BP, it would be less efficient than the specialized range proof protocol. In the BP protocol for circuits, the prover constructs a vector valued polynomial commitment to some $(v(X), x(X), y(X))$ and wants to show that when we apply the inner product equation to this witness, the X^2 term of the polynomial $t(X) = v(X) - \langle x(X), y(X) \rangle$ vanishes. To show this, the prover commits to all the other "error" terms of $t(X)$ in Pedersen scalar commitments in T_1, T_3, T_4, T_5, T_6.

BP++ arithmetic circuits avoids these extra commitments, as well as the two final commitments necessary to blind in both BP and BP+. Rather than committing to these other terms in scalar commitments, we commit to them as a vector in the final blinding commitment. This comes at no cost, and conveniently generalizes to larger polynomials without increasing proof size. The norm linear argument naturally allows us to evaluate the committed $t(X)$ at a random X by placing the coefficients in l and changing the c vector to be powers of X. We are then able to use the other commitments in the proof to blind these error terms at no additional cost in terms of proof size. This procedure is responsible for the much of the reduction in proof size.

BP++ also modifies the circuit protocol so that instead of the constraint $w_L \circ w_R = w_O$, the arithmetic circuit checks that $w_L \circ w_R$ equals a linear combination of the entire witness.

This makes it efficient to formulate reciprocal constraints, where the denominators occur in w_L, the reciprocals in w_R, and the numerators can be any linear combination on the right hand side. This new arithmetic circuit protocol allows encoding reciprocal range proofs and MACT more efficiently than existing protocols without the use of specialized protocols.

4   Norm Linear Argument

Unlike BP and BP+ which show inner product relations, BP++ is an argument of knowledge for the weighted norm linear relation

$$\mathcal{R}_{nl} = \left\{ \begin{pmatrix} H \in \mathbb{G}^l, G \in \mathbb{G}^n, G \in \mathbb{G}; \\ C \in \mathbb{G}, c \in \mathbb{F}^l, \mu \in \mathbb{F}; \\ l \in \mathbb{F}^l, n \in \mathbb{F}^n \end{pmatrix} : \begin{array}{l} v = \langle c, l \rangle + |n|_\mu^2 \\ C = vG + \langle l, H \rangle + \langle n, G \rangle \end{array} \right\}. \qquad (11)$$

4.1   Reducing the Vectors

We note that the norm linear relation $\mathcal{R}_{nl}$ is equivalent in expressiveness to the weighted inner product relation $\mathcal{R}_{ip}$, in the sense that both are capable of proving arithmetic circuit satisfiability and more narrowly in the sense that one could, in principle, write the norm linear relation as an inner product and thus construct a norm linear argument by reducing directly to an inner product argument. However, the latter approach requires committing to the vector n twice, in as both x and y from the inner product relation (see Sect. 3.1). While it is possible to simplify the initial commitment by computing $\langle n, G + H \rangle$ in the inner product commitment, the vectors x and y will be reduced asymmetrically following such an approach. This means that even if $x = y$, it will not be the case that $x' = y'$.

This makes clear what we want from a norm linear argument: given a commitment C to vectors as defined in the relation, we want to reduce this commitment to a new commitment to vectors l' and n' of half the length of the original vectors. To this end, we need a folding relation for a pair of vectors that treats both vectors symmetrically. That is, instead of scaling the halves of x and y by complementary γ and γ^{-1}, we would like to use reduced vectors that are folded in the same way, such as

$$x' = \rho^{-1}[x]_0 + \gamma[x]_1 \qquad y' = \rho^{-1}[y]_0 + \gamma[y]_1. \tag{12}$$

Now if $x = y$ then $x' = y'$. Here the value is defined as $\rho^2 = \mu$ for weight μ. Taking the weighted inner product of these vectors by μ we can work out a relation that includes the original weighted inner product $\langle x, y \rangle_\mu$ as one coefficient of a polynomial in γ

$$v_x = \rho^{-1}(\langle [x]_0, [y]_1 \rangle_{\mu^2} + \langle [x]_1, [y]_0 \rangle_{\mu^2}) \qquad v_r = \langle [x]_1, [y]_1 \rangle_{\mu^2}$$
$$\langle x', y' \rangle_{\mu^2} = \langle x, y \rangle_\mu + v_x \gamma + v_r(\gamma^2 - 1). \tag{13}$$

Note that this reduction is sound because the polynomials $1, \gamma, \gamma^2 - 1 \in \mathbb{F}[\gamma]$ are linearly independent. As in BP(+), the protocol follows straightforwardly from this relation by applying it to all the inner products in the commitment and grouping alike terms. The prover can commit to the γ and $\gamma^2 - 1$ coefficients (X, R) and then the verifier can select a random γ to evaluate the relation. Because this relation is symmetric, the prover can apply it to the $x = y = n$ case and reduce n to a single n'.

4.2   Norm Linear Argument

In the norm linear relation, there are 4 inner products that the prover needs to reduce: $|n|^2_\mu$, $\langle n, G \rangle$, $\langle c, l \rangle$, and $\langle l, H \rangle$. Since n participates in a weighted inner product (norm), we need to modify the relation for G slightly, and since l, c, and H only participate in unweighted relations, there are no weights present. The reduced vectors are thus

$$v' = |n'|^2_{\mu^2} + \langle c', l' \rangle \qquad c' = [c]_0 + \gamma[c]_1$$
$$l' = [l]_0 + \gamma[l]_1 \qquad n' = \rho^{-1}[n]_0 + \gamma[n]_1 \tag{14}$$
$$G' = \rho[G]_0 + \gamma[G]_1 \qquad H' = [H]_0 + \gamma[H]_1.$$

The commitments X and R follow directly from expanding all the reduced inner products and gathering γ and $\gamma^2 - 1$ coefficients. Explicitly

$$v_x = 2\rho^{-1} \langle [\boldsymbol{n}]_0, [\boldsymbol{n}]_1 \rangle_{\mu^2} + \langle \boldsymbol{c}, ([\boldsymbol{l}]_1, [\boldsymbol{l}]_0) \rangle \tag{15}$$

$$v_r = |[\boldsymbol{n}]_1|^2_{\mu^2} + \langle [\boldsymbol{c}]_1, [\boldsymbol{l}]_1 \rangle \tag{16}$$

$$X = v_x G + \langle ([\boldsymbol{l}]_1, [\boldsymbol{l}]_0), \boldsymbol{H} \rangle + \langle (\rho[\boldsymbol{n}]_1, \rho^{-1}[\boldsymbol{n}]_0), \boldsymbol{G} \rangle \tag{17}$$

$$R = v_r G + \langle [\boldsymbol{l}]_1, [\boldsymbol{H}]_1 \rangle + \langle [\boldsymbol{n}]_1, [\boldsymbol{G}]_1 \rangle . \tag{18}$$

Evaluating the polynomial commitment at γ yields a commitment on the reduced basis to the reduced witness, i.e., we have

$$C + \gamma X + (\gamma^2 - 1)R = v'G + \langle \boldsymbol{l}', \boldsymbol{H}' \rangle + \langle \boldsymbol{n}', \boldsymbol{G}' \rangle . \tag{19}$$

The full protocol applies this reduction recursively until doing so does not reduce the overall proof size. This occurs when $|\boldsymbol{l}| + |\boldsymbol{n}| \leq 6$, at which point the prover sends the reduced $\boldsymbol{l}$ and $\boldsymbol{n}$ to the verifier. If these vectors satisfy the norm linear relation for the reduced $\boldsymbol{c}$ and μ, then it follows by induction that the original commitment satisfies the relation.

Completeness follows directly from this equation holding and soundness from the linear independence of the polynomials $1, \gamma, \gamma^2 - 1 \in \mathbb{F}[\gamma]$. Linear independence can be used to construct a round extractor, which as in BP can be used to construct an extractor for the entire protocol.

Theorem 1. *The weighted norm linear argument has perfect completeness. Assuming the expected-PPT hardness of the discrete logarithm relation problem, the argument has CWEE and is therefore an argument of knowledge for the weighted norm linear relation.*

See the full version [20] for the proof.

4.3   Full Protocol Description

The setup protocol for the norm linear argument $\mathcal{K}$ simply chooses all group elements $G, \boldsymbol{H}, \boldsymbol{G}$ uniformly at random.

Weighted Norm Linear Argument $\langle \mathcal{P}_{nl}, \mathcal{V}_{nl} \rangle$

Common input: $G, \boldsymbol{G}, \boldsymbol{H}, \boldsymbol{c}, C, \rho$ and $\mu = \rho^2$

$\mathcal{P}$'s input: $(\boldsymbol{l}, \boldsymbol{n})$ and $v = \langle \boldsymbol{c}, \boldsymbol{l} \rangle + |\boldsymbol{n}|^2_\mu$ such that $C = vG + \langle \boldsymbol{l}, \boldsymbol{H} \rangle + \langle \boldsymbol{n}, \boldsymbol{G} \rangle$

1. If $|\boldsymbol{l}| + |\boldsymbol{n}| < 6$:
   1.1 $\mathcal{P} \to \mathcal{V} : \boldsymbol{l}, \boldsymbol{n}$
   1.2 $\mathcal{V}$ computes $v := \langle \boldsymbol{c}, \boldsymbol{l} \rangle + |\boldsymbol{n}|^2_\mu$
   1.3 $\mathcal{V}$ accepts if $C \overset{?}{=} vG + \langle \boldsymbol{l}, \boldsymbol{H} \rangle + \langle \boldsymbol{n}, \boldsymbol{G} \rangle$, otherwise rejects
2. Else:
   2.1 $\mathcal{P} \to \mathcal{V} : X, R$
   2.2 $\mathcal{V} \to \mathcal{P} : \gamma \leftarrow_\$ \mathbb{F}$
   2.3 $\mathcal{P}$ computes $\boldsymbol{l}', \boldsymbol{n}'$
   2.4 $\mathcal{P}, \mathcal{V}$ compute $\boldsymbol{G}', \boldsymbol{H}', \boldsymbol{c}'$ and $\rho' := \mu, \mu' := \mu^2, C' := C + \gamma X + (\gamma^2 - 1)R$
   2.5 Run $\langle \mathcal{P}_{nl}, \mathcal{V}_{nl} \rangle$ with $(G, \boldsymbol{G}', \boldsymbol{H}', \boldsymbol{c}', C', \rho', \mu'; \boldsymbol{l}', \boldsymbol{n}')$.

As in BP, it is not necessary for the verifier to actually compute the intermediate (G, H, c, C) values and the final verification check can be replaced with a single linear combination of public curve points. Letting k be the number of rounds before stopping and the vectors γ_l and γ_n be defined as

$$\gamma_l = \bigotimes_{i=0}^{k-1}(1, \gamma_i) \qquad \gamma_n = \bigotimes_{i=0}^{k-1}(\rho^{2^i}, \gamma_i), \tag{20}$$

the (G, H, c, C) in the final verification equation can be rewritten in terms of the original (G, H, c, C) as

$$v = \langle c, \gamma_l \otimes l \rangle + |n|_\mu^2 \tag{21}$$

$$vG + \langle \gamma_l \otimes l, H \rangle + \langle \gamma_n \otimes n, G \rangle \overset{?}{=} C + \sum_{i=0}^{k-1} \gamma_i X_i + (\gamma_i^2 - 1)R_i. \tag{22}$$

Also as in BP, when verifying multiple proofs simultaneously, the verifier can take a random linear combination of the equations and combine the $\gamma_l \otimes l$ and $\gamma_n \otimes n$ from different proofs if the G and H are the same. Thus the marginal cost of verifying an additional proof is only $O(\log n)$ additional scalar multiplications and $O(n)$ field operations. There are additional optimizations that help reduce prover work, as we discuss in the full version [20].

5   Arithmetic Circuits

In BP, arithmetic circuits are represented using four public matrices and one public vector (W_L, W_R, W_O, W_V, c) and four witness vectors (w_L, w_R, w_O, v), which must satisfy Eq. (10). For each multiplication in a BP arithmetic circuit, the prover commits to the left input in $w_{L,i}$, the right input in $w_{R,i}$ and the output in $w_{O,i}$. In some cases, this leads to the prover committing to redundant information. Specifically, if an output of a multiplication is immediately subject to a linear constraint, the prover could avoid committing to it by instead showing

$$w_L \circ w_R = W_{m,L}w_L + W_{m,R}w_R + W_{m,O}w_O. \tag{23}$$

This motivates the BP++ circuit encoding, where we make exactly this change. It turns out that effectively every multiplication gate in reciprocal range proofs (Sect. 6.2) and MACTs is of this form. This change makes it more efficient to represent these protocols as arithmetic circuits, rather than using bespoke range proof protocols like other Bulletproof based constructions. We also modify the circuits to accept input vectors from Pedersen vector commitments, rather than just scalars, which removes the matrix W_V.

Concretely, an arithmetic circuit $\mathcal{C}$ will be encoded into two matrices (W_l, W_m) and two vectors (a_l, a_m) which constrain a witness $w = (w_L, w_R, w_O)$. The vectors w_L and w_R are the left and right inputs to each multiplication, as in BP. The input vector is the concatenation of vectors

$w_V = (v_i)_{i=0}^k$, each of which comes from a Pedersen vector commitment V_i. The circuit is satisfied if both

$$0 = W_l w + w_V + a_l \qquad w_L \circ w_R = W_m w + a_m. \qquad (24)$$

The arithmetic circuit protocol is therefore a proof of knowledge for the relation

$$\mathcal{C} = \left(W_l \in \mathbb{F}^{N_l \times N_w}, a_l \in \mathbb{F}^{N_l}, W_m \in \mathbb{F}^{N_m \times N_w}, a_m \in \mathbb{F}^{N_m} \right) \qquad (25)$$

$$\mathcal{R}_{ac} = \left\{ \left(\begin{array}{c} G \in \mathbb{G}, H \in \mathbb{G}^{N_v+7}, G \in \mathbb{G}^{N_m}; \\ \mathcal{C}, V \in \mathbb{G}^k; v_i \in \mathbb{F}^{N_v} : i = [0,k), \\ s_V \in \mathbb{F}^k, w_O \in \mathbb{F}^{N_O} w_L, w_R \in \mathbb{F}^{N_m} \end{array} \right) : \begin{array}{c} V_i = \mathsf{Com}(v_i; s_{V,i}) \\ \mathrm{Eq.~(24)} \end{array} \right\} \qquad (26)$$

This new arithmetic circuit format can encode satisfiability of BP circuits and is therefore capable of representing any arithmetic circuit, see the full version [20] for details.

5.1   Protocol Overview

We defer the explicit details of how the arithmetic circuit protocol encodes the statement into the norm linear argument to the full version [20] and limit ourselves to a high-level description here. First, the prover will commit to (w_L, w_R, w_O) in (C_L, C_R, C_O) and send these to the verifier. There is some freedom in how the prover can organize the witness into these three norm linear commitments. Specifically, in some cases it may be more efficient to commit to some of w_O in the linear portion of C_L and C_R.

Then, the verifier will choose two challenges λ and μ to combine the linear and multiplicative constraints respectively using the vectors of powers $e_{N_l}(\lambda)$ and $e_{N_m}(\mu)$. The verifier will also choose challenges β and δ, which will be necessary for blinding. These allow us to transform equations Eq. (24) into a single scalar equation

$$0 = e_{N_l}(\lambda)^\top (W_l w + w_V + a_l) + \langle w_L, w_R \rangle_\mu - e_{N_m}(\mu)^\top (W_m w + a_m). \qquad (27)$$

We want to construct a triple of polynomials $(\hat{v}(T), \hat{l}(T), \hat{n}(T))$ so that when we apply the norm linear relation and get $\hat{f}(T) = \hat{v}(T) - \langle c(T), l(T) \rangle - |\hat{n}(T)|_\mu^2$ exactly one term of $\hat{f}(T)$ encodes these randomized constraints. We call this term the value term and the other terms the error terms. To show that the constraints are satisfied, it suffices to show that the value term vanishes, and prove knowledge of the error terms.

To construct this polynomial, we first assign a unique T term to each commitment. The product of the T terms for C_L and C_R will be the value term. Each constraint will be placed on the unique T term so that when multiplied with the T term of the commitment to the witness it acts on, the result will be the value term. So, if T multiplies C_L and $T^2 C_R$, then the value term is T^3 and $e_{N_l}(\lambda)^\top W_L$ should be multiplied by T^2. The challenge δ will be used to prevent the norm portion of the w_V commitments from interfering with $f(X)$.

Then, the prover sends C_S to blind. For the portions of the commitments that commit to w, C_S will consist of uniformly random values. We need to choose a T term for C_S so that none of these random values can interfere with the value term. Our goal now is to introduce some additional elements to the linear portion of C_S to subtract off the non-value terms from $\hat{f}(T)$ and the additional terms that arise from the blinding. If the result of this is zero, then the value term must be zero.

This can have two problems: it might allow interference with the value term and it will not be zero knowledge as it may reveal information about the error terms. The second problem is fixed by allowing the commitments C_L, C_R, C_O to blind the error terms in C_S. The first is fixed by using the challenge δ to prevent interference. Showing that the result is zero knowledge is somewhat more involved than other protocols, and is ultimately reducible to showing that by manipulating the error term blinding in C_L, C_R, C_O can produce any valid opening. Equivalently that a certain matrix is full rank.

Finally, the verifier will send a challenge $T = \tau$. Because of how the blinding was constructed, the prover and verifier can take a linear combination of C_L, C_R, C_S, C_O and public information to produce a valid norm linear instance. Without the blinding protocol, the protocol would need an additional round of interaction. At this point, since the witness is blinded the prover and verifier can run the norm linear argument and complete the protocol.

Arithmetic Circuit Protocol $\langle \mathcal{P}_{ac}, \mathcal{V}_{ac} \rangle$

1. $\mathcal{P} \to \mathcal{V} : C_L, C_R, C_O$ // Choose blinding r_L, r_R, r_O and commit to w
2. $\mathcal{V} \to \mathcal{P} : \rho, \lambda, \beta, \delta \leftarrow_\$ \mathbb{F}$
3. $\mathcal{P} \to \mathcal{V} : C_S$ // C_S is chosen s.t. all error terms cancel and w is blinded
4. $\mathcal{V} \to \mathcal{P} : \tau \leftarrow_\$ \mathbb{F}$
5. $\mathcal{P}$ computes $v(\tau), l(\tau), n(\tau)$ // Compute opening of $C(\tau)$.
   (Since all error terms cancel, norm linear relation is satisfied.)
6. $\mathcal{P}, \mathcal{V}$ run the weighted norm linear argument $\langle \mathcal{P}_{nl}, \mathcal{V}_{nl} \rangle = b$ with common input $(c(\tau), C(\tau), \mu = \rho^2)$ and prover input $(l(\tau), n(\tau), v(\tau))$.

Theorem 2 (Arithmetic Circuits). *The arithmetic circuit protocol (whose pseudocode can be found in the full version [20]) has perfect completeness and perfect honest verifier zero-knowledge. Assuming the expected-PPT hardness of the discrete logarithm relation problem, the protocol has computational witness-extended emulation.*

See the full version [20] for the proof.

6 Reciprocal Argument

Initially, zero knowledge proof arithmetizations, including that of the original Bulletproof AC protocol, supported only additions and multiplications. This was sufficient to encode all arithmetic circuits, but more modern proof systems like Halo2 [49] incorporate so called "custom gates" directly into the arithmetization. These custom gates allow circuit designers to "factor out" certain features into the arithmetization, which has a number of benefits for circuit designers. For example, a custom gate to compute x^5 avoids adding the values x^2 and x^4 to the witness.

Another more powerful type of custom gate is the so called "lookup gate", which is implemented using a variant of plookup [21] in Halo2 [49]. This allows circuit designer to incorporate lookup arguments into their circuits. Unlike raising to the fifth power, this gate cannot be conveniently implemented as a low degree expression since it requires an additional round of prover, verifier interaction. In particularly, this means it is not possible to efficiently perform plookup, or the reciprocal argument, inside simpler arithmetizations like BP++ AC. This motivates adding the reciprocal argument directly to BP++ AC, which we call reciprocal form circuits. By formalizing this modification of the protocol, we are also able to provide a single knowledge soundness proof.

To demonstrate the power of this approach, we use the new reciprocal form circuit protocol to define a range proof and a MACT protocol. Since these protocol are simply reciprocal from arithmetic circuits, zero-knowledge and knowledge soundness will follow without the need for additional security proofs.

6.1 Warmup: Reciprocal Argument Protocol

Recall from Sect. 3.2 that the reciprocal argument is an interactive protocol by which the prover can convince a verifier that a *collection* A vanishes.

Definition 6. *Let A be a set of pairs (m_i, s_i) of multiplicities $m_i \in \mathbb{F}$ and symbols $s_i \in \mathbb{F}$. Let the* total multiplicity *of a symbol $s \in \mathbb{F}$ in A be*

$$\hat{m}_s = \sum_{i:\, s_i = s} m_i.$$

We call A a collection, *and we say that A vanishes if $\forall s \in \mathbb{F} : \hat{m}_s = 0$.*

Let $S = \{s_i : \exists m : (m, s_i) \in A\}$ be the set of symbols in A, and further recall that reciprocal argument encodes A as a rational function f_A defined as

$$f_A(X) := \sum_{i=0}^{|A|-1} \frac{m_i}{X + s_i} = \sum_{s \in S} \frac{\hat{m}_v}{X + s}. \tag{28}$$

To demonstrate the core idea of the reciprocal argument, we present an informal protocol in which the prover sends the verifier the witness explicitly. This protocol is not used in a blackbox manner by BP++; we will instead embed it into an arithmetic circuit and make additional modifications, e.g., some of s or m may be known to the verifier.

The (informal) protocol works as follows: First, the prover sends multiplicities m and symbols s in A. Next the verifier selects a random challenge α, and the prover responds by sending the "reciprocals" $r_i = m_i/(\alpha + s_i)$. Finally, the verifier checks that each reciprocal is properly formed and that the sum of all the reciprocals vanish, i.e., if $(\alpha + s_i)r_i = m_i$ and $\sum_i r_i = 0$.

Reciprocal Argument Protocol $\langle \mathcal{P}_{ra}, \mathcal{V}_{ra} \rangle$

1. $\mathcal{P} \to \mathcal{V} : \boldsymbol{m}, \boldsymbol{s}$
2. $\mathcal{V} \to \mathcal{P} : \alpha \leftarrow_\$ \mathbb{F}$
3. $\mathcal{P} \to \mathcal{V} : \boldsymbol{r}$ s.t. $r_i = m_i/(\alpha + s_i)$
4. $\mathcal{V}$ accepts if $(\alpha + s_i)r_i = m_i$ for $i = 0 .. |\boldsymbol{r}| - 1$ and $\sum_i r_i = 0$

This protocol lacks perfect completeness because if $\alpha = -s_i$ for any s_i then r_i is not well-defined. However, this only occurs with negligible probability since $\alpha \leftarrow_\$ \mathbb{F}$. Informally, soundness follows from the structure of the sum of the reciprocals. If $(\alpha + s_i)r_i = m_i$, then either $\alpha = -s_i$ and $m_i = 0$, or $r_i = m_i/(\alpha + s_i)$. So, with overwhelming probability, if $\sum_i r_i = 0$ we have that $f_A(\alpha) = 0$.

We can show that if $f_A(\alpha_j) = 0$ for $2|S|$ distinct challenges α_j then $\hat{m}_s$ must be zero for all $s \in S$.

Lemma 1 (Reciprocal Argument Vanishing). *Let A be a collection of pairs of multiplicities and symbols. If there exist $2|A|$ accepting transcripts of the reciprocal argument protocol for A with pairwise distinct challenges α_j, then A vanishes (Definition 6).*

Proof. There are at most $|S|$ values α such that there exists $s_i \in S$ for which $\alpha = -s_i$. Let $\boldsymbol{\alpha}'$ be a vector of $|S|$ challenges α_j from the transcripts such that $\alpha_j' \neq -s_i$ for any i, j. Let $\boldsymbol{s}$ be the vector of elements in S, and note that the components of vector $-\boldsymbol{s}$ are pairwise distinct and the components in $\boldsymbol{\alpha}'$ are pairwise distinct. This means the $|S| \times |S|$ Cauchy matrix C formed from $-\boldsymbol{s}$ and $\boldsymbol{\alpha}'$ is well-defined and therefore invertible. Let $f_j = f_A(\alpha_j')$ for f_A as defined in Eq. (28) and note that $\boldsymbol{f} = C\hat{m}_s = \boldsymbol{0}$. Since C is invertible, $\hat{m}_s = \boldsymbol{0}$ and therefore A vanishes.

6.2 Reciprocal Form Circuits

Reciprocal form circuits extend the BP++ AC protocol to support the reciprocal argument. As in the protocol outlined above, this requires an additional round of interaction, where the verifier chooses α, and will require the prover to commit to the witness in several stages. Once we have α and the entire witness, we can use a BP++ AC to verify step 4 of the reciprocal argument protocol.

Suppose we have an arithmetic circuit $\mathcal{C}$ and the arithmetic circuit witness $(\boldsymbol{w}_L, \boldsymbol{w}_R, \boldsymbol{w}_O, \boldsymbol{w}_V)$. To integrate the reciprocal argument, we want to show that this circuit is satisfied and that some set of rational functions $\boldsymbol{f}(X)$ vanishes, where each rational function encodes a reciprocal argument instance. In general, we want the symbols and multiplicities to be able to depend on the arithmetic circuit witness $\boldsymbol{w}$ and ultimately would like to be able to compile the $\boldsymbol{f}(X)$ vanishing check into an arithmetic circuit for a particular $X = \alpha$.

Let $\boldsymbol{w}_D$ be the vector of private denominators for all the reciprocal argument instances, and let $\boldsymbol{w}_P(X)$ be the vector of all the reciprocals associated to each $w_{D,i}$. Define the "initial witness" $\boldsymbol{w}_I = \boldsymbol{w}_O \,||\, \boldsymbol{w}_L \,||\, \boldsymbol{w}_D$ and the "entire witness" to be $\boldsymbol{w}(X) = \boldsymbol{w}_D \,||\, \boldsymbol{w}_L \,||\, \boldsymbol{w}_P(X) \,||\, \boldsymbol{w}_R \,||\, \boldsymbol{w}_O$. We can specify all the reciprocal argument instances using three matrices $(W_n, W_d, W_p(X))$

$$w_{P,i}(X) = \frac{(W_n\boldsymbol{w}_I + \boldsymbol{a}_n)_i}{X + w_{D,i}} \tag{29}$$

$$W_d\boldsymbol{w}_I + \boldsymbol{w}_V + \boldsymbol{a}_d = \boldsymbol{0} \tag{30}$$

$$\boldsymbol{f}(X) = W_p(X)\boldsymbol{w}(X) + \boldsymbol{a}_p(X). \tag{31}$$

The intuition here is as follows. First, we take all the reciprocals that occur in all the $\boldsymbol{f}(X)$ instances and partition them into two groups. The first are the reciprocals with public denominators, and the second are those with denominators that depend on the witness. Those with public denominators do not require multiplicative constraints and can be encoded via $W_p(X)$. The second set are organized into a vector, and $\boldsymbol{w}_D$ is their denominators. We allow the prover to constrain these values via Eq. (30). The numerators of these reciprocals are encoded via $W_n\boldsymbol{w}_I + \boldsymbol{a}_n$, and the reciprocals themselves will be committed via $\boldsymbol{w}_P(\alpha)$. Finally, we map each reciprocal to its reciprocal argument instance via $W_p(X)$ and add any that consist of entirely public information via $\boldsymbol{a}_p(X)$.

Following commitment to $\boldsymbol{w}_I$, the verifier chooses α, and the prover commits to $\boldsymbol{w}_R$ and $\boldsymbol{w}_P(\alpha)$. We can now define the new arithmetic circuit $\mathcal{C}'$ for α. First, prepend the vector $\boldsymbol{w}_D$ onto $\boldsymbol{w}_L$ and the vector $\boldsymbol{w}_P(\alpha)$ onto $\boldsymbol{w}_R$ to produce $\boldsymbol{w}'_L$ and $\boldsymbol{w}'_R$ for $\mathcal{C}'$. We keep $\boldsymbol{w}'_O = \boldsymbol{w}_O$, and can let $\boldsymbol{w}' = \boldsymbol{w}'_L \,||\, \boldsymbol{w}'_R \,||\, \boldsymbol{w}'_O$. To verify that the committed vector $\boldsymbol{w}'_P$ is correctly constructed as $\boldsymbol{w}_P(\alpha)$, we can clear the denominator of Eq. (29) and check

$$w_{D,i}w'_{P,i} = (W_n\boldsymbol{w}_I + \boldsymbol{a}_n)_i - \alpha w'_{P,i}. \tag{32}$$

This is satisfied if $w'_{P,i} = w_{P,i}(\alpha)$ or if $w_{D,i} = -\alpha$ and the numerator is zero. The latter occurs with negligible probability, so this is sufficient to check $\boldsymbol{w}'_P$ is correctly constructed. The rest of the constraints can be appended onto the W_l and W_m matrices to construct the W'_l and W'_m matrices for $\mathcal{C}'$ as

$$W'_l\boldsymbol{w}' = (W_d\boldsymbol{w}_I) \,||\, (W_p(\alpha)\boldsymbol{w}(X)) \,||\, (W_l\boldsymbol{w}) \tag{33}$$

$$W'_m\boldsymbol{w}' = (W_n\boldsymbol{w}_I - \alpha\boldsymbol{w}_P(\alpha)) \,||\, (W_m\boldsymbol{w}). \tag{34}$$

Formally, the reciprocal form arithmetic circuit protocol shows that the reciprocal form arithmetic circuit relation is satisfied for the circuit $\mathcal{RC}$. In the relation, A_i refers to the collection for the ith instance of the reciprocal argument. That is, the collection A_i is encoded as in Eq. (28) by $f_i(X)$ in Eq. (31).

$$\mathcal{RC} = \begin{pmatrix} \mathcal{C}, W_n \in \mathbb{F}^{N_p \times N_I}, W_d \in \mathbb{F}^{N_d \times N_I}, \\ W_p(X) \in \mathbb{F}(X)^{N_p \times N'_w} \\ \boldsymbol{a}_n \in \mathbb{F}^{N_p}, \boldsymbol{a}_d \in \mathbb{F}^{N_d}, \boldsymbol{a}_p(X) \in \mathbb{F}(X)^{N_p} \end{pmatrix} \tag{35}$$

$$\mathcal{R}_{rf} = \left\{ (\sigma; x, \mathcal{RC}; w, \boldsymbol{w}_D \in \mathbb{F}^{N_p}) : A_i \text{ vanishes}, \text{Eq. (30)}, (\sigma; x; w) \in \mathcal{R}_{ac} \right\} \tag{36}$$

Given that we can compile reciprocal form circuits to arithmetic circuits for a particular α, the security proofs are able to inherit most of the structure of those of arithmetic circuits. Zero-knowledge follows immediately, and soundness requires one additional level in the transcript tree for α to extract the vanishing of $f(\alpha)$.

Theorem 3 (Reciprocal Form Arithmetic Circuits). *The arithmetic circuit protocol for circuits in reciprocal form (whose pseudocode can be found in the full version [20]) has completeness and perfect honest verifier zero-knowledge. Assuming the expected-PPT hardness of the discrete logarithm relation problem, the protocol has computational witness-extended emulation.*

See the full version [20] for the proof.

6.3   Reciprocal Range Proofs

Given the reciprocal argument and reciprocal form arithmetic circuits, we can now construct a range proof as an argument of knowledge for

$$\mathcal{R}_{rp} = \left\{ \left(\begin{matrix} G, H \in \mathbb{G}; \\ V \in \mathbb{G}^k, A, B \in \mathbb{Z}^k, B_i - A_i \in [1,p); \\ v, s \in \mathbb{F}^k \end{matrix} \right) : \begin{matrix} \forall i : v_i \in [A_i, B_i), \\ V_i = \mathsf{Com}(v_i; s_i) \end{matrix} \right\}. \quad (37)$$

For simplicity, assume each range $[A_i, B_i)$ uses the same base b. To show that each value lies in the range the prover can break down v_i into digits d_i, show that each digit is a valid base b digit, and show that for some vector of public constants b_i, the following linear relation is satisfied $\langle b_i, d_i \rangle = v_i - A_i$. To show each d_i is a valid digit we can use the reciprocal argument and let w_D consist of all the digits for all the range proofs.

We will also assume for simplicity of presentation that the size of the range is a power of b. That is $B - A = b^k$ for some integer k. This simplifies the range proof description, and is typically sufficient in practice. Especially in cryptocurrencies range proofs are typically used to enforce that a value is not "negative" rather than that it lies in a specific range. It is straightforward to adapt the protocol to support arbitrary ranges using the work of Chaabouni, Lipmaa, shelat [12] and we defer a detailed description to the full version [20].

BP++ arithmetic circuits, as mentioned before, allow placing the vector w_O of witness elements that participate only linear constraints either in the l_X portion of the witness, or in the n_O portion of the witness. For reciprocal range proofs, it makes sense to either place them in n_O, which we will call "inline" multiplicity range proofs, or in l_L, which we will call "shared" multiplicity range proofs. The terminology refers to the fact that in the multiparty setting when multiplicities are placed in the linear portion of the witness multiple provers can reuse the same basis points in their separate proofs. Inline range proofs are so called because in the multiparty setting, multiplicities must be represented over the basis elements used by each prover to commit to their digits, so the multiplicities are inline with the digits.

Arithmetic Circuit. In both the inline and reciprocal cases, the vector $\boldsymbol{w}_D$ consists of the concatenation of the digit vectors for all the ranges. The numerator for each digit reciprocal is always 1, so the numerator matrix is simply zero and $a_n = 1$. The vector of reciprocals $\boldsymbol{w}_P(X)$ is the concatenation of the values $r_{i,j} = 1/(\alpha + d_{i,j})$ so they align with $\boldsymbol{w}_D$ per value that verifies the range using

$$\langle W_{d,i}, \boldsymbol{w}_D \rangle = \langle \boldsymbol{b}_i, \boldsymbol{d}_i \rangle \qquad a_{d,i} = A_i \tag{38}$$

Now all that remains is to describe the matrix $W_p(X)$ in terms of the multiplicities. In both the inline and shared cases, the prover shows that the set membership check is satisfied for all the digits of each base. Let the vector $\boldsymbol{m}_i$ be the number of times each value in $[1, b_i)$ occurs in $\boldsymbol{d}_i$. Note this does not include a multiplicity for zero, as this multiplicity is equal to the number of digits minus the sum of the other multiplicities. Let the total multiplicity be $\hat{\boldsymbol{m}} = \sum_i \boldsymbol{m}_i$ and the total number of digits be $\hat{n} = \sum_i |\boldsymbol{d}_i|$. In both the inline and the shared cases, the prover uses the vectors of reciprocals to prove each digit is a valid base b digit

$$\sum_i \langle \boldsymbol{1}, \boldsymbol{r}_i \rangle = \frac{\hat{n} - \langle \boldsymbol{1}, \hat{\boldsymbol{m}} \rangle}{X} + \sum_{j=0}^{b-2} \frac{\hat{m}_j}{X + j + 1}. \tag{39}$$

The difference arises in how the prover commits to the multiplicities in the inline case, the prover commits to the vector $\boldsymbol{m}$ in $\boldsymbol{w}_O$ padded so that they align with $\boldsymbol{d}_i$. The partition function $\mathcal{F}$ in the inline case maps all of $\boldsymbol{w}_O$ to $\boldsymbol{n}_O$. Since the $\hat{\boldsymbol{m}}$ are a linear function of the $\boldsymbol{m}_i$, the matrix $W_p(X)$ is defined to compute this function and then the right hand side of Eq. (39).

In the shared case, the prover commits to the all the $\hat{\boldsymbol{m}}$ directly in $\boldsymbol{w}_O$ and the partition function maps these values to $\boldsymbol{l}_L$. In this case, since neither $\boldsymbol{l}_O$ or $\boldsymbol{n}_O$ are used, the commitment can be safely dropped from the protocol. The matrix $W_p(X)$ once again encodes Eq. (39) but now uses the committed total multiplicities.

Theorem 4 (Reciprocal Range Proofs). *Both the inline and shared multiplicity reciprocal range proofs and zero knowledge arguments of knowledge for the reciprocal range proof relation $\mathcal{R}_{rp}$ Eq. (37) assuming the expected-PPT hardness of the discrete logarithm relation problem.*

Proof. The reciprocal range proof protocols are both instances of the reciprocal form arithmetic circuit protocol, so they have SHVZK, CWEE, and completeness. To show they are arguments for Eq. (37), we must establish that the circuit is satisfiable only if the inputs $\boldsymbol{v}$ satisfy the relation. The protocol applies the reciprocal form circuit protocol to $A = \{(-1, d_i) : i\} \cup \{(m_j, t_j) : j\}$. By the soundness of the reciprocal form circuit protocol, A vanishes. So long as the number of digits is less than $\mathbb{F}$, which is the case by assumption, this implies all d_i are valid base b digits. Therefore $v_i = \langle \boldsymbol{b}_i, \boldsymbol{d}_i \rangle + A_i$ implies that $v_i \in [A_i, B_i)$. Thus, the reciprocal range proof protocol is a zero knowledge argument of knowledge for Eq. (37). ∎

6.4 Multi-asset Confidential Transactions

In a MACT, the prover wants to prove a closely related relation to that of an aggregated range proof. Given a transaction with a set of inputs I ($o_i = 0$) and outputs O ($o_i = 1$), each with a type and amount, the prover wants to show that the amount of input tokens of each type equals the amount of tokens output of each type and that all the output token amounts are "positive." This is because if one of the outputs were negative it would be possible to secretly create new tokens, by adding more tokens to one of the other outputs to be larger. It is typically not necessary to check that the inputs are positive since they are the outputs of some other transaction.

In a finite field, the positivity condition is checked by bounding each output ($o_i = 1$) by a range much smaller than the field characteristic. More precisely, it must be the case that any negligible amount of inputs and outputs cannot wrap around in the field to create a "negative" value. For simplicity, we can assume that all transaction outputs use the same range in the range proof $[0, B)$, and in practice we can assume that $B = 2^{64}$. The MACT relation is thus

$$
\mathcal{R}_{ct} = \left\{ \begin{pmatrix} G, H_0, H_1 \in \mathbb{G}; o \in \{0,1\}^k, \\ V \in \mathbb{G}^k, B \in \mathbb{Z}, kB < p, \\ \forall i : o_i = 0 \Rightarrow v_i \in [0, B); \\ v, t, s \in \mathbb{F}^k \end{pmatrix} : \begin{array}{l} \forall i : V_i = v_i G + t_i H_0 + s_i H_1 \\ \forall i : o_i = 1 \Rightarrow v_i \in [0, B) \\ \forall t : \sum_{i:t_i=t} (-1)^{o_i} v_i = 0 \end{array} \right\}.
$$

(40)

To check the range proof part of the relation, we can use any reciprocal range proof over all the transaction outputs, i.e. $o_i = 1$, for the optimal base b and range $[0, B)$. Checking that all the amounts of each type net to zero in $\mathbb{F}$ is essentially a multiset permutation check with large multiplicities, and can be stated in the form of the reciprocal argument as

$$
f(X) = \sum_{i=1}^{k} \frac{(-1)^{o_i} v_i}{X + t_i} = 0.
$$

(41)

From Lemma 1 it follows that if $f(\alpha) = 0$ for a uniformly random α then with overwhelming probability the total multiplicity associated to each t_i must be zero in $\mathbb{F}$. From the structure of the function, this total multiplicity is the sum of all the inputs of that type minus the sum of all the outputs of that type, and so the total multiplicity is zero in $\mathbb{F}$ if and only if the amounts net to zero in $\mathbb{F}$.

Taking these together, we can show that the total amount (i.e., multiplicity) of each type of asset nets to zero in $\mathbb{Z}$. We know by assumption that each transaction input amount lies in $[0, B)$, and we know from the range proof that each transaction output amount lies in $[0, B)$. Therefore, the total multiplicity $\hat{v}_t$ of any type of asset lies in $(-kB, kB)$, which occurs in a transaction with k inputs or k outputs all of the same type and maximum amount. Since $kB < p$, this value cannot wrap around the field, so if $\hat{v}_t = 0$ in $\mathbb{F}$ and $\hat{v}_t \in (-kB, kB)$, then the amounts net to zero in $\mathbb{Z}$.

Arithmetic Circuit. Each input and each output commit to two values, so $N_v = 2$. As in the reciprocal range proofs, all multiplicative constraints are reciprocal constraints and the matrices W_L, W_R have zero rows. The protocol can use any reciprocal range proof, and for the purposes of this protocol assume one is fixed by a reciprocal form circuit $\mathcal{RC}$ for either a shared or inline digit range proof for all v_i with $o_i = 1$ for the range $[0, B)$.

We will append the vector t of types to w_D from the range proof, and we will add copy constraints to check that these are the same values from the input commitments. Note these copy constraints should be interleaved with the range proof linear constraints to line up with t in w_V. Each reciprocal in Eq. (41) has $v_i(-1)^{o_i}$ as its numerator and $X + t_i$ as its denominator. We will define $w_{P,i}(X)$ to be the unsigned reciprocals $w_{P,i}(X) = v_i/(X + t_i)$. Since multiplicative constraints cannot directly access inputs, we also need to add constraints to copy v_i into w_I and modify W_n such that This lets us simplify $(W_n w_I + a_n)_i = v_i$. We can insert dummy constraints that check $t_i = t_i$ in the linear constraints so that the inputs align with the constraint matrix. To check that Eq. (41) holds, we can then append a row $W_p(X)$ so that

$$\langle W_p(X)_0, w \rangle = \sum_{i=1}^{k} (-1)^{o_i} w_{P,i}(X).$$

This completes the MACT arithmetic circuit. In total, each input adds only one element to w_D and $w_P(X)$, one copy constraint to W_d and one, trivial, row to W_n. There is also one constraint in $W_p(X)$ to check Eq. (41).

The marginal cost of a MACT over an aggregated range proof is negligible in prover time, verifier time, and proof size. This is in stark contrast to existing protocols which either require large proofs, complex circuits, and require trading off multi-party proving for the full relation.

Theorem 5 (Multi-Asset Confidential Transactions). *The confidential transaction protocol, instantiated with any of the reciprocal range proofs is a zero-knowledge argument of knowledge for the MACT relation Eq. (40) assuming the expected-PPT hardness of the discrete logarithm relation problem.*

Proof. Since the MACT protocol is an instantiation of the reciprocal form arithmetic circuit protocol, it has completeness and perfect SHVZK and CWEE. Therefore, it is sufficient to show that this circuit is satisfied if and only if the protocol inputs v and t satisfy the relation. By Theorem 4, we know that all the transaction output commitments commit to values in $[0, B)$ if they satisfy the circuit, and we know by assumption that all inputs lie in this range. Since $kB < p$, the magnitude of the total multiplicity of any type of asset cannot exceed p. The circuit invokes the reciprocal argument on the collection A formed as $\{(v, t) : (v, t) \in I\} \cup \{(-v, t) : (v, t) \in O\}$. By the soundness of the reciprocal form circuits, A vanishes, so total multiplicity of each token type must be zero in $\mathbb{F}$. Therefore, the total multiplicity of each type of asset must be 0 as an integer.

7   Implementation and Benchmarks

To demonstrate the real-world performance of BP++, we provide a reference implementation in C [19] as well as benchmarks. Our implementation builds on top of the libsecp256k1-zkp library [44] and thus uses secp256k1, the elliptic curve used in Bitcoin and many other cryptocurrencies. All operations on secret data performed by the prover implementation are constant-time. The experiments were performed on an Intel i7-10510U system at 1.80 GHz using a single thread. The implementation uses a single multi-exponentiation algorithm and scalar

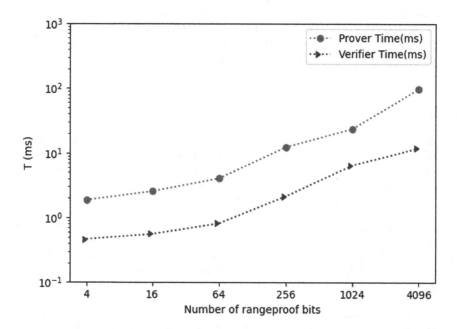

Fig. 1. Proving and verification time for BP++ range proofs. X-axis shows the total number of bits in the range proof. For $x > 64$ bits, we consider an aggregation of 64-bit range proofs. Y-axis shows the time in milliseconds.

Table 2. Proving and verification time compared to prior work.

	BP++	BP+ ([14])	BP ([17])	BP ([42])
Curve	secp256k1	Ristretto255	Ristretto255	secp256k1
Range	Prover time (ms)			
1 × 64	4.041	11.851	12.136	19.241
32 × 64	52.108	307.26	384.20	499.060
Range	Verifier time (ms)			
1 × 64	0.840	1.815	1.907	2.223
32 × 64	6.424	28.920	29.490	33.548

precomputation optimizations. In summary, verifying a 64-bit range proof took about 0.9 ms and proving about 4 ms. Figure 1 shows the proving and verification time as a function of the total number of range proof bits.

In order to compare the performance of BP++ with existing implementations of BP and BP+, we ran a BP implementation on secp256k1 [42], a BP implementation on Ristretto255 [17] and a BP+ implementation on Ristretto255 [14]. The results are summarized in Table 2. Despite secp256k1 having slower group operations than Ristretto255, for a 64-bit range proof, the BP++ prover is about 3 times and the verifier about 2.2 times faster than the BP+ implementation. The performance improvement in BP++ is amplified when aggregating multiple range proofs, e.g., when aggregating 32 64-bit range proofs, the BP++ prover and verifier are about 5–6 times faster than BP+. Moreover, based on SwiftRange's [52] comparison to BP, we anticipate BP++ to outperform Swift-Range significantly, with roughly 3 times faster proving speed and 1.3 times faster verification speed.[3]

References

1. Attema, T., Cramer, R.: Compressed Σ-protocol theory and practical application to plug & play secure algorithmics. In: Micciancio, D., Ristenpart, T. (eds.) CRYPTO 2020, Part III. LNCS, vol. 12172, pp. 513–543. Springer, Cham (2020). https://doi.org/10.1007/978-3-030-56877-1_18
2. Attema, T., Fehr, S., Klooß, M.: Fiat-Shamir transformation of multi-round interactive proofs. In: Kiltz, E., Vaikuntanathan, V. (eds.) TCC 2022, Part I. LNCS, vol. 13747, pp. 113–142. Springer, Cham (2022). https://doi.org/10.1007/978-3-031-22318-1_5
3. Bayer, S., Groth, J.: Efficient zero-knowledge argument for correctness of a shuffle. In: Pointcheval, D., Johansson, T. (eds.) EUROCRYPT 2012. LNCS, vol. 7237, pp. 263–280. Springer, Heidelberg (2012). https://doi.org/10.1007/978-3-642-29011-4_17
4. Bellare, M., Rogaway, P.: Random oracles are practical: a paradigm for designing efficient protocols. In: ACM CCS 93 (1993). https://doi.org/10.1145/168588.168596
5. Bootle, J., Cerulli, A., Chaidos, P., Groth, J., Petit, C.: Efficient zero-knowledge arguments for arithmetic circuits in the discrete log setting. In: Fischlin, M., Coron, J.-S. (eds.) EUROCRYPT 2016. LNCS, vol. 9666, pp. 327–357. Springer, Heidelberg (2016). https://doi.org/10.1007/978-3-662-49896-5_12
6. Bowe, S., Grigg, J., Hopwood, D.: Halo: recursive proof composition without a trusted setup. Cryptology ePrint Archive, Report 2019/1021 (2019). https://eprint.iacr.org/2019/1021
7. Bowe, S., Hornby, T., Wilcox, N.: Zcash protocol specification (2023). Version 2023.4.0 https://github.com/zcash/zips/blob/main/protocol/protocol.pdf
8. Bünz, B., Bootle, J., Boneh, D., Poelstra, A., Wuille, P., Maxwell, G.: Bulletproofs: short proofs for confidential transactions and more. In: 2018 IEEE Symposium on Security and Privacy (2018). https://doi.org/10.1109/SP.2018.00020

---

[3] A direct comparison has only limited meaning due to the use of different programming languages, but our BP++ C implementation is about 20x times faster than the SwiftRange Java implementation for 64-bit range proof proving and verification.

9. Bünz, B., Chiesa, A., Mishra, P., Spooner, N.: Recursive proof composition from accumulation schemes. In: Pass, R., Pietrzak, K. (eds.) TCC 2020, Part II. LNCS, vol. 12551, pp. 1–18. Springer, Cham (2020). https://doi.org/10.1007/978-3-030-64378-2_1

10. Bünz, B., Fisch, B., Szepieniec, A.: Transparent SNARKs from DARK compilers. In: Canteaut, A., Ishai, Y. (eds.) EUROCRYPT 2020, Part I. LNCS, vol. 12105, pp. 677–706. Springer, Cham (2020). https://doi.org/10.1007/978-3-030-45721-1_24

11. Camenisch, J., Chaabouni, R., shelat, A.: Efficient protocols for set membership and range proofs. In: Pieprzyk, J. (ed.) ASIACRYPT 2008. LNCS, vol. 5350, pp. 234–252. Springer, Heidelberg (2008). https://doi.org/10.1007/978-3-540-89255-7_15

12. Chaabouni, R., Lipmaa, H., Shelat, A.: Additive combinatorics and discrete logarithm based range protocols. In: Steinfeld, R., Hawkes, P. (eds.) ACISP 2010. LNCS, vol. 6168, pp. 336–351. Springer, Heidelberg (2010). https://doi.org/10.1007/978-3-642-14081-5_21

13. Chen, B., Bünz, B., Boneh, D., Zhang, Z.: HyperPlonk: plonk with linear-time prover and high-degree custom gates. In: Hazay, C., Stam, M. (eds.) EUROCRYPT 2023, Part II. LNCS, vol. 14005, pp. 499–530. Springer, Cham (2023). https://doi.org/10.1007/978-3-031-30617-4_17

14. Chung, H., Han, K., Ju, C., Kim, M., Seo, J.H.: Bulletproofs+ implementation. https://github.com/KyoohyungHan/BulletProofsPlus/commit/2c9dd40

15. Chung, H., Han, K., Ju, C., Kim, M., Seo, J.H.: Bulletproofs+: shorter proofs for a privacy-enhanced distributed ledger. IEEE Access **10** (2022)

16. Couteau, G., Klooß, M., Lin, H., Reichle, M.: Efficient range proofs with transparent setup from bounded integer commitments. In: Canteaut, A., Standaert, F.-X. (eds.) EUROCRYPT 2021, Part III. LNCS, vol. 12698, pp. 247–277. Springer, Cham (2021). https://doi.org/10.1007/978-3-030-77883-5_9

17. Dalek Cryptography Bulletproofs. https://github.com/dalek-cryptography/bulletproofs/commit/be67b6d5f5ad1c1f54d5511b52e6d645a1313d07

18. Eagen, L., Fiore, D., Gabizon, A.: CQ: cached quotients for fast lookups. Cryptology ePrint Archive, Report 2022/1763 (2022). https://eprint.iacr.org/2022/1763

19. Eagen, L., Kanjalkar, S., Ruffing, T., Nick, J.: Bulletproofs++ C implementation used for benchmarks. https://github.com/sanket1729/secp256k1-zkp/commit/785f9d728086dd5b9c697ca4d452c517b8243a85

20. Eagen, L., Kanjalkar, S., Ruffing, T., Nick, J.: Bulletproofs++: next generation confidential transactions via reciprocal set membership arguments. Cryptology ePrint Archive, Paper 2022/510 (2022). https://eprint.iacr.org/2022/510

21. Gabizon, A., Williamson, Z.J.: plookup: A simplified polynomial protocol for lookup tables. Cryptology ePrint Archive, Report 2020/315 (2020). https://eprint.iacr.org/2020/315

22. Gabizon, A., Williamson, Z.J., Ciobotaru, O.: PLONK: permutations over lagrange-bases for oecumenical noninteractive arguments of knowledge. Cryptology ePrint Archive, Report 2019/953 (2019). https://eprint.iacr.org/2019/953

23. Ganesh, C., Orlandi, C., Pancholi, M., Takahashi, A., Tschudi, D.: Fiat-Shamir bulletproofs are non-malleable (in the random oracle model). Cryptology ePrint Archive, Report 2023/147 (2023). https://eprint.iacr.org/2023/147

24. Ghesmati, S., Fdhila, W., Weippl, E.R.: SoK: how private is bitcoin? Classification and evaluation of bitcoin privacy techniques. In: ARES 2022 (2022)

25. Ghoshal, A., Tessaro, S.: Tight state-restoration soundness in the algebraic group model. In: Malkin, T., Peikert, C. (eds.) CRYPTO 2021, Part III. LNCS, vol. 12827, pp. 64–93. Springer, Cham (2021). https://doi.org/10.1007/978-3-030-84252-9_3

26. Gibson, A.: An Investigation into Confidential Transactions (2016). https://github.com/AdamISZ/ConfidentialTransactionsDoc/raw/master/essayonCT.pdf
27. Grin. https://www.grin-tech.org/
28. Groth, J.: Non-interactive zero-knowledge arguments for voting. In: Ioannidis, J., Keromytis, A., Yung, M. (eds.) ACNS 2005. LNCS, vol. 3531, pp. 467–482. Springer, Heidelberg (2005). https://doi.org/10.1007/11496137_32
29. Groth, J.: On the size of pairing-based non-interactive arguments. In: Fischlin, M., Coron, J.-S. (eds.) EUROCRYPT 2016. LNCS, vol. 9666, pp. 305–326. Springer, Heidelberg (2016). https://doi.org/10.1007/978-3-662-49896-5_11
30. Groth, J., Ishai, Y.: Sub-linear zero-knowledge argument for correctness of a shuffle. In: Smart, N. (ed.) EUROCRYPT 2008. LNCS, vol. 4965, pp. 379–396. Springer, Heidelberg (2008). https://doi.org/10.1007/978-3-540-78967-3_22
31. Haböck, U.: Multivariate lookups based on logarithmic derivatives. Cryptology ePrint Archive, Report 2022/1530 (2022). https://eprint.iacr.org/2022/1530
32. Jaeger, J., Tessaro, S.: Expected-time cryptography: generic techniques and applications to concrete soundness. In: Pass, R., Pietrzak, K. (eds.) TCC 2020, Part III. LNCS, vol. 12552, pp. 414–443. Springer, Cham (2020). https://doi.org/10.1007/978-3-030-64381-2_15
33. Lee, J.: Dory: efficient, transparent arguments for generalised inner products and polynomial commitments. In: Nissim, K., Waters, B. (eds.) TCC 2021, Part II. LNCS, vol. 13043, pp. 1–34. Springer, Cham (2021). https://doi.org/10.1007/978-3-030-90453-1_1
34. Lindell, Y.: Parallel coin-tossing and constant-round secure two-party computation. J. Cryptol. 16(3) (2003). https://doi.org/10.1007/s00145-002-0143-7
35. Lipmaa, H.: On diophantine complexity and statistical zero-knowledge arguments. In: Laih, C.-S. (ed.) ASIACRYPT 2003. LNCS, vol. 2894, pp. 398–415. Springer, Heidelberg (2003). https://doi.org/10.1007/978-3-540-40061-5_26
36. Maxwell, G.: CoinJoin: Bitcoin privacy for the real world (2013). BitcoinTalk post, https://bitcointalk.org/index.php?topic=279249.0
37. Maxwell, G.: Confidential Transactions (2015). https://web.archive.org/web/20190502140939/https://people.xiph.org/~greg/confidential_values.txt
38. Meiklejohn, S., et al.: A fistful of bitcoins: characterizing payments among men with no names. In: Internet Measurement Conference (IMC). https://doi.org/10.1145/2504730.2504747
39. Monero. https://monero.org/
40. Nakamoto, S.: Bitcoin: a peer-to-peer electronic cash system (2008). https://bitcoin.org/bitcoin.pdf
41. Nick, J., Poelstra, A., Sanders, G.: Liquid: a bitcoin sidechain. Technical report (2020). https://blockstream.com/assets/downloads/pdf/liquid-whitepaper.pdf
42. Poelstra, A.: Bulletproofs implementation in libsecp256k1-zkp. https://github.com/BlockstreamResearch/secp256k1-zkp/pull/23/commits/6fb7e05
43. Poelstra, A., Back, A., Friedenbach, M., Maxwell, G., Wuille, P.: Confidential assets. In: Zohar, A., et al. (eds.) FC 2018. LNCS, vol. 10958, pp. 43–63. Springer, Heidelberg (2019). https://doi.org/10.1007/978-3-662-58820-8_4
44. Poelstra, A. et al.: libsecp256-zkp. See https://github.com/ElementsProject/secp256k1-zkp
45. Posen, J., Kattis, A.A.: Caulk+: table-independent lookup arguments. Cryptology ePrint Archive, Report 2022/957 (2022). https://eprint.iacr.org/2022/957
46. Ruffing, T., Moreno-Sanchez, P.: ValueShuffle: mixing confidential transactions for comprehensive transaction privacy in bitcoin. In: Brenner, M., et al. (eds.) FC

2017. LNCS, vol. 10323, pp. 133–154. Springer, Cham (2017). https://doi.org/10.1007/978-3-319-70278-0_8

47. sethforprivacy: Monero will undergo a network upgrade on 13th August, 2022 (2022). https://web.getmonero.org/2022/04/20/network-upgrade-july-2022.html

48. Spagnuolo, M., Maggi, F., Zanero, S.: BitIodine: extracting intelligence from the bitcoin network. In: Christin, N., Safavi-Naini, R. (eds.) FC 2014. LNCS, vol. 8437, pp. 457–468. Springer, Heidelberg (2014). https://doi.org/10.1007/978-3-662-45472-5_29

49. The Halo 2 Developers: Halo2 (2020). https://zcash.github.io/halo2/

50. Valence, H. de, Yun, C., Andreev, O.: Cloak (2019). https://github.com/stellar/slingshot/blob/main/spacesuit/spec.md

51. Wang, N., Chau, S.C.-K.: Flashproofs: efficient zero-knowledge arguments of range and polynomial evaluation with transparent setup. In: Agrawal, S., Lin, D. (eds.) ASIACRYPT 2022, Part II. LNCS, vol. 13792, pp. 219–248. Springer, Cham (2022). https://doi.org/10.1007/978-3-031-22966-4_8

52. Wang, N., Chau, S.C.-K., Liu, D.: SwiftRange: a short and efficient zero-knowledge range argument for confidential transactions and more. Cryptology ePrint Archive, Paper 2023/1185 (2023). https://eprint.iacr.org/2023/1185

53. Wikström, D.: Special soundness in the random oracle model. Cryptology ePrint Archive, Report 2021/1265 (2021). https://eprint.iacr.org/2021/1265

54. Zapico, A., Buterin, V., Khovratovich, D., Maller, M., Nitulescu, A., Simkin, M.: Caulk: lookup arguments in sublinear time. In: ACM CCS 2022 (2022). https://doi.org/10.1145/3548606.3560646

Perfect Asynchronous MPC with Linear Communication Overhead

Ittai Abraham[1], Gilad Asharov[2], Shravani Patil[3], and Arpita Patra[3(✉)]

[1] Intel Labs, Hillsboro, USA
ittai.abraham@intel.com
[2] Department of Computer Science, Bar-Ilan University, Ramat Gan, Israel
Gilad.Asharov@biu.ac.il
[3] Indian Institute of Science, Bangalore, Bengaluru, India
{shravanip,arpita}@iisc.ac.in

Abstract. We study secure multiparty computation in the asynchronous setting with perfect security and optimal resilience (less than one-fourth of the participants are malicious). It has been shown that every function can be computed in this model [Ben-OR, Canetti, and Goldreich, STOC'1993]. Despite 30 years of research, all protocols in the asynchronous setting require $\Omega(n^2 C)$ communication complexity for computing a circuit with C multiplication gates. In contrast, for nearly 15 years, in the synchronous setting, it has been known how to achieve $\mathcal{O}(nC)$ communication complexity (Beerliova and Hirt; TCC 2008). The techniques for achieving this result in the synchronous setting are not known to be sufficient for obtaining an analogous result in the asynchronous setting.

We close this gap between synchronous and asynchronous secure computation and show the first asynchronous protocol with $\mathcal{O}(nC)$ communication complexity for a circuit with C multiplication gates. Linear overhead forms a natural barrier for general secret-sharing-based MPC protocols. Our main technical contribution is an asynchronous weak binding secret sharing that achieves rate-1 communication (i.e., $\mathcal{O}(1)$-overhead per secret). To achieve this goal, we develop new techniques for the asynchronous setting, including the use of *trivariate polynomials* (as opposed to bivariate polynomials).

Keywords: Perfect Secure Computation · Asynchronous networks · Secret sharing

1   Introduction

Secure multiparty computation (MPC) protocols can be divided into two broad categories: *synchronous* and *asynchronous*, depending on their resilience to network conditions. In the *synchronous* model of MPC, the assumption is that all messages sent between honest parties arrive after some known bounded delay. This delay bound needs to be fixed in advance and must hold for the lifetime of

M. Joye and G. Leander (Eds.): EUROCRYPT 2024, LNCS 14655, pp. 280–309, 2024.
https://doi.org/10.1007/978-3-031-58740-5_10

the system. Fixing a large delay bound may cause the protocol to be inefficient and slow. More worrisome, using a delay that is smaller than the actual delay the adversary can impose may lead to non-termination. In many real world settings it is very hard to guess in advance a bound on the maximum delay the adversary can impose.

The second category of protocols is the *asynchronous* model, where each message sent between honest parties arrives after some finite delay. This model allows protocols to dynamically adjust to any adversarial network conditions, and obtain termination (with probability 1) even under very powerful adversaries that can adaptively manipulate network delays.

In this paper we consider the most demanding setting: *perfect security with optimal resilience in the asynchronous model.* From the lower bound of [3,9,10], perfect security implies that the number of corruptions in this setting is at most $t < n/4$, so optimal resilience is when $n = 4t + 1$ (this is in contrast to $n = 3t + 1$ in the synchronous setting). The seminal work of [9,13] obtains perfect security with optimal resilience in the asynchronous model.

Communication Complexity of Asynchronous MPC

The communication efficiency of MPC protocols is measured by the (amortized) cost of their communication complexity per multiplication gate. In the perfectly secure, optimally-resilient synchronous model, $\mathcal{O}(n \log n)$ communication complexity per multiplication gate was obtained nearly 15 years ago by the work of [7] (recently [1] improves the round complexity from $\mathcal{O}(D + n)$ to expected $\mathcal{O}(D)$ for circuits of depth D). Linear communication complexity per multiplication gate seems to be a natural barrier. While there is no lower bound, getting $o(n)$ per multiplication gate seems to require fundamentally different techniques and comes at the cost of trading off optimal threshold (e.g., see [20]).

Progress in the (perfectly secure, optimally resilient) asynchronous model over the last 30 years has been slower. The work of [9] obtained $\tilde{\mathcal{O}}(n^6)$ per gate. [25,26] improve to $\tilde{\mathcal{O}}(n^5)$ per gate. [6] improves to $\tilde{\mathcal{O}}(n^3)$ per gate. The best current bounds are by [23,24] that obtained $\tilde{\mathcal{O}}(n^2)$ communication complexity per multiplication gate. A natural question remained open for 30 years:

Is there a perfectly secure, optimally-resilient asynchronous MPC with
$\tilde{\mathcal{O}}(n)$ *communication complexity per multiplication gate?*
Or is there an inherent lower bound due to asynchrony?

Our Main Result

Our main result is a perfectly secure, optimally-resilient asynchronous MPC protocol that achieves $\widetilde{\mathcal{O}}(n)$ communication per multiplication gate.

Theorem 1.1 (Main Result). *For a circuit with C multiplication gates and depth D there exists a perfectly-secure, optimally-resilient asynchronous MPC protocol with $\mathcal{O}((Cn + Dn^2 + n^5) \log n)$ communication complexity and $\mathcal{O}(D)$ expected run-time.*

Previously, the best-known result required $\mathcal{O}((Cn^2 + Dn^2 + n^5)\log n)$ communication complexity [23].

Main Technical Result

Our main technical result is a new Asynchronous Weak-Binding Secret Sharing that costs just $\mathcal{O}(\log n)$ bits of communication complexity per secret of size $\log n$ bits. It is perfectly secure, resilient to $t < n/4$, and has constant round complexity and polynomial computation complexity. For our MPC purposes, we do not need the reconstruction of those shares; we just need the dealer to commit to a well-defined polynomial. We call this property as "weak-binding".

Theorem 1.2 (Asynchronous Weak-binding Secret Sharing (informal)). *There exists a perfectly secure, optimally resilient protocol for asynchronous weak-binding secret sharing that can share $\mathcal{O}(n^4)$ secrets in constant time, with communication complexity of $\mathcal{O}(\log n)$ bits per secret of size $\log n$ bits.*

Many forms of verifiable secret sharing, both in the synchronous and asynchronous settings, rely on bivariate polynomial sharing. Our protocol is based on *trivariate polynomial* sharing. Our use of trivariate polynomial sharing approach follows the recent work of Appelbaum and Kachlon [4]. Nevertheless, we show how to reconstruct the trivariate polynomial for future reference and for independent interest. This variant is "weak" in the sense that reconstruction might fail (or not terminate). In that case, however, the honest dealer can shun a set of $t/2 + 1$ corrupted parties. Nonetheless, we remark again that we do not use reconstruction, and in particular, our final MPC construction does not shun parties and does not use player elimination.

The first asynchronous verifiable secret sharing protocol [8] achieves $\mathcal{O}(n^4)$ (amortized) overhead per secret. In comparison, our trivariate-based asynchronous weak-binding secret sharing achieves $\mathcal{O}(1)$ (amortized) overhead per secret. Nevertheless, we remark again that our primitive is weaker as it does not guarantee reconstruction. Despite this fact, we show that this weak primitive suffices for the crux of our MPC, which is a distributed ZK proof of multiplication triplets. The aim of the ZK proof is to prove that some (secret) polynomial $p(x)$ possesses a certain degree. To accomplish this, the prover incorporates the coefficients of $p(x)$ as secrets in the trivariate polynomial and distributes shares on this trivariate polynomial. Since the trivariate polynomial can contain a predetermined number of secrets, the mere success of the sharing process and the existence of a well-defined trivariate polynomial are sufficient evidence to confirm that $p(x)$ indeed has the desired degree. Here, there is no need for reconstruction. Reconstruction would also reveal the coefficients of the polynomial $p(x)$, which have to remain secret.

1.1   Related Work

In the setting of perfect security with a synchronous network, the work of [7,22] achieved $\tilde{\mathcal{O}}(n)$ communication per multiplication gate. A lower bound of $\tilde{\mathcal{O}}(n)$

was later established in [21] for a resilience of $t < n/3$ which is known to be necessary in this setting. The recent work of [1] improves the round complexity of [7,22] from $\mathcal{O}(D + n)$ to $\mathcal{O}(D)$ in expectation while maintaining linear communication complexity in the number of parties.

The results in the perfect asynchronous setting have been mentioned earlier and we avoid repetition here. We simply summarize that there is no linear overhead protocol in this setting thus far. Nonetheless, linear-overhead protocols have been achieved earlier in two weaker setting– (a) statistical security with non-optimal resilience of $t < n/4$ over asynchronous networks[1] [19] (b) perfect security with $t < n/4$ over hybrid network where the network permits a single synchronous round before turning to fully asynchronous mode [18,19].

As mentioned, our trivariate secret sharing protocol is inspired by the work of Applebaum and Kachlon [4]. This work uses trivariate polynomial for constructing error-correcting code with quasipolynomial-time conflict-decoder.

2 Technical Overview

In this section, we provide a technical overview of our work. We give some background on basic asynchronous verifiable secret sharing (basically covering previous work) in Sect. 2.1, and proceed to our asynchronous weak-binding secret sharing in Sect. 2.2. We overview our MPC protocol in Sect. 2.3. Lastly, we conclude our triple secret sharing protocol in Sect. 2.4 which acts as the building block for MPC and builds upon our asynchronous weak-binding secret sharing.

The Model. Before we proceed, let us first introduce the model. We assume asynchronous communication, which means the adversary can arbitrarily delay messages sent between honest parties. However, such messages are eventually received. It is important to note that the adversary does not see the content of the messages (as we assume ideal channels between the honest parties), but it can see the type of messages that are being sent (e.g., identifying whether it's the first, second, or third message of the protocol). Since the adversary controls the corrupted parties, messages that are supposed to be sent by the corrupted parties to the honest parties might never be sent. Honest parties cannot distinguish whether a message is merely delayed or has not been sent altogether. Consequently, honest parties must continue waiting, with the potential consequence of certain foundational processes never reaching completion. However, it's important to highlight that the complete MPC protocol guarantees termination. This means that it possesses mechanisms to recognize non-terminating sub-protocols and take appropriate measures to bring them to a halt.

Besides the point-to-point channels, we assume for now the existence of a broadcast channel with the guarantee that (1) If the sender is honest and broadcasts M then eventually all honest parties will receive M; (2) If some honest party received a message M (in an instance of a corrupted sender), then

---

[1] The optimal resilience for statistical asynchronous MPC is $t < n/3$ [10].

eventually all honest parties will receive M. This can be implemented by asynchronous broadcast or A-cast primitive [11]. The cost is $\mathcal{O}(n^2|M|)$ for broadcasting the message M.

2.1 Basic Asynchronous Verifiable Secret Sharing

Our starting point is a variant of the verifiable secret sharing due to Ben-Or, Canetti, and Goldreich [9]. In asynchronous verifiable secret sharing (AVSS), the dealer holds some secret s, and its goal is to distribute the shares to the parties. The parties then verify that the shares define a unique secret. At a later point, the parties might reconstruct the secret s. The properties that the AVSS offers are:

- **Validity:** If the dealer is honest, then the protocol must terminate. At the end of the reconstruction phase, all honest parties output s, the input of the dealer in the sharing phase;
- **Secrecy:** The view of the adversary in the sharing phase in the case of an honest dealer is independent of s;
- **Binding:** The view of the honest parties at the end of the sharing phase (if terminated) uniquely defines some secret s'.

For simplicity, we assume for now that the dealer can efficiently solve the problem of finding the maximal clique in a graph. At a high level, the secret-sharing protocol proceeds as follows:

1. The dealer: Choose a random bivariate polynomial $S(\mathbf{x}, \mathbf{y})$ of degree-t in both variables such that $S(0,0) = s$. Send over the private channels to each party P_i its shares $(S(\mathbf{x}, i), S(i, \mathbf{y}))$.
2. Each party P_i: Upon receiving the shares $(f_i(\mathbf{x}), g_i(\mathbf{y}))$ from the dealer, send to P_j the sub-shares $(f_i(j), g_i(j))$.
3. Each party P_i: Upon receiving $(u_{j,i}, v_{j,i})$ from party P_j, verify that $u_{j,i} = g_i(j)$ $(= f_j(i))$ and $v_{j,i} = f_i(j)$ $(= g_j(i))$. If so, then P_i broadcasts $\mathsf{Good}(i,j)$.
4. The dealer: Initialize an undirected graph G over the vertices $V = [n]$. Upon seeing $\mathsf{Good}(i,j)$ broadcasted by P_i and $\mathsf{Good}(j,i)$ broadcasted by P_j, add the edge (i,j) to the graph. If a clique $K \subseteq [n]$ of cardinality at least $3t + 1$ is found in G, then broadcast (Clique, K).
5. Each party P_i: Initialize a similar graph as the dealer in the previous step. Upon seeing a broadcasted message (Clique, K) from the dealer, verify that K is a $3t + 1$ clique in the graph. If not, continue to listen to Good messages broadcast and update the graph. Once K is verified:
   (a) If $i \in K$, then halt and output $(f_i(x), g_i(y))$.
   (b) If $i \notin K$, then wait to receive all sub-shares from parties in K (received from Step 3.), and reconstruct the polynomials $f_i(x)$, $g_i(y)$ using Reed-Solomon decoding.

We do not specify the reconstruction phase, as it is immediate and less relevant to our discussion. Moreover, note that the protocol might never terminate in a case of a corrupted dealer. E.g., the parties might wait forever for the dealer to broadcast the message (Clique, K). A party cannot decide whether to abort or whether this message will eventually arrive.

We first claim that if one honest party terminates, all honest parties eventually terminate. An honest party terminates only after the dealer has broadcasted a clique K, and it validated that the clique exists in its graph. Since those are all broadcasted messages if one honest party saw this, all honest parties would eventually see the same property.

If a clique of $3t+1$ parties is found, the clique must contain at least $2t+1$ honest parties. All the messages of those honest parties are broadcasted; therefore, we know that their shares agree. Their shares define a unique bivariate polynomial $S(\mathbf{x}, \mathbf{y})$ of degree-t in both variables. It is also guaranteed that all honest parties eventually output shares on the same bivariate polynomial. Specifically, when running the Reed-Solomon decoding on messages received from parties in K, there are $2t+1$ shares on the polynomial $S(\mathbf{x}, \mathbf{y})$ and at most t errors. Reed Solomon decoding results in shares on the bivariate polynomial. Finally, validity holds from the fact that when the dealer is honest, all honest parties agree with each other, and therefore a $3t+1$-clique must appear in the graph.

Making it Polynomial Time – The STAR Algorithm. The problem with the above protocol is that the dealer has to solve clique, which is an NP-hard problem. A beautiful idea in the work of Ben-Or, Canetti, and Goldreich [9] (credit within is given to Canetti's thesis [14]) shows that an *approximation* of clique suffices to bind a unique bivariate polynomial. Specifically, the dealer searches for a (C, D)-star, which is defined as follows:

> **(C, D)-Star:** sets C, D $\subseteq [n]$ are Star in G if (1): C $\subseteq$ D; (2) $|C| \geq 2t+1$ and $|D| \geq n-t$; (3) For every $c \in$ C and $d \in$ D it holds that $(c,d) \in G$.

Note that C is a clique, whereas nodes in D agree with all nodes in C, but not necessarily with each other. The main idea is that if there exists a clique K of size $n-t \geq 3t+1$ in G, it might be hard to find it, but it is easy to find smaller cliques of size $n - 2t \geq 2t+1$. For example, to find such a clique, look at the complement graph $\overline{G}$. The clique K is now an independent set; Find a maximal matching in the graph $\overline{G}$; let M be that maximal matching. The set $[n] \setminus M$ is an independent set in $\overline{G}$ and, therefore, a clique in G. Moreover, when the dealer is honest, since all the edges are between honest parties and corrupted parties, or between corrupted parties, then M is of size at most $2t$. Therefore, $[n] \setminus M$ is of size $n - 2t$ and is a clique in the graph G. Canetti [14] shows a procedure that, if a $3t + 1$ clique exists, then it efficiently finds a (C, D)-STAR in a graph – i.e., a smaller clique (C) of size $2t+1$, together with a larger set D where each $d \in$ D is connected to all of C.

The verifiable secret sharing is slightly more involved when the dealer finds a (C, D)-star and not a $3t + 1$-clique. We do not get into the exact details. Yet, the main ideas why the STAR structure suffices are as follows:

– Validity: When the dealer is honest, then the dealer must eventually find a STAR. That is, when the dealer is honest, then eventually, we will have a clique K of size $3t+1$ in the graph. In that case, the STAR algorithm always finds a (C,D)-star.

- Binding: If a (C,D)-star was found (either when the dealer is honest or corrupted), then a unique bivariate polynomial is defined from the shares of the honest parties in C. Since the size of C is at least $2t+1$, it contains at least $t+1$ honest parties. The shares of those honest parties uniquely define a bivariate polynomial. Moreover, the honest parties in D agree with all the honest parties in C; therefore, their shares lie on the same bivariate polynomial. At this point, we have at least $2t+1$ honest parties that hold correct shares, and therefore all honest parties can eventually reconstruct correct shares.

Communication Complexity. Before we proceed, let us first elaborate on the communication complexity of the protocol above. It is easy to see that the parties exchange a total of $\mathcal{O}(n^2 \log n)$ bits over the point-to-point channels and additional $\mathcal{O}(n^2 \log n)$ bits over the broadcast channel. This is translated to $\mathcal{O}(n^4 \log n)$ total communication complexity over point-to-point channels and no broadcast (using the broadcast protocol of [11]). That is, we have an overhead of $\mathcal{O}(n^4 \log n)$ for sharing just a single value!

2.2   Our Asynchronous Weak-Binding Secret Sharing

Our Goal: $\mathcal{O}(1)$ Overhead per Secret. To achieve secure computation with linear communication complexity, our ultimate goal is to reach $\mathcal{O}(1)$ overhead per secret. This necessitates a substantial enhancement of the basic scheme by a factor of $\mathcal{O}(n^4)$. Borrowing ideas from the synchronous MPC [1], this goal is achieved via two routes: (1) batching; and (2) packing. However, packing in the asynchronous case gets an intriguing turn and requires borrowing new ideas.

Reducing the Communication Complexity by Batching. It is immediate to reduce the communication complexity using a batching technique: The dealer will invoke m instances of AVSS in parallel. At the same time, the broadcasted information will be shared for all m instances. That is, a party P_i will broadcast $\mathsf{Good}(i,j)$ only after it receives from P_j the sub-shares in all m instances and verifies that they agree with the share it received from the dealer in each one of the m instances. This reduces the total cost to $\mathcal{O}(m \cdot n^2 \log n)$ over point-to-point plus $\mathcal{O}(n^2 \log n)$ broadcast (notice that the broadcast cost is independent of m). Setting $m = n^2$, we obtain a protocol that runs in total communication complexity of $\mathcal{O}(n^4 \log n)$ bits for sharing n^2 secrets (each is of size $\log n$ bits). At this point, we have an overhead of $\mathcal{O}(n^2)$ per secret.

Reducing the Communication Complexity by Packing. Packing in the asynchronous case turns out to be radically different than in the synchronous case. The main reason for the $\mathcal{O}(n^2)$ overhead in the secret sharing is because a single secret is hidden in a structure of size $\mathcal{O}(n^2)$, i.e., a bivariate polynomial. To achieve $\mathcal{O}(1)$ overhead, we have to pack $\mathcal{O}(n^2)$ secrets in a single bivariate polynomial or use a different structure.

In the basic AVSS protocol, a single secret is shared using a (t,t)-bivariate polynomial.[2] The adversary, which controls at most t parties, receives $f_i(\mathbf{x}) = S(\mathbf{x}, i)$ and $g_i(\mathbf{y}) = S(i, \mathbf{y})$ for every $i \in I$, when I is the set of corrupted parties, and assume for simplicity that $|I| = t$ (and not smaller). The f-shares give the adversary a total of $t(t+1)$ points on the polynomial. Since $f_i(k) = g_k(i)$ for every $i, k \in I$, the g-shares gives the adversary just additional $t(t+1) - t^2 = t$ "new" points on the polynomial (those are $g_i(0)$ for $i \in I$), and thus the adversary gets a total of $t^2 + 2t$. The polynomial $S(\mathbf{x}, \mathbf{y}) = \sum_{i=0}^{t} \sum_{j=0}^{t} a_{i,j} x^i y^j$ contains a total of $(t+1)^2$ points, and thus we have just a single degree of freedom, i.e., we can hide just a single secret.

The main idea of packing is to use a polynomial of a higher degree while maintaining the same cost for the sharing and verification:

Using $(t+t/2) \times t$–Bivariate Polynomial.[3] If we use a bivariate polynomial of degree, e.g., $(t+t/2, t)$, then there are in total $(t+t/2+1)(t+1)$ values on the polynomial. The important part of this particular choice of parameters is that the degree of the $\mathbf{y}$ is t, which still allows using Reed-Solomon decoding as part of the protocol. Similar calculation as in the (t,t) case leads to the adversary's shares revealing a total of $t(t+t/2+1)+t$ values. The bivariate polynomial, therefore, contains $t/2+1$ degrees of freedom, i.e., we can hide $\mathcal{O}(n)$ values in a single bivariate polynomial.

Packing $\mathcal{O}(n)$ values instead of $\mathcal{O}(1)$ reduced the overhead per secret from $\mathcal{O}(n^2)$ to $\mathcal{O}(n)$. The important message here is that the STAR algorithm still suffices. Specifically, a (C, D)-star defines a unique bivariate polynomial: Recall that C is a clique of $2t+1$ parties, and therefore it must contain at least $t+1$ honest parties with their shares agreeing with each other. Moreover, all the honest parties in C are consistent with all the parties in D where D contains at least $2t+1$ honest parties. The shares f shares of honest parties in C together with the g-shares of honest parties in D define a unique bivariate polynomial $S(\mathbf{x}, \mathbf{y})$ that satisfies $S(\mathbf{x}, c) = f_c(\mathbf{x})$ for every $c \in \mathsf{C}$ (recall that each f_c has degree $t + t/2$). Moreover $S(d, \mathbf{y}) = g_d(\mathbf{y})$ holds for every honest party $d \in \mathsf{D}$. Guaranteeing these parties will also hold correct f-shares requires some additional work, which was already shown in previous works (see [19]).

This protocol plays a pivotal role in our final construction, but for our ultimate goal, we still need to go one step further and push for $\mathcal{O}(1)$-word overhead per secret. Note, however, that this one step forward will not give us verifiable secret sharing, but only some weaker form of sharing.

Using $(t + t/2) \times (t + t/2)$–Bivariate Polynomial. If we use a bivariate polynomial of degree $(t + t/2, t + t/2)$, there are $(t + t/2 + 1)^2$ total values on the polynomial. Similar calculations as above lead to $(t/2 + 1)^2$ values that we can pack in the polynomial, i.e., $\mathcal{O}(n^2)$ secrets.

---

[2] We use (q, ℓ)-bivariate polynomial to denote a bivariate polynomial which is of degree at most q in $\mathbf{x}$ and at most ℓ in $\mathbf{y}$.

[3] We use $t + t/2$ just as an example. The above works for any $t \times (t + d)$-bivariate polynomial for $d \leq t$ and $d \in O(n)$.

However, here the STAR technique does not give us a binding guarantee. A (C, D)-star provides a clique C of size $2t + 1$, which contains, in the worst case, $t + 1$ honest parties. Their f-shares, their g-shares, separately or combined, do not uniquely define a $(t + t/2) \times (t + t/2)$-bivariate polynomial. Since the parties in D do not necessarily agree with each other, we cannot use their shares to define the bivariate polynomial before we have a unique one that is defined by the parties in C.

It is easy to see that an alternative, stronger guarantee, would suffice for binding:

(C, D)-BigStar: sets $C, D \subseteq [n]$ are BigStar in G if: (1) $C \subseteq D$; (2) $|C| \geq 2t + t/2 + 1$ and $|D| \geq n - t$; (3) For every $c \in C$ and $d \in D$ it holds that $(c, d) \in G$.

Note that the only difference between BigStar and Star is that C is of size $2t + t/2 + 1$ instead of $2t + 1$ as in Star. Such a larger set C ensures $t + t/2 + 1$ honest parties that agree with each other, hence defining a unique bivariate polynomial. However, we are unaware of any polynomial-time algorithm that finds BigStar in a graph. At this point, we can potentially reach the $\mathcal{O}(1)$ overhead in communication complexity, but at the expense of having the dealer find a large clique in exponential time. This is clearly not ideal.

Exponential-Time Improvement Using Trivariate Polynomials. To solve the above problem, we add one more dimension, which will allow us, in particular, to pack $\mathcal{O}(n^3)$ secrets and find a BigStar efficiently, if it exists. Instead of using a bivariate polynomial $S(\mathbf{x}, \mathbf{y})$ of degree $t + t/2$ in both variables $\mathbf{x}, \mathbf{y}$, the dealer will use a *trivariate* polynomial $\mathbf{S}(\mathbf{x}, \mathbf{y}, \mathbf{z})$ of degree $t + t/2$ in all three variables $\mathbf{x}, \mathbf{y}, \mathbf{z}$. We then naturally extend the protocol to trivariate sharing. E.g., the share of each party P_i is now *three* bivariate polynomials:

$$\mathbf{S}(\mathbf{x}, \mathbf{y}, i), \quad \mathbf{S}(\mathbf{x}, i, \mathbf{z}), \quad \mathbf{S}(i, \mathbf{y}, \mathbf{z}) \ .$$

Two parties, P_i and P_j then exchange *six* univariate polynomials:

$$\mathbf{S}(\mathbf{x}, j, i), \quad \mathbf{S}(\mathbf{x}, i, j), \quad \mathbf{S}(i, \mathbf{y}, j) \ ,$$
$$\mathbf{S}(j, \mathbf{y}, i), \quad \mathbf{S}(j, i, \mathbf{z}), \quad \mathbf{S}(i, j, \mathbf{z}) \ .$$

and a party P_i broadcasts $\mathsf{Good}(i, j)$ if the shares it receives from P_j (i.e., the six univariate polynomials) agree with those it received from the dealer.

The dealer then constructs a graph G as in the basic AVSS scheme. However, as mentioned, we are now looking for a more robust condition on the graph since our polynomials are of degree $t + t/2$. Thus, we need a clique of size $2t + t/2 + 1$, which will imply having at least $t + t/2 + 1$ honest parties. BigStar now also suffices for binding, but it is unclear how to find it just as in the bivariate sharing case. However, at this point, some seemingly weaker property on the graph also suffices to achieve binding, which was insufficient in bivariate sharing. The property is (We note that an L of size $2t + t/2 + 1$ would, in fact, suffice for defining a unique trivariate polynomial. However, we are able to find a larger set of size $3t + 1$ in polynomial time.):

> Dense: *A set of vertices $L \subseteq [n]$ is called* Dense *if it is of cardinality at least $3t + 1$, and each node in L has at least degree $3t + t/2 + 1$.*

This is clearly a property that is easy to find in a graph G. The intuition is that the set L contains at least $2t + 1$ honest parties. Moreover, two honest parties P_k, P_ℓ that have degree $3t + t/2 + 1$ *must agree with each other, even though they did not necessarily hear the shares of one another* due to communication delays (we will see why this holds soon). The honest parties in Dense therefore define a clique of at least $2t + 1$ honest parties, and their shares define a unique trivariate polynomial.

Binding: For binding, it suffices to have one of the two following properties:

1. Dense: which essentially defines a clique of $2t + 1$ honest parties;
2. BigStar: where $|C| \geq 2t + t/2 + 1$, and $|D| \geq n - t$. The set C defines a clique of $t + t/2 + 1$ honest parties that agree with each other, which defines a unique trivariate polynomial. Moreover, the set D defines overall $2t + 1$ honest parties that have correct shares.

Therefore, whenever one of those properties occurs in the graph, we are satisfied and can terminate the protocol. We show a poly-time algorithm that finds those properties.

Validity. For validity, we have to guarantee that when the dealer is honest, it must find one of these two properties (Dense or BigStar) in the graph. In the honest dealer case, the graph will eventually contain a clique of size $3t + 1$. At this point, the following algorithm must find either Dense or BigStar:

1. The dealer looks for a Dense set L in the graph. If found, output (Dense, L).
2. If the graph does not contain a dense set L, then it implies that there is at least one honest party, say P_j, whose degree is less than $3t + t/2 + 1$. Moreover, all missing edges in the graph are between honest parties and corrupted parties, or between corrupted parties. We then consider the graph G while considering only the neighbors of P_j (including P_j). We will obtain a graph of size $n' = 3t + t/2 + 1$ vertices, where all removed vertices correspond to corrupted parties, and so we have $t' = t/2$ corrupted parties remaining. Moreover, this graph contains a clique of size $3t + 1$. The standard (C, D)-star returns a clique $|C| \geq n' - 2t' \geq 2t + t/2 + 1$, and a set $|D| \geq n' - t' \geq 3t + 1$, which is essentially a BigStar in G. The dealer does the above for every low-degree party P_j until it hits on a BigStar, and this procedure is efficient.

Therefore, once we have a clique of $3t + 1$ honest parties, the dealer is guaranteed to find either a Dense or a BigStar in polynomial time.

Why Do Bivariate Polynomials Not Suffice? A natural question is why we could not find the same property on the graph with bivariate polynomials, and we have to work with trivariates. This is an idea we borrow from [4], and is the crux of this part of the paper. The property we need here is *transitivity*.

Suppose P_k and P_j are both honest, and they agree with a common set E of at least $2t+1$ honest parties, but they did not hear the sub-shares from each other since the adversary delays their communication. Do their shares agree?

Note that in the setting of the Dense graph, P_k and P_j are two honest parties that have a high degree of $3t + t/2 + 1$. This means they have at least $3t + 1$ parties in their intersection, which implies that they agree with some common set E of at least $2t + 1$ honest parties. To see whether or not their shares agree, let's consider bivariate sharing versus trivariate sharing:

1. **Bivariate:** In bivariate sharing, the parties hold univariate polynomials as shares, and they exchange points. It is easy to see that the shares of P_k and P_j do not necessarily agree with each other, even if they agree with a common set E of cardinality $2t + 1$. We can set P_k to have $f_k(\mathbf{x}), g_k(\mathbf{y})$ and P_j to have $f_j(\mathbf{x}), g_j(\mathbf{y})$ such that $f_k(j) \neq g_j(k)$ and $f_j(k) \neq g_k(j)$. Yet, we can give a set E of cardinality $2t + 1$ arbitrary shares such that $f_j(e) = g_e(j)$ and $g_j(e) = f_e(j)$ for every $e \in E$, and likewise, $f_k(e) = g_e(k)$ and $g_k(e) = f_e(k)$ for every $e \in E$. This does not impose many constraints on the polynomials $f_e(\mathbf{x}), g_e(\mathbf{y})$ for every $e \in E$. Therefore, the existence of the property Dense does not necessarily imply a clique of honest parties of large cardinality that agree with each other.

2. **Trivariate:** In trivariate sharing, the parties hold bivariate polynomials as shares, and they exchange univariate polynomials. If P_j and P_k have a common set of neighbors E of cardinality $2t+1$, then *they necessarily hold shares that agree with each other*[4]. The key idea is that P_k exchanges with each party P_e for $e \in E$ univariate polynomials. Since the univariate polynomials agree, they also agree on the index j. The $2t + 1$ points of parties in E on the index j uniquely define the univariate polynomials that P_k expects to receive from P_j. Thus, even though P_k did not hear yet the message from P_j, and P_j is honest, it knows that the shares would agree, even if the dealer is corrupted. A similar argument holds for P_j. The formal argument appears in the full version.

To conclude, to share the trivariate polynomial, we have a total of $\mathcal{O}(n^3 \log n)$ bits over point-to-point channel together with $\mathcal{O}(n^2 \log n)$ bits over the broadcast channel. If we batch n instances together, we get a total of $\mathcal{O}(n^4 \log n)$ bits over point-to-point channels and no broadcast for sharing $\mathcal{O}(n^4)$ secrets, each of $\log n$ bits. I.e., we obtain an overhead of $\mathcal{O}(1)$.

Note, however, that the sharing is weak. Namely, we know that there is a well-defined trivariate polynomial, but we cannot necessarily reconstruct it robustly. In particular, even in the case of an honest dealer, reconstruction might fail. In that case, however, the dealer can shun at least $t/2 + 1$ corrupted parties. We show the reconstruction in Sect. 5.

---

[4] In fact, as shown in [4], having a common set of honest neighbors of size $t + t/2 + 1$ suffices for P_j and P_k to hold shares that are consistent with the same trivariate polynomial of degree $t + t/2$ in each variable.

However, as we will see, the reconstruction is not required for our MPC, and the sharing itself suffices. We gave it for completeness and as it might be useful as an independent primitive.

2.3   Our MPC Protocol

Our MPC protocol follows the following structure: an offline phase in which the parties generate Beaver triplets [5], and an online phase in which the parties compute the circuit while consuming those triples.

Beaver Triplets Generation. Our goal is to distribute (Shamir, univariate degree-t) shares of random secret values a, b, and c, such that $c = ab$. If the circuit contains C multiplication gates, we need C such triplets. Towards that end, we follow the same steps as in [19], and generate such triplets in three stages:

1. **Triplets with a dealer:** Each party generates shares of a_i, b_i, c_i such that $c_i = a_i \cdot b_i$. We generate all the triplets in parallel using expected $\mathcal{O}(1)$ rounds. We overview this step below in Sect. 2.4. Our main contribution is in improving this step using the asynchronous weak-binding secret sharing with $\mathcal{O}(1)$-overhead. Despite the fact that this secret sharing with $\mathcal{O}(1)$-overhead is not robust, it suffices since it is used as part of a perfect zero-knowledge proof where the dealer proves that the shares it generated indeed correspond to a product relation. If the sharing fails, then we can simply ignore the contribution of that dealer.
   In our protocol, each party acts as a dealer to generate C/n triplets. This step requires a cost of $\mathcal{O}(n^4 \log n + C \log n)$ communication for a single party and an overall cost of $\mathcal{O}(n^5 \log n + Cn \log n)$ for all the parties together.
2. **Agreeing on a core set (ACS):** All triplet generations of honest dealers eventually terminate, whereas those of corrupted dealers might never terminate. However, if one honest party sees that the triplet generation of some player P_i terminates, then all the honest parties will eventually receive output in that triplet generation.

   As t instances might never terminate, the parties proceed with the protocol once at least $n - t$ parties successfully complete the triplet generation. Since parties might receive messages in different orders, they have to agree on the set of parties for which their triplet generation was successful.
   The set Core of at least $n - t$ parties (who have successfully completed the triple sharing) will be chosen using the agreement on core set (ACS) protocol. The communication cost of ACS from [14] is $\mathcal{O}(n^7 \log n)$, and its run-time is $\log n$. In [2], the communication is improved to $\mathcal{O}(n^5 \log n)$, and run-time is expected constant time. We use the latter to quote our complexity.[5]

---

[5] Without [2], the cost of our entire MPC is $\mathcal{O}((Cn + Dn^2 + n^7) \log n)$ and $\mathcal{O}(D + \log n)$ expected-time.

3. **Triplets with no dealer:** Once agreed which triplets to consider (Core), using triplet extraction of [19], we can extract from a total of $\frac{C(n-t)}{n}$ triplets generated by the dealers in Core, $\mathcal{O}(C)$ triplets where no party knows the underlying values. This step costs $\mathcal{O}(n^2 \log n + Cn \log n)$.

In summary, for generating C triplets we pay a total of $\mathcal{O}(n^5 \log n + Cn \log n)$.

The MPC protocol follows the standard structure where each party shares its input, and the parties evaluate the circuit gate-by-gate, or more exactly, layer-by-layer. In each multiplication gate, the parties have to consume one multiplication triple. Using the method of [19], if the ith layer of the circuit contains C_i multiplications (for $i \in [D]$, where D is the depth of the circuit), the evaluation costs $\mathcal{O}(n^2 \log n + C_i \cdot n \log n)$. Summing over all layers, this is $\sum_{i \in [D]} (n^2 + nC_i) \log n = (Dn^2 + Cn) \log n$. Together with the generation of the triplets, we get the claimed $\mathcal{O}((Cn + Dn^2 + n^5) \log n)$ cost as in Theorem 1.1. We refer the reader to Sect. 7 for further details on our MPC protocol.

One point worth addressing is that we parallelize the input-sharing phase to the triplet generation. In that case, the ACS protocol selects the parties for which their triplet generation and input sharing were successful. Moreover, the input-sharing phase uses the robust secret-sharing with $\mathcal{O}(n)$ overhead and not the non-robust $\mathcal{O}(1)$. After the parties obtain robust shares (either sharing inputs or of product relations), all other computations are merely reconstructions and linear combinations of shared values. Since messages of honest parties are guaranteed to be delivered, and we have at least $2t + 1$ honest parties in Core with at most t corruptions, all reconstructions are guaranteed to terminate successfully and asynchrony has no effect.

2.4   Multiplication Triplets with a Dealer

The goal is that a dealer wishes to distribute shares of secret values $\vec{a}, \vec{b}, \vec{c}$ such that for every i it holds that $c_i = a_i b_i$. Towards this end, the dealer plants $\vec{a}$ into some bivariate polynomial $A(\mathbf{x}, \mathbf{y})$ using the asynchronous VSS scheme that employs a bivariate polynomial of degree-$(t + t/2, t)$. Such a VSS is given in [19], which we slightly simplify in the full version and give it for completeness. Specifically, $\vec{a}$ is placed at $(A(-\beta, 0))_{\beta \in 0, \ldots, t/2}$. Similarly, the dealer plants $\vec{b}$ into $B(\mathbf{x}, \mathbf{y})$ and $\vec{c}$ into $C(\mathbf{x}, \mathbf{y})$. It is important to note that we deploy robust AVSS here, to ensure that the triplets are shared via degree-t polynomials (which is utilized by our MPC protocol). So we can plant only $\mathcal{O}(n)$ values in each bivariate polynomial. Specifically, the ith secret in $\vec{a}$ is shared via the t-degree polynomial $A(-i, \mathbf{y})$.

Next, the dealer has to prove, using a distributed zero-knowledge protocol, that indeed $c_i = a_i b_i$ for every i (i.e., that $C(-\beta, 0) = A(-\beta, 0) \cdot B(-\beta, 0)$ for every $\beta \in \{0, \ldots, t/2\}$). The input of each party P_j is a point on the univariate polynomials $A(-\beta, \mathbf{y}), B(-\beta, \mathbf{y})$ and $C(-\beta, \mathbf{y})$. The zero-knowledge proof shares and operates on the coefficients of the polynomials used for sharing $\vec{a}, \vec{b}, \vec{c}$. If the dealer shared $\mathcal{O}(M)$ triplets, then the zero-knowledge involves sharing of $\mathcal{O}(Mn)$ values. For simplicity, assume hereafter that $M = \mathcal{O}(n^2)$.

Verifying Product Relation. We now provide a detailed disposition of the zero-knowledge for product relations via the asynchronous weak-binding secret sharing. For simplicity of notation, the dealer has already (verifiably) shared, for every $u \in U = \{0, \ldots, t/2\}^2$, degree-$t$ polynomial $A^u(\mathbf{x}), B^u(\mathbf{x}), C^u(\mathbf{x})$. Each party P_j holds shares $A^u(j), B^u(j), C^u(j)$. The goal of the dealer is to prove that $A^u(0) \cdot B^u(0) = C^u(0)$. The zero-knowledge proof shares and operates on the coefficients of the polynomials used for sharing. Since $|U| \in \mathcal{O}(n^2)$ and each product polynomial has $\mathcal{O}(n)$ coefficients, we have a total of $\mathcal{O}(n^3)$ coefficients to pack. We now need $\mathcal{O}(1)$ trivariate polynomials to pack all needed coefficients. This sharing does not need to produce t-sharing of the secrets. Rather the mere confirmation that the dealer commits to a unique set of secrets is good enough. Hence, as discussed in the previous section, we can utilize the asynchronous weak-binding secret sharing with light-enhanced features.

Constructing the Trivariate Polynomials. For every $u \in U$, define:

$$E^u(\mathbf{x}) := A^u(\mathbf{x}) \cdot B^u(\mathbf{x}) - C^u(\mathbf{x}) .$$

We redefine $U = V \times V$ where $V = \{0, \ldots, t/2\}$. Then, we need to verify that for every $(\beta, \gamma) \in V \times V$ it holds that

$$E^{(\beta,\gamma)}(0) = A^{(\beta,\gamma)}(0) \cdot B^{(\beta,\gamma)}(0) - C^{(\beta,\gamma)}(0) = 0 ,$$

which implies that $A^{(\beta,\gamma)}(0) \cdot B^{(\beta,\gamma)}(0) = C^{(\beta,\gamma)}(0)$. Since $A^{(\beta,\gamma)}(\mathbf{x}), B^{(\beta,\gamma)}(\mathbf{x})$, and $C^{(\beta,\gamma)}(\mathbf{x})$ are polynomials of degree-t, the polynomial $E^{(\beta,\gamma)}(\mathbf{x})$ is of degree-$2t$. We explicitly write

$$E^{(\beta,\gamma)}(\mathbf{x}) = e_1^{(\beta,\gamma)}\mathbf{x} + \ldots + e_{2t}^{(\beta,\gamma)}\mathbf{x}^{2t} .$$

Since the constant term of this polynomial is supposed to be 0 (if indeed $A^{(\beta,\gamma)}(0) \cdot B^{(\beta,\gamma)}(0) = C^{(\beta,\gamma)}(0)$) we do not specify it. The dealer embeds the $2t$ coefficients of each of those $(t/2+1)^2$ polynomials in four trivariate polynomials, each of degree $t+t/2$ in $\mathbf{x}, \mathbf{y}$ and $\mathbf{z}$. Note that each trivariate polynomial can pack $(t/2+1)^3$ values, where we have a total of $(t/2+1)^2 \cdot 2t$ values to pack; We therefore need four trivariate polynomial $\mathbf{S}_1, \mathbf{S}_2, \mathbf{S}_3, \mathbf{S}_4$ (in each we pack $t/2(t/2+1)^2$ while we can pack $(t/2+1)^3$ values; i.e., we do not fully pack it). Specifically (where in all of the following rows we quantify over all $k \in [1, \ldots, t/2]$, and $(\beta, \gamma) \in V \times V$):

The coefficients	Embedded in the trivariate	The embedding
$e_1^{(\beta,\gamma)}, \ldots, e_{t/2}^{(\beta,\gamma)}$	$\mathbf{S}_1(\mathbf{x}, \mathbf{y}, \mathbf{z})$	$\mathbf{S}_1(-\beta, -k, -\gamma) = e_k^{(\beta,\gamma)}$
$e_{t/2+1}^{(\beta,\gamma)}, \ldots, e_t^{(\beta,\gamma)}$	$\mathbf{S}_2(\mathbf{x}, \mathbf{y}, \mathbf{z})$	$\mathbf{S}_2(-\beta, -k, -\gamma) = e_{t/2+k}^{(\beta,\gamma)}$
$e_{t+1}^{(\beta,\gamma)}, \ldots, e_{t+t/2}^{(\beta,\gamma)}$	$\mathbf{S}_3(\mathbf{x}, \mathbf{y}, \mathbf{z})$	$\mathbf{S}_3(-\beta, -k, -\gamma) = e_{t+k}^{(\beta,\gamma)}$
$e_{t+t/2+1}^{(\beta,\gamma)}, \ldots, e_{2t}^{(\beta,\gamma)}$	$\mathbf{S}_4(\mathbf{x}, \mathbf{y}, \mathbf{z})$	$\mathbf{S}_4(-\beta, -k, -\gamma) = e_{t+t/2+k}^{(\beta,\gamma)}$

This fixes $t/2(t/2+1)^2$ points on each trivariate polynomial. The dealer chooses random trivariate polynomials under the above constraints. It then "secret shares" those trivariate polynomials among the parties. Each party P_i receives the share:

$$\text{share}_i = (\mathbf{S}_r(\mathbf{x}, \mathbf{y}, i),\ \mathbf{S}_r(\mathbf{x}, i, \mathbf{y}),\ \mathbf{S}_r(i, \mathbf{y}, \mathbf{z}))_{r \in [4]} \ .$$

Let us assume for simplicity that share$_i$s are distributed such that *all* the honest parties' share$_i$s uniquely define four trivariate polynomials of degree at most $t + t/2$ in each variable. We have to perform the following checks:

1. The shares that the dealer distributes uniquely define four trivariate polynomials of degree at most $t + t/2$ in each variable.
2. The trivariate polynomials define coefficients of polynomials $E^{(\beta,\gamma)}(\mathbf{x})$ for every $(\beta, \gamma) \in V \times V$. It should hold that for at least $2t + 1$ indices i:

$$a_i^{(\beta,\gamma)} \cdot b_i^{(\beta,\gamma)} - c_i^{(\beta,\gamma)} = E^{(\beta,\gamma)}(i) = i \cdot e_1^{(\beta,\gamma)} + i^2 \cdot e_2^{(\beta,\gamma)} + \ldots + i^{2t} \cdot e_{2t}^{(\beta,\gamma)} \quad (1)$$

Since each $A^{(\beta,\gamma)}(\mathbf{x}), B^{(\beta,\gamma)}(\mathbf{x}), C^{(\beta,\gamma)}(\mathbf{x})$ is of degree-t, the polynomial $A^{(\beta,\gamma)}(\mathbf{x}) \cdot B^{(\beta,\gamma)}(\mathbf{x}) - C^{(\beta,\gamma)}(\mathbf{x})$ is of degree-$2t$. If Eq. (1) holds for at least $2t + 1$ indices i, then this polynomial is exactly $E^{(\beta,\gamma)}(\mathbf{x})$. Since $E^{(\beta,\gamma)}(0) = 0$, we have that $A^{(\beta,\gamma)}(0) \cdot B^{(\beta,\gamma)}(0) = C^{(\beta,\gamma)}(0)$. To require that the above verification holds for at least $2t + 1$ honest parties, we actually require that it holds for at least $3t + 1$ parties.

To check that the trivariate shares pack the correct values, each P_i must be able to reconstruct $E^{(\beta,\gamma)}(i)$, where

$$E^{(\beta,\gamma)}(i) = \sum_{k=1}^{t/2} \Big(i^k \cdot \underbrace{\mathbf{S}_1(-\beta, -k, -\gamma)}_{e_k^{(\beta,\gamma)}} + i^{t/2+k} \cdot \underbrace{\mathbf{S}_2(-\beta, -k, -\gamma)}_{e_{t/2+k}^{(\beta,\gamma)}}$$

$$+ i^{t+k} \cdot \underbrace{\mathbf{S}_3(-\beta, -k, -\gamma)}_{e_{t+k}^{(\beta,\gamma)}} + i^{t+t/2+k} \cdot \underbrace{\mathbf{S}_4(-\beta, -k, -\gamma)}_{e_{t+t/2+k}^{(\beta,\gamma)}} \Big)$$

We therefore let P_i get the bivariate polynomial from the dealer in addition to share$_i$, which embeds $(E^{(\beta,\gamma)}(i))_{(\beta,\gamma) \in V \times V}$:

$$T_i(\mathbf{x}, \mathbf{z}) = \sum_{r=1}^{4} \sum_{k=1}^{t/2} i^{(r-1) \cdot (t/2)+k} \cdot \mathbf{S}_r(\mathbf{x}, -k, \mathbf{z}). \quad (2)$$

Note that for every (β, γ), $T_i(-\beta, -\gamma) = E^{(\beta,\gamma)}(i)$.

We now need a mechanism for P_i to verify that the dealer indeed passes on a correct bivariate polynomial T_i consistent with the unique trivariate polynomials $(\mathbf{S}_r)_{r \in \{1,2,3,4\}}$ defined by share$_j$s of the honest parties. We observe that $T_i(\mathbf{x}, j)$ can be computed by P_j based on share$_j$. Since the degree of T_i is $t + t/2$ in both variables, it is enough if $t + t/2 + 1$ honest parties or alternatively a total of $2t + t/2 + 1$ parties confirm that their $T_i(\mathbf{x}, j)$ is consistent with P_i's received T_i. So, to let P_i verify $T_i(\mathbf{x}, \mathbf{z})$, the parties jointly perform the following:

1. On holding $(\mathbf{S}_r(\mathbf{x}, \mathbf{y}, j))_{r \in [4]}$ as part of share$_j$, for every $r \in [4]$, P_j evaluates $\mathbf{S}_r(\mathbf{x}, \mathbf{y}, j)$ on $t/2$ values $\mathbf{y} = -1, \ldots, -t/2$ to obtain $\mathbf{S}_r(\mathbf{x}, -1, j), \ldots,$ $\mathbf{S}_r(\mathbf{x}, -t/2, j)$.

2. Define $t_i^j(\mathbf{x}) = \sum_{r=1}^{4} \sum_{k=1}^{t/2} i^{(r-1) \cdot (t/2)+k} \cdot \mathbf{S}_r(\mathbf{x}, -k, j)$.

3. Send P_i the univariate polynomial $t_i^j(\mathbf{x})$.

P_i can then verify if $t_i^j(\mathbf{x}) = T_i(\mathbf{x}, j)$ for at least $2t + t/2 + 1$ P_js.

We require the dealer to find a set of size at least $3t + 1$ such that: (a) the honest parties in it must define four unique trivariate polynomials; (b) every honest party in it holds T_i that is consistent with every honest party in the set; and (c) every honest party in it must have successfully verified Equation (1). We note that an honest dealer will always be able to find eventually such a set.

Modeling. We describe our protocol in the Simple UC (SUC) framework due to Canetti, Cohen, and Lindell [16]. This implies standard UC security [15]. We try to avoid over-formalism in the protocol descriptions (e.g., we ignore sid while those are implicit). As standard secret-shared protocols in the perfect setting, we conjecture that our protocols are also adaptively secure.

Organization. The rest of the paper is organized as follows. In Sect. 3, we provide the preliminaries, mainly overview the SUC framework. Additional preliminaries are deferred to the full version. In Sect. 4, we provide full details of our zero-knowledge protocol, i.e., verifying product relation. In Sect. 5, we provide our rate-1, asynchronous weak-binding secret sharing. We remark again that we do not use this secret sharing directly, and we provide it just for completeness. In Sect. 6, we show verifiable triple sharing, followed by the MPC protocol in Sect. 7.

3   Preliminaries

Notations. Our protocols are defined over a finite field $\mathbb{F}$ where $|\mathbb{F}| > n + t + 1$. We denote the elements by $\{-t, \ldots, 0, 1 \ldots, n\}$. We use $\langle v \rangle$ to denote the degree-t Shamir-sharing of a value v among parties in $\mathcal{P}$, and $\langle v \rangle_i$ to denote the share held by a party P_i.

3.1   Asynchronous Secure Computation and SUC

We consider an asynchronous network where the parties are $\mathcal{P} = \{P_1, \ldots, P_n\}$. The parties are connected via pairwise ideal private channels. To model asynchrony, messages sent on a channel can be arbitrarily delayed, however, they are guaranteed to be eventually received after some finite number of activations of the adversary. In general, the order in which messages are received might be different from the order in which they were sent. Yet, to simplify notation and improve readability, we assume that the messages that a party receives from a channel are guaranteed to be delivered in the order they were sent. This can be achieved using standard techniques – counters, and acknowledgements, and so we just make this simplification assumption.

We prove our protocols in this simplified universally composable setting (SUC), which is a simplified UC model aimed for modeling secure protocols, formalized by Canetti, Cohen and Lindell [17], and implies UC security. We briefly review the definitions, but many details are left out, see [17] for additional information. We refer the readers to the full version for the security proofs and more details.

Main Difference from SUC. The SUC model allows the adversary to also drop messages, and the adversary is not limited to eventually deliver all messages. To model "eventual delivery" (which is the essence of the asynchronous model), we limit the capabilities of the adversary and quantify over adversaries that eventually transmit each message in the network (i.e., they do not drop messages). Formally, any message sent must be delivered after some finite number of activations of the adversary.

As in SUC, the parties are modeled as interactive Turing machines, with code tapes, input tapes, outputs tapes, incoming communication tapes, outgoing communication tape, random tape and work tape.

Communication. In each execution there is an *environment* $\mathcal{Z}$, an *adversary* $\mathcal{A}$, participating *parties* $P_1, \ldots, P_n$, and possibly an *ideal functionality* $\mathcal{F}$ and a *simulator* $\mathcal{S}$. The parties, adversary and ideal functionality are connected in a star configuration, where all communication is via an additional *router machine* that takes instructions from the adversary. That is, each entity has one outgoing channel to the router and one incoming channel. When P_i sends a message to P_j, it sends it to the router, and the message is stored by the router. The router delivers to the adversary a general information about the message (i.e., "a header" but not the "content". That is, the adversary can know the type of the message and its size, but cannot see its content). When the adversary allows the delivery of the message, the router delivers the message to P_j. As mentioned, we quantify only over all adversaries that eventually deliver all messages. In particular, even in an execution with an ideal functionality, communication between the parties and this functionality is done via the router machine and is subject to (finite) delivery delays imposed by the adversary.

Note that the router machine is also part of the ideal model. When the functionality gives for instance, some output to party P_j, then this is performed via the router, and the simulator is notified. Thus, if the adversary, for instance, delays the delivery of the output of some party P_j, we do not explicitly mention that in the functionality (e.g., "wait to receive OK_j from the adversary and then deliver the output to P_j"), yet it is captured by the model.

Finally, the environment $\mathcal{Z}$ communicates with the adversary directly and not via the router. In particular, the environment can communicate only with the adversary (and it cannot communicate even with the ideal functionality $\mathcal{F}$). In addition, $\mathcal{Z}$ can *write* inputs to the honest parties' input tapes and can *read* their output tapes.

Execution in the Ideal Model. In the ideal model we consider an execution of the environment $\mathcal{Z}$, dummy parties $P_1, \ldots, P_n$, the router, a functionality $\mathcal{F}$ and a simulator $\mathcal{S}$. In the ideal model with a functionality $\mathcal{F}$ the parties follow a fixed ideal-model protocol. The environment is first activated with some input z. The environment delivers the inputs to the dummy honest parties, which forward the inputs to the functionality (recall that this is done via the router, which then gives some leakage about the message header to $\mathcal{S}$, which can adaptively delay the delivery by any finite amount). Moreover, $\mathcal{Z}$ can also give some initial inputs to the corrupted parties via $\mathcal{S}$. At a later stage where the dummy parties receive output from the functionality $\mathcal{F}$, they just write the outputs on their output tapes (and $\mathcal{Z}$ can read those outputs). The simulator $\mathcal{S}$ can send messages to $\mathcal{Z}$ and to the functionality $\mathcal{F}$. The simulator cannot directly communicate with the participating parties. We stress that in the ideal model, the simulator $\mathcal{S}$ interacts with $\mathcal{Z}$ in an online way, and the environment can essentially read the outputs of the honest parties, and query the simulator (i.e., can see the view of the adversary) at any point of the execution. At the end of the interaction, $\mathcal{Z}$ outputs some bit b. We denote by $\text{IDEAL}_{\mathcal{F}, \mathcal{S}, \mathcal{Z}}(z)$ an execution of this ideal model of the functionality $\mathcal{F}$ with a simulator $\mathcal{S}$ and environment $\mathcal{Z}$, which starts with an input z.

Execution in the Real Model with Protocol π. In the real model, there is no ideal functionality and the participating parties are $\mathcal{Z}$, the parties $P_1, \ldots, P_n$, the router and the real-world adversary $\mathcal{A}$. The environment is first activated with some input z, and it can give inputs to the honest parties, as well as some initial inputs to the corrupted parties controlled by the adversary $\mathcal{A}$. The parties run the protocol π as specified, while the corrupted parties are controlled by $\mathcal{A}$. The environment can see at any point the outputs of the honest parties, and communicate directly with the adversary $\mathcal{A}$ (and see, without loss of generality, its partial view). At the end of the execution, the environment outputs some bit b. We denote by $\text{REAL}_{\pi, \mathcal{A}, \mathcal{Z}}(z)$ an execution of this real model with the protocol π, the real-world adversary $\mathcal{A}$ and the environment $\mathcal{Z}$, which starts with some input z.

Definition 3.1. *We say that an adversary $\mathcal{A}$ is an* asynchronous *adversary if any message that it receives from the router, it allows its delivery within some finite number of activations of $\mathcal{A}$.*

Definition 3.2. *Let π be a protocol and let $\mathcal{F}$ be an ideal functionality. We say that π securely computes $\mathcal{F}$ in the asynchronous setting if for every real-model asynchronous adversary $\mathcal{A}$ there exists an ideal-world adversary $\mathcal{S}$ that runs in polynomial time in $\mathcal{A}$'s running time, such that for every $\mathcal{Z}$:*

$$\left\{\text{IDEAL}_{\mathcal{F}, \mathcal{S}, \mathcal{Z}}(z)\right\}_z \equiv \left\{\text{REAL}_{\pi, \mathcal{A}, \mathcal{Z}}(z)\right\}_z$$

Additional Preliminaries. We review in the full version some additional preliminaries, such as hybrid model and composition. We also provide some known primitives – such as asynchronous broadcast, asynchronous agreement on a common set, finding a STAR in a graph, and some properties of bivariate and trivariate polynomials.

4   Verifying Product Relation

In this section, we show how to realize the product-relation verification functionality. Assume that a dealer owns and preshares $\mathcal{O}(n^2)$ Shamir-sharings of triples, such that each of the triples are supposed to satisfy a product relation. That is, for a triple (a, b, c), c must be equal to ab. The parties input shares of those shared triples to the functionality, and the functionality checks that shares define triples satisfying product relations.

Functionality 4.1: Verifying Product Relation

The functionality is parameterized by a set of corrupted parties $I \subseteq [n]$.

1. Let $U = [(t/2 + 1)^2]$. Each party P_j sends to the functionality a set of points $(a_j^u, b_j^u, c_j^u)_{u \in U}$.
2. For every $u \in U$, the functionality reconstructs the unique degree-t univariate polynomials $A^u(\mathbf{x}), B^u(\mathbf{x}), C^u(\mathbf{x})$ satisfying

$$A^u(j) = a_j^u, \qquad B^u(j) = b_j^u, \qquad C^u(j) = c_j^u .$$

   If the dealer is honest, then the dealer also sends $A^u(\mathbf{x}), B^u(\mathbf{x}), C^u(\mathbf{x})$.
3. If the dealer is honest, then give the adversary the shares $A^u(i), B^u(i)$ and $C^u(i)$ for every $i \in I$. If the dealer is corrupted, then give the adversary the reconstructed $A^u(\mathbf{x}), B^u(\mathbf{x}), C^u(\mathbf{x})$.
4. The functionality verifies that for every $u \in U$ it holds that

$$A^u(0) \cdot B^u(0) = C^u(0).$$

   If yes, then it sends OK to all parties and halts. Otherwise, the functionality never terminates.

4.1   Trivariate Polynomial Verification – Functionality

We overviewed the ZK property in Sect. 2.4. Towards realizing Functionality 4.1, we introduce an aiding functionality. To recall, we write $U = V \times V$ where $V = \{0, \ldots, t/2\}$, and the dealer embeds the coefficients of the polynomials $A^{(\beta, \gamma)}, B^{(\beta, \gamma)}, C^{(\beta, \gamma)}$ in four trivariate polynomials. We abstract some computations that the parties perform to improve readability by considering general predicates. Specifically:

1. Each party P_i also receives from the dealer the bivariate polynomial $T_i(\mathbf{x}, \mathbf{z})$ as part of its share; each party P_j computes from its share share$_j$ a univariate polynomial that is supposed to be $T_i(\mathbf{x}, j)$ by applying some linear combination over its shares. We abstract this linear combination as "linear circuit", formally defined below. Note that the same computation that the dealer performs on the trivariate shares to obtain $T_i(\mathbf{x}, \mathbf{y})$, each party performs on its share share$_j$ to obtain $T_i(\mathbf{x}, j)$.

2. Each party P_i also checks that for every (β, γ) it holds that $T_i(-\beta, -\gamma) = a_i^{(\beta,\gamma)} \cdot b_i^{(\beta,\gamma)} - c_i^{(\beta,\gamma)}$. We abstract this check as an "external validity" predicate that P_i enters as input.

Linear Circuits. We consider a circuit L_j that receives as an input a bivariate polynomial $F(\mathbf{x}, \mathbf{y})$ and it has the following structure:

1. Evaluate $F(\mathbf{x}, \mathbf{y})$ on several constants $\mathbf{y} = \alpha_1, \ldots, \alpha_k$ in the field. The results are univariate polynomials $f_1(\mathbf{x}) = F(\mathbf{x}, \alpha_1), \ldots, f_k(\mathbf{x}) = F(\mathbf{x}, \alpha_k)$.
2. Output the univariate polynomial $f^{L_j}(\mathbf{x}) = \sum_{\ell=1}^{k} \lambda_\ell \cdot f_\ell(\mathbf{x})$ for some constants $\lambda_1, \ldots, \lambda_k$. That is, output a fixed linear combination of $f_1(\mathbf{x}), \ldots, f_k(\mathbf{x})$.

We write $f^{L_j(F)}(\mathbf{x}) = L_j(F(\mathbf{x}, \mathbf{y}))$. We also evaluate the circuit L_j on a trivariate polynomial $\mathbf{F}(\mathbf{x}, \mathbf{y}, \mathbf{z})$. In that case:

1. Evaluate $\mathbf{F}(\mathbf{x}, \mathbf{y}, \mathbf{z})$ on the same constants $\mathbf{y} = \alpha_1, \ldots, \alpha_k$. The results are bivariate polynomials $(F_1(\mathbf{x}, \mathbf{z}), \ldots, F_k(\mathbf{x}, \mathbf{z})) = (\mathbf{F}(\mathbf{x}, \alpha_1, \mathbf{z}), \ldots, \mathbf{F}(\mathbf{x}, \alpha_k, \mathbf{z}))$.
2. Output the bivariate polynomial which is a fixed linear combination $F^{L_j}(\mathbf{x}, \mathbf{z}) := \sum_{\ell=1}^{k} \lambda_\ell \cdot F_\ell(\mathbf{x}, \mathbf{z})$.

We write $F^{L_j(\mathbf{F})}(\mathbf{x}, \mathbf{y}) = L_j(\mathbf{F}(\mathbf{x}, \mathbf{y}, \mathbf{z}))$. For every $i \in [n]$, consider $F_i(\mathbf{x}, \mathbf{y}) = \mathbf{F}(\mathbf{x}, \mathbf{y}, i)$, and let $f^{L_j(F_i)}(\mathbf{x}) = L_j(F_i(\mathbf{x}, \mathbf{y}))$. Then clearly it holds that

$$f^{L_j(F_i)}(\mathbf{x}) = L_j(F_i(\mathbf{x}, \mathbf{y})) = L_j(\mathbf{F}(\mathbf{x}, \mathbf{y}, i)) = F^{L_j(\mathbf{F})}(\mathbf{x}, i) .$$

The specific linear circuit that we use is given below in Circuit 4.2.

External Validity. The predicate $\mathsf{ExternalValidity}_j$ receives as input the share of P_j and outputs 0 or 1. The exact predicate that we use is given in Algorithm 4.3.

Linear Circuit 4.2 (The circuit L_i:).

- **Input:** *Trivariate polynomials* $\mathbf{S}_1, \mathbf{S}_2, \mathbf{S}_3, \mathbf{S}_4$.
  1. *For* $r \in [1, \ldots, 4]$, *evaluate* $\mathbf{S}_r(\mathbf{x}, \mathbf{y}, \mathbf{z})$ *on the constants* $\mathbf{y} = -1, \ldots, -t/2$.
  2. *Obtain* $\mathbf{S}_r(\mathbf{x}, -k, \mathbf{z})$ *for* $k \in [1, \ldots, t/2]$ *and* $r \in [1, \ldots, 4]$.
  3. *Define* $T_i(\mathbf{x}, \mathbf{z}) := \sum_{r=1}^{4} \sum_{k=1}^{t/2} i^{(r-1) \cdot (t/2) + k} \cdot \mathbf{S}_r(\mathbf{x}, -k, \mathbf{z})$.
- **Output:** *The bivariate polynomial* $T_i(\mathbf{x}, \mathbf{z})$.

Algorithm 4.3: The predicate $\mathsf{ExternalValidity}_i$

- **Input:** The share share_i of P_i, which consists of shares on each one of the polynomials $\mathbf{S}_1, \ldots, \mathbf{S}_4$ and bivariate polynomial $T_i(\mathbf{x}, \mathbf{z})$.
- **Parameters:** For every $(\beta, \gamma) \in V \times V$ the algorithm is hardwired with values $a_i^{(\beta,\gamma)}, b_i^{(\beta,\gamma)}, c_i^{(\beta,\gamma)} \in \mathbb{F}$.
- **The algorithm:** Output 1 iff for every $\beta, \gamma \in V$ it holds that:

$$T_i(-\beta, -\gamma) = a_i^{(\beta,\gamma)} \cdot b_i^{(\beta,\gamma)} - c_i^{(\beta,\gamma)} .$$

We are now ready to provide the functionality which the product-relation verification protocol uses as its main building block:

Functionality 4.4: Trivariate Polynomial Verification

The functionality is parameterized by (1) The set of corrupted parties $I \subseteq [n]$; (2) Some linear circuits $L_1, \ldots, L_n$ as defined above. The functionality works as follows:

1. The dealer sends four trivariate polynomials $\mathbf{S}_1(\mathbf{x}, \mathbf{y}, \mathbf{z}), \ldots, \mathbf{S}_4(\mathbf{x}, \mathbf{y}, \mathbf{z})$.
2. Define the share of each party P_i to be

$$\mathsf{share}_i = \left((\mathbf{S}_r(\mathbf{x}, \mathbf{y}, i), \mathbf{S}_r(\mathbf{x}, i, \mathbf{z}), \mathbf{S}_r(\mathbf{x}, \mathbf{y}, i))_{r \in [4]}, L_i(\mathbf{S}_1, \mathbf{S}_2, \mathbf{S}_3, \mathbf{S}_4) \right) .$$

   If the dealer is honest, then for every $i \in I$ send P_i the share share_i.
3. The honest parties send to the functionality their external validity predicates $\mathsf{ExternalValidity}_j$ to the functionality. Each $\mathsf{ExternalValidity}_j$ takes as input share_j and outputs 0 or 1.
4. If the dealer is corrupted, then send $(\mathsf{ExternalValidity}_j)_{j \notin I}$ to the adversary.
5. If each one of the four trivariate polynomials $\mathbf{S}_1, \ldots, \mathbf{S}_4$ is of degree $t + t/2$ in each one of the three variables, and $\mathsf{ExternalValidity}_j(\mathsf{share}_j) = 1$ holds for at least $2t + 1$ honest parties, then send OK to all parties and halt. Otherwise, the functionality does not terminate.

4.2 Verifying Product Relation Using Trivariate Polynomial

We now proceed to show how to implement Functionality 4.1, using the trivariate sharing as a building block (i.e., Functionality 4.4). We then provide the theorem statement which we prove in the full version.

Protocol 4.5: Verifying the Product Relation

- **Input:** The dealer holds $A^{(\beta,\gamma)}(\mathbf{x}), B^{(\beta,\gamma)}(\mathbf{x}), C^{(\beta,\gamma)}(\mathbf{x})$ for every $(\beta, \gamma) \in V \times V$. Each party P_i holds the points $A^{(\beta,\gamma)}(i), B^{(\beta,\gamma)}(i), C^{(\beta,\gamma)}(i)$ for every $(\beta, \gamma) \in V \times V$.
- **The protocol:**
  1. The dealer computes $E^{(\beta,\gamma)}(\mathbf{x}) = A^{(\beta,\gamma)}(\mathbf{x}) \cdot B^{(\beta,\gamma)}(\mathbf{x}) - C^{(\beta,\gamma)}(\mathbf{x})$ for every $(\beta, \gamma) \in V \times V$ and define the coefficients $e_1^{(\beta,\gamma)}, \ldots, e_{2t}^{(\beta,\gamma)}$.
  2. The dealer chooses four trivariate polynomials $\mathbf{S}_1, \ldots, \mathbf{S}_4$ of degree $t + t/2$ in all three variables uniformly at random while embedding the coefficients $e_1^{(\beta,\gamma)}, \ldots, e_{2t}^{(\beta,\gamma)}$ as described in the text in Section 2.4.
  3. The parties invoke Functionality 4.4 where the dealer inputs $\mathbf{S}_1, \ldots, \mathbf{S}_4$ and each party P_i (eventually) inputs its private $\mathsf{ExternalValidity}_i$ as defined in Algorithm 4.3. The functionality is parameterized by the linear circuits $L_1, \ldots, L_n$, each is defined as in Circuit 4.2.
  4. Each party P_i: upon receiving an output OK from Functionality 4.4, then terminate and output OK.

Theorem 4.6. *Let $n \geq 4t+1$. Protocol 4.5 securely computes Functionality 4.1 in the presence of a malicious adversary controlling at most t parties. It requires communication of $\mathcal{O}(n^3 \log n)$ bits over point-to-point channels and $\mathcal{O}(n^2 \log n)$ bits of broadcast. Each party broadcasts at most $\mathcal{O}(n \log n)$ bits.*

4.3 Trivariate Polynomial Verification – Protocol

In the remainder of this sub-section, we show how to implement Functionality 4.4. To ease notations, we show how to implement the functionality with general linear functions $L_1, \ldots, L_n$ and general ExternalValidity$_j$. Moreover, we assume that the dealer sends just one trivariate polynomial $\mathbf{S}$ instead of four; generalizing for the case of four polynomial is straightforward. This construction is essentially our asynchronous weak-binding trivariate secret sharing, for which we provided an extensive overview in Sect. 2.2.

Definition 4.7. *We say that the share that P_i received from the dealer*

$$\mathsf{share}_i = (Q_i(\mathbf{x}, \mathbf{y}), \quad W_i(\mathbf{x}, \mathbf{z}), \quad R_i(\mathbf{y}, \mathbf{z}), \quad T_i(\mathbf{x}, \mathbf{z}))$$
$$(= (\mathbf{S}(\mathbf{x}, \mathbf{y}, i), \quad \mathbf{S}(\mathbf{x}, i, \mathbf{z}), \quad \mathbf{S}(i, \mathbf{y}, \mathbf{z}), \quad L_i(\mathbf{S}(\mathbf{x}, \mathbf{y}, \mathbf{z}))))$$

is consistent with an exchange sub-share message $m_{j \to i}$ that P_j sends to P_i,

$$m_{j \to i} := \left(\mathsf{exchange}, j, i, f_i^{Q_j}(\mathbf{x}), g_i^{Q_j}(\mathbf{y}), f_i^{W_j}(\mathbf{x}), g_i^{W_j}(\mathbf{z}), f_i^{R_j}(\mathbf{y}), g_i^{R_j}(\mathbf{z}), t^{L_i(Q_j)}(\mathbf{x}) \right) ,$$

denoted as consistent(share$_i$, $m_{j \to i}$) $= 1$, *if the following conditions hold:*

$$f_i^{Q_j}(\mathbf{x}) = W_i(\mathbf{x}, j) \quad (= \mathbf{S}(\mathbf{x}, i, j)), \qquad g_i^{Q_j}(\mathbf{y}) = R_i(\mathbf{y}, j) \quad (= \mathbf{S}(i, \mathbf{y}, j)),$$
$$f_i^{W_j}(\mathbf{x}) = Q_i(\mathbf{x}, j) \quad (= \mathbf{S}(\mathbf{x}, j, i)), \qquad g_i^{W_j}(\mathbf{z}) = R_i(j, \mathbf{z}) \quad (= \mathbf{S}(i, j, \mathbf{z})),$$
$$f_i^{R_j}(\mathbf{y}) = Q_i(j, \mathbf{y}) \quad (= \mathbf{S}(j, \mathbf{y}, i)), \qquad g_i^{R_j}(\mathbf{z}) = W_i(j, \mathbf{z}) \quad (= \mathbf{S}(j, i, \mathbf{z})) ,$$

and,

$$t^{L_i(Q_j)}(\mathbf{x}) = T_i(\mathbf{x}, j)$$

Protocol 4.8: Trivariate Polynomial Verification

Input: The input of the dealer is some trivariate polynomial $\mathbf{S}(\mathbf{x}, \mathbf{y}, \mathbf{z})$. The input of each party P_j is some predicate ExternalValidity$_j$.

Public parameters: The protocol is parameterized by linear circuits $L_1, \ldots, L_n$.

The protocol:

1. **(Share Distribution)** For each party P_i, the dealer sends the share:

$$(\mathsf{share}, \ i, \ \mathbf{S}(\mathbf{x}, \mathbf{y}, i), \ \mathbf{S}(\mathbf{x}, i, \mathbf{z}), \ \mathbf{S}(i, \mathbf{y}, \mathbf{z}), \ L_i(\mathbf{S}(\mathbf{x}, \mathbf{y}, \mathbf{z})))$$

2. **(Exchange sub-share)** Each party P_i:

(a) Upon receiving (share, i, $Q_i(\mathbf{x}, \mathbf{y})$, $W_i(\mathbf{x}, \mathbf{z})$, $R_i(\mathbf{y}, \mathbf{z})$, $T_i(\mathbf{x}, \mathbf{z})$) from the dealer, check if: $\mathsf{ExternalValidity}_i \left(Q_i(\mathbf{x}, \mathbf{y}), W_i(\mathbf{x}, \mathbf{z}), R_i(\mathbf{y}, \mathbf{z}), T_i(\mathbf{x}, \mathbf{z}) \right)$ $= 1$.

(b) If the above condition holds, then for every P_j define the following seven polynomials:

$$f_j^{Q_i}(\mathbf{x}) \overset{\text{def}}{=} Q_i(\mathbf{x}, j) \quad (= \mathbf{S}(\mathbf{x}, j, i)), \qquad g_j^{Q_i}(\mathbf{y}) \overset{\text{def}}{=} Q_i(j, \mathbf{y}) \quad (= \mathbf{S}(j, \mathbf{y}, i)),$$
$$f_j^{W_i}(\mathbf{x}) \overset{\text{def}}{=} W_i(\mathbf{x}, j) \quad (= \mathbf{S}(\mathbf{x}, i, j)), \qquad g_j^{W_i}(\mathbf{z}) \overset{\text{def}}{=} W_i(j, \mathbf{z}) \quad (= \mathbf{S}(j, i, \mathbf{z})),$$
$$f_j^{R_i}(\mathbf{y}) \overset{\text{def}}{=} R_i(\mathbf{y}, j) \quad (= \mathbf{S}(i, \mathbf{y}, j)), \qquad g_j^{R_i}(\mathbf{z}) \overset{\text{def}}{=} R_i(j, \mathbf{z}) \quad (= \mathbf{S}(i, j, \mathbf{z})),$$

and

$$t^{L_j(Q_i)}(\mathbf{x}) = L_j(Q_i(\mathbf{x}, \mathbf{y})) .$$

Then, define the message:

$$m_{i \to j} := \left(\mathsf{exchange}, i, j, f_j^{Q_i}(\mathbf{x}), g_j^{Q_i}(\mathbf{y}), f_j^{R_i}(\mathbf{x}), g_j^{R_i}(\mathbf{z}), f_j^{W_i}(\mathbf{y}), g_j^{W_i}(\mathbf{z}), t^{L_j(Q_i)}(\mathbf{x}) \right) .$$

(c) Verify that $\mathsf{consistent}(\mathsf{share}_i, m_{i \to i}) = 1$ (as per Definition 4.7), i.e., the share that P_i received from the dealer is consistent with itself.

(d) If all the above conditions hold, then P_i sends to each P_j its sub-share $m_{i \to j}$.

(e) Upon receiving a message $m_{j \to i}$ from P_j, verify that it is consistent with share_i (i.e., $\mathsf{consistent}(\mathsf{share}_i, m_{j \to i}) = 1$), where share_i received from the dealer and $\mathsf{consistent}$ is as Definition 4.7. If so, then broadcast $\mathsf{Good}(i, j)$.

3. **(Identifying Star or Clique)** The dealer does as follows. Initalize a dynamic undirected graph $G = (V, E)$ with $V = [n]$. Upon receiving broadcasted messages $\mathsf{Good}(i, j)$ from P_i and $\mathsf{Good}(j, i)$ from P_j, add the edge (i, j) to E. Run Algorithm 4.9 and if the output is not $\perp$ then broadcast the output and output OK. Otherwise, continue to listen to Good messages and repeat.

4. **(Verifying Star or Clique)** Each party P_i:

(a) Initialize an undirected graph $G_i = (V_i, E_i)$ with $V_i = [n]$. Upon receiving broadcasted messages $\mathsf{Good}(i, j)$ from P_i and $\mathsf{Good}(j, i)$ from P_j, add the edge (i, j) to E_i.

  i. If $(\mathsf{Dense}, \mathsf{C})$ is received from the broadcast of the dealer, validate that $|\mathsf{C}| \geq n - t$, and that each node $i \in \mathsf{C}$ has a degree at least $3t + t/2 + 1$ in G_i. If the conditions hold, output OK.

  ii. If $(\mathsf{BigStar}, \mathsf{C}, \mathsf{D})$ is received from the broadcast of the dealer, P_i verifies that $\mathsf{C} \subset \mathsf{D}$, $|\mathsf{C}| \geq 2t + t/2 + 1$, $|\mathsf{D}| \geq n - t$ and that for every $c \in \mathsf{C}$ and $d \in \mathsf{D}$ the edge (c, d) is in G_i. If the conditions hold, then output OK.

(b) Otherwise, continue to listen to Good messages, and with each message it updates the graph G_i and repeats the above checks.

Algorithm 4.9: Finding a BigStar or a Clique

- **Input:** An undirected graph G over $[n]$.
  1. Initialize a set $\mathsf{C} = \emptyset$.
  2. For each node i that has degree higher than $3t + t/2 + 1$, add i to C.
  3. If $|\mathsf{C}| \geq 3t + 1$ then output $(\mathsf{Dense}, \mathsf{C})$.
  4. Otherwise, let $\overline{\mathsf{C}} = [n] \setminus \mathsf{C}$, i.e., the set of all nodes with degree less than $3t + t/2 + 1$. For each node $i \in \overline{\mathsf{C}}$:
     (a) Consider the graph $G[\Gamma(i)]$ which consists of all vertices in G that have an edge to i (including i). If $G[\Gamma(i)]$ consists of less than $3t + t/2 + 1$ vertices, then add arbitrary vertices in G (say the lexicographically first one) to have a graph with exactly $3t + t/2 + 1$ vertices.
     (b) Run STAR algorithm on input $(G[\Gamma(i)], n', t/2)$ where n' is the number of vertices in $G[\Gamma(i)]$ (i.e., at least $3t+t/2+1$). If the output is (C, D), then output $(\mathsf{BigStar}, \mathsf{C}, \mathsf{D})$.
  5. Otherwise, output $\perp$.

Theorem 4.10. *Let $n \geq 4t+1$. Protocol 4.8 securely computes Functionality 4.4 in the presence of a malicious adversary controlling at most t parties. It has a communication complexity of $\mathcal{O}(n^3 \log n)$ bits over point-to-point channels and $\mathcal{O}(n^2 \log n)$ bits of broadcast. Each party broadcasts at most $\mathcal{O}(n \log n)$ bits.*

5 Rate-1 Asynchronous Weak-Binding Secret Sharing

Protocol 4.8 provides a secret sharing of a trivariate polynomial with $\mathcal{O}(1)$ overhead. Along the way, it also allows some external verification (ExternalValidity) and some computation on the trivariate shares. This section describes our weak-binding secret-sharing protocol with a shunning reconstruction. We remark again that we do not use this protocol in the paper. Nevertheless, we provide it as an independent primitive for completeness and as it might be useful as an independent primitive.

Protocol 5.1: Asynchronous Weak-binding Secret Sharing

Input: The input of the dealer is some trivariate polynomial $\mathbf{S}(\mathbf{x}, \mathbf{y}, \mathbf{z})$. Each other party has no input.
Sharing phase:

1. Each party P_i and the dealer: Run Protocol 4.8 with $\mathsf{ExternalValidity}_i(\cdot)$ as the predicate that always returns 1, and each $L_j(\cdot) = \perp$ for every share$_j$.
2. If the protocol terminates with output OK, then:
   (a) If $(\mathsf{Dense}, \mathsf{C})$ was received as the broadcasted message from the dealer: if $i \in \mathsf{C}$ then store $X = \mathsf{C}$ and share$_i$. (excluding the last element – which is $\perp$.)

(b) If (BigStar, C, D) was received as the broadcasted message from the dealer:
   if $i \in$ D then store $X =$ D and share$_i$. (excluding the last element.)
(c) Otherwise, store $X =$ C if Dense and $X =$ D if BigStar.

Shunning Reconstruction phase:

1. **(Broadcasting the Polynomial)** The dealer:
   (a) Initialise a shunning list Shun $= X$.
   (b) Broadcast a trivariate polynomial $\mathbf{S}(\mathbf{x}, \mathbf{y}, \mathbf{z})$.
2. **(Verifying the Dealer's Polynomial)** Each party P_i:
   (a) Upon receiving a polynomial $\mathbf{S}(\mathbf{x}, \mathbf{y}, \mathbf{z})$ from the dealer, verify that the polynomial is of degree at most $t + t/2$ in each variable. If not, then discard the dealer and terminate.
   (b) If $i \in X$, then verify that $\mathbf{S}(\mathbf{x}, \mathbf{y}, i) = Q_i(\mathbf{x}, \mathbf{y})$, $\mathbf{S}(\mathbf{x}, i, \mathbf{z}) = W_i(\mathbf{x}, \mathbf{z})$ and $\mathbf{S}(i, \mathbf{y}, \mathbf{z}) = R_i(\mathbf{y}, \mathbf{z})$ holds. If all the conditions hold, then P_i broadcasts OK.
3. **(Output)**
   (a) Upon receiving the OK from the broadcast of P_i, the dealer updates Shun $=$ Shun $\setminus \{i\}$.
   (b) Upon receiving OK from at least $2t + t/2 + 1$ parties in X, party P_i outputs $\mathbf{S}(\mathbf{x}, \mathbf{y}, \mathbf{z})$ and terminates. Otherwise, it continues to wait for OK messages.

We use the term "shunning" for reconstruction to indicate that the reconstruction phase offers the following guarantees: either the reconstruction succeeds, or the dealer can identify at least $t/2 + 1$ parties thereafter.

Essentially, in an honest dealer case, termination of the sharing phase is guaranteed. However, since the set X does not necessarily contain $2t + t/2 + 1$ honest parties, for reconstruction, we might need the adversary's help. This is why the reconstruction is either guaranteed, or the dealer shuns at least $t/2 + 1$ parties. In the case of a corrupted dealer, once the sharing terminates, reconstruction must be to the same polynomial (or discard the dealer, or not terminate, but cannot be ended successfully with a different polynomial). We formalize the properties of this protocol in the full version.

6   Verifiable Triple Sharing

In this section, we build upon packed VSS and Functionality 4.1 to show how a dealer can verifiably share $\mathcal{O}(n^2)$ triples simultaneously. We model the packed VSS in Functionality 6.1 below. A protocol realizing it and the complete simulation proof appear in the full version.

Functionality 6.1: Packed VSS Functionality

The functionality is parameterized by the set of corrupted parties $I \subseteq [n]$.

1. The dealer sends to the functionality its input $S(\mathbf{x}, \mathbf{y})$.
2. The functionality verifies that S is of degree at most $3t/2$ in $\mathbf{x}$ and degree at most t in $\mathbf{y}$. If not, it does not terminate.
3. If the above condition does hold, then the functionality sends to the ideal adversary the shares $S(\mathbf{x}, i), S(i, \mathbf{y})$ for every $i \in I$, and for each honest party P_j it sends $S(\mathbf{x}, j), S(j, \mathbf{y})$.

The functionality for verifiable triple sharing appears below, followed by the protocol. The Shamir-shares of party P_j for the $(t/2 + 1)^2$ multiplication triples are as follows, following the invocation of the functionality or the protocol: $(A^u(-\beta, j), B^u(-\beta, j), C^u(-\beta, j))$ for every $u, \beta \in \{0, \ldots, t/2\}$.

Functionality 6.2: Verifiable Triple Secret Sharing

The functionality is parameterized by a set of corrupted parties $I \subseteq [n]$.

1. The dealer sends to the functionality 3 sets of $t/2 + 1$ polynomials $\{A^u(\mathbf{x}, \mathbf{y})\}$, $\{B^u(\mathbf{x}, \mathbf{y})\}$ and $\{C^u(\mathbf{x}, \mathbf{y})\}$ for each $u \in \{0, \ldots, t/2\}$.
2. The functionality verifies that each polynomial is of degree at most $t + t/2$ in $\mathbf{x}$ and t in $\mathbf{y}$. If not, it does not terminate.
3. If the dealer is honest, then for each $u \in \{0, \ldots, t/2\}$, give adversary the shares $(A^u(\mathbf{x}, i), A^u(i, \mathbf{y})), (B^u(\mathbf{x}, i), B^u(i, \mathbf{y}))$ and $(C^u(\mathbf{x}, i), C^u(i, \mathbf{y}))$ for every $i \in I$.
4. The functionality verifies that for every $u, \beta \in \{0, \ldots, t/2\}$ it holds that

$$A^u(-\beta, 0) \cdot B^u(-\beta, 0) = C^u(-\beta, 0) .$$

If yes, then it sends $(A^u(\mathbf{x}, j), A^u(j, \mathbf{y})), (B^u(\mathbf{x}, j), B^u(j, \mathbf{y}))$ and $(C^u(\mathbf{x}, j), C^u(j, \mathbf{y}))$ for every $u \in \{0, \ldots, t/2\}$ to each party P_j and halts. Otherwise, the functionality never terminates.

Protocol 6.3: Verifiable Triple Secret Sharing Protocol

- **Input:** The dealer holds the polynomials $A^u(\mathbf{x}, \mathbf{y})$, $B^u(\mathbf{x}, \mathbf{y})$ and $C^u(\mathbf{x}, \mathbf{y})$ of degree $t + t/2$ in $\mathbf{x}$ and t in $\mathbf{y}$ for every $u \in \{0, \ldots, t/2\}$ such that $A^u(-\beta, 0) \cdot B^u(-\beta, 0) = C^u(-\beta, 0)$ holds for every $\beta \in \{0, \ldots, t/2\}$.
- **The protocol:**
  1. The dealer invokes Functionality 6.1 with its polynomials $A^u(\mathbf{x}, \mathbf{y})$, $B^u(\mathbf{x}, \mathbf{y})$ and $C^u(\mathbf{x}, \mathbf{y})$ for every $u \in \{0, \ldots, t/2\}$ in a batched manner.
  2. The dealer invokes Functionality 4.1 with the input $A^u(-\beta, \mathbf{y}), B^u(-\beta, \mathbf{y})$ and $C^u(-\beta, \mathbf{y})$ for every $u, \beta \in \{0, \ldots, t/2\}$.
  3. Upon receiving an output $(A^u(\mathbf{x}, j), A^u(j, \mathbf{y})), (B^u(\mathbf{x}, j), B^u(j, \mathbf{y}))$ and $(C^u(\mathbf{x}, j), C^u(j, \mathbf{y}))$ from the functionality, each P_j invokes the Functionality 4.1 with the inputs $(A^u(-\beta, j), B^u(-\beta, j), C^u(-\beta, j))$ for every $u, \beta \in \{0, \ldots, t/2\}$.

4. Upon receiving an output OK from the Functionality 4.1, P_j outputs $(A^u(\mathbf{x}, j), A^u(j, \mathbf{y}))$, $(B^u(\mathbf{x}, j), B^u(j, \mathbf{y}))$ and $(C^u(\mathbf{x}, j), C^u(j, \mathbf{y}))$, where $(A^u(-\beta, j), B^u(-\beta, j), C^u(-\beta, j))$ for every $u, \beta \in \{0, \ldots, t/2\}$ defines P_j's degree-t Shamir-share of the $(t/2 + 1)^2$ multiplication triples.

Theorem 6.4. *Let* $n \geq 4t + 1$*. Protocol 6.3 securely computes Functionality 6.2 in the presence of a malicious adversary controlling at most t parties. It has a communication complexity of $\mathcal{O}(n^3 \log n)$ bits over point-to-point channels and $\mathcal{O}(n^2 \log n)$ bits of broadcast for sharing $\mathcal{O}(n^2)$ triples simultaneously. Each party broadcasts at most $\mathcal{O}(n \log n)$ bits.*

6.1 Batching for Linear Overhead per Triple

We note that the overall communication of one instance of verifiable triple sharing protocol is $\mathcal{O}(n^3 \log n)$ over point-to-point channels and $\mathcal{O}(n^2 \log n)$ using broadcast. Using the broadcast of [12], the total cost turns out to be $\mathcal{O}(n^4 \log n)$ for sharing $\mathcal{O}(n^2)$ triples. We make the cost linear per triple by simply batching n instances of the triple sharing protocol under the same dealer. Since all the instances have the same dealer, the broadcasts communication can be common for all. For instance, P_i can send a single broadcast of $\mathsf{Good}(i, j)$ after checking consistency with P_j in all the instances of AVSS and triple sharing. Similarly, the dealer can run the Star algorithm just once for all the AVSSs and broadcast one common Star. Likewise, Algorithm 4.9 also is run for all the trivariate sharings together and the output is broadcast once for all.

This batching allows us to keep the broadcast communication the same as before i.e. $\mathcal{O}(n^4 \log n)$. The point-to-point communication increases by a factor of n and now becomes $\mathcal{O}(n^4 \log n)$. However, we are now able to share n^3 triplets, and thus achieve a linear overhead.

7   The MPC Protocol

We now describe our MPC protocol building upon the packed VSS (Functionality 6.1) and the verifiable triple sharing (Sect. 6) protocol, as well as existing building blocks from the literature such as ACS, reconstruction (Π_{Rec}), triple extraction ($\Pi_{\mathsf{tripleExt}}$) and batched Beaver multiplication (Π_{bBeaver}) (see the full version for details). The protocol relies on Beaver's circuit randomization technique [5] and at a high level works as follows:

1. *Preparing the Beaver Triples and Input Sharing:* Here, parties generate C degree-t Shamir-shared multiplication triples where C denotes the number of multiplication gates in the circuit. Towards this, each party first uses the verified triple-sharing protocol (Sect. 6) to share the required number of multiplication triples. In addition, the input holding parties share their inputs using the packed VSS (Functionality 6.1).

To ensure termination while accounting for the asynchronous nature of the network, parties cannot wait for all the parties to conclude their triple sharing and input sharing. Hence, each party waits for at least $n - t$ instances to terminate. This set of instances may, however, differ across parties. Parties thus need to agree on a common set of at least $n - t$ parties, say Core, whose shared triples will be utilized for subsequent computation. For this purpose, they invoke an instance of ACS. Upon identifying this set, a triple extraction protocol "merges" the triples shared by the parties in Core and extracts "random" triples (unknown to any party), which will be consumed for evaluation in the second phase. The set also defines the parties who contribute their inputs to the computation. For the remaining parties, a default sharing of 0 is considered during computation.

2. *Circuit Evaluation:* This phase corresponds to the shared evaluation of the circuit in a predetermined topological order. The addition and multiplication by constant operations are local owing to the linearity of our sharing. For the multiplication of shared values, parties consume the Beaver triples generated during the first phase. Finally, the outputs are provided to the designated parties via reconstruction to complete the circuit evaluation.

Protocol 7.1: AMPC – Π_{AMPC}

Common input: The description of a circuit, the field $\mathbb{F}$, n non-zero distinct elements $1, \ldots, n$ and a parameter h where $n - t = 2h + 1$. Let $m = \lceil \frac{C}{h+1-t} \rceil$.
Input: Parties hold their inputs (belonging to $\mathbb{F} \cup \{\bot\}$) to the circuit.
(Beaver triple generation and Input sharing:)

1. **(Beaver Triple generation with a dealer)** Each P_i chooses m random multiplication triples and executes $\lceil \frac{m}{(t/2+1)^2} \rceil$ instances of Protocol 6.3 (Section 6) in a batched manner each with $(t/2+1)^2$ triples.
2. **(Input sharing)** Each party P_i holding k_i inputs to the circuit executes the VSS protocol (Functionality 6.1) in a batched manner, packing $\lceil \frac{k_i}{t/2+1} \rceil$ inputs in one instance.
3. **(ACS Execution)** Parties invoke ACS protocol to agree on a set , of at least $n - t$ parties whose instances of triple sharing and input sharing will terminate eventually all the honest parties. Let $(\langle a_i^j \rangle, \langle b_i^j \rangle, \langle c_i^j \rangle)$ for $j \in [m]$ denote the triples shared by $P_i \in$,. The input sharing for the parties outside , is take as default sharing of 0.
4. **(Beaver Triple Extraction)** Parties execute m instances of the triple extraction protocol, $\Pi_{\mathsf{tripleExt}}$, with , as the common input and additionally $(\langle a_i^j \rangle, \langle b_i^j \rangle, \langle c_i^j \rangle)$ for every $P_i \in$, as the input for the jth instance. Let $(\langle \mathbf{a}_i \rangle, \langle \mathbf{b}_i \rangle, \langle \mathbf{c}_i \rangle)$ for $i \in [C]$ denote the random multiplication triples generated.

(Circuit computation:)

1. **(Linear Gates)** Parties locally apply the linear operation on their respective shares of the inputs.

2. **(Multiplication Gates)** Let $(\langle a_i \rangle, \langle b_i \rangle, \langle c_i \rangle)$ be the multiplication triple associated with the ith multiplication gate with shared inputs $(\langle x_i \rangle, \langle y_i \rangle)$. Parties invoke the batched Beaver protocol, Π_{bBeaver}, with $\{\langle x_i \rangle, \langle y_i \rangle, \langle a_i \rangle, \langle b_i \rangle, \langle c_i \rangle\}$ for all gates i at the same layer of the circuit and obtain the corresponding $\langle z_i \rangle$ as the output sharing for every gate i.
3. **(Output)** For each output gate j with the associated sharing $\langle v_j \rangle$, parties execute private reconstruction protocol, Π_{Rec}, towards every party P_i who is supposed to receive the output v_j.

The functionality, theorem statement and proof of security appear in the full version.

Acknowledgements. Gilad Asharov is sponsored by the Israel Science Foundation (grant No. 2439/20), by JPM Faculty Research Award, and by the European Union's Horizon 2020 research and innovation programme under the Marie Skłodowska-Curie grant agreement No. 891234. Shravani Patil would like to acknowledge the support of C3iHub IIT Kanpur 2020–2025. Arpita Patra would like to acknowledge the support of C3iHub IIT Kanpur 2020–2025, Google India Faculty Award, and JPM Faculty Research Award.

References

1. Abraham, I., Asharov, G., Patil, S., Patra, A.: Detect, pack and batch: perfectly-secure MPC with linear communication and constant expected time. In: Hazay, C., Stam, M. (eds.) EUROCRYPT 2023. LNCS, vol. 14005, pp. 251–281. Springer, Cham (2023). https://doi.org/10.1007/978-3-031-30617-4_9
2. Abraham, I., Asharov, G., Patra, A., Stern, G.: Perfectly secure asynchronous agreement on a core set in constant expected time. IACR Cryptol. ePrint Arch., p. 1130 (2023). https://eprint.iacr.org/2023/1130
3. Abraham, I., Dolev, D., Stern, G.: Revisiting asynchronous fault tolerant computation with optimal resilience. Distrib. Comput. 35(4), 333–355 (2022)
4. Applebaum, B., Kachlon, E.: Conflict checkable and decodable codes and their applications. IACR Cryptol. ePrint Arch., p. 627 (2023)
5. Beaver, D.: Efficient multiparty protocols using circuit randomization. In: Feigenbaum, J. (ed.) CRYPTO 1991. LNCS, vol. 576, pp. 420–432. Springer, Heidelberg (1992). https://doi.org/10.1007/3-540-46766-1_34
6. Beerliová-Trubíniová, Z., Hirt, M.: Simple and efficient perfectly-secure asynchronous MPC. In: Kurosawa, K. (ed.) ASIACRYPT 2007. LNCS, vol. 4833, pp. 376–392. Springer, Heidelberg (2007). https://doi.org/10.1007/978-3-540-76900-2_23
7. Beerliová-Trubíniová, Z., Hirt, M.: Perfectly-secure MPC with linear communication complexity. In: Canetti, R. (ed.) TCC 2008. LNCS, vol. 4948, pp. 213–230. Springer, Heidelberg (2008). https://doi.org/10.1007/978-3-540-78524-8_13
8. Ben-Or, M.: Another advantage of free choice: completely asynchronous agreement protocols (extended abstract). In: PODC (1983)
9. Ben-Or, M., Canetti, R., Goldreich, O.: Asynchronous secure computation. In: ACM Symposium on Theory of Computing (1993)

10. Ben-Or, M., Kelmer, B., Rabin, T.: Asynchronous secure computations with optimal resilience (extended abstract). In: Proceedings of the Thirteenth Annual ACM Symposium on Principles of Distributed Computing, PODC 1994, pp. 183–192. Association for Computing Machinery, New York (1994)
11. Bracha, G.: An asynchronous [(n-1)/3]-resilient consensus protocol. In: PODC, pp. 154–162 (1984)
12. Bracha, G.: Asynchronous byzantine agreement protocols. Inf. Comput. **75**(2), 130–143 (1987)
13. Canetti, R.: Studies in secure multiparty computation and applications (1996). https://www.wisdom.weizmann.ac.il/~oded/PSX/ran-phd.pdf
14. Canetti, R.: Studies in secure multiparty computation and applications. Ph.D. thesis, Citeseer (1996)
15. Canetti, R.: Universally composable security: a new paradigm for cryptographic protocols. In: FOCS (2001)
16. Canetti, R., Cohen, A., Lindell, Y.: A simpler variant of universally composable security for standard multiparty computation. In: Gennaro, R., Robshaw, M. (eds.) CRYPTO 2015, Part II. LNCS, vol. 9216, pp. 3–22. Springer, Heidelberg (2015). https://doi.org/10.1007/978-3-662-48000-7_1
17. Canetti, R., Cohen, A., Lindell, Y.: A simpler variant of universally composable security for standard multiparty computation. In: Gennaro, R., Robshaw, M. (eds.) CRYPTO 2015. LNCS, vol. 9216, pp. 3–22. Springer, Heidelberg (2015). https://doi.org/10.1007/978-3-662-48000-7_1
18. Choudhury, A., Hirt, M., Patra, A.: Unconditionally secure asynchronous multiparty computation with linear communication complexity. In: DISC (2013)
19. Choudhury, A., Patra, A.: An efficient framework for unconditionally secure multiparty computation. IEEE Trans. Inf. Theory **63**, 428–468 (2016)
20. Damgård, I., Ishai, Y., Krøigaard, M.: Perfectly secure multiparty computation and the computational overhead of cryptography. In: Gilbert, H. (ed.) EUROCRYPT 2010. LNCS, vol. 6110, pp. 445–465. Springer, Heidelberg (2010). https://doi.org/10.1007/978-3-642-13190-5_23
21. Damgård, I., Schwartzbach, N.I.: Communication lower bounds for perfect maliciously secure MPC. Cryptology ePrint Archive (2020)
22. Goyal, V., Liu, Y., Song, Y.: Communication-efficient unconditional MPC with guaranteed output delivery. In: Boldyreva, A., Micciancio, D. (eds.) CRYPTO 2019. LNCS, vol. 11693, pp. 85–114. Springer, Cham (2019). https://doi.org/10.1007/978-3-030-26951-7_4
23. Patra, A., Choudhury, A., Rangan, C.P.: Communication efficient perfectly secure VSS and MPC in asynchronous networks with optimal resilience. In: Bernstein, D.J., Lange, T. (eds.) AFRICACRYPT 2010. LNCS, vol. 6055, pp. 184–202. Springer, Heidelberg (2010). https://doi.org/10.1007/978-3-642-12678-9_12
24. Patra, A., Choudhury, A., Pandu Rangan, C.: Efficient asynchronous verifiable secret sharing and multiparty computation. J. Cryptol. **28**(1), 49–109 (2015)
25. Prabhu, B., Srinathan, K., Rangan, C.P.: Asynchronous unconditionally secure computation: an efficiency improvement. In: Menezes, A., Sarkar, P. (eds.) INDOCRYPT 2002. LNCS, vol. 2551, pp. 93–107. Springer, Heidelberg (2002). https://doi.org/10.1007/3-540-36231-2_9
26. Srinathan, K., Pandu Rangan, C.: Efficient asynchronous secure multiparty distributed computation. In: Roy, B., Okamoto, E. (eds.) INDOCRYPT 2000. LNCS, vol. 1977, pp. 117–129. Springer, Heidelberg (2000). https://doi.org/10.1007/3-540-44495-5_11

Perfect (Parallel) Broadcast in Constant Expected Rounds via Statistical VSS

Gilad Asharov$^{(\boxtimes)}$ and Anirudh Chandramouli

Department of Computer Science, Bar-Ilan University, Ramat Gan, Israel
{Gilad.Asharov,Anirudh.Chandramouli}@biu.ac.il

Abstract. We study broadcast protocols in the information-theoretic model under optimal conditions, where the number of corruptions t is at most one-third of the parties, n. While worst-case $\Omega(n)$ round broadcast protocols are known to be impossible to achieve, protocols with an expected constant number of rounds have been demonstrated since the seminal work of Feldman and Micali [STOC'88]. Communication complexity for such protocols has gradually improved over the years, reaching $O(nL)$ plus expected $O(n^4 \log n)$ for broadcasting a message of size L bits.

This paper presents a perfectly secure broadcast protocol with expected constant rounds and communication complexity of $O(nL)$ plus expected $O(n^3 \log^2 n)$ bits. In addition, we consider the problem of parallel broadcast, where n senders, each wish to broadcast a message of size L. We show a parallel broadcast protocol with expected constant rounds and communication complexity of $O(n^2 L)$ plus expected $O(n^3 \log^2 n)$ bits. Our protocol is optimal (up to expectation) for messages of length $L \in \Omega(n \log^2 n)$.

Our main contribution is a framework for obtaining *perfectly* secure broadcast with an expected constant number of rounds from a *statistically* secure verifiable secret sharing. Moreover, we provide a new statistically secure verifiable secret sharing where the broadcast cost per participant is reduced from $O(n \log n)$ bits to only $O(\text{poly} \log n)$ bits. All our protocols are adaptively secure.

Keywords: Perfect Secure Computation · Broadcast · Byzantine Agreement · Verifiable Secret Sharing

1 Introduction

Broadcast is a fundamental building block in secure computation, serving as a crucial primitive. It enables a designated party (a sender) to transmit a message

This research is sponsored by the Israel Science Foundation (grant No. 2439/20). Asharov is additionally sponsored by JPM Faculty Research Award, and by the European Union's Horizon 2020 research and innovation programme under the Marie Skłodowska-Curie grant agreement No. 891234.

M. Joye and G. Leander (Eds.): EUROCRYPT 2024, LNCS 14655, pp. 310–339, 2024.
https://doi.org/10.1007/978-3-031-58740-5_11

while ensuring that all participants receive an identical message and reach a consensus on its content. However, this task becomes particularly challenging when dealing with potentially corrupted parties, as they may deceive others about the messages they have received, or a corrupted sender may transmit inconsistent messages.

The primary focus of this paper is to address the realization of the broadcast primitive over point-to-point (ideal private) channels, in the most demanding scenario: achieving perfect security with optimal resilience. Perfect security means that the protocol cannot rely on any computational assumption and that the error probability is zero. Optimal resilience means that the number of corrupted parties is at most $t < n/3$, which is tight by the lower bounds of [28,33].

For broadcasting a message of size L, the best one can hope for is $O(nL)$; since each party has to receive a message of size L, then the total bits transmitted is at least nL. Broadly, broadcast protocols can be characterized into two categories:

- **Succinct protocols but with a high number of rounds:** In this family, broadcasting a message of size L takes $O(nL + n^2 \log n)$ total communication complexity with $\Theta(n)$ rounds [11,14,16]. Broadcasting a single bit requires $\Omega(n^2)$ bits of communication, when the protocol is deterministic [19], or randomized, against strongly-adaptive adversaries[1] [4].

- **More communication, but with an expected constant number of rounds:** It has been shown that for any broadcast protocol with perfect security, there exists an execution that requires $t+1$ rounds [22]. This implies that a protocol with a strict constant number of rounds is impossible to achieve, and this limitation can be overcome by using randomization [8,34]. This family of protocols, originated by Feldman and Micali [20] followed by the impressive improvement of Katz and Koo [25], results in $O(n^2L)$ bits plus expected $O(n^6 \log n)$ bits in expectation for broadcasting a message of size L, with an expected constant number of rounds. This result was recently improved by Abraham et al. [2], which requires communication complexity of $O(nL)$ bits plus expected $O(n^4 \log n)$ bits, with an expected constant number of rounds.

Since broadcast is such a fundamental primitive, narrowing the gap between these two families of protocols is of high importance. This has a potential impact on the complexity of secure computation protocols.

Parallel Broadcast. In secure protocols, we often witness the communication pattern in which n parties have to broadcast messages in parallel at the same round. For instance, in verifiable secret sharing, the parties often complain (in parallel) about messages sent by the dealer, or vote (in parallel) whether to accept or reject the shares of the dealer. Since each party has to receive $O(nL)$ bits in total, the best we can hope for is $O(n^2L)$ communication complexity, with an expected constant number of rounds, and in that case, we say that the

---

[1] Strongly adaptive adversary means that at the same round, the adversary can see the message sent by an honest party, corrupt it, and remove (and switch) the other messages being sent at the same round by that party.

protocol is "asymptotically-free". The protocol of [25] shows an asymptotically-free parallel broadcast for messages of size $\approx n^4$, while [2] is asymptotically-free for messages of size $\approx n^2$. Explicitly, the former is a parallel broadcast with expected $O(n^2 L + n^6 \log n)$ communication complexity and the latter is $O(n^2 L + n^4 \log n)$.

1.1 Our Results

Our main result is an asymptotically-free parallel broadcast for messages of size $\approx n$. We show:

Theorem 1.1. *There exists a perfectly secure, balanced, parallel-broadcast protocol with optimal resilience which allows n senders to distribute each a message of size L, at the communication cost of $O(n^2 L)$ bits plus expected $O(n^3 \log^2 n)$ bits, and expected constant number of rounds.*

By "balanced" we mean that each party sends or receives roughly the same amount of information, and so each party sends or receives $O(nL)$ bits plus expected $O(n^2 \log^2 n)$ bits in our protocol. On the other hand, we mentioned that every parallel broadcast protocol must incur $\Omega(n^2 L)$. In addition, strict constant round parallel broadcast is impossible [22], and so our protocol is optimal up to logarithmic factor and expectation for messages of size $L \geq \Omega(n \log^2 n)$.

The best prior requires either $O(n^2 L)$ plus expected $O(n^4 \log n)$ with constant expected number of rounds [2], or $O(n^2 L + n^3 \log n)$ but with $O(n)$ rounds (easily derived from [14]).

Giving a coarse analysis, and just evaluating the terms in the asymptotic notation, for 1024 parties, even if each party has to broadcast just a single bit (e.g., voting whether to accept the shares of the dealer), in the protocol of [2] each party has to send or receive about 1.34 GB whereas in our protocol it has to send or receive about 13 MB.

Ordinary Broadcast. In classical broadcast, where there is a single sender, we provide an improvement of almost a factor of n in the communication complexity of broadcast with perfect security and optimal resilience. Our protocol is asymptotically free for messages of size $\approx n^2$:

Theorem 1.2 (Informal). *There exists a perfectly secure, balanced, broadcast protocol with optimal resilience that requires communication of $O(nL)$ plus expected $O(n^3 \log^2 n)$ bits for broadcasting a message of size L bits, with an expected constant number of rounds.*

That is, our protocol falls in the second category of protocols where the best previous result is that of Abraham et al. [2], which requires $O(nL)$ bits plus expected $O(n^4 \log n)$ bits. As such, our protocol is asymptotically-free also for much shorter messages.

The protocol of Abraham et al. [2] is asymptotically free for messages of size $L \in \Omega(n^3 \log n)$. Our protocol is asymptotically free for messages of smaller size

$L \in \Omega(n^2 \log^2 n)$. E.g., ignoring constant factors and just evaluating the terms in the asymptotic notation, for broadcasting 1 KB and 512 parties, each party in [2] has to send or receive ≈144 MB; ours is ≈2.65 MB.

Main Technical Contributions

Our result is obtained from the following technical contributions.

Efficient Oblivious Leader Election (OLE). The broadcast protocols in [2, 20, 25] rely on a primitive called oblivious leader election (OLE). The goal in OLE is that all parties would randomly pick one of them as a leader, and reach an agreement on the identity of that leader. The desired outcome is that the chosen leader would be one of the honest parties. The protocol might fail with some constant probability (either, a non-honest leader is chosen, or there is no agreement on who is the chosen leader). We show:

Theorem 1.3. *There exists a perfectly secure, oblivious leader election, with total communication of $O(n^3 \log^2 n)$ bits over point-to-point channels and strict constant number of rounds.*

The oblivious leader election of [25] requires $O(n^6 \log n)$ bits over point-to-point channels; the leader election of [2] requires $O(n^4 \log n)$ cost over point-to-point channels. Our conceptual contribution is that, at least at the intuitive level, the embedded error in the functionality of OLE allows it to be implemented from weaker primitives. Our improved OLE is achieved via two improvements:

- **OLE from Statistical VSS:** OLE uses verifiable secret sharing as a sub-protocol. Since the oblivious leader election may fail regardless with some constant probability, it becomes possible to build it using a statistically secure VSS as a sub-protocol rather than a perfectly secure one. Essentially, the negligible security error introduced to the statistical VSS is shifted into the constant failure probability of the oblivious leader election, resulting in negligible degradation in the round complexity (which still remains constant in expectation).
- **Less VSSes:** The oblivious leader election in [2,25] requires all parties to run VSS in parallel, while each party has to share $O(n)$ secrets. That is, a total of $O(n^2)$ secrets being shared. Our OLE requires each party to share only $O(\text{poly} \log n)$ secrets. This introduces an error, which is again shifted into the constant failure probability of the OLE.

Those improvements open the door to significantly reducing the communication complexity.

Broadcast Efficient Statistically-Secure Verifiable Secret Sharing. The protocol of [3] has low overhead per secret – but only for a relatively high number of secrets. Even if we use an ideal broadcast (that is impossible to achieve – i.e., $O(nL)$ and constant round) in the protocol of [3], we get $O(n^3 \log n)$ total communication for sharing $O(n^2)$ secrets, i.e., overhead of $O(n)$ per secret. But if one wants to share only, say $O(\log n)$ secrets, the cost, even when using an ideal broadcast, still remains $O(n^3 \log n)$, i.e., overhead of $O(n^3)$ per secret. The same is true also for other VSS protocols such as [2,10,21] in the perfect setting and in the statistical setting [32]. We show a protocol that has low overhead also for small number of secrets.

Theorem 1.4. *There exists a verifiable secret sharing protocol that allows a dealer to distribute m secrets of $O(\log n)$ bits each, with a total communication complexity of $O(m \cdot n^2 \log n)$ bits over the point-to-point channels; the dealer broadcasts $O(n \log n)$ bits, and each party broadcasts $O((m + \log(n/\epsilon)) \cdot \log n)$ bits. The protocol has an error probability of ϵ in case of a corrupted dealer. The protocol tolerates up to $t < n/3$ malicious parties and is adaptively secure.*

Putting it differently, using an ideal broadcast, our protocol achieves a lower cost than [3] when the number of secrets $m \in o(n)$. Specifically, for our oblivious leader election, each one of the n parties shares $m = \log n$ secrets. Using the VSS of [3] this results in $O(n^4 \log n)$ bits in total (for all n dealers). Using our VSS, this results in $O(n^3 \log^2 n)$, which leads to the cost of the OLE mentioned in Theorem 1.3. We achieve this improvement by letting all parties broadcast together $\tilde{O}(n)$ bits over the broadcast channel, instead of $\tilde{\Omega}(n^2)$ by previous works.

For our OLE, it suffices to have VSS that fails with probability $\epsilon = 1/\mathsf{poly}(n)$. We also use $m = \log n$, and thus we get that each participant broadcasts $O((m + \log(n/\epsilon)) \cdot \log n = O(\log^2 n)$ bits. Theorem 1.2 is reported in that light.

An important challenge that we overcome is that the protocol is *adaptively* secure (even strongly-adaptively secure). Existing statistically-secure VSS protocols [18,26,31,35] are not suitable for our needs due to either not being adaptively secure (see [18]) or not incurring the above costs. Furthermore, several common techniques for achieving statistical security, such as dynamically electing a *small* (for instance, of size $o(n)$) committee are also not acceptable, as an adaptive adversary can corrupt the elected committee dynamically.

Discussions

Applications. Protocols in the MPC literature are usually given in the broadcast hybrid model, and improving broadcast automatically improves the complexity of protocols or other building blocks. For example, the VSS protocol of [3], when using the broadcast protocol of [2], results in $O(m \cdot n \log n + n^4 \log n)$ for sharing m secrets. In particular, it means that if one has to share $m = n^2 \log^2 n$ secrets, the protocol runs in $O(n^4 \log n)$, i.e., an overhead of $\approx O(n^2)$ per secret. The same protocol of [3], using our broadcast, results in $O(m \cdot n \log n + n^3 \log^2 n)$ bits for sharing m secrets, that is, for the same m as before it runs in $O(n^3 \log^2 n)$, i.e., an overhead of $O(n)$ per secret.

Worst-Case Number of Rounds. Broadcast protocols [2,20,25] in expected constant number of rounds work by repeating some randomized process (oblivious leader election) that succeeds with a constant probability. If not succeeded, there is a repetition. This leads to a protocol that might never terminate. Such protocols can be transformed into protocols in strict polynomial time, using the approach of Goldreich and Petrank [24]. E.g., after $O(\log n)$ unsuccessful iterations, the parties can run the $O(n)$ rounds protocol for broadcast with guaranteed termination. This results in a protocol that is perfectly secure and runs in an expected constant number of rounds, and $O(n)$ rounds in the worst case.

Adaptive Security. It is well known that any perfectly secure protocol that is secure against a static adversary, (and in addition satisfies some natural properties) is also adaptively secure [13]. Therefore, at first sight, it seems unclear why in Theorem 1.4 we require that the statistically-secure protocol would be adaptively secure. We remark that the approach of [13] does not necessarily preserves the communication complexity. Moreover, we obtain perfect security (and thus also adaptive security) only after following the approach of Goldreich and Petrank [24]. For instance, assume an OLE which is not adaptively secure, and thus a corrupted adversary can make the OLE to always fail (we stress that this is not the case in our protocol, but we give it just as an example). As a result, after $O(n)$ unsuccessful iterations, the parties would always have to run the $O(n)$ rounds protocol with guaranteed termination. The resulting protocol is perfectly secure with an expected $O(1)$ rounds against a static adversary, but with $\Theta(n)$ rounds against an adaptive adversary. Using adaptively-secure VSS guarantees that we successfully terminate after (expected) $O(1)$ rounds even when the adversary is adaptive. This is why in all statistically-secure sub-protocols that we have, we explicitly require adaptive security.

Simultaneous Termination. Any broadcast protocol with $o(t)$ expected rounds cannot guarantee simultaneous termination. This raises a difficulty when sequentially composing such protocols – parties are not necessarily synchronized. This issue was addressed in Lindell, Lysyanskaya and Rabin [29], Katz and Koo [25] and Cohen, Coretti, Garay and Zikas [17], and we refer the reader there for further details.

We use a standalone, simulation-based definition as in [12]. This definition does not capture rounds in the ideal functionality or that there is no simultaneous termination. The work of [17] shows that one can compile a protocol using deterministic termination hybrids (as the ideal functionality that we provide) into a protocol that uses an expected constant number of rounds protocol for emulating those hybrids.

1.2   Related Work

Broadcast is an essential primitive and was studied extensively over the years. It is known that perfect byzantine agreement and broadcast are impossible for $t \geq n/3$ [28,33]. Fischer and Lynch [22] showed that in any deterministic broadcast, there exists an execution that takes at least $t + 1$ rounds. Rabin [34] and Ben-Or [8] studied the effect of randomization on round complexity, and Feldman and Micali [20] gave the first protocol with an expected constant round protocol for byzantine agreement with optimal resilience. We report the progress of broadcast protocols over the years in Table 1.

Table 1. The complexity of our protocols and comparison to previous works of broadcast and parallel broadcast. Total communication is given in bits.

Protocol	Total Communication	Rounds
Broadcast		
Coan et al. [16], Berman et al. [11]	$O(n^2 L)$	$O(n)$
[11,16]+Chen [14]	$O(nL + n^2 \log n)$	
Katz and Koo [25]	$O(n^2 L) + E(O(n^6 \log n))$	
[25] + Nayak et al. [30]	$O(nL) + E(O(n^7 \log n))$	Expected
Abraham et al. [2]	$O(nL) + E(O(n^4 \log n))$	Constant
Our Work	$O(nL) + E(O(n^3 \log^2 n))$	
Parallel Broadcast		
Chen [14]	$O(n^2 L + n^3 \log n)$	$O(n)$
Katz and Koo [25]	$O(n^2 L) + E(O(n^6 \log n))$	
Abraham et al. [2]	$O(n^2 L) + E(O(n^4 \log n))$	Expected Constant
Our Work	$O(n^2 L) + E(O(n^3 \log^2 n))$	

Gradecast was introduced by Feldman and Micali [20], and was improved over the years (e.g., [1,2]). Gradecast is used as a building block for multiple consensus algorithms, e.g., multi-consensus, approximate agreement [9], or for Phase-King [5].

Verifiable secret sharing was introduced by Chor et al. [15]. The first perfectly secure verifiable secret sharing was presented by Ben Or, Goldwasser, and Wigderson [10] and by Feldman [21]. Abraham et al. [2] showed how to distribute $O(n)$ secrets at the same cost as one VSS invocation, which led to reduce the cost of Broadcast as well. In another work, Abraham et al. [3] showed how to batch many instances of VSS together while keeping the same broadcast cost among all instances as just a single instance, to reduce the cost of MPC protocols in the perfect settings. The protocol of [3] serves as our starting point for the VSS protocol, as it reduces the broadcast cost of the dealer from $O(n^2 \log n)$ to $O(n \log n)$.

The parallel broadcast protocol of [36] for $L = 1$, incurs a total communication $O(n^2 \kappa^4)$ assuming a trusted PKI, where κ is the security parameter.

2   Technical Overview

The construction of broadcast in an expected constant number of rounds is quite complex and consists of several different building blocks. For a brief overview of the structure of such protocols, we refer the reader to the full version [6], which provides a glossary for the different primitives used and can be used as a reference when reading other parts of the paper. In the following, we overview our contributions in two primitives, each can be studied and analyzed independently and regardless to broadcast. We overview our oblivious leader election (Sect. 2.1) and our statistically secure VSS (Sect. 2.2). We provide some conclusions in Sect. 2.3.

2.1   Efficient Oblivious Leader Election

Oblivious leader election is a protocol where the parties try to elect one of them as a leader, uniformly at random. Each party has no input, and each party outputs an index in $\{1, \ldots, n\}$. We might have three possible outcomes: (1) All parties output the same index $j \in \{1, \ldots, n\}$, and P_j is honest; (2) All parties agree on the same index $i \in \{1, \ldots, n\}$, but P_i is corrupted; (3) There is no agreement on the output index. The goal is to achieve outcome (1) with some constant probability (and a strict constant number of rounds). Once outcome (1) occurs, then the broadcast protocol terminates successfully. If (2) or (3) occur, then we re-run OLE, leading to an overall broadcast protocol that runs in expected constant number of rounds.

The main idea in [2,20,25] to elect a leader is to pick a random value c_j for each one of the parties P_j. The value c_j is chosen collectively by all parties. Then, the elected leader is the one for which c_j is minimal. Towards that end, in [2,20, 25] each party P_i chooses n random values uniformly at random, $c_{i \to 1}, \ldots, c_{i \to n}$, where each $c_{i \to j}$ should be interpreted as the contribution of P_i to P_j. The parties define the value $c_j = \sum_{i=1}^{n} c_{i \to j}$ to be the random value associated with P_j. This guarantees that even if some corrupted parties contribute values that are not uniformly random, each c_j is still random.

To make this idea work and prevent the corrupted parties from biasing those random values, we need to implement a mechanism that achieves hiding and binding, like a commitment scheme. A mechanism that allows exactly that in the information-theoretic setting is a verifiable secret sharing. Each party P_i verifiably secret shares $c_{i \to 1}, \ldots, c_{i \to n}$. Then, after all parties share their values, all parties reconstruct all secrets. Hiding guarantees that the shares do not provide any information about the secrets, which means that the adversary must choose its contributions independently of the contributions of the honest parties. Binding guarantees that once the sharing phase is concluded, the dealer cannot change its decision, and reconstruction is always guaranteed. Therefore, the adversary cannot bias the result by either opening different values than what it initially committed to, or selectively failing particular reconstructions.

Our OLE. Our conceptual contribution is that, at least at the intuitive level, the embedded error in the functionality of OLE allows us to use statistically secure building blocks to realize OLE. Specifically, all we care about is that outcome (1) occurs with a constant probability. Therefore, we can relax the requirements from the protocol, and achieve a more efficient construction.

Reducing the Amount of Secrets. When designing a perfectly secure protocol, we have to guarantee that for each party P_i, there is at least one *honest* party P_j that contributed to the value c_i. Since the number of corrupted parties might be up to $n/3$, it implies that each party must receive at least $n/3 + 1$ contributions, i.e., we have $O(n^2)$ secrets in total that have to be shared. This is why each party just contributes to all other parties in the protocols of [2,20,25]. However, when designing a statistically secure protocol, it suffices that *with high enough probability*, for each party P_i there is at least one *honest* party P_j that contributed $c_{j \to i}$ to the value c_i. This guarantees that c_i is uniform.

Towards that end, instead of each P_j picking n random values, we instruct it to just pick $O(\text{poly} \log n)$ random values, together with $O(\text{poly} \log n)$ random parties that it contributes to. The identities of which parties P_j contributes to are secret shared as well to guarantee that the adversary cannot pick which parties to contribute to after seeing the choices made by the honest parties. We show that this simple mechanism suffices to guarantee that with high probability, all parties have at least one honest party that contributed to their value, and therefore, all values $c_1, \ldots, c_n$ are random.

Moderated VSS. The above description is oversimplified. Specifically, one problem that arises is that the VSS itself uses broadcast as a primitive while we use OLE to implement broadcast. To avoid this circularity, the broadcast inside the VSS is replaced with a weaker primitive called gradecast. Gradecast (see the glossary in [6]) is a relaxation of broadcast where the sender sends a message M to all parties, and each party P_i outputs some message together with a grade. The guarantee is that if the sender is honest, then all honest parties output the same message (agreement) and with a high grade; but this is not necessarily true if the sender is corrupted. In that case, different parties might receive different messages (and with low grades). It is essential to note that the substitution of gradecast for broadcast within the VSS framework introduces a degree of uncertainty. This uncertainty stems from the fact that parties may not unanimously agree on whether to accept or reject the shared information, leading to potential divergence of outcomes within the VSS protocol.

The protocol of [25] works by having a designated party, called "a moderator", to be responsible for all gradecasts, so that if something goes wrong, we can know who is to blame (somewhat similar to the concept of identifiable abort in secure computation). Namely, whenever the VSS instructs a party to broadcast a message – that party gradecasts it; Moreover, the moderator then has to repeat the message (i.e., gradecast it), and parties proceed with the message gradecasted by the moderator. At the end of the sharing phase, each party outputs, together with the shares, a grade for the moderator in $\{0,1\}$. For instance, if a party P_j sees that the moderator repeats a different message than the one gradecsated by some party P_k (and was previously received with a high grade) – then clearly the moderator is malicious, and P_j sets the grade of the moderator to be 0.

At the end of this step, we have the guarantee that if the moderator is honest, all honest parties give grade 1 to the moderator, and we will always have an agreement on the VSSes it moderates. This is true for both the case where the dealer is honest, or the case where the dealer is corrupted, regardless of whether the parties accept or reject the shares. If the moderator is dishonest, then we might not have an agreement, but it is enough that one honest party believes that the moderation was successful to guarantee that the underlying VSS was successful (i.e., all parties do agree whether to accept or reject the shares, but some might be uncertain of whether moderation was successful).

The protocol of [25] proceeds as follows:

1. For every $(i, j) \in [n^2]$ run a moderated VSS where P_i is the dealer and P_j is the moderator, and the secret is some random $c_{i \to j}$ chosen by P_i.
2. Reconstruct all secrets.
3. Each P_k sets $\mathsf{Successful}_k = \emptyset$; Add j to $\mathsf{Successful}_k$ if P_j successfully moderated all the n instances it moderated, and set $c_j = \sum_{\ell=1}^{n} c_{\ell \to j}$.
4. Each P_k chooses as a leader P_j for which c_j is minimal among all indices in $\mathsf{Successful}_k$.

All honest parties are included in all $\mathsf{Successful}_k$ for every honest k, and they see the same value c_j. If some honest party added to $\mathsf{Successful}_k$ some corrupted party P_i, then c_i must be uniform. A simple argument shows that an honest leader is chosen and agreed upon among all honest parties with some constant probability.

Reducing the Amount of VSSes. In [25] there are n^2 independent instances of moderated VSS. As mentioned, we reduced the number of different secrets to $O(n \log n)$. Moreover, each party (a dealer) chooses randomly which $O(\log n)$ parties (moderators) it contributes to. Furthermore, we mentioned that which parties P_j contributes to must be kept secret at the sharing phase. This means that a party cannot know in advance which instances it has to moderate – those are chosen dynamically by the different dealers.

We address this challenge by implementing a novel moderation approach. Instead of assigning a single moderator to oversee each instance of VSS, all participating parties collectively assume the role of moderators for every instance. That is, we can envision each VSS execution as n parallel executions, with the same dealer, the same secret, but each instance is moderated by a different moderator. The moderation mechanism relies on the fact that at least two-thirds of the moderators are honest. As a result, we can look at the majority of the n different executions. If the dealer is honest, then all honest parties output, at the end of the reconstruction phase, the secret that the dealer shared. If the dealer is dishonest, then we might have disagreements as different moderators can make the VSS go into different directions. However, if one honest party believes that the moderation of some P_j was successful, then all honest parties unanimously output the same secret in the instance where P_j moderated.

Efficiency. The above mechanism is now problematic from an efficiency perspective. In particular, we tried to reduce the number of VSS executions from n^2 to $O(n \log n)$; instead, in each instance we have n moderators, and so we get $O(n^2 \log n)$ executions! Each VSS has $O(n^2 \log^2 n)$ bits over point-to-point and $O(n \log n)$ bits gradecasted, which results in a total of $O(n^4 \log n)$ bits over point-to-point.

To circumvent this issue, we first note that the point-to-point messages should not be repeated between the n different moderators inside a VSS execution. Moreover, following the idea of [2], we let the dealer moderate all messages except for the last message in which the execution "forks" into n different executions, corresponding to the n moderators. Each moderator echos just the last round (a vote on whether to accept or reject the shares of the dealer).

However, this idea alone does not fully address our requirements. Even echoing the last message proves to be prohibitively costly. To put it into perspective, echoing n bits of votes across n dealers, overseen by n moderators, results in the gradecast of n^3 bits. When accounting for the inherent overhead of gradecast, we are confronted once again with a total communication cost of $O(n^4)$.

To achieve the desired communication efficiency, we implement a batching mechanism wherein a single message is echoed by each moderator, applicable to the n distinct dealers they oversee. In essence, this identical message is utilized across multiple VSS executions, providing a substantial reduction in communication complexity. In [20], there are n^2 independent executions, one for each $(i, j) \in [n]^2$ where P_i is the dealer, and P_j is the moderator. In [2], there are n independent executions, for every P_i, $i \in [n]$, where each execution is one dealer with n moderators at the same time. In our case, we have one big execution that contains $O(n \log n)$ secrets. That is, in our case, all the different VSSes intertwine - the same message of the moderator is used across the different dealers.

More precisely, each moderator gradecasts a single message of size $O(n)$, and this message is shared across all executions, serving as a universal indicator for which dealers' shares should be accepted or rejected. In the context of the n moderators, our approach results in a gradecast of $\tilde{O}(n^2)$ bits, which, when factoring the gradecast overhead, totals to $\tilde{O}(n^3)$. This optimization substantially improves the overall communication complexity. We refer the reader to Sects. 5 and 6 for more details.

2.2 Efficient Statistical VSS

We show a statistically secure VSS with low broadcast cost. We start with a brief overview of the VSS protocol of Ben Or, Goldwasser and Wigderson [10]; we then overview the VSS protocol of Abraham et al. [3] and proceed to our protocol. At a very high level, in [10], each party broadcasts $O(n \log n)$ bits and the dealer might broadcast up to $O(n^2 \log n)$ bits. The work of [3] shows how to reduce the broadcast cost of the dealer to $O(n \log n)$. Our goal is to reduce the cost of all parties except the dealer to $O(\log^2 n)$ bits, albeit achieving only statistical security (or even $O(\log n)$ bits, with a one over poly error probability). Thus, in total we have $O(n \log n)$ bits broadcasted.

In this overview, we describe a statistically-secure protocol with negligible error probability (in n), while for our OLE it suffices to have a one over poly error.

Overview of the VSS of [10]. To share a secret s, the dealer chooses a bivariate polynomial $S(x,y) = \sum_{k=0}^{t} \sum_{\ell=0}^{t} s_{k,\ell} x^k y^\ell$ of degree t in both x and y, where $s_{0,0} = s$. The protocol is as follows:

1. **Sharing:** The dealer gives to each P_i its shares $(f_i(x), g_i(y)) = (S(x,i), S(i,y))$.
2. **Pairwise consistency check:** P_i sends to P_j the points $(f_i(j), g_i(j)) = (S(j,i), S(i,j)) = (g_j(i), f_j(i))$. If P_i sees that the shares it received from the dealer do not agree with the points it received from P_j it publicly **broadcasts** a complaint $\mathsf{complaint}(i,j,f_i(j),g_i(j))$.
3. **The dealer resolves complaints:** Note that in each complaint, P_i is supposed to provide the values it received from the dealer, not those that it received from P_j. If the dealer notices some public complaint that is wrong, i.e., contains points that it did not provide P_i, it completely reveals the shares of that complaining party, by **broadcasting** $(i, S(x,i), S(i,y))$.
4. If a party P_j sees that (1) all polynomials that the dealer made public agree with its private share; (2) its share was not made public; (3) if there is a joint complaint - two parties P_k and P_ℓ that disagree with one another, then the dealer must publicly reveal the share of one of them. If all those conditions are met, then P_i is happy. If there are $2t+1$ parties that are happy, then the shares are accepted.

If the dealer is honest, then their shares are always consistent and honest parties never complain on honest parties; Moreover, all honest parties are happy. Furthermore, the adversary learns nothing new in the verification process – note that all possibly revealed shares are shares of corrupted parties, which the adversary has anyways.

If the dealer is corrupted, then $2t+1$ parties that are happy implies that there is a core set of at least $t+1$ honest parties that are happy. The shares of these honest parties must agree with each other; otherwise, those parties would have raised a complaint and the dealer must have publicly reveal one of them. The shares of those happy honest parties uniquely define a bivariate polynomial $S'(x,y)$ of degree t in both variables. Moreover, all other honest parties must hold shares on that polynomial – if some honest P_i initially held a polynomial that disagrees with some P_j that is in the core set, then both P_i and P_j raised a complaint. Since P_j is in the core set, then the dealer must have resolved this complaint by revealing the share of P_i, and the entire core verified this polynomial (and therefore, it must agree with $S'(x,y)$).

Costs, and the VSS Protocol of [3]. All broadcasts in the above protocol are marked in **bold**: Each party might broadcast up to $O(n)$ complaints; The dealer might broadcast $O(n^2 \log n)$ bits (e.g., revealing the shares of t parties). The protocol of [3] provides a key improvement that we borrow: it reduces the broadcast cost of the dealer from $O(n^2 \log n)$ to $O(n \log n)$. The goal was to allow batching of many parallel instances of VSS (with the same dealer) with the same broadcast cost of just one instance. Towards that end, all broadcasts made by the dealer should not be instance specific (e.g., revealing shares), but information that is useful across multiple instances. We use batching and benefit from this reduction in the broadcast cost of the dealer.

To elaborate further, instead of the dealer broadcasting the shares of each party that falsely complained, [3] let the dealer just broadcast a set CONFLICTS of the identities of parties that raised false complaints. In a sense, the dealer "revokes" the shares of all parties in CONFLICTS. Yet, the parties cannot conclude the protocol unless all parties in CONFLICTS receive correct shares. At this point, there are three possible outcomes:

1. Discard the dealer - this might occur when there is a joint complaint that was not resolved (P_i complaint against P_j but none of them is in CONFLICTS), or when the dealer broadcasts a set CONFLICTS that contains more than t parties.
2. If $|\text{CONFLICTS}| > t/2$ then there are too many shares "to correct". Instead of publicly broadcasting the shares of those parties, they are all just set to be 0, and the protocol is restarted while the dealer chooses a new bivariate polynomial where all the shares of all parties in CONFLICTS are set to be 0. In that case, the dealer, in a sense, publicly reveals their shares, but without broadcasting them. In the next iteration, parties do not expect to receive shares from parties in CONFLICTS, and each party P_i verifies that $f_i(j) = g_i(j) = 0$ for $j \in$ CONFLICTS. Formally, the parties maintain a public set ZEROS of parties whose shares are set to be 0 and before the next iteration ZEROS is updated to ZEROS $\cup$ CONFLICTS. Note that we can restart only once as restarting twice means that the dealer tries to revoke $> t/2 + t/2 = t$ parties ($|\text{ZEROS}| > t/2$ and $|\text{CONFLICTS}| > t/2$) and is being discarded.
3. Otherwise, the parties proceed to a sub-protocol where they reconstruct all shares of parties in CONFLICTS, with the help of the dealer. We elaborate on this part later below.

Our Goal: Reducing the Broadcast Cost. Note that if the parties decide to proceed, then we have binding – there is a unique bivariate polynomial $S(x, y)$ of degree at most t in x and y, such that all honest parties that are not in CONFLICTS hold shares on $S(x, y)$. This is because each pair of honest parties that disagree with each other must have raised a joint complaint, and the dealer must have included at least one of them in CONFLICTS. Therefore, all shares of honest parties not in CONFLICTS must agree, and thus define a bivariate polynomial of the appropriate degree. Moreover, note that all honest parties that are not in CONFLICTS have shares, and that $|\text{CONFLICTS}| < t/2$; as such, at least $t + t/2 + 1$ honest parties have shares (as opposed to just $t + 1$ as the core set in [10]) – not only that there is a well defined polynomial, but there is also some redundancy.

For reconstructing the shares of parties in CONFLICTS, it is crucial that all honest parties that are not in CONFLICTS have shares that agree with each other. However, this is achieved using the fact that each party complains against each party that they did not agree with. But this requires a high broadcast cost.

To reduce the broadcast cost, we instruct each party to limit the number of complaints they file. Specifically, each party now randomly samples $O(\log^2 n)$ complaints out of the $O(n)$ that it might have. This raises two questions – (1) why $O(\log^2 n)$ complaints suffice; (2) What if P_i chooses P_j but P_j picked other parties? In that case, we would not have a joint complaint, and the dealer can just ignore complaints without being discarded.

Addressing the second question is easy. We just add one more round of complaints – if a party P_i complains against P_j, and P_j did not choose to complain against P_i in the first round of complaints, then it complains against it at the second round of complaints. This approach effectively doubles the number of complaints, maintaining the overall count at $O(\log^2 n)$ per party. However, this additional step guarantees that if two honest parties disagree, and one picks the other in its random choices, then all parties will see a joint complaint, forcing the dealer to resolve it.

To address the first question, we claim that with high probability – $O(\log^2 n)$ complaints by each party suffice to have binding with overwhelming probability (in n). To see why it holds, consider for simplicity the case where all honest parties (that are not in CONFLICTS) agree with each other, except for some party P_i. In that case, we have a set of $t + t/2$ honest parties that agree with each other. Moreover, P_i has a polynomial of degree t – and therefore, *it must disagree with at least $t/2$ parties* in the core, and not just one. Each one of these parties picks $O(\log^2 n)$ random complaints – the probability that none of those random choices made by either i, or by those $t/2$ parties that disagree with P_i, is bounded by $((1 - 1/n)^{t/2})^{\log^2 n}$, which is negligible in n. This argument is generalized to other cases beyond this simple case of all honest parties agreeing but one. We remark again that for our purpose of broadcast, it suffices that each party chooses $O(\log n)$ complaints out of the $O(n)$ that it might have; this results in an error probability of $O(1/\text{polyn})$.

Reconstruction of Shares for Parties in CONFLICTS. In the second stage of the protocol, the parties face the challenge of reconstructing the shares of all parties within the CONFLICTS set on the bivariate polynomial $S(x, y)$. We cannot simply adopt the approach used in [10], where the dealer broadcasts these shares, because doing so would require a broadcast of $O(n^2 \log n)$ bits by the dealer. Moreover, it's not feasible for each party P_k (for $k \notin$ CONFLICTS) to directly transmit the value $f_k(j)$ to each party P_j (for $j \in$ CONFLICTS), as in the worst-case scenario, where we have $t+t/2+1$ correct points and possibly t errors, party P_j might fail to decode its share. Similarly, public reconstruction (utilizing the dealer to eliminate errors) is not viable either, as it would necessitate each party ($k \notin$ CONFLICTS) to broadcast $O(n \log n)$ bits, once again resulting in a total broadcast of $O(n^2 \log n)$ bits. We remark that public reconstruction is the approach taken in [3]. Here we take a different route to reduce the broadcast complexity.

Instead of reconstructing the f and g polynomials of parties in CONFLICTS as in [3], we reconstruct just the points $g_j(0) = S(j, 0)$ for each party $j \in$ CONFLICTS. This suffices, as together with the shares of the parties that are in CONFLICTS, the parties can reconstruct the polynomial $S(x, 0)$ in the reconstruction phase, which suffices for reconstructing $S(0, 0)$. As an immediate consequence, our protocol for the reconstruction of the shares for parties in CONFLICTS requires each of the parties to broadcast only $O(\log n)$ bits.

Assume without loss of generality, and for simplicity of notation, that the set CONFLICTS $= \{1, \ldots, c\}$ where $c \leq t/2$. Consider the $c \times t$ bivariate polynomial $V(x, y) = \sum_{j=1}^{c} x^{j-1} \cdot S(j, y)$. Our goal is to publicly reconstruct the degree c univariate polynomial $f_0^V(x) := V(x, 0) := \sum_{j=1}^{c} x^{j-1} \cdot S(j, 0)$. Observe that the coefficients for this polynomial are $S(j, 0)$ for every $j \in$ CONFLICTS. The parties will reconstruct this polynomial $V(x, 0)$ publicly, and then they can recover $S(1, 0), \ldots, S(c, 0)$, as required. Moreover, note that this is a polynomial of degree at most $c \leq t/2$.

Towards that end, each party P_k for $k \notin$ CONFLICTS can locally compute

$$f_k^V(x) := V(x, k) = \sum_{j=1}^{c} x^{j-1} \cdot S(j, k) = \sum_{j=1}^{c} x^{j-1} \cdot f_k(j) .$$

Each P_k sends $f_k^V(i)$ to each party P_i for $i \notin$ CONFLICTS. Now each such party P_i tries to reconstruct $V(i, y)$ from all the points $(f_k^V(i))_{k \notin \mathsf{CONFLICTS}}$ that it received. Note that $V(i, y)$ is of degree t, and since $|\mathsf{CONFLICTS}| \leq t/2$, P_i receives at least $t + t/2 + 1$ correct points, but might receive up to t incorrect points. Once received more than $t/2$ incorrect points, there is no unique reconstruction. In that case, P_i broadcasts complaint(i). If P_i successfully learns $V(i, y)$, then it can compute $f_0^V(i) = V(i, 0)$ and publish it. The dealer (which knows $V(x, y)$) listen to all published messages, and add to a set Bad all parties that complaints or that published incorrect values. The dealer broadcasts Bad.

The parties discard the dealer if Bad is too large, or restart the protocol if $|\mathsf{Bad}| > t/2$. Otherwise, $|\mathsf{Bad}| \leq t/2$, and the dealer "confirmed" $n - |\mathsf{CONFLICTS}| - |\mathsf{Bad}| \geq n - t/2 - t/2 \geq 2t + 1$ points on a univariate polynomial $f_0^V(x)$. All the points on this polynomial are public, and the dealer must take care that all points (for those it did not include in Bad) must lie on a unique univariate polynomial of degree at most $c \leq t/2$ (by including parties in Bad if some point is incorrect). If not, then the dealer is publicly discarded. Therefore, we are guaranteed that all parties have $f_0^V(x)$, and from its coefficients, all parties learn the values $g_1(0), \ldots, g_c(0)$.

We note that the above share reconstruction protocol is *perfectly* secure (as opposed to the first part, which was just statistically secure). Moreover, each party broadcasts just $O(\log n)$ bits, and the dealer broadcasts $O(n \log n)$ bits, leading to a total of $O(n \log n)$ bits broadcasted.

2.3 Putting It All Together

We now present our overall broadcast protocol, which follows the paradigm of [20, 25]. We also refer the reader to [6] for an overview of the different primitives. To broadcast a message L:

1. The sender gradecasts the message L. Each party receives a message L_i with a grade $g_i \in \{0, 1, 2\}$.
2. The parties run Byzantine agreement on the grade g_i. If $g_i = 2$ then the input of the Byzantine agreement is 1. Otherwise, it is 0. Byzantine agreement intuitively works as follows:
   (a) The parties try to see if they all hold the same bit as input. Along the way, they send to each other the input bit. If they agree - they halt and output that bit.
   (b) If there is no agreement – they obliviously elect a leader. They run the protocol again with the leader's value that was sent in the previous step.

Gradecasting a message of size L requires $O(nL + n^2 \log n)$ communication [37]. Our OLE requires $O(n^3 \log^2 n)$, and the additional messages of Byzantine agreement require $O(n^2)$ bits per iteration. Overall we get $O(nL)$ plus expected $O(n^3 \log^2 n)$ with an expected constant number of rounds. The costs are described in Fig. 1. We denote the costs that we improve in red in Fig. 1a and in green in Fig. 1b.

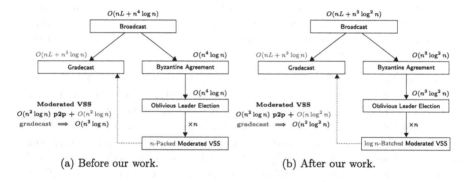

(a) Before our work.   (b) After our work.

Fig. 1. The structure of Broadcast, including costs before and after our improvements. Our improvements are in oblivious leader election and in (moderated) batched VSS. We use the gradecast protocol of [37] which we denote in blue. (Color figure online)

Parallel Broadcast. For our parallel broadcast, we can follow the idea of Fitzi and Garay [23] and use a single election across all instances. That is, each party gradecasts its message, and then the parties run n instances of Byzantine agreement where they use the same leader across all n instances. Once an honest leader is chosen, all instances can reach agreement. Since we have n gradecasts, we get cost of $O(n^2 L + n^3 \log n)$ for the gradecasts, and in addition $O(n^3 \log^2 n)$ per instance of OLE, leading to $O(n^2 L)$ plus expected $O(n^3 \log^2 n)$ with expected constant number of rounds.

Organization. The rest of the paper is organized as follows. In Sect. 3, we provide the preliminaries, while some are deferred to the full version [6]. In Sect. 4 we provide our statistical verifiable secret sharing, and in Sect. 5 we provide our batched multi-moderated VSS. We present the OLE protocol in Sect. 6 and the broadcast protocol and parallel broadcast in Sect. 7.

3 Preliminaries

We consider the set of parties represented by identities in $[n] := \{1, \ldots, n\}$ who are connected by pair-wise private and authenticated channels. We alternate as convenient between referring to parties by their identity $i \in [n]$ or as P_i where $i \in [n]$. In our verifiable secret sharing protocol we assume the parties have access to a broadcast channel as well. Up to $t < n/3$ of the parties are maliciously corrupted by a *computationally unbounded* active adversary $\mathcal{A}$. Our security proofs are all in the standalone model for a static adversary. The standalone security implies adaptive security with inefficient simulation [13] and universal composability [12] due to [27]. We provide the formal security definition in the full version [6].

We also assume for our protocols the existence of a finite field $\mathbb{F}$ where $|\mathbb{F}| > n+1$ and the set of values $\{0, 1, \ldots, n\}$ is a distinct set of elements known apriori to all the parties.

In the full version [6], we provide additional definitions, including statistical security, hybrid model and composition, and some properties on bivariate polynomials. We also provide the ideal functionalities for our final primitives – Broadcast and Byzantine agreement.

Adaptive Security. As mentioned, we need to prove the security of our statistical primitives against an adaptive adversary (otherwise, since parts of our protocol are just statistically secure, adaptive security of those parts cannot be derived for free from [13]). We follow the definition of adaptive corruptions from [7]. However, our statistical primitives are *reactive* and we need to make slight changes to the definition from [7]. [7, Sect. 2.4] defines adaptive corruptions for a computation at each of the following stages: (1) before inputs; and (2) after inputs and computation; and (3) post-execution. It thus suffices to allow the adaptive ideal world adversary perform adaptive corruptions (1) before a reactive interaction; and (2) after the reactive interaction; and (3) after the ideal functionality has finished executing. Note that for an ideal functionality with exactly one interaction (non-reactive) the above is identical to the adaptive definition of [7].

4 Statistical Verifiable Secret Sharing

In this section, we provide our statistically secure verifiable secret sharing, which has low broadcast cost. In Sect. 4.1, we give the *sharing attempt* protocol, where the dealer tries to share its secret, but it might fail. At the end of an execution of the sharing attempt, there exists a set CONFLICTS of parties of size at most $t/2$ such that each honest party $P_j \notin$ CONFLICTS holds $f_j(x), g_j(y)$ where $f_j(x) = S(x, j)$, $g_j(y) = S(j, y)$ for some unique degree-(t, t) bivariate polynomial $S(x, y)$. Furthermore, if the dealer was honest, no honest party is included in CONFLICTS. Specifically, at the end of a sharing attempt, one of the following outcomes occurs:

1. If $|\text{CONFLICTS}| > t/2$, then the protocol is restarted (after publicly fixing the shares of the parties in CONFLICTS).
2. The dealer is discarded;
3. $|\text{CONFLICTS}| \leq t/2$. In this case, the protocol proceeds to reconstruct the shares of the parties in CONFLICTS. See Sect. 4.2.

4.1 Sharing Attempt

We realize the sharing attempt functionality (see the full version [6]) with only statistical security and hence we need to additionally prove the adaptive security of our protocol. In the ideal execution, the adversary may adaptively corrupt parties after each interaction between the parties and the ideal functionality.

Protocol 4.1: $\Pi_{\text{ShareAttempt}}$

Input: All parties input $\text{ZEROS} \subset [n]$. The dealer, denoted as the party P for simplicity, inputs a polynomial $S(x,y)$ with degree t in x and y, such that for each $P_i \in \text{ZEROS}$ it holds that $S(x,i) = 0$ and $S(i,y) = 0$.

The protocol:

1. **(Dealing shares)**: The dealer P sends $(f_i(x), g_i(y)) = (S(x,i), S(i,y))$ to $P_i \notin \text{ZEROS}$. Each $P_i \in \text{ZEROS}$ sets $(f_i(x), g_i(y)) = (0,0)$.

2. **(Pairwise Consistency Checks)**:
   (a) Each $P_i \notin \text{ZEROS}$ sends $(f_i(j), g_i(j))$ to every $P_j \notin \text{ZEROS}$. Let (f_{ji}, g_{ji}) be the values received by P_i from P_j.
   (b) Initialize a set $\text{Complaints}_i = \emptyset$. If it holds that $f_{ji} \neq g_i(j)$ or $g_{ji} \neq f_i(j)$ then add j to Complaints_i.
   (c) If there exists a $j \in \text{ZEROS}$ for which $f_i(j) \neq 0$ or $g_i(j) \neq 0$, then broadcast $(\text{complaint}, i)$.

3. **(Random Complaints)**:
   (a) P_i samples a set S_i by choosing m elements from $[n]$ (with replacements).
   (b) For every $j \in \text{Complaints}_i \cap S_i$, the party P_i broadcasts $(\text{complaint}, i, j, f_i(j), g_i(j))$.

4. **(Confirming Random Complaints)**:
   (a) For each P_j that broadcast $(\text{complaint}, j, i, \cdot, \cdot)$, if $j \in \text{Complaints}_i$ and P_j broadcasted at most R complaints in the previous step, then P_i also broadcasts $(\text{complaint}, i, j, f_i(j), g_i(j))$.

5. **(Conflict Resolution)**:
   (a) P sets $\text{CONFLICTS} = \phi$. Add $i \notin \text{ZEROS}$ to CONFLICTS if one of the following occurs: (a) P_i broadcasted $(\text{complaint}, i)$; (b) P_i broadcasted more than m complaints in Step 3b; (c) P_i broadcasted $(\text{complaint}, i, j, u, v)$ such that $u \neq S(j,i)$ or $v \neq S(i,j)$.
   (b) P broadcasts CONFLICTS.

6. **(Output)**:

(a) Each P_i outputs discard if any one of the following does not hold: (i) ZEROS $\cap$ CONFLICTS $= \phi$; (ii) |ZEROS $\cup$ CONFLICTS| $\leq t$; (iii) if P_i broadcasts (complaint, i) but $i \notin$ CONFLICTS; (iv) If P_i broadcasted more than m complaints in Step 3b but $i \notin$ CONFLICTS; (v) If P_i broadcasted (complaint, i, j, u_i, v_i) and P_j broadcasted (complaint, i, j, u_j, v_j) with $u_i \neq v_j$ or $v_i \neq u_j$, and neither i or j in CONFLICTS.

(b) If |CONFLICTS| $> t/2$, then each P_i outputs (detect, CONFLICTS).

(c) Else, $P_i \in$ CONFLICTS outputs (proceed, $\perp, \perp$, CONFLICTS) and $P_i \notin$ CONFLICTS outputs (proceed, $f_i(x), g_i(y)$, CONFLICTS).

The simulation for the sharing attempt protocol of [3] can be repurposed to work for our protocol; however, it is conditioned on the following event: *all conflicts between honest parties is resolved by the dealer.* Towards that end, we provide the following upper bound on the probability that the above event occurs and defer the proof for the security of Protocol 4.1 to the full version [6].

To formalize the above event, we first define a *clique*. A set $C \subseteq [n]$ is a clique if for each ordered pair $i, j \in C$ it holds that the parties P_i and P_j agreed with each other in Step 2c, i.e., P_i did not include P_j in Complaints$_i$.

Claim 4.2. *The probability that all honest parties (at the end of the protocol) output* proceed *but there is no clique $C \subseteq H$ among the honest parties (H is the set of parties that remain honest until the end of the protocol) that are not in* CONFLICTS *is at most $\epsilon = n \cdot e^{-m/6}$. Recall that m is the size of the set S_i chosen by each party P_i in Step 3b.*

Proof. Let $K = H \setminus$ CONFLICTS where H is the set of honest parties at the end of the protocol. Since |CONFLICTS| $\leq t/2$ and $|H| \geq 2t+1$, we have that $|K| \geq t + t/2 + 1$. Let Bad denote the following events:

Bad: *The parties output* proceed *but there is no clique among K; Namely, all parties in K output* proceed *but the maximal clique $C \subseteq K$ is of size $< |K|$, where C is a clique if for every $i, j \in C$ it holds that $i \notin$ Complaints$_j$ and $j \notin$ Complaints$_i$.*

Bad$_c$: *The parties output* proceed *but the maximal clique $C \subseteq K$ is of size c, where C is a clique if for every $i, j \in C$ it holds that $i \notin$ Complaints$_j$ and $j \notin$ Complaints$_i$.*

It is easy to see that Bad $= \bigcup_{c=1}^{|K|-1}$ Bad$_c$.

Bounding the Probability of Bad$_c$. We define different cases according to the size of c (the maximal clique). We start as a warm up with the case of $c = |K|-1$:

The Case of $c = |K| - 1$. In this case, the shares of the parties in C define a unique bivariate polynomial of degree $t \times t$. In particular, this means that there exists some P_j that can agree with at most t parties in C, that is, |Complaints$_j \cap C$| $\geq |C| - t = |K| - 1 - t$. When P_j broadcasts its complaints, it did not pick any one of those parties, and likewise, those $|K| - 1 - t \geq t + t/2 + 1 - 1 - t \geq t/2$ parties did not complain against P_j. Otherwise, we must have a joint complaint, and the dealer must have included one of the two parties in CONFLICTS or be discarded. In particular, each one of those $\geq t/2$ chose m elements in $[n]$, none of them is j. Therefore,

$$\Pr\left[\mathsf{Bad}_{|K|-1}\right] \leq \left(\left(\frac{n-1}{n}\right)^m\right)^{t/2} \leq \left(\left(1 - \frac{1}{n}\right)^n\right)^{m/6} \leq e^{-m/6}.$$

The Case of $c \geq t + 1$. As in the previous case, the shares of the parties in C define a unique bivariate polynomial of degree $t \times t$. Moreover, there is a set J of at least $|K| - c$ honest parties that are not in the clique C. Each one of those P_j, for $j \in J$ has $|\mathsf{Complaints}_j \cap C| \geq 1$, as otherwise we would have a larger clique. In fact, since the degree of the polynomial is t, P_j can agree with at most t parties in C. As such, $|\mathsf{Complaints}_j \cap C| \geq c - t\ (\geq 1)$ When randomly choosing the complaints, each P_j did not pick the $c - t$ parties it disagreed with from C. Likewise, there are at least $c - t$ parties in C that did not pick a corresponding (at least one) element in J, and the parties in C did not pick those parties in J. We get:

$$\Pr\left[\mathsf{Bad}_c\right] \leq \left(\left(\frac{n-1}{n}\right)^m\right)^{|K|-c} \cdot \left(\left(\frac{n-1}{n}\right)^m\right)^{c-t} \leq \left(\left(\frac{n-1}{n}\right)^m\right)^{t/2} \leq e^{-m/6},$$

where we use the fact that $|K| \geq t + t/2 + 1$ and so $|K| - t \geq t/2$.

The Case of $c < t + 1$. In that case, there is a set of $|K| - c \geq t/2$ parties, and each one of them disagrees with at least one party in C, and does not pick a disagreeing party when complaining. We have:

$$\Pr\left[\mathsf{Bad}_c\right] \leq \left(\left(\frac{n-1}{n}\right)^m\right)^{t/2} \cdot e^{-m/6}.$$

Putting It All Together. By a simple union bound, we can bound:
$\Pr\left[\mathsf{Bad}\right] \leq \sum_{c=1}^{|K|-1} \Pr\left[\mathsf{Bad}_c\right] \leq n \cdot e^{-m/6} = \epsilon.$ □

As mentioned before, the simulator constructed in the proof of security for the sharing attempt protocol of [3] can be re-purposed to work for our protocol. However, as our protocol is only statistically secure we cannot derive adaptive security directly from [13]. We provide the *adaptive* simulation security proof for our statistical sharing attempt protocol in the full version [6].

Theorem 4.3. *Protocol $\Pi_{\mathsf{ShareAttempt}}$ (Protocol 4.1), securely computes the functionality $\mathcal{F}_{\mathsf{ShareAttempt}}$ (see [6]) with statistical security, in the presence of a malicious* **adaptive** *adversary controlling at most $t < n/3$ except with probability $\epsilon = n \cdot e^{-m/6}$. The total communication complexity is $O(n^2 \log n)$ bits over point-to-point channels; The dealer broadcasts $O(n \log n)$ bits, and each other party broadcasts $O(m \log n)$ bits.*

4.2   Reconstructing Shares

In the reconstruction phase, each party $j \in$ CONFLICTS is able to reconstruct a share $s_j = S(j, 0)$. Note that the parties not in CONFLICTS do not learn their entire share but just s_j. Moreover, this is sufficient to guarantee reconstruction of $S(0, 0)$. Looking ahead, one of the following is possible after an execution of Protocol 4.4:

1. The parties in CONFLICTS successfully reconstruct their shares. In this case, the parties hold a sharing on the polynomial $q(x) = S(x, 0)$ (where the secret is $q(0) = S(0, 0)$ as required).
2. At most $t/2$ additional conflicts are identified. In this case, the protocol is restarted from the sharing attempt (Protocol 4.1).
3. More than $t/2$ additional conflicts are identified. In this case, the dealer is discarded.

Protocol 4.4: $\Pi_{\text{rec-shares}}$: A Protocol for Reconstructing the shares

Input: All parties hold the same set CONFLICTS and ZEROS. Each honest party not in CONFLICTS holds a pair of polynomials $(f_i(x), g_i(y))$, and it is guaranteed that all the shares of honest parties lie on the same bivariate polynomial $S(x, y)$ with degree at most t in x and y. Without loss of generality, let CONFLICTS = $\{1, \ldots, c\}$ where $c \leq t/2$.

The protocol:

1. Every party sets HAVE-SHARES = $[n] \setminus$ (ZEROS $\cup$ CONFLICTS).
2. **Computing $f_i^V(x)$:**
   (a) Each party $P_i \notin$ CONFLICTS computes the degree c polynomial:

$$f_i^V(x) := \sum_{k=1}^{c} x^{k-1} \cdot f_i(k) \ .$$

   It sends to each party P_j for $j \notin$ CONFLICTS the value $u_{i \to j} = f_i^V(j)$.
3. **Computing $g_i^V(y)$:**
   (a) Let $u_{j \to i}$ be the value that P_j sent P_i in the previous step (and take $u_{j \to i} = 0$ for $j \in$ ZEROS). P_i attempts to find a unique polynomial $g_i^V(y)$ of degree at most t satisfying $g_i^V(j) = u_{j \to i}$ for every $j \notin$ CONFLICTS, with at most $t/2$ errors.
   (b) If there is no unique reconstruction, then P_i broadcasts complaint(i).
   (c) If there is a unique reconstruction, then P_i broadcasts reveal($i, g_i^V(0)$).
4. **Dealer – Complaint Resolution**
   (a) The dealer sets Bad = ϕ. For each complaint(i) broadcasted by P_i, add i to Bad.
   (b) For every reveal(i, u_i) broadcasted by P_i, the dealer checks if

$$u_i = \sum_{k=1}^{c} i^{k-1} \cdot S(k, 0)$$

   If not, then it adds i to Bad. The dealer broadcasts Bad.

5. **Output:**
   (a) **Discard:** discard the dealer if any one of the following holds: (1) There exists P_i that broadcasted complaint(i) but $i \notin$ Bad; (2) If ZEROS $\cap$ Bad $\neq \emptyset$; (3) |ZEROS $\cup$ CONFLICTS $\cup$ Bad| $> t$; (4) If the set of points $K = \{(j, u_j)\}_{j \notin (\text{CONFLICTS} \cup \text{Bad} \cup \text{ZEROS})} \cup \{(j, 0)\}_{j \in \text{ZEROS}}$ not all lie on a univariate polynomial $f_0^V(y)$ of degree c.
   If any one of the above holds, output discard.
   (b) **Large detection:** Otherwise, if |Bad| $> t/2$ then output (detect, Bad).
   (c) **Proceed:** Otherwise, if P_i for $i \notin$ CONFLICTS outputs $g_i(0)$. P_i for $i \in$ CONFLICTS reconstructs $f_0^V(x)$ from the set of points K as above, and outputs the coefficient of the x^{i-1} term.

For brevity, we present the corresponding ideal functionality and the proof of the following theorem in the full version [6].

Theorem 4.5. $\Pi_{\text{rec-shares}}$ *(Protocol 4.4) securely computes the functionality* $\mathcal{F}_{\text{rec-shares}}$ *(see [6]) with perfect security, in the presence of a malicious adversary controlling at most $t < n/3$ parties. The total communication complexity is $O(n^2 \log n)$ bits over point-to-point channels; The dealer broadcasts $O(n \log n)$ bits and each other party broadcasts $O(\log n)$ bits.*

4.3   Statistical VSS Protocol

In the entire VSS protocol, the dealer first attempt to share its secret using the sharing attempt protocol. The parties then either proceed to discarding the dealer, or to another sharing attempt, or to reconstruct the shares of parties in CONFLICTS. We present the entire VSS protocol and the proof of secure in the full version [6].

Statistical Security After Composition. In the full version, we also show that our protocol actually achieves **adaptive** security, and realizes an $\mathcal{F}_{\text{VSS}}$ functionality (which is also formally defined in the full version). We obtain the following corollary:

Corollary 4.6. *There exists a protocol that statistically realizes the functionality $\mathcal{F}_{\text{VSS}}$ against $t < n/3$ **adaptive** corruptions such that the statistical error for the protocol is $\epsilon < 2n \cdot e^{-m/6}$.*

Note that in each invocation to Π_{VSS}, there is a statistical error of at most $n \cdot e^{-m/6}$ and due to the repetitions the number of invocations to $\mathcal{F}_{\text{ShareAttempt}}$ is at most 2. From the definition of statistical security, it holds that the statistical error for the composed sharing protocol is at most $2n \cdot e^{-m/6}$.

Batching. The protocol Π_{VSS} that we discussed so far incurs a communication complexity of $O(n^2 \log n)$ bits over the point-to-point channels. Additionally, each party broadcasts $O(m \log n)$ bits ($=$ poly $\log n$) and the dealer broadcasts $O(n \log n)$ bits. Towards reducing the cost, we batch the broadcast costs among multiple instances.

1. **Batching broadcast in the sharing attempt.** The dealer inputs L bivariate polynomials, and the same set ZEROS is used across all instances, that is, each bivariate has zero shares for parties in the set ZEROS. The parties chooses R elements and broadcasts complaints with respect to one of the bivariates where there was a conflict. The complaint is now of the form (complaint, $i, j, \ell, f_i^\ell(j), g_i^\ell(j)$) where $S^\ell(x, y)$ is the ℓth bivariate. The parties confirm the random complaints as before with ℓ included in the complaint. The dealer then computes a single CONFLICTS set after checking the complaints with each bivariate. As discussed in [3], a joint complaint in some instance (say the lexicographically smallest index) must be resolved by the dealer and consistency must hold across all bivariates.

2. **Batching dealer's broadcast in the share reconstruction.** We note that our share reconstruction protocol already batches the reconstruction of the shares of parties in CONFLICTS by embedding all the shares of parties in CONFLICTS in a polynomial $u(y)$ and robustly reconstructing $u(0)$. Thus, our protocol already performs a batching of the reconstruction of $|\text{CONFLICTS}| = O(n)$ values and it is unclear how the same technique can be extended to the reconstruction of $O(nL)$ values. However, the dealer computes a single Bad set by checking the parties' broadcasted values with each bivariate. After removing the parties in the dealer's broadcasted Bad set, the broadcasted values must determine a unique polynomial for each instance (else, the dealer is discarded). Hence, all the reconstructed shares must be correct on each bivariate. The dealer broadcasts $O(n \log n)$ bits however each party broadcasts $O(m \log n)$ bits.

The cost of the batched VSS is $O(Ln^2 \log n)$ bits on the point-to-point channels, the dealer broadcasts $O(n \log n)$ bits and each party broadcasts $O(m \log n)$ bits. Looking ahead, we will set $m = \text{poly} \log n$ and $L = m$ which allows us to achieve the reduced cost for oblivious leader election. The protocol is statistically secure, with statistical error $\epsilon < 2n \cdot e^{-m/6}$. The exact details appear in the full version [6].

5   Batched Multi-moderated Verifiable Secret Sharing

As mentioned in the overview (Sect. 2.1), we replace the broadcast in the VSS with a gradecast [37]. However, we need the help of moderators to make this substitution more robust. We use all parties as moderators. Corresponding to each moderator M_j, each party P_k holds a pair of flags $v_{M_j}^k$ and $d_{M_j}^k$:

- The flag $v_{M_j}^k \in \{0, 1\}$ indicates if P_k believes that M_j *moderated* the broadcasts correctly, that is, if the parties agree on the outputs of the moderated broadcasts. If at least one honest party P_k holds $v_{M_j}^k = 1$, then the moderated broadcast of M_j are identical to the actual broadcast. If M_j is honest, then each honest party P_k holds $v_{M_j}^k = 1$.
- The flag $d_{M_j}^k \in \{0, 1\}$ indicates if P_k accepts the dealer's share based on the simulated broadcast messages of M_j.

see the formal description of the functionality in the full version [6].

The Protocol. Our multi-moderated VSS protocol below is exactly the same as our VSS protocol with the broadcasts carefully replaced by simulated broadcasts. Until the output has to be computed, the dealer acts as the moderator for the broadcasts of the parties, that is, for each message m that needs to be broadcasted by a party, the party gradecasts m followed by the dealer's gradecast of the same message. Once the protocol reaches the output stage, we artificially add an additional round of public voting by the parties which is then moderated by every other party acting as a moderator. This additional round allows us to compress the size of the messages that the different n parties have to moderate.

Each party gradecasts the decision on the dealer (accept or reject). Each party acting as a moderator, then gradecasts the decision d on the dealer and a set of parties Bad such that:

1. d $= 1$ if and only if $t + 1$ at least accept votes were received with grade 2.
2. $k \in$ Bad if and only if P_k's vote was received with a grade < 2.

The flags for each moderator are then set by the parties based on the grades in the gradecast decisions and (d, Bad). Specifically, an honest party sets a high grade for a moderator if and only if any party that sent a vote with grade 0 is included in Bad and the decision d is consistent with the votes of parties not in Bad. We provide the ideal functionality $\mathcal{F}_{\text{mm-VSS}}$, the protocol, and the proof of the security of our protocol in the full version [6].

Corollary 5.1. *There exists a protocol that statistically realizes the functionality $\mathcal{F}_{\text{mm-VSS}}$ against $t < n/3$ corruptions such that the statistical error for the protocol is $\epsilon < 2n \cdot e^{-m/6}$.*

Efficiency: The protocol $\Pi_{\text{mm-VSS}}$ (defined in the full version) incurs a communication complexity of $O(n^3 \log n)$ bits over the point-to-point channels. However, we will utilize certain batching techniques to maintain a communication complexity of $O(n^3 \log n)$ bits when running $\Pi_{\text{mm-VSS}}$ in parallel for multiple dealers.

5.1   Reconstruction with Moderators

Protocol 5.2: $\Pi_{\text{mm-VSS}}^{\text{Rec}}$

Input: Each party P_i holds $s_i, (d_M^i)_{M \in [n]}$ and $(v_M^i)_{M \in [n]}$.

1. Each party sends s_i to all. Let $(s_1', \dots, s_n')$ be the shares received.
2. If $d_{M_j}^i = 1$ for at least $n - t$ parties M_j acting as the moderator, then use Reed-Solomon decoding to reconstruct the unique degree t polynomial $g(y)$ that agrees with at least $2t+1$ values $s_1', \dots, s_n'$ and set $s^i = g(0)$. If no unique decoding exists or if less than $n - t$ moderators rejected, then set $s^i = 0$.
3. **Output:** Output s^i.

We provide the proof of the following theorem in the full version [6].

Theorem 5.3. *If the dealer is honest, then all honest parties output the dealer's secret s. Else, if for each party $M_j \in [n]$ acting as a moderator, there exists an honest party P_k with $v_{M_j}^k = 1$, then each honest party P_k outputs the same secret $s^k = s'$.*

Efficiency: The protocol $\Pi_{\text{mm-VSS}}^{\text{Rec}}$ (Protocol 5.2) incurs a communication complexity of $O(n^2 \log n)$ bits over the point-to-point channels.

5.2 Batching

Looking ahead in our oblivious leader election, each party P_ℓ is required to share m ($=$ poly $\log n$) uniformly random values. We now show how each moderator M_j can batch the gradecast in the moderation phase (**Phase II**) across multiple instances of (moderated) sharing where each party P_ℓ acts as a dealer.

1. Before the moderation phase (**Phase II**), each party P_k gradecasts a bit a_k^ℓ denoting the decision on the instance of sharing where P_ℓ acts as a dealer.
2. M_j computes a single set Bad_{M_j} across all the instances. Specifically, M_j includes $i \in \text{Bad}_{M_j}$ if the gradecast of a_i^ℓ for any $\ell \in [n]$ by P_i yielded a grade < 2 for the moderator M_j.
3. M_j computes the majority decision among a_k^ℓ for each $\ell \in [n]$ and $k \notin \text{Bad}_{M_j}$ and denotes it as $d_{M_j}^\ell$.
4. M_j gradecasts $\left(d_{M_j}^\ell \right)_{\ell=1}^n$, Bad_{M_j}.

Each moderator M_j gradecasts $\Theta(n)$ bits (the n decisions $d_{M_j}^\ell$ and the set Bad_{M_j}) which incurs a total communication of $O(n^2 \log n)$ bits for M_j and $O(n^3 \log n)$ bits across all moderators. Naively gradecasting n different sets Bad_{M_j} requires each moderator M_j to gradecast $\Theta(n^2)$ bits which yields a total communication $O(n^3 \log n)$ bits for M_j and $O(n^4 \log n)$ bits across all moderators (which is not suitable in our case).

We denote the batched multi-moderated secret sharing as $\Pi_{\text{mm-bVSS}}$. For brevity, we present the corresponding batched ideal functionality and theorem in the full version [6].

6   Oblivious Leader Election

As mentioned before, we realize the same oblivious leader election functionality as in [2]. We describe the functionality in detail in the full version [6].

Protocol 6.1: Π_{OLE}

---

1. **Choose random hidden moderators:** Each party P_i samples a set of hidden moderators $\mathcal{M}_i$ by choosing $m < n$ elements from $[n]$ (with replacements).
2. **Choose and commit weights:** Each party P_i acts as a dealer and chooses $c_{i \to j}$ as random values in $\{1, \ldots, n^4\}$, for every $j \in \mathcal{M}_i$. P_i then runs the following m times in parallel, for each $\ell \in [m]$, where P_i acts as a dealer in each instance:
   (a) The dealer distributes the values $(j, c_{i \to j})$ for each $j \in \mathcal{M}_i$ using $\mathcal{F}_{\mathsf{mm\text{-}VSS}}$ where P_i is the dealer.
   (b) Each party P_k gets as output a share $s_k^{i,\ell}$, outputs $\mathsf{d}_{i,j}^k$ and a flag $v_{i,j}^k$ for each party P_j acting as moderator.
   Note that the above is run for all dealers $P_1, \ldots, P_n$ in parallel, where each dealer has m parallel instances (in total $m \cdot n$ invocations). Upon completion, let $\mathsf{Successful}_i$ be the set of moderators for which P_i holds a flag $v = 1$ in all executions, that is, $\mathsf{Successful}_i = \{j \mid v_{d,j}^i = 1 \text{ for all dealers } d \in [n]\}$.
3. **Reconstruct the weights and recipients and pick a leader:** The reconstruction phase, $\Pi_{\mathsf{mm\text{-}VSS}}^{\mathsf{Rec}}$ (Protocol 5.2) of each of the above mn instances of multi-moderated secret sharing is run in parallel to reconstruct the secrets previously shared.
   (a) Let $\mathcal{M}_i^k$ and the values $c_{i \to j}$ for each $i \in [n], j \in \mathcal{M}_i^k$ denote P_k's view of the set R_i and $c_{i \to j}$ for each $i \in [n], j \in \mathcal{M}_i$, that is, the reconstructed value for the instance where P_i was the dealer and chose $j \in \mathcal{M}_i$ as a hidden moderator (included in the reconstructed value for P_i's instance).
   (b) P_k sets $c_j^k = \sum\limits_{i, j \in \mathcal{M}_i^k} c_{i \to j} \mod n^4$ and outputs j that minimizes c_j^k among all $j \in \mathsf{Successful}_k$ (break ties arbitrarily).

The proof from [2,25] carries over almost verbatim in our case, conditioned on the following event: *For each party P_j which succeeds in the moderation, some honest party P_k included P_j in its hidden moderator set $\mathcal{M}_i$.* We present only the bound on the above event and defer the details of the proof to the full version [6]. To that end, we first define: $\mathsf{Successful} = \bigcup_{k \in H} \mathsf{Successful}_k$, where H is the set of all parties that were honest at the end of phase 2.. We now define Bad_j for $j \in \mathsf{Successful}$ which defines the event that the party j was not chosen as a hidden moderator by any honest dealer.

$\underline{\mathsf{Bad}_j}$: No $P_k \in H$ chose $j \in \mathcal{M}_k$.

We then define the event Bad as the disjunction of the events Bad_j over all $j \in \mathsf{Successful}$. If Bad does not occur, then for each $j \in \mathsf{Successful}$ there exists some honest party P_k that chose P_j as a hidden moderator, that is, $j \in \mathcal{M}_i$. Note that this is exactly the informal event we describe above.

$\underline{\mathsf{Bad}}$: $\bigcup_{j \in \mathsf{Successful}} \mathsf{Bad}_j$.

We now give a bound on the probability of Bad occurring.

Claim 6.2. *The probability that* Bad *occurs is at most* $n \cdot e^{-2m/3}$ *where each party chooses* m *hidden moderators in Protocol 6.1.*

Proof. We first upper bound $\Pr[\mathsf{Bad}_j]$ and use a union bound over all parties in Successful to give an upper bound on $\Pr[\mathsf{Bad}]$. The probability that no $k \in H$ chooses $j \in \mathcal{M}_k$ is $1 - 1/n$ for each independent sample. For $t < n/3$, it holds that $|H| \geq 2n/3$ and hence,

$$\Pr[\mathsf{Bad}_j] \leq \left(\left(1 - \frac{1}{n}\right)^m \right)^{|H|} \leq \left(\left(1 - \frac{1}{n}\right)^n \right)^{2m/3} \leq e^{-2m/3}.$$

From the definition of Bad and the fact that $|H| \leq n$, it must hold that $\Pr[\mathsf{Bad}] \leq n \cdot \Pr[\mathsf{Bad}_j] \leq n \cdot e^{-2m/3}$. □

For brevity, we present the proof of the following theorem in the full version [6], and formally define the $\mathcal{F}_{\mathsf{OLE}}$ functionality:

Theorem 6.3. *Protocol* Π_{OLE} *(Protocol 6.1), perfectly securely computes the functionality* $\mathcal{F}_{\mathsf{OLE}}$, *in the presence of a malicious adversary controlling at most* $t < n/3$ *parties.*

Efficiency: Each instance of $\Pi_{\mathsf{mm\text{-}VSS}}$ incurs a cost of $O(n^2 \log n)$ bits on the point-to-point channels and gradecast of $O(m \log n)$ bits by each party. Since there are $O(mn)$ instances (which have the required batching modifications), the total cost is thus $O(mn^3 \log n)$ bits. Fixing $m = 6 \log 4n$ (suffices to realize oblivious leader election) yields a total communication complexity of $O(n^3 \log^2 n)$.

7   Broadcast, and Parallel Broadcast

The protocols for Byzantine agreement, broadcast and parallel broadcast are identical to the protocols of [2,23,25] and we present them in the full version [6] for the completeness of our result.

Theorem 7.1. *There exists a perfect Byzantine agreement protocol that in the presence of a malicious adversary controlling at most* $t < n/3$ *parties and incurs a communication complexity of* $O(n^3 \log^2 n)$ *bits in expectation.*

Theorem 7.2. *There exists a perfect broadcast protocol in the presence of a malicious adversary controlling at most* $t < n/3$ *parties. For an input message* M *of length* L *bits, the protocol incurs a communication complexity of* $O(nL)$ *bits and an additional* $O(n^3 \log^2 n)$ *bits in expectation with* $O(1)$ *rounds in expectation.*

Parallel Broadcast. Consider the case when each party wishes to broadcast some message of size L bits each. As in [2,23], a single election can be used across the instances. Hence, we have the following corollary:

Corollary 7.3. *There exists a perfectly secure parallel-broadcast in the presence of a malicious adversary controlling at most $t < n/3$ parties. For n parties to each broadcast L bits, the protocol incurs a communication complexity of $O(n^2 L)$ bits and an additional $O(n^3 \log^2 n)$ bits in expectation with $O(1)$ rounds in expectation.*

Acknowledgements. We are grateful to Ittai Abraham and Eylon Yogev for helpful discussions.

References

1. Abraham, I., Asharov, G.: Gradecast in synchrony and reliable broadcast in asynchrony with optimal resilience, efficiency, and unconditional security. In: PODC 2022: ACM Symposium on Principles of Distributed Computing, Salerno, Italy, 25–29 July 2022, pp. 392–398. ACM (2022)
2. Abraham, I., Asharov, G., Patil, S., Patra, A.: Asymptotically free broadcast in constant expected time via packed VSS. In: Kiltz, E., Vaikuntanathan, V. (eds.) Theory of Cryptography - 20th International Conference, TCC 2022. LNCS, vol. 13747, pp. 384–414. Springer, Cham (2022). https://doi.org/10.1007/978-3-031-22318-1_14
3. Abraham, I., Asharov, G., Patil, S., Patra, A.: Detect, pack and batch: perfectly-secure MPC with linear communication and constant expected time. In: Hazay, C., Stam, M. (eds.) Advances in Cryptology - EUROCRYPT 2023. LNCS, vol. 14005, pp. 251–281. Springer, Cham (2023). https://doi.org/10.1007/978-3-031-30617-4_9
4. Abraham, I., et al.: Communication complexity of Byzantine agreement, revisited. Distrib. Comput. **36**(1), 3–28 (2023)
5. Abraham, I., Lewis-Pye, A.: Phase-king through the lens of gradecast: a simple unauthenticated synchronous Byzantine agreement protocol. Decentralized Thoughts, Blog Post (2022). https://decentralizedthoughts.github.io/2022-06-09-phase-king-via-gradecast/
6. Asharov, G., Chandramouli, A.: Perfect (parallel) broadcast in constant expected rounds via statistical VSS. IACR Cryptol. ePrint Arch. Paper 2024/376 (2024)
7. Asharov, G., Cohen, R., Shochat, O.: Static vs. adaptive security in perfect MPC: a separation and the adaptive security of BGW. In: 3rd Conference on Information-Theoretic Cryptography, ITC 2022. LIPIcs, vol. 230, pp. 15:1–15:16. Schloss Dagstuhl - Leibniz-Zentrum für Informatik (2022)
8. Ben-Or, M.: Another advantage of free choice: completely asynchronous agreement protocols (extended abstract). In: Proceedings of the Annual Symposium on Principles of Distributed Computing (PODC) (1983)
9. Ben-Or, M., Dolev, D., Hoch, E.N.: Brief announcement: simple gradecast based algorithms. In: Lynch, N.A., Shvartsman, A.A. (eds.) Distributed Computing, 24th International Symposium, DISC 2010, Cambridge, MA, USA, 13–15 September 2010. Proceedings. LNCS, vol. 6343, pp. 194–197. Springer, Cham (2010). https://doi.org/10.1007/978-3-642-15763-9_18
10. Ben-Or, M., Goldwasser, S., Wigderson, A.: Completeness theorems for non-cryptographic fault-tolerant distributed computation (extended abstract). In: Proceedings of Annual ACM Symposium on Theory of Computing (1988)

11. Berman, P., Garay, J.A., Perry, K.J.: Bit optimal distributed consensus. In: Baeza-Yates, R., Manber, U. (eds.) Computer Science. Springer, Cham (1992). https://doi.org/10.1007/978-1-4615-3422-8_27

12. Canetti, R.: Security and composition of multiparty cryptographic protocols. J. Cryptol. **13**(1), 143–202 (2000)

13. Canetti, R., Damgaard, I., Dziembowski, S., Ishai, Y., Malkin, T.: On adaptive vs. non-adaptive security of multiparty protocols. In: Pfitzmann, B. (ed.) EURO-CRYPT 2001. LNCS, vol. 2045, pp. 262–279. Springer, Heidelberg (2001). https://doi.org/10.1007/3-540-44987-6_17

14. Chen, J.: Optimal error-free multi-valued Byzantine agreement. In: DISC 2021. LIPIcs, vol. 209, pp. 17:1–17:19. Schloss Dagstuhl - Leibniz-Zentrum für Informatik (2021)

15. Chor, B., Goldwasser, S., Micali, S., Awerbuch, B.: Verifiable secret sharing and achieving simultaneity in the presence of faults (extended abstract). In: 26th Annual Symposium on Foundations of Computer Science, Portland, Oregon, USA, 21–23 October 1985, pp. 383–395. IEEE Computer Society (1985)

16. Coan, B.A., Welch, J.L.: Modular construction of nearly optimal byzantine agreement protocols. In: ACM Symposium on Principles of Distributed Computing (1989)

17. Cohen, R., Coretti, S., Garay, J.A., Zikas, V.: Probabilistic termination and composability of cryptographic protocols. J. Cryptol. **32**(3), 690–741 (2019)

18. Cramer, R., Damgård, I., Dziembowski, S., Hirt, M., Rabin, T.: Efficient multiparty computations secure against an adaptive adversary. In: Stern, J. (ed.) EURO-CRYPT 1999. LNCS, vol. 1592, pp. 311–326. Springer, Heidelberg (1999). https://doi.org/10.1007/3-540-48910-X_22

19. Dolev, D., Reischuk, R.: Bounds on information exchange for Byzantine agreement. In: ACM SIGACT-SIGOPS Symposium on Principles of Distributed Computing, Ottawa, Canada, 18–20 August 1982, pp. 132–140. ACM (1982)

20. Feldman, P., Micali, S.: Optimal algorithms for Byzantine agreement. In: Proceedings of the 20th Annual ACM Symposium on Theory of Computing (1988)

21. Feldman, P.N.: Optimal algorithms for Byzantine agreement. Ph.D. thesis, Massachusetts Institute of Technology (1988)

22. Fischer, M.J., Lynch, N.A.: A lower bound for the time to assure interactive consistency. Inf. Process. Lett. **14**, 183–186 (1982)

23. Fitzi, M., Garay, J.A.: Efficient player-optimal protocols for strong and differential consensus. In: PODC (2003)

24. Goldreich, O., Petrank, E.: The best of both worlds: guaranteeing termination in fast randomized Byzantine agreement protocols. Inf. Process. Lett. **36**(1), 45–49 (1990)

25. Katz, J., Koo, C.: On expected constant-round protocols for Byzantine agreement. In: Annual International Cryptology Conference (2006)

26. Kumaresan, R.: Broadcast and verifiable secret sharing: new security models and round optimal constructions. University of Maryland, College Park (2012)

27. Kushilevitz, E., Lindell, Y., Rabin, T.: Information-theoretically secure protocols and security under composition. In: Proceedings of the 38th Annual ACM Symposium on Theory of Computing (2006)

28. Lamport, L., Shostak, R., Pease, M.: The Byzantine generals problem. ACM Trans. Program. Lang. Syst. **4**, 382–401 (1982)

29. Lindell, Y., Lysyanskaya, A., Rabin, T.: Sequential composition of protocols without simultaneous termination. In: Proceedings of the Twenty-First Annual ACM Symposium on Principles of Distributed Computing, PODC 2002, Monterey, California, USA, 21–24 July 2002, pp. 203–212. ACM (2002)
30. Nayak, K., Ren, L., Shi, E., Vaidya, N.H., Xiang, Z.: Improved extension protocols for byzantine broadcast and agreement. arXiv preprint arXiv:2002.11321 (2020)
31. Kumaresan, R., Patra, A., Rangan, C.P.: The round complexity of verifiable secret sharing: the statistical case. In: Abe, M. (ed.) ASIACRYPT 2010. LNCS, vol. 6477, pp. 431–447. Springer, Heidelberg (2010). https://doi.org/10.1007/978-3-642-17373-8_25
32. Patra, A., Choudhary, A., Rangan, C.P.: Round efficient unconditionally secure multiparty computation protocol. In: Chowdhury, D.R., Rijmen, V., Das, A. (eds.) Progress in Cryptology - INDOCRYPT 2008, 9th International Conference on Cryptology in India, Kharagpur, India, 14–17 December 2008. Proceedings. LNCS, vol. 5365, pp. 185–199. Springer, Cham (2008). https://doi.org/10.1007/978-3-540-89754-5_15
33. Pease, M., Shostak, R., Lamport, L.: Reaching agreement in the presence of faults. J. ACM (JACM) 27, 228–234 (1980)
34. Rabin, M.O.: Randomized Byzantine generals. In: 2013 IEEE 54th Annual Symposium on Foundations of Computer Science (1983)
35. Rabin, T.: Robust sharing of secrets when the dealer is honest or cheating. J. ACM (JACM) 41(6), 1089–1109 (1994)
36. Tsimos, G., Loss, J., Papamanthou, C.: Gossiping for communication-efficient broadcast. In: Advances in Cryptology - CRYPTO 2022 - 42nd Annual International Cryptology Conference, CRYPTO 2022, Santa Barbara, CA, USA, 15–18 August 2022, Proceedings, Part III. LNCS, vol. 13509, pp. 439–469. Springer, Cham (2022). https://doi.org/10.1007/978-3-031-15982-4_15
37. Zhu, J., Li, F., Chen, J.: Communication-efficient and error-free gradecast with optimal resilience. In: 2023 IEEE International Symposium on Information Theory (ISIT), pp. 108–113 (2023). https://doi.org/10.1109/ISIT54713.2023.10206579

Fuzzy Private Set Intersection with Large Hyperballs

Aron van Baarsen[1,2] and Sihang Pu[3]([✉]) [iD]

[1] Cryptology Group, CWI, Amsterdam, The Netherlands
`aronvanbaarsen@gmail.com`
[2] Mathematical Institute, Leiden University, Leiden, The Netherlands
[3] CISPA Helmholtz Center for Information Security, Saarbrücken, Germany
`sihang.pu@gmail.com`

Abstract. Traditional private set intersection (PSI) involves a receiver and a sender holding sets X and Y, respectively, with the receiver learning only the intersection $X \cap Y$. We turn our attention to its fuzzy variant, where the receiver holds $|X|$ hyperballs of radius δ in a metric space and the sender has $|Y|$ points. Representing the hyperballs by their center, the receiver learns the points $x \in X$ for which there exists $y \in Y$ such that $\mathsf{dist}(x, y) \leq \delta$ with respect to some distance metric. Previous approaches either require general-purpose multi-party computation (MPC) techniques like garbled circuits or fully homomorphic encryption (FHE), leak details about the sender's precise inputs, support limited distance metrics, or scale poorly with the hyperballs' volume.

This work presents the first black-box construction for fuzzy PSI (including other variants such as PSI cardinality, labeled PSI, and circuit PSI), which can handle polynomially large radius and dimension (i.e., a potentially exponentially large volume) in two interaction messages, supporting general $L_{\mathsf{p} \in [1, \infty]}$ distance, without relying on garbled circuits or FHE. The protocol excels in both asymptotic and concrete efficiency compared to existing works. For security, we solely rely on the assumption that the Decisional Diffie-Hellman (DDH) holds in the random oracle model.

1 Introduction

Private set intersection (PSI) is a cryptographic primitive that allows two parties to compute the intersection $X \cap Y$ of their private datasets X and Y, without revealing any information about items not in the intersection. The first PSI protocol is often dated back to Meadows [30] and many modern protocols still have the same structure using an oblivious pseudorandom function (OPRF) [28, 35, 36]. Recent PSI protocols are very practical and can for example compute the intersection of sets of 2^{20} elements in ≈ 0.37 s [35]. Many richer PSI functionalities have also been explored, such as: *PSI cardinality* [16,18,27], where only the cardinality of the intersection is revealed; *labeled PSI* [10,13,14], which allows

---

A. van Baarsen—Research partially funded by NWO/TKI Grant 628.009.014.

M. Joye and G. Leander (Eds.): EUROCRYPT 2024, LNCS 14655, pp. 340–369, 2024.
https://doi.org/10.1007/978-3-031-58740-5_12

the parties to learn labels associated to the items in the intersection; *circuit PSI* [24,34,36], which only reveals secret shares of the intersection and allows the parties to securely evaluate any function on the intersection.

Recently Garimella et al. [20,21] introduced the concept of *structure-aware PSI*, where the receiver's input set has some publicly known structure. For example, the receiver holds N balls of radius δ and dimension d and the sender holds a set of M points, and the sender learns which of the sender's points lie within one of their balls. This special case is often referred to as *fuzzy PSI* and is the focus of our work. Using a standard PSI protocol for this task leads to a rather inefficient solution since the communication and computation complexity usually scale at least linearly in the cardinality of the input sets, i.e., the total volume of the balls $N \cdot \delta^d$. Garimella et al. can overcome this barrier in terms of communication in the semi-honest [20] as well as in the malicious [21] setting. However, the receiver's computation is still proportional to the total volume of the input balls, which makes their protocols scale poorly with the dimension d. Moreover, their protocols are limited to the L_∞ and L_1[1] distance and only realize a *standard PSI* functionality, where the receiver learns exactly which of the sender's points lie in the intersection. Other works are either limited to the Hamming distance [37], Hamming and L_2 distance [26] or Hamming distance and one-dimensional L_1 distance [8], and often require heavy machinery or yield non-negligible correctness error.

In this work, we present fuzzy PSI protocols in the semi-honest setting for general L_∞ and L_p distance with $p \in [1, \infty)$, and present several optimized variants for low as well as high dimensions. Notably, the communication as well as computation complexity of our high-dimension protocols scales linearly or quadratically with the dimension d. We moreover extend our protocols to various richer fuzzy PSI functionalities including PSI cardinality, labeled PSI, PSI with sender privacy, and circuit PSI. Our protocols have comparable performance to [20] in the low-dimensional setting and significantly outperform other approaches when the dimension increases. Finally, our protocols rely only on the decisional Diffie-Hellman (DDH) assumption.

1.1 Our Contributions

Fuzzy Matching. The main building block for our fuzzy PSI constructions is a fuzzy matching protocol, which on input a point $\mathbf{w} \in \mathbb{Z}^d$ from the receiver and a point $\mathbf{q} \in \mathbb{Z}^d$ from the sender, outputs 1 to the receiver if $\mathsf{dist}(\mathbf{w}, \mathbf{q}) \leq \delta$ and 0 otherwise. Here dist can either be L_∞ distance or L_p distance for $p \in [1, \infty)$. It results in a two-message protocol for L_∞ distance with communication complexity $O(\delta d)$, computation complexity $O(\delta d)$ for the receiver and $O(d)$ for the sender when $\mathsf{dist} = L_\infty$; For L_p distance, it has communication complexity $O(\delta d + \delta^p)$, computation complexity $O(\delta d)$ for the receiver, and $O(d + \delta^p)$ for the sender.

---

[1] The overhead of L_1 balls would be $\frac{2^d}{d}$ times larger than that of L_∞ balls in their protocols.

Table 1. Asymptotic complexities of fuzzy PSI protocols, where the receiver holds N hyperballs of radius δ and the sender holds M points in $\mathbb{Z}^d$. $\rho \leq 1/c$ is a parameter to the LSH scheme if the receiver's points are distance $> c\delta$ apart. We ignore multiplicative factors of the computational security parameter λ and statistical parameter κ.

Setting [protocol]		Communication	Comp. (receiver)	Comp. (sender)
L_∞	trad. PSI [35]	$O\left((2\delta)^d N + M\right)$	$O\left((2\delta)^d N\right)$	$O\left((2\delta)^d N + M\right)$
	$> 2\delta$ [ours]	$\mathbf{O\left(\delta dN + 2^d M\right)}$	$\mathbf{O\left(\delta dN + 2^d M\right)}$	$\mathbf{O\left(2^d dM)\right)}$
	$> 2\delta$ [20]	$O\left((4\log\delta)^d N + M\right)$	$O\left((2\delta)^d N\right)$	$O\left((2\log\delta)^d M\right)$
	$> 4\delta$ [ours]	$O\left(\delta 2^d dN + M\right)$	$\mathbf{O\left(\delta 2^d dN + M\right)}$	$\mathbf{O\left(dM\right)}$
	$> 4\delta$ [20]	$O\left(2^d dN \log\delta + M\right)$	$O\left((2\delta)^d N\right)$	$O\left(dM \log\delta\right)$
	$> 8\delta$ [21]	$O\left(dN \log\delta + M\right)$	$O\left((2\delta)^d N\right)$	$O\left(dM \log\delta\right)$
	$\exists$disj. proj. [ours]	$O\left((\delta d)^2 N + M\right)$	$O\left((\delta d)^2 N + M\right)$	$O\left(d^2 M\right)$
	$\forall$disj. proj. [20]	$O\left(dN \log\delta + M\right)$	$O\left((2\delta)^d N\right)$	$O\left(dM \log\delta\right)$
L_p	$> 2\delta(d^{1/p}+1)$[ours]	$O\left(\delta 2^d dN + \delta^p M\right)$	$O\left(\delta 2^d dN + M\right)$	$O\left((d+\delta^p)M\right)$
	LSH [ours]	$O\left(\delta dN^{1+\rho} + \delta^p MN^\rho \log N\right)$	$O\left(\delta dN^{1+\rho} + MN^\rho \log N\right)$	$O\left((d+\delta^p)MN^\rho \log N\right)$

Fuzzy PSI in Low-Dimensions. Using a fuzzy matching protocol we can trivially obtain a fuzzy PSI protocol by letting the sender and receiver run the fuzzy matching protocol for every combination of inputs, but this leads to an undesirable $N \cdot M$ blowup in communication and computation complexity. To circumvent this blowup for a low dimension d, we develop a new spatial hashing technique for disjoint L_∞ balls which incurs only a $O(2^d)$ factor to the receiver's communication and sender's computational complexity. To support L_p balls, we extend the "shattering" idea from [20] to generalized L_p setting. The asymptotic complexities are given in Table 1. It is worth noting that, unlike to [20,21], the computation complexity of our protocols scale *sublinearly* to the volume of balls.

Fuzzy PSI in High-Dimensions. Unfortunately, the above spatial hashing approaches still yield a 2^d factor in the communication and computation complexities, which becomes prohibitive for large dimensions d. The earlier work [20] proposes a protocol that can overcome this factor, for communication costs, in the L_∞ setting under the *globally disjoint* assumption that the projections $[w_{k,i} - \delta, w_{k,i} + \delta]$ of the sender's balls $k \in [N]$ are disjoint *for all* dimensions $i \in [d]$, which the authors themselves mention is a somewhat artificial assumption. We present a two-message protocol with comparable communication and much lower computation complexity under a milder assumption that for each $k \in [N]$ *there exists* a dimension $i \in [d]$ where the projection is disjoint from all other $k' \in [N]$, namely, not necessary to be globally disjoint. We argue that this is a more realistic assumption since points in high dimensions tend to be sparser and show that it is satisfied with a high probability if the points $\mathbf{w}_k$ are uniformly distributed.

We moreover present a two-message protocol in the L_p setting which can circumvent this exponential factor in the dimension d, while achieving subquadratic complexity in the number of inputs. The key idea of this protocol is to use locality-sensitive hashing (LSH) to perform a coarse mapping such that points close to each other end up in the same bucket with high probability, and subsequently use our fuzzy matching protocol for L_p distance to compare the items in each bucket. See Table 1 for the asymptotic complexities of our protocols.

Extensions to Broader Functionalities. By default, all our protocols except for the LSH-based protocol realize the stricter PSI functionality where the receiver only learns how many of the sender's points lie close to any of the receiver's points, which we call *PSI cardinality* (PSI-CA). Earlier works [20,21] realize the functionality where the receiver learns exactly which of the sender's points are in the intersection. We refer to this functionality as *standard PSI*.

For all of our protocols discussed above, except for the LSH-based protocol, we show that we can extend them to realize the following functionalities: standard PSI; *PSI with sender privacy* (PSI-SP), where the receiver only learns which of the receiver's balls are in the intersection; *labeled PSI*, where the receiver only learns some label associated to the sender's points in the intersection; *circuit PSI*, where the parties only learn secret shares of the intersection and optional data associated to each input point, which they can use as the input to any secure follow-up computation. We can realize these extensions without increasing the asymptotic complexities of the protocols and without needing to introduce additional computational assumptions. With the only exception that for the circuit PSI extension we need a generic MPC functionality to compute a secure comparison circuit at the end of the protocol, which is common for traditional (non-fuzzy) circuit PSI protocols [34,36].

Performance. Our experimental results demonstrate that it requires only 1.2 GB bandwidth and 432 s in total to complete a standard fuzzy PSI protocol when parties have thousands of L_∞ balls and millions of points in a 5-dimensional space. As a comparison, prior works need $\gg 4300$ s (conservative estimate).

1.2   Related Work

Traditional PSI protocols have become very efficient [9,28,35], but are optimized for the setting where the parties' input sets have approximately the same size, and their communication and computation costs scale linearly with the input size. This leads to an inefficient fuzzy PSI protocol since the receiver's input size is $N \cdot \delta^d$ when the receiver holds N hyperballs of dimension d and radius δ. Asymmetric (or unbalanced) PSI protocols [1,10,11,14] target the setting where one party's set is much larger than the other's and can achieve communication complexity sublinear in the large set size, but $O(\sqrt{N} \cdot \delta^{d/2})$ computational complexity, using fully homomorphic encryption [14]. For traditional PSI there exist many efficient protocols realizing richer functionalities such as PSI cardinality [16,27], labeled PSI [10,14] and circuit PSI [24,34,36], but all of these suffer from the same limitations as discussed above when applied to the fuzzy PSI setting.

There exists another line of works concerning threshold PSI [3,7,22,23], where the fuzziness is measured by the number of *exact* matches between items.

Secure fuzzy matching was introduced by Freedman et al. [18] as the problem of identifying when two tuples have a Hamming distance below a certain threshold. They propose a protocol based on additively homomorphic encryption and polynomial interpolation, which was later shown to be insecure [12]. Follow-up works focus on the Hamming distance as well and use similar oblivious polynomial evaluation techniques [12,38]. Indyk and Woodruff [26] construct a fuzzy PSI protocol for L_2 and Hamming distance using garbled circuits. Uzun et al. [37] give a protocol for fuzzy labeled PSI for Hamming distance using garbled circuits and fully homomorphic encryption. Chakraborti et al. [8] propose a fuzzy PSI protocol for Hamming distance based on additively homomorphic encryption and vector oblivious linear evaluation (VOLE), which has a non-negligible false positive rate. They moreover present a protocol for one-dimensional L_1 distance, which can be constructed using any $O(N)$ communication PSI protocol for sets of size N, and has resulting communication complexity $O(N \log \delta)$ [8]. It is an interesting question whether their techniques can be extended to higher dimensions. Since the focus of our work is to construct fuzzy PSI protocols for general L_p and L_∞ distances, general dimension d, and with negligible error rate, it is not possible to make a meaningful comparison with these works.

Garimella et al. [20,21] initiated the study of structure-aware PSI, which covers fuzzy PSI as a special case. They introduce the definition of weak boolean function secret sharing (bFSS) for set membership testing and give a general protocol for structure-aware PSI from bFSS. They develop several new bFSS techniques, focusing on the case where the input set is the union of N balls of radius δ with respect to the L_∞ norm in d-dimensional space, which results in a fuzzy PSI protocol as the ones we concern ourselves with in this work. The techniques used in their protocols are fundamentally different from ours, except that we use similar spatial hashing techniques to obtain efficient fuzzy matching protocols in the low-dimensional setting. Moreover, their protocols are limited to the L_∞ and L_1 distance setting and only realize the standard PSI functionality where the receiver learns the exact sender's points in the intersection. Finally, the receiver's computational complexity in their protocols scales as $O((2\delta)^d N)$, which makes them unsuitable in the high-dimensional setting. See Table 1 for a more detailed comparison of communication and computational complexities.

1.3   Applications

Private Proximity Detection. There exist certain contexts where individuals need to know the proximity of others for varying purposes: In the realm of contact tracing, where individuals may seek to determine if they are in the vicinity of an infected person; Within the scope of ride-sharing platforms, users might wish to identify available vehicles in their surroundings. In both scenarios, the privacy of all involved parties should preserved and fuzzy PSI protocols provide a direct solution to this problem.

Biometric and Password Identification. Fuzzy matching could also be useful in authentication or identification scenarios. Notable applications of this technique can be observed in the matching of similar passwords to enhance usability or security. A case in point is Facebook's authentication protocol, which auto-corrects the capitalization of the initial character in passwords [31]. Similarly, it can be useful to check if a user's password is similar to a leaked password [33]. Furthermore, fuzzy matching can be employed to match biometric data, such as fingerprint and iris scans, thereby facilitating a blend of convenience and security [17]. In general, a fuzzy unbalanced PSI protocol is more useful since the server usually holds a large database of clients' passwords (or biometric samples).

Illegal Content Detection. Recently, Bartusek et al. [4] introduced the study of illegal content detection within the framework of end-to-end secure messaging, focusing particularly on the detection of child sexual abuse material, encompassing photographs and videos. Central to their protocol is a two-message PSI protocol, wherein the initial message is reusable and published once for the receiver's database. After this, the computational overhead for both parties is rendered independent of the database size. The research notably leverages Apple's PSI protocol [5], which, while only facilitating exact matches, serves its purpose effectively. Ideally, matching should be sufficiently fuzzy to ensure that illegal images remain detectable even following rotation or mild post-processing. Our fuzzy PSI constructions, encapsulated within two-round protocols and featuring a reusable initial message, may find potential applicability in such contexts.

2 Technical Overview

Before heading for the details of our fuzzy matching and PSI protocols, let us start by discussing a standard PSI protocol proposed by Apple [5].

2.1 Recap: Apple's PSI Protocol

We simplify Apple's PSI protocol to the basic setting where the receiver holds a set $W := \{w_1, \ldots, w_n\}$, the sender holds an item q, and the receiver wants to learn q if $q \in W$ and nothing otherwise. Their main idea is a novel usage of random self-reduction of DDH tuples from Naor and Reingold [32] in PSI contexts. Given a cyclic group $\mathbb{G} := \langle g \rangle$ of prime order p, the tuple (g, h, h_1, h_2) can be re-randomized into (g, h, u, v) such that u, v are uniformly random over $\mathbb{G}$ as long as (g, h, h_1, h_2) is *not* a well-formed DDH tuple (i.e., there is no $s \in \mathbb{Z}_p^*$ to satisfy $g^s = h \wedge h_1^s = h_2$). Otherwise, both (g, h, h_1, h_2) and the re-randomized tuple (g, h, u, v) are valid DDH tuples. This re-randomization basically utilizes two random coins $a, b \leftarrow_\$ \mathbb{Z}_p^*$ to output

$$(u := g^a h_1^b, v := h^a h_2^b).$$

Now to obtain a PSI protocol, the receiver could sample $s \leftarrow_s \mathbb{Z}_p^*$ and publish

$$(g, h := g^s, \mathsf{H}(w_1)^s, \ldots, \mathsf{H}(w_n)^s),$$

where H is a hash-to-group function. Then the sender returns pairs

$$(u_i, \mathsf{ct}_i := \mathsf{Enc}_{v_i}(q))_{i \in [n]},$$

where (u_i, v_i) is the re-randomization output for each tuple $(g, h, \mathsf{H}(q), \mathsf{H}(w_i)^s)$, and Enc is some symmetric-key encryption scheme (e.g., a one-time pad). The receiver can try to decrypt each ct_i using the key u_i^s to learn q. For the sender's privacy, the random self-reduction of DDH tuples guarantees that when $q \neq w_i$, the secret key v_i is uniformly random from the receiver's view and thus q is hidden according to the security of this symmetric-key encryption. For the receiver's privacy, $(\mathsf{H}(w_1)^s, \ldots, \mathsf{H}(w_n)^s)$ is pseudorandom according to the generalized DDH assumption when H is modelled as a random oracle.

2.2 Fuzzy Matching for Infinity Distance

Our crucial observation is that the above approach can be naturally applied in fuzzy matching protocols where the receiver holds a point $\mathbf{w} \in \mathbb{Z}^d$ in a d-dimensional space, the sender holds a point $\mathbf{q} \in \mathbb{Z}^d$, and the receiver learns if $\mathsf{dist}(\mathbf{w}, \mathbf{q}) \leq \delta$. Here, δ is the maximal allowed distance between $\mathbf{w}$ and $\mathbf{q}$. For the moment, let us focus on the simplest case where the distance is calculated over L_∞, which means the receiver gets 1 if

$$\forall i \in [d] : w_i - \delta \leq q_i \leq w_i + \delta,$$

and gets 0 otherwise. This problem is equivalent to the following: The receiver holds d sets $\{W_1, \ldots, W_d\}$ where $W_i := \{w_i - \delta, \ldots, w_i + \delta\}$, the sender holds d items $\{q_1, \ldots, q_d\}$, and they want to run a membership test for each dimension simultaneously, without leaking the results for individual dimensions. Though the receiver can publish $\mathsf{H}(w_i + j)^s$ for each $i \in [d], j \in [-\delta, +\delta]$ as above, the sender has to use random self-reduction for each possible match, which yields too much communication and computation effort for the sender. Namely, the entire volume of a d-dimensional δ-radius ball $O\left((2\delta + 1)^d\right)$.

Reducing the Complexity. There is a standard trick to significantly reduce the complexity by using an oblivious key-value store (OKVS). Recall that an OKVS [19] will encode a key-value list $\{(\mathsf{key}_j, \mathsf{val}_j)\}_{j \in [n]}$ into a data structure E, such that decoding with a correct key_* returns the corresponding val_*, where the encoding time scales linearly to the list size and decoding a single key takes only a constant number of operations. So the above protocol can be improved as follows:

1) The receiver publishes $(g, h, E_i \leftarrow \mathsf{Encode}(\{(w_i + j, \quad \mathsf{H}(w_i + j)^s)\}_{j \in [-\delta, +\delta]}))$ for each $i \in [d]$;

2) The sender retrieves $h_i \leftarrow \mathsf{Decode}(E_i, q_i)$ for each $i \in [d]$ and sends the rerandomized tuple $(u := g^a \prod_{i=1}^{d} \mathsf{H}(q_i)^b, v := h^a \prod_{i=1}^{d} h_i^b)$, where $a, b \leftarrow_\$ \mathbb{Z}_p^*$, to the receiver;

3) The receiver checks if (g, h, u, v) is a valid DDH tuple.

The protocol is correct when $\mathsf{dist}(\mathbf{q}, \mathbf{w}) \leq \delta$, according to the correctness of the underlying OKVS scheme, which says that decoding the structure E_i with a correct encoding key q_i will return the encoded value $h_i := \mathsf{H}(q_i)^s$; When $\mathsf{dist}(\mathbf{q}, \mathbf{w}) > \delta$, we typically need to rely on the independence property of OKVS, which says that decoding with a non-encoded key will yield a uniformly random result. Therefore, in this case, there exists at least one h_{i^*} that is uniformly random; hence $(g, h, \mathsf{H}(q_{i^*}), h_{i^*})$ is not a DDH tuple except with negligible probability. The sender's privacy can be established as before from the random self-reduction of DDH tuples. To argue the receiver's privacy, we rely on the obliviousness property of the OKVS, namely, the encoded keys $\{w_i + j\}$ are completely hidden as long as the encoded values $\{\mathsf{H}(w_i + j)^s\}$ are uniformly random. Since $(h, \mathsf{H}(w_i + j), \mathsf{H}(w_i + j)^s)$ is pseudorandom by the DDH assumption, then according to the obliviousness of OKVS, the receiver's message can be simulated by encoding random key-value pairs.

Note that our real construction shown in Sect. 5.1, is slightly different from what we described here. We encode the OKVS "over the exponent" to reduce heavy public-key operations over $\mathbb{G}$ because our encoded values are pseudorandom over a *structured* group $\mathbb{G}$ (i.e., the elliptic curves).

So far, we have obtained a two-message fuzzy matching protocol for L_∞ distance, with $O(d\delta)$ communication and computation complexity.

2.3 Generalized Distance Functions

When the distance function is calculated in L_p, the receiver would get 1 if

$$\mathsf{dist}_\mathsf{p}(\mathbf{w}, \mathbf{q}) := \left(\sum_{i=1}^{d} |w_i - q_i|^\mathsf{p} \right)^{1/\mathsf{p}} \leq \delta,$$

and 0 otherwise. To make the problem easier, we consider the p-powered L_p distance, namely, we check if $\sum_{i=1}^{d} |w_i - q_i|^\mathsf{p} \leq \delta^\mathsf{p}$. Thanks to the homomorphism of DDH tuples, the sender can homomorphically evaluate the distance function. Moreover, since an $L_{\mathsf{p} \geq 1}$ ball must be confined in an L_∞ ball, namely, $|w_i - q_i| \leq \delta$ for any $i \in [d]$ if $\mathsf{dist}_\mathsf{p}(\mathbf{w}, \mathbf{q}) \leq \delta$, the protocol could work as follows:

1) The receiver publishes

$$\left(g, h, E_i \leftarrow \mathsf{Encode}\left(\left\{ (w_i + j, \quad \mathsf{H}(w_i + j)^s \cdot g^{|j|^\mathsf{p}}) \right\}_{j \in [-\delta:\delta]} \right) \right),$$

for each $i \in [d]$;

2) The sender retrieves $h_i \leftarrow \mathsf{Decode}(E_i, q_i)$ for each $i \in [d]$, and computes

$$\left(u := g^a \prod_{i=1}^{d} \mathsf{H}(q_i)^b, v := h^a \prod_{i=1}^{d} h_i^b \right),$$

for random $a, b \leftarrow_\$ \mathbb{Z}_p^*$;
3) The sender generates a list $\mathsf{list} := \{g^{b \cdot j}\}_{j \in [0:\delta^p]}$ and outputs (u, v, list);
4) The receiver checks if there is any $x \in \mathsf{list}$ such that $v = u^s \cdot x$.

Denote $t := \mathsf{dist}_p(\mathbf{w}, \mathbf{q})$. If $\forall i \in [d]$, $|w_i - q_i| \leq \delta$, then the correctness holds naturally since each retrieved $h_i := \mathsf{H}(q_i)^s \cdot g^{|w_i - q_i|^p}$, implying that

$$\frac{v}{u^s} = g^{b \cdot t^p},$$

which would be included in list if and only if $t \leq \delta^2$. On the other hand, if there exists $i^* \in [d]$ such that $|w_{i^*} - q_{i^*}| > \delta$, then according to the independence property of OKVS the decoded h_{i^*} as well as v would be uniformly random over $\mathbb{G}$, such that $v/u^s \in \mathsf{list}$ with only negligible probability.

Subtle Issues and the Fix. The receiver's privacy is almost the same as before, relying on the generalized DDH assumption and the obliviousness of OKVS. It is a little bit subtle to argue the sender's privacy: Currently, list would leak information on the sender's input. Precisely, given (u, v, list), the receiver could check, for example, if $\frac{v}{u^s \cdot g^b} \in \mathsf{list}$ to learn if $t^p = \delta^p + 1$ or not, since $g^b \in \mathsf{list}$. Moreover, even in the case that $t \leq \delta$, the receiver could still deduce the *exact* t by checking which index is matched. The latter can be solved by shuffling the list, so we focus on the former issue. One approach is to hash each list item as $\mathsf{list} := \{\mathsf{H}'(g^{b \cdot j})\}_{j \in [0:\delta^p]}$. By modeling $\mathsf{H}' : \mathbb{G} \mapsto \{0, 1\}^*$ as a random oracle, the group structure is erased and the adversary cannot utilize $g^{b \cdot j}$ anymore. However, the issue still exists since the adversary could check if $\mathsf{H}'\left((\frac{v}{u^s})^{1/\alpha}\right) \in \mathsf{list}$ to learn if $t^p \in \{0, \alpha, 2\alpha, \ldots, \delta^p \alpha\}$ for any α. Therefore, we have to apply a random linear function over t^p to make sure that $\frac{v}{u^s} = g^{b \cdot t^p + c}$ where b, c are random scalars. The details can be found in Sect. 5.2.

Regarding the complexity, the communication and computation are increased by an additive term $O(\delta^p)$ from the infinity distance setting.

2.4 Fuzzy PSI in Low Dimensions

For the moment, let us consider the fuzzy PSI *cardinality* problem, where the receiver holds a union of d-dimensional balls of radius δ represented by their centers $\{\mathbf{w}_1, \ldots, \mathbf{w}_N\}$, the sender holds a set of points $\{\mathbf{q}_1, \ldots, \mathbf{q}_M\}$ in the same space, and the receiver learns *the number of* sender's points located inside the balls. When the dimension d of the space is low, e.g., $O(\log(\lambda))$, we can exploit

---

[2] Assuming the group order p is large enough that $t^p < p$.

the geometric structure of the space to efficiently match balls and points to avoid the quadratic blowup mentioned in the introduction. The high-level idea is to tile the entire space by d-dimensional hypercubes of side-length 2δ (also called *cells*, together a *grid*), then the receiver can encode a ball (represented by its center $\mathbf{w}_i$) in a way that the sender can efficiently match it with a point $\mathbf{q}_j$, without enumerating all balls. After that, both parties can run a fuzzy matching protocol between $\mathbf{w}_i$ and $\mathbf{q}_j$ as before.

The idea of Garimella et al. [20] is to "shatter" each receiver's ball into its intersected cells, however, to guarantee each cell is intersected with a single ball (otherwise collisions appear during encoding an OKVS[3]), the receiver's balls typically need to be at least 4δ apart from each other. To tackle the case of disjoint balls, the authors improved their techniques [21] by observing that each grid cell can only contain the center of a single receiver's ball. Thus, the receiver could encode the identifier of each cell which contains a ball center, and the sender can try to decode the OKVS by iterating over all neighborhood cells[4] surrounding its point. This approach yields a $O(3^d)$ factor for the sender's computation and communication costs: Given a point $\mathbf{q}$, the center of any L_∞ ball intersected with $\mathbf{q}$ is located in at most 3^d cells surrounding the cell containing $\mathbf{q}$.

New Spatial Hashing Ideas. Here we provide a new hashing technique to reduce this blowup from 3^d to 2^d. Note that the 3^d factor comes from the fact that the entire neighborhood of the point $\mathbf{q}$ is too large (i.e., a hypercube of side-length 6δ), but we only need to care about the neighbor cells that intersected with the receiver's balls already. Specifically, if the grid is set properly, an L_∞ ball will intersect *exactly* 2^d cells, which constitute a hypercube of side-length 4δ, denoted as a *block*. Our crucial observation is that each block is *unique* for each disjoint ball, i.e., two disjoint balls must be associated with different blocks, as detailed in Lemma 6. Given this, the receiver could encode the identifier of each block, and the sender would decode by iterating all potential blocks. There are in total 2^d possible blocks for each sender's point due to each block being comprised of 2^d cells and each cell contains at most a single ball's center.

Compatible with L_p Balls. Though we only considered L_∞ balls so far, we can generalize the "shattering" idea from [20] to L_p balls as well. We still tile the space with hypercubes, but we show that as long as L_p balls are at least $2\delta(d^{1/p}+1)$ apart from each other, then each grid cell intersects at most one L_p ball, as detailed in Lemma 5. Particularly, when $p = \infty$, $2\delta(d^{1/p}+1)$ degrades to the original 4δ. Combining it with our fuzzy matching protocols for L_p distance, we immediately obtain fuzzy PSI for precise L_p distance (i.e., without approximation or metric embedding). One important step different from the L_∞ setting is to pad the key-value list to size $2^d N$ with random pairs since an L_p ball could intersect with a various number of cells. Otherwise, the receiver's privacy would be compromised.

---

[3] Note that this is not a problem in their setting as they use the function secret sharing (FSS) to handle each grid cell.

[4] The neighborhood is a hypercube of side-length 6δ.

2.5   Extending to High Dimensions

To overcome the 2^d factor in complexities, we first focus our attention on L_∞ distances: Ideally, if the receiver's balls are *globally disjoint* on every dimension, namely, the projection of the balls on each dimension never overlaps, then the "collision" issue mentioned above would disappear. In this way, for each dimension $i \in [d]$, the receiver could encode the OKVS as

$$E_i \leftarrow \mathsf{Encode}\Big(\big\{\big(w_{k,i} + j, \quad \mathsf{H}(w_{k,i} + j)^s\big)\big\}_{j \in [-\delta,+\delta]}\Big),$$

where $w_{k,i}$ is the projection of the ball center $\mathbf{w}_k$ on dimension i. The sender just behaves the same as in Sect. 2.2. This approach results in $O(\delta dN + M)$ communication and computation costs. However, as stated in [20], this ideal setting is somewhat artificial and unrealistic.

Weaker Assumptions by Leveraging Dummy OKVS Instances. After taking a closer look at this approach, we realized that the global disjointness is not necessary to be satisfied on *every* dimension, as we actually could tolerate some collisions. Specifically, the value h_i decoded from E_i for some point $\mathbf{q}$ (lying in one of the receiver's balls) would constitute a tuple $(g, h, \mathsf{H}(q_i), h_i)$. However, this tuple does not necessarily need to be a DDH tuple. We only need the final product

$$\left(g, h, \prod_{i=1}^{d} \mathsf{H}(q_i), \prod_{i=1}^{d} h_i\right)$$

to be a valid DDH tuple for correctness.

Suppose there exists *at least one* dimension on which the projections of *all* balls are disjoint. This gives each ball a unique way to identify it from others. Our idea is to leverage OKVS instances recursively: For each ball $\mathbf{w}_k$, the receiver encodes an *outer* OKVS for dimension i by

$$E_i \leftarrow \mathsf{Encode}\Big(\big\{\big(w_{k,i} + j, \quad \mathsf{val}_{k,i,j}\big)\big\}_{j \in [-\delta,+\delta]}\Big),$$

where $\mathsf{val}_{k,i,j}$ differs in two cases:

- If the current dimension i is the globally separated dimension for all balls, then $\mathsf{val}_{k,i,j}$ is an *inner* OKVS instance for fuzzy matching with $\mathbf{w}_k$, namely,

$$\mathsf{val}_{k,i,j} \leftarrow \mathsf{Encode}\Big(\big\{\big(i' \,\|\, w_{k,i'} + j', \quad h_{i',j'} \,\|\, h_{i',j'}^s\big)\big\}_{i' \in [d], j' \in [-\delta,+\delta]}\Big),$$

  where $h_{i',j'} \leftarrow_{\$} \mathbb{G}$;
- Otherwise, the $\mathsf{val}_{k,i,j} := (\mathbf{r} \,\|\, \mathbf{r}^s)$ is a *dummy* instance where $\mathbf{r} \leftarrow_{\$} \mathbb{G}^m$ and m is the size of the inner OKVS instance.

For each point $\mathbf{q}$, the sender first decodes the outer OKVS to obtain a list $\{\mathsf{val}_1, \ldots, \mathsf{val}_d\}$, then runs the decoding function on each $\mathsf{val}_{j \in [d]}$ to get

$$(u_j \,\|\, v_j) := \prod_{i=1}^{d} \mathsf{Decode}(\mathsf{val}_j, q_i).$$

In the end, the sender re-randomizes the result from the tuple $(g, h, \prod_{j=1}^{d} u_j, \prod_{j=1}^{d} v_j)$.

For correctness, we expect that decoding a dummy instance on any key would output a valid DDH pair all the time. This can be guaranteed if the inner OKVS has a linear decoding function. Clearly, in this way, each $\mathbf{q}$ would get either an inner OKVS instance or random garbage from *the globally separated* dimension. The latter results in valid DDH tuples with negligible probability, so we focus on the case that the sender gets an inner OKVS instance in the end. This reduces the fuzzy PSI problem to the fuzzy matching problem as other dummy instances won't affect the correctness. For security, the inner OKVS has to be doubly oblivious, namely, the encoded structure itself is uniformly random. Regarding the complexity, the receiver's communication and computation costs would be $O(d\delta)$ times larger.

Further Weaken the Assumption. The above assumption is weaker and milder than what was used in prior works, but it is still somewhat artificial. Here we show that we can even weaken this assumption to the following: For each ball, there *exists* at least one dimension on which *its* projection is separated from others. Note that the above approach doesn't work yet in this setting: There might exist a point whose projection on *each* dimension is inside the projection of a *non-separated* interval from some ball. In other words, the sender would get a list of dummy instances after decoding the outer OKVS. This results in a false positive since dummy instances always output a match. To rule out these false positives, we realize that we could encode additional information into each $\mathsf{val}_{k,i,j}$.

For simplicity, let's assume the decoding function of the OKVS is determined by a binary vector with some *fixed hamming weight*, that is, given an instance $\mathbf{r} \in \mathbb{G}^m$ and some key, the decoding function outputs

$$\mathsf{Decode}(\mathbf{r}, \mathsf{key}) = \langle \mathbf{d}, \mathbf{r} \rangle = \prod_{i=1}^{m} r_i^{d_i},$$

where $\mathbf{d} \in \{0,1\}^m$ is deterministically sampled by the key, and $\mathsf{HammingWeight}(\mathbf{d}) = t$. The receiver samples two random shares $\zeta_\perp, \zeta_\top$ such that $\zeta_\perp \cdot \zeta_\top = 1$. We denote as I_k the *first* dimension on which $\mathbf{w}_k$ projects a separated interval. Then the receiver could set $\mathsf{val}_{k,i,j}$ for each $\mathbf{w}_k$ in this way:

– If the current dimension $i = I_k$, then $\mathsf{val}_{k,i,j}$ is an inner OKVS instance defined by

$$\mathsf{val}_{k,i,j} \leftarrow \mathsf{Encode}\left(\left\{\left(i' \,\|\, w_{k,i'} + j', \;\; h_{i',j'} \,\|\, h^s_{i',j'} \cdot \zeta_\perp^{t \cdot (d-1)}\right)\right\}_{i' \in [d], j' \in [-\delta, +\delta]}\right),$$

where $h_{i',j'} \leftarrow_\$ \mathbb{G}$ and t is the hamming weight of $\mathbf{d}$;
- Otherwise, the $\mathsf{val}_{k,i,j} := (\mathbf{r} \,\|\, \mathbf{r}^s \cdot \zeta_\mathsf{T})$ for $\mathbf{r} \leftarrow_\$ \mathbb{G}^m$.

The security follows as before, whereas the correctness is non-trivial. First, consider the sender's point $\mathbf{q}$ intersecting some receiver's ball. After decoding the inner OKVS instance, the sender gets a pair $(u_* \,\|\, u_*^s \cdot \zeta_\perp^{td \cdot (d-1)})$ for some u_*; After decoding a dummy instance, the sender gets $(r_* \,\|\, r_*^s \cdot \zeta_\mathsf{T}^{td})$ for some r_* instead. Now, by multiplying them together, the final tuple

$$\left(g, h, v \,\|\, v^s \cdot \zeta_\perp^{td \cdot (d-1)} \cdot \zeta_\mathsf{T}^{td \cdot (d-1)}\right) = (g, h, v \,\|\, v^s)$$

is a valid DDH tuple for some $v \in \mathbb{G}$.

Then consider the case that the sender's point $\mathbf{q}$ is outside of all balls. The only way to report a match is to get a list of all dummy instances after decoding the outer OKVS instance, otherwise the inner OKVS instance will output a random garbage result. However, since dummy instances only encode ζ_T, the product of them equals 1 with negligible probability due to ζ_T being randomly sampled and $td^2 \ll p$ if $t = O(\kappa)$.

Recall that we assume the decoding vector $\mathbf{d}$ to have fixed hamming weight. This is not ideal since most modern OKVS instantiations (e.g., [6,19,35]) don't satisfy this requirement, whereas the only exception is the garbled bloom filters [15] whose efficiency is not satisfactory. We managed to get rid of this assumption in our real protocol in the end, please refer to Sect. 7.1 for details.

Locality-Sensitive Hashing. The above approaches are heavily tailored to the L_∞ distance. To support L_p distance in high dimensions, we utilize locality-sensitive hashing (LSH) to identify matching balls. An LSH family with parameters $(\delta, c\delta, p_1, p_2)$ guarantees the following:

- If two points $\mathbf{w}$ and $\mathbf{q}$ are close enough, i.e., $\mathsf{dist}_p(\mathbf{w}, \mathbf{q}) \leq \delta$, they would be hashed into the same bucket with at least p_1 probability;
- If they are far apart, i.e., $\mathsf{dist}_p(\mathbf{w}, \mathbf{q}) > c\delta$, then the probability of hashing them into the same bucket is at most p_2.

In other words, an LSH family bounds the false-positive and false-negative probability to p_2 and $1 - p_1$, respectively. Usually, false-positive and false-negative cannot be reduced to negligible simultaneously. However, given the existence of our fuzzy matching protocols, we can tolerate false positives by running fuzzy matching on each positive match. Therefore, the high-level strategy is that the receiver hashes each ball center via LSH to some LSH entry, and the sender would identify multiple positive LSH entries for each of its points. If we set the parameters properly, the total number of false positives for each sender's point can be upper-bounded by $O(N^\rho)$ for some $\rho < 1$ which gives us just a *sub-quadratic* blowup in total communication and computation complexities.

One caveat is that there is a constant gap between the calculation of false positives and false negatives mentioned above, namely, false positives are calculated when points are $c\delta$-apart, whereas false negatives are calculated when points are δ-close. Fortunately, when the receiver's balls are disjoint (i.e., centers are 2δ-part), this gap can be filled by setting $c = 2$. Another caveat is that this approach does not support fuzzy PSI cardinality anymore due to the rationale behind the LSH: To guarantee a negligible false-negative rate, we typically have to prepare multiple LSH tables where a true positive might appear more than once.

For the formal details of this construction, we refer to the full version of the paper [2].

3 Preliminaries

We represent the computational security parameter as $\lambda \in \mathbb{N}$, the statistical security parameter as $\kappa \in \mathbb{N}$ and the output of the algorithm $\mathcal{A}$ on input in using $r \leftarrow \{0, 1\}$ as its randomness by $x \leftarrow \mathcal{A}(\text{in}; r)$. The randomness is often omitted and only explicitly mentioned when necessary. Efficient algorithms are considered to be *probabilistic polynomial time* (PPT) machines. We use $\approx_c$ to denote computational indistinguishability and $\approx_s$ to denote statistical indistinguishability of probability distributions. The notation $[n]$ signifies a set $\{1, \ldots, n\}$ and $[a : b]$ the set $\{a, a + 1, \ldots b - 1, b\}$. We use $\mathbf{c}[i : j]$ to represent a vector with a defined length of $[c_i, \ldots, c_j]$ and $\mathbf{c}$ to indicate a vector of c.

All the protocols presented in this work are two-party protocols. Security is proven against semi-honest adversaries via the standard simulation-based paradigm (see e.g., [29]).

3.1 Oblivious Key-Value Store (OKVS)

The concept of an oblivious key-value store (OKVS) was introduced by Garimella et al. [19] to capture the properties of data structures commonly used in PSI protocols. Subsequent works proposed OKVS constructions offering favorable trade-offs between encoding/decoding time and encoding size [6, 35].

Definition 1 (Oblivious Key-Value Store). *An oblivious key-value store* OKVS *is parameterized by a key space* $\mathcal{K}$, *a value space* $\mathcal{V}$, *computational and statistical security parameters* λ, κ, *respectively, and consists of two algorithms:*

- Encode : *takes as input a set of key-value pairs* $L \in (\mathcal{K} \times \mathcal{V})^n$ *and randomness* $\theta \in \{0, 1\}^\lambda$, *and outputs a vector* $P \in \mathcal{V}^m$ *or a failure indicator* $\perp$.
- Decode : *takes as input a vector* $P \in \mathcal{V}^m$, *a key* $k \in \mathcal{K}$ *and randomness* $\theta \in \{0, 1\}^\lambda$, *and outputs a value* $v \in \mathcal{V}$.

That satisfies:

- **Correctness:** *For all* $L \in (\mathcal{K} \times \mathcal{V})^n$ *with distinct keys and* $\theta \in \{0, 1\}^\lambda$ *for which* Encode$(L; \theta) = P \neq \perp$, *it holds that* $\forall (k, v) \in L$: Decode$(P, k; \theta) = v$.
- **Low failure probability:** *For all* $L \in (\mathcal{K} \times \mathcal{V})^n$ *with distinct keys:* $\Pr_{\theta \leftarrow_{\$} \{0,1\}^\lambda}[\text{Encode}(L; \theta) = \perp] \leq 2^{-\kappa}$.

354   A. van Baarsen and S. Pu

- **Obliviousness:** For any $\{k_1, \ldots, k_n\}, \{k_1', \ldots, k_n'\} \subseteq \mathcal{K}$ of n distinct keys and any $\theta \in \{0,1\}^\lambda$, if Encode does not output $\perp$, then for $v_1, \ldots, v_n \leftarrow_\$ \mathcal{V}$: $\{P \leftarrow \mathsf{Encode}(\{(k_i, v_i)_{i \in [n]})\}; \theta)\} \approx_c \{P' \leftarrow \mathsf{Encode}(\{(k_i', v_i)_{i \in [n]}\}; \theta)\}$.
- **Double obliviousness:** For all sets of n distinct keys $\{k_1, \ldots, k_n\} \subseteq \mathcal{K}$ and n values $\{v_1, \ldots, v_n\} \leftarrow_\$ \mathcal{V}$, there is $\mathsf{Encode}(\{(k_i, v_i)_{i \in [n]})\}; \theta)\}$ statistically indistinguishable from uniformly random element from $\mathcal{V}^m$.

The efficiency of OKVS is characterized by: (1) the time it takes to encode n key-value pairs; (2) the time it takes to decode a single key; (3) the ratio n/m between the number of key-value pairs n and the encoding size m, also called the *rate*. Recent OKVS constructions [6,19,35] achieve: (1) encoding time $O(n\kappa)$; (2) decoding time $O(\kappa)$; (3) constant rate.

For this work, we will need OKVS to support the value space $\mathcal{V}$ being equal to a cyclic group $\mathbb{G}$ of prime order p. A sufficient condition for this, which is satisfied by the efficient constructions of [6,19,35] is:

- $\mathbb{F}_p$-**Linear:** There exists a function $\mathsf{dec} : \mathcal{K} \times \{0,1\}^\lambda \to \mathbb{F}_p^m$ such that for all $P \in \mathbb{G}^m$, $k \in \mathcal{K}$ and $\theta \in \{0,1\}^\lambda$ it holds that $\mathsf{Decode}(P, k; \theta) := \langle \mathsf{dec}(k; \theta), P \rangle$, where for $\mathbf{d} \in \mathbb{F}_p^m$ and $\mathbf{g} \in \mathbb{G}^m$ we define $\langle \mathbf{d}, \mathbf{g} \rangle := g_1^{d_1} \cdots g_m^{d_m}$.

Lemma 1 (Independence). *If OKVS satisfies $\mathbb{F}_p$-linearity and $\mathsf{negl}(\kappa)$ failure probability, and θ is uniformly randomly chosen, then for any $L := \{(k_i, v_i)_{i \in [n]}\}$ with distinct keys, and any key $k \notin \{k_i\}_{i \in [n]}$, it holds that $\mathsf{Decode}(\mathsf{Encode}(L; \theta), k)$ is indistinguishable from random.*

3.2 Random Self-reductions of DDH Tuples

The well-known decisional Diffie-Hellman (DDH) assumption for a cyclic group $\mathbb{G} = \langle g \rangle$ of prime order p states that the distribution of Diffie-Hellman (DH) tuples $(g, h := g^s, h_1, h_2 := h_1^s)$, where $s \leftarrow_\$ \mathbb{Z}_p$, $h_1 \leftarrow_\$ \mathbb{G}$, is computationally indistinguishable from the distribution of random tuples $(g, h := g^s, h_1, h_2)$, where $s \leftarrow_\$ \mathbb{Z}_p$, $h_1, h_2 \leftarrow_\$ \mathbb{G}$. Naor and Reingold [32] show that deciding whether an arbitrary tuple (g, h, h_1, h_2) with $h, h_1, h_2 \in \mathbb{G}$ is a DH tuple can be reduced to breaking the DDH assumption. For this work, we consider a special case of this reduction where $h := g^s$ is fixed.

Lemma 2 (Random Self-Reduction [32]). *Let $\mathbb{G} := \langle g \rangle$ be a cyclic group of order p, let $h := g^s$ for $s \in \mathbb{Z}_p$ and $h_1, h_2 \in \mathbb{G}$. If $h_1' := g^a \cdot h_1^b$ and $h_2' := h^a \cdot h_2^b$, where $a, b \leftarrow_\$ \mathbb{Z}_p$, then:*

- h_1' *is uniformly random in $\mathbb{G}$ and $h_2' = (h_1')^s$ if $h_2 = h_1^s$.*
- (h_1', h_2') *is a uniformly random pair of group elements otherwise.*

$\mathcal{F}_{\text{FuzzyMatch}}$

Parameters : dimension d, radius δ, and a distance function $\text{dist}(\cdot, \cdot)$.

Functionality :

- RECEIVER inputs $\mathbf{w} \in \mathbb{Z}^d$.
- SENDER inputs $\mathbf{q} \in \mathbb{Z}^d$.
- Output 1 to RECEIVER if $\text{dist}(\mathbf{w}, \mathbf{q}) \leq \delta$, and 0 otherwise.

Possible Distance Functions

$\text{dist}(\mathbf{w}, \mathbf{q})$ is defined as:

- L_∞ Distance: $\text{dist}(\mathbf{w}, \mathbf{q}) = \max_{i \in [d]} |w_i - q_i|$
- Hamming Distance: $\text{dist}(\mathbf{w}, \mathbf{q}) = \sum_{i=1}^{d} (w_i \neq q_i)$
- Conjunction of Hamming Distance and L_∞ on δ_∞:
  $\text{dist}(\mathbf{w}, \mathbf{q}) = \sum_{i=1}^{d} (|w_i - q_i| > \delta_\infty)$
- L_p Distance: $\text{dist}(\mathbf{w}, \mathbf{q}) = \left(\sum_{i=1}^{d} |w_i - q_i|^p \right)^{1/p}$

Fig. 1. Ideal Functionality of Fuzzy Matching

4 Definitions and Functionalities

We define the two-message protocol as below, consisting of three algorithms:

- $\text{Receiver}_1(\text{INPUT}_R)$: The algorithm takes the RECEIVER's INPUT_R, outputs the first message msg_1 and its secret state st;
- $\text{Sender}_1(\text{INPUT}_S, \text{msg}_1)$: The algorithm takes the SENDER's INPUT_S and msg_1, outputs the second message msg_2;
- $\text{Receiver}_2(\text{st}, \text{msg}_2)$: The algorithm takes the state st and the second message msg_2, outputs the final OUTPUT.

4.1 Definition of Fuzzy Matching

We define the functionality of fuzzy matching between two points in Fig. 1, with different distance functions including both infinity (L_∞) and Minkowski (L_p) distance where $p \in [1, \infty)$.

4.2 Definition of Fuzzy (Circuit) Private Set Intersection

We define the functionality of fuzzy PSI and fuzzy circuit PSI in Figs. 2 and 3, respectively. Note that for standard fuzzy PSI, we also consider a slightly stronger functionality (compared to prior works) where the receiver only learns whether their points are in the intersection, but not the sender's exact points, which we call PSI with sender privacy (PSI-SP). We extend the functionality of fuzzy PSI to many closely related variants including PSI cardinality (PSI-CA), labeled PSI, and circuit PSI.

$\mathcal{F}_{\text{FuzzyPSI}}$

Parameters : dimension d, radius δ, cardinality of sets N, M, a distance function $\text{dist}(\cdot, \cdot)$, a leakage function $\text{leakage}(\cdot, \cdot)$, label length σ, and a concise description for receiver's and sender's points $\mathcal{D}_R, \mathcal{D}_S$, respectively.

Funtionality :

- RECEIVER inputs $\mathbf{W} \in \mathbb{Z}^{d \times N}$ according to $\mathcal{D}_R$.
- SENDER inputs $\mathbf{Q} \in \mathbb{Z}^{d \times M}$ according to $\mathcal{D}_S$.
  For Labeled PSI, SENDER inputs $\text{Label}_{\mathbf{Q}} \in \{0,1\}^{\sigma \times M}$.
- Return $\text{leakage}(\mathbf{W}, \mathbf{Q})$ to RECEIVER.

Possible Leakage Functions

$\text{leakage}(\mathbf{W}, \mathbf{Q})$ is defined as:

- PSI-CA: $\text{leakage}(\mathbf{W}, \mathbf{Q}) = \sum_{i \in [N], j \in [M]} (\text{dist}(\mathbf{w}_i, \mathbf{q}_j) \leq \delta)$.
- PSI: $\text{leakage}(\mathbf{W}, \mathbf{Q}) = \{\mathbf{q}_j \mid \exists i \in [N], \text{dist}(\mathbf{w}_i, \mathbf{q}_j) \leq \delta\}$.
- PSI-SP: $\text{leakage}(\mathbf{W}, \mathbf{Q}) = \{\mathbf{w}_i \mid \exists j \in [M], \text{dist}(\mathbf{w}_i, \mathbf{q}_j) \leq \delta\}$.
- Labeled PSI: $\text{leakage}(\mathbf{W}, \mathbf{Q}) = \{\text{label}_j \mid \exists i \in [N], \text{dist}(\mathbf{w}_i, \mathbf{q}_j) \leq \delta\}$, where label_j is the label associated with $\mathbf{q}_j$.

Fig. 2. Ideal Functionality of Fuzzy PSI

$\mathcal{F}_{\text{FuzzyCPSI}}$

Parameters : dimension d, radius δ, cardinality of sets N, M, a distance function $\text{dist}(\cdot, \cdot)$, a leakage function $\text{leakage}(\cdot, \cdot)$, associated data length σ, and a concise description for receiver's and sender's points $\mathcal{D}_R, \mathcal{D}_S$, respectively.

Funtionality :

- RECEIVER inputs $\mathbf{W} \in \mathbb{Z}^{d \times N}$ according to $\mathcal{D}_R$ and associated data $\bar{\mathbf{W}} \in \{0,1\}^{\sigma \times N}$.
- SENDER inputs $\mathbf{Q} \in \mathbb{Z}^{d \times M}$ according to $\mathcal{D}_S$ and associated data $\tilde{\mathbf{Q}} \in \{0,1\}^{\sigma \times M}$.
- For each $j \in [M]$, sample $r_j, s_j \leftarrow_{\$} \{0,1\}^{1+2\sigma}$ such that:
  $r_j \oplus s_j = 1\|\tilde{\mathbf{w}}_i\|\tilde{\mathbf{q}}_j$ if $\exists i \in [N]$ s.t. $\text{dist}(\mathbf{w}_i, \mathbf{q}_j) \leq \delta$, and $r_j \oplus s_j = 0^{1+2\sigma}$ otherwise.
- Return $(r_j)_{j \in [M]}$ to RECEIVER and $(s_j)_{j \in [M]}$ to SENDER.

Fig. 3. Ideal Functionality of Fuzzy Circuit PSI

5 Fuzzy Matching

We start by presenting a fuzzy matching protocol for two points in hyperspace with infinity distance (L_∞) and hamming distance, then we extend it into a more general setting with Minkowski distance ($L_{\mathsf{p} \in [1,\infty)}$).

5.1 Fuzzy Matching for Infinity Distance

We provide the protocol for infinity distance in Fig. 4. We also show how to generalize the above approach to support the conjunction of infinity and hamming distance in the full version of the paper [2]. The proofs of the following theorems can be found in the full version of the paper [2].

Theorem 1 (Correctness). *The protocol provided in Fig. 4 is correct with* $1 - \text{negl}(\kappa)$ *probability if* OKVS *satisfies perfect correctness defined in Sect. 3.1*

$\mathsf{GetList}_\infty(h, s, \mathbf{w}, \Delta_w)$ | $\mathsf{GetTuple}_\infty(g, h, \mathbf{q}, \Delta_q, \mathbf{E})$

For each $i = 1 \ldots d$:
  For each $j = -\delta \ldots \delta$:
    Set $\mathsf{key}_j \leftarrow \mathsf{H}_\gamma(\Delta_w \| w_i + j)$
    Set $h_j \leftarrow\!\!\$\ \mathbb{G}$
    Set $\mathsf{val}_j = (h_j \| h_j^s)$
    Set $\mathsf{list}_i = \{(\mathsf{key}_j, \mathsf{val}_j)_{j \in [-\delta:\delta]}\}$
  Return $\mathsf{list}_1, \ldots, \mathsf{list}_d$

For each $i = 1 \ldots d$:
  Set $\mathsf{key}_i \leftarrow \mathsf{H}_\gamma(\Delta_q \| q_i)$
  $(u_i \| v_i) \leftarrow \mathsf{Decode}(E_i, \mathsf{key}_i)$
Sample $a, b \leftarrow\!\!\$\ \mathbb{Z}_p$
Set $u_* = g^a \cdot \left(\prod_{i=1}^d u_i\right)^b$
Set $v' = h^a \cdot \left(\prod_{i=1}^d v_i\right)^b$
Set $v_* \leftarrow \mathsf{H}_{\kappa'}(v')$
Return (u_*, v_*)

$\mathsf{Receiver}_1(\mathbf{w} \in \mathbb{Z}^d)$ | $\mathsf{Sender}_1(\mathbf{q} \in \mathbb{Z}^d, \mathsf{msg}_1)$

Sample $g \leftarrow\!\!\$\ \mathbb{G}, s \leftarrow\!\!\$\ \mathbb{Z}_p$
Compute $h = g^s$
Get $\{\mathsf{list}_i\}_{i \in [d]} \leftarrow \mathsf{GetList}_\infty(h, s, \mathbf{w}, 0^\kappa)$
Set $E_i \leftarrow \mathsf{Encode}(\mathsf{list}_i)$ for each $i \in [d]$
Set $\mathbf{E} = \{E_1, \ldots, E_d\}$
Output $\mathsf{msg}_1 := (g, h, \mathbf{E}), \mathsf{st} := s$

Parse $\mathsf{msg}_1 := (g, h, \mathbf{E})$
$(u_*, v_*) \leftarrow \mathsf{GetTuple}_\infty(g, h, \mathbf{q}, 0^\kappa, \mathbf{E})$
Output $\mathsf{msg}_2 := (u_*, v_*)$

$\mathsf{Receiver}_2(\mathsf{st}, \mathsf{msg}_2)$

Parse $\mathsf{msg}_2 := (u_*, v_*)$ and $\mathsf{st} := s$
Output 1 if $\mathsf{H}_{\kappa'}(u_*^s) = v_*$ and 0 otherwise

Fig. 4. Fuzzy Matching for L_∞ Distance

and independence property from Lemma 1, and $\mathsf{H}_\gamma : \{0,1\}^* \mapsto \{0,1\}^\gamma, \mathsf{H}_{\kappa'} :$ $\mathbb{G} \mapsto \{0,1\}^{\kappa'}$ *are universal hash functions where* $\gamma = \kappa + \log\delta$ *and* $\kappa' = \kappa$.

Theorem 2 (Security). *The protocol provided in Fig. 4 realizes the functionality defined in Fig. 1 for* L_∞ *distance function against semi-honest adversaries if* OKVS *is oblivious and the DDH assumption holds.*

Theorem 3 (Complexity). *The communication complexity is* $O(2\delta d\lambda + \lambda + \kappa)$ *where* λ, κ *are the security and statistical parameters; The computational complexity is* $O(2\delta d)$ *for the receiver and* $O(d)$ *for the sender.*

5.2 Fuzzy Matching for Minkowski Distance

We provide the protocol for L_p distance where $1 \leq p < \infty$ in Fig. 5. For simplicity, we assume p is an integer for the moment. The proofs of the following theorems can be found in the full version of the paper [2].

Theorem 4 (Correctness). *The protocol provided in Fig. 5 is correct with* $1 - \mathsf{negl}(\kappa)$ *probability if* OKVS *satisfies perfect correctness defined in Sect. 3.1 and independence property from Lemma 1, and* $\mathsf{H}_\gamma : \{0,1\}^* \mapsto \{0,1\}^\gamma, \mathsf{H}_\kappa : \mathbb{G} \mapsto \{0,1\}^\kappa$ *are universal hash functions where* $\gamma = \kappa + \log\delta$ *and* $\kappa' = \kappa + p\log\delta$.

$\mathsf{GetList}_\mathsf{p}(h, s, \mathbf{w}, \Delta_w)$

For each $i = 1 \ldots d$:
  For each $j = -\delta \ldots \delta$:
    Set $\mathrm{key}_j \leftarrow \mathsf{H}_\gamma(\Delta_w \| w_i + j)$
    Set $h_j \leftarrow_\$ \mathbb{G}$
    Set $\mathrm{val}_j = (h_j \| h_j^s \cdot g^{|j|^\mathsf{p}})$
    Set $\mathrm{list}_i = \big\{ (\mathrm{key}_j, \mathrm{val}_j)_{j \in [-\delta:\delta]} \big\}$
Return $\mathrm{list}_1, \ldots, \mathrm{list}_d$

$\mathsf{GetTuple}_\mathsf{p}(g, h, \mathbf{q}, \Delta_q, \mathbf{E})$

For each $i = 1 \ldots d$:
  Set $\mathrm{key}_i \leftarrow \mathsf{H}_\gamma(\Delta_q \| q_i)$
  $(u_i \| v_i) \leftarrow \mathsf{Decode}(E_i, \mathrm{key}_i)$
Sample $a, b, c \leftarrow_\$ \mathbb{Z}_p$
Set $f_* = g^c \cdot \left(\prod_{i=1}^d u_i \right)^b$
Set $h_* = h^c \cdot \left(\prod_{=1}^d v_i \right)^b \cdot g^a$
Set $\mathrm{list}_* = \varnothing$
For each $j = 0 \ldots \delta^\mathsf{p}$:
  Set $x_j = \mathsf{H}_{\kappa'}(g^{a+b \cdot j})$
  Set $\mathrm{list}_* = \mathrm{list}_* \cup x_j$
Shuffle list_*
Return $(f_*, h_*, \mathrm{list}_*)$

$\mathsf{Receiver}_1(\mathbf{w} \in \mathbb{Z}^d)$

Sample $g \leftarrow_\$ \mathbb{G}, s \leftarrow_\$ \mathbb{Z}_p$
Compute $h = g^s$
Get $\{\mathrm{list}_{i \in [d]}\} \leftarrow \mathsf{GetList}_\mathsf{p}(h, s, \mathbf{w}, 0^\kappa)$
Get $E_i \leftarrow \mathsf{Encode}(\mathrm{list}_i)$ for each $i \in [d]$
Set $\mathbf{E} = \{E_1, \ldots, E_d\}$
Output $\mathrm{msg}_1 := (g, h, \mathbf{E}), \mathrm{st} := s$

$\mathsf{Sender}_1(\mathbf{q} \in \mathbb{Z}^d, \mathrm{msg}_1)$

Parse $\mathrm{msg}_1 := (g, h, \mathbf{E})$
$(f_*, h_*, \mathrm{list}_*) \leftarrow \mathsf{GetTuple}_\mathsf{p}(g, h, \mathbf{q}, 0^\kappa, \mathbf{E})$
Output $\mathrm{msg}_2 := (f_*, h_*, \mathrm{list}_*)$

$\mathsf{Receiver}_2(\mathrm{st}, \mathrm{msg}_2)$

Parse $\mathrm{msg}_2 := (f_*, h_*, \mathrm{list}_*)$ and $\mathrm{st} := s$
Set $x = \mathsf{H}_{\kappa'}(f_*^{-s} \cdot h_*)$
Output 1 if $x \in \mathrm{list}_*$ and 0 otherwise

Fig. 5. Fuzzy Matching for L_p Distance

Theorem 5 (Security). *The protocol provided in Fig. 5 realizes the functionality defined in Fig. 1 for L_p distance function, against semi-honest adversaries if OKVS is oblivious, the hash function $\mathsf{H}_{\kappa'} : \mathbb{G} \mapsto \{0,1\}^{\kappa'}$ is modeled as a random oracle, and the DDH assumption holds.*

Theorem 6 (Complexity). *The communication complexity is $O(2\delta d\lambda + 2\lambda + \delta^\mathsf{p}\kappa)$ where λ, κ are the security and statistical parameters; The computational complexity is $O(2\delta d)$ for the receiver and $O(d + \delta^\mathsf{p})$ for the sender.*

6 Fuzzy PSI in Low-Dimension Space

Clearly, with a fuzzy matching protocol in hand, we could straightforwardly execute a protocol instance for every pair of points from both the sender and receiver. Yet, this approach would lead to a quadratic increase in computational and communicative overheads. In the following sections, we depict some methods to circumvent this quadratic overhead, addressing both low-dimensional (in Sect. 6) and high-dimensional (in Sect. 7) spaces separately. We will deal with PSI-CA first (i.e., only let the receiver learn the cardinality of the intersection), then show how to extend PSI-CA to broader functionalities in Sect. 8, including standard PSI, labeled PSI, and circuit PSI.

6.1 Spatial Hashing Techniques

Consider the case that points are located in a low-dimension space $\mathcal{U}^d$ (e.g., $d = o(\log(\lambda))$ where $\mathcal{U}$ is the universe for each dimension. We use a similar idea from [20] to tile the entire space into hypercubes with side length 2δ, but we consider a more general L_p distance setting. That is, we consider L_p distance over a space tiled by L_∞ hypercubes. We denote each hypercube as a *cell*. Specifically, given a point $\mathbf{w} \in \mathcal{U}^d$, the index id_i of each cell $\mathcal{C}$ on each dimension $i \in [d]$ is determined by $\mathrm{id}_i = \lfloor \frac{w_i}{2\delta} \rfloor$ and each cell is labeled by $\mathrm{id}_0 \| \ldots \| \mathrm{id}_d$. The proofs of the following results are given in the full version of the paper [2].

Lemma 3 (Maximal Distance in a Cell). *Given two points* $\mathbf{w}, \mathbf{q} \in \mathcal{U}^d$ *located in the same cell with side length* 2δ, *then the distance between them is* $\mathrm{dist}_p(\mathbf{w}, \mathbf{q}) < 2\delta d^{\frac{1}{p}}$ *where* $p \in [1, \infty]$. *Specifically, if* $p = \infty$, $\mathrm{dist}_\infty(\mathbf{w}, \mathbf{q}) < 2\delta$.

Lemma 4 (Unique Center). *Suppose there are multiple* L_p *balls* ($p \in [1, \infty]$) *with radius* δ *lying in a d-dimension space which is tiled by hypercubes (i.e., cells) with side length* 2δ. *If these balls' centers are at least* $2\delta d^{\frac{1}{p}}$ *apart, then for each cell, there is at most one center of the balls lying in this cell. Specifically, if* $p = \infty$, *then the unique center holds for disjoint balls since* $2\delta d^{\frac{1}{p}}$ *degrades to* 2δ *in this case.*

Lemma 5 (Unique Ball). *Suppose there are multiple* δ-*radius* L_p *balls* ($p \in [1, \infty]$) *distributed in a d-dimension space which is tiled by hypercubes (cells) of side length* 2δ. *If these balls' centers are at least* $2\delta(d^{\frac{1}{p}} + 1)$ *apart from each other, then there exists at most one ball intersecting with the same cell. Specifically, if* $p = \infty$, *this holds for* L_∞ *balls with* 4δ-*apart centers.*

Lemma 6 (Unique Block). *Any* L_∞ *ball with radius* δ *will intersect with **exactly** 2^d cells with side length 2δ in a d-dimension space. Moreover, if we denote such 2^d cells together as a block (which is a hypercube with side length 4δ), then each block is unique for each disjoint ball. In other words, any two disjoint balls must be associated with different blocks.*

6.2 Fuzzy PSI-CA for Infinity Distance

We provide the detailed protocol in Fig. 6 realizing fuzzy PSI-CA for infinity distance where the receiver's points are 2δ apart from each other (i.e., the receiver's δ-radius balls are disjoint). In the figure, $\mathrm{block}_{4\delta}$ returns the label of the block of side-length 4δ, $\mathrm{cell}_{2\delta}$ returns the label of the cell of side-length

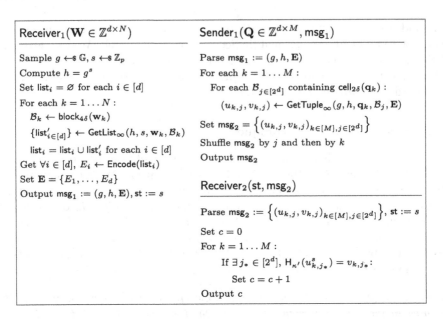

Fig. 6. Fuzzy PSI-CA, infinity distance, receiver's points are 2δ apart (i.e., disjoint balls)

2δ, and GetList, GetTuple are provided in Fig. 4. The proofs of the following theorems can be found in the full version of the paper [2], and we also generalize this approach to the setting where both parties hold a structured set of hyperballs.

Theorem 7 (Correctness). *The protocol presented in Fig. 6 is correct with probability $1 - \mathsf{negl}(\kappa)$ if OKVS satisfies perfect correctness defined in Sect. 3.1 and the independence property from Lemma 1, $\mathsf{H}_\gamma : \{0,1\}^* \mapsto \{0,1\}^\gamma, \mathsf{H}_{\kappa'} : \mathbb{G} \mapsto \{0,1\}^{\kappa'}$ used in GetList, GetTuple are universal hash functions where $\gamma = \kappa + \log(MN\delta)$, $\kappa' = \kappa + d\log M$, and the receiver's points are 2δ apart.*

Theorem 8 (Security). *The protocol presented in Fig. 6 realizes the fuzzy PSI-CA functionality defined in Fig. 2 for infinity distance against semi-honest adversaries if OKVS is oblivious, and the DDH assumption holds.*

Theorem 9 (Complexity). *The protocol provided in Fig. 6 has communication complexity $O(2\delta dN\lambda + 2^d M(\lambda + \kappa'))$ where $\lambda, \kappa = \kappa' - d\log M$ are the security and statistical parameters; The computational complexity is $O(2\delta dN + 2^d M)$ for the receiver and $O(2^d dM)$ for the sender.*

6.3 Fuzzy PSI-CA for Minkowski Distance

Assuming that the receiver's points are spaced $2\delta(d^{\frac{1}{p}} + 1)$ apart, we can allow the receiver to iterate through each possible location, as depicted in Fig. 7. The proofs of the following theorems can be found in the full version of the paper [2]

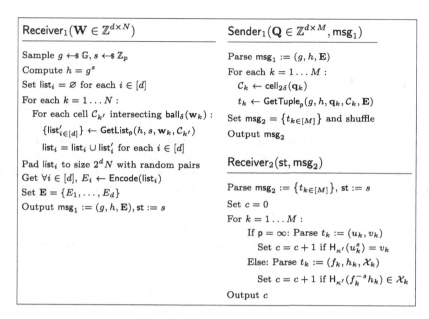

Fig. 7. Fuzzy PSI-CA, L_p distance with $p \in [1, \infty]$, receiver's points are $2\delta(d^{\frac{1}{p}} + 1)$ apart

Theorem 10 (Correctness). *The protocol presented in Fig. 7 is correct with probability $1 - \mathsf{negl}(\kappa)$ if OKVS satisfies the perfect correctness defined in Sect. 3.1 and the independence property from Lemma 1, $\mathsf{H}_\gamma : \{0,1\}^* \mapsto \{0,1\}^\gamma, \mathsf{H}_{\kappa'} : \mathbb{G} \mapsto \{0,1\}^{\kappa'}$ used in GetList, GetTuple are universal hash functions where $\gamma = \kappa + d\log(\delta N) + \log M$, $\kappa' = \kappa + p\log(M\delta)$ if $p < \infty$ and $\kappa' = \kappa + \log M$ if $p = \infty$, and the receiver's points are $2\delta(d^{\frac{1}{p}} + 1)$ apart for $p \in [1, \infty]$.*

Theorem 11 (Security). *The protocol presented in Fig. 7 realizes the fuzzy PSI-CA functionality defined in Fig. 2 for $L_{p \in [1, \infty]}$ distance against semi-honest adversaries if OKVS is oblivious and the DDH assumption holds. Additionally, if $p < \infty$, the hash function $\mathsf{H}_{\kappa'} : \mathbb{G} \mapsto \{0,1\}^{\kappa'}$ is modeled as a random oracle.*

Theorem 12 (Complexity). *The protocol provided in Fig. 7 has communication complexity $O(2\delta d2^d N\lambda + M(\lambda + \kappa'))$ when $L_p = L_\infty$ and $O(2\delta d2^d N\lambda + M(2\lambda + \delta^p \kappa'))$ when $p \in [1, \infty)$ where λ, κ are the security and statistical parameters. Specifically, $\kappa = \kappa' - \log M$ if $p = \infty$ and $\kappa = \kappa' - p\log(M\delta)$ otherwise. The receiver's computational complexity is $O(2\delta d2^d N + M)$; The sender's computational complexity is $O(dM)$ if $p = \infty$, and $O(dM + \delta^p)$ otherwise.*

7 Fuzzy PSI in High-Dimension Space

In this section, we construct an efficient fuzzy PSI protocol in a high-dimensional space, i.e., of a polynomially large dimension. For infinity distance, we provide a fuzzy PSI-CA protocol in Sect. 7.1 and extend it to richer functionalities in Sect. 8; For Minkowski distance, please refer to the full version of the paper [2] for details.

7.1 Infinity Distance

Suppose we assume the receiver's set has good distribution in a high-dimensional space, particularly if each ball has disjoint projections (i.e., separated) from others on *at least one* dimension. In this case, we can get communication and computation complexity both scaling *polynomially* in the dimension. For instance, if balls are uniformly distributed, then it satisfies this predicate with overwhelming probability. The proof of this can be found in the full version of the paper [2].

Definition 2 (Separated Balls). *The set of δ-radius balls are separated in a d-dimension space if and only if the projections are separated on at least one dimension for each ball. Specifically, for the center $\mathbf{w}_k$ of each ball in the set, there exists some dimension $i_* \in [d]$ such that*

$$\forall j \in [-\delta : \delta], \; w_{k,i_*} + j \notin \{w_{k',i_*} + j'\}_{k' \neq k, j' \in [-\delta:\delta]},$$

where $\{w_{k',i_*} + j'\}$ is the set of projections from other balls.

Lemma 7 (Uniform Distribution). *If centers of the balls are uniformly distributed $(\mathbf{W} \leftarrow_{\$} \mathcal{U}^{d \times N})$ where $\mathcal{U} := \mathbb{Z}_{2^u}$, then it has the property defined in Definition 2 with probability $1 - \mathsf{negl}(d)$.*

Given the receiver's balls are separated as defined in Definition 2, we provide an efficient protocol in Fig. 8 which gets rid of the 2^d term for both communication and computation. The proofs of the following theorems can be found in the full version of the paper [2].

Theorem 13 (Correctness). *The protocol presented in Fig. 8 is correct with probability $1 - \mathsf{negl}(\kappa)$ if OKVS satisfies the perfect correctness, $\mathbb{F}_p$-linearity defined in Sect. 3.1 and the independence property from Lemma 1, $\mathsf{H}_\gamma : \{0,1\}^* \mapsto \{0,1\}^\gamma$, $\mathsf{H}_{\kappa'} : \mathbb{G} \mapsto \{0,1\}^{\kappa'}$ are universal hash functions where $\gamma = \kappa + \log NM\delta$, $\kappa' = \kappa + \log M$, and the receiver's set are separated as defined in Definition 2. Particularly, we require that the decoding vector satisfies $\mathsf{dec}(\cdot) \in \{0,1\}^m$ and $\mathsf{HammingWeight}(\mathsf{dec}(\cdot)) = O(\kappa)$ where m is the size of the OKVS.*

Theorem 14 (Security). *The protocol presented in Fig. 8 satisfies the fuzzy PSI-CA functionality defined in Fig. 2 for infinity distance against semi-honest adversaries if OKVS is doubly oblivious, and the DDH assumption holds.*

Theorem 15 (Complexity). *The protocol presented in Fig. 8 has communication complexity $O\left((2\delta d)^2 N\lambda + M(\lambda + \kappa)\right)$ where λ, $\kappa = \kappa' - \log M$ are computational and statistical parameters; The computational complexity is $O((2\delta d)^2 N + M)$ for the receiver and $O(2d^2 M)$ for the sender.*

Receiver$_1$($\mathbf{W} \in \mathbb{Z}^{d \times N}$)

Sample $g \leftarrow_\$ \mathbb{G}$, $s \leftarrow_\$ \mathbb{Z}_p$, compute $h = g^s$, and set list$_i = \varnothing$ for each $i \in [d]$

Set $m = (2\delta + 1)d \cdot (1 + \epsilon)$ where ϵ is the expansion factor of the OKVS scheme

Denote dec for the $\mathbb{F}_p$-linear decoding function of the OKVS scheme

Denote as I_k the *first* separated dimension for the ball $\mathbf{w}_k \in \mathbf{W}$

Sample $\zeta \leftarrow_\$ \mathbb{G}$

For each $k = 1 \ldots, N$:

  For each $i = 1 \ldots d$:

    For each $j \in [-\delta, +\delta]$:

      If $i = I_k$:

        Set val$_j \leftarrow \mathsf{Encode}\Big(\big\{(\mathsf{H}_\gamma(i', w_{k,i'} + j'), \quad h_{i',j'} \| h^s_{i',j'} \cdot \zeta^{-x_{i',j'}})\big\}_{i' \in [d], j' \in [-\delta, +\delta]}\Big)$

        where $h_{i',j'} \leftarrow_\$ \mathbb{G}$ and $x_{i',j'} := (d-1) \cdot \sum_{\ell=1}^m \mathsf{dec}(\mathsf{H}_\gamma(i', w_{k,i'} + j))_\ell$

      Else:

        Set val$_j := (\mathbf{r}_j \| \zeta \cdot \mathbf{r}^s_j)$ where $\mathbf{r}_j \leftarrow_\$ \mathbb{G}^m$

        Set list$_i = $ list$_i \cup (\mathsf{H}_\gamma(i, w_{k,i} + j), \quad$ val$_j)$

Pad each list$_i$ to size $(2\delta + 1)N$ with random key-val pairs

Set $E_i \leftarrow \mathsf{Encode}(\mathsf{list}_i)$ for each $i \in [d]$, and $\mathbf{E} = \{E_1, \ldots, E_d\}$

Output msg$_1 := (g, h, \mathbf{E})$, st $:= s$

Sender$_1$($\mathbf{Q} \in \mathbb{Z}^{d \times M}$, msg$_1$)

Parse msg$_1 := (g, h, \mathbf{E})$

For each $k = 1 \ldots M$:

  Sample $a, b \leftarrow_\$ \mathbb{Z}_p$

  For each $i = 1 \ldots d$:

    Set $\mathbf{e}_i \leftarrow \mathsf{Decode}(E_i, \mathsf{H}_\gamma(i, q_{k,i}))$

    For each $j = 1 \ldots d$:

    Set $(f'_j \| h'_j) \leftarrow \mathsf{Decode}(\mathbf{e}_i, \mathsf{H}_\gamma(j, q_{k,j}))$

  Set $f_i := \prod_{j=1}^d f'_j$, $h_i := \prod_{j=1}^d h'_j$

  Set $u_k = g^a \cdot \prod_{i=1}^d f^b_i$, $v'_k = h^a \cdot \prod_{i=1}^d h^b_i$, and $v_k = \mathsf{H}_{\kappa'}(v'_k)$

Set msg$_2 = \{(u_k, v_k)_{k \in [M]}\}$

Shuffle and output msg$_2$

Receiver$_2$(st, msg$_2$)

Parse msg$_2 := \{(u_k, v_k)_{k \in [M]}\}$, st $:= s$

Set $c = 0$

For each $k = 1 \ldots M$:

  If $\mathsf{H}_{\kappa'}(u^s_k) = v_k$, set $c = c + 1$

Output c

Fig. 8. Fuzzy PSI-CA, infinity distance, each ball is separated on at least one dimension

8 Extending to Broader Functionalities

We show above protocols can be extended to a broader class of functionalities, including standard PSI, PSI with sender privacy, labeled PSI, and circuit PSI, with small tweaks and therefore preserving the efficiency. We describe extensions for all protocols in this work except for the L_p distance protocol in high dimensional space since currently, the simulator for a corrupt receiver needs to know the points of the sender that lie in the intersection, i.e., only works for the standard PSI functionality. We describe the main idea behind the extensions and give the formal details for the different protocol settings (including PSI with sender privacy and circuit PSI) in the full version of the paper [2].

Labeled PSI. For labeled PSI, the sender has some labels $\mathsf{label}_k \in \{0,1\}^\sigma$ attached to their input points $\mathbf{q}_k$, $k \in [M]$, and the receiver wishes to learn the labels of the points for which there exists an $i \in [N]$ such that $\mathsf{dist}(\mathbf{w}_i, \mathbf{q}_k) \leq \delta$ (see Fig. 2 for the ideal functionality). It can be realized for the protocol in Fig. 6 (and similar for the protocols in Figs. 7 and 8 by ignoring the index j in these cases) by letting the sender use $v_{k,j}$ as a one-time pad to encrypt label_k together with a special prefix, e.g., 0^κ, indicating that the label belongs to a valid match. For the protocol in Fig. 7 with $\mathsf{p} \neq \infty$, the sender instead uses the $x_{k,j} \in \mathcal{X}_k$ as a one-time pad to encrypt $0^\kappa \| \mathsf{label}_k$.

Standard PSI. By letting the labels be a description of the sender's points, we can realize standard PSI, where the receiver learns the sender's points $\mathbf{q}_k$ for which there exists an $i \in [N]$ such that $\mathsf{dist}(\mathbf{w}_i, \mathbf{q}_k) \leq \delta$ (see Fig. 2 for the ideal functionality).

9 Performance Evaluation

In this section, we provide a micro-benchmark for our fuzzy PSI protocols for $L_{\mathsf{p} \in \{1,2,\infty\}}$ in low-dimension settings.

Implementation. We implement the standard fuzzy PSI variant (i.e., the receiver learns the sender's points in the intersection) in three different metrics (L_∞, L_1, L_2) in a d-dimension space where $d = \{2,3,5,10\}$, following the Figs. 6, and 7. The proof-of-concept implementation[5] is written in Rust, with less than 1000 lines of code. We use Risttreto and curve25519-dalek to instantiate the underlying group $\mathbb{G}$, use FxHash and Blake3 to instantiate the hash function $\mathsf{H}_\gamma, \mathsf{H}_{\kappa'}$. We choose the security parameter $\lambda = 128$ and statistical parameter $\kappa = 40$ as usual. To instantiate the OKVS, we follow the construction from [6] but working in $\mathbb{F}_p$ and the expansion rate $\epsilon = 0.5$ to make sure we have $2^{-\kappa}$ correctness error rate. Though it can be optimized to $\epsilon = 0.1 \sim 0.25$ to have a more compact size, the encoding and decoding time would also increase accordingly.

Environment. We run the experiments on an ordinary laptop over a single thread: Macbook Air (M1 2020) with 8 GB RAM and a 2.1 GHz CPU, without using SIMD (e.g., AVX, NEON) optimizations. We measure the entire protocol time in a local network setting (i.e., LAN-like) without considering latency.

9.1 Concrete Performance

Fuzzy PSI. We mainly consider three cases for fuzzy PSI protocols: The receiver's points are 2δ-apart (shown in Table 2), and $2\delta(d^{\frac{1}{p}} + 1)$-apart (shown in Table 3). It is worth noting that, any distribution of the receiver's points can

---

[5] The open-sourced repository: https://github.com/sihangpu/fuzzy_PSI

Table 2. Fuzzy PSI when points are $>2\delta$ (i.e., disjoint balls)

Metric	Radius δ	Dimension d	Receiver's N	Sender's M	Bandwidth	Total Time
L_∞ [20]	30	2	2^{11}	2^{20}	$\approx 9865^{b}$ MB	$\gg 1500^{a}$ s
L_∞	30	2	2^{11}	2^{20}	173 MB	257.25 s
L_∞	30	5	2^{13}	2^{11}	231 MB	177.18 s
L_∞	1000	2	2^{11}	2^{11}	753 MB	303.59 s

[a] Estimated by assuming each PRG evaluation is about 4.8 ns and hash evaluation is about 4.8 ns/byte [25]. Only consider the computational costs at the receiver's side.
[b] Estimated by the concrete bFSS size provided in [20].

Table 3. Fuzzy PSI when points are $>2\delta(d^{\frac{1}{p}}+1)$

Metric	Radius δ	Dimension d	Receiver's N	Sender's M	Bandwidth	Total Time
L_∞ [20]	10	5	2^{11}	2^{20}	-	$\gg 4300^{a}$ s
L_∞ [20]	30	10	2^{5}	2^{20}	$\approx 10^{11\ b}$ MB	$\gg 10^{13\ a}$ s
L_∞	30	2	2^{11}	2^{20}	134 MB	99.28 s
L_∞	10	5	2^{11}	2^{20}	1240 MB	432.42 s
L_∞	30	10	2^{5}	2^{20}	1844 MB	1135.63 s
L_1	10	2	2^{11}	2^{20}	107 MB	94.10 s
L_1	30	2	2^{11}	2^{20}	369 MB	111.07 s
L_2	10	2	2^{11}	2^{20}	467 MB	97.37 s
L_2	30	2	2^{11}	2^{20}	3727 MB	121.21 s

[a] Estimated by assuming each PRG evaluation is about 4.8 ns and hash evaluation is about 4.8 ns/byte [25]. Only consider the computational costs at the receiver's side.
[b] Estimated by the concrete bFSS size provided in [20].

be reduced to the disjoint setting by varying the radius. Specifically, for the L_∞ metric, the second case degrades to 4δ-apart points; For the $L_{\{1,2\}}$ metric, our protocol only supports the second case. Our protocols can support large volume balls since our computation and communication cost scaled only sub-linearly to the total volume. In the full version of the paper [2] we also explore the setting where both receiver and sender hold a structured set consisting of hyperballs.

For comparison, we estimate the concrete communication cost for [20] based on their concrete bFSS size table reported in the paper. For the disjoint balls setting we use the reported share sizes for their spatial hash ∘ sum ∘ tensor ∘ ggm $(0.5, 1)$-bFSS, assume bFSS evaluation to cost $(2 \log \delta)^d$ PRG calls, estimate PRG calls to take 10 machine cycles using AES-NI, and put $\ell = 440$. For the distance $> 4\delta$ setting we use the reported share sizes for their spatial hash ∘ concat ∘ tt $(1 - 1/2^d, d)$-bFSS, assume bFSS evaluation to cost 1 machine cycle and put $\ell = 162$ for dimension $d = 5$, $\ell = 139$ for dimension $d = 10$. In all settings we estimate the correlation-robust hash calls at the end of the protocol to take around 10 machine cycles/byte, based on the fastest performance reported in [25] on 64-byte inputs. We assume a universe size of 32-bit integers for each dimension. Note that here we report the most conservative estimates for their running time and can only be considered as a loose lower bound.

10   Conclusion

In this work, we explored the fuzzy PSI in a more general setting, including higher dimensional space, comprehensive L_p distance metric, and extended functionality variants. We also demonstrate the practicality of our protocols by experimental results. However, there are still many open problems to be solved, such as, our L_p protocols have an additional $O(\delta^p)$ communication overhead for each sender's point which might be expensive when δ or p is too large. Another interesting problem to think is how to get a more efficient protocol in polynomially large dimension space for L_2 distance, or if we can weaken the separated assumption further for L_∞ distance? We leave them as well as the concrete efficiency optimization to future works. Also, current fuzzy PSI protocols with negligible correctness error require disjoint balls at least. What if the receiver's balls are intersected? Any non-trivial approaches without quadratic overhead would be interesting to explore.

References

1. Alamati, N., Branco, P., Döttling, N., Garg, S., Hajiabadi, M., Pu, S.: Laconic private set intersection and applications. In: Nissim, K., Waters, B. (eds.) TCC 2021. LNCS, vol. 13044, pp. 94–125. Springer, Cham (2021). https://doi.org/10.1007/978-3-030-90456-2_4

2. van Baarsen, A., Pu, S.: Fuzzy private set intersection with large hyperballs. Cryptology ePrint Archive, Paper 2024/330 (2024). https://eprint.iacr.org/2024/330

3. Badrinarayanan, S., Miao, P., Raghuraman, S., Rindal, P.: Multi-party threshold private set intersection with sublinear communication. In: Garay, J.A. (ed.) PKC 2021, Part II. LNCS, vol. 12711, pp. 349–379. Springer, Cham (2021). https://doi.org/10.1007/978-3-030-75248-4_13

4. Bartusek, J., Garg, S., Jain, A., Policharla, G.V.: End-to-end secure messaging with traceability only for illegal content. In: Hazay, C., Stam, M. (eds.) Advances in Cryptology – EUROCRYPT 2023. LNCS, Part V, Germany, Lyon, France, 23–27 April 2023, vol. 14008, pp. 35–66. Springer, Heidelberg (2023). https://doi.org/10.1007/978-3-031-30589-4_2

5. Bhowmick, A., Boneh, D., Myers, S., Talwar, K., Tarbe, K.: The Apple PSI system (2021). https://www.apple.com/child-safety/pdf/Apple_PSI_System_Security_Protocol_and_Analysis.pdf

6. Bienstock, A., Patel, S., Seo, J.Y., Yeo, K.: Near-optimal oblivious key-value stores for efficient PSI, PSU and volume-hiding multi-maps. In: USENIX Security Symposium, pp. 301–318. USENIX Association (2023)

7. Branco, P., Döttling, N., Pu, S.: Multiparty cardinality testing for threshold private intersection. In: Garay, J. (ed.) 24th International Conference on Theory and Practice of Public Key Cryptography, PKC 2021. LNCS, Part II, Virtual Event, 10–13 May 2021, vol. 12711, pp. 32–60. Springer, Heidelberg (2011). https://doi.org/10.1007/978-3-030-75248-4_2

8. Chakraborti, A., Fanti, G., Reiter, M.K.: Distance-aware private set intersection. In: USENIX Security Symposium. USENIX Association (2023)
9. Chase, M., Miao, P.: Private set intersection in the internet setting from lightweight oblivious PRF. In: Micciancio, D., Ristenpart, T. (eds.) CRYPTO 2020, Part III. LNCS, vol. 12172, pp. 34–63. Springer, Cham (2020). https://doi.org/10.1007/978-3-030-56877-1_2
10. Chen, H., Huang, Z., Laine, K., Rindal, P.: Labeled PSI from fully homomorphic encryption with malicious security. In: Lie, D., Mannan, M., Backes, M., Wang, X. (eds.) 25th Conference on Computer and Communications Security, ACM CCS 2018, Toronto, ON, Canada, 15–19 October 2018, pp. 1223–1237. ACM Press (2018). https://doi.org/10.1145/3243734.3243836
11. Chen, H., Laine, K., Rindal, P.: Fast private set intersection from homomorphic encryption. In: Thuraisingham, B.M., Evans, D., Malkin, T., Xu, D. (eds.) 24th Conference on Computer and Communications Security, ACM CCS 2017, Dallas, TX, USA, 31 October–November 2 2017, pp. 1243–1255. ACM Press (2017). https://doi.org/10.1145/3133956.3134061
12. Chmielewski, L., Hoepman, J.: Fuzzy private matching (extended abstract). In: ARES, pp. 327–334. IEEE Computer Society (2008)
13. Chor, B., Gilboa, N., Naor, M.: Private information retrieval by keywords. Cryptology ePrint Archive, Report 1998/003 (1998). https://eprint.iacr.org/1998/003
14. Cong, K., et al.: Labeled PSI from homomorphic encryption with reduced computation and communication. In: Vigna, G., Shi, E. (eds.) 28th Conference on Computer and Communications Security, ACM CCS 2021, Virtual Event, Republic of Korea, 15–19 November 2021, pp. 1135–1150. ACM Press (2021). https://doi.org/10.1145/3460120.3484760
15. Dong, C., Chen, L., Wen, Z.: When private set intersection meets big data: an efficient and scalable protocol. In: Sadeghi, A.R., Gligor, V.D., Yung, M. (eds.) 20th Conference on Computer and Communications Security, ACM CCS 2013, Berlin, Germany, 4–8 November 2013, pp. 789–800. ACM Press (2013). https://doi.org/10.1145/2508859.2516701
16. Duong, T., Phan, D.H., Trieu, N.: Catalic: delegated PSI cardinality with applications to contact tracing. In: Moriai, S., Wang, H. (eds.) ASIACRYPT 2020, Part III. LNCS, vol. 12493, pp. 870–899. Springer, Cham (2020). https://doi.org/10.1007/978-3-030-64840-4_29
17. Dupont, P.-A., Hesse, J., Pointcheval, D., Reyzin, L., Yakoubov, S.: Fuzzy password-authenticated key exchange. In: Nielsen, J.B., Rijmen, V. (eds.) EUROCRYPT 2018. LNCS, vol. 10822, pp. 393–424. Springer, Cham (2018). https://doi.org/10.1007/978-3-319-78372-7_13
18. Freedman, M.J., Nissim, K., Pinkas, B.: Efficient private matching and set intersection. In: Cachin, C., Camenisch, J.L. (eds.) EUROCRYPT 2004. LNCS, vol. 3027, pp. 1–19. Springer, Heidelberg (2004). https://doi.org/10.1007/978-3-540-24676-3_1
19. Garimella, G., Pinkas, B., Rosulek, M., Trieu, N., Yanai, A.: Oblivious key-value stores and amplification for private set intersection. In: Malkin, T., Peikert, C. (eds.) CRYPTO 2021, Part II. LNCS, vol. 12826, pp. 395–425. Springer, Cham (2021). https://doi.org/10.1007/978-3-030-84245-1_14
20. Garimella, G., Rosulek, M., Singh, J.: Structure-aware private set intersection, with applications to fuzzy matching. In: Dodis, Y., Shrimpton, T. (eds.) Advances in Cryptology, CRYPTO 2022, Part I. LNCS, Santa Barbara, CA, USA, 15–18 August 2022, vol. 13507, pp. 323–352. Springer, Heidelberg (2022). https://doi.org/10.1007/978-3-031-15802-5_12

21. Garimella, G., Rosulek, M., Singh, J.: Malicious secure, structure-aware private set intersection. In: Handschuh, H., Lysyanskaya, A. (eds.) Advances in Cryptology, CRYPTO 2023, Part I. LNCS, Santa Barbara, CA, USA, 20–24 August 2023, vol. 14081, pp. 577–610. Springer, Heidelberg (2023). https://doi.org/10.1007/978-3-031-38557-5_19

22. Ghosh, S., Simkin, M.: The communication complexity of threshold private set intersection. In: Boldyreva, A., Micciancio, D. (eds.) CRYPTO 2019, Part II. LNCS, vol. 11693, pp. 3–29. Springer, Cham (2019). https://doi.org/10.1007/978-3-030-26951-7_1

23. Ghosh, S., Simkin, M.: Threshold private set intersection with better communication complexity. In: Boldyreva, A., Kolesnikov, V. (eds.) 26th International Conference on Theory and Practice of Public Key Cryptography, PKC 2023, Part II. LNCS, Atlanta, GA, USA, 7–10 May 2023, vol. 13941, pp. 251–272. Springer, Heidelberg (2023). https://doi.org/10.1007/978-3-031-31371-4_9

24. Huang, Y., Evans, D., Katz, J.: Private set intersection: are garbled circuits better than custom protocols? In: ISOC Network and Distributed System Security Symposium, NDSS 2012, San Diego, CA, USA, 5–8 February 2012. The Internet Society (2012)

25. ECRYPT II: eBACS: ECRYPT Benchmarking of Cryptographic Systems (2023). https://bench.cr.yp.to/results-sha3

26. Indyk, P., Woodruff, D.P.: Polylogarithmic private approximations and efficient matching. In: Halevi, S., Rabin, T. (eds.) 3rd Theory of Cryptography Conference, TCC 2006. LNCS, New York, NY, USA, 4–7 March 2006, vol. 3876, pp. 245–264. Springer, Heidelberg (2006). https://doi.org/10.1007/11681878_13

27. Ion, M., et al.: On deploying secure computing: private intersection-sum-with-cardinality. In: EuroS&P, pp. 370–389. IEEE (2020)

28. Kolesnikov, V., Kumaresan, R., Rosulek, M., Trieu, N.: Efficient batched oblivious PRF with applications to private set intersection. In: Weippl, E.R., Katzenbeisser, S., Kruegel, C., Myers, A.C., Halevi, S. (eds.) 23rd Conference on Computer and Communications Security, ACM CCS 2016, Vienna, Austria, 24–28 October 2016, pp. 818–829. ACM Press (2016). https://doi.org/10.1145/2976749.2978381

29. Lindell, Y.: How to simulate it - a tutorial on the simulation proof technique. Cryptology ePrint Archive, Report 2016/046 (2016). https://eprint.iacr.org/2016/046

30. Meadows, C.: A more efficient cryptographic matchmaking protocol for use in the absence of a continuously available third party. In: S&P, pp. 134–137. IEEE Computer Society (1986)

31. Muffett, A.: Facebook: password hashing & authentication (2015). https://rwc.iacr.org/2015/program.html

32. Naor, M., Reingold, O.: Number-theoretic constructions of efficient pseudo-random functions. In: 38th Annual Symposium on Foundations of Computer Science, Miami Beach, Florida, 19–22 October 1997, pp. 458–467. IEEE Computer Society Press (1997). https://doi.org/10.1109/SFCS.1997.646134

33. Pal, B., et al.: Might I Get Pwned: a second generation compromised credential checking service. In: USENIX Security Symposium, pp. 1831–1848. USENIX Association (2022)

34. Pinkas, B., Schneider, T., Tkachenko, O., Yanai, A.: Efficient circuit-based PSI with linear communication. In: Ishai, Y., Rijmen, V. (eds.) EUROCRYPT 2019. LNCS, vol. 11478, pp. 122–153. Springer, Cham (2019). https://doi.org/10.1007/978-3-030-17659-4_5

35. Raghuraman, S., Rindal, P.: Blazing fast PSI from improved OKVS and subfield VOLE. In: Yin, H., Stavrou, A., Cremers, C., Shi, E. (eds.) 29th Conference on Computer and Communications Security, ACM CCS 2022, Los Angeles, CA, USA, 7–11 November 2022, pp. 2505–2517. ACM Press (2022). https://doi.org/10.1145/3548606.3560658

36. Rindal, P., Schoppmann, P.: VOLE-PSI: fast OPRF and circuit-PSI from vector-OLE. In: Canteaut, A., Standaert, F.-X. (eds.) EUROCRYPT 2021, Part II. LNCS, vol. 12697, pp. 901–930. Springer, Cham (2021). https://doi.org/10.1007/978-3-030-77886-6_31

37. Uzun, E., Chung, S.P., Kolesnikov, V., Boldyreva, A., Lee, W.: Fuzzy labeled private set intersection with applications to private real-time biometric search. In: Bailey, M., Greenstadt, R. (eds.) 30th USENIX Security Symposium, USENIX Security 2021, 11–13 August 2021, pp. 911–928. USENIX Association (2021)

38. Ye, Q., Steinfeld, R., Pieprzyk, J., Wang, H.: Efficient fuzzy matching and intersection on private datasets. In: Lee, D., Hong, S. (eds.) ICISC 2009. LNCS, vol. 5984, pp. 211–228. Springer, Heidelberg (2010). https://doi.org/10.1007/978-3-642-14423-3_15

Fast Batched Asynchronous Distributed Key Generation

Jens Groth[1]([✉]) [iD] and Victor Shoup[2] [iD]

[1] Nexus, New York, USA
jens@nexus.xyz
[2] Offchain Labs, New York, USA
victor@shoup.net

Abstract. We present new protocols for threshold Schnorr signatures that work in an *asynchronous* communication setting, providing *robustness* and *optimal resilience*. These protocols provide unprecedented performance in terms of communication and computational complexity. In terms of communication complexity, for each signature, a single party must transmit a few dozen group elements and scalars across the network (independent of the size of the signing committee). In terms of computational complexity, the amortized cost for one party to generate a signature is actually less than that of just running the standard Schnorr signing or verification algorithm (at least for moderately sized signing committees, say, up to 100).

For example, we estimate that with a signing committee of 49 parties, at most 16 of which are corrupt, we can generate *50,000 Schnorr signatures per second* (assuming each party can dedicate one standard CPU core and 500 Mbs of network bandwidth to signing). Importantly, this estimate includes both the cost of an offline precomputation phase (which just churns out message independent "presignatures") and an online signature generation phase. Also, the online signing phase can generate a signature with very little network latency (just one to three rounds, depending on how throughput and latency are balanced).

To achieve this result, we provide two new innovations. One is a new secret sharing protocol (again, asynchronous, robust, optimally resilient) that allows the dealer to securely distribute shares of a large batch of ephemeral secret keys, and to publish the corresponding ephemeral public keys. To achieve better performance, our protocol minimizes public-key operations, and in particular, is based on a novel technique that does *not* use the traditional technique based on "polynomial commitments". The second innovation is a new algorithm to efficiently combine ephemeral public keys contributed by different parties (some possibly corrupt) into a smaller number of secure ephemeral public keys. This new algorithm is based on a novel construction of a so-called "super-invertible matrix" along with a corresponding highly-efficient algorithm for multiplying this matrix by a vector of group elements.

As protocols for verifiably sharing a secret key with an associated public key and the technology of super-invertible matrices both play a major role in threshold cryptography and multi-party computation, our two new innovations should have applicability well beyond that of threshold Schnorr signatures.

M. Joye and G. Leander (Eds.): EUROCRYPT 2024, LNCS 14655, pp. 370–400, 2024.
https://doi.org/10.1007/978-3-031-58740-5_13

1 Introduction

The main motivation for our work is to design efficient protocols for threshold Schnorr signatures that work in an *asynchronous* communication setting, providing *robustness* and *optimal resilience*. As will be explained in detail below, our results and techniques result in threshold Schnorr protocols with extremely high throughput and low latency. These protocols follow the usual offline/online paradigm, where higher-latency, message-independent precomputations are performed in the offline phase, and lower-latency, message-dependent computations are performed in the online phase. The resulting protocol has linear communication complexity per signature in both phases—each party in the signing committee essentially transmits and receives a total number of 18 scalars and 9 group elements per signature in the offline phase, and 6 scalars per signature in the online phase.[1] Moreover, for moderately sized signing committees (in the range 10–100), they enjoy extremely good computational complexity. In particular, over a group of order $q \approx 2^\lambda$, and with a signing committee of size n, the running time per signature of each party in the signing committee in the offline phase is dominated by the cost of performing $O(n + \lambda/n)$ group additions (we use additive notation and terminology throughout), and in the online phase is dominated by the cost of $O(n)$ arithmetic operations mod q. Note that these estimates assume some batching is done in the offline phase and a small amount of batching is done in the online phase. Somewhat surprisingly, this result says that for such moderately sized n, the running time per party decreases as n increases, and is actually less than the time used to just compute a Schnorr signature. Note that our results and techniques have much broader applicability. For example, they can also be applied to threshold ECDSA signatures and other problems in threshold cryptography.

   The big-O constants here are quite small. For example, with $n = 49$ and $\lambda = 256$, the number of group additions per party per signature in the offline phase is just 23. Note that this group addition count does not presume an exorbitant amount of batching in the offline phase, nor does it assume a particularly sophisticated multi-scalar/group multiplication algorithm. If the group is an elliptic curve such as secp2565k1 [9], a single group addition can be performed by a reasonably good library in well under $0.5\mu s$ on commonly available machines (see details in Appendix A.1 of the full version of this paper [20]). This translates to a total of $11.5\mu s$ per signature, and we will conservatively round this up to $20\mu s$ to account for other overheads. This translates to a throughput of 50,000 signatures per second. Now, as mentioned above each party transmits a total of 24 scalars and 9 group elements per signature, so roughly 10Kb (10,000 bits). So in order to sustain a throughput of 50,000 signatures per second, a network bandwidth of 500Mbs suffices, which is not unreasonable.

---

[1] We stress that we are not assuming any type of "broadcast channel": when we say P transmits a certain amount of data, we are counting the sum over all parties Q of the amount of data that P sends to Q over a point-to-point channel.

1.1   An MPC Engine Geared Towards Schnorr

Let us first recall the Schnorr signature scheme. Let E be a group of prime order q generated by $\mathcal{G} \in E$. As mentioned already, we use additive notation for the group operation of E, and denote the identity element of E by $\mathcal{O}$. The secret key is a random $x \in \mathbb{Z}_q$ an the public key is $\mathcal{X} \leftarrow x\mathcal{G} \in E$. To sign a message m, the signer chooses $r \in \mathbb{Z}_q$ at random, computes $\mathcal{R} \leftarrow r\mathcal{G} \in E$, $h \leftarrow \mathsf{Hash}(\mathcal{X}, \mathcal{R}, m) \in \mathbb{Z}_q$, $s \leftarrow r + xh \in E$, and outputs the signature $(\mathcal{R}, s) \in E \times \mathbb{Z}_q$.

The approach we take to designing a threshold Schnorr signing protocol in the asynchronous communication setting is to build it on top of a highly optimized **MPC (multi-party computation) engine**. That is, rather than designing and analyzing a monolithic protocol, we design an MPC engine that supports operations well suited to threshold Schnorr signatures (and other threshold cryptography tasks as well), and that can be efficiently implemented while providing robustness and optimal resilience in an asynchronous communication setting.

At a high level, we need an MPC engine that, as an ideal functionality $\mathfrak{F}_{\mathrm{MPC}}$, supports the following operations:

- $([r], \mathcal{R}) \leftarrow \mathsf{RandomKeyGen}()$:
  $\mathfrak{F}_{\mathrm{MPC}}$ chooses $r \in \mathbb{Z}_q$ at random, computes $\mathcal{R} \leftarrow r\mathcal{G} \in E$, gives $\mathcal{R}$ immediately to the adversary, and gives $\mathcal{R}$ to each party as a delayed output (i.e., the adversary indicates when the output is given to any given party). The ideal functionality $\mathfrak{F}_{\mathrm{MPC}}$ also stores r for future use.
- $[z] \leftarrow \mathsf{LinearOp}(a, [x], b, [y])$:
  For public inputs $a, b \in \mathbb{Z}_q$, and previously stored values $x, y \in \mathbb{Z}_q$, $\mathfrak{F}_{\mathrm{MPC}}$ computes $z \leftarrow ax + by \in \mathbb{Z}_q$ and stores z for future use.
  This is typically implemented as a local computation.
- $z \leftarrow \mathsf{Open}([z])$:
  For a previously stored value $z \in \mathbb{Z}_q$, $\mathfrak{F}_{\mathrm{MPC}}$ gives z to each party as a delayed output.

We assume we have n parties $P_1, \ldots, P_n$, at most $t < n/3$ of which may be corrupt. We also assume static corruptions—that is at the beginning of the attack and before the start of the protocol the adversary corrupts some subset of $t^* \leq t$ parties. We envision a signing protocol that is driven by a blockchain or any other BFT protocol that orders the signing requests and the execution of the $\mathfrak{F}_{\mathrm{MPC}}$-operations, so that each party receives the same signing requests and initiates the same $\mathfrak{F}_{\mathrm{MPC}}$-operations in the same order. It is not important here which method is used for the parties to agree on request and activation ordering.

Using the above MPC engine, we can easily implement threshold Schnorr signatures as follows. The protocol to generate the key is:

$([x], \mathcal{X}) \leftarrow \mathsf{RandomKeyGen}()$

The protocol to sign a message m is:

$([r], \mathcal{R}) \leftarrow \mathsf{RandomKeyGen}()$
$h \leftarrow \mathsf{Hash}(\mathcal{X}, \mathcal{R}, m) \in \mathbb{Z}_q$ // local computation
$[s] \leftarrow \mathsf{LinearOp}(1, [r], h, [x])$ // local computation
$s \leftarrow \mathsf{Open}([s])$
output $(\mathcal{R}, s)$

While the above is very simple, it is typically not very efficient. The problem is that in a typical implementation of $\mathfrak{F}_{\mathrm{MPC}}$, the $\mathsf{RandomKeyGen}$ operation is fairly expensive. One way of improving this situation is to observe that the value r is independent of m, and so we might move the computation of $([r], \mathcal{R}) \leftarrow \mathsf{RandomKeyGen}()$ to an "offline" precomputation phase. In this case, we refer to the pair $([r], \mathcal{R})$ as a "presignature". Moreover, we might be able to exploit "batching" techniques to more efficiently produce such presignatures in batches, and then consume them in an "online" phase as signing requests are made.

The problem with this approach is that by computing these presignatures $([r], \mathcal{R})$ in advance and revealing the group element $\mathcal{R}$ to the adversary before the corresponding signing request is made, the signature scheme becomes insecure. This is a well-known problem and a number of good mitigation strategies have been devised. See [28] for details on how this can be done efficiently and securely (see also Sect. 7.2 of the full version [20]).

So we can safely ignore these issues for now and focus on the remaining challenge: how to generate large batches of presignatures efficiently. In computing batches of presignatures, we are not so much concerned about the latency of producing a batch, as this occurs in the "offline" phase. We are, however, concerned about the throughput, that is, the rate at which we can produce presignatures, as this will be the limiting factor on the signing throughput, that is, the rate at which we can process signing requests.

So the problem we focus on is this: *high-throughput generation of presignatures*. This problem may be simplified by the observation that for a presignature $([r], \mathcal{R})$, we do not require that the value r is perfectly random. In fact, as was first observed in a specific context in [16], and then again in an another specific context in [3], and then more recently in a much more general context in [28], the threshold signing protocol will still be secure even if the adversary is allowed to *bias* the presignatures in a particular *benign* way, and moreover, it is much easier to generate such benignly biased presignatures than it is to generate unbiased presignatures.

One form of biased presignature that is relevant can be captured by the following operation, which we can add to our MPC engine:

- $([r'], \mathcal{R}') \leftarrow \mathsf{BiasedKeyGen}()$:
  $\mathfrak{F}_{\mathrm{MPC}}$ chooses $r \in \mathbb{Z}_q$ at random, computes $\mathcal{R} \leftarrow r\mathcal{G} \in E$, gives $\mathcal{R}$ immediately to the adversary.
  The adversary later responds with a "bias" $(a, b) \in \mathbb{Z}_q^* \times \mathbb{Z}_q$.
  $\mathfrak{F}_{\mathrm{MPC}}$ then computes $r' \leftarrow ar + b \in \mathbb{Z}_q$ and $\mathcal{R}' \leftarrow r'\mathcal{G} \in E$, and gives $\mathcal{R}'$ to each party as a delayed output. $\mathfrak{F}_{\mathrm{MPC}}$ also stores r' for future use.

One can securely realize this functionality based on a simpler operation and a consensus protocol. The simpler operation is this:

- $([r_i], \mathcal{R}_i) \leftarrow \mathsf{InputKey}_i(r_i)$:
  Party P_i inputs $r_i \in \mathbb{Z}_q$ to $\mathfrak{F}_{\mathrm{MPC}}$, who computes $\mathcal{R}_i \leftarrow r_i \mathcal{G} \in E$, gives $\mathcal{R}_i$ immediately to the adversary, and gives $\mathcal{R}_i$ to each party as a delayed output. $\mathfrak{F}_{\mathrm{MPC}}$ also stores r_i for future use.

To implement BiasedKeyGen with this operation, each party P_i inputs a random secret key r_i to the ideal functionality via $\mathsf{InputKey}_i$ so that every party, including the adversary, learns the public key $\mathcal{R}_i$. Note that while honest parties input random secret keys, the corrupt parties may choose arbitrary secret keys in a way that depends on the public keys of the honest parties. The parties then use a consensus protocol to agree on a set $\mathcal{I}$ of $t + 1$ indices, where for each $i \in \mathcal{I}$, the operation $\mathsf{InputKey}_i$ has successfully completed.[2] The resulting biased key-pair is $([r'], \mathcal{R}')$, where $r' = \sum_{i \in \mathcal{I}} r_i$ and $\mathcal{R}' = \sum_{i \in \mathcal{I}} \mathcal{R}_i$. This is computed locally, using LinearOp to compute $[r']$ from $\{[r_i]\}_{i \in \mathcal{I}}$, and computing $\mathcal{R}'$ directly using the known values $\{\mathcal{R}_i\}_{i \in \mathcal{I}}$ as output by $\{\mathsf{InputKey}\}_{i \in \mathcal{I}}$. That this securely realizes BiasedKeyGen is fairly straightforward to see (this was observed implicitly in [18] and explicitly in Section A.3.6 of [19]).

Yet better performance can be obtained by utilizing the well-known "batch randomness extraction" technique — an idea that goes back at least to [21], but first applied to Schnorr signatures in [3], and then analyzed more fully in the context of Schnorr signatures in [28]. Here, we choose a certain $M \times N$ matrix W over $\mathbb{Z}_q$ (whose entries are public constants — see below), where $M = n - 2t$ and $N = n - t$. As above, each party P_i inputs a random secret key r_i to the ideal functionality via $\mathsf{InputKey}_i$, so that every party, including the adversary, learns the public key $\mathcal{R}_i$. As above, while honest parties input random secret keys, the corrupt parties may choose arbitrary secret keys in a way that depends on the public keys of the honest parties. The parties then use a consensus protocol to agree on a set $\mathcal{I}$ of N indices, where for each $i \in \mathcal{I}$, the operation $\mathsf{InputKey}_i$ has successfully completed. Let us write $\mathcal{I} = \{i_1, \ldots, i_N\}$. The parties then locally compute M biased key-pairs $([r'_1], \mathcal{R}'_1), \ldots, ([r'_M], \mathcal{R}'_M)$ where $(r'_1, \ldots, r'_M)^\mathsf{T} = W \cdot (r_{i_1}, \ldots, r_{i_N})^\mathsf{T}$ and $(\mathcal{R}'_1, \ldots, \mathcal{R}'_M)^\mathsf{T} = W \cdot (\mathcal{R}_{i_1}, \ldots, \mathcal{R}_{i_N})^\mathsf{T}$. This is computed locally, using LinearOp to compute $[r'_1], \ldots, [r'_M]$ from $[r_1], \ldots, [r_N]$, and computing $\mathcal{R}'_1, \ldots, \mathcal{R}'_M$ directly using the known values $\{\mathcal{R}_i\}_{i \in \mathcal{I}}$.

The property that the matrix W must satisfy is called **super-invertibility**, which simply means that every subset of M columns of A is linearly independent.

The security property that the above protocol satisfies can be elegantly captured by adding the following operation to our MPC engine, where we define

---

[2] More specifically, the parties run an ACS (Agreement on a Common Set) protocol. See [11] for a state-of-the art ACS protocol and for useful historical context. In a practical implementation, it may be perfectly reasonable to use PBFT [8] or one of its modern descendants (such as [25]) that work in a the *partially* synchronous communication model.

$M := n - 2t$ and $N^* := n - t^*$, where $t^* \leq t$ is the number of actual corrupted parties.

- $(([r'_1], \mathcal{R}'_1), \ldots, ([r'_M], \mathcal{R}'_M)) \leftarrow$ BatchedBiasedKeyGen():
  $\mathfrak{F}_{\text{MPC}}$ chooses $r_1, \ldots, r_{N^*} \in \mathbb{Z}_q$ at random, computes
  $\mathcal{R}_1 \leftarrow r_1\mathcal{G}, \ldots, \mathcal{R}_{N^*} \leftarrow r_{N^*}\mathcal{G}$ and gives these group elements immediately to the adversary.
  The adversary later responds with a "bias" $(A, \mathbf{b})$, where $A \in \mathbb{Z}_q^{M \times N^*}$ is a full rank matrix and $\mathbf{b} \in \mathbb{Z}_q^{M \times 1}$ is an arbitrary vector.
  $\mathfrak{F}_{\text{MPC}}$ then computes $(r'_1, \ldots, r'_M)^\intercal = A \cdot (r_1, \ldots, r_{N^*})^\intercal + \mathbf{b}$ and
  $\mathcal{R}'_1 \leftarrow r'_1\mathcal{G}, \ldots, \mathcal{R}'_M \leftarrow r'_M\mathcal{G}$ and gives $(\mathcal{R}'_1, \ldots, \mathcal{R}'_M)$ to each party as a delayed output. $\mathfrak{F}_{\text{MPC}}$ also stores the values $r'_1, \ldots, r'_M$ for future use.

Note that one can define this operation more generally, in that the parameter M could be set to a different value, possibly determined adaptively by the adversary. This can be useful to model variations on the above protocol for batch randomness extraction.

1.2 Two Problems

So we now have reduced the problem of building threshold Schnorr to the following two problems:

Problem 1: Securely and efficiently implementing the $\mathfrak{F}_{\text{MPC}}$-operations InputKey, LinearOp, and Open.

Problem 2: Designing a super-invertible matrix equipped with an efficient algorithm for multiplication on the right by a vector of group elements.

Indeed, with solutions to both of these problems, we can directly implement BiasedKeyGen and BatchedBiasKeyGen, as outlined above. Now, the papers [28] and [3] do not analyze the usage of biased keys as signing keys, but only as presignatures. However, the analysis in [28] can be extended to allow for biased signing keys. That said, it is arguably not that important, since we presumably generate signing keys very occasionally, and so we could afford to use a more expensive implementation of an unbiased key. Moreover, for other applications, such as ECDSA, the use of an unbiased signing key is essential — see Sect. 3.6 of [19]. Note that to support ECDSA, we would also have to extend our MPC engine to include a multiplication operations. That is an issue we do not consider in the paper. Nevertheless, our techniques here can be extended to cover this as well, although with certain limitations. In any case, in this paper we do not consider any implementation of RandomKeyGen, as it is not needed to implement threshold Schnorr, but in any case, it is easy enough to implement in a way that is (a) not too horribly inefficient, and (b) is compatible with the other operations in our MPC engine.

2 Our Contributions

We present new solutions to Problems 1 and 2 above.

2.1   Solution to Problem 1

Our new solution to Problem 1 is a new type of protocol, which we call a **GoAVSS protocol**. Here, GoAVSS stands for **group-oriented asynchronous verifiable secret sharing**. We assume parties $P_1, \ldots, P_n$, one of which is designated as the dealer, and at most $t < n/3$ of which may be (statically) corrupted. We also assume we have fixed evaluation points $e_1, \ldots, e_n$, which are distinct, nonzero elements of $\mathbb{Z}_q$. A GoAVSS protocol should securely realize the following ideal functionality.

- The dealer inputs polynomials $f_1, \ldots, f_L \in \mathbb{Z}_q[x]$ to the GoAVSS functionality, each of which must have degree at most t (this condition is enforced by the functionality).
- For each $\ell \in [L]$, the polynomial f_ℓ defines a secret key $s_\ell := f_\ell(0) \in \mathbb{Z}_q$ and a public key $\mathcal{S}_\ell := s_\ell \mathcal{G} \in E$, and the GoAVSS functionality immediately reveals the public keys $\mathcal{S}_1, \ldots, \mathcal{S}_L$ to the adversary.
- The GoAVSS functionality gives to each party P_j as a delayed output the public keys $\mathcal{S}_1, \ldots, \mathcal{S}_L$, as well as its shares of the secret keys $s_1, \ldots, s_L$, that is, the values $f_1(e_j), \ldots, f_L(e_j)$.

In addition, a GoAVSS protocol should satisfy a **completeness property**, which means that if the dealer is honest or any honest party outputs a value, then all honest parties eventually output a value. Here, "eventually" means if and when all honest parties initiate the protocol and all messages sent between honest parties are delivered.

Any GoAVSS protocol gives a solution to Problem 1. Indeed, such a protocol can be used directly to implement the InputKey operation of our MPC engine. In fact, one run of the GoAVSS protocol actually yields L instances of InputKey. For our application to threshold signatures, such batching is perfectly fine, as parties just input random secret keys. Moreover, such batching can be used to get much more efficient protocols. Since a GoAVSS protocol distributes traditional Shamir shares of the secrets, the LinearOp is also easily and efficiently implemented.

As for the Open operation, the reader may notice that our GoAVSS functionality does not make any explicit mention of a "polynomial commitment" of any form that can be used to verify the secret shares revealed during the Open operation. This is intentional: our new GoAVSS protocol is very efficient precisely because it does not use a polynomial commitment at all. This is also very different from just about every other DKG protocol in the literature (going back to Feldman [14] and Pedersen [26]).[3] Nevertheless, since we are assuming $n > 3t$ (which is necessary in the asynchronous setting), we do not need to use polynomial commitments to verify the secret shares revealed during the Open

---

[3] One notable exception to this is the DKG protocol in the very recent work [1], which presents a DKG protocol in the synchronous model. We compare our work to theirs in the full version [20].

operation—we can instead just use error correcting codes. This is a standard technique in the field of information-theoretic asynchronous MPC.[4]

As already mentioned, our GoAVSS protocol achieves very good performance by avoiding polynomial commitments. Instead, at a very high level, it works as follows.

First, the dealer runs a "plain" AVSS protocol, which just works with scalars, rather than group elements, to distribute shares of the polynomials $f_1, \ldots, f_\ell \in \mathbb{Z}_q[x]$. The dealer then simply broadcasts the group elements $\mathcal{S}_1, \ldots, \mathcal{S}_L$ to the receivers.

To get very high performance for this step, we may use the recently developed AVSS protocol from [29], which uses very lightweight cryptography (i.e., hash functions) and generally has very good communication and computational complexity.

At this point, we may assume that the "plain" AVSS protocol ensures that receivers are holding shares of polynomials $f_1, \ldots, f_\ell$ of the right degree. However, there is no guarantee that $f_\ell(0)\mathcal{G} = \mathcal{S}_\ell$ for all $\ell \in [L]$. So we run another subprotocol that performs a simple statistical test. Moreover, this test is designed so that we can distribute the work among the receivers, so that each party performs a *very* small number of group additions — just $O(\lambda/n)$ additions per individual sharing, if $q \approx 2^\lambda$. The work actually decreases as n increases! This is, of course, too good to be true. Indeed, there is a trade-off, in that each party must perform $O(n)$ *very* simple scalar operations per individual sharing (each such operation is not much more expensive than the addition of two λ-bit numbers, and we estimate that such a scalar operation takes just a few percentage points of the time to perform a single group addition). For moderately sized n, this turns out to be an excellent trade-off.

We analyze in detail both the computational and communication complexity of our GoAVSS protocol, with certain subprotocols implemented as in [29]. These subprotocols have an "optimistic path", where no party misbehaves in a publicly provable way, and we only consider the cost on this optimistic path. Arguably, over a long run of the system where parties that provably misbehave are effectively removed from the system, this is the only cost that matters. Now, each run of our GoAVSS protocol produces L "raw sharings" created by a single dealer. In the intended usage as a subprotocol in our implementation of the BatchedBiasedKeyGen, every party will run the GoAVSS protocol n times: once playing role of both dealer and receiver, and $n-1$ times just as a receiver, and this will yield a total of $L \cdot (n-2t) \geq L \cdot n/3$ "processed sharings". So we naturally measure the amortized cost per "processed sharing", which in the application to threshold signatures, represents the amortized cost per presignature of the offline

---

[4] In Sect. 7.1 of the full version [20], we review this technique, and discuss how this impacts the practical performance of the online phase of a threshold signing protocol. As discussed there, to get the best throughput in the online phase, we have to increase the latency of the online phase just a bit (but this is not because we use error correcting codes). Note that the completeness property of our GoAVSS protocol is essential to make it possible to forgo polynomial commitments and rely on error correction.

phase contributed by the GoAVSS protocol (but does not include the computational cost of applying the super-invertible matrix). Our stated amortized costs assume that n is not too big relative to L and λ. In particular, to achieve the stated amortized costs, we require $L = \Omega(n^2)$ and $\lambda = \Omega(n)$—actually, for larger n, we can use a variant of our main protocol for which we only require $L = \Omega(n \log n)$, rather than $L = \Omega(n^2)$.

2.1.1 Communication Complexity

We define *communication complexity* as the sum, over all honest parties P and all parties Q, of the total number of bits that P sends to Q over a point-to-point channel.

The amortized communication complexity per processed sharing of our GoAVSS protocol is $O(n\lambda)$, where $q \approx 2^\lambda$ and we assume group elements are encoded as $O(\lambda)$-bit strings. Also, the communication complexity is well balanced: each party sends (and receives) $O(\lambda)$ bits per of data per processed sharing. In fact, each party essentially transmits (and receives) a total of 18 scalars and 9 group elements per processed sharing.

2.1.2 Computational Complexity

We define *computational complexity* to be the maximum running time of any one individual honest party.

The amortized computational complexity per processed sharing of our GoAVSS protocol is dominated by the cost of performing $O(n/\lambda + 1)$ additions in the group E, and $O(n)$ arithmetic operations in $\mathbb{Z}_q$.

To state the computational complexity more precisely, we introduce some terminology.

Full Scalar/Group Multiplication: This is a scalar/group multiplication, where the scalar is a secret, full-sized element of $\mathbb{Z}_q$, and the group element is the generator $\mathcal{G}$. This means that (a) we can use precomputation on $\mathcal{G}$ to make the algorithm faster, but (b) we have to be careful to use a constant-time algorithm. For typical parameter settings and implementations, we can estimate the cost of a full scalar/group multiplication to be about 64 group additions (see Appendix A of the full version [20]).

Tiny Scalar/Group Multiplication: Let ρ be a parameter (usually clear from context). This is a scalar/group multiplication where the scalar is a public, random ρ-bit number, and the group element is variable and public. Moreover, the resulting products are only used as terms in a long summation, so special optimized algorithms may be used. Using Pippenger's simple "bucket method" (see Appendix B of the full version [20]), for typical parameter settings, the amortized cost of each tiny/scalar group multiplication is just 1 or 2 group additions.

Tiny Scalar/Scalar Multiplication: Again, let ρ be a parameter (usually clear from context). This is a scalar/scalar multiplication where one scalar input is a public, random ρ-bit number, and the other scalar input is a secret, full-sized element of $\mathbb{Z}_q$. Moreover, the resulting products are only used as terms in a long summation, so special optimized algorithms may be used. In particular, the cost of such an operation is essentially that of multiplying a ρ-bit integer by a λ-bit integer (without a modular reduction). For typical parameter settings, the amortized cost of each tiny scalar/scalar group multiplication is just a very small fraction (less than $1/40$) of the cost of a group addition.

Let σ be a statistical security parameter (typically $\sigma = 80$). Set the parameter $\rho = \lceil 3\sigma/n \rceil + 2$, used in defining tiny scalar/group and scalar/scalar multiplications, as above. The amortized computational complexity per processed sharing of our GoAVSS protocol can be stated as follows: (i) $3/n$ full scalar/group multiplications, (ii) 3 tiny scalar/group multiplications, and (iii) $4n$ tiny scalar/scalar multiplications.

In addition to the communication and computational complexity of our GoAVSS protocol, also of interest is the **round complexity**. This is a (reasonably small) constant. Because of this, any performance degradation caused by network latency (which could cause the network and CPU bandwidth to be under-utilized) can be minimized by increasing the batch size L. We also present a variation of our main GoAVSS protocol that achieves even better round complexity — at the cost of relying on the random oracle model and a slightly higher computational complexity.

2.2   Solution to Problem 2

Our solution to problem two can be stated very simply. For any $M \leq N \leq q$, we give an explicit construction of an $M \times N$ super-invertible matrix over $\mathbb{Z}_q$, along with an algorithm for multiplying this matrix on the right by an $N \times 1$ column vector over the group E that uses precisely $M \cdot (N - 1 - (M + 1)/2) + 1$ additions in the group E. In the application to batch randomness extraction, where $M = n - 2t$ and $N = n - t$, this contributes a amortized cost of about $n/2 - 3/2$ group additions per processed sharing. Moreover, as we discuss, in some special cases, this amortized cost can be reduced a bit further, to just t group additions per processed sharing.

2.3   Combining the Two Solutions

Combining our solutions to Problems 1 an 2, we immediately get a protocol for computing presignatures for Schnorr threshold signing with the following properties: (i) its amortized communication complexity per presignature is $O(n\lambda)$, i.e., $O(\lambda)$ bits per party and (ii) a party's amortized computational complexity per presignature is dominated by the cost of performing $O(n + \lambda/n)$ additions in the group E.

The online complexity of the resulting protocol depends on a number of design choices with regard to how the Open protocol is implemented. If we insist on one round of communication in the online phase, we obtain (i) an amortized communication complexity per signature of $O(n^2\lambda)$, with each party essentially transmitting n scalars per signature, and (ii) an amortized computational complexity per signature dominated by the cost of performing $O(n^2)$ arithmetic operations in $\mathbb{Z}_q$.

If we allow two rounds of communication in the online phase, and also allow for some batching of signing requests (which is reasonable in a heavily loaded system), we obtain (i) an amortized communication complexity per signature of $O(n\lambda)$, with each party essentially transmitting 6 scalars per signature, and (ii) an amortized computational complexity per signature dominated by the cost of performing $O(n)$ arithmetic operations in $\mathbb{Z}_q$. This is discussed in more detail in the full version [20].

All of the above computational estimates assume only naive, quadratic-time polynomial arithmetic.

2.4   The Rest of the Paper

In Sect. 3, we present the precise security definitions of AVSS and GoAVSS that we will use throughout the paper. In Sect. 4, we review the subprotocols we use to build our new GoAVSS protocol. In Sect. 5, we present our new GoAVSS protocol, providing a security analysis in Sect. 5.1 and a complexity analysis in Sect. 5.2. In Sect. 5.3, we present a variant that may be preferred in when n is very large. In Sect. 6, we present our new constructions of super-invertible matrices with corresponding algorithms for multiplying such a matrix on the right by a vector of group elements.

In the full version [20]: (i) we provide several other variations on our main GoAVSS protocols, including variants that do not rely on a "random beacon" (these "beacon free" variants also achieve better round complexity, but also rely on the random oracle model and have slightly higher computational complexity); (ii) we discuss in more detail the online signing phase of the threshold Schnorr signature derived from our protocols; (iii) we make an in-depth comparison (with numerical examples) with our closest competitor, SPRINT [3], and also combine various ideas (from [19] as well as from this paper) to get the best possible "batch Feldman" GoAVSS protocol based on polynomial commitments, and compare its performance to that of our new GoAVSS protocol; (iv) we compare our techniques to those in [1], which presents (among other things) DKG and threshold Schnorr protocols that work in the synchronous communication model (while the goals and results of that paper are in many ways incomparable with our results, there is some overlap in techniques).

3   Preliminaries

3.1   Asynchronous Verifiable Secret Sharing

We recall the notion of *asynchronous verifiable secret sharing (AVSS)*. We have n parties $P_1, \ldots, P_n$, of which at most $t < n/3$ may be corrupt. We assume *static* corruptions. Let $\mathcal{H}$ denote the indices of the honest parties, and let $\mathcal{C}$ denote the indices of the corrupt parties.

We assume the parties are connected by secure point-to-point channels, which provide both privacy and authentication. As we are working exclusively in the

---

$\mathfrak{F}_{\text{AVSS}}$

Input($f_1, \ldots, f_L$): this operation is invoked once by the dealer D, who inputs polynomials $f_1, \ldots, f_L \in \mathbb{Z}_q[x]_{<d}$ to $\mathfrak{F}_{\text{AVSS}}$. In response, $\mathfrak{F}_{\text{AVSS}}$ sends the message NotifyInput() to the ideal-world adversary.

RequestOutput(j): after the input has been received, this operation may be invoked by the ideal-world adversary, who specifies $j \in [n]$. In response, $\mathfrak{F}_{\text{AVSS}}$ sends to P_j the message Output($\{ f_\ell(e_j) \}_{\ell \in [L]}$).

Fig. 1. The AVSS Ideal Functionality (parameterized by n, d, L, $\mathbb{Z}_q$, $\vec{e}$, and D)

asynchronous communication model, there is no bound on the time required to deliver messages between honest parties.

Let $\mathbb{Z}_q$ be finite field with q elements. Let $\vec{e} = (e_1, \ldots, e_n) \in \mathbb{Z}_q^n$ be a sequence of distinct, nonzero elements of $\mathbb{Z}_q$. Let d be a positive integer, and let $\mathbb{Z}_q[x]_{<d}$ denote the $\mathbb{Z}_q$-subspace of $\mathbb{Z}_q[x]$ consisting of all polynomials of degree less than d. Let L be a positive integer.

An (n, d, L)-**AVSS protocol** over $\mathbb{Z}_q$ (with respect to $\vec{e}$) allows a dealer $D \in \{P_1, \ldots, P_n\}$ to share a polynomials $f_1, \ldots, f_L \in \mathbb{Z}_q[x]_{<d}$ in such a way that each party P_j learns only $f_1(e_j), \ldots, f_L(e_j)$. More precisely, it should satisfy a *security* property and a *completeness* property. The security property is captured by the ideal functionality $\mathfrak{F}_{\text{AVSS}}$ in Fig. 1. Note that $\mathfrak{F}_{\text{AVSS}}$ enforces the constraint that the polynomials $f_1, \ldots, f_L$ must be of degree less than d. The completeness property is as follows: if the dealer is honest or any honest party outputs a value, then all honest parties eventually output a value. Here, "eventually" means if and when all honest parties initiate the protocol and all messages sent between honest parties are delivered.

3.2 Group-Oriented AVSS

We now introduce the notion of a **group-oriented AVSS (GoAVSS)**. In this setting, q is a prime, and we are working over a group E of order q generated by $\mathcal{G} \in E$. We use additive notation for the group operation of E, and denote the identity element of E by $\mathcal{O}$.

Essentially, an (n, d, L)-**GoAVSS protocol** over E (with respect to $\vec{e}$) is the same as an (n, d, L)-GoAVSS protocol over $\mathbb{Z}_q$, but where each party (including the adversary) also obtains $\mathcal{S}_\ell := f_\ell(0)\mathcal{G} \in E$ for each $\ell \in [L]$.

The security property of a GoAVSS protocol is captured by the ideal functionality $\mathfrak{F}_{\text{GoAVSS}}$ in Fig. 2. We also require a completeness property, which is identical to that for an AVSS protocol.

4 Subprotocols

In this section, we review the subprotocols that our new GoAVSS protocol will need.

4.1   AVSS

Our GoAVSS protocol over E will be built using an ordinary AVSS protocol over $\mathbb{Z}_q$ (as defined above in Sect. 3.1). In principle, any such AVSS protocol could be used. However, the protocol in [29] is well suited to the task, as it uses only "lightweight" cryptography (namely, hash functions) and is quite efficient, both in terms of communication and computational complexity, especially on the so-called "optimistic path", where no party provably misbehaves. More concretely, on the "optimistic path", if $q \approx 2^\lambda$, the communication complexity (total number of bits transmitted in aggregate by all honest parties) $6nL\lambda + O(\lambda \cdot n^2 \log n + n^3)$. Also, the computational complexity (running time of any one individual honest party) is as follows, assuming $L = \Omega(n \log n)$. For a party acting in its role as a receiver, the cost of decoding, encoding, hashing, and decrypting $O(L\lambda)$ bits of data, performing $O(L(1 + n/\lambda))$ arithmetic operations in $\mathbb{Z}_q$, and generating $O(\lambda L(1 + n/\lambda))$ pseudorandom bits. For a party acting in its role as a dealer, the cost of encrypting, encoding, and hashing $O(nL\lambda)$ bits of data, performing $O(dL(1 + n/\lambda))$ arithmetic operations in $\mathbb{Z}_q$, and generating $O(d\lambda L(1 + n/\lambda))$ pseudorandom bits. Note that the dealer plays a role both as a dealer and as a receiver. Here, encoding and decoding refers to encoding and decoding data using an $(n, n - 2t)$-erasure code.

$\mathfrak{F}_{\text{GoAVSS}}$

Input($f_1, \ldots, f_L$): this operation is invoked once by the dealer D, who inputs polynomials $f_1, \ldots, f_L \in \mathbb{Z}_q[x]_{<d}$ to $\mathfrak{F}_{\text{GoAVSS}}$. In response, $\mathfrak{F}_{\text{GoAVSS}}$ sends the message NotifyInput($\{\mathcal{S}_\ell\}_{\ell \in [L]}$) to the ideal-world adversary, where $\mathcal{S}_\ell := f_\ell(0)\mathcal{G}$, for $\ell \in [L]$.

RequestOutput(j): after the input has been received, this operation may be invoked by the ideal-world adversary, who specifies $j \in [n]$. In response, $\mathfrak{F}_{\text{GoAVSS}}$ sends to P_j the message Output($\{ (\mathcal{S}_\ell, f_\ell(e_j)) \}_{\ell \in [L]}$).

Fig. 2. The GoAVSS Ideal Functionality (parameterized by n, d, L, E (which defines $\mathbb{Z}_q$), $\vec{e}$, and D)

Note that this protocol makes use of a collision resistant hash function with a κ-bit output and a statistical security parameter σ, and we assume $\max\{\kappa, \sigma\} \leq \lambda$. This protocol uses a statistical test that has error bound of $2^n/q$, For large n, this test must be repeated several times, and this is what gives rise to the additive term n^3 appearing in the communication complexity bound and the additive term n/λ appearing in the computational complexity bounds.

Note that when the protocol falls off the "optimistic path", the communication and computational complexity may increase by a factor of $O(n)$. However, at least one misbehaving party will be identified and can be effectively removed from participating any further in the protocol.

$\mathfrak{F}_{\text{ReliableBroadcast}}$

Input(m): this operation is invoked once by the sender S, who inputs a message m. In response, $\mathfrak{F}_{\text{ReliableBroadcast}}$ sends the message NotifyInput(m) to the ideal-world adversary.

RequestOutput(j): after the input has been received, this operation may be invoked by the ideal-world adversary, who specifies $j \in [n]$. In response, $\mathfrak{F}_{\text{ReliableBroadcast}}$ sends to P_j the message Output(m).

Fig. 3. The Reliable Broadcast Ideal Functionality (parameterized by S)

In the above computational complexity estimates, we have not included the cost for the dealer of actually computing the shares $f_\ell(e_j)$ for $\ell \in [L]$, $j \in [n]$, which is a part of any AVSS protocol. For very large n, an asymptotically fast multi-point evaluation algorithm may be useful. However, for small to moderate sized n, it is more practical to use a simple Horner's rule evaluation, which adds to the dealer's cost $\approx dnL$ multiplications and additions mod q. Moreover, if the evaluation points are $1, \ldots, n$ (which is typical), we can run many steps of Horner without any reductions mod q, making these steps relatively inexpensive.

4.2 Reliable Broadcast

A **reliable broadcast** protocol allows a sender S to broadcast a single message m to $P_1, \ldots, P_n$ in such a way that all parties are guaranteed to receive the same message. More precisely, it should satisfy a *security* property and a *completeness* property. The security property is captured by the ideal functionality $\mathfrak{F}_{\text{ReliableBroadcast}}$ in Fig. 3. The completeness property says that: if one honest party outputs a message, then every honest party eventually outputs a message; moreover, if S is honest, then every honest party eventually outputs a message.

A well-known Reliable Broadcast protocol is due to Bracha [6]. However, its communication complexity (total number of bits transmitted in aggregate by all honest parties) is $O(n^2 \cdot |m|)$. Better communication complexity can be obtained using a protocol based on erasure codes. This approach was initially considered in [7]. For our complexity estimates, we shall rely on a variation of this protocol given in [29], which has somewhat better communication complexity than the protocol in [7]. That protocol, called $\Pi_{\text{CompactBroadcast}}$, has communication complexity $3n|m| + O(\kappa \cdot n^2 \log n)$, where κ is the output length of a collision-resistant hash. Also, the computational complexity (running time of any one individual honest party) is as follows, assuming $|m| = \Omega(\kappa \cdot n \log n)$. For a party acting in its role as a receiver, the cost of decoding, encoding, and hashing $O(|m|)$ bits of data. For a party acting in its role as a dealer, the cost of encoding and hashing $O(n|m|)$ bits of data operations in $\mathbb{Z}_q$. Note that the dealer plays a role both as a dealer and as a receiver. Here, encoding and decoding refers to encoding and decoding data using an $(n, n - 2t)$-erasure code.

4.3 One-Sided Voting

A degenerate version of Bracha broadcast can be used as a simple *one-sided voting* protocol. Each party may initiate the protocol and may output the value done. This is a simple two-round protocol with $O(n^2)$ communication complexity. See, for example, $\Pi_{\mathrm{OneSidedVote}}$ in Sect. 3.2.5 of [29]. The *security* property for this protocol is captured by the ideal functionality $\mathfrak{F}_{\mathrm{OneSidedVote}}$ in Fig. 4. The main idea is that if any honest party outputs done, then at least $n-t-t'$ honest parties must have initiated the protocol, where $t' \leq t$ is the actual number of corrupt parties. This protocol also satisfies the following *completeness* property: if all honest parties initiate the protocol or some honest party outputs done, then every honest party eventually outputs done.

$\mathfrak{F}_{\mathrm{OneSidedVote}}$

Input(init): This operation may be invoked once by each party P_j. In response, $\mathfrak{F}_{\mathrm{OneSidedVote}}$ sends NotifyInput(j) to the ideal-world adversary.

RequestOutput(j): after $n-t-t'$ honest parties have received input init (where $t' \leq t$ is the number of corrupt parties), this operation may be invoked by the ideal-world adversary, who specifies $j \in [n]$. In response, $\mathfrak{F}_{\mathrm{OneSidedVote}}$ sends to P_j the message Output(done).

Fig. 4. The One-Sided Voting Ideal Functionality $\mathfrak{F}_{\mathrm{OneSidedVote}}$

$\mathfrak{F}_{\mathrm{Beacon}}$

Input(init): This operation may be invoked once by each party P_j. If this is the first time this is invoked by any honest party, $\mathfrak{F}_{\mathrm{Beacon}}$ chooses $\omega \in \Omega$ at random and sends NotifyInput(j, ω) to the ideal-world adversary; otherwise, $\mathfrak{F}_{\mathrm{Beacon}}$ sends NotifyInput(j) to the ideal-world adversary.

RequestOutput(j): after the value ω has been generated, this operation may be invoked by the ideal-world adversary, who specifies $j \in [n]$. In response, $\mathfrak{F}_{\mathrm{AVSS}}$ sends to P_j the message Output(ω).

Fig. 5. The Random Beacon Functionality $\mathfrak{F}_{\mathrm{Beacon}}$ (parameterized by output space Ω)

4.4 Random Beacon

This is a protocol that reveals a value ω chosen at random from an **output space** Ω, in such a way that satisfies a *security* property and a *completeness* property. The security property is captured by the ideal functionality $\mathfrak{F}_{\mathrm{Beacon}}$ in Fig. 5. The main idea is that the adversary learns nothing about ω until after at least one honest party initiates the protocol. The completeness property says that if all honest parties initiate the protocol, every honest party eventually outputs a value.

A random beacon may be efficiently implemented using any AVSS protocol and any consensus protocol, using the standard technique of agreeing on a set of $t+1$ secret sharings, and then opening all of them and adding them up. This will yield a beacon output that is an element of a finite field. If the output of the random beacon needs to be longer, it can be passed through a PRG or a hash function. In a practical implementation, it may also be reasonable to implement a random beacon using a threshold BLS signature scheme [4,5].

Note that while our main GoAVSS protocol requires a random beacon, we give a variant in Sect. 5.5 of the full version [20] that does not.

5   Our New GoAVSS Protocol

Our new GoAVSS protocol is presented in Fig. 6. The protocol is parameterized by a subset $R \subseteq \mathbb{Z}_q$ and makes use of

- an instance of an AVSS subprotocol (see Sects. 3.1 and 4.1), which is invoked as an ideal functionality $\mathfrak{F}_{\text{AVSS}}$;
- two instances of a reliable broadcast subprotocol (see Sect. 4.2), which are invoked as ideal functionalities $\mathfrak{F}_{\text{ReliableBroadcast}}^{(1)}$ and $\mathfrak{F}_{\text{ReliableBroadcast}}^{(2)}$;
- an instance of a one-sided voting protocol (see Sect. 4.3), which is invoked as an ideal functionality $\mathfrak{F}_{\text{OneSidedVote}}$;
- an instance of a random beacon (see Sect. 4.4), which is invoked as an ideal functionality $\mathfrak{F}_{\text{Beacon}}$; this beacon outputs $\{\gamma_\ell^{(k)}\}_{\ell \in [L], k \in [n]}$, where each $\gamma_\ell^{(k)} \in R \subseteq \mathbb{Z}_q$; an implementation may choose to instead use a beacon that outputs a short seed to a PRG, and then use the PRG to derive these values.

We express the logic for the dealer as a separate process, even though the dealer is also one of the receiving parties. In particular, the dealer will receive an output from the random beacon, just like the receiving parties.

The protocol starts when the dealer D is initiated with inputs $f_1, \ldots, f_L \in \mathbb{Z}_q[x]_{<d}$. The dealer generates random "blinding" polynomials $g^{(k)} \in \mathbb{Z}_q[x]_{<d}$ for $k \in [n]$, and then disseminates shares of all of these polynomials using an AVSS protocol. The dealer also computes and reliably broadcasts the group elements $\mathcal{T}^{(k)} := g^{(k)}(0)\mathcal{G}$ for $k \in [n]$ and $\mathcal{S}_\ell := f_\ell(0)\mathcal{G}$ for $\ell \in [L]$

Upon receiving its share $w_j^{(k)}$ of each $g^{(k)}$ and its share of $v_{\ell,j}$ of each f_ℓ, as well as the group elements $\{\mathcal{T}^{(k)}\}_{k \in [n]}$ and $\{\mathcal{S}_\ell\}_{\ell \in [L]}$, party P_j in will initiate the random beacon subprotocol. The random beacon will eventually output to each party $\{\gamma_\ell^{(k)}\}_{\ell \in [L], k \in [n]}$, where each $\gamma_\ell^{(k)}$ is a random element of R. The random beacon output serves as a random "challenge".

Given the random "challenge" from the beacon, the dealer D computes "response" polynomials $h^{(k)} := g^{(k)} + \sum_{\ell \in [L]} \gamma_\ell^{(k)} \cdot f_\ell \in \mathbb{Z}_q[x]_{<d}$ for $k \in [n]$, and then reliably broadcasts these polynomials to all parties.

386 J. Groth and V. Shoup

Π_{GoAVSS1}

    // **Dealer D with input $f_1, \ldots, f_L \in \mathbb{Z}_q[x]_{<d}$**
        for all $k \in [n]$: choose random $g^{(k)} \in \mathbb{Z}_q[x]_{<d}$
        invoke operation $\mathsf{Input}(\{g^{(k)}\}_{k\in[n]}, \{f_\ell\}_{\ell\in[L]})$ on $\mathfrak{F}_{\text{AVSS}}$
        for all $k \in [n]$: compute $\mathcal{T}^{(k)} \leftarrow g^{(k)}(0)\mathcal{G} \in E$
        for all $\ell \in [L]$: compute $\mathcal{S}_\ell \leftarrow f_\ell(0)\mathcal{G} \in E$
  (1) invoke operation $\mathsf{Input}(\{\mathcal{T}^{(k)}\}_{k\in[n]}, \{\mathcal{S}_\ell\}_{\ell\in[L]})$ on $\mathfrak{F}^{(1)}_{\text{ReliableBroadcast}}$
        wait for $\mathfrak{F}_{\text{Beacon}}$ to deliver a message $\mathsf{Output}(\{\gamma_\ell^{(k)}\}_{\ell\in[L],k\in[n]})$
        for all $k \in [n]$: compute $h^{(k)} \leftarrow g^{(k)} + \sum_{\ell\in[L]} \gamma_\ell^{(k)} \cdot f_\ell \in \mathbb{Z}_q[x]_{<d}$
        invoke operation $\mathsf{Input}(\{h^{(k)}\}_{k\in[n]})$ on $\mathfrak{F}^{(2)}_{\text{ReliableBroadcast}}$

    // **Receiving party P_j**
        wait for $\mathfrak{F}_{\text{AVSS}}$ to deliver a message $\mathsf{Output}(\{w_j^{(k)}\}_{k\in[n]}, \{v_{\ell,j}\}_{\ell\in[L]})$
        wait for $\mathfrak{F}^{(1)}_{\text{ReliableBroadcast}}$ to deliver a message
            $\mathsf{Output}(\{\mathcal{T}^{(k)}\}_{k\in[n]}, \{\mathcal{S}_\ell\}_{\ell\in[L]})$
        invoke operation $\mathsf{Input}(\text{init})$ on $\mathfrak{F}_{\text{Beacon}}$
        wait for $\mathfrak{F}_{\text{Beacon}}$ to deliver a message $\mathsf{Output}(\{\gamma_\ell^{(k)}\}_{\ell\in[L],k\in[n]})$
        wait for $\mathfrak{F}^{(2)}_{\text{ReliableBroadcast}}$ to deliver a message $\mathsf{Output}(\{h^{(k)}\}_{k\in[n]})$
  (2) if $h^{(j)}(0)\mathcal{G} = \mathcal{T}^{(j)} + \sum_{\ell\in[L]} \gamma_\ell^{(j)} \mathcal{S}_\ell$ and
  (3)   for all $k \in [n]$: $h^{(k)} \in \mathbb{Z}_q[x]_{<d}$ and $h^{(k)}(e_j) = w_j^{(k)} + \sum_{\ell\in[L]} \gamma_\ell^{(k)} \cdot v_{\ell,j}$
        then
            invoke operation $\mathsf{Input}(\text{init})$ on $\mathfrak{F}_{\text{OneSidedVote}}$
        wait for $\mathfrak{F}_{\text{OneSidedVote}}$ to deliver $\mathsf{Output}(\text{done})$
        output $\{(\mathcal{S}_\ell, v_{\ell,j})\}_{\ell\in[L]}$

Fig. 6. A GoAVSS protocol

Upon receiving these "response" polynomials, each party P_j performs a local validity check. It checks two conditions. The first condition is $h^{(j)}(0)\mathcal{G} = \mathcal{T}^{(j)} + \sum_{\ell\in[L]} \gamma_\ell^{(j)} \mathcal{S}_\ell$, which requires P_j to compute a number of group operations. The second condition is $h^{(k)} \in \mathbb{Z}_q[x]_{<d}$ and $h^{(k)}(e_j) = w_j^{(k)} + \sum_{\ell\in[L]} \gamma_\ell^{(k)} \cdot v_{\ell,j}$ (for all $k \in [n]$), which requires P_j to compute a (larger) number of (cheaper) scalar operations. If these checks pass, party P_j will initiate the one-sided voting subprotocol. Finally — and even if these checks fail — if and when the one-sided voting subprotocol outputs done, party P_j will output the group elements $\{\mathcal{S}_\ell\}_{\ell\in[L]}$ and the shares $\{v_{\ell,j}\}_{\ell\in[L]}$.

5.1 Security Analysis of Protocol Π_{GoAVSS1}

Let $S_{N,p}$ be the number of successes among N independent Bernoulli trials, each with success probability p. Let M be a nonnegative integer. We define

$$\text{Tail}(N, M, p) := \Pr[S_{N,p} \geq M]. \tag{1}$$

Theorem 1 (Security of $\Pi_{GoAVSS1}$). *Suppose that $t < d \leq n - 2t$ and $|R| \geq 2^{\rho}$, and assume that*

$$\text{Tail}(n - t, n - 2t, 1/|R|) \leq 2^{-n \cdot (\rho - 2)/3} \tag{2}$$

is negligible. Then we have:

(i) *$\Pi_{GoAVSS1}$ securely realizes $\mathfrak{F}_{GoAVSS}$ in the $(\mathfrak{F}_{AVSS}, \mathfrak{F}_{ReliableBroadcast}, \mathfrak{F}_{OneSidedVote}, \mathfrak{F}_{Beacon})$-hybrid model.*

(ii) *If $\Pi_{GoAVSS1}$ is instantiated with concrete protocols for $\mathfrak{F}_{AVSS}$, $\mathfrak{F}_{ReliableBroadcast}$, $\mathfrak{F}_{OneSidedVote}$, and $\mathfrak{F}_{Beacon}$, that are secure (i.e., securely realize the corresponding functionality) and complete (i.e., satisfy the corresponding completeness property), then the resulting concrete protocol (a) securely realizes $\mathfrak{F}_{GoAVSS}$, and (b) satisfies the AVSS completeness property.*

Proof. We start with statement (i) of the theorem. To that end, we need to show that there is a simulator that interacts with $\mathfrak{F}_{GoAVSS}$ in the ideal world such that no environment can effectively distinguish the ideal world from the hybrid world.

Without loss of generality, we may assume that in the hybrid world, the adversary is a "dummy" adversary that essentially acts as a "router" between the environment and the hybrid functionalities. In addition, in the ideal world, our simulator is actually in charge of implementing the hybrid functionalities. In particular, in the ideal world, any messages sent from (resp., to) the adversary to (resp., from) these hybrid functionalities are actually sent directly to (resp., from) our simulator — this including the inputs (resp., outputs) of corrupt parties.

If the dealer is honest, we just have to show how to simulate the information that the protocol leaks to the adversary, given the information leaked by $\mathfrak{F}_{GoAVSS}$, which is $\{v_{\ell,j}\}_{\ell \in [L], j \in \mathcal{C}}$ and $\{\mathcal{S}_\ell\}_{\ell \in [L]}$, and given the fact that the simulator is also allowed to generate the output $\{\gamma_\ell^{(k)}\}_{\ell \in [L], k \in [n]}$ of the random beacon in advance. This is straightforward. For each $k \in [n]$, the simulator can simply generate the polynomial $h^{(k)}$ at random, and then compute the adversary's shares of $g^{(k)}$ as $w_j^{(k)} \leftarrow h^{(k)}(e_j) - \sum_{\ell \in [L]} \gamma_\ell^{(k)} v_{\ell,j}$ for $j \in \mathcal{C}$, and the group element $\mathcal{T}^{(k)}$ as $\mathcal{T}^{(k)} \leftarrow h^{(k)}(0)\mathcal{G} - \sum_{\ell \in [L]} \gamma_\ell^{(k)} \mathcal{S}_\ell$.

Now assume the dealer is corrupt. The dealer must submit polynomials $\{g^{(k)}\}_{k \in [n]}$ and $\{f_\ell\}_{\ell \in [L]}$ of degree less than d to $\mathfrak{F}_{AVSS}$ and group elements $\{\mathcal{T}^{(k)}\}_{k \in [n]}$ and $\{\mathcal{S}_\ell\}_{\ell \in [L]}$ before the random beacon values are revealed. If and when an honest party produces an output, the simulator will submit $\{f_\ell\}_{\ell \in [L]}$ to the ideal functionality $\mathfrak{F}_{GoAVSS}$. Let $\mathfrak{E}$ be the event that $\mathcal{S}_\ell \neq f_\ell(0)\mathcal{G}$ for some $\ell \in [L]$. The simulation is perfect unless $\mathfrak{E}$ occurs. We argue that the probability that $\Pr[\mathfrak{E}]$ occurs is at most (2).

Consider the point in time where some honest party produces an output. By the security property of one-sided voting, at least $n - 2t$ out of a set of $n - t$ honest parties must have found that all checks passed in Steps (2)–(3). Call these parties "accepting" parties. Since $n - 2t \geq d$, and all polynomials here have degree less than d, this means all of the polynomials $h^{(k)}$ for $k \in [n]$ were correctly computed, that is, $h^{(k)} = g^{(k)} + \sum_{\ell \in [L]} \gamma_\ell^{(k)} f_\ell$ for all $k \in [n]$. Therefore, for each "accepting" party P_j, we have

$$T^{(j)} + \sum_{\ell \in [L]} \gamma_\ell^{(j)} \mathcal{S}_\ell = h^{(j)}(0)\mathcal{G} = g^{(j)}(0)\mathcal{G} + \sum_{\ell \in [L]} \gamma_\ell^{(j)} f_\ell(0)\mathcal{G}.$$

Here, the first equality holds by the logic of test in Step (2), and the second holds because of the fact that the polynomials $h^{(k)}$ for $k \in [n]$ were correctly computed.

For each $k \in [n]$, if the values $\{f_\ell\}_{\ell \in [L]}$, $\{\mathcal{S}_\ell\}_{\ell \in [L]}$, $T^{(k)}$, and $g^{(k)}$ are fixed, and $\mathcal{S}_\ell \neq f_\ell(0)\mathcal{G}$ for some $\ell \in [L]$, and if we choose the values $\gamma_\ell^{(k)} \in R$ at random for $\ell \in [L]$, then the probability that

$$T^{(k)} + \sum_{\ell \in [L]} \gamma_\ell^{(k)} \mathcal{S}_\ell = g^{(k)}(0)\mathcal{G} + \sum_{\ell \in [L]} \gamma_\ell^{(k)} f_\ell(0)\mathcal{G}$$

is clearly at most $2^{-\rho}$.

Thus, if $\mathfrak{E}$ is to occur, at least $n - 2t$ parties out of a set of $n - t$ honest parties must each find that a certain event occurs, where these events are independent of one another and each occurs with probability $\leq 2^{-\rho}$. Therefore, $\Pr[\mathfrak{E}] \leq \text{Tail}(n - t, n - 2t, 1/|R|)$. Setting $\theta := t/n \leq 1/3$, the bound (2) can be derived by simply using the union bound:

$$\begin{aligned}
\text{Tail}(n - t, n - 2t, 1/|R|) &\leq (1/|R|)^{n-2t} \cdot \binom{n-t}{n-2t} \\
&\leq (1/|R|)^{n-2t} \cdot 2^{n-t} = 2^{-n \cdot (\rho \cdot (1-2\theta) - (1-\theta))} \\
&\leq 2^{-n \cdot (\rho - 2)/3},
\end{aligned}$$

where the last inequality follows from the fact that $\rho \cdot (1 - 2\theta) - (1 - \theta)$ is a decreasing function of θ, and so is minimized at $\theta = 1/3$.

That proves statement (i) of the theorem. Statement (ii)(a) is a direct consequence of statement (i) and the UC composition theorem. Statement (ii)(b) follows fairly easily from the security and completeness properties of the concrete subprotocols, and the logic of Π_{GoAVSS1}. □

Remark 1. The error bound (2) is the probability that a corrupt dealer breaks the security of the protocol. So to achieve an error bound of $2^{-\sigma}$, where σ is a statistical security parameter, we can set $\rho := \lceil 3\sigma/n \rceil + 2$. In a typical implementation, R will be chosen to be the set of all ρ-bit numbers. For a typical setting such as $\sigma = 80$, and with a network of size, say, $n = 49 = 3 \cdot 16 + 1$, we can set $\rho = 7$. By using such small numbers, we get a protocol that is very attractive from a computational complexity perspective. We analyze the computational complexity of this protocol in detail below in Sect. 5.2. □

Remark 2. Note that the analysis here is in the static corruption model, and the error bound (2) reflects that. If we carried out the analysis in an adaptive corruption model, it would be $\text{Tail}(n, n - 2t, 1/|R|) \leq 2^{-n \cdot (\rho - 3)/3}$. Indeed, in a adaptive corruption model, before corrupting any parties, the adversary could then hope that $n - 2t$ of these parties cast a positive vote, and then corrupt t of the remaining parties and make them cast positive votes as well. While our recommended implementation of the AVSS subprotocol in [29] is only analyzed in the static corruption model, it is suggested there that it may be secure against adaptive corruptions in the random oracle model. If this adaptive error bound is used, we would have to add 1 to the value of ρ to achieve the same level of security, so this would generally have a mild impact on the performance of the protocol.   □

Remark 3. The random beacon may output a short seed, which is passed to a PRG to derive all of the challenge values $\gamma_\ell^{(k)}$. When we do this, we need to add to the error probability in Theorem 1 a term that measures advantage of a certain adversary (whose running time is essentially the same as that of the original adversary) in distinguishing the PRG output from random.   □

5.2   Complexity Analysis of Protocol Π_{GoAVSS1}

We analyze both computational and communication complexity. For each complexity metric, we consider the cost contributed by the body of the protocol, as well the cost contributed by the recommended implementation of the subprotocols. For subprotocols that have an "optimistic path", where no party provably misbehaves, we consider only the cost on this optimistic path. Arguably, over a long run of the system where parties that provably misbehave are effectively removed from the system, this is the only cost that matters. To simplify matters, we assume the $d = t + 1$ and $n = 3t + 1$.

We will also consider the "amortized" cost, in two different senses.

- One is the amortized cost per "raw sharing" in one run of Π_{GoAVSS1}, where one party is the designated dealer, and the other parties are receivers. As there are L sharings generated in one run of Π_{GoAVSS1}, and it is assumed that L is very large, we can effectively ignore the cost of any protocol steps and subprotocols whose cost does not grow with L (such as the random beacon). We will generally assume that $L = \Omega(n^2)$. This assumption is needed only to account for the overhead associated with the polynomials $h^{(k)}$ for $k \in [n]$. Otherwise, we could get by just under the weaker assumption that $L = \Omega(n \log n)$ to account for the overheads in the subprotocols. For large n, we can use the protocol in Sect. 5.3 to get by with a weaker assumption on L.
- The other is the amortized cost per "processed sharing". This is the sum of the amortized cost per "raw sharing" over n runs of the protocol, with different designated dealer in each run, divided by the number of sharings output by the batch randomness extraction procedure (which is at least $t + 1$). This is ultimately the number of interest in applications.

Throughout this section, $\lambda := \lceil \log_2(q) \rceil$ and σ is a statistical security parameter. We assume $\sigma \leq \lambda$. In typical settings, we will have $\lambda = 256$ and $\sigma = 80$.

5.2.1 Communication Complexity

As usual, we measure communication complexity as the sum, over all honest parties P and all parties Q, of the total number of bits that P sends to Q over a point-to-point channel. With AVSS and reliable broadcast implemented as described in Sect. 4, it is easily seen that the amortized communication complexity per processed sharing is $O(n\lambda)$. This assumes elements of E can be encoded in $O(\lambda)$ bits. Also, the communication complexity is well balanced: each party transmits (and receives) $O(\lambda)$ bits of data per processed sharing. In fact, it is easy to see from the estimates given in Sect. 4 that (for large enough L), each party essentially transmits (and receives) a total of 18 scalars and 9 group elements per processed sharing.

5.2.2 Computational Complexity

To state computational costs, we use the terms "full scalar/group multiplication", "tiny scalar/group multiplication", and "tiny scalar/scalar multiplication" introduced in Sect. 2.1.

Amortized cost per raw sharing. For a party acting in its role as a receiver, the amortized cost per raw sharing in the body of our protocol is:

- 1 tiny scalar/group multiplication and addition;
- n tiny scalar/scalar multiplications.

For a party acting in its role as a dealer, the amortized cost per raw sharing in the body of our protocol is:

- 1 full scalar/group multiplication;
- $n(t+1)$ tiny scalar/scalar multiplications.

Note that the dealer plays a role both as a dealer and as a receiver.

Amortized cost per processed sharing. The amortized cost per processed sharing is equal to $n/(t+1)$ times the amortized receiver cost per raw sharing plus $1/(t+1)$ times the amortized dealer cost per raw sharing. This gives us an amortized cost per processed sharing of:

- $1/(t+1)$ full scalar/group multiplications;
- 3 tiny scalar/group multiplications;
- $4n$ tiny scalar/scalar multiplications.

Example 1. Consider $n = 49 = 3 \cdot 16 + 1$ and we set the statistical security parameter $\sigma := 80$. So we set $\rho := 7$. Let us also assume that $\lambda = 256$. We compute the amortized cost per processed sharing. This is:

- $1/17$ full scalar/group multiplications.
  We will assume that we can compute a full scalar/group multiplication using 64 group additions (see Appendix A of the full version [20] for justification). Dividing by 17, we get an amortized cost per processed sharing of less than 4 group additions.

- 3 tiny scalar/group multiplications.
  Using Pippenger's simple "bucket method" bucket method (see Appendix B of the full version [20]), using just a single window of size 7, the amortized cost of one tiny scalar/group multiplication is just one group addition. Multiplying by 3, we get an amortized cost per processed sharing of 3 group additions.
- 196 tiny scalar/scalar multiplications.

So we get a total of 7 group additions plus 196 tiny scalar/scalar multiplications.

Now let us add in the amortized cost of applying our new constructions super-invertible matrices (see Sect. 6). Using the construction $U'_{17,32,q}$ in Sect. 6.2, this amortized cost is $(17 \cdot (32 - 9) + 1)/17 \approx 23$ group additions. However, because t is small enough, we can use the better construction $S'_{17,16,q}$ is Sect. 6.3, which has an amortized of just 16 group additions.

This is 16 group additions and 16 additions in $\mathbb{Z}_q$ per processed sharing. So this gives us:

- $23 = 7 + 16$ group additions;
- 196 tiny scalar/scalar multiplications;
- 16 additions in $\mathbb{Z}_q$.

Note that we perform almost 10 times as many tiny scalar/scalar multiplications as we do group additions. However, each of these is tiny scalar/scalar multiplications relatively cheap (essentially, the cost of multiplying a ρ-bit integer by a λ-bit integer, with no modular reduction), so that in any reasonably optimized implementation, the cost of these should be significantly less than the cost of the group additions.

Indeed, we conservatively estimate that each tiny scalar/scalar multiplication is about 1/40th the cost of a group addition over an elliptic curve such as secp2565k1. In such a group addition, we have to perform several multiplications mod p, where p is also a 256-bit prime. We estimate the number of such multiplications mod p to be about 10 (although this depends on many factors). On a 64-bit machine, assuming 256 bit numbers are represented as four 64-bit limbs (i.e., four base-2^{64} digits), one multiplication mod p costs four 1-limb-by-4-limb multiplications. While reduction mod p is not free, we ignore that cost here. In contrast, a tiny scalar/scalar multiplication should take about the same cost as one 1-limb-by-4-limb multiplication. This is where we get the factor of $40 = 10 \cdot 4$. Thus, we estimate the cost of the tiny scalar/scalar multiplications to be the equivalent of about 5 group additions.

Note that if we use the adaptive error bound as discussed in Remark 2, we have to use $\rho = 8$. However, this does not change the amortized cost of our algorithm at all (but we may have to use a slightly somewhat larger batch size to compensate). □

Other Costs. The above cost analysis left out some costs that we shall now discuss. As we shall see, these other costs should not have any significant impact on the overall performance.

392 J. Groth and V. Shoup

Cost of Subprotocols. In terms of amortized computational complexity per sharing (raw or processed), the only subprotocols that matter are AVSS and reliable broadcast (specifically, the reliable broadcast at Step (1)). We assume all subprotocols are implemented as in [29]. We focus here on the AVSS subprotocol, as this is the most expensive.

This protocol uses a statistical test that has error bound of $2^n/q$. For n of the size we are mostly interested in here, this error probability will be sufficiently small, and the test only needs to be repeated once. If we count the number of arithmetic operations in $\mathbb{Z}_q$ performed by this AVSS protocol, the amortized number of such operations per processed sharing is easily seen to be 4. Thus, this will not have any measurable impact on the overall GoAVSS protocol.

For larger values of n, this test has to be repeated several times. However, for $\lambda = 256$ and $\sigma = 80$, and for n up to 1000, we have to repeat the test at most 5 times, giving an amortized cost per processed sharing of 20 arithmetic operations in $\mathbb{Z}_q$, which still has no measurable impact on the overall GoAVSS protocol.

The above does not take into account the cost for the dealer of actually computing the shares $f_\ell(e_j)$ for $\ell \in [L]$, $j \in [n]$, which is a part of any AVSS protocol. As discussed in Sect. 4.1, for small to moderate size n, we can use Horner's rule, which will add the cost of performing $\approx n$ multiplications and additions mod q to the amortized cost per processed sharing. Moreover, if the evaluation points are $1, \ldots, n$ (which is typical), we can run many steps of Horner without any reductions mod q, making these steps relatively inexpensive (similar in cost to a tiny scalar/scalar multiplication).

Cost of Erasure Codes. We also consider the cost of performing the encoding and decoding operations for the erasure codes used in the reliable broadcast protocol and similar subprotocols used in the AVSS protocol in [29]. Per processed sharing, the amortized amount of data that each party (i) encodes is 6 scalars and $3 + 1/(t + 1)$ group elements, and (ii) decodes is 3 scalars and 3 group elements. Note that all of these encoding and decoding operations work only on public data, so there are no restrictions on the type of codes and algorithms that may be used. This cost should not greatly impact the overall cost of GoAVSS, if one uses a good implementation of erasure coding algorithms. One such implementation is the `reed-solomon-simd` library at https://github.com/AndersTrier/reed-solomon-simd, which is based on [23,24]. We ran some benchmarks on various machines (x86 and Arm) using this library, with parameters corresponding to those in Example 1, and a batch size of $L = 5000$ (the amortized cost of decoding gets better with large batch sizes). With these parameters, on commonly available machines, we can encode at a rate of about 2 GB per second and decode at a rate of about 200–350 MB per second. With these estimates, the amortized cost per processed sharing for all encoding and decoding is roughly equivalent to that of (at most) 3–5 group additions on similar machines, adding about 10–20% to the overall amortized cost per processed sharing.

Cost of PRGs and Hashing. We also must consider the cost of generating pseudorandom bits as a the output for the random beacon, both in the GoAVSS protocol and in the implementation of the AVSS subprotocol. In typical settings, where $n = O(\lambda)$, the amortized number of bits per processed sharing that need to generated is $O(\lambda)$. It seems likely that with any good implementation of a pseudorandom bit generator, especially on a CPU with good cryptographic hardware support [10,13], this cost will not greatly impact the overall cost of GoAVSS.

Similarly, in the underlying AVSS and reliable broadcast subprotocols, much of the data sent and received needs to be hashed. The amortized number of bits per processed sharing that need to be hashed is $O(\lambda)$. It seems likely that with any good implementation of a hash function, especially on a CPU with good cryptographic hardware support [13], this cost will not greatly impact the overall cost of GoAVSS.

5.3 A Variation for Large n

For large n, the following variation of Π_{GoAVSS1} may be preferred.

Suppose that instead of having k range over $[n]$ in Π_{GoAVSS1}, it instead ranges over $[K]$ for some parameter K in the range $1, \ldots, n$. Moreover, in Step (2) of the protocol, Party P_j checks that

$$h^{(k)}(0)\mathcal{G} = \mathcal{T}^{(k)} + \sum_{\ell \in [L]} \gamma_\ell^{(k)} \mathcal{S}_\ell, \qquad (3)$$

where $k := (j \bmod K) + 1 \in [K]$. Let us call this variation Π_{GoAVSS2}.

Theorem 2 (Security of $\Pi_{GoAVSS2}$). *Suppose that $t < d \leq n - 2t$ and $|R| \geq 2^\rho$, and assume that*

$$\text{Tail}\left(K, \lceil (n - 2t)/\lceil n/K \rceil \rceil, 1/|R| \right) \qquad (4)$$

is negligible. Then we have:

(i) Π_{GoAVSS2} *securely realizes* $\mathfrak{F}_{\text{GoAVSS}}$ *in the* $(\mathfrak{F}_{\text{AVSS}}, \mathfrak{F}_{\text{ReliableBroadcast}}, \mathfrak{F}_{\text{OneSidedVote}}, \mathfrak{F}_{\text{Beacon}})$- *hybrid model.*

(ii) *If* Π_{GoAVSS2} *is instantiated with concrete protocols for* $\mathfrak{F}_{\text{AVSS}}$, $\mathfrak{F}_{\text{ReliableBroadcast}}$, $\mathfrak{F}_{\text{OneSidedVote}}$, *and* $\mathfrak{F}_{\text{Beacon}}$, *that are secure (i.e., securely realize the corresponding functionality) and complete (i.e., satisfy the corresponding completeness property), then the resulting concrete protocol (a) securely realizes* $\mathfrak{F}_{\text{GoAVSS}}$, *and (b) satisfies the AVSS completeness property.*

Proof. The main thing we have to do is to bound the probability that a corrupt dealer "wins" by breaking the security of the protocol. As it simplifies the proof, we will assume the adversary adaptively corrupts parties. For an index $k \in [K]$, let us say that party P_j is "associated with" k if $k = (j \bmod K) + 1$, and let us say that k is "good" if the equality (3) holds. To win, there must be at least

$n-2t$ parties associated with good indices, and the adversary can corrupt t other parties. Since there are at most $\lceil n/K \rceil$ parties associated with any one index, this means there must be at least $\lceil (n - 2t)/\lceil n/K \rceil \rceil$ good indices.   □

Remark 4. The error bound (4) is the probability that a corrupt dealer breaks the security of the protocol.   □

Remark 5. The point of this protocol is that when $n = 3t + 1$ amortized computational cost of this protocol per processed sharing becomes

- $1/(t+1)$ full scalar/group multiplications,
- 3 tiny scalar/group multiplications,
- $4K$ tiny scalar/scalar multiplications,

instead of

- $1/(t+1)$ full scalar/group multiplications,
- 3 tiny scalar/group multiplications,
- $4n$ tiny scalar/scalar multiplications.

However, the value of ρ defining the size of the "tiny" scalars may be smaller in Π_{GoAVSS1} than in Π_{GoAVSS2}.   □

Example 2. Let us return to the parameters in Example 1, with $n = 49 = 3 \cdot 16 + 1$, $\lambda = 256$, and $\sigma = 80$. We will estimate the amortized cost per processed sharing contributed by the tiny scalar/group multiplications and the tiny scalar/scalar multiplications. In that example, we estimated this cost to be (the equivalent of) 8 group additions (3 for the tiny scalar/group multiplications and the equivalent of at most 5 for the tiny scalar/scalar multiplications). In this example, we shall estimate the amortized cost per tiny scalar/group multiplication for a given value of ρ to be $\lceil \rho/8 \rceil$, using Pippenger's simple "bucket method" (see Appendix B of the full version [20]), with a window size of 8.

We can set $K = 1$ and $\rho = 80$, and the amortized cost per cost per tiny scalar/group multiplication is 10 group additions, which contributes a total of 30 group additions to the amortized cost per processed sharing. The cost contributed by the tiny scalar/scalar multiplications may be safely ignored.

We can set $K = 16$ and $\rho = 16$—although the statement of Theorem 2 does not directly imply an error bound of 2^{-80}, the proof is easily adapted (one sees that at least 6 out of 16 indices must be good in order for the adversary to win). So the amortized cost per cost per tiny scalar/group multiplication is 2 group additions, which contributes a total of 6 group additions to the amortized cost per processed sharing. As we did in Example 1, we may safely estimate the cost of the 64 tiny scalar/scalar multiplications per processed sharing to be the equivalent of less than 2 group additions. So this setting yields roughly the same computational performance as the settings in Example 1.   □

As the above example illustrates, for large values of n, and $\lambda \approx 256$, it probably makes sense to use Π_{GoAVSS2} with values of K in the range 10–20 rather than Π_{GoAVSS1}. One advantage of doing so is that in order to achieve the stated amortized complexity bounds, we only need to assume $L = \Omega(n \cdot \max\{\log n, K\})$, rather $L = \Omega(n^2)$ as we did with Π_{GoAVSS1}. (See also Sect. 5.6 of the full version [20].) Perhaps in many situations it even makes sense to just use $K = 1$, which is the simplest version of any of our protocols and still achieves quite good performance.

6   Super-Invertible Matrices from Pascal

Let $A \in \mathbb{Z}_q^{M \times N}$ be a matrix with M rows and $N \geq M$ columns. The matrix A is called **super-invertible** if every collection of M of its columns is linearly independent. The definition of super-invertible matrices and their application to multi-party computation comes from [21]. Such matrices also have been studied in the context of error-correcting codes, as they are precisely the generator matrices of MDS (maximum distance separable) codes—see, for example, [27].

6.1   The Symmetric Pascal Matrix

The well-known symmetric Pascal matrix $S_N \in \mathbb{Z}^{N \times N}$ is an $N \times N$ matrix whose i, j entry is defined to be

$$S_{i,j} := C_{i+j,i} = C_{i+j,j} = \frac{(i+j)!}{i!j!},$$

where the indices i, j start at 0 and $C_{n,k}$ is the binomial coefficient $C_{n,k} = \binom{n}{k}$.

Define the matrix $S_{M,N,q} \in \mathbb{Z}_q^{M \times N}$ to be the matrix consisting of the first M rows of S_N with entries mapped from $\mathbb{Z}$ to $\mathbb{Z}_q$.

Theorem 3 (The symmetric Pascal matrix is super-invertible). *Assuming $q \geq N$, the matrix $S_{M,N,q}$ is super-invertible.*

Proof. First, for $i = 0, 1, \ldots, M - 1$ define the polynomial

$$p_i(x) := \frac{(x+1)(x+2) \cdots (x+i)}{1 \cdot 2 \cdot \cdots \cdot i} \in \mathbb{Z}_q[x].$$

Note that since $M \leq N \leq q$, the denominator in the definition of $p_i(x)$, which is the image of $i!$ in $\mathbb{Z}_q$, is nonzero and hence invertible. So we see that $p_i(x)$ is a polynomial of degree i.

Second, for $j = 0, 1, \ldots, N - 1$, observe that the i, j entry of $S_{M,N,q}$ is equal to $p_i(j)$. This follows from the definition, as the i, j entry of $S_{M,N,q}$ is

$$\frac{(i+j)!}{i!j!} = \frac{(j+1)(j+2) \cdots (j+i)}{1 \cdot 2 \cdot \cdots \cdot i} = p_i(j).$$

So now consider any subset $\mathcal{J} \subseteq \{0, \ldots, N-1\}$ of cardinality M and form the matrix $R \in \mathbb{Z}_q^{M \times M}$ consisting of the columns of $S_{M,N,q}$ indexed by $j \in \mathcal{J}$. By the above observations, we can write

$$R = P \cdot V, \tag{5}$$

where $P \in \mathbb{Z}_q^{M \times M}$ is the matrix whose ith row, for $i = 0, 1, \ldots, M-1$, is the coefficient vector of the polynomial $p_i(x)$, and $V \in \mathbb{Z}_q^{M \times M}$ is the Vandermonde matrix whose ith column, for $i = 0, 1, \ldots, M-1$, is $(1, j_i, \ldots, j_i^{M-1})^\mathsf{T}$. Since $N \leq q$, the entries $j_1, \ldots, j_M \in \mathcal{J}$ are distinct when mapped to $\mathbb{Z}_q$ and hence V is nonsingular. Since P is a lower diagonal matrix with nonzero entries along the diagonal, P is also nonsingular. Since R is a product of nonsingular matrices, it follows that R is nonsingular, which proves the theorem.   □

Now suppose we are given as input a column vector of group elements $\mathbf{x} = (\mathcal{X}_0, \ldots, \mathcal{X}_{N-1})^\mathsf{T} \in E^{N \times 1}$ and want to compute a column vector of group elements $\mathbf{y} = (\mathcal{Y}_0, \ldots, \mathcal{Y}_{M-1})^\mathsf{T} \in E^{M \times 1}$, where $\mathbf{y} = S_{M,N,q}\mathbf{x}$. We next show how this can be done using $M \cdot (N-1)$ group additions.

Define group elements $\mathcal{X}_k^{(i)}$ for $k = 0, \ldots, N-1$ and $i = -1, 0, \ldots, M-1$, as follows:

$$\mathcal{X}_k^{(-1)} := \mathcal{X}_k \quad \text{for } k = 0, \ldots, N-1 \tag{6}$$

and for $i = 0, \ldots, M-1$

$$\mathcal{X}_{N-1}^{(i)} := \mathcal{X}_{N-1}^{(i-1)} \quad \text{and} \quad \mathcal{X}_k^{(i)} := \mathcal{X}_k^{(i-1)} + \mathcal{X}_{k+1}^{(i)} \quad \text{for } k = N-2, \ldots, 1, 0. \tag{7}$$

Then for $i = 0, \ldots, M-1$ and $k = 0, \ldots, N-1$, we have:

$$\mathcal{X}_k^{(i)} = \sum_{j=k}^{N-1} C_{i+j-k,i} \mathcal{X}_j. \tag{8}$$

This follows from a simple induction proof and Pascal's rule $C_{a,b} = C_{a-1,b-1} + C_{a-1,b}$. It follows that $\mathcal{Y}_i = \mathcal{X}_0^{(i)}$ for $i = 0, \ldots, M-1$. Using (7) we can therefore compute $\mathcal{Y}_0, \ldots, \mathcal{Y}_{M-1}$ using $M \cdot (N-1)$ group additions.

6.2   The Upper-Triangular Pascal Matrix

The upper-triangular Pascal matrix $U_N \in \mathbb{Z}^{N \times N}$ is an $N \times N$ upper-triangular matrix whose i, j entry is defined to be $U_{i,j} := C_{j,i}$, where the indices i, j start at 0 and we define $C_{j,i} := 0$ for $j < 0$.

Define the matrix $U_{M,N,q} \in \mathbb{Z}_q^{M \times N}$ to be the matrix consisting of the first M rows of U_N with entries mapped from $\mathbb{Z}$ to $\mathbb{Z}_q$.

Theorem 4 (The upper Pascal matrix is super-invertible). *Assuming* $q \geq N$, *the matrix* $U_{M,N,q}$ *is super-invertible.*

The proof is the same as that of Theorem 3, except we define

$$p_i(x) := \frac{(x-0)(x-1)\cdots(x-(i-1))}{1\cdot 2 \cdots \cdot i} \in \mathbb{Z}_q[x].$$

Now suppose we are given as input a column vector of group elements $\mathbf{x} = (\mathcal{X}_0, \ldots, \mathcal{X}_{N-1})^\mathsf{T} \in E^{N\times 1}$ and want to compute a column vector of group elements $\mathbf{y} = (\mathcal{Y}_0, \ldots, \mathcal{Y}_{M-1})^\mathsf{T} \in E^{M\times 1}$, where $\mathbf{y} = U_{M,N,q}\mathbf{x}$. We next show how this can be done using $M \cdot (N - (M+1)/2)$ group additions.

Define group elements $\mathcal{X}_k^{(i)}$ as in (6) and (7). Then by (8), we have $\mathcal{Y}_i = \mathcal{X}_i^{(i)}$ for $i = 0, \ldots, M - 1$. These values can therefore be computed using $(N - 1) + (N - 2) + \cdots + (N - M) = M \cdot (N - (M+1)/2)$ group additions.

Theorem 4 was already proved in [22]. They also prove that if one augments $U_{M,N,q}$ by adding the column $(0, \ldots, 0, 1)^\mathsf{T}$, the resulting $M \times (N+1)$ matrix $U'_{M,N,q}$ is also super-invertible. This result is easily seen to apply to any $M \times N$ super-invertible matrix A with the property that the $(M-1) \times N$ submatrix consisting of the first $M - 1$ rows of A is also super-invertible.

The augmented matrix $U'_{M,N,q}$, then, is an $M \times (N+1)$ super-invertible matrix that we can multiply on the right by a vector of group elements using just $M \cdot (N - (M+1)/2) + 1$ group additions. In our application to batch randomness extraction, we need an $(n-2t) \times (n-t)$ super-invertible matrix. We can therefore apply the construction $U'_{M,N,q}$ with $M = n - 2t$ and $N = n - t - 1$, and we get a cost of $(n - 2t) \cdot (n/2 - 3/2) + 1$ group additions.

6.3   Better Super-Invertible Matrices from Hyper-invertible Matrices

Let $A \in \mathbb{Z}_q^{M\times N}$ be a matrix with M rows and N columns. The matrix A is called **hyper-invertible** if every square submatrix is invertible — that is, if for every $k \in [\min\{M, N\}]$, and every subset $\mathcal{I} \subseteq [M]$ of size k and every subset $\mathcal{J} \subseteq [N]$ of size k, the $k \times k$ submatrix of A with rows indexed by $\mathcal{I}$ and columns indexed by $\mathcal{J}$ is invertible. The definition of hyper-invertible matrices and their application to multi-party computation comes from [2]. Such matrices also have been studied in the context of error-correcting codes, where they are (sometimes) called *super-regular matrices* — see, for example, [27]. In coding theory, one of the main features of such a matrix, as observed, for example, in [27], is that if I is the $M \times M$ identity matrix, then $A' := [I \mid A]$ is a generator matrix for a systematic MDS code. In the language of cryptographers, A' is a super-invertible matrix. One of the nice features of A' is that the cost of multiplying A' on the right by a vector of group elements is just M additions plus the cost of multiplying A on the right by a vector of group elements. This feature was noted in [3], and used to get a more efficient batch randomness extraction algorithm.

An interesting question to which do not know a very good answer is: under what conditions is the symmetric Pascal matrix S_N hyper-invertible mod q (i.e., $S_{N,N,q}$ hyper-invertible)? An obvious necessary condition is that $q \geq 2N$ (this is clear from the decomposition (5), as otherwise some entries of S_N are zero mod

q). We do know that S_N is *(strictly) totally positive*, meaning that every square submatrix of S_N has positive determinant — this follows from the corresponding result for U_N (see [17]), along with the Cauchy-Binet identity and the fact that $S_N = U_N^\mathsf{T} U_N$ (see [12], who also outlines a direct proof of the total positivity of S_N based on bidiagonal decomposition [15]). Thus, we can trivially show that S_N is hyper-invertible mod q if every square submatrix of S_N has determinant less than q. A convenient fact about totally positive matrices is that we can bound the determinant of such a matrix by the product of its diagonal entries — this is a special case of Fischer's inequality (see [12]). Because of the fact that entries of S_N only increase as we move down or to the right, we may conclude that every square submatrix of S_N has determinant at most $B_N := C_{2,1} \cdot C_{4,2} \cdot C_{2(N-1),N-1}$. By direct calculation, one can verify that $B_N < 2^{237}$ for $N \le 17$. This means that for $N \le 17$ and $q > 2^{237}$, the symmetric Pascal matrix S_N is hyper-invertible mod q. These ranges of N and q are already useful in a range of practical cryptographic applications.

Generalizing the above argument, the matrix $S_{M,N,q}$ is hyper-invertible provided $\prod_{j=1}^{\min(M,N)} C_{M+N-2j,N-j} < q$. In any case, for those values of M, N, and q for which $S_{M,N,q}$ is hyper-invertible, if I is the $M \times M$ identity matrix, the augmented $M \times (M+N)$ matrix $S'_{M,N,q} := [I \mid S_{M,N,q}]$ is super-invertible, and the cost of multiplying $S'_{M,N,q}$ on the right by a vector of group elements is just $M \cdot N$ group additions. In our application to batch randomness extraction, we need an $(n-2t) \times (n-t)$ super-invertible matrix. We can therefore apply the construction $S'_{M,N,q}$ with $M = n-2t$ and $N = t$, and we get a cost of $(n-2t) \cdot t$ group additions.

Acknowledgment. This work was partially done while both authors were employed at DFINITY. The first author thanks Melissa Chase for discussions about cryptographic applications of the symmetric Pascal matrix. The second author thanks Daniel Bernstein for discussions on algorithms for multi-scalar/group multiplication.

References

1. Atapoor, S., Baghery, K., Cozzo, D., Pedersen, R.: VSS from distributed ZK proofs and applications. Cryptology ePrint Archive, Paper 2023/992 (2023). https://eprint.iacr.org/2023/992
2. Beerliová-Trubíniová, Z., Hirt, M.: Perfectly-secure MPC with linear communication complexity. In: Canetti, R. (ed.) TCC 2008. LNCS, vol. 4948, pp. 213–230. Springer, Heidelberg (2008). https://doi.org/10.1007/978-3-540-78524-8_13
3. Benhamouda, F., Halevi, S., Krawczyk, H., Ma, Y., Rabin, T.: SPRINT: high-throughput robust distributed SCHNORR signatures. Cryptology ePrint Archive, Paper 2023/427 (2023). https://eprint.iacr.org/2023/427
4. Boldyreva, A.: Threshold signatures, multisignatures and blind signatures based on the Gap-Diffie-Hellman-Group signature scheme. In: Desmedt, Y.G. (ed.) PKC 2003. LNCS, vol. 2567, pp. 31–46. Springer, Heidelberg (2003). https://doi.org/10.1007/3-540-36288-6_3
5. Boneh, D., Lynn, B., Shacham, H.: Short signatures from the Weil pairing. In: Boyd, C. (ed.) ASIACRYPT 2001. LNCS, vol. 2248, pp. 514–532. Springer, Heidelberg (2001). https://doi.org/10.1007/3-540-45682-1_30

6. Bracha, G.: Asynchronous byzantine agreement protocols. Inf. Comput. **75**(2), 130–143 (1987)
7. Cachin, C., Tessaro, S.: Asynchronous verifiable information dispersal. In: Fraigniaud, P. (ed.) DISC 2005. LNCS, vol. 3724, pp. 503–504. Springer, Heidelberg (2005). https://doi.org/10.1007/11561927_42
8. Castro, M., Liskov, B.: Practical byzantine fault tolerance. In: Seltzer, M.I., Leach, P.J. (eds.) Proceedings of the Third USENIX Symposium on Operating Systems Design and Implementation (OSDI), pp. 173–186. USENIX Association (1999)
9. Certicom Research: Sec 2: Recommended elliptic curve domain parameters (2010), version 2.0. http://www.secg.org/sec2-v2.pdf
10. Drucker, N., Gueron, S., Krasnov, V.: Making AES great again: the forthcoming vectorized AES instruction. Cryptology ePrint Archive, Paper 2018/392 (2018). https://eprint.iacr.org/2018/392
11. Duan, S., Wang, X., Zhang, H.: FIN: practical signature-free asynchronous common subset in constant time. Cryptology ePrint Archive, Paper 2023/154 (2023). https://eprint.iacr.org/2023/154
12. Fallat, S.M.: Bidiagonal factorizations of totally nonnegative matrices. Am. Math. Mon. **108**(8), 697–712 (2001). http://www.jstor.org/stable/2695613
13. Faz-Hernández, A., López-Hernández, J.C., de Oliveira, A.K.D.S.: SoK: a performance evaluation of cryptographic instruction sets on modern architectures. In: Proceedings of the 5th ACM on ASIA Public-Key Cryptography Workshop, pp. 9–18. ACM (2018)
14. Feldman, P.: A practical scheme for non-interactive verifiable secret sharing. In: 28th Annual Symposium on Foundations of Computer Science, Los Angeles, California, USA, 27-29 October 1987, pp. 427–437. IEEE Computer Society (1987)
15. Gasca, M., Peña, J.M.: On factorizations of totally positive matrices. In: Gasca, M., Micchelli, C.A. (eds.) Total Positivity and Its Applications, pp. 109–130. Springer, Netherlands (1996). https://doi.org/10.1007/978-94-015-8674-0_7
16. Gennaro, R., Jarecki, S., Krawczyk, H., Rabin, T.: Secure distributed key generation for discrete-log based cryptosystems. J. Cryptol. **20**(1), 51–83 (2007)
17. Gessel, I., Viennot, G.: Binomial determinants, paths, and hook length formulae. Adv. Math. **58**, 300–321 (1985)
18. Groth, J.: Non-interactive distributed key generation and key resharing. Cryptology ePrint Archive, Report 2021/339 (2021). https://ia.cr/2021/339
19. Groth, J., Shoup, V.: Design and analysis of a distributed ECDSA signing service. Cryptology ePrint Archive, Report 2022/506 (2022). https://ia.cr/2022/506
20. Groth, J., Shoup, V.: Fast batched asynchronous distributed key generation. Cryptology ePrint Archive, Paper 2023/1175 (2023). https://eprint.iacr.org/2023/1175
21. Hirt, M., Nielsen, J.B.: Robust multiparty computation with linear communication complexity. In: Dwork, C. (ed.) CRYPTO 2006. LNCS, vol. 4117, pp. 463–482. Springer, Heidelberg (2006). https://doi.org/10.1007/11818175_28
22. Hua, M., Damelin, S.B., Sun, J., Yu, M.: The truncated & supplemented Pascal matrix and applications (2016). http://arxiv.org/abs/1506.07437
23. Lin, S., Al-Naffouri, T.Y., Han, Y.S., Chung, W.: Novel polynomial basis with fast Fourier transform and its application to Reed-Solomon erasure codes. IEEE Trans. Inf. Theory **62**(11), 6284–6299 (2016)
24. Lin, S., Chung, W.: An efficient (n, k) information dispersal algorithm for high code rate system over Fermat fields. IEEE Commun. Lett. **16**(12), 2036–2039 (2012)
25. Malkhi, D., Nayak, K.: Extended abstract: HotStuff-2: Optimal two-phase responsive BFT. Cryptology ePrint Archive, Paper 2023/397 (2023). https://eprint.iacr.org/2023/397

26. Pedersen, T.P.: A threshold cryptosystem without a trusted party (extended abstract). In: Davies, D.W. (ed.) EUROCRYPT 1991. LNCS, vol. 547, pp. 522–526. Springer, Heidelberg (1991). https://doi.org/10.1007/3-540-46416-6_47

27. Roth, R.M., Lempel, A.: On MDS codes via cauchy matrices. IEEE Trans. Inf. Theory **35**(6), 1314–1319 (1989)

28. Shoup, V.: The many faces of Schnorr. Cryptology ePrint Archive, Paper 2023/1019 (2023). https://eprint.iacr.org/2023/1019

29. Shoup, V., Smart, N.P.: Lightweight asynchronous verifiable secret sharing with optimal resilience. Cryptology ePrint Archive, Paper 2023/536 (2023). https://eprint.iacr.org/2023/536

Toward Malicious Constant-Rate 2PC via Arithmetic Garbling

Carmit Hazay[1]([✉]) [ID] and Yibin Yang[2] [ID]

[1] Bar-Ilan University, Ramat Gan, Israel
Carmit.Hazay@biu.ac.il
[2] Georgia Institute of Technology, Atlanta, USA
yyang811@gatech.edu

Abstract. A recent work by Ball, Li, Lin, and Liu [Eurocrypt'23] presented a new instantiation of the arithmetic garbling paradigm introduced by Applebaum, Ishai, and Kushilevitz [FOCS'11]. In particular, Ball et al.'s garbling scheme is the first *constant-rate* garbled circuit over large enough *bounded integer computations*, inferring the first constant-round constant-rate secure two-party computation (2PC) over bounded integer computations in the presence of *semi-honest* adversaries.

The main source of difficulty in lifting the security of garbling schemes-based protocols to the malicious setting lies in proving the correctness of the underlying garbling scheme. In this work, we analyze the security of Ball et al.'s scheme in the presence of malicious attacks.

- We demonstrate an *overflow attack*, which is inevitable in this computational model, even if the garbled circuit is *fully* correct. Our attack follows by defining an adversary, corrupting *either* the garbler or the evaluator, that chooses a bad input and causes the computation to overflow, thus leaking information about the honest party's input. By utilizing overflow attacks, we show that 1-bit leakage is necessary for achieving security against a malicious garbler, discarding the possibility of achieving full malicious security in this model. We further demonstrate a wider range of overflow attacks against a malicious evaluator with more than 1 bit of leakage.
- We boost the security level of Ball et al.'s scheme by utilizing two variants of Vector Oblivious Linear Evaluation, denoted by VOLEc and aVOLE. We present the *first constant-round constant-rate* 2PC protocol over bounded integer computations, in the presence of a malicious garbler with 1-bit leakage and a semi-honest evaluator, in the {VOLEc,aVOLE}-hybrid model and being black-box in the underlying group and ring. Compared to the semi-honest variant, our protocol incurs only a constant factor overhead, both in computation and communication. The constant-round and constant-rate properties hold even in the plain model.

Keywords: Arithmetic GC · Constant-rate 2PC · Malicious security

© International Association for Cryptologic Research 2024
M. Joye and G. Leander (Eds.): EUROCRYPT 2024, LNCS 14655, pp. 401–431, 2024.
https://doi.org/10.1007/978-3-031-58740-5_14

1   Introduction

Secure two-party computation (2PC) [41] allows two mutually untrusting parties to jointly compute arbitrary public functions with their private inputs while only revealing the output. It has been deployed in many real-world use cases, including medicine, privacy-preserving machine learning, and many more.

While 2PC can be built based on multiple approaches, instantiating it using *garbled circuits* is one of the most popular methods due to its simplicity, flexibility, and high practicality in constant-round 2PC. In these protocols, a garbler (denoted by G) generates an encoded version of the publicly agreed circuit $\mathcal{C}$, referred to as a garbled circuit (GC). G further generates a set of *garbled labels* encoding all potential wire values of every input wire. Next, an evaluator (denoted by E) can evaluate the GC on a single input to get the corresponding output upon obtaining the GC and the garbled input labels.

A garbled circuit is a cryptographic object consisting of three algorithms: (1) circuit encoding, (2) input encoding, and (3) evaluation, where security is followed by privacy and correctness. Namely, privacy implies that the former two encoding algorithms can be simulated without accessing the input to the computation x, whereas correctness ensures that the evaluator learns $\mathcal{C}(x)$. Garbled circuits easily imply passive (semi-honest) 2PC, given that the parties have access to parallel semi-honest oblivious-transfer [30] or oblivious linear evaluation, where the communication rate is $\mathcal{O}(\kappa)$ for a security parameter κ.[1]

Yao's Boolean GC. The classic approach for designing garbled circuits, commonly known as Yao's GC, considers garbling Boolean circuits consisting of AND and XOR gates. It was first introduced by Yao in 1986 [41] and later refined in [30] as a scheme requiring 4κ bits of communication per gate. Following these, a long line of work has devoted substantial effort to improving the communication overhead. Notable improvements include *row reduction* (GRR3) [33], which reduced the communication per gate to 3κ; *free XOR* [27], which eliminated the communication for XOR gates; *half-gates* [42], which reduced the communication per AND gate to 2κ while being compatible with free XOR; and most recently, the *three halves* [37], which achieves state of the art 1.5κ bits per AND gate. This great effort did not improve the asymptotic communication rate for arbitrary circuits. Namely, the communication rate remained $\mathcal{O}(\kappa)$.

Arithmetic GC over Bounded Integer Computations. To break the barrier of $\mathcal{O}(\kappa)$ rate, a natural attempt is to design garbling schemes for computations defined beyond Boolean circuits, e.g., a circuit defined over some ring $\mathcal{R}$. One such endeavor led by Ball et al. [4] to generalize free XOR to the *bounded integer computations*. The model of computation considers circuits defined over the

---

[1] Communication rate for passive protocols compares the number of bits transferred within the protocol execution vs. the size of the computed circuit. In this work, we use the terminology "rate" to express the overhead from insecure execution to passive/active secure execution *in communication only*.

integer ring $\mathbb{Z}$ with addition and multiplication gates and a pre-defined bound B, where *any* wire value falls within $[-B, B]$. Nevertheless, this effort did not achieve any asymptotic rate improvement due to employing bit decomposition techniques. Other attempts (e.g. [1,25]) studied new approaches for arithmetic GC. However, their scope was limited to arithmetic formulas and branching programs. The first construction for arbitrary arithmetic circuits over bounded integer computations, which took a different route from Yao's paradigm, was proposed by Applebaum, Ishai, and Kushilevitz (AIK) [2]. Their construction is based on the *Learning With Errors* (LWE) assumption while still requiring $\mathcal{O}(\kappa)$ rate. This rate is due to a so-called key extension (KE) gadget that enables E to expand a short garbled label to a long one while encoding the same value. At the core of this construction lies a key and message homomorphic encryption scheme, and AIK illustrated how to instantiate this encryption scheme with LWE. Building on [2], a recent work by Ball et al. [3] improved over the AIK paradigm by introducing an alternative instantiation of their KE gadget based on the *Decisional Composite Residuosity* (DCR) assumption over Paillier groups [13,35]. Notably, [3]'s GC over B-bounded integer computations achieves $\mathcal{O}(1)$ rate for a large enough bound $B = B(\lambda)$. This implies the first semi-honest constant-round constant-rate 2PC protocol in this computational model. Henceforth, we use the term *BLLL's GC* to denote the constant-rate GC scheme in [3]. We note that [3] additionally proposed GC schemes for other models, but only the GC for bounded integer computations achieves a constant rate.

Active 2PC via Yao's GC. Lifting the security of the Yao semi-honest protocols to the active (aka, *malicious*) setting is challenging due to the intricate task of proving the correctness of a garbled circuit. In theory, boosting passive to active is feasible with a constant communication overhead due to the GMW compiler [19] and succinct proofs. Nevertheless, its high computation cost keeps encouraging researchers to develop more desirable solutions. Many of these works, explicitly or implicitly, exploit the fact that Yao's GC is naturally secure against a malicious E. Namely, the main focus becomes forcing a malicious G to provide a correct GC. Within the developed methods, the *cut-and-choose* paradigm [23,28,29] addresses some of the practicality concerns by repeating the garbling procedure multiple times but inflates the overheads by a factor of statistical parameter λ to achieve $2^{-\lambda}$ error. A different approach applies authentication to the wire labels [12,14,20,24,39], while achieving constant communication overhead.

With the aim of reducing the concrete communication overhead, another line of work weakens the standard security notion, allowing the adversary to learn one bit of information about the honest party's input. This notion is denoted by security with 1-bit leakage. Several variants of this notion have been considered in the literature, such as the *dual execution* paradigm [22,26,32,36] and one-sided leakage [20]. This security relaxation enables constant communication factor overheads where the concrete factors are smaller than 2.

1.1 Our Contributions

Motivated by the recent breakthrough achieved by BLLL's GC, we focus on constructing constant-rate constant-round 2PC over bounded integer computations in the presence of static malicious adversaries. Our focus is not only feasibility but also practicality. We list our following contributions:

- **Observing a security subtlety in the bounded computational model.** We discuss an issue in the bounded integer computation model, which is inherited by the nature of the computation. Namely, a B-bounded input may still cause an internal wire value to overflow. Nevertheless, the model does not specify what should be the output in case of an inadmissible input, partly because a party cannot tell whether an input is admissible without viewing the other party's input. While this is not required in the semi-honest setting, it eliminates the possibility of obtaining full security in the active setting, as an adversary may choose its input maliciously. We stress that this issue holds even if the attack is limited to only modifying the input to the computation.
- **Understanding the active security of BLLL garbling.** We demonstrate a new class of attacks coined *overflow attacks* and show that these attacks are *inevitable* in BLLL's GC because even with a fully correct GC, both G and E can exploit this attack to compromise the privacy of the honest party's inputs. This attack implies that the *best notion of security* in the bounded integer model via BLLL's GC in the presence of a malicious G and a semi-honest E is security with 1-bit leakage, as the leakage boils down to whether E aborted or not. We further show that this is not necessarily the case in the presence of a malicious E, which may leak the entire input of G by demonstrating a larger class of attacks overflowing multiple wires.
- **Lifting BLLL's GC to the active setting.** We construct a practical 2PC protocol over bounded integer computations, achieving the above best notion of security using two hybrids (see Theorem 1). The first hybrid refers to Vector Oblivious Linear Evaluation correlations[2] (VOLEc) functionality [10,11,31] that can be instantiated based on the LPN assumption with sublinear communication cost, whereas the second hybrid refers to the so-called authenticated VOLE[3] (aVOLE) functionality that our protocol uses to allow the evaluator to learn his garbled input labels. We do not instantiate the aVOLE functionality since its effect on the overall cost vanishes with the circuit's size as its complexity grows with E's input size. Therefore, even general malicious 2PC can be used here. Overall, our protocol is *constant-round* and maintains both *constant computation* and *communication* multiplicative overheads compared to the semi-honest variant in the {VOLEc, aVOLE}-hybrid model, where the

---

[2] Where VOLE correlations over ring $\mathbb{Z}_{N^\zeta}$ sample correlated randomness for the sender and receiver. The sender will obtain $\boldsymbol{u}, \boldsymbol{w} \in \mathbb{Z}_{N^\zeta}^n$ and the receiver will obtain $\Delta \in \mathbb{Z}_{N^\zeta}, \boldsymbol{v} \in \mathbb{Z}_{N^\zeta}^n$ such that $\boldsymbol{v} = \boldsymbol{w} + \boldsymbol{u}\Delta$. See Fig. 1 and Sect. 1.2 for details.

[3] Authenticated VOLE works similarly to (non-randomized) VOLE. In aVOLE, the sender inputs four vectors $\boldsymbol{a}, \boldsymbol{b}, \boldsymbol{c}, \boldsymbol{d}$ and the receiver sends two elements x, Δ to learn $\boldsymbol{a}x + \boldsymbol{b}, \boldsymbol{a}\Delta + \boldsymbol{c}, \boldsymbol{b}\Delta + \boldsymbol{d}$. See Fig. 4 and Sect. 5.3 for details.

VOLE correlations can be generated in a circuit-independent pre-processing phase. Moreover, our protocol achieves a constant communication rate even in the plain model and only uses *black-box* access to the underlying group and ring. To construct our protocol, we transfer the VOLE-based ZK (e.g., [15]) to the integer ring $\mathbb{Z}_{N^\zeta}$ where N is an RSA modulus and $\zeta \in \mathbb{Z}^+$, as well as design a customized Σ-protocol [38], which could have independent interests.

Theorem 1 (Informal, Main). *Assuming DCR assumption over $\mathbb{Z}^*_{N^{\zeta+1}}$ where $N = pq$ is a safe RSA modulus and ζ is a sufficiently large integer. There exists a constant-rate constant-round secure two-party computation protocol for any circuit $\mathcal{C}$ over B-bounded integer computations in the $\{VOLEc, aVOLE\}$-hybrid model instantiated via BLLL's GC [3], where the computation is linear in $|\mathcal{C}|$. The protocol is secure against malicious G with 1-bit leakage and semi-honest E.*

1.2   Technical Overview

In this section, we informally explain our techniques while neglecting less important details; we refer to Sect. 3 for a complete overview of BLLL's GC.

Overflow Attacks. We begin with an overview of the subtlety within the bounded integer computation model. While considering active adversaries, we noticed that B-bounded inputs do not guarantee that all wires will be B-bounded, where an intermediate wire can overflow. Such an overflow may occur even if the garbled circuit is constructed correctly and, in the presence of corrupting, either G or E. I.e., the adversary can set B-bounded inputs but try to cause the evaluation of GC to suffer from overflows on intermediate wires. We call these inputs *legal* but *inadmissible*. Now, since the evaluation procedure of BLLL's GC heavily relies on all wires being B-bounded, overflow attacks can help a malicious E to break the privacy guarantee of BLLL's GC scheme and a malicious G to cause an input-dependent select-failure abort as follows:

- **Malicious E (see Sect. 4.1):** While evaluating a BLLL's GC, E obtains a garbled label encoding a private value on each wire. There are $\mathcal{O}(|\mathcal{C}|)$ wires in the BLLL's GC having the following property: if the wire encoding a value w, the garbled label during evaluation will reveal $w + r$ to E where r is uniformly chosen from a larger fixed bound B_e such that $w + r$ statistically hides w. Note that $w + r$ can only be leaked to E if w is bounded by B. When E uses bad inputs and w overflows, $w + r$ no longer hides w, so it should not be leaked to E. Essentially, E can select his inputs and monitor whether each wire overflows to make G's inputs leak.
- **Malicious G (see Sect. 4.2):** While evaluating a BLLL's GC, E needs to decode $\mathcal{O}(|\mathcal{C}|)$ garbled labels from domain $\mathbb{Z}_{N^\zeta}$ to $\mathbb{Z}$.[4] In particular, E can decode these labels because they are B-bounded, so they will not wrap around the domain $\mathbb{Z}_{N^\zeta}$. When G uses bad inputs, the value could wrap around if

---

[4] The computation in this scheme is embedded into a sufficiently large integer ring $\mathbb{Z}_{N^\zeta}$ where N is an RSA modulus.

Functionality $\mathcal{F}_{\mathsf{VOLEc}}^{N,\zeta}$

Let $\mathbb{Z}_{N^\zeta}$ denote the ring of integers modulus N^ζ where $N = pq$ is an RSA modulus and $\zeta \in \mathbb{Z}^+$. Functionality interacts with G, E and the adversary $\mathcal{A}$ as follows:

Initialize. Upon receiving (init) from G and E, if E is honest, sample $\Delta \xleftarrow{\$} \mathbb{Z}_{N^\zeta}$, else receive Δ from $\mathcal{A}$. Store Δ and send it to E. Ignore subsequent (init).

Extend. Upon receiving (extend, n) from G and E, do the following:

- If E is honest, sample $\boldsymbol{v} \xleftarrow{\$} \mathbb{Z}_{N^\zeta}^n$, else receive $\boldsymbol{v} \in \mathbb{Z}_{N^\zeta}^n$ from $\mathcal{A}$.
- If G is honest, sample $\boldsymbol{u} \xleftarrow{\$} \mathbb{Z}_{N^\zeta}^n$ and compute $\boldsymbol{w} := \boldsymbol{v} - \boldsymbol{u}\Delta \in \mathbb{Z}_{N^\zeta}^n$, else receive $\boldsymbol{u} \in \mathbb{Z}_{N^\zeta}^n$ and $\boldsymbol{w} \in \mathbb{Z}_{N^\zeta}^n$ from $\mathcal{A}$ and compute $\boldsymbol{v} := \boldsymbol{w} + \boldsymbol{u}\Delta \in \mathbb{Z}_{N^\zeta}^n$.
- Send $(\boldsymbol{u}, \boldsymbol{w})$ to G and $\boldsymbol{v}$ to E.

Fig. 1. The VOLE correlation functionality

some wire overflows. Hence, E might incorrectly decode the garbled labels and fail to evaluate the garbled tables, which will abort the execution. Thus, G can cause a selective failure attack, learning whether an overflow occurs, which can be captured as applying a predicate on E's inputs.

VOLE Correlations and Authenticated VOLE over $\mathbb{Z}_{N^\zeta}$ as Hybrid Functionalities. Vector Oblivious Linear Evaluation (VOLE) allows a receiver (E in our protocol) to learn a linear combination of two vectors held by a sender (G in our protocol). In the case where the sender's vectors and the receiver's evaluation point are (pseudo-)random, known as VOLE correlation (VOLEc)[5], recent works (e.g., [10]) show that it can be instantiated via the *Learning Parity with Noise* (LPN) assumption with sublinear communication cost, known as the *Pseudorandom Correlation Generator* (PCG) paradigm. Our 2PC protocol relies on "authenticating" G's randomness in BLLL's GC using VOLE correlations. In particular, we need to use VOLE correlations defined over $\mathbb{Z}_{N^\zeta}$ where N is an RSA modulus and $\zeta \in \mathbb{Z}^+$. Recently, Liu et al. [31] showed that the decisional LPN problem over the integer ring $\mathbb{Z}_{N^\zeta}$ is as hard as the LPN problems over the fields $\mathbb{F}_p$ and $\mathbb{F}_q$. Therefore, it is sufficient to generate VOLE correlations over $\mathbb{Z}_{N^\zeta}$ via the standard PCG paradigm to achieve sublinear cost in communication. Formally, this functionality is defined in Fig. 1.

Our protocol also uses another hybrid functionality called authenticated VOLE (aVOLE) to allow E to learn his input garbled labels (as the OT in Yao). The authenticated VOLE is just a small modification over the standard (non-randomized) VOLE where G holds 4 vectors $\boldsymbol{a}, \boldsymbol{b}, \boldsymbol{c}, \boldsymbol{d}$ and E holds two elements x, Δ such that E can learn $\boldsymbol{a}x + \boldsymbol{b}, \boldsymbol{a}\Delta + \boldsymbol{c}, \boldsymbol{b}\Delta + \boldsymbol{d}$. Crucially, the cost of instantiating this functionality is only proportional to E's input size, so we do not instantiate it. See Fig. 4 and Sect. 5.3 for more discussions.

---

[5] We note that prior works use this terminology interchangeably.

Our Protocol. Overflow attacks imply that the best we can hope while boosting the security of BLLL's GC is 1-bit leakage security in the presence of malicious G and a semi-honest E. We notice that to achieve this security notion, we only need to guarantee that E must obtain a result of the intended computation whenever it evaluates the circuit and does not abort. This means that a malicious G can either learn the output of $\mathcal{C}$ or that E had aborted.

Interestingly, we observe that this can be guaranteed by an almost correct rather than fully correct BLLL's GC (see Sect. 4.2). By simplifying the statements, we can design custom zero-knowledge proofs (ZKP) at a very low cost. To see how it works, recall that the BLLL garbling procedure includes the following operations: (1) sample uniform randomness in $\mathbb{Z}_{N^\varsigma}$; (2) add two random samples over $\mathbb{Z}_{N^\varsigma}$; (3) multiply two random samples over $\mathbb{Z}_{N^\varsigma}$; and (4) use two random samples a, b to construct an element in the group $\mathbb{Z}^*_{N^{\varsigma+1}}$ as $\tau^a(N+1)^b$ where τ is a public uniform $2N^\varsigma$-th residue. The operation (4) generates the garbled tables for the KE gadgets. BLLL's GC utilizes the homomorphism of this ciphertext format where $(\tau^{a_1}(N+1)^{b_1})^k(\tau^{a_2}(N+1)^{b_2}) = \tau^{a_1 k+b_1}(N+1)^{a_2 k+b_2}$. By obtaining $k, a_1 k + b_1$ from the GC evaluation, E can obtain $a_2 k + b_2$ by solving the discrete logarithm of $(N+1)^{a_2 k+b_2}$ to the base $N+1$, which is known to be easy and commonly used in the Paillier cryptosystem [13,35].

Inspired by the authenticated garbling method of [39], we observe that the randomness used in the garbling procedure of BLLL's GC can be generated in an authenticated manner by VOLE correlations over $\mathbb{Z}_{N^\varsigma}$ in a circuit-independent pre-processing phase. Namely, the ideal functionality $\mathcal{F}^{N,\varsigma}_{\mathsf{VOLEc}}$ can be used to generate a pool of committed randomness over $\mathbb{Z}_{N^\varsigma}$, which can replace operation (1). Later, during the GC generation procedure, G and E consume the committed randomness to *authenticate* the garbled circuit. I.e., G will use the committed randomness to produce correlated (and new committed) randomness for operations (2–3), and use special-purpose ZK proofs to validate that the computation of (4) is done almost correctly. In slightly more detail:

- **To support operations (2–3):** We transform the existing VOLE-based ZK proofs to the ring $\mathbb{Z}_{N^\varsigma}$ domain (see Sect. 5.1), used to prove the correctness of addition/multiplication operations. The proof of each operation requires sending only $\mathcal{O}(1)$ elements and performing $\mathcal{O}(1)$ ring operations.
- **To support operation (4):** We observe that as long as a committed random element $b \in \mathbb{Z}_{N^\varsigma}$ is indeed used to generate a garbled table ciphertext $\tau^a(N+1)^b \in \mathbb{Z}^*_{N^{\varsigma+1}}$ of some KE gadget, it ensures that E will perform an intended computation of the KE gadget upon evaluating it. Namely, an erroneous garbled table of form $\varepsilon(N+1)^b$ is *harmless* under 1-bit leakage where ε can be an arbitrary error that is not dividable by $N+1$ in $\mathbb{Z}^*_{N^{\varsigma+1}}$. By exploiting the order of $N+1$ in the group $\mathbb{Z}^*_{N^{\varsigma+1}}$ is exactly N^ς, we adjust the well-known Schnorr's Σ-protocol [38] for the knowledge of the discrete logarithm to achieve this (see Sect. 5.2). Roughly speaking, the crucial adjustment requires G to open the committed randomness in the response phase of Σ-protocol. The adjusted Σ-protocol is also very cheap and requires sending only $\mathcal{O}(1)$ group elements, and performing $\mathcal{O}(1)$ exponentiation in $\mathbb{Z}^*_{N^{\varsigma+1}}$ (and $\mathcal{O}(1)$ additions/multiplications in $\mathbb{Z}_{N^\varsigma}$).

To conclude, our protocol is constant-round[6] and constant-rate, with constant factor blowup in both computation and communication (compared to [3]) in the $\{\mathcal{F}_{\mathsf{VOLEc}}^{N,\varsigma}, \mathcal{F}_{\mathsf{aVOLE}}^{N,\varsigma}\}$-hybrid model, and only uses black-box access to the underlying group $\mathbb{Z}_{N^\varsigma}$ and ring $\mathbb{Z}_{N^{\varsigma+1}}^*$. The cost of our protocol is dominated by a total number of $\mathcal{O}(|\mathcal{C}|)$ operations (4), achieving constant factor blowup. Finally, by using LPN assumption over $\mathbb{Z}_{N^\varsigma}$ to instantiate $\mathcal{F}_{\mathsf{VOLEc}}^{N,\varsigma}$ with sublinear communication cost in $\mathcal{O}(|\mathcal{C}|)$, our protocol preserves a constant rate of communication, and constant-round, even in the plain model.

Full Version. Full version of this paper is available at [21].

2   Notations and Definitions

Our work uses the following notations:

λ is the statistical security parameter (e.g., 40).

κ is the computational security parameter (e.g., 128).

$x \triangleq y$ denotes that x is *defined* as y. $x := y$ denotes that y is assigned to x.

We denote that x is uniformly drawn from a set S by $x \xleftarrow{\$} S$.

We denote $\{1, \ldots, n\}$ by $[n]$, $\{a, \ldots, b\}$ by $[a, b]$.

We denote vectors by bold lower-case letters (e.g., $\boldsymbol{a}$), where a_i (or $a[i]$) denotes the ith component of $\boldsymbol{a}$ (starting from 1).

We denote sets by bold upper-case letters (e.g., $\boldsymbol{A}$). In some cases, the elements in the set will be indexed via integer tuples (e.g., $A_{i,j,k}$).

N denotes a safe RSA modulus. That is, $N = pq$ where p, q are equal-length large primes (e.g., 1024-bits). Moreover $p = 2p' + 1$ and $q = 2q' + 1$ where p', q' are also primes. W.l.o.g., we assume $p < q$. Formally, p, q are sampled according to the security parameter λ.

$\approx_c$ denotes the computational indistinguishability. $\approx_s$ denotes the statistical indistinguishability; see [18] for more details.

Due to space limitations, we defer the following definitions to our full version:

We extend the classic security definition of 2PC and define secure two-party computation with 1-bit leakage in the Ideal/Real simulation paradigm, which is adopted from [20]. The main modification allows the adversary to submit a predicate to the ideal functionality.

We include the DCR and LPN hardness assumptions. We include the hardness lemma regarding the LPN over $\mathbb{Z}_{N^\varsigma}$, which is adopted from [31].

We include the definitions for arithmetic garbling scheme over bounded integer computations and communication rate, adopted from [3].

---

[6] In the random oracle model, our protocol only requires 2 rounds by applying the Fiat-Shamir transformation [16], in the $\{\mathcal{F}_{\mathsf{VOLEc}}^{N,\varsigma}, \mathcal{F}_{\mathsf{aVOLE}}^{N,\varsigma}\}$-hybrid model, when both parties receive the output.

Gadget for addition gate

Consider an addition gate with inputs wire x, y and out wire z where $z = x + y$:

- **Gb:** Let the key pair assigned to z be $(k_0^z, k_1^z) \in \mathcal{R}^n \times \mathcal{R}^n$ for some $n \in \mathbb{Z}^+$. G uniformly samples $r \in \mathcal{R}^n$, then sets key pairs of x and y as:

$$(k_0^x, k_1^x) := (k_0^z, r) \quad (k_0^y, k_1^y) := (k_0^z, k_1^z - r)$$

- **Ev:** If E obtains $L^x = k_0^z x + r \in \mathcal{R}^n$ and $L^y = k_0^z y + k_1^z - r \in \mathcal{R}^n$, E calculates:

$$L^z := L^x + L^y = k_0^z(x + y) + k_1^z, \text{ note that } L^z \in \mathcal{R}^n$$

Gadget for multiplication gate

Consider an addition gate with inputs wire x, y and out wire z where $z = x \cdot y$:

- **Gb:** Let the key pair assigned to z be $(k_0^z, k_1^z) \in \mathcal{R}^n \times \mathcal{R}^n$ for some $n \in \mathbb{Z}^+$. G uniformly samples $r, u \in \mathcal{R}^n$ and $s \in \mathcal{R}$, and sets the key pairs of x and y as:

$$(k_0^x, k_1^x) := ((k_0^z, k_0^z s), (r, u)) \quad (k_0^y, k_1^y) := ((1, r), (s, rs - k_1^z - u))$$

- **Ev:** If E obtains

$$L^x = (L_0^x = k_0^z x + r \in \mathcal{R}^n, L_1^x = k_0^z xs + u \in \mathcal{R}^n)$$
$$L^y = (L_0^y = y + s \in \mathcal{R}, L_1^y = r(y + s) - k_1^z - u \in \mathcal{R}^n)$$

E calculates L^z:

$$L^z := L_0^x \cdot L_0^y - L_1^x - L_1^y = k_0^z(x \cdot y) + k_1^z, \text{ note that } L^z \in \mathcal{R}^n$$

Fig. 2. Information-theoretic add/mult gadgets from the AIK paradigm [2]

3   A Review of Constant-Rate BLLL's GC

Given that BLLL's GC, building on AIK, dramatically deviates from the standard Yao's paradigm, we provide a concise overview of this scheme in this section. Recall that the bounded integer computation model requires that, for a class of admissible inputs over $\mathbb{Z}$, *all* wire values fall within the range $[-B, B]$ for some predefined positive integer B. Naturally, the computation can be embedded into a large enough modular integer ring.

The AIK Paradigm for Arithmetic Garbling. BLLL's GC follows the AIK paradigm [2] for arithmetic garbling. Unlike Yao's GC, the AIK paradigm generates the GC backward, i.e., in the reverse topology order. To garble a circuit $\mathcal{C}$ defined over some integer ring $\mathcal{R}$ (i.e., the computation is defined over the integer ring $\mathcal{R}$), the AIK paradigm generates GC from the following components:

- **Affine garbled labels:** The AIK GC encodes garbled labels using affine functions. That is, for each wire w in $\mathcal{C}$, G assigns it with a pair of keys $(\boldsymbol{k}_0^w, \boldsymbol{k}_1^w) \in \mathcal{R}^n \times \mathcal{R}^n$ for some positive integer n. During the evaluation, E obtains a garbled label encoding w defined by $\boldsymbol{L}^w \triangleq \boldsymbol{k}_0^w w + \boldsymbol{k}_1^w$. The key pair $(\boldsymbol{k}_0^w, \boldsymbol{k}_1^w)$ is denoted by the *garbled key pair*[7] for wire w. In particular, $n = |\boldsymbol{k}_0^w| = |\boldsymbol{k}_0^w|$ denotes the length of the garbled key pair.
- **Information-theoretic addition/multiplication gadgets:** For a gate with input wires x, y and output wire z, E holding $\boldsymbol{L}^x$ and $\boldsymbol{L}^y$ should learn $\boldsymbol{L}^z$. The AIK GC achieves this in an information-theoretic way *without communication*. Essentially, G selects the garbled key pairs of two input wires after the garbled key pair of the output wire is assigned. The complete scheme is presented in Fig. 2. Note that the gate can have unlimited fan-out. Hence, the garbled key pair of wire z is constructed as the concatenation of all garbled key pairs of the wire z provided as inputs to the next layer.
- **Key extension gadgets:** While the constructions for addition/multiplication gadgets are information-theoretic, the length of the garbled key pairs grows exponentially *backward* because (1) the length for one garbled key pair of the inputs of a multiplication gate doubles and (2) a gate (including an input gate) can have unlimited fan-out. Thus, transferring garbled labels of inputs of $\mathcal{C}$ from G to E will require exponential costs. To tackle this issue, the AIK GC scheme introduced a garbled gadget called the key extension (KE) gadget. A KE gadget allows E to expand a short, so-called "version-A", gabled label $\boldsymbol{L}^{w,A} \in \mathcal{R}^{n_s}$ to a longer "version-B" garbled label $\boldsymbol{L}^{w,B} \in \mathcal{R}^{n_l}$ (where $n_l > n_s$ and n_s is a small constant), while encoding an *identical* value w. In other words, it can be viewed as augmenting $\mathcal{C}$ with extra "identical" gates. Recursively applying the KE gadgets will result in a KE gadget that allows E to expand a length n garbled label into any length. We emphasize that, since G garbles the circuit *backward*, a KE gadget helps G to *shrink* the length of the garbled key pair. That is, the length of the garbled key pair will *no longer* grow exponentially. Unlike the addition and multiplication gadgets, a KE gadget requires garbled tables to be transferred from G to E. [2] showed how to build KE gadgets from the *Learning With Errors* (LWE) assumption. Building on [2,3] further showed how to build them based on the DCR assumption. Essentially, optimizing the communication cost requires building improved KE gadgets.

The complete garbling procedure of the AIK paradigm can be roughly viewed as follows: G assigns the output wires with garbled key pair $(1, 0)$.[8] G assigns the corresponding garbled key pair to each gate *backward* in a gate-by-gate manner. For the output wire of each gate (including an input gate), G applies a KE gadget to shrink the length of the garbled key pair to a value smaller than (or equal to) n_s. Finally, G obtains garbled key pairs for the input wires of input gates, each of a maximum length of n_s, where n_s is a small constant. Then E can evaluate the circuit by obtaining the garbled labels of the inputs and the truth tables generated by the KE gadgets.

---

[7] We note that unlike in Yao's GC where, $\boldsymbol{k}_0^w$ and $\boldsymbol{k}_1^w$ respectively represent the bits 0 and 1, in the AIK paradigm, these keys have nothing related to encoding 0 and 1.

[8] Thus, the output label encoding wire w is just w.

A General Paradigm to Construct KE. Both [2] and [3] utilize an encryption scheme with *linear homomorphism* to implement the KE gadget. Consider an integer ring $\mathcal{R}$ and an encryption scheme with the procedures enc and dec, where enc takes a key $k \in \mathcal{R}$ and a vector of messages $\boldsymbol{m} \in \mathcal{R}^n$ $(n > 2)$ as its input and outputs a ciphertext denoted by $\text{enc}(k, \boldsymbol{m})$. The encryption scheme supports linear evaluation over keys and plaintexts. Namely, given a constant element $\beta \in \mathcal{R}$, a ciphertext $\text{enc}(k_1, \boldsymbol{m_1})$ that encrypts $\boldsymbol{m_1}$ under the key k_1 and a ciphertext $\text{enc}(k_2, \boldsymbol{m_2})$ that encrypts $\boldsymbol{m_2}$ under the key k_2, one can compute a ciphertext $\text{enc}(k_1\beta + k_2, \boldsymbol{m_1}\beta + \boldsymbol{m_2})$ by computing $(\beta \boxtimes \text{enc}(k_1, \boldsymbol{m_1})) \boxplus \text{enc}(k_2, \boldsymbol{m_2})$ where β is embedded inside the ciphertext space and $\boxtimes, \boxplus$ are operations defined over the ciphertext space. Recall that our goal is to let E with $\boldsymbol{L}^{w,A} \triangleq \boldsymbol{a}w + \boldsymbol{b}$ obtain $\boldsymbol{L}^{w,B} \triangleq \boldsymbol{c}w + \boldsymbol{d}$ where $(\boldsymbol{a}, \boldsymbol{b})$ and $(\boldsymbol{c}, \boldsymbol{d})$ are garbled key pairs assigned to the input and output wires of the KE gadget. Assume that E obtains the garbled label $\boldsymbol{L}^{w,A} = \boldsymbol{a}w + \boldsymbol{b} = (w + r, s_1(w + r) + s_2)$ during the evaluation, where $\boldsymbol{a} \triangleq (1, s_1)$ and $\boldsymbol{b} \triangleq (r, s_1 r + s_2)$, and r, s_1, s_2 are sampled by G (the precise way of sampling r, s_1, s_2 is instantiated per GC and it will be addressed soon). In addition, G sends E the following ciphertexts as the garbled tables:

$$\text{enc}(s_1, \boldsymbol{c}) \quad \text{enc}(s_2, -\boldsymbol{c} \cdot r + \boldsymbol{d})$$

E can first utilize the linear homomorphism to obtain a new ciphertext:

$$(w + r) \boxtimes \text{enc}(s_1, \boldsymbol{c}) \boxplus \text{enc}(s_2, -\boldsymbol{c} \cdot r + \boldsymbol{d}) \triangleq \text{enc}(s_1(w + r) + s_2, \boldsymbol{c} \cdot w + \boldsymbol{d})$$

then decrypts the new ciphertext using key $s_1(w + r) + s_2$ and learns $\boldsymbol{c} \cdot w + \boldsymbol{d}$. This achieves a KE gadget that can expand a length-2 garbled label to a length-n garbled label. While the paradigm is simple and elegant, instantiating it is non-trivial. This is mainly because we need to ensure $x + r$ and $s_1(x + r) + s_2$ are allowed to be revealed without compromising privacy.

BLLL's GC for the Bounded Integer Computation. The crucial observation of the BLLL's GC is that the AIK paradigm for bounded computation can be instantiated by carefully selecting the integer ring $\mathcal{R}$ accompanied by a customized KE gadget that is instantiated via a lightweight, customized encryption scheme defined based on the DCR assumption. Consider two large enough (e.g., 1024-bits) primes $p = 2p' + 1$ and $q = 2q' + 1$ of equal length,[9] where p', q' are also primes, and the corresponding RSA modulus $N = pq$. Given that the computation is B-bounded, select $B_e = B\lambda^{\omega(1)}$, $B_{\text{msg}} = NB_e\lambda^{\omega(1)}$ and some sufficiently large integer ζ such that $N^\zeta > 2B_{\text{msg}} + 1$. For a small constant Ψ (e.g., 10), G and E sample $\tau_1, \ldots, \tau_\Psi \xleftarrow{\$} \left\{ a^{2N^\zeta} \mid a \in \mathbb{Z}_{N^{\zeta+1}}^* \right\}$ as part of the encryption parameters.

BLLL's GC embeds the B-bounded integers into the integer modular ring $\mathbb{Z}_{N^\zeta}$. This is allowed because $N^\zeta > 2B + 1$. Essentially, BLLL's GC applies the AIK paradigm over $\mathbb{Z}_{N^\zeta}$ and further shows a KE gadget that can expand the garble label defined over $\mathbb{Z}_{N^\zeta}$. To achieve this, BLLL's GC relies on an encryption

---

[9] Formally, p, q are selected with the security parameter λ given as an argument.

scheme where the enc algorithm takes a key $k \in \mathbb{Z}$ and a vector message $\boldsymbol{m} \in \mathbb{Z}_{N^{\varsigma}}^{\Psi}$ as input and outputs a ciphertext in $(\mathbb{Z}_{N^{\varsigma+1}}^*)^{\Psi}$. More specifically, consider $\boldsymbol{m} = (m_1, \ldots, m_\Psi)$, procedure enc is defined as[10]:

$$\text{enc}(k, \boldsymbol{m}) \triangleq \left(\tau_1^k (N+1)^{2m_1}, \ldots, \tau_n^k (N+1)^{2m_n} \right) \text{ over } \mathbb{Z}_{N^{\varsigma+1}}^*$$

Note that the order of $N+1$ within the group $\mathbb{Z}_{N^{\varsigma+1}}^*$ is N^{ς}. The decryption procedure is done by element-wise (1) multiplication each term with $\tau_{i\in[n]}^{-k}$, and (2) solving the discrete logarithm to the base $N+1$ in the group $\mathbb{Z}_{N^{\varsigma+1}}^*$, which is known to be easy [13,35]. Moreover, this encryption scheme supports linear evaluations over keys and plaintexts. Namely, given an integer $\beta \in \mathbb{Z}$.

$$\begin{aligned}
&\text{enc}(k_1\beta + k_2, \beta\boldsymbol{m}_1 + \boldsymbol{m}_2) \\
&= \left(\tau_1^{k_1\beta+k_2}(N+1)^{2m_{1,1}\beta+2m_{2,1}}, \ldots, \tau_n^{k_1\beta+k_2}(N+1)^{2m_{1,n}\beta+2m_{2,n}} \right) \\
&= \left(\tau_1^{k_1\beta}(N+1)^{2m_{1,1}\beta}, \ldots, \tau_n^{k_1\beta}(N+1)^{2m_{1,n}\beta} \right) \\
&\otimes \left(\tau_1^{k_2}(N+1)^{2m_{2,1}}, \ldots, \tau_n^{k_2}(N+1)^{2m_{2,n}} \right) \\
&= \text{enc}(k_1, \boldsymbol{m}_1)^{\beta} \otimes \text{enc}(k_2, \boldsymbol{m}_2)
\end{aligned}$$

where $\otimes$ is the element-wise product over $\mathbb{Z}_{N^{\varsigma+1}}^*$. Recall that we still need to address how to select r, s_1, s_2 in the paradigm for constructing the KE gadget we presented above. Here, for each KE gadget expanding a length-2 garbled label to a length-Ψ garbled label, G samples $r \xleftarrow{\$} [-B_e, B_e]$, $s_1 \xleftarrow{\$} \{0, \ldots, N\}$ and $s_2 \xleftarrow{\$} [-B_{\mathsf{msg}}, B_{\mathsf{msg}}]$. Crucially, for any $w \in [-B, B]$, (1) $w + r$ statistically hides w; and (2) $s_1(x + r) + s_2$ statistically hides $s_1(x + r)$. Hence, $x + r$ and $s_1(x + r) + s_2$ can be revealed to E.

A small subtlety arises here as the garbled labels are defined over $\mathbb{Z}_{N^{\varsigma}}$. However, the key (and the homomorphism operation) is defined over $\mathbb{Z}$. Interestingly, this is not an issue because N^{ς} is large enough *and* w is B-bounded. For example, since $w \in [-B, B]$, we have $w + r \in [-B - B_e, B + B_e]$. Now, since $N^{\varsigma} > 2B + 2B_e + 1$, by obtaining the value $w + r \in \mathbb{Z}_{N^{\varsigma}}$, E can recover $w + r$ value in $\mathbb{Z}$. Henceforth, we will use $(\alpha)_{\mathbb{Z}}$ to denote the procedure to map a value α in $\mathbb{Z}_{N^{\varsigma}}$ to a value in $\mathbb{Z}$, specified by BLLL's GC.

Finally, note that the encryption scheme above is not a standard Paillier encryption [35]. In fact, it is not even a randomized encryption. However, it is sufficient because each key is used in a single instance of enc.[11]

Constant-Rate Property. The constant-rate property of BLLL's GC comes from that the garbled truth tables of the KE gadget are constant-rate. Namely, element in $\mathbb{Z}_{N^{\varsigma+1}}^*$ has length $\log N^{\varsigma+1}$ and:

---

[10] The factor 2 in the equation is guided by the DCR assumption.

[11] We note that "the single instance" term views enc as a complete object. Indeed, a key k will be reused by different $\tau_{i\in[\Psi]}$ *within a single* enc.

$$\log N^{\zeta+1} = \mathcal{O}(\log N + \log B_{\mathsf{msg}}) = \mathcal{O}(\log N + \log NB\lambda^{\omega(1)})$$
$$= \mathcal{O}(\log N + \log B + \omega(\log \lambda))$$
$$= \mathcal{O}(\kappa + \log B)$$

4   Overflow Attacks via BLLL's GC

In this section, we demonstrate why the natural 2PC protocol for bounded integer computations, instantiated via BLLL's GC, is *not* secure against a malicious adversary, corrupting either G or E. In contrast, the 2PC semi-honest protocol instantiated via Yao Boolean GC implies security against a malicious E; see a discussion in our full version regarding the reasons for these differences.

Ill-Defined Computation Model. Before showing concrete attacks, we note that B-bounded integer computation regarding malicious 2PC is not well-defined. This is because the computational model should properly define what should happen if the computation is applied to an inadmissible input (where intermediate wires overflow B). This is not required in the semi-honest setting since the definitions can condition over an admissible input. Nevertheless, what we show in this section eliminates the possibility of defining the result of computing on inadmissible inputs as abort when instantiating the garbling scheme with the BLLL GC. Also, it is insufficient to output the computation result over $\mathbb{Z}_{N^\zeta}$.

4.1   Overflow Attacks by Malicious E: A Toy Example

We present a concrete toy example attack that explains how a malicious E* could compromise the privacy of the honest G by carefully selecting his inputs. Our attack indicates the challenges in boosting security for E beyond semi-honest. In the rest of this paper, we will only focus on a malicious G.

Consider 2PC over B-bounded integer computations where $B = 2$. That is, the parties use inputs within $[-2, 2]$ and compute the circuits over $\mathbb{Z}$ where all the intermediate wires fall within $[-2, 2]$ as well. Recall that in BLLL's GC, the parties need to set up some public parameters, including $B_{\mathsf{e}} = B\lambda^{\omega(1)}$. Let $\lambda = 40$ and $B_{\mathsf{e}} = 2^{80}$. Now, consider a circuit $\mathcal{C}$ that includes an intermediate wire w holding the value $w = (xy)^{80}$ where x is G's input, and y is E's input. Assume that w is used as an input of a KE gadget. Namely, E learns $w + r$ (over large enough $\mathbb{Z}_{N^\zeta}$) where r is sampled from $[-2^{80}, 2^{80}]$. Let the honest E hold the input $y = 0$. This implies $w = 0$ no matter what G inputs for x. Indeed, any $x \in [-2, 2]$ with $y = 0$ forms an admissible input. In particular, $w + r$ will always be just r as a uniform distribution over $[-2^{80}, 2^{80}]$ so E should not obtain any information on x by observing $(xy)^{80} + r$.

However, a malicious E* can simply use $\widetilde{y} = 1$ as his input. Namely, $w = (x\widetilde{y})^{80} = x^{80}$. Obviously, if $x \in \{0, \pm 1\}$, $w + r$ will be within $[-B_{\mathsf{e}}, B_{\mathsf{e}}]$ with overwhelming probability over r. However, if $x \in \{\pm 2\}$, $w + r$ will be within $[-B_{\mathsf{e}}, B_{\mathsf{e}}]$ with probability roughly $\frac{1}{2}$ over r. Say differently, if E* observes that $w + r$ does not belong to $[-B_{\mathsf{e}}, B_{\mathsf{e}}]$, he learns that $x \in \{\pm 2\}$. Thus, E* gains information about x simply by setting his input to 1 and monitoring $(x\widetilde{y})^{80} + r$. We remark that $1 \in [-2, 2]$, so this input is legal. We denote this attack by an *overflow attack* because E^* compromises G's privacy by causing an overflow by maliciously choosing his B-bounded inputs.

One might think that the above toy example is contrived. Specifically, when $B = 2$, by setting $\widetilde{y} = 1$, E learns whether $(x, \widetilde{y})$ is admissible. Namely, if $x \in \{0, \pm 1\}$, $(x, \widetilde{y})$ is an admissible input; otherwise, if $x \in \{\pm 2\}$, it is not. Therefore, this leakage may already be covered by the intended computation. We emphasize that the leakage of an overflow attack is beyond the intended computation. In particular, consider the same attack with x_1, x_2, y_1, y_2 where there are wires $w_1 = (x_1 y_1)^{80}$ and $w_2 = (x_2 y_2)^{80}$. By changing the honest input $(y_1, y_2) = (0, 0)$ to $(\widetilde{y_1}, \widetilde{y_2}) = (1, 1)$, E can use overflow to distinguish the following three cases regarding G's inputs (x_1, x_2): (a) $(\{0, \pm 1\}, \{\pm 2\})$, (b) $(\{\pm 2\}, \{0, \pm 1\})$, or (c) $(\{\pm 2\}, \{\pm 2\})$. This leakage is beyond learning whether $((x_1, x_2), (1, 1))$ is an inadmissible input, which does not help to distinguish the above three cases. We conclude with the following remark:

Remark 1 (Generality). The above example can be generalized to any bound B. Consider $B_e = B^{2\lambda}$ and a circuit $\mathcal{C}$ where there exists an intermediate wire $w = (xy)^{2\lambda}$ such that x is G's input, y is E's input and $y = 0$ in the honest case. By injecting $\widetilde{y} = 1$, a malicious E^* can gain information regarding the range of x based on whether $w + r$ overflows B_e, which should not happen when $y = 0$ because $w + r$ should be uniform and always bounded by B_e. Note that this attack is not restricted to a power of xy and is feasible for other computations.

Notably, the overflow attack breaks privacy but may also harm correctness, as it may prevent E^* from obtaining the correct next garbled labels. Nevertheless, in some cases, the overflow does not prevent E^* from continuing to evaluate the KE gadgets. To further see this point, recall that the garbled tables of a KE gadget (for a single entry) are of the form:

$$\tau^{s_1}(N+1)^{2c_1} \quad \tau^{s_2}(N+1)^{-2c_1 r + 2d_1} \quad \text{over } \mathbb{Z}^*_{N^{\varsigma+1}}$$

where the garbled label of the input obtained by E will be:

$$w + r \quad s_1(w+r) + s_2 \quad \text{over } \mathbb{Z}_{N^\varsigma}$$

In the honest execution, E can recover $w + r$ and $s_1(w + r) + s_2$ from the $\mathbb{Z}_{N^\varsigma}$ domain and use homomorphism to obtain $c_1 w + d_1$ over $\mathbb{Z}_{N^\varsigma}$, as the garbled output labels of the KE gadget. Now, when an overflow happens, recovering $w + r$ and $s_1(w + r) + s_2$ can be more challenging as they may wrap around the domain of $\mathbb{Z}_{N^\varsigma}$. Nevertheless, it does not mean that E^* fails to recover these values since the wrapping may be small and E^* can just brute force it.

An interesting case happens when w indeed overflows over integers, however, due to the computation being taken over the ring $\mathbb{Z}_{N^\varsigma}$, it wraps around the space and ends up as $[-B, B]$ over $\mathbb{Z}_{N^\varsigma}$. In this case, a malicious E^* cannot detect whether an overflow occurred *regardless of the choice of randomness* r, s_1, s_2.

We denote this type of overflow an *undetectable* overflow. It is easy to see that, in this case, the security of a malicious E* can be reduced to the privacy of BLLL's GC since the simulator can use the simulator of BLLL's GC to generate faked garbled tables and faked garbled labels of inputs.

Given the above discussion, a malicious E may learn $\mathcal{O}(|\mathcal{C}|)$ leaked bits regarding G's inputs since he can observe whether each wire overflows. In our full version, we include a conjecture (strongest) ideal world that captures the 2PC naïvely instantiated via BLLL's GC for a malicious E.

4.2 Overflow Attacks by Malicious G: The Lower Bound

We already presented how a malicious E can utilize overflow attacks to compromise the privacy of the honest G's inputs. Indeed, a malicious G can also launch a similar attack by using some legal B-bounded inputs, *even while providing a correct BLLL's GC*. However, the consequence of this attack changes.

Consider a malicious G* that provides a correct garbled BLLL's GC but uses some bad inputs. In this case, G* may observe whether the honest E aborts the execution, which implies whether an overflow occurred, even without identifying the precise wire that overflowed. Note that aborting the execution may be inevitable because E may not be able to evaluate the KE gadget when the overflow is too large. This attack rules out achieving full security against a malicious G since this abort event is correlated with E's input. More precisely, the best security notion we can hope to achieve in the presence of a malicious G is security with leakage. In this work, we observe that this leakage can be as small as only 1-bit, capturing the malicious G attacks. That is, a malicious G cannot change the intended computation circuit but rather learn whether E aborted.

Leakage Class of Predicates in the Presence of a Correct GC. Recall that 1-bit leakage is captured by allowing the ideal adversary to submit a leakage predicate. We first analyze what class of leakage predicates can be submitted if we assume that the malicious G* constructs a correct BLLL's GC, which naturally serves as a lower bound on the class of leakage predicates that a malicious 2PC protocol via BLLL's GC can tolerate as the attacks are only selective due to bad inputs.

Note that the only parameters G* can specify for *each* KE gadget are r, s_1, s_2. Now, since the BLLL's GC is constructed correctly, E must obtain the garbled labels $(L_0, L_1) = (w + r, s_1(w + r) + s_2)$ for the input wire of the KE gadget, where w is a value defined by the circuit $\mathcal{C}$. If either L_0 or L_1 overflows, E aborts. We notice that when r, s_1, s_2 are selected within the correct bounds (see Sect. 3), even if the computation can wrap around the domain $\mathbb{Z}_{N^\varsigma}$, a well-bounded L_0 implies a well-bounded L_1. Here, the well-bounded notion includes the scenario of undetectable overflows. I.e., $w + r \in [-B - B_e + N^\varsigma T, B + B_e + N^\varsigma T]$ for some integer T. Moreover, when E decodes these two values in $\mathbb{Z}$ as $(L_0)_\mathbb{Z}$ and $(L_1)_\mathbb{Z}$, it implies that E can use $(L_1)_\mathbb{Z}$ as the key to correctly decrypt Ψ ciphertexts:

$$\left\{ (\tau_i^{s_1}(N+1)^{2c_i})^{(L_0)_\mathbb{Z}} \cdot (\tau_i^{s_2}(N+1)^{-2c_i r + 2d_i}) \right\}_{i \in [\Psi]}$$

where (c, d) are the garbled key pair of the output wire of this KE gadget, and $\tau_1, \ldots, \tau_\Psi$ are public parameters sampled from $\left\{ a^{2N^\varsigma} \mid a \in \mathbb{Z}_{N^{\varsigma+1}}^* \right\}$ (which will be reused across different KE gadgets). Thus, E aborts if and only if L_0 overflows. Hence, the predicate that the ideal malicious G can submit to the ideal functionality is a disjunction of the following predicate clauses:

- For each KE gadget[12] over wire $w = w(\boldsymbol{x}, \boldsymbol{y})$ defined by the circuit $\mathcal{C}$, a malicious G can select $r \in [-B_e, B_e]$ to add a clause checking whether:

$$L_0(\boldsymbol{x}, \boldsymbol{y}) \triangleq w(\boldsymbol{x}, \boldsymbol{y}) + r \stackrel{?}{\in} [-B - B_e, B + B_e] \text{ over } \mathbb{Z}_{N^\varsigma}.$$

Note that the above leakage predicate is a disjunction of small predicate clauses. In particular, if there are two wires being overflowed, while there are 2 clauses being set to 1, the adversary can only learn that there exists *at least* one 1-clause.

Enlarging the Class of Leakage Predicates by Relaxing Correctness. Ensuring correct garbling with respect to the above class of leakage predicates is challenging. In this work, we circumvent this difficulty by allowing a larger class of predicates, *where the leakage a malicious G can obtain remains a single bit.*

Specifically, we present in Sect. 5 a non-trivial 2PC protocol via BLLL's GC that is secure against a malicious G with 1-bit leakage, preserving constant-rate with low cost. This comes at the price of tolerating a slightly larger class of 1-bit leakage predicates. The crucial observation lies in allowing G to inject some small errors inside GC, which will not affect the correct evaluation if E does not abort. In other words, we will only force a malicious G to provide an almost correct BLLL's GC rather than a fully correct one. We observe that if we can force G to provide garbled tables (of a KE gadget) that encrypt the correct intended plaintexts, it is already sufficient to ensure that E will obtain a correct garbled label for the KE output wire. In slightly more detail, recall that the garbled tables of a KE gadget (for a single entry) are of the form:

$$\tau^{s_1}(N+1)^{2c_1} \quad \tau^{s_2}(N+1)^{-2c_1 r + 2d_1} \quad \text{over } \mathbb{Z}_{N^{\varsigma+1}}^*$$

where (c_1, d_1) is one entry of the garbled output key pair and r, s_1, s_2 are selected by G. Assume that E holds the garbled input label $(L_0, L_1) = (w + r, s_1(w + r) + s_2)$ over $\mathbb{Z}_{N^\varsigma}$. We notice that if we can ensure that (1) L_0 equals to $w + r - N^\varsigma T$ for some integer T (i.e., a correct input garbled label); and (2) the garbled tables encrypt the values $2c_1$ and $-2c_1 r + 2d_1$, then we have:

$$(L_0)_{\mathbb{Z}} = w + r - N^\varsigma T - N^\varsigma t \text{ where } t \in \{0, 1\}$$
$$(N+1)^{2c_1(L_0)_{\mathbb{Z}}} \cdot (N+1)^{-2c_1 r + d_1} = (N+1)^{2c_1 w + d}$$

since $\text{ord}(N+1) = N^\varsigma$ in $\mathbb{Z}_{N^{\varsigma+1}}^*$. This implies that E must obtain $c_1 w + d$ as the garbled output label of the KE gadget *given that E can decrypt the ciphertext,*

---

[12] Due to the unlimited fan-out, each wire can have many KE gadgets assigned to it.

which already provides a correct KE gadget. Namely, G cannot force E to output an ill-formed garbled label (e.g., $w + 1$). As a result, we do not need to force G to provide bounded r, s_1, s_2 or even bind s_1, s_2 within τ^{s_1}, τ^{s_2} in the garbled tables. We remark that additional details to explain why this is true, e.g., how to ensure E obtains a correct L_0 and how we utilize this fact, will be covered and discussed explicitly in Sect. 5. Informally, since the garbled labels are defined over $\mathbb{Z}_{N^\varsigma}$ and the order of $N + 1$ is also N^ς modulus $\mathbb{Z}^*_{N^{\varsigma+1}}$, we can operate over the space $\mathbb{Z}_{N^\varsigma}$ to "authenticate" an almost correct BLLL's GC.

We conclude this discussion by emphasizing that an almost correct BLLL's GC will allow a malicious G to specify a leakage predicate of a slightly larger class than the one induced by a fully correct BLLL's GC. This is because a malicious G can further select unbounded r, s_1, s_2 and use ill-formed multiplication terms $\tau^{s_{i \in [2]}}$ in the garbled tables to trigger E's abort. Note that this implies that the leakage predicate will include more clauses but will still be defined as a disjunction. Namely, our protocol complements the lower bound of 1-bit leakage but leaves a gap concerning the minimal leakage predicate class. Given that the GMW compiler, instantiated with succinct proofs, can complement this tighter leakage class of predicate (again, with an undesirable non-black-box computation cost), we leave it as a valuable open problem to extend our protocol to support the tighter leakage predicate class or show that this expansion on the leakage predicate class is harmless. We will further discuss the challenges in Sect. 5.

5   Secure Two-Party Computation over Bounded Integer Computations for Malicious G with 1-Bit Leakage

We formally describe how to design secure two-party computation for bounded integer computation based on BLLL GC and several non-trivial correctness mechanisms to achieve malicious security for G with 1-bit leakage. Informally, our protocol forces G to provide an almost correct BLLL's GC (see Sect. 4.2).

Deferred Proofs. All proofs are deferred to our full version [21].

5.1   IT-MACs over $\mathbb{Z}_{N^\varsigma}$

Our protocol requires G to commit the randomness she used to select the garbled key pairs for each wire. As the garbled key pairs of two different wires can be correlated (e.g., the garbled key pairs of an input and an output wires of a multiplication gate), we use ZK proofs to ensure the correctness of the GC. To run these proofs, G and E should be able to perform some basic operations over the commitments, instantiated by VOLE correlation.

IT-MAC Commitments over $\mathbb{Z}_{N^\varsigma}$. VOLE correlations (see Fig. 1) can be viewed as random *Information Theoretic Message Authentication Codes* (IT-MACs) [9, 34]. An IT-MAC of $x \in \mathbb{Z}_{N^\varsigma}$ is a correlated distributed tuple where G holds a value x and a MAC of x as $\mathsf{mac}(x) \xleftarrow{\$} \mathbb{Z}_{N^\zeta}$, and E holds a *global key*[13] $\Delta \xleftarrow{\$} \mathbb{Z}_{N^\zeta}$ and a local key of x as $\mathsf{key}(x) = x\Delta + \mathsf{mac}(x)$. We denote the IT-MAC of x as $[x]_\Delta = \langle \mathsf{mac}(x), x; \mathsf{key}(x) \rangle$ or $[x]$. Each VOLE correlation over $\mathbb{Z}_{N^\zeta}$ is an IT-MAC $[r]$ where r is a uniform sample. A random IT-MAC $[r]$ can be "consumed" and updated into an IT-MAC $[x]$ using a standard technique [8]. Namely, G can send $x - r$ to E, and then both parties can adjust $[r]$ to $[x]$. IT-MACs (in particular, over $\mathbb{Z}_{N^\zeta}$) hold the following notable properties:

- **Perfect hiding:** For $[x]$, $\mathsf{key}(x)$ and Δ include no information among x since $\mathsf{key}(x)$ is one-time padded by a uniform $\mathsf{mac}(x)$.
- **Statistical binding:** For $[x]$, G can open it by sending $x, \mathsf{mac}(x)$ where E can check $\mathsf{key}(x) \stackrel{?}{=} x\Delta + \mathsf{mac}(x)$. A malicious G can only open x to a different value x' with probability up to $\frac{1}{p}$ as proven in Lemma 1. This is sufficient for our security argument since p is a large enough prime (in λ).
- **Linear homomorphism:** IT-MACs can be linearly evaluated locally as:
  - Holding $[x]$ and $[y]$, two parties can *locally* generate $[x+y]_\Delta$ as $\langle \mathsf{mac}(x) + \mathsf{mac}(y), x + y; \mathsf{key}(x) + \mathsf{key}(y) \rangle$.
  - Holding $c \in \mathbb{Z}_{N^\zeta}$, two parties can *locally* generate $[c]_\Delta$ as $\langle 0, c; c\Delta \rangle$.
  - Holding $c \in \mathbb{Z}_{N^\zeta}$ and $[x]$, two parties can *locally* generate $[cx]$ as $\langle c \cdot \mathsf{mac}(x), cx; c \cdot \mathsf{key}(x) \rangle$.

Lemma 1 (Statistical Binding for IT-MACs over $\mathbb{Z}_{N^\zeta}$). *Let $N = pq$ be an RSA modulus where $p < q$ and $\zeta \in \mathbb{Z}^+$. An IT-MAC $[x]$ over $\mathbb{Z}_{N^\zeta}$ can only be opened to a different value $x' \neq x$ with probability up to $\frac{1}{p}$.*

Zero-Knowledge Proofs for Multiplication Triples of IT-MACs over $\mathbb{Z}_{N^\zeta}$. While G and E can evaluate IT-MACs linearly without communication, in our protocol, we also need G and E to multiply two IT-MACs. This can be done by the standard commit-and-prove paradigm. Formally, this means that G and E holding $[x], [y], [z]$ over $\mathbb{Z}_{N^\zeta}$ where G needs to convince E in ZK that $z = xy$. While there are many different techniques to do this, e.g. [6,15,40], we find that a technique called *Line-point Zero-Knowledge* (LPZK) over fields [15] can also support rings $\mathbb{Z}_{N^\zeta}$. LPZK only requires 2 ring elements of communications to prove each multiplication triple. We note that the LPZK does not directly work for some rings, e.g., $\mathbb{Z}_{2^k}$ (see [5]). We defer the details of LPZK to our full version. Crucially, it relies on Lemma 2 to achieve a $\frac{2}{p}$ soundness error.

Lemma 2 (Number of Roots for Quadratic Equations over $\mathbb{Z}_{N^\zeta}$). *Let $N = pq$ be an RSA modulus where $p < q$ and $\zeta \in \mathbb{Z}^+$. For any $a, b, c \in \mathbb{Z}$ such that $N^\zeta \nmid a$, the following equation has at most $2p^{\zeta-1}q^\zeta$ solutions.*

$$a\chi^2 + b\chi + c \equiv 0 \pmod{N^\zeta} \tag{1}$$

In summary, in the $\mathcal{F}_{\mathsf{VOLEc}}^{N,\zeta}$-hybrid, G and E can:

---

[13] I.e., Δ is identical and reused among all IT-MACs.

- Generate IT-MAC $[r]$ from $\mathcal{F}_{\mathsf{VOLEc}}^{N,\varsigma}$ where r is uniform and unknown to E.
- Generate IT-MAC $[x]$ where x is G-chosen by communicating 1 element.
- Open IT-MAC $[x]$ to x by communicating 2 elements.
- Perform linear operations over IT-MACs for free.
- Obtain IT-MAC $[xy]$ given $[x]$ and $[y]$ by communicating 3 elements.

The communication of the above operations is uni-directional once the VOLE correlations are generated. The computation complexity for both parties is $\mathcal{O}(1)$ additions/multiplications in $\mathbb{Z}_{N^\varsigma}$. We conclude by remarking that our arguments hold only when G has no knowledge of Δ, which is the case in our protocol.

5.2 Protocol to Bind IT-MACs with Key Extension Gadgets

The operations presented in Sect. 5.1 allow G and E to perform additions and multiplications on the IT-MACs. However, to garble a circuit as in BLLL's GC, G must also use the randomness committed within the IT-MACs to construct the garbled tables of KE gadgets. Clearly, a malicious G can provide badly generated garbled tables, so we need to design a mechanism to force G to use the committed randomness. Recall that for KE gadgets (see Sect. 3), G sends ciphertexts Cs defined over $\mathbb{Z}_{N^\varsigma+1}^*$. Let the public parameter τ be $\tau \xleftarrow{\$} \{a^{2N^\varsigma} | a \in \mathbb{Z}_{N^\varsigma+1}^*\}$ then, each ciphertext C is defined as[14] $\tau^s \cdot (N+1)^m$ over $\mathbb{Z}_{N^\varsigma+1}$, where s and m are determined (over $\mathbb{Z}_{N^\varsigma}$) by the randomness of G. Therefore, s and m can also be committed within the IT-MACs as $[s]$ and $[m]$. We now present a protocol to ensure that G indeed uses $[m]$ to construct the garbled tables for the KE gadgets. We note that a malicious G can use a different $[s]$ or even an element in $\mathbb{Z}_{N^\varsigma+1}$ that is not generated by τ. In Sect. 4.2, we have already informally justified why the evaluator does not need to monitor this attack, and why it affects neither privacy (up to 1 bit of leakage) nor correctness. Our observation is crucial for feasibility and reducing communication overhead, which leads to a non-trivial Σ-protocol formalization discussed below.

Remark 2 (A gap between soundness and correctness). Our special-purpose object (Definition 1) can be viewed as a customized interactive proof rather than a classical one. More specifically, unlike a classical proof, the language recognized by the correctness property in our customized interactive proof is a subset of the language recognized by the soundness property. That is, given $[s], [\Gamma], C$, correctness holds for $C = \tau^s(N+1)^\Gamma$, while soundness only prevents a malicious G* from using $C = C_U(N+1)^{\Gamma'}$ where $C_U \in U$ and $\Gamma' \neq \Gamma$. In particular, for a $C = C_U(N+1)^\Gamma$ where $C_U \in U$, our definition does not explicitly say whether E will output C. Say differently; we only need to prevent a malicious G* from using a ciphertext (i.e., the KE gadget) that encrypts a wrong message but not using a wrong key. This suffices since (1) a corrupting key will only cause up to 1-bit leakage, and (2) a correct message ensures a correct execution.

Before continuing with the definition and protocol, we recall the decomposition property of an element in $\mathbb{Z}_{N^\varsigma+1}^*$.

---

[14] We recall that there are Ψ different τ values.

LU decomposition over $\mathbb{Z}^*_{N^{\zeta+1}}$. Recall that $\mathbb{Z}^*_{N^{\zeta+1}}$, is a direct product $L \times U$, where L is the cyclic of order N^ζ generated by $(N+1)$ and U is isomorphic to $\mathbb{Z}^*_N$ of order $(p-1)(q-1)$. That is, given an element C in $\mathbb{Z}^*_{N^{\zeta+1}}$, it can be *uniquely* decomposed into $C_L \in L$ and $C_U \in U$ such that $C_L \cdot C_U = C$. Moreover, $C_L = (N+1)^{k_C}$ for some *unique* $k_C \in \mathbb{Z}_{N^\zeta}$. We define auxiliary functions LU, returning C_L, C_U given an element $C \in \mathbb{Z}^*_{N^{\zeta+1}}$, and LU_k that outputs the discrete logarithm of C_L to the base $N+1$[15]. Clearly, for any $C \in \mathbb{Z}^*_{N^{\zeta+1}}$, let $(C_L, C_U) := \mathsf{LU}(C)$, we have $\mathsf{LU}_k(C_L) = \mathsf{LU}_k(C)$ and $\mathsf{LU}_k(C_U) = 0$.

Special-purpose Σ-protocol in the VOLEc-hybrid. To ensure correctness on the garbler's side, we abstract out the following guarantees. Assume that G and E hold an IT-MAC $[\Gamma]$ and an element $C \in \mathbb{Z}^*_{N^{\zeta+1}}$ generated by the KE gadget forwarded from G. Then G can convince E in ZK that $\mathsf{LU}_k(C) = \Gamma$. The syntax and security properties of this cryptographic object are defined in Definition 1.

Definition 1 (Special-purpose Σ-protocol in the VOLEc-hybrid). *G and E have access to all public parameters* pp *including* $\lambda, N = pq, \zeta, \tau \xleftarrow{\$} \left\{ a^{2N^\zeta} | a \in \mathbb{Z}^*_{N^{\zeta+1}} \right\}$ *and an ideal access to* $\mathcal{F}^{N,\zeta}_{\mathsf{VOLEc}}$ *(Fig. 1) where* $\mathcal{F}^{N,\zeta}_{\mathsf{VOLEc}}$ *outputs a global key* $\Delta \in \mathbb{Z}_{N^\zeta}$ *to E. G and E hold an IT-MAC* $[\Gamma]_\Delta \in \mathbb{Z}_{N^\zeta}$ *(which is generated from the basic IT-MAC operations presented in Sect. 5.1, and in particular, only requires communication from G to E), and G has an additional input* $s \in \mathbb{Z}_{N^\zeta}$. *Interactive PPT algorithms* $\langle G^{\mathsf{pp},\mathcal{F}^{N,\zeta}_{\mathsf{VOLEc}}}([\Gamma], s), E^{\mathsf{pp},\mathcal{F}^{N,\zeta}_{\mathsf{VOLEc}}}([\Gamma]) \rangle$ *form a special-purpose Σ-protocol (for KE gadgets) in the VOLEc-hybrid (or in short, SP Σ-protocol), if after the execution, G outputs nothing and E outputs either* abort *or* $C \in \mathbb{Z}^*_{N^{\zeta+1}}$, *and the following properties hold.*

1. **Correctness.** *A special-purpose Σ-protocol (for KE gadgets) in the VOLEc-hybrid is correct if*

$$\Pr\left[\langle G^{\mathsf{pp},\mathcal{F}^{N,\zeta}_{\mathsf{VOLEc}}}([\Gamma], s), E^{\mathsf{pp},\mathcal{F}^{N,\zeta}_{\mathsf{VOLEc}}}([\Gamma]) \rangle = \tau^s (N+1)^\Gamma \right] = 1$$

2. **Statistical soundness.** *A special-purpose Σ-protocol (for KE gadgets) in the VOLEc-hybrid is sound if, for any malicious algorithm G^**

$$\Pr\left[\mathsf{LU}_k(C) \neq \Gamma \;\middle|\; \langle G^*, E^{\mathsf{pp},\mathcal{F}^{N,\zeta}_{\mathsf{VOLEc}}}([\Gamma]) \rangle = C \in \mathbb{Z}^*_{N^{\zeta+1}} \right] < \mathsf{negl}(\lambda)$$

   where $\mathsf{negl}(\cdot)$ *is some negligible function.*

3. **Statistical honest verifier zero-knowledge (SHVZK).** *A special-purpose Σ-protocol (for KE gadgets) in the VOLEc-hybrid is SHVZK if there exists a PPT algorithm $\mathcal{S}^E$ that takes public parameters* pp, *E's inputs, and* $\tau^s(N+1)^\Gamma$ *over* $\mathbb{Z}^*_{N^{\zeta+1}}$ *as inputs that can output a view satisfying:*

$$\left. \begin{array}{l} \mathcal{S}^E(\mathsf{pp}, \mathsf{key}(\Gamma), \Delta, C) \\ \approx_s \mathrm{VIEW}^E \end{array} \right| \begin{array}{l} C := \langle G^{\mathsf{pp},\mathcal{F}^{N,\zeta}_{\mathsf{VOLEc}}}([\Gamma], s), E^{\mathsf{pp},\mathcal{F}^{N,\zeta}_{\mathsf{VOLEc}}}([\Gamma]) \rangle, \\ \mathrm{VIEW}^E = \mathrm{VIEW}^E \langle G^{\mathsf{pp},\mathcal{F}^{N,\zeta}_{\mathsf{VOLEc}}}([\Gamma], s), E^{\mathsf{pp},\mathcal{F}^{N,\zeta}_{\mathsf{VOLEc}}}([\Gamma]) \rangle \end{array}$$

---

[15] Functions LU and LU_k are purely used for explanation and analysis. Note that the DCR assumption implies there is no computationally efficient way to calculate them.

Remark 3 (Coping with multiple correlated instances). In Definition 1, we say G and E hold an IT-MAC $[\Gamma]$. Formally, this means that G and E agree on some IT-MAC tuple generated by the operations defined in Sect. 5.1, which only requires uni-directional communication from G to E in the VOLEc-hybrid. Note that G and E can hold many other IT-MACs besides $[\Gamma]$ while they should not affect the correctness/security properties. E.g., even though a malicious G^* can have many instances of IT-MACs, this should not break the soundness. Informally, this is because the VOLE correlations G^* received from $\mathcal{F}_{\mathsf{VOLEc}}^{N,\varsigma}$ are independent of the global key Δ held by E, as each VOLE correlation is one-time padded by a uniform sample (i.e., the local key chosen by $\mathcal{F}_{\mathsf{VOLEc}}^{N,\varsigma}$).

Our SP Σ-protocol shares similarities with the classic discrete logarithm proof [38], where the differences are (1) there are two bases τ and $N + 1$, and (2) we need to bind G's discrete logarithm on $N + 1$ to $[\Gamma]$. We adjust Schnorr's protocol as follows: (1) G needs to provide two answers for the random challenge from E, one for the base τ and one for the base $N + 1$, and (2) G also needs to open the IT-MAC to authenticate its answer with respect to the base $N + 1$. We formally define the protocol in Fig. 3 and the security claim in Theorem 2. We remark that since G needs to reply with $\nu s + \sigma$ over $\mathbb{Z}$ and s must be kept private, σ has to be sampled from a large enough domain such that $\nu s + \sigma$ statistically hides νs. Note that $\nu s \in \{0, \ldots, (N^\varsigma - 1)^2\}$ over $\mathbb{Z}$, and we can select σ from $\{0, \ldots, B_\sigma\}$ where $B_\sigma = N^{2\varsigma}\lambda^{\omega(1)}$. Essentially, this does not affect the rate.

Theorem 2. *Protocol in Fig. 3 is a SP Σ-protocol in the VOLEc-hybrid per Definition 1 with the following efficiency features: $\mathcal{O}(1)$ communication in $\mathbb{Z}_{N^{\varsigma+1}}^*$, $\mathcal{O}(1)$ computation of exponentiation in $\mathbb{Z}_{N^{\varsigma+1}}^*$, and 3 rounds.*

Parallel SP Σ-Protocol Instances. Our 2PC protocol requires multiple parallel instances of the SP Σ-protocol. Indeed, this can be done directly with multiple parallel instances of the protocol defined in Fig. 3 where E issues a new random challenge ν per instance.[16] We observe that ν can be reused across different parallel instances simply because each check performed by E is done separately. For completeness, see our full version for the formal definition.

Sufficiency of Binding Only Discrete Logarithm to the Base $N + 1$. Consider the event that E outputs $C \in \mathbb{Z}_{N^{\varsigma+1}}^*$ and let $(C_L, C_U) := \mathsf{LU}(C)$.[17] Indeed, the soundness of this protocol only guarantees that $(N + 1)^\Gamma = C_L$ and does *not* guarantee that $\tau^s = C_U$. This is what we refer to as an almost correct BLLL's GC in Sect. 4.2. Looking ahead, this is the only place where a malicious G can inject errors in BLLL's GC to specify a leakage predicate. Recall that this does not weaken the 1-bit leakage privacy as it guarantees that the KE gadget will operate correctly, as formally defined in Lemma 3.

---

[16] A small subtlety arises here since we also need to argue that Δ is independent of each ν in the proof, which is trivially true.

[17] We note that this does *not* imply that E can factor C into C_L and C_U.

Special-purpose Σ-protocol in the VOLEc-hybrid

G and E have access to all public parameters including $N = pq, \zeta, \tau \overset{\$}{\leftarrow} \left\{ a^{2N^\zeta} | a \in \mathbb{Z}^*_{N^{\zeta+1}} \right\}$ and hybrid access to $\mathcal{F}^{N,\zeta}_{\mathsf{VOLEc}}$. Let G and E hold IT-MACs $[\Gamma]$ over $\mathbb{Z}_{N^\zeta}$. G holds $s \in \mathbb{Z}_{N^\zeta}$. G and E proceed as follows:

Commit Phase

1. G samples $\sigma \overset{\$}{\leftarrow} \{0, \ldots, B_\sigma\}$ where B_σ is large enough such that σ statistically hides $y \in \{0, \ldots, (N^\zeta - 1)^2\}$. I.e., $B_\sigma = N^{2\zeta} \lambda^{\omega(1)}$.
2. G and E obtain a fresh random IT-MAC $[\Lambda]$ over $\mathbb{Z}_{N^\zeta}$ generated by $\mathcal{F}^{N,\zeta}_{\mathsf{VOLEc}}$.
3. G sends $C = \tau^s (N+1)^\Gamma$ and $D = \tau^\sigma (N+1)^\Lambda$ over $\mathbb{Z}^*_{N^{\zeta+1}}$.

Challenge Phase

4. E samples a random challenge $\nu \in \mathbb{Z}_{N^\zeta}$ and sends ν to G.

Response Phase

5. G and E locally calculate $[\eta] := [\nu\Gamma + \Lambda] = \nu[\Gamma] + [\Lambda]$ over $\mathbb{Z}_{N^\zeta}$.
6. G sends $\phi = \nu s + \sigma$ over $\mathbb{Z}$; and opens $[\eta] = [\nu\Gamma + \Lambda]$ over $\mathbb{Z}_{N^\zeta}$ to E. If the opening fails, E outputs **abort** and halts permanently.
7. E checks $C^\nu \cdot D \overset{?}{=} \tau^\phi (N+1)^\eta \mod N^{\zeta+1}$. If so, E outputs C. Otherwise, E outputs **abort** and halts permanently.

Fig. 3. Special-purpose Σ-protocol in the VOLEc-hybrid

Lemma 3 (Almost Correct KE Gadgets). *Given two ciphertexts $CT_0, CT_1 \in \mathbb{Z}^*_{N^{\zeta+1}}$ of some KE gadget, which is used to encode the entry (c_1, d_1) of the output garbled key pair where $c_1, d_1 \in \mathbb{Z}_{N^\zeta}$. Let $(CT_{0,L}, CT_{0,U}) := \mathsf{LU}(CT_0)$ and $(CT_{1,L}, CT_{1,U}) := \mathsf{LU}(CT_1)$. If $\mathsf{LU}_k(CT_0) = c_1$ and $\mathsf{LU}_k(CT_1) = -c_1 r + d$ where $r \in \mathbb{Z}_{N^\zeta}$, assume that E obtains $(L_0 = w + r, \epsilon)$ over $\mathbb{Z}_{N^\zeta}$ as the garbled label of this KE gadget input, conditioned on E not aborting. Then E must obtain $c_1 w + d_1$ over $\mathbb{Z}_{N^\zeta}$ as the garbled label of this KE gadget output, independent of the concrete values within $CT_{0,U}, CT_{1,U}, \epsilon, r$.*

Challenges for Achieving a Fully Correct KE. Recall that our protocol complements the lower bound of 1-bit leakage but does not meet the minimal class leakage predicate. To bridge this gap, it is sufficient to upgrade our almost correct KE gadget to a fully correct one. See our full version for the challenges behind upgrading our protocol to achieve this, which we pose as open problems.

5.3 Our 2PC Protocol

We are now ready to present our 2PC protocol for bounded integer computations instantiated by BLLL's GC. Due to space limitations, we focus on the key components and defer additional details to our full version.

Functionality $\mathcal{F}_{\mathsf{aVOLE}}^{N,\zeta}$

Let $\mathbb{Z}_{N^\zeta}$ denote the ring of integers modulus N^ζ. Functionality interacts with G, E, and the adversary $\mathcal{A}$ as follows:

Evaluate. Upon receiving $(\texttt{evaluate}, n, \boldsymbol{u}_0, \boldsymbol{w}_0, \boldsymbol{u}_1, \boldsymbol{w}_1)$ from G and $(\texttt{evaluate}, n, \Delta, x)$ from E where $\boldsymbol{u}_0, \boldsymbol{w}_0, \boldsymbol{u}_1, \boldsymbol{w}_1 \in \mathbb{Z}_{N^\zeta}^n$ and $\Delta, x \in \mathbb{Z}_{N^\zeta}$:
  - Output $\boldsymbol{v}_0 := \boldsymbol{u}_0 \Delta + \boldsymbol{w}_0, \boldsymbol{v}_1 := \boldsymbol{u}_1 \Delta + \boldsymbol{w}_1, \boldsymbol{y} := \boldsymbol{u}_0 x + \boldsymbol{u}_1$ to E.

Fig. 4. The authenticated VOLE functionality

Generating the Public Parameters. Our protocol starts with securely generating the public parameters for establishing the trusted setup (e.g. [17] for securely generating RSA modulus). We refer readers to [3] for the details on selecting these parameters. Besides the public parameters for BLLL's GC, G and E need to generate the public parameters for the special-purpose Σ-protocol we presented in Sect. 5.2. Overall, for a given security parameter λ and bound $B = B(\lambda)$, G and E jointly sample the following public parameters:

1. A sufficiently large RSA modulus $N = pq$.
2. A bound $B_e = B\lambda^{\omega(1)}$; a bound $B_{\mathsf{msg}} = NB_e\lambda^{\omega(1)}$.
3. A sufficiently large integer ζ such that $N^\zeta > 2B_{\mathsf{msg}} + 1$.
4. A bound $B_\sigma = N^{2\zeta}\lambda^{\omega(1)}$.
5. $\tau_1, \ldots, \tau_\Psi \overset{\$}{\leftarrow} \left\{ a^{2N^\zeta} \mid a \in \mathbb{Z}_{N^{\zeta+1}}^* \right\}$ where Ψ is a constant (e.g., 10).

These public parameters are selected before the circuit $\mathcal{C}$ is known. In particular, they are independent of the circuit size $|\mathcal{C}|$ and can be reused across several instances of (different) B-bounded circuits.

Authenticated VOLE. Similar to the role of *oblivious transfer* (OT) in Yao's GC protocol, G and E use VOLE for E to learn his garbled input labels, even in the semi-honest case. Recall that in the VOLE functionality (over $\mathbb{Z}_{N^\zeta}$), G holds two length-n vectors $\boldsymbol{u}_0, \boldsymbol{u}_1$ and E holds an input x, where E learns $\boldsymbol{u}_0 x + \boldsymbol{u}_1$. To further force G to use consistent garbled key pairs with the IT-MACs (i.e., G and E hold $[\boldsymbol{u}_0], [\boldsymbol{u}_1]$), we need a slightly modified version of VOLE. Namely, G holds two extra length-n vectors $\boldsymbol{w}_0, \boldsymbol{w}_1$ and E holds Δ (the global key of the IT-MACs), where E learns $\boldsymbol{u}_0 \Delta + \boldsymbol{w}_0$ and $\boldsymbol{u}_1 \Delta + \boldsymbol{w}_1$. Note that these two vectors are exactly the local key vectors of the IT-MACs held by E (i.e., $\mathsf{key}(\boldsymbol{u}_0)$ and $\mathsf{key}(\boldsymbol{u}_1)$), where E can abort if G cheats by providing wrong garbled key pairs (which are not authenticated using the IT-MACs). Figure 4 presents this functionality. In this work, we do not instantiate this functionality but use it as a hybrid[18]. We emphasize that our protocol only uses this functionality with length vectors proportional to the input size, independent of the circuit size.

---

[18] Indeed, $\mathcal{F}_{\mathsf{aVOLE}}^{N,\zeta}$ can be reduced to two $\mathcal{F}_{\mathsf{VOLE_c}}^{N,\zeta}$ instances in a classic way [7], this reduction only works in the presence of *passive* adversaries.

Sub-procedure: Expand. Our protocol makes function calls to a sub-procedure Expand. Essentially, this sub-procedure packs the (recursively used) KE gadgets of BLLL's GC into a parallel SP Σ-protocol. The sub-procedure implements three algorithms:

- Expand.Gb: This is a sub-protocol capturing the generation of garbled tables of each KE gadget. Compared to BLLL's GC, the difference lies in that G will also prepare the messages related to the commit phase of the parallel SP Σ-protocol. The communication is uni-directional from G to E. E will abort w.h.p. if G tries to cheat in operating IT-MACs.
- Expand.Sigma: This is a sub-protocol capturing the challenge and response phases of the parallel SP Σ-protocol. Essentially, this happens after *all* Expand.Gbs finish. The communication is uni-directional from G to E after E issues a single uniform challenge. Note that the random challenge can be replaced by the Fiat-Shamir heuristic [16] assuming *random oracle* (RO). E will abort w.h.p. if some garbled table of a KE gadget provided by G (in a call to Expand.Gb) is not almost correct.
- Expand.Ev: This is a sub-procedure used by E only to (recursively) evaluate KE gadgets. Compared to BLLL's GC, the difference lies in that E will abort if E detects some errors (e.g., overflow or inability to evaluate).

See our full version for the fined-grained descriptions and formalization.

Our protocol Π: primary components. We formalize our protocol algorithmically. G and E start with public parameters, a circuit $\mathcal{C}$ as a sequence of tuples under the standard gate-by-gate representation. We only consider single-output circuits to simplify the presentation, but our protocol can be trivially generalized to multiple outputs. Our protocol Π is composed of three primary components:

0. **G and E generate VOLE correlations.** In Step 0 (embedded in the first primary component in Fig. 5), G and E instantiate the VOLE correlation functionality over $\mathbb{Z}_{N^\zeta}$ to generate enough (pseudo-)random VOLE instances. These VOLE correlations are used as (pseudo-)random IT-MACs, to set up a pool of committed randomness that G and E can consume. The overall number of VOLE correlations required by the parties need is $\mathcal{O}(|\mathcal{C}|)$. This step is a circuit-independent pre-processing phase.

1. **G garbles an almost correct BLLL's GC (see Fig. 5).** In the first primary component, G generates a BLLL's GC in an authenticated manner. Step 1 is adjusted from the BLLL's GC garbling procedure – the difference lies in that each operation insides is replaced by either an IT-MAC operation or the commit phase of the parallel SP Σ-protocol (captured by sub-protocol Expand.Gb). Step 1 only requires uni-directional communication from G to E. Step 2 captures the challenge and response phases of the parallel SP Σ-protocol (captured by sub-protocol Expand.Sigma), which requires a round-trip communication. By Fiat-Shamir transform, assuming RO, this can be achieved with uni-directional communication from G to E. If E aborts in the first component, the abort is independent of E's inputs; otherwise, it means that E holds an almost correct BLLL's GC.

2. **E obtains the garbled labels of the input (see Fig. 6a).** In the second primary component, E obtains garbled labels of inputs of C. In this component, E can abort if G fails to provide correct garbled labels generated from the committed garbled key pairs. The communication is uni-directional from G to E in the $\mathcal{F}_{aVOLE}^{N,\zeta}$-hybrid model. If E aborts in the second component, the abort is independent of E's inputs.

3. **E evaluates the circuit (see Fig. 6b).** E evaluates the GC as BLLL's GC. The difference lies in E may abort if E catches overflows on garbled labels or incorrectly evaluates some KE gadget (captured by sub-protocol Expand.Ev). The communication is uni-directional from E to G. If E aborts in the third component, the abort depends on E's inputs.

See our full version for the fined-grained descriptions.

Proof Overview. The security of Π can be shown using the following arguments:

Correct Execution (see Lemma 4). Intuitively, to argue our protocol is secure against malicious G with 1-bit leakage, we need to argue: if E does not abort and output *res*, *res* w.h.p. must be calculated using the malicious G's chosen inputs $\tilde{x}$ and E's inputs y over the intended computation C. I.e., a malicious G cannot forge the intended computation task. Informally, this is because if G does not use an almost correct BLLL's GC, she will be caught before E starts the evaluation, i.e., before the third component of Π. Conditioned over the GC is almost correct, we need to argue that the garbled labels obtained by E are "well-formed". Namely, they indeed encode a value generated from committed garbled key pairs. This trivially holds because we require G (1) to prove the correctness of the committed IT-MAC values related to E's input garbled key pair (see Step 3); (2) to open IT-MACs of gabled labels of her inputs (see Step 4).

Well-Defined Leakage Predicate. Note that E's abort before evaluation (i.e., the third component of Π) is independent of E's inputs. Thus, the leakage predicate is well-defined by the evaluation procedure of BLLL's GC. In particular, a malicious G^* can choose some parameters (i.e., errors in an almost correct GC). Note that these parameters can be extracted by a simulator because all the randomness G^* used is committed under IT-MACs. The simulator, by emulating $\mathcal{F}_{VOLE_c}^{N,\zeta}$ hybrid for G^*, can extract them trivially as the hiding property of the IT-MAC no longer holds. See our full version for a formal captured leakage predicate using a family of wrapper functions.

Simulatable E's View. To ensure that our protocol preserves security for the semi-honest E, we need to construct a simulator to sample the entire views of E from knowing the computation result. This can be easily reduced to the security of BLLL's GC and SHVZK property of the parallel SP Σ-protocol. Informally, the simulator can first use the simulator of BLLL's GC to generate fake garbled tables and fake garbled labels, then call the simulator of SHVZK to generate the fake proofs. By knowing the global key Δ, the simulator can easily open an IT-MACs commitment to any value and perform wrong multiplication operations. Formally, the security claims of our protocols are provided in Theorems 3 and 4. The overall efficiency analysis of our protocol is discussed in Sect. 1.2, where a detailed cost accounting is included in our full version.

Protocol Π: First Component

G and E have access to all public parameters, including N, ζ. G and E have ideal access to $\mathcal{F}_{\mathsf{VOLEc}}^{N,\zeta}, \mathcal{F}_{\mathsf{aVOLE}}^{N,\zeta}$. G and E with a circuit $\mathcal{C}$, proceed as follows:

0. <u>Initialize:</u> G and E send (init) to $\mathcal{F}_{\mathsf{VOLEc}}^{N,\zeta}$, which returns Δ to E. G and E send (extend, $n = \mathcal{O}(|\mathcal{C}|)$) to $\mathcal{F}_{\mathsf{VOLEc}}^{N,\zeta}$ to generate enough VOLE correlations.

1. G garbles an authenticated <u>BLLL's GC</u>: G and E set up committed garbled key pairs on each wire gate-by-gate backward. in the following way:

   - The output gate: For the output gate (output, $outputid$, wid_o), save tuple $(\mathsf{gb}, \mathsf{output}, outputid, wid_o, 1, ([1], [0]))$.

   - Addition gates: For an addition gate (add, $addid$, wid_x, wid_y, wid_z), G and E set up two empty vectors $[\boldsymbol{k}_0]$ and $[\boldsymbol{k}_1]$ of IT-MACs. For each successor gates using wid_z as inputs in the pre-determined order:

     • For a saved tuple $(\mathsf{gb}, \mathsf{output}, -, wid_z, -, ([\boldsymbol{L}], [\boldsymbol{R}]))$, let $[\boldsymbol{k}_0] := [\boldsymbol{k}_0] \,\|\, [\boldsymbol{L}]$ and $[\boldsymbol{k}_1] := [\boldsymbol{k}_1] \,\|\, [\boldsymbol{R}]$.

     • For a saved tuple $(\mathsf{gb}, \mathsf{add/mult}, -, wid_z, -, -, -, ([\boldsymbol{L}], [\boldsymbol{R}]), -)$, let $[\boldsymbol{k}_0] := [\boldsymbol{k}_0] \,\|\, [\boldsymbol{L}]$ and $[\boldsymbol{k}_1] := [\boldsymbol{k}_1] \,\|\, [\boldsymbol{R}]$.

     • For a saved tuple $(\mathsf{gb}, \mathsf{add/mult}, -, -, wid_z, -, -, -, ([\boldsymbol{L}], [\boldsymbol{R}]))$, let $[\boldsymbol{k}_0] := [\boldsymbol{k}_0] \,\|\, [\boldsymbol{L}]$ and $[\boldsymbol{k}_1] := [\boldsymbol{k}_1] \,\|\, [\boldsymbol{R}]$.

     Finally, let $|\boldsymbol{k}_0| = |\boldsymbol{k}_1| = m$. G and E call the sub-protocol Expand.Gb (add, $addid, m, [\boldsymbol{k}_0], [\boldsymbol{k}_1]$), which (*if not halt*) returns shrunk $[\boldsymbol{k}_0^z]$ and $[\boldsymbol{k}_1^z]$. Let $n = |\boldsymbol{k}_0^z| = |\boldsymbol{k}_1^z| \leq 2$. G and E fetch and consume fresh VOLE correlations $[\boldsymbol{r}]$ where $|\boldsymbol{r}| = n$. Let

     $$[\boldsymbol{k}_0^x] = [\boldsymbol{k}_0^y] := [\boldsymbol{k}_0^z], [\boldsymbol{k}_1^x] := [\boldsymbol{r}], [\boldsymbol{k}_1^y] := [\boldsymbol{k}_1^z] - [\boldsymbol{r}] \qquad (2)$$

     Save $(\mathsf{gb}, \mathsf{add}, addid, wid_x, wid_y, n, n, ([\boldsymbol{k}_0^x], [\boldsymbol{k}_1^x]), ([\boldsymbol{k}_0^y], [\boldsymbol{k}_1^y]))$.

   - Multiplication gates: For a multiplication gate (mult, $multid$, wid_x, wid_y, wid_z), G and E generate $[\boldsymbol{k}_0]$ and $[\boldsymbol{k}_1]$ the same as the addition gate (traversing successor gates using wid_z as inputs). Let $|\boldsymbol{k}_0| = |\boldsymbol{k}_1| = m$. G and E call the sub-protocol Expand.Gb(mult, $multid, m, [\boldsymbol{k}_0], [\boldsymbol{k}_1]$), which (*if not halt*) returns shrunk $[\boldsymbol{k}_0^z]$ and $[\boldsymbol{k}_1^z]$. Let $n = |\boldsymbol{k}_0^z| = |\boldsymbol{k}_1^z| \leq 2$. G and E fetch and consume fresh VOLE correlations $[\boldsymbol{r}], [\boldsymbol{u}], [\boldsymbol{s}]$ where $|\boldsymbol{r}| = |\boldsymbol{u}| = n$. Let

     $$[\boldsymbol{k}_0^x] := [\boldsymbol{k}_0^z] \,\|\, [\boldsymbol{k}_0^z] \cdot [\boldsymbol{s}] \qquad\qquad [\boldsymbol{k}_1^x] := [\boldsymbol{r}] \,\|\, [\boldsymbol{u}] \qquad (3)$$

     $$[\boldsymbol{k}_0^y] := [1] \,\|\, [\boldsymbol{r}] \qquad\qquad [\boldsymbol{k}_1^y] := [\boldsymbol{s}] \,\|\, ([\boldsymbol{r}] \cdot [\boldsymbol{s}] - [\boldsymbol{k}_1^z] - [\boldsymbol{u}]) \qquad (4)$$

     Save $(\mathsf{gb}, \mathsf{mult}, multid, wid_x, wid_y, 2n, n+1, ([\boldsymbol{k}_0^x], [\boldsymbol{k}_1^x]), ([\boldsymbol{k}_0^y], [\boldsymbol{k}_1^y]))$.

   - Input gates: For an input gate (input, $inputid$, wid_i), G and E generate $[\boldsymbol{k}_0]$ and $[\boldsymbol{k}_1]$ the same as the addition gate (traversing successor gates using wid_i as inputs). Let $|\boldsymbol{k}_0| = |\boldsymbol{k}_1| = m$. G and E call the sub-procedure Expand.Gb(input, $inputid, m, [\boldsymbol{k}_0], [\boldsymbol{k}_1]$) which (*if not halt*) will return $[\boldsymbol{k}_0^z]$ and $[\boldsymbol{k}_1^z]$. Let $n = |\boldsymbol{k}_0^z| = |\boldsymbol{k}_1^z| \leq 2$. Save $(\mathsf{gb}, \mathsf{input}, inputid, wid_i, n, ([\boldsymbol{k}_0^z], [\boldsymbol{k}_1^z]))$.

2. G and E executes the sub-protocol Expand.Sigma() to check the KE gadgets are generated almost correctly. Note that E may halt in this step.

Fig. 5. The first component of our protocol Π. Note that Eqs. (2) to (4) are the same as add/mult gadgets from the AIK paradigm presented in Fig. 2.

Protocol Π: Second Component

G and E continue from Figure 5 as follows:

3. E obtains garbled labels of E's input gates: For each input gate (input, $inputid$, wid_i) owned by E, G and E fetch the tuple (gb, input, $inputid$, wid_i, n_i, $([\mathbf{k}_0^i], [\mathbf{k}_1^i])$). Note that E has an input on this gate as $y \in [-B, B]$ (and embedded in $\mathbb{Z}_{N^\varsigma}$). G sends (evaluate, n_i, mac($\mathbf{k}_0^i$), $\mathbf{k}_0^i$, mac($\mathbf{k}_1^i$), $\mathbf{k}_1^i$) to $\mathcal{F}_{\mathsf{aVOLE}}^{N,\varsigma}$. E sends (evaluate, n_i, Δ, y) to $\mathcal{F}_{\mathsf{aVOLE}}^{N,\varsigma}$ and obtains $v_0, v_1, \mathbf{L}^i$ from $\mathcal{F}_{\mathsf{aVOLE}}^{N,\varsigma}$. If $v_0 \neq$ key($\mathbf{k}_0^i$) or $v_1 \neq$ key($\mathbf{k}_1^i$), E outputs abort and halts permanently; otherwise, E saves the tuple (ev, input, $inputid$, $\mathbf{L}^i$).

4. E obtains garbled labels of G's input gates: For each input gate (input, $inputid$, wid_i) owned by G, G and E fetch the tuple (gb, input, $inputid$, wid_i, n_i, $([\mathbf{k}_0^i], [\mathbf{k}_1^i])$). G commits x as $[x]$ where x is the input of G (via consuming 1 VOLE correlation). G and E compute $[\mathbf{L}^i] := [\mathbf{k}_0^i] \cdot [x] + [\mathbf{k}_1^i]$. G then opens $[\mathbf{L}^i]$. If G fails to open the IT-MACs, E outputs abort and halts permanently. Otherwise, E will obtain $\mathbf{L}^i := \mathbf{k}_0^i \cdot x + \mathbf{k}_1^i$. E saves the tuple (ev, input, $inputid$, $\mathbf{L}^i$).

(a) The second component

Protocol Π: Third Component

5. E evaluates the garbled circuit: E evaluates the circuit gate-by-gate forward in the following ways:
   - Input gates: For an input gate (input, $inputid$, wid_i), E fetches the tuple (ev, input, $inputid$, $\mathbf{L}^i$). E calls the sub-procedure Expand.Ev(input, $inputid$, $-$, $\mathbf{L}^i$), which (if not halt) will return expanded $\mathbf{L}^{\mathsf{ex}}$. For each successor gates using wid_i as inputs in the pre-determined order:
     • For a saved tuple (gb, output, $outputid$, wid_i, $1, \cdots$), let $\mathbf{L}^{\mathsf{ex}} = \mathbf{L}^o \| \mathbf{L}'$ where $|\mathbf{L}^o| = 1$. Save (ev, output, $outputid$, $\mathbf{L}^o$). Let $\mathbf{L}^{\mathsf{ex}} := \mathbf{L}'$.
     • For a saved tuple (gb, op = add/mult, $opid$, wid_i, $-$, $n_x, \cdots$), let $\mathbf{L}^{\mathsf{ex}} = \mathbf{L}^x \| \mathbf{L}'$ where $|\mathbf{L}^x| = n_x$. Save (ev, op, $opid$, le, $\mathbf{L}^x$). Let $\mathbf{L}^{\mathsf{ex}} := \mathbf{L}'$.
     • For a saved tuple (gb, op = add/mult, $opid$, $-$, wid_i, $-$, $n_y, \cdots$), let $\mathbf{L}^{\mathsf{ex}} = \mathbf{L}^y \| \mathbf{L}'$ where $|\mathbf{L}^y| = n_y$. Save (ev, op, $opid$, ri, $\mathbf{L}^y$). Let $\mathbf{L}^{\mathsf{ex}} := \mathbf{L}'$.
   - Addition/Multiplication gates: For an add/mult gate (op = add/mult, $opid$, wid_x, wid_y, wid_z), E fetches the tuples (ev, op, $opid$, le, $\mathbf{L}^x$) and (ev, op, $opid$, ri, $\mathbf{L}^y$). E evaluates the addition/multiplication gadget using $\mathbf{L}^x$ and $\mathbf{L}^y$ (see Figure 2) and obtains $\mathbf{L}$. E calls the sub-procedure Expand.Ev (op, $opid$, $\mathbf{L}$), which (if not halt) will return expanded $\mathbf{L}^{\mathsf{ex}}$. For each successor gates using wid_z as inputs in the pre-determined order, split $\mathbf{L}^{\mathsf{ex}}$ into correct positions using the similar procedure of input gates.

6. E sends the circuit's output: For the output gate (output, $outputid$, wid_o), E fetches the tuple (ev, output, $outputid$, res). If res is not in range $[-B, B]$ (over $\mathbb{Z}_{N^\varsigma}$), E outputs abort and halts permanently; otherwise, E sends res to G.

7. G and E output res (decoded to $\mathbb{Z}$).

(b) The third component

Fig. 6. The second and third components of our protocol Π

Lemma 4 (Correct Execution). *For every protocol execution between an adversary G^* and E, as defined in our full version Figs. 5, 6a and 6b, such that E outputs res (embedded into $\mathbb{Z}_{N^\varsigma}$), there exists a well defined $\widetilde{x}$ that correspond to the committed values in Step 4, and y that denote E's inputs, such that $res = C(\widetilde{x}, y)$ with overwhelming probability.*

Theorem 3 (Malicious G). *Let pp denote the public parameters for any circuit C defined over B-bounded integer computations. Then protocol Π specified in our full version and Figs. 5, 6a and 6b securely computes C (embedded within $\mathbb{Z}_{N^\varsigma}$) with 1-bit leakage in the presence of malicious G in the $\{\mathcal{F}_{\mathsf{VOLEc}}^{N,\varsigma}, \mathcal{F}_{\mathsf{aVOLE}}^{N,\varsigma}\}$-hybrid model, where the leakage predicate is defined by the wrapper function $\mathsf{Wrap}^{\mathsf{pp},C}$ specified in our full version.*

Theorem 4 (Semi-honest E). *Let pp denote that public parameters, for any circuit C defined over B-bounded integer computations and assume the DCR assumption. Then protocol Π specified in our full version Figs. 5, 6a and 6b securely computes C (embedded within $\mathbb{Z}_{N^\varsigma}$) in the presence of semi-honest E in the $\{\mathcal{F}_{\mathsf{VOLEc}}^{N,\varsigma}, \mathcal{F}_{\mathsf{aVOLE}}^{N,\varsigma}\}$-hybrid model.*

Acknowledgments. The first author was partially supported by the Algorand Centres of Excellence programme managed by Algorand Foundation. Any opinions, findings, and conclusions or recommendations expressed in this material are those of the author(s) and do not necessarily reflect the views of the Algorand Foundation and the United States-Israel Binational Science Foundation (BSF) through Grant No.@ 2020277. The second author was supported by Visa research award, Cisco research award, and NSF awards CNS-2246354, and CCF-2217070. The authors thank Yunmeng Chen and Srinivasan Raghuraman for useful discussions.

References

1. Applebaum, B., Ishai, Y., Kushilevitz, E.: Cryptography in NC⁰. In: 45th FOCS, pp. 166–175. IEEE Computer Society Press, Rome, Italy (2004). https://doi.org/10.1109/FOCS.2004.20

2. Applebaum, B., Ishai, Y., Kushilevitz, E.: How to garble arithmetic circuits. In: Ostrovsky, R. (ed.) 52nd FOCS, pp. 120–129. IEEE Computer Society Press, Palm Springs, CA, USA (2011). https://doi.org/10.1109/FOCS.2011.40

3. Ball, M., Li, H., Lin, H., Liu, T.: New ways to garble arithmetic circuits. In: Hazay, C., Stam, M. (eds.) EUROCRYPT 2023, Part II. LNCS, vol. 14005, pp. 3–34. Springer, Heidelberg, Germany, Lyon, France (2023).https://doi.org/10.1007/978-3-031-30617-4_1

4. Ball, M., Malkin, T., Rosulek, M.: Garbling gadgets for Boolean and arithmetic circuits. In: Weippl, E.R., Katzenbeisser, S., Kruegel, C., Myers, A.C., Halevi, S. (eds.) ACM CCS 2016. pp. 565–577. ACM Press, Vienna, Austria (2016). https://doi.org/10.1145/2976749.2978410

5. Baum, C., Braun, L., Munch-Hansen, A., Scholl, P.: MozZ_{2^k}arella: efficient vector-OLE and zero-knowledge proofs over Z_{2^k}. In: Dodis, Y., Shrimpton, T. (eds.) CRYPTO 2022, Part IV. LNCS, vol. 13510, pp. 329–358. Springer, Heidelberg, Germany, Santa Barbara, CA, USA (2022). https://doi.org/10.1007/978-3-031-15985-5_12

6. Baum, C., Malozemoff, A.J., Rosen, M.B., Scholl, P.: Mac'n'Cheese: zero-knowledge proofs for boolean and arithmetic circuits with nested disjunctions. In: Malkin, T., Peikert, C. (eds.) CRYPTO 2021. LNCS, vol. 12828, pp. 92–122. Springer, Cham (2021). https://doi.org/10.1007/978-3-030-84259-8_4

7. Beaver, D.: Multiparty protocols tolerating half faulty processors. In: Brassard, G. (ed.) CRYPTO 1989. LNCS, vol. 435, pp. 560–572. Springer, New York (1990). https://doi.org/10.1007/0-387-34805-0_49

8. Beaver, D.: Precomputing oblivious transfer. In: Coppersmith, D. (ed.) CRYPTO 1995. LNCS, vol. 963, pp. 97–109. Springer, Heidelberg (1995). https://doi.org/10.1007/3-540-44750-4_8

9. Bendlin, R., Damgård, I., Orlandi, C., Zakarias, S.: Semi-homomorphic encryption and multiparty computation. In: Paterson, K.G. (ed.) EUROCRYPT 2011. LNCS, vol. 6632, pp. 169–188. Springer, Heidelberg (2011). https://doi.org/10.1007/978-3-642-20465-4_11

10. Boyle, E., Couteau, G., Gilboa, N., Ishai, Y.: Compressing vector OLE. In: Lie, D., Mannan, M., Backes, M., Wang, X. (eds.) ACM CCS 2018. pp. 896–912. ACM Press, Toronto, ON, Canada (2018). https://doi.org/10.1145/3243734.3243868

11. Boyle, E., Couteau, G., Gilboa, N., Ishai, Y., Kohl, L., Scholl, P.: Efficient pseudorandom correlation generators from ring-LPN. In: Micciancio, D., Ristenpart, T. (eds.) CRYPTO 2020. LNCS, vol. 12171, pp. 387–416. Springer, Cham (2020). https://doi.org/10.1007/978-3-030-56880-1_14

12. Cui, H., Wang, X., Yang, K., Yu, Y.: Actively secure half-gates with minimum overhead under duplex networks. In: Hazay, C., Stam, M. (eds.) EUROCRYPT 2023, Part II. LNCS, vol. 14005, pp. 35–67. Springer, Heidelberg, Germany, Lyon, France (2023). https://doi.org/10.1007/978-3-031-30617-4_2

13. Damgård, I., Jurik, M.: A generalisation, a simplification and some applications of paillier's probabilistic public-key system. In: Kim, K. (ed.) PKC 2001. LNCS, vol. 1992, pp. 119–136. Springer, Heidelberg (2001). https://doi.org/10.1007/3-540-44586-2_9

14. Dittmer, S., Ishai, Y., Lu, S., Ostrovsky, R.: Authenticated garbling from simple correlations. In: Dodis, Y., Shrimpton, T. (eds.) CRYPTO 2022, Part IV. LNCS, vol. 13510, pp. 57–87. Springer, Heidelberg, Germany, Santa Barbara, CA, USA (2202). https://doi.org/10.1007/978-3-031-15985-5_3

15. Dittmer, S., Ishai, Y., Ostrovsky, R.: Line-point zero knowledge and its applications. In: 2nd Conference on Information-Theoretic Cryptography (2021)

16. Fiat, A., Shamir, A.: How to prove yourself: practical solutions to identification and signature problems. In: Odlyzko, A.M. (ed.) CRYPTO 1986. LNCS, vol. 263, pp. 186–194. Springer, Heidelberg (1987). https://doi.org/10.1007/3-540-47721-7_12

17. Frederiksen, T.K., Lindell, Y., Osheter, V., Pinkas, B.: Fast distributed RSA key generation for semi-honest and malicious adversaries. In: Shacham, H., Boldyreva, A. (eds.) CRYPTO 2018. LNCS, vol. 10992, pp. 331–361. Springer, Cham (2018). https://doi.org/10.1007/978-3-319-96881-0_12

18. Goldreich, O.: Foundations of cryptography: volume 2, basic applications. Cambridge University Press (2009)

19. Goldreich, O., Micali, S., Wigderson, A.: How to play any mental game or a completeness theorem for protocols with honest majority. In: Aho, A. (ed.) 19th ACM STOC, pp. 218–229. ACM Press, New York City, NY, USA (1987). https://doi.org/10.1145/28395.28420

20. Hazay, C., Ishai, Y., Venkitasubramaniam, M.: Actively secure garbled circuits with constant communication overhead in the plain model. In: Kalai, Y., Reyzin, L. (eds.) TCC 2017. LNCS, vol. 10678, pp. 3–39. Springer, Cham (2017). https://doi.org/10.1007/978-3-319-70503-3_1

21. Hazay, C., Yang, Y.: Toward malicious constant-rate 2PC via arithmetic garbling. Cryptology ePrint Archive, Paper 2024/283 (2024). https://eprint.iacr.org/2024/283

22. Huang, Y., Katz, J., Evans, D.: Quid-Pro-Quo-tocols: strengthening semi-honest protocols with dual execution. In: 2012 IEEE Symposium on Security and Privacy, pp. 272–284. IEEE Computer Society Press, San Francisco, CA, USA (2012). https://doi.org/10.1109/SP.2012.43

23. Huang, Y., Katz, J., Evans, D.: Efficient secure two-party computation using symmetric cut-and-choose. In: Canetti, R., Garay, J.A. (eds.) CRYPTO 2013. LNCS, vol. 8043, pp. 18–35. Springer, Heidelberg (2013). https://doi.org/10.1007/978-3-642-40084-1_2

24. Ishai, Y., Kushilevitz, E., Ostrovsky, R., Prabhakaran, M., Sahai, A.: Efficient non-interactive secure computation. In: Paterson, K.G. (ed.) EUROCRYPT 2011. LNCS, vol. 6632, pp. 406–425. Springer, Heidelberg (2011). https://doi.org/10.1007/978-3-642-20465-4_23

25. Ishai, Y., Wee, H.: Partial garbling schemes and their applications. In: Esparza, J., Fraigniaud, P., Husfeldt, T., Koutsoupias, E. (eds.) ICALP 2014. LNCS, vol. 8572, pp. 650–662. Springer, Heidelberg (2014). https://doi.org/10.1007/978-3-662-43948-7_54

26. Kolesnikov, V., Mohassel, P., Riva, B., Rosulek, M.: Richer efficiency/security trade-offs in 2PC. In: Dodis, Y., Nielsen, J.B. (eds.) TCC 2015. LNCS, vol. 9014, pp. 229–259. Springer, Heidelberg (2015). https://doi.org/10.1007/978-3-662-46494-6_11

27. Kolesnikov, V., Schneider, T.: Improved garbled circuit: free XOR gates and applications. In: Aceto, L., Damgård, I., Goldberg, L.A., Halldórsson, M.M., Ingólfsdóttir, A., Walukiewicz, I. (eds.) ICALP 2008. LNCS, vol. 5126, pp. 486–498. Springer, Heidelberg (2008). https://doi.org/10.1007/978-3-540-70583-3_40

28. Lindell, Y.: Fast cut-and-choose-based protocols for malicious and covert adversaries. J. Cryptol. 29(2), 456–490 (2016). https://doi.org/10.1007/s00145-015-9198-0

29. Lindell, Y., Pinkas, B.: An efficient protocol for secure two-party computation in the presence of malicious adversaries. In: Naor, M. (ed.) EUROCRYPT 2007. LNCS, vol. 4515, pp. 52–78. Springer, Heidelberg (2007). https://doi.org/10.1007/978-3-540-72540-4_4

30. Lindell, Y., Pinkas, B.: A proof of security of Yao's protocol for two-party computation. J. Cryptol. 22(2), 161–188 (2009). https://doi.org/10.1007/s00145-008-9036-8

31. Liu, H., Wang, X., Yang, K., Yu, Y.: The hardness of LPN over any integer ring and field for PCG applications. Cryptology ePrint Archive, Report 2022/712 (2022). https://eprint.iacr.org/2022/712

32. Mohassel, P., Franklin, M.: Efficiency tradeoffs for malicious two-party computation. In: Yung, M., Dodis, Y., Kiayias, A., Malkin, T. (eds.) PKC 2006. LNCS, vol. 3958, pp. 458–473. Springer, Heidelberg (2006). https://doi.org/10.1007/11745853_30

33. Naor, M., Pinkas, B., Sumner, R.: Privacy preserving auctions and mechanism design. In: Proceedings of the 1st ACM Conference on Electronic Commerce, pp. 129–139 (1999)

34. Nielsen, J.B., Nordholt, P.S., Orlandi, C., Burra, S.S.: A new approach to practical active-secure two-party computation. In: Safavi-Naini, R., Canetti, R. (eds.) CRYPTO 2012. LNCS, vol. 7417, pp. 681–700. Springer, Heidelberg (2012). https://doi.org/10.1007/978-3-642-32009-5_40

35. Paillier, P.: Public-key cryptosystems based on composite degree Residuosity classes. In: Stern, J. (ed.) EUROCRYPT 1999. LNCS, vol. 1592, pp. 223–238. Springer, Heidelberg (1999). https://doi.org/10.1007/3-540-48910-X_16

36. Rindal, P., Rosulek, M.: Faster malicious 2-party secure computation with online/offline dual execution. In: Holz, T., Savage, S. (eds.) USENIX Security 2016, pp. 297–314. USENIX Association, Austin, TX, USA (2016)

37. Rosulek, M., Roy, L.: Three halves make a whole? Beating the half-gates lower bound for garbled circuits. In: Malkin, T., Peikert, C. (eds.) CRYPTO 2021. LNCS, vol. 12825, pp. 94–124. Springer, Cham (2021). https://doi.org/10.1007/978-3-030-84242-0_5

38. Schnorr, C.P.: Efficient identification and signatures for smart cards. In: Brassard, G. (ed.) CRYPTO 1989. LNCS, vol. 435, pp. 239–252. Springer, New York (1990). https://doi.org/10.1007/0-387-34805-0_22

39. Wang, X., Ranellucci, S., Katz, J.: Authenticated garbling and efficient maliciously secure two-party computation. In: Thuraisingham, B.M., Evans, D., Malkin, T., Xu, D. (eds.) ACM CCS 2017, pp. 21–37. ACM Press, Dallas, TX, USA (2017). https://doi.org/10.1145/3133956.3134053

40. Weng, C., Yang, K., Katz, J., Wang, X.: Wolverine: fast, scalable, and communication-efficient zero-knowledge proofs for Boolean and arithmetic circuits. In: 2021 IEEE Symposium on Security and Privacy, pp. 1074–1091. IEEE Computer Society Press, San Francisco, CA, USA (2021). https://doi.org/10.1109/SP40001.2021.00056

41. Yao, A.C.C.: How to generate and exchange secrets (extended abstract). In: 27th FOCS, pp. 162–167. IEEE Computer Society Press, Toronto, Ontario, Canada (1986). https://doi.org/10.1109/SFCS.1986.25

42. Zahur, S., Rosulek, M., Evans, D.: Two halves make a whole. In: Oswald, E., Fischlin, M. (eds.) EUROCRYPT 2015. LNCS, vol. 9057, pp. 220–250. Springer, Heidelberg (2015). https://doi.org/10.1007/978-3-662-46803-6_8

Closing the Efficiency Gap Between Synchronous and Network-Agnostic Consensus

Giovanni Deligios$^{(\boxtimes)}$ and Mose Mizrahi Erbes$^{(\boxtimes)}$

ETH Zurich, Zürich, Switzerland
{gdeligios,mmizrahi}@ethz.ch

Abstract. In the consensus problem, n parties want to agree on a common value, even if some of them are corrupt and arbitrarily misbehave. If the parties have a common input m, then they must agree on m.

Protocols solving consensus assume either a *synchronous* communication network, where messages are delivered within a known time, or an *asynchronous* network with arbitrary delays. Asynchronous protocols only tolerate $t_a < n/3$ corrupt parties. Synchronous ones can tolerate $t_s < n/2$ corruptions with setup, but their security completely breaks down if the synchrony assumptions are violated.

Network-agnostic consensus protocols, as introduced by Blum, Katz, and Loss [TCC'19], are secure regardless of network conditions, tolerating up to t_s corruptions with synchrony and t_a without, under provably optimal assumptions $t_a \leq t_s$ and $2t_s + t_a < n$. Despite efforts to improve their efficiency, all known network-agnostic protocols fall short of the asymptotic complexity of state-of-the-art purely synchronous protocols.

In this work, we introduce a novel technique to compile *any* synchronous and *any* asynchronous consensus protocols into a network-agnostic one. This process only incurs a small constant number of overhead rounds, so that the compiled protocol matches the optimal round complexity for synchronous protocols. Our compiler also preserves under a variety of assumptions the asymptotic communication complexity of state-of-the-art synchronous and asynchronous protocols. Hence, it closes the current efficiency gap between synchronous and network-agnostic consensus.

As a plus, our protocols support ℓ-bit inputs, and can be extended to achieve communication complexity $\mathcal{O}(n^2\kappa + \ell n)$ under the assumptions for which this is known to be possible for purely synchronous protocols.

1 Introduction

1.1 Motivation

Consensus, or byzantine agreement, is a fundamental problem in distributed computing and cryptography. A consensus protocol enables n parties with inputs

---

A full version of this paper is available at https://eprint.iacr.org/2024/317.

© International Association for Cryptologic Research 2024
M. Joye and G. Leander (Eds.): EUROCRYPT 2024, LNCS 14655, pp. 432–461, 2024.
https://doi.org/10.1007/978-3-031-58740-5_15

to agree on a common output by communicating via bilateral channels, even when some parties maliciously deviate from the protocol. Pre-agreement among honest parties on a common input must be preserved by a consensus protocol.

The problem has a decades-long research history [7,9,12,26] and consensus protocols serve as building blocks for more complex tasks, such as distributed key generation and multi-party computation. In the last decade, the emergence of blockchain applications [25,31] sparked renewed interest in the problem, and the number of consensus protocols implemented and deployed is now higher than ever. Interestingly, the security of deployed protocols relies on assumptions on the underlying communication network which are, in practice, not always satisfied, leading to serious security failures [22].

The two dominant communication abstractions are known as the *synchronous* model and the *asynchronous* model. In the synchronous model, messages are delivered within some publicly known time Δ after being sent, and parties have access to a global clock. This is in contrast to the asynchronous setting, where messages are delivered with arbitrary (finite) delays decided by an adversary, and parties' local clocks need not be synchronized.

Protocol design is significantly simpler in the synchronous model: communication can proceed in rounds where each party waits for messages from *all* other parties before computing their next message. Consensus protocols in this model can with setup achieve statistical or cryptographic security against less than $\frac{n}{2}$ malicious parties, but their security completely breaks down if even a *single* message is dropped or delayed.

The unpredictability of the asynchronous model requires a more involved protocol design, as one cannot differentiate between a corrupt party not sending a message and an honest party whose message is delayed. Given the minimal assumptions of this model, the achievable security guarantees are unsurprisingly weaker: asynchronous consensus protocols can tolerate less than $\frac{n}{3}$ malicious parties. On the positive side, in the real world, asynchronous protocols are resilient to very adverse network conditions.

Starting with [5], a recent line of works tries to marry the better resiliency of synchronous protocols with the tolerance of asynchronous protocols to adverse network conditions. The goal is to design *network-agnostic* protocols in which parties are unaware of the network conditions at execution time. If synchrony is satisfied throughout the execution, then the protocol should be secure if up to a threshold t_s of parties misbehave. However, even if some of the synchrony assumptions are violated during the execution, the protocol should still tolerate a lower threshold t_a of corruptions.

In this setting, consensus (with setup) is possible if and only if $t_a \leq t_s$ and $2t_s + t_a < n$ [5]. Observe that if the threshold t_a is set to 0, one has the optimal resilience of synchronous consensus protocols. Furthermore, even if the network is asynchronous, the protocol still achieves security when all parties honestly follow it. This is not true for purely synchronous protocols, where an adversary who controls the network can typically disrupt the execution of a protocol by simply delaying a *single* message.

Currently, known network-agnostic protocols for consensus and multi-party computation mostly follow some variation of the following approach: 1) Identify a synchronous and an asynchronous protocol for the task at hand, 2) Enhance both so that the synchronous protocol provides *some* weak guarantees even when the network is not synchronous and the asynchronous protocol provides *some* stronger guarantees (than it normally would) if synchrony holds, and finally 3) Run some clever combination of the two enhanced protocols to obtain a network-agnostic protocol with full security.

Despite proving quite effective, this design approach has two major downsides. First, if one wishes to replace the synchronous or asynchronous components with different protocols (because more efficient constructions are discovered, or because for a specific application the cryptographic primitives or setup assumptions required are not available), then the enhancement step 2) above must be carried out from scratch. This step is typically the most technically involved, and even if successful, new security proofs are required. Second, solving the design challenges of step 2) typically incurs a large complexity overhead.

These observations naturally lead to the following question:

Is there a complexity-preserving way to combine in a black-box fashion synchronous and asynchronous consensus protocols into a network-agnostic protocol?

For round complexity, we answer this question affirmatively with a compiler for network-agnostic consensus which makes only a single *black-box* use of *any* synchronous and asynchronous consensus protocols. The compiler only incurs a *constant* overhead in the number of rounds, and it does *not* run the asynchronous protocol if the network happens to be synchronous. Hence, we close up to a constant number of rounds any round complexity gap between purely synchronous and network-agnostic consensus protocols, including the asymptotic gap that remained open between [10, 19].

Our construction is the most efficient known, and it preserves the asymptomatic communication complexity of the best-known synchronous and asynchronous protocols when they are used in the compiler. As a plus, it supports long inputs natively and more efficiently than previous network-agnostic protocols, despite only invoking consensus protocols for single-bit inputs. For security we rely on the (provably necessary) trade-off $2t_s + t_a < n$ and the existence of unforgeable signatures, which can be instantiated from any setup necessary for honest majority synchronous consensus.

There is no known result or heuristic evidence implying that network-agnostic protocols should be inherently less efficient than purely synchronous protocols *for the same task*, assuming network synchrony holds. Recent work [3] shows that network-agnostic distributed key generation incurs no such loss. Our work goes in the same direction, and shows that no inherent efficiency loss is incurred for the network-agnostic security of consensus.

1.2   Technical Overview

Starting Point. A consensus protocol is run among n parties: each party holds an input m in some alphabet $\mathcal{M}$. A consensus protocol achieves *consistency* if all honest parties (parties following the prescribed protocol) output the same value. It achieves *validity* if whenever all honest parties have the same input m, they all output m (informally, we say that pre-agreement is preserved).

If a protocol achieves a property, for example consistency, only if the assumptions of the synchronous model are satisfied, we say that it achieves *synchronous consistency*. We say it simply achieves *consistency* if it achieves consistency regardless of the assumptions on the network (in particular, in the weakest model possible, the asynchronous model). Similarly, we say it achieves *t-consistency* if consistency holds only if at most t parties deviate from the protocol.

Protocols with synchronous t_s-validity and synchronous t_s-consistency (that we denote by SBA) exist for all $t_s < \frac{n}{2}$ assuming setup [12], while consensus protocols with t_a-validity and t_a-consistency *even in asynchronous networks* (which we denote by ABA) only exist for $t_a < \frac{n}{3}$, even with setup [9].

Blum, Katz, and Loss [5] first proposed a way to adapt such SBA and ABA protocols to obtain a network-agnostic protocol. Assuming $2t_s + t_a < n$ (which they prove to be necessary) they obtain a protocol HBA with the following properties 1) synchronous t_s-validity 2) t_a-validity 3) synchronous t_s-consistency, and 4) t_a-consistency.

The paradigm they use has been adopted in later works [3,10]. The idea is to run SBA and ABA in succession. First, the input to HBA is used as input to SBA, and then the output from SBA as input to ABA. Finally, the output from ABA is taken to be the output from HBA. However, without modifications, this simple procedure does not provide the wanted guarantees. The first problem is that SBA provides no security guarantees whatsoever if the network is not synchronous. In particular, it does not preserve pre-agreement between honest parties; so, t_a-validity does not hold in the overall protocol HBA. The second problem is that when the network is synchronous but $t_s > t_a$, protocol ABA provides no security guarantees. This means that synchronous t_s-validity and synchronous t_s-consistency do not hold for HBA.

Their solution is clever. Consider the following weaker notion of validity, which we call *fallback validity*: if all honest parties have the same input $m \in \mathcal{M}$, then they all output m or abort the protocol. Assume the existence of a protocol SBA* which, in addition to the properties of SBA, achieves t_a-fallback validity.

Now, run in succession SBA* and ABA, but any party who aborts in SBA* uses their original input as input to ABA. Now, even if the network is asynchronous, pre-agreement on an input m among honest parties is preserved: thanks to t_a-fallback validity, all parties output m from SBA* or abort. Either way, they all input m to ABA, and pre-agreement is preserved by the t_a-validity of ABA.

To fix the second problem, assume the existence of a protocol ABA* which, in addition to the properties of ABA achieves synchronous t_s-validity,[1] and replace ABA with ABA* in HBA. Observe that, if the network is synchronous, by the synchronous t_s-consistency of SBA*, honest parties are always in pre-agreement before executing ABA* (either on the pre-agreed upon input, or on some arbitrary value if no pre-agreement was present before executing SBA*). Therefore, the synchronous t_s-validity of ABA* suffices for the security of HBA.

Constructing protocols SBA* and ABA* with the required properties is a significant design challenge which fundamentally exploits the assumption $2t_s + t_a < n$. In [5], Dolev-Strong broadcast [12] and the asynchronous consensus protocol from [28] are used as starting points. The resulting network-agnostic protocol requires setup for unique threshold signatures and runs in $\mathcal{O}(n)$ rounds when the network is synchronous. In [10], Deligios and Hirt design a new SBA* by modifying the synchronous protocol from [14]. Again, unique threshold signatures are needed, but the new protocol runs in a constant (in n) number of rounds when the network is synchronous, with an error probability $\mathcal{O}(c^{-r})$ in r rounds for some constant $c > 1$. At the time, this matched the asymptotic round complexity of the most efficient purely-synchronous protocols known. However, more recently, [19] showed an SBA protocol which under appropriate assumptions can achieve an error probability of $\mathcal{O}((c \cdot r)^{-r})$ in r rounds for some constant $c > 0$, which has long been known to be optimal [23], thus reopening the gap between synchronous and network-agnostic protocols. This gap remained, until now, open.

Closing the Round-Efficiency Gap. Design-wise, it is clearly sub-optimal to repeat the process of enhancing SBA with t_a-validity and rewriting security proofs to obtain a corresponding SBA* whenever *any new synchronous protocol* is published. To make matters worse, certain SBA protocols (including [19]) seem to be inherently less friendly to such adaptations.

For this reason, we propose a new enhancing technique to obtain a protocol with the properties required from SBA* that invokes *any* SBA protocol in a black-box fashion, and only introduces a constant overhead in the number of rounds required. We stress that this construction can be instantiated with any SBA protocol, including [19]. We begin by adding t_a-fallback validity to a weaker agreement primitive (a flavor of *graded consensus*), whose security only relies on an abstract form of digital signatures (which can also be instantiated with information theoretic security [34]). Our graded-consensus intuitively provides the validity guarantees required from SBA* when synchrony does not hold, so that the role of the underlying SBA is reduced to providing full agreement when the network is synchronous. This allows us to use SBA in a black-box way.

However, plugging the SBA from [19] into our construction for SBA* does not suffice: to achieve network-agnostic security, protocol HBA requires running both the SBA* and the ABA* sub-protocols regardless of the network conditions. Unfortunately, a classical lower bound shows that in r rounds, an asynchronous

---

[1] The protocol ABA* should also have certain termination properties if the network is synchronous, but such details are not needed to appreciate this technical overview.

consensus protocol can only achieve consistency and validity with error probability $\mathcal{O}(c^{-r})$ for some constant $c > 1$ [2]. This means that even running an *optimal* ABA* protocol when the network is synchronous would increase the error of the overall protocol from $\mathcal{O}((c \cdot r)^{-r})$ to $\mathcal{O}(c^{-r})$ in r rounds.

To fix this, we propose a new way to enhance *any* ABA protocol to fulfill the properties of ABA* that only requires black-box access to the underlying ABA protocol. We observe that when the network is synchronous, the SBA* protocol guarantees that honest parties are always in pre-agreement upon entering the protocol ABA*. We exploit this by designing a termination procedure that, when the network is synchronous, is triggered within a small constant number of rounds, causing ABA* to terminate *without* running the underlying ABA. This means that the underlying ABA protocol is only run when the network is asynchronous, which in turn allows us to use it in a black-box way.

Multi-valued Inputs. Our protocols actually support inputs from any alphabet $\mathcal{M}$. When $\mathcal{M} = \{0,1\}$, validity guarantees that the common output of honest parties is the input of at least one honest party. For large input spaces, this desirable property is unattainable unless $t \cdot |\mathcal{M}| < n$. Instead, it is common to only require that the common output is either the input of some honest party or a special symbol $\perp$: this property is called intrusion tolerance. Since it requires no extra work, our consensus protocols guarantee that the common output is the input of at least δn honest parties whenever $2t_s + t_a \leq (1 - \delta)n$ and δn is a positive integer. This is without loss of generality, as the requirement that t_a, t_s and n are integers allows us to simply take δn to be $n - 2t_s - t_a$.

Overview of our Construction. Our novel SBA* construction has two components: the first is *any* SBA protocol, and the second is a weaker agreement primitive we call SGC^2 (2-graded consensus), which provides the network-agnostic security guarantees. We build increasingly strong agreement primitives towards SGC^2. All these primitives achieve the validity and fallback validity properties, but provide increasingly strong consistency guarantees. SGC^2 is sufficiently strong so that combining it with SBA one finally obtains full security. We then mimic this approach for our ABA* protocol.

Protocol SWC. We begin with SWC (synchronous weak consensus). The protocol is simple: in the first round parties sends their signed inputs (with some signature scheme) to everyone. Any party receiving less than $n - t_s$ messages is *sure* that the network is asynchronous (or they would have received messages from all honest parties) and it simply aborts the protocol. Otherwise, in the second round, if a party has received at least $t_s + \delta n$ copies of the same validly signed value m from different parties, it sets its tentative output to m, combines the signatures on m into a *certificate*, and sends the certificate to everyone in an effort to prevent inconsistencies. Upon seeing a certificate on a value different from its tentative output, a party changes its output to $\perp$. In a synchronous network the protocol achieves t_s-validity and a weaker notion of t_s-consistency: there is some $m \in \mathcal{M}$ such that each honest party outputs either m or $\perp$, because before outputting some $m \in \mathcal{M}$, a party sends a certificate on m to everyone, preventing other parties from outputting any $m' \in \mathcal{M} \setminus \{m\}$. Notice that the protocol also achieves t_a-fallback validity: informally, if the network is asynchronous but honest parties have pre-agreement on m, an honest party who does not abort in the first round has received at least $n - t_s$ validly signed messages, and of these, at most t_a come from corrupted parties. Therefore, the assumption $2t_s + t_a \leq (1 - \delta)n$ guarantees that at least $n - t_s - t_a \geq t_s + \delta n$ of the signed inputs hail from honest parties, who all sign the input m.

Protocol SProp. The next building block for SGC^2 is the protocol SProp (synchronous proposal). In a proposal protocol, honest parties have inputs in some common set $S = \{x, \perp\} \subseteq \mathcal{M}^\perp = \mathcal{M} \cup \{\perp\}$, and they output either x, $\perp$, or the set $\{x, \perp\}$. The protocol description and the security properties achieved are similar to SWC: pre-agreement on an input should be preserved, and it should not happen that an honest party outputs x while another outputs $\perp$. However, it is allowed that an honest party outputs x or $\perp$ while another outputs $\{x, \perp\}$. Indeed, the mapping $(x, \{x, \perp\}, \perp) \longrightarrow (0, \perp, 1)$ *actually* yields a weak-consensus protocol for binary inputs. The crucial difference which we exploit is that for proposal, the set $S = \{x, \perp\}$ doesn't have to be known a priori: honest parties with the input $\perp$ do not need to know what x is.

Protocols SGC^1 and SGC^2. Protocols SGC^1 and SGC^2 are different flavors of a primitive called graded consensus. They invoke SWC and SProp as sub-protocols. In graded consensus, each party has an input $x \in \mathcal{M}^\perp$ and outputs a value $y \in \mathcal{M}^\perp$, together with a grade $g \in [0, k]$. Intuitively, the grade measures "how certain" a party is of its output. The grades of honest parties must differ by *at most* 1, and if an honest party has a non-zero grade, then all honest parties must have the same value y (graded consistency). In addition, if the honest parties are in pre-agreement on a value y, then all honest parties must output y with the *maximum grade* $g = k$ (graded validity). The higher k is, the harder it is to achieve these properties.

Protocol SGC^1 has a maximum grade $k = 1$. First, the parties run an instance of SWC on their inputs. If their outputs here matches their inputs, they repeat their inputs to an instance of SProp. Otherwise, they input $\perp$ to SProp. Finally, the mapping $(m, \{m, \perp\}, \perp) \longrightarrow ((m, 1), (m, 0), (\perp, 0))$ is applied to the SProp outputs. Protocol SWC guarantees that the inputs of honest parties are valid inputs for SProp, and then SProp provides graded consistency. Indeed, if a party outputs a value x with grade 1, this means that it output x from SProp, and no honest party has output $\perp$ from SProp. This shows all honest parties output x with grade 1 or 0. Other properties, including t_a-fallback validity, are inherited from the sub-protocols in a straightforward way.

Protocol SGC^2 has a maximum grade $k = 2$. The protocol is similar to SGC^1, but invokes SGC^1 instead of SWC and SWC instead of SProp. The output *value* of SGC^2 is simply taken to be the output value from SGC^1, but an instance of SWC is run on the output *grades* from SGC^1 in order to increase k from 1 to 2 via the mapping $(0, \perp, 1) \longrightarrow (0, 1, 2)$ on the outputs of SWC. The weak consistency of SWC guarantees that the grades of honest parties differ by at most by 1, and the validity of SWC guarantees that non-zero SGC^2 grades only occur if some honest parties obtained the grade 1 from SGC^1, implying agreement on the output values.[2]

***Protocol* SBA*.** We combine SGC^2 together with any fixed-round synchronous binary consensus protocol SBA to obtain our enhanced synchronous consensus protocol SBA*. The construction is simple. First, the parties run SGC^2 on their inputs, and then they run SBA to decide whether agreement has been reached, inputting 1 to SBA if they have non-zero grades. The parties with the grade 2 just ignore SBA and output their SGC^2 output values. From this follows validity and fallback validity. The remaining parties use SBA for consistency. If SBA outputs 1, then they output their SGC^2 output values; otherwise, they output $\bot$. For synchronous consistency, there are three scenarios to consider. If some party has the grade 2, then by graded consistency, every party has the grades 2 or 1, and therefore, by validity, SBA outputs 1, leading to everyone outputting the common SGC^2 output value. If every party has the grade 0, then by validity SBA outputs 0, and so everyone outputs $\bot$. Finally, if some parties have the grade 1 while others the grade 0, then either SBA outputs 1 and everyone outputs the common SGC^2 output value, or SBA outputs 0 and everyone outputs $\bot$.

***Protocol* AProp.** Our AProp (asynchronous proposal) protocol is an adaption of $\Pi_{\mathsf{prop}}^{t_s}$ from [5]. For simplicity, here we only consider the case $\delta n = 1$; if $\delta n > 1$, some care must be taken to achieve $(t_s, \delta n)$-intrusion tolerance. As in SProp, the honest parties have inputs in a set $S = \{x, \bot\} \in \mathcal{M}^\bot$. They start by simply sending their inputs to everyone (AProp does not need signatures). If a party receives an input v from $t_s + 1$ parties, then it learns that v is the input of an honest party, and therefore sends the input v to everyone, even if v is not its own input. If a party P_i receives an input v from $n - t_s$ parties, then it adds v to a set V_i. Upon adding a first value v to V_i, party P_i *proposes* to everyone that they should output v, and upon adding a second value to V_i, party P_i outputs $V_i = S$. Alternatively, a party will output v upon receiving from $n - t_s$ parties proposals to output v. If everyone has a common input v, then v will be the unique value everyone will add to V_i; therefore, everyone will propose and output v. A standard quorum-intersection argument on proposals shows t_a-consistency. The trickiest property is t_a-liveness, meaning that all parties obtain output. Since $n - t_a > 2t_s$, there exists an input held by at least $t_s + 1$ parties. Furthermore, if $t_s + 1$ parties send everyone an input v, then every party P_i sends everyone the input v and adds v to V_i; thus, there exists an input that every party P_i adds to V_i. Finally, if some P_i adds v to V_i, then at least $n - t_s - t_a \geq t_s + 1$ parties must have sent everyone the input v, meaning that every P_j adds v to V_j. Therefore, either every party P_i adds both x and $\bot$ to V_i and can output $\{x, \bot\}$, or there is a unique v which every party P_i adds to V_i, proposes, and outputs. Protocol AProp is non-terminating; it is designed to be run forever. Termination is guaranteed by the outer protocol ABA*.

---

[2] Grades 0 and 1 suffice for SBA* with binary inputs. Expanding the grade range is only necessary for multi-valued inputs, but incurs no asymptotic round or communication complexity overhead, which is why we do not consider the cases separately.

Protocol AWC. The asynchronous weak consensus protocol AWC is the counterpart of SWC. In theory, AProp can be used as a weak-consensus protocol for binary inputs via the mapping $(x, \{x, \bot\}, \bot) \longrightarrow (0, \bot, 1)$. This provides a simple way to obtain weak consensus on ℓ-bit messages by simply running ℓ parallel instances of AProp, one instance per bit. Then, any honest party that obtained $\bot$ from any instance would output $\bot$, and any honest party that obtained bits from all instances would output the concatenation of the bits. This design would increase message complexity by a multiplicative ℓ-factor, and the messages would need $(\log \ell)$-bit tags that indicate which AProp instance they belong to. To keep the complexity low, we parallelize the AProp instances in a more refined way, by batching/combining messages of different instances.

Protocols AGC^1 ***and*** AGC^2. These graded consensus protocols are simple message-driven adaptations of their synchronous counterparts SGC^1 and SGC^2. They invoke AWC and AProp as sub-protocols rather than SWC and SProp.

Protocol ABA*. Our asynchronous consensus protocol with t_s-validity ABA* combines AGC^2 and *any* asynchronous binary consensus protocol ABA secure against t_a corruptions. The composition is similar to that in SBA*, but since we can no longer rely on having a fixed running time, we need to rethink termination. We avoid the termination technique of sending certificates on tentative outputs (as done in some previous work [3,5,10]), and instead opt for an approach similar to Bracha's classical protocol from [7]. This keeps the communication complexity quadratic rather than cubic, and makes ABA* a signature-free reduction of asynchronous multi-valued consensus to binary consensus [30]. To keep the communication complexity low, we ensure that the honest parties do not send ABA messages when the network is synchronous. We do so by requiring that when the network is synchronous, the honest parties know a common input $m \in \mathcal{M}$ by some publicly known time $r_s \cdot \Delta$, which triggers the termination rules and guarantees the termination of ABA* within a few additional rounds, by some publicly known time T. Before local time T, honest parties do not send ABA messages. Hence they terminate without ever sending ABA messages if the network is synchronous.

Protocol HBA. We obtain HBA by composing SBA* and ABA* as described previously. The t_a-fallback validity of SBA* and the synchronous t_s-validity (with termination) of ABA* make the composition sound.

1.3   Contributions

Theorem 1. *Let* SBA *be any synchronous consensus protocol for binary inputs achieving error probability ϵ in k rounds, and* ABA *be any asynchronous consensus protocol for binary inputs. Under the provably optimal assumptions $2t_s + t_a < n$ and $t_a \leq t_s$, there exists a network-agnostic consensus protocol* HBA *for any inputs which invokes* SBA *and* ABA *in a black-box way and that, when the network is synchronous, achieves error probability ϵ in $k + 13$ rounds.*

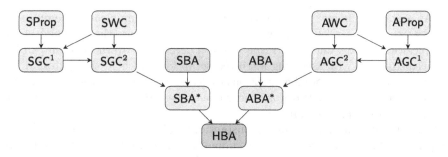

Fig. 1. An overview of how sub-protocols are composed for HBA.

Theorem 1 reduces the synchronous round complexity of network-agnostic consensus protocols to the round complexity of purely synchronous consensus protocols, up to a small additive constant. Concretely, HBA can take full advantage of a round-optimal λ-round SBA with an error probability decreasing superexponentially with λ [19], improving over the state-of-the-art [10] (in which the error decreases exponentially) and finally matching the known lower bound for purely synchronous protocols [23]. Note that to achieve consensus for honest-majority when the network is synchronous, some sort of setup is *provably* necessary [26]. Our protocol also needs setup. Concretely, it can be instantiated from a variety of setup assumptions such as threshold signatures, bulletin-PKI or even correlated randomness for information theoretic pseudo-signatures.

Below, we compare the communication complexity (in terms of bits) of our construction with that of previous network-agnostic protocols, when we use the most efficient SBA and ABA protocols at hand. We denote with κ a computational security parameter and with ε a positive constant. Since [3] only has an ABA* component, we pair it with our SBA*. For fairness, we consider variants of previous protocols optimized to take full advantage of threshold signatures.

Table 1. Communication complexities of previous network-agnostic consensus protocols and ours, under assumptions that have been considered for network-agnostic consensus.

Assumptions Protocols	Bulletin-PKI	Bulletin-PKI & $2t_s \leq (1-\varepsilon)n$	Threshold Signatures
Blum, Katz, Loss [5]	—	—	$\mathcal{O}(n^4\kappa)$ (Bit Consensus)
Deligios, Hirt, Liu-Zhang [10]	—	—	$\mathcal{O}(n^2\kappa)$ (Bit Consensus)
Bacho, Collins, Liu-Zhang, Loss [3]	$\mathcal{O}(n^3\kappa + \ell n^3)$	$\mathcal{O}(n^3\kappa + \ell n^3)$	$\mathcal{O}(n^2\kappa + \ell n^3)$
Our Work	$\mathcal{O}(n^3\kappa + \ell n^2)$	$\mathcal{O}(n^2\kappa + \ell n^2)$ if network synchronous, else $\mathcal{O}(n^3\kappa + \ell n^2)$	$\mathcal{O}(n^2\kappa + \ell n^2)$

As a starting point, our protocol HBA has the communication complexity $\mathcal{O}(n^3\kappa + \ell n^2 + \mathsf{CC}_{\mathsf{SBA}} + \mathsf{CC}_{\mathsf{ABA}})$, where $\mathsf{CC}_{\mathsf{SBA}}$ and $\mathsf{CC}_{\mathsf{ABA}}$ are the communication complexities of SBA and ABA respectively. The $\mathcal{O}(n^3\kappa)$ overhead term can be reduced to $\mathcal{O}(n^2\kappa)$ by assuming a trusted setup for threshold signatures, or by slightly lowering the allowed corruptions to $2t_s \leq (1-\varepsilon)n$ for a positive constant ε. Furthermore, if the network is synchronous, then ABA messages are not sent and the term $\mathsf{CC}_{\mathsf{ABA}}$ is eliminated.

To minimize communication, we instantiate SBA with the protocol from [27] which in its base form achieves the communication complexity $\mathcal{O}(n^3\kappa)$, but can achieve the complexity $\mathcal{O}(n^2\kappa)$ with threshold signatures if they are available, or with expander graphs if $2t_s \leq (1-\varepsilon)n$. As for ABA, we instantiate it with the state-of-the-art cubic protocol from [18],[3] or, if setup for unique threshold signatures is available, with [28] using the coin protocol[4] from [8] to achieve quadratic complexity. When these instantiations are used, the asymptotic communication complexity of HBA for binary inputs matches that the complexity of its state-of-the-art[5] SBA component if the network is synchronous, and the complexity of its its state-of-the-art ABA component otherwise.

If bulletin-PKI is available and $2t_s \leq (1-\varepsilon)n$, then we achieve the complexity $O(n^2\kappa + \ell n^2)$ with expander graphs. We do so with 3-round variants of SWC and SProp, inspired by the graded consensus protocol in [27]. Due to a lack of space, we only present these variants in the full version.

When considering ℓ-bit inputs, the $\mathcal{O}(\ell n^2)$ term is already a strict improvement over the $\mathcal{O}(\ell n^3)$ term from [3] and over any straightforward adaptation of known protocols. Using techniques from the literature on extension protocols together with some novel ideas, it is possible to bring this all the way down to $\mathcal{O}(\ell n)$, which is the best possible even for purely synchronous protocols [17]. We discuss network-agnostic consensus extension protocols later in more detail, and we present such extension protocols in the full version.

The efficiency improvements are facilitated by our new black-box construction of HBA which allows us to instantiate the sub-protocols SBA and ABA with the most efficient known protocols from the literature. We consider this new approach to be a contribution of independent interest, and hope that analogous constructions will unlock similar efficiency gains for other network-agnostic distributed tasks.

1.4 Related Work

Network-agnostic protocols were first considered by Blum, Katz and Loss [5]; in this work, the authors showed the first network-agnostic consensus protocol. The first network-agnostic full multi-party computation protocol (MPC)

---

[3] The ABA in [18] is secure statically, or adaptively with a one-time CRS.

[4] This coin protocol is secure in the random oracle model.

[5] An SBA protocol concurrent with our work uses threshold signatures to achieve $\mathcal{O}(nf\kappa)$ complexity, where $f \leq t_s \leq \frac{(1-\varepsilon)n}{2}$ is the actual number of malicious parties [13]. Our work only considers the worst case $f = t_s$.

was shown in [6]. There has since been a significant interest in the field. Other network-agnostic MPC protocols include [1,11]. Network-agnostic approximate agreement has been investigated in [20,21]. Most related to our work are [10], which contains an efficient network-agnostic consensus protocol which at the time matched the round complexity of the best known synchronous protocols, and [3], that deals with distributed-key-generation but also constructs an ABA* counterpart.

The round complexity of consensus protocols has a long research history. Without setup, consensus among n parties is possible (both in synchronous and asynchronous networks) if less than $n/3$ parties are corrupted [7,26]. In this setting, the first synchronous consensus protocol with a number of rounds independent from n was [14], and the first asynchronous one was [9]. Constant-round protocols, regardless of the network assumptions, cannot be deterministic [12,15], and they fail with negligible probability. Assuming setup (like a PKI, or correlated randomness) consensus tolerating up to $n/2$ corruptions is possible [12]. One can also obtain constant round constructions in this setting [24]. Until recently, constant-round consensus protocols in any corruption setting failed with probability at least c^{-r} in r rounds for some constant $c > 1$. A long standing lower bound from [23] shows that, even in synchronous networks and assuming setup, one cannot hope to reduce the failure probability to less than $(c \cdot r)^{-r}$ in r rounds. The first synchronous protocol matching this lower bound is [19], and in this work we match its optimal round complexity when synchrony holds, while also ensuring consensus if the network is asynchronous. Our construction must not (and does not) run an asynchronous consensus protocol if the network is asynchronous, in order to circumvent another lower bound [2] which shows that error c^{-r} in r rounds is actually optimal for asynchronous protocols.

2   Preliminaries

2.1   Model

Adversary. We consider n parties $P_1, P_2, \ldots, P_n$ who communicate over a complete network of point-to-point authenticated channels. We consider an active threshold adversary bound by the integer thresholds t_s and t_a such that $t_a \leq t_s$ and $2t_a + t_s \leq (1 - \delta)n$, where δn is a positive integer.[6] The adversary may corrupt up to t_s parties in an adaptive fashion (depending on information learned during the execution) if the network is synchronous and t_a parties if the network is asynchronous, making them deviate arbitrarily from the prescribed protocol in a coordinated and malicious manner. We call a party who is never corrupted throughout the execution of a protocol *honest*.

Network. We consider different network models. If the network is *synchronous*, then all messages sent by honest parties must be delivered within a fixed time

---

[6] Since $2t_s + t_a < n$ is required, this assumption is without loss of generality. One can simply consider $\delta = (n - 2t_s - t_a)/n$.

bound Δ, known to all honest parties. Subject to this rule, the adversary can arbitrarily schedule the delivery of messages. Furthermore, we assume that the honest parties have synchronized local clocks, which means that they can start a protocol simultaneously and that their local clocks progress at the same rate. In this setting, the adversary is allowed to corrupt up to t_s parties for a fixed threshold t_s known to all parties. If the network is *asynchronous*, then the adversary can arbitrarily schedule the delivery of messages, with the restriction that messages sent by honest parties must eventually be delivered. Additionally, honest parties need not have synchronized local clocks. In this setting, the adversary is allowed to corrupt up to t_a parties for a fixed threshold t_a known to all parties. Finally, in the network-agnostic setting, the network may be synchronous or asynchronous. Honest parties do not know the network condition. Depending on the network type, the rules for the synchronous setting or the asynchronous setting are in effect, and the parameters Δ, t_s and t_a are all known to all parties. This is the setting in which we analyze our protocols.

Some of our protocols are *round-based*. The round r should be understood to be the local time interval between $(r-1)\Delta$ and $r\Delta$. In round r, each honest party sends messages at time $(r-1)\Delta$, listens to messages throughout the round, and makes decisions depending on received messages at time $r\Delta$. The scheduling powers of the adversary make it *rushing*, which means that it can choose its round r messages depending on the honest parties' round r messages.

In our protocols, something we very commonly direct parties to do is to send a message m to *all* parties. We call this "multicasting the message m."

2.2 Building Blocks

Security Parameter. We denote by κ a security parameter.

Signatures and Bulletin-PKI. For a bulletin-PKI setup, before the execution of the protocol, each party P_i generates a key pair $(\mathsf{sk}_i, \mathsf{vk}_i)$, where sk_i is for signing messages and vk_i is for verifying them. Party P_i keeps sk_i private, and posts vk_i on a public board. If P_i is corrupted before the execution of a protocol, then it can freely choose its public vk_i; e.g. it can duplicate the key vk_j of an honest party P_j. We denote with $\sigma = \mathsf{Sgn}_{\mathsf{sk}_i}(m)$ that σ is a signature of length $\mathcal{O}(\kappa)$ obtained by signing m with sk_i, and say $\mathsf{Vfy}_{\mathsf{vk}_i}(m, \sigma) = 1$ if σ is a valid signature on m with respect to vk_i. We idealize the signature scheme (consisting of efficient key generation, signing and verification algorithms) to have perfect existential unforgeability, so that for any honestly generated key pair $(\mathsf{sk}_i, \mathsf{vk}_i)$, an adversary can't forge a signature σ such that $\mathsf{Vfy}_{\mathsf{vk}_i}(m, \sigma) = 1$ without sk_i.

Certificates. A certificate is a collection of valid signatures on a message. We formally define a certificate on a message $m \in \mathcal{M}$ to be a pair (m, L), where L is a list $(l_1, \ldots, l_n)$ such that either $l_i = \sigma_i$ and $\mathsf{Vfy}_{\mathsf{vk}_i}(m, \sigma_i) = 1$ for some signature σ_i, or $l_i = \bot$, where $\bot$ is a special value which indicates the absence of a signature. A k-certificate on m contains at least k signatures on m.

Common Coins. Given an instance number k and a corruption threshold t, an idealized common coin protocol emulates a trusted entity which, upon receiving the message (**coin request**, k) from $t+1$ distinct parties, samples the bit $\mathbf{coin}_k$ uniformly at random and sends the message $(k, \mathbf{coin}_k)$ to all parties.

Unique Threshold Signatures. Appropriate trusted setup makes it possible for a party to compress any f-certificate (where e.g. $f = t_s + 1$) into a single threshold signature of length $\mathcal{O}(\kappa)$. This provides complexity savings whenever the party needs to send a certificate. Uniqueness is the desirable property that all f-certificates on a message m compress into the same threshold signature. While not needed for certificate compression, it is essential for the construction of a common coin protocol against up to $t < \frac{n}{2}$ corruptions with $\mathcal{O}(n^2)$ messages of length $\mathcal{O}(\kappa)$ in the random oracle model (wherein one models a cryptographic hash function as a random function from its domain to its range) [8].

2.3 Definitions of Primitives and Security Properties

Notions of Validity. For multi-valued consensus, one can consider different notions of validity.

Validity: The most typical notion is that if all honest parties have the same input m, then all honest parties must output m.

Strong Validity: A stronger notion of validity is that the common output m must be the input of some honest party. While this is equivalent to regular validity for binary inputs, it is indeed stronger for multi-valued consensus: if two honest parties run consensus with the distinct inputs m_1 and m_2, then only regular validity permits the common output to be $m_3 \notin \{m_1, m_2\}$. Unfortunately, to achieve strong validity, even in the synchronous setting and for computational security, one needs $t < \frac{n}{2^\ell}$ [16]. Intuitively, the problem is that if all honest parties have different inputs, there is no secure way to choose the input of an honest party against even a single corruption.

Intrusion Tolerance: An alternative weakening of strong validity is that the common output should either be the input of some honest party, or a special output $\perp$ outside the domain of inputs. This property has been considered both explicitly [3,29] and implicitly [4,17,32], and it can be achieved together with optimal resilience for consensus. One can obtain it trivially by having all parties output $\perp$, but not when (regular) validity is also required.

Protocol Syntax. We primarily concern ourselves with protocols to reach consensus on ℓ-bit inputs, where ℓ is a publicly known length parameter. Hence, we define $\mathcal{M} = \{0,1\}^\ell$ to be the input space, and $\mathcal{M}^\perp = \mathcal{M} \cup \{\perp\}$ to be the input space with a special value $\perp$ added to it.

Security Properties. We consider property-based security for our protocols. Recall that we use the prefix "t-" to mean that a property only holds if at most t parties can be corrupted, and the prefix "synchronous" to mean that a property only holds if the network is synchronous. For round complexity, we sometimes also use the prefix "r-round". With it, we mean that if the network is synchronous and all honest parties know their inputs by some time $k\Delta$, then the guarantees of the prefixed property are achieved by time $(k+r)\Delta$.

With notational conventions out of the way, let us first define some properties shared by many primitives.

- **t-termination:** If all honest parties participate in the protocol with input, and they don't stop participating until termination, then all honest parties terminate the protocol with output.
- **t-liveness:** If all honest parties participate in the protocol with input without ever stopping, then all honest parties obtain output from the protocol.
- **t-robustness:** No honest party aborts the protocol.

Our round-based protocols all have fixed numbers of rounds, so that honest parties who do not abort trivially terminate. Because in this case termination follows from robustness, we only consider robustness for these protocols. Also, we do not consider robustness for protocols where honest parties cannot abort.

We define some agreement primitives together with relevant security properties below. The "fallback validity" properties refer to honest parties who provide input. This is because our round-based protocols permit honest parties to not have any input and abort immediately if the network is asynchronous.

Note that our parameterized notion of intrusion tolerance is related to the differential validity studied in [16]. Against t corruptions, a consensus protocol with (t,q)-intrusion tolerance automatically has $(n-2q)$-differential validity.

Weak Consensus. In a weak consensus protocol, each honest party P_i has an input $m_i \in \mathcal{M}$ and outputs some $y_i \in \mathcal{M}^\perp$. Below are the relevant properties:

- **(t,q)-intrusion tolerance:** Suppose less than q honest parties have the input m for some $m \in \mathcal{M}$. Then no honest party outputs m.
- **t-validity:** Suppose all honest parties have the same input $m \in \mathcal{M}$. Then honest parties can only output m.
- **t-weak consistency:** If some honest party outputs some $m \in \mathcal{M}$, then honest parties can only output m or $\perp$.
- **t-fallback validity:** Suppose all honest parties who provide input have the same input $m \in \mathcal{M}$. Then honest parties either abort or output m.
- **t-validity with liveness:** Suppose all honest parties participate in the protocol with a common input $m \in \mathcal{M}$, and they never stop participating. Then all honest parties output m.

Proposal. In a proposal protocol, there exists some set $S = \{x, \perp\} \subseteq \mathcal{M}^\perp$ such that each honest party P_i has an input $v_i \in S$, and each honest party P_i outputs some $y_i \in \{x, \{x, \perp\}, \perp\}$. The relevant properties are the following:

- **(t,q)-intrusion tolerance:** Suppose less than q honest parties have the input m for some $m \in \mathcal{M}$. Then no honest party outputs m or $\{m, \perp\}$. Note that for any proposal protocol, this property with $q \geq 1$ implies that honest parties can only obtain outputs in $\{x, \{x, \perp\}, \perp\}$, as required above.

- **t-validity:** Suppose all honest parties have the same input $v \in S$. Then honest parties can only output v.
- **t-weak consistency:** If some honest party outputs x, then no honest party outputs $\perp$.
- **t-fallback validity:** Suppose all honest parties who provide input have the same input $v \in S$. Then honest parties either abort or output v.
- **t-validity with liveness:** Suppose all honest parties participate in the protocol with a common input $v \in S$, and they never stop participating. Then all honest parties output v.

k-Graded Consensus. In a k-graded consensus protocol, each honest party P_i has an input $m_i \in \mathcal{M}$ and outputs a tuple (y_i, g_i), where $g_i \in \{0, 1, \ldots, k\}$. The relevant properties are the following:

- **(t,q)-intrusion tolerance:** Suppose less than q honest parties have the input m for some $m \in \mathcal{M}$. Then no honest party P_i obtains $y_i = m$.
- **t-graded validity:** Suppose all honest parties have the same input $m \in \mathcal{M}$. Then honest parties can only output (m, k).
- **t-graded consistency:** Suppose honest parties P_i and P_j output (y_i, g_i) and (y_j, g_j). Then, $|g_i - g_j| \leq 1$, and if $g_i \geq 1$, then $y_j = y_i$.
- **t-fallback graded validity:** If all honest parties who provide input have the same input $m \in \mathcal{M}$, then honest parties either abort or output (m, k).
- **t-graded validity with liveness:** Suppose all honest parties participate in the protocol with a common input $m \in \mathcal{M}$, and they never stop participating. Then all honest parties output (m, k).

Consensus. In a consensus protocol, each honest party P_i has an input $m_i \in \mathcal{M}$ and outputs some $y_i \in \mathcal{M}^{\perp}$. The relevant properties are the following:

- **(t,q)-intrusion tolerance:** Suppose less than q honest parties have the input m for some $m \in \mathcal{M}$. Then no honest party outputs m.
- **t-validity:** Suppose all honest parties have the same input $m \in \mathcal{M}$. Then honest parties can only output m.
- **t-consistency:** Honest parties do not obtain different outputs in $v \in \mathcal{M}^{\perp}$.
- **t-fallback validity:** Suppose all honest parties who provide input have the same input $m \in \mathcal{M}$. Then honest parties either abort or output m.
- **t-validity with termination:** Suppose all honest parties participate in the protocol with a common input $m \in \mathcal{M}$, and they never stop participating until termination. Then all honest parties terminate with the output m.

3   Synchronous Consensus with Fallback Validity

In this section, we show how to compile *any* fixed-round consensus protocol SBA for binary inputs with synchronous t_s-robustness, synchronous t_s-validity and synchronous t_s-consistency, into a fixed-round multi-valued consensus protocol SBA* with $(t_s, \delta n)$-intrusion tolerance, synchronous t_s-robustness, synchronous t_s-validity, synchronous t_s-consistency and t_a-fallback validity.

3.1 Synchronous Weak Consensus (SWC)

We begin with SWC: an adaptation of a protocol from [10], modified to support multi-valued inputs and have increased intrusion tolerance. The security of the protocol is captured by the lemma below it. All missing proofs can be found in the full version of this paper.

Protocol SWC

Input: Party P_i has an input $m_i \in \mathcal{M}$ which it knows at the beginning, or it may have no input if the network is asynchronous.

Output: Party P_i either aborts or outputs $y_i \in \mathcal{M}^\perp$.

Initialization: If P_i has input, then P_i sets $y_i = \perp$. Else, P_i aborts.

Round 1: P_i computes $\sigma_i = \mathsf{Sgn}_{\mathsf{sk}_i}(m_i)$ and multicasts (m_i, σ_i). At the end of the round,

- If P_i hasn't received validly signed messages from $n - t_s$ parties, P_i aborts.
- Else, if the messages P_i received are so that P_i can form a $(t_s + \delta n)$-certificate on a unique $m \in \mathcal{M}$, then P_i sets $y_i = m$.

Round 2: If P_i possesses a $(t_s + \delta n)$-certificate on a unique $m \in \mathcal{M}$, then P_i multicasts a $(t_s + \delta n)$-certificate on m. At the end of the round, if P_i has seen a $(t_s + \delta n)$-certificate on some $m \neq y_i$, then P_i sets $y_i = \perp$.

Lemma 1 (Security of SWC). *If $t_a \leq t_s$ and $2t_s + t_a \leq (1 - \delta)n$, then SWC is a weak consensus protocol with $(t_s, \delta n)$-intrusion tolerance, synchronous t_s-robustness, synchronous t_s-validity, synchronous t_s-weak consistency and t_a-fallback validity.*

Complexity of SWC: The message complexity is $\mathsf{MC}_{\mathsf{SWC}} = \mathcal{O}(n^2)$, and the communication complexity is $\mathsf{CC}_{\mathsf{SWC}} = \mathcal{O}(n^3 \kappa + \ell n^2)$.

3.2 Synchronous Proposal (SProp)

We continue with SProp, which we obtain by modifying SWC to fit the mold of a proposal protocol. Proposal protocols require there to exist some set $S = \{x, \perp\} \subseteq \mathcal{M}^\perp$ such that honest parties can only have inputs in S. We assume such a set $S = \{x, \perp\}$ exists, and use it in our description of SProp below.

Protocol SProp

Input: Party P_i has an input $v_i \in S$ which it knows at the beginning, or it may have no input if the network is asynchronous

Output: Party P_i either aborts or outputs $y_i \in \{x, \{x, \bot\}, \bot\}$.

Initialization: If P_i has input, then P_i sets $y_i = \bot$. Else, P_i aborts.

Round 1: If $v_i = \bot$, then P_i multicasts $\bot$. Else, P_i computes $\sigma_i = \mathsf{Sgn}_{\mathsf{sk}_i}(v_i)$ and multicasts (v_i, σ_i). At the end of the round,

  – If P_i hasn't received valid messages from $n - t_s$ parties, then P_i aborts.
  – Else, if the messages P_i received are so that P_i can form a $(t_s + \delta n)$-certificate on a unique $m \in \mathcal{M}$, then P_i sets $y_i = m$.

Round 2: If P_i possesses a $(t_s + \delta n)$-certificate on a unique $m \in \mathcal{M}$, then P_i multicasts it. At the end of the round, if P_i had $v_i = \bot$ but received a $(t_s + \delta n)$-certificate on some $m \in \mathcal{M}$, then P_i sets $y_i = \{m, \bot\}$.

Lemma 2 (Security of SProp). *If $t_a \leq t_s$ and $2t_s + t_a \leq (1 - \delta)n$, then SProp is a proposal protocol with $(t_s, \delta n)$-intrusion tolerance, synchronous t_s-robustness, synchronous t_s-validity, synchronous t_s-weak consistency and t_a-fallback validity.*

Complexity of SProp: The message and communication complexities of SProp are also respectively $\mathsf{MC}_{\mathsf{SProp}} = \mathcal{O}(n^2)$ and $\mathsf{CC}_{\mathsf{SProp}} = \mathcal{O}(n^3\kappa + \ell n^2)$.

3.3 Synchronous 1-Graded Consensus (SGC^1)

Now that we have SWC and SProp, we compose them into SGC^1. When instantiated with the protocols SWC and SProp above, SGC^1 runs in 4 rounds.

Protocol SGC^1

Input: Party P_i has an input $m_i \in \mathcal{M}$ which it knows at the beginning, or it may have no input if the network is asynchronous.

Output: Party P_i either aborts or outputs (y_i, g_i), where $y_i \in \mathcal{M}^\bot$ is the output value and $g_i \in \{0, 1\}$ is the output grade.

Phase 1: P_i participates in a common SWC instance with the input m_i. If P_i aborts SWC, P_i aborts the protocol. Else, let v_i be P_i's output.

Phase 2: P_i participates in a common SProp instance with the input v_i if $v_i = m_i$, and the input $\bot$ otherwise. If P_i aborts SProp, P_i aborts the protocol. Else, let z_i be P_i's output.

  – If $z_i = m$, then P_i outputs $(m, 1)$.
  – If $z_i = \{m, \bot\}$, then P_i outputs $(m, 0)$.
  – If $z_i = \bot$, then P_i outputs $(\bot, 0)$.

Lemma 3 (Security of SGC^1). *Let SWC and SProp respectively be a weak consensus protocol and a proposal protocol, both with fixed numbers of rounds, such that they both have synchronous t_s-robustness, synchronous t_s-validity, synchronous t_s-weak consistency and t_a-fallback validity. Furthermore, suppose SProp has $(t_s, \delta n)$-intrusion tolerance. Then, SGC^1 is a 1-graded consensus protocol with $(t_s, \delta n)$-intrusion tolerance, synchronous t_s-robustness, synchronous t_s-graded validity, synchronous t_s-graded consistency and t_a-fallback graded validity.*

Complexity of SGC^1: We have $\mathsf{MC}_{\mathsf{SGC}^1} = \mathsf{MC}_{\mathsf{SWC}} + \mathsf{MC}_{\mathsf{SProp}} = \mathcal{O}(n^2)$ and $\mathsf{CC}_{\mathsf{SGC}^1} = \mathsf{CC}_{\mathsf{SWC}} + \mathsf{CC}_{\mathsf{SProp}} = \mathcal{O}(n^3 \kappa + \ell n^2)$.

3.4 Synchronous 2-Graded Consensus (SGC^2)

Using SGC^1 as a basis and SWC as a weak consensus protocol for binary inputs, we construct SGC^2. When instantiated with sub-protocols from previous sections, the protocol runs in 6 rounds when the network is synchronous.

Protocol SGC^2

Input: Party P_i has an input $m_i \in \mathcal{M}$ which it knows at the beginning, or it may have no input if the network is asynchronous.

Output: Party P_i either aborts or outputs (y_i, g_i), where $y_i \in \mathcal{M}^\perp$ is the output value and $g_i \in \{0, 1, 2\}$ is the output grade.

Phase 1: P_i participates in a common SGC^1 instance with the input m_i. If P_i aborts SGC^1, P_i aborts the protocol. Else, let (z_i, h_i) be P_i's output. P_i sets $y_i = z_i$.

Phase 2: P_i participates in a common SWC instance with the input h_i. If P_i aborts SWC, then P_i aborts the protocol. Else, let v_i be P_i's output.

- If $v_i = 0$, then P_i sets $g_i = 0$.
- If $v_i = \perp$, then P_i sets $g_i = 1$.
- If $v_i = 1$, then P_i sets $g_i = 2$.

Lemma 4 (Security of SGC^2). *Let SGC^1 and SWC respectively be a 1-graded consensus protocol and a weak binary consensus protocol, both with fixed numbers of rounds, such that SGC^1 has $(t_s, \delta n)$-intrusion tolerance, synchronous t_s-robustness, synchronous t_s-graded validity, synchronous t_s-graded consistency and t_a-fallback graded validity, and SWC has synchronous t_s-robustness, synchronous t_s-validity, synchronous t_s-weak consistency and t_a-fallback validity. Then, SGC^2 is a 2-graded consensus protocol with $(t_s, \delta n)$-intrusion tolerance, synchronous t_s-robustness, synchronous t_s-graded validity, synchronous t_s-graded consistency and t_a-fallback graded validity.*

Complexity of SGC^2: We have $\mathsf{MC}_{\mathsf{SGC}^2} = \mathsf{MC}_{\mathsf{SGC}^1} + \mathsf{MC}_{\mathsf{SWC}} = \mathcal{O}(n^2)$ and $\mathsf{CC}_{\mathsf{SGC}^2} = \mathsf{CC}_{\mathsf{SGC}^1} + \mathsf{CC}_{\mathsf{SWC}} = \mathcal{O}(n^3 \kappa + \ell n^2)$.

3.5 Synchronous Consensus (SBA*)

Finally, we take *any* fixed-round binary consensus protocol SBA and combine it with SGC^2 to obtain SBA*: the synchronous component of HBA. Again, SBA* is a two-phase protocol. The first phase lasts sufficiently long for SGC^2 (6 rounds with our constructions). The number of rounds for the second phase depends on the specific SBA protocol chosen.

Protocol SBA*

Input: Party P_i has an input $m_i \in \mathcal{M}$ which it knows at the beginning, or it may have no input if the network is asynchronous.

Output: Party P_i either aborts or outputs $y_i \in \mathcal{M}^\perp$.

Phase 1: P_i participates in a common SGC^2 instance with the input m_i. If P_i aborts SGC^2, P_i aborts the protocol. Else, let (z_i, g_i) be P_i's output.

Phase 2: P_i participates in a common SBA instance with the input 1 if $g_i \in \{1, 2\}$ and 0 otherwise. If P_i fails to obtain output from SBA for any reason, then P_i outputs z_i and terminates. Else, let h_i be P_i's output.

- If $g_i = 2$ or $h_i = 1$, then P_i outputs z_i.
- Otherwise, P_i outputs $\perp$.

Theorem 2 (Security of SBA*). *Let SGC^2 and SBA respectively be 2-graded consensus protocol and a binary consensus protocol, both with fixed numbers of rounds, such that SGC^2 has $(t_s, \delta n)$-intrusion tolerance, synchronous t_s-robustness, synchronous t_s-graded validity, synchronous t_s-graded consistency and t_a-fallback graded validity, and SBA has synchronous t_s-robustness, synchronous t_s-validity and synchronous t_s-consistency. Then, SBA^* is a consensus protocol with $(t_s, \delta n)$-intrusion tolerance, synchronous t_s-robustness, synchronous t_s-validity, synchronous t_s-consistency and t_a-fallback validity.*

Complexity of SBA*: We have $\mathsf{MC_{SBA^*}} = \mathsf{MC_{SGC^2}} + \mathsf{MC_{SBA}} = \mathcal{O}(\mathsf{MC_{SBA}} + n^2)$ and $\mathsf{CC_{SBA^*}} = \mathsf{CC_{SGC^2}} + \mathsf{CC_{SBA^*}} = \mathcal{O}(\mathsf{CC_{SBA}} + n^3\kappa + \ell n^2)$. Note that if SBA is designed to be run synchronously, then it might suffer from increased complexity when run asynchronously. This is not an issue for any protocol that we cite.

The $\mathcal{O}(n^3\kappa)$ term in the complexity is the consequence of certificate multicasting in SWC and SProp. One straightforward option to reduce this term by a factor of n is to assume a $(t_s + \delta n - 1)$-threshold signature setup. Then, individual parties' signatures are replaced by signature shares, and $(t_s + \delta n)$-certificates by signatures of size $\mathcal{O}(\kappa)$. Another option, only assuming a bulletin-PKI setup, is to use expander graph based techniques [27]. One imposes an n-vertex expander graph on the parties, with each party corresponding to a vertex. In SWC and SProp parties just send the $\mathcal{O}(n)$ sized certificates to their (constant sized) set of neighbors in the graph. This modification breaks weak consistency, which can be regained with the introduction of an additional round. However, with expander graphs, security requires the slightly stronger assumption $2t_s \leq (1 - \varepsilon)n$ for a constant $\varepsilon > 0$. In the full version, we present 3-round expander-based variants of SWC and SProp with which the communication complexity of SBA^* can be reduced to $\mathcal{O}(\mathsf{CC}_{\mathsf{SBA}} + n^2\kappa + \ell n^2)$ when $2t_s \leq (1 - \varepsilon)n$ for a constant $\varepsilon > 0$.

4   Asynchronous Consensus with High Validity

We now leave round-based protocols behind, and switch to message-driven protocols. In this section we take a (possibly non-terminating) consensus protocol ABA with t_a-validity, t_a-consistency and t_a-liveness, and combine it with our AGC^2 protocol to obtain a protocol ABA^* with $(t_s, \delta n)$-intrusion tolerance, t_s-validity[7], synchronous t_s-validity with termination, t_a-consistency and t_a-termination.

4.1   Asynchronous Proposal (AProp)

We begin with AProp. The "Conflict Echoing" rule is asymmetrically biased to make the output $\perp$ more likely than x or $\{x, \perp\}$. This lets us obtain $(t_s, \delta n)$-intrusion tolerance rather than $(t_s, \lceil \frac{\delta n}{2} \rceil)$-intrusion tolerance.

As AProp is a proposal protocol, we assume there exists some set $S = \{x, \perp\} \in \mathcal{M}^{\perp}$ such that honest parties have inputs in S.

Protocol AProp

Input: Party P_i has an input $v_i \in S$ which it can eventually learn.

Output: Party P_i outputs $y_i \in \{x, \{x, \perp\}, \perp\}$. P_i only outputs once, so P_i only takes into account its first outputting directive.

Initialization: P_i lets $V_i = \varnothing$.

Input Acquisition: When P_i knows v_i, P_i multicasts $(\textbf{input}, v_i)$.

Conflict Echoing: Upon receiving the message $(\textbf{input}, v)$ for some $v \neq v_i$ for the first time from some party,

- If $v = \perp$ and P_i has received the message $(\textbf{input}, v)$ from exactly $t_s + 1$ parties, P_i multicasts $(\textbf{input}, \perp)$.
- If $v \in \mathcal{M}$ and P_i has received the message $(\textbf{input}, v)$ from exactly $t_s + \delta n$ parties, P_i multicasts $(\textbf{input}, v)$.

Value Rule: Upon receiving the message $(\textbf{input}, v)$ for some v from exactly $n - t_s$ parties, P_i adds v to V_i. Then,

- If this rule has been activated for the first time, P_i multicasts $(\textbf{propose}, v)$.
- If this rule has been activated for the second time, P_i outputs V_i.

Certify Rule: Upon receiving the message $(\textbf{propose}, v)$ for some v from exactly $n - t_s$ parties, P_i outputs v.

---

[7] Actually, t_a-validity from ABA^* suffices for HBA.

Lemma 5 (Security of AProp). *If $t_a \le t_s$ and $2t_s + t_a \le (1-\delta)n$, then AProp is a proposal protocol with $(t_s, \delta n)$-intrusion tolerance, 2-round t_s-validity with liveness, t_a-weak consistency and t_a-liveness.*

Complexity of AProp: AProp is designed so that honest parties only send **input** messages on inputs held by honest parties. As the honest parties have inputs in $S = \{x, \bot\}$, they multicast at most two **input** messages. Furthermore, by the design of AProp, honest parties may only multicast a single **propose** message. So, honest parties multicast at most three messages (two **input** messages and one **propose** message), and all of these messages are of size $\mathcal{O}(\ell)$. Therefore, the message complexity is $\mathsf{MC}_{\mathsf{AProp}} = \mathcal{O}(n^2)$ and the communication complexity is $\mathsf{CC}_{\mathsf{AProp}} = \mathcal{O}(\ell n^2)$.

4.2 Asynchronous Weak Consensus (AWC)

Now, we present our weak consensus protocol AWC. To improve efficiency, we parallelize ℓ instances of AProp in a refined way. We batch together **input** messages from the "Input Acquisition" rule and **propose** messages from the "Value Rule." The "Conflict Echoing" rule is not amenable to such batching; therefore, any message sent as a result of the rule affects all instances. Although this introduces dependency among instances, we still get security for AWC *without* intrusion tolerance, which we do not need in any case.

Protocol AWC

Input: Party P_i has an input $m_i \in \mathcal{M}$ which it can eventually learn.

Output: Party P_i outputs $y_i \in \mathcal{M}^\bot$. P_i only outputs once, so P_i only takes into account its first outputting directive.

Initialization: P_i lets $V_i^1, V_i^2, \ldots, V_i^\ell = \varnothing, \varnothing, \ldots, \varnothing$.

Input Acquisition: When P_i knows m_i, P_i multicasts $(\textbf{input}, m_i)$.

Conflict Echoing: Upon receiving from exactly $t_s + 1$ parties inputs with the kth bit $1 - b_i^k$ or the message **conflict**, P_i multicasts **conflict**.

Value Rule: For each k, upon receiving from exactly $n - t_s$ parties inputs with the kth bit b or the message **conflict**, P_i adds b to V_i^k. Then,

- If each of the sets $V_i^1, V_i^2, \ldots, V_i^\ell$ contain exactly one bit, then P_i crafts the ℓ-bit message m which as its kth bit has the unique bit in V_i^k, and P_i multicasts $(\textbf{propose}, m)$.
- If $V_i^k = \{0, 1\}$, then P_i outputs $\bot$.

Certify Rule: Upon receiving the message $(\textbf{propose}, m)$ for some $m \in \mathcal{M}$ from exactly $n - t_s$ parties, P_i outputs m.

Theorem 3 (Security of AWC). *If $t_a \leq t_s$ and $2t_s + t_a < n$, then AWC is a weak consensus protocol with 2-round t_s-validity with liveness, t_a-weak consistency and t_a-liveness.*

Complexity of AWC: Honest parties multicast at most three messages (one **input** message, one **conflict** message and one **propose** message), and all of these messages are of size $\mathcal{O}(\ell)$. Therefore, the message complexity is $\mathsf{MC_{AWC}} = \mathcal{O}(n^2)$ and the communication complexity is $\mathsf{CC_{AWC}} = \mathcal{O}(\ell n^2)$.

4.3 Asynchronous Graded Consensus

Recall that in the previous section, we obtained SGC^1 by composing SWC and SProp, and then obtained SGC^2 by composing SGC^1 and SWC. These compositions translate very well to the asynchronous setting: we can easily compose AWC and AProp to obtain the 1-graded consensus protocol AGC^1, and then compose AGC^1 and AWC to obtain the 2-graded consensus protocol AGC^1.

Since AGC^1 and AGC^2 are almost identical (although message-driven) copies of SGC^1 and SGC^2, here we only state the security guarantees they achieve. The full protocols AGC^1 and AGC^2 can be found in the full version.

Lemma 6 (Security of AGC^1). *Let AProp and AWC respectively be a proposal protocol and a weak consensus protocol such that AProp has $(t_s, \delta n)$-intrusion tolerance, r_p-round t_s-validity with liveness, t_a-weak consistency and t_a-liveness, and AWC has r_w-round t_s-validity with liveness, t_a-weak consistency and t_a-liveness. Then, AGC^1 is a 1-graded consensus protocol with $(t_s, \delta n)$-intrusion tolerance, $(r_w + r_p)$-round t_s-graded validity with liveness, t_a-graded consistency and t_a-liveness.*

Lemma 7 (Security of AGC^2). *Let AGC^1 and AWC respectively be a 1-graded consensus protocol and a weak binary consensus protocol such that AGC^1 has $(t_s, \delta n)$-intrusion tolerance, r_g-round t_s-graded validity with liveness, t_a-graded consistency and t_a-liveness, and AWC has r_w-round t_s-graded validity with liveness, t_a-weak consistency and t_a-liveness. Then, AGC^2 is a 2-graded consensus protocol with $(t_s, \delta n)$-intrusion tolerance, $(r_g + r_w)$-round t_s-graded validity with liveness, t_a-graded consistency and t_a-liveness.*

Complexity of AGC^1 and AGC^2: Both composed protocols involve no messages other than those of their sub-protocols. Thus, we have $\mathsf{MC_{AGC^1}} = \mathsf{MC_{AWC}} + \mathsf{MC_{AProp}} = \mathcal{O}(n^2)$, $\mathsf{CC_{AGC^1}} = \mathsf{CC_{AWC}} + \mathsf{CC_{AProp}} = \mathcal{O}(\ell n^2)$, $\mathsf{MC_{AGC^2}} = \mathsf{MC_{AGC^1}} + \mathsf{MC_{AWC}} = \mathcal{O}(n^2)$, and $\mathsf{CC_{AGC^2}} = \mathsf{CC_{AGC^1}} + \mathsf{CC_{AWC}} = \mathcal{O}(\ell n^2)$.

4.4 Asynchronous Consensus (ABA*)

To conclude this section, we construct ABA^* by composing AGC^2 and a binary consensus protocol ABA with just t_a-validity, t_a-consistency and t_a-liveness. The protocol ABA actually does not even need to provide termination, as this is guaranteed by a separate termination procedure in ABA*. For maximum generality, we let r_g be the number of rounds in which AGC^2 achieves t_s-validity with liveness; the r_g-round t_s-graded validity with liveness of AGC^2 lets us prove synchronous $(r_g + 1)$-round t_s-validity with termination for ABA*. Note that if AGC^2 is based on our AProp and AWC protocols, then $r_g = 6$.

Protocol ABA*

Start Round: The parties have an agreed upon "start round" r_s.

Input: Party P_i has an input $m_i \in \mathcal{M}$ which it can eventually learn.

Output: Party P_i outputs $y_i \in \mathcal{M}^\perp$.

Initialization: Party P_i starts participating in a common instance of AGC^2 and a common instance of ABA. Before time $(r_s + r_g + 1)\Delta$, P_i runs ABA passively, not processing the messages it receives.

Input Acquisition: When P_i knows m_i, P_i sets it as its input for AGC^2.

Graded Output: Upon outputting (z_i, g_i) from AGC^2,

- If $g_i = 2$, then P_i multicasts (**commit**, z_i) if it hasn't done so previously.
- If $g_i \in \{2, 1\}$, P_i sets its ABA input to 1. Else, P_i sets its ABA input to 0.

Late Output: Upon outputting (z_i, g_i) from AGC^2 where $g_i \neq 2$ and outputting h_i from ABA, P_i sets x_i to z_i if $h_i = 1$, and to $\perp$ otherwise. Then, P_i multicasts (**commit**, x_i) if it hasn't done so previously.

Commit Processing: Upon receiving (**commit**, x) for some $x \in \mathcal{M}^\perp$,

- If P_i has received (**commit**, x) from exactly $t_s + 1$ parties, then P_i multicasts (**commit**, x) if it hasn't done so previously.
- If P_i has received (**commit**, x) from exactly $n - t_s$ parties, then P_i terminates with the output x if $(r_s + r_g)\Delta$ time has passed, and sets itself up to terminate with the output x at time $(r_s + r_g)\Delta$ otherwise.

Theorem 4 (Security of ABA*). *Let $t_a \leq t_s$ and $2t_s + t_a \leq (1 - \delta)n$, and suppose honest parties must know their inputs by time $r_s\Delta$ when the network is synchronous. Let AGC^2 and ABA respectively be a 2-graded consensus protocol and a binary consensus protocol such that AGC^2 has $(t_s, \delta n)$-intrusion tolernace, r_g-round t_s-graded validity with liveness, t_a-graded consistency and t_a-liveness, and ABA has t_a-validity, t_a-consistency and t_a-liveness. Then, ABA* is a consensus protocol with $(t_s, \delta n)$-intrusion tolerance, t_s-validity, t_a-consistency, t_a-termination and synchronous $(r_g + 1)$-round t_s-validity with termination.*

Complexity of ABA*: One can prove that honest parties commit at most once. With that in mind, the complexity depends on the network type.

- If the network is asynchronous, then we sum up the complexities of AGC^2 and ABA together with the complexities arising from the **commit** messages. Hence, we get $\mathsf{MC}_{\mathsf{ABA}^*}^{\mathsf{Async}} = \mathsf{MC}_{\mathsf{ABA}} + \mathsf{MC}_{\mathsf{AGC}^2} + \mathcal{O}(n^2) = \mathcal{O}(\mathsf{MC}_{\mathsf{ABA}} + n^2)$ and $\mathsf{CC}_{\mathsf{ABA}^*}^{\mathsf{Async}} = \mathsf{CC}_{\mathsf{ABA}} + \mathsf{CC}_{\mathsf{AGC}^2} + \mathcal{O}(\ell n^2) = \mathcal{O}(\mathsf{CC}_{\mathsf{ABA}} + \ell n^2)$.
- If the network is synchronous, then the synchronous (r_g+1)-round t_s-validity of ABA^* ensures that all honest terminate by time $(r_s + r_g + 1)\Delta$ without ever sending ABA messages. Thus, we get the reduced $\mathsf{MC}_{\mathsf{ABA}^*}^{\mathsf{Sync}} = \mathsf{MC}_{\mathsf{AGC}^2} + \mathcal{O}(n^2) = \mathcal{O}(n^2)$ and $\mathsf{CC}_{\mathsf{ABA}^*}^{\mathsf{Sync}} = \mathsf{CC}_{\mathsf{AGC}^2} + \mathcal{O}(\ell n^2) = \mathcal{O}(\ell n^2)$.

5 The Network-Agnostic Protocol (HBA)

Finally, in this section we compose SBA^* and ABA^* to construct our network-agnostic consensus protocol HBA. Intrusion tolerance here is a challenge: SBA^* allows honest parties to output $\bot$, but ABA^* doesn't allow them to input $\bot$. Thus, we extend inputs for ABA^*, making them $(\ell+1)$ bits long rather than ℓ bits long; the first bit is reserved to indicate whether the SBA^* output is $\bot$ or not. Notationally, we write $b \parallel m$ to represent $m \in \mathcal{M}$ with the bit b prepended.

We present HBA as a two-phase protocol. The first phase begins at time 0 and lasts sufficiently long for SBA^*; the second phase begins after the first and lasts indefinitely.

Protocol HBA

Input: Party P_i has an input $m_i \in \mathcal{M}$ which it must know at the beginning of the protocol if the network is synchronous.

Output: Party P_i outputs $y_i \in \mathcal{M}^\bot$.

Initialization: P_i starts participating in a common instance of ABA^*, set to achieve consensus on $(\ell+1)$-bit inputs. Also, P_i sets $v_i = \bot$.

Phase 1: If P_i knows its input m_i, then P_i participates in a common instance of SBA^* with the input m_i. If P_i doesn't abort it, let z_i be the output P_i obtains from it. If $z_i = \bot$, then P_i sets $v_i = (0,0,\dots,0) \in \{0,1\}^{\ell+1}$. Otherwise, P_i sets $v_i = 1 \parallel z_i$.

Phase 2: If $v_i \neq \bot$, then P_i sets v_i as its input for ABA^*. Else, P_i sets $1 \parallel m_i$ as its ABA^* input once P_i knows m_i. Upon terminating ABA^* with the output $x_i = (x_i^1, x_i^2, \dots, x_i^{\ell+1})$,

- If $x_i^1 = 0$, then P_i outputs $\bot$ and terminates.
- If $x_i^1 = 1$, then P_i outputs $(x_i^2, \dots, x_i^{\ell+1}) \in \mathcal{M}$ and terminates.

Note that to use the particular ABA^* protocol presented in Sect. 4.4, we would need to set its "start round r_s" to be the round count of SBA^*.

Theorem 5 (Security of HBA). *Let SBA* * *be an* r_s-*round consensus protocol with* $(t_s, \delta n)$-*intrusion tolerance, synchronous* t_s-*robustness, synchronous* t_s-*validity, synchronous* t_s-*consistency and* t_a-*fallback validity, and let ABA* * *be a consensus protocol with* $(t_s, \delta n)$-*intrusion tolerance,* t_a-*validity, synchronous* r_a-*round* t_s-*validity with termination,* t_a-*consistency and* t_a-*termination. Then, HBA is a consensus protocol with* $(t_s, \delta n)$-*intrusion tolerance, synchronous* t_s-*validity, synchronous* t_s-*consistency, synchronous* $(r_s + r_a)$-*round* t_s-*termination,* t_a-*validity,* t_a-*consistency and* t_a-*termination.*

Proof. We use the synchronous t_s-robustness of SBA * implicitly.

- $(\mathbf{t_s}, \boldsymbol{\delta n})$-**intrusion tolerance:** Suppose less than δn honest parties have some $m \in \mathcal{M}$ as input. By the $(t_s, \delta n)$-intrusion tolerance of SBA *, honest parties do not output m from SBA *. This ensures that only honest parties who abort SBA * and have the input m may provide the input $1 \| m$ to ABA *. As there can only be less than δn such honest parties, by the $(t_s, \delta n)$-intrusion tolerance of ABA *, honest parties do not output $1 \| m$ from ABA *. This implies that honest parties do not output m.
- **synchronous properties:** Suppose the network is synchronous, and suppose the adversary can corrupt at most t_s parties. Since the network is synchronous, all honest participate in SBA * with input. They all terminate it by time r_s, with some common output $z \in \mathcal{M}^\perp$ by the synchronous t_s-consistency of SBA *. Afterwards, all honest parties participate in ABA * with the common input z', where $z' = (0, 0, \ldots, 0) \in \{0, 1\}^{\ell+1}$ if $z = \perp$, and $z' = 1 \| z$ otherwise. By time $(r_s + r_a)\Delta$, the synchronous r_a-round t_s-validity with termination of ABA * guarantees that they terminate ABA * with the common output z' and hence terminate HBA with a common output. This gives us synchronous t_s-consistency and synchronous $(r_s + r_a)$-round t_s-termination. Additionally, suppose all honest parties have the same input $m \in \mathcal{M}$. Then, the synchronous t_s-validity of SBA * implies that $z = m$ and hence that $z' = 1 \| m$, which means that the honest parties all terminate with the output m. Thus, we also obtain synchronous t_s-validity.
- $\mathbf{t_a}$-**termination and** $\mathbf{t_a}$-**consistency:** All honest parties eventually provide ABA * input, and run it until they terminate it with consistent outputs. Thus, HBA inherits the t_a-termination and the t_a-consistency of ABA *.
- $\mathbf{t_a}$-**validity:** Suppose all honest parties have the same input $m \in \mathcal{M}$. By the t_a-fallback validity of SBA *, any honest party that doesn't abort SBA * outputs m from it. This ensures that all honest parties participate in ABA * with the input $1 \| m$. Finally, by the t_a-validity and the t_a-termination of ABA *, all honest parties terminate ABA * with the output $1 \| m$ and therefore terminate HBA with the output m.

Complexity of HBA: Note that the extension of ABA * inputs to $\ell + 1$ bits doesn't affect asymptotic complexity.

- If the network is synchronous, then the message complexity is $\mathsf{MC}_{\mathsf{HBA}}^{\mathsf{Sync}} = \mathsf{MC}_{\mathsf{SBA}^*} + \mathsf{MC}_{\mathsf{ABA}^*}^{\mathsf{Sync}} = \mathcal{O}(\mathsf{MC}_{\mathsf{SBA}} + n^2)$, and if the network is asynchronous, then it is $\mathsf{MC}_{\mathsf{HBA}}^{\mathsf{Async}} = \mathsf{MC}_{\mathsf{SBA}^*} + \mathsf{MC}_{\mathsf{ABA}^*}^{\mathsf{Async}} = \mathcal{O}(\mathsf{MC}_{\mathsf{SBA}} + \mathsf{MC}_{\mathsf{ABA}} + n^2)$.

- As discussed in the technical overview, if threshold signatures are available or if $2t_s < (1 - \varepsilon)n$ for a constant $\varepsilon > 0$, then we get $\mathsf{CC}_{\mathsf{HBA}} = \mathcal{O}(\mathsf{CC}_{\mathsf{SBA}} + \mathsf{CC}_{\mathsf{ABA}} + n^2\kappa + \ell n^2)$. Else, we get $\mathsf{CC}_{\mathsf{HBA}} = \mathcal{O}(\mathsf{CC}_{\mathsf{SBA}} + \mathsf{CC}_{\mathsf{ABA}} + n^3\kappa + \ell n^2)$. Finally, if the network is synchronous, then the term $\mathsf{CC}_{\mathsf{ABA}}$ is eliminated.
- We also concretely state the synchronous round complexity of HBA. Recall that we build SBA^* by composing SGC^2 (6 rounds) and a fixed-round synchronous consensus protocol SBA (k rounds), so that SBA^* requires $k + 6$ rounds. Protocol AGC^2 achieves 6-round t_s-validity with liveness, and hence ABA^* attains synchronous 7-round t_s-validity with termination. Combining the round complexities of SBA^* and ABA^*, we conclude that HBA terminates in at most $k + 13$ rounds when the network is synchronous.

Reducing $\mathcal{O}(\ell n^2)$ to $\mathcal{O}(\ell n)$. For ℓ-bit consensus, the optimal communication complexity is $\mathcal{O}(\ell n + \dots)$ [17]. There is a rich literature *extending* consensus protocols to handle ℓ-bit inputs in clever ways to meet this bar [4,17,32,33].

To the best of our knowledge, [32] presents the state-of-the-art adaptively secure consensus extension protocol.[8] The protocol requires the parties to agree on κ-bit values in an intrusion-tolerant manner. Intrusion tolerance is achieved via two instances of consensus (one to decide the a κ-bit value, the other to decide if this value was the input of some honest party), but we observe that this is superfluous if the underlying consensus protocol is already intrusion-tolerant. In the full version, we present an adaptation of the protocol which makes only one black-box invocation of HBA on κ-bit inputs, and has an overhead of two rounds when the network is synchronous, $\mathcal{O}(n^2)$ messages, and $\mathcal{O}(n^2\kappa + \ell n)$ or $\mathcal{O}(n^2\kappa \log n + \ell n)$ bits of communication depending on the availability of trusted setup. We follow it with a novel setup-free expander-based extension protocol which makes full use of $(t_s, \delta n)$-intrusion tolerance to reduce the overhead $\mathcal{O}(n^2\kappa \log n + \ell n)$ to $\mathcal{O}(n^2\kappa + \ell n)$ when $\delta = \Theta(1)$.

Note that the $\mathcal{O}(\ell n^2)$ term in the communication complexity of HBA (as opposed to the $\mathcal{O}(\ell n^3)$ in [3]) permits extensions for long inputs with the total complexity $\mathcal{O}(n^2\kappa + \ell n)$ whenever HBA achieves the complexity $\mathcal{O}(n^2\kappa + \ell n^2)$. Thus, with HBA, one can match the complexity of state-of-the-art synchronous protocols.

References

1. Appan, A., Chandramouli, A., Choudhury, A.: Perfectly-secure synchronous mpc with asynchronous fallback guarantees. In: Proceedings of the 2022 ACM Symposium on Principles of Distributed Computing, pp. 92–102 (2022)
2. Attiya, H., Censor, K.: Lower bounds for randomized consensus under a weak adversary. In: Bazzi, R.A., Patt-Shamir, B. (eds.) 27th ACM Symposium Annual on Principles of Distributed Computing, pp. 315–324. Association for Computing Machinery (Aug 2008). https://doi.org/10.1145/1400751.1400793

---

[8] Adaptively secure sub-quadratic extension is possible in the atomic-send model [4].

3. Bacho, R., Collins, D., Liu-Zhang, C.D., Loss, J.: Network-agnostic security comes (almost) for free in DKG and MPC. In: Handschuh, H., Lysyanskaya, A. (eds.) Advances in Cryptology – CRYPTO 2023, Part I. LNCS, vol. 14081, pp. 71–106. Springer, Heidelberg (Aug 2023). https://doi.org/10.1007/978-3-031-38557-5_3

4. Bhangale, A., Liu-Zhang, C.D., Loss, J., Nayak, K.: Efficient adaptively-secure byzantine agreement for long messages. In: Agrawal, S., Lin, D. (eds.) Advances in Cryptology – ASIACRYPT 2022, Part I. LNCS, vol. 13791, pp. 504–525. Springer, Heidelberg (Dec 2022). https://doi.org/10.1007/978-3-031-22963-3_17

5. Blum, E., Katz, J., Loss, J.: Synchronous consensus with optimal asynchronous fallback guarantees. In: Hofheinz, D., Rosen, A. (eds.) TCC 2019. LNCS, vol. 11891, pp. 131–150. Springer, Cham (2019). https://doi.org/10.1007/978-3-030-36030-6_6

6. Blum, E., Liu-Zhang, C.-D., Loss, J.: Always have a backup plan: fully secure synchronous MPC with asynchronous fallback. In: Micciancio, D., Ristenpart, T. (eds.) CRYPTO 2020. LNCS, vol. 12171, pp. 707–731. Springer, Cham (2020). https://doi.org/10.1007/978-3-030-56880-1_25

7. Bracha, G.: Asynchronous byzantine agreement protocols. Inf. Comput. **75**(2), 130–143 (1987). https://doi.org/10.1016/0890-5401(87)90054-X

8. Cachin, C., Kursawe, K., Shoup, V.: Random oracles in constantipole: Practical asynchronous byzantine agreement using cryptography (extended abstract). In: Proceedings of the Nineteenth Annual ACM Symposium on Principles of Distributed Computing, p. 123–132. PODC '00, Association for Computing Machinery, New York, NY, USA (2000). https://doi.org/10.1145/343477.343531

9. Canetti, R., Rabin, T.: Fast asynchronous byzantine agreement with optimal resilience. In: 25th Annual ACM Symposium on Theory of Computing, pp. 42–51. ACM Press (May 1993). https://doi.org/10.1145/167088.167105

10. Deligios, G., Hirt, M., Liu-Zhang, C.-D.: Round-efficient byzantine agreement and multi-party computation with asynchronous fallback. In: Nissim, K., Waters, B. (eds.) TCC 2021. LNCS, vol. 13042, pp. 623–653. Springer, Cham (2021). https://doi.org/10.1007/978-3-030-90459-3_21

11. Deligios, G., Liu-Zhang, C.D.: Synchronous perfectly secure message transmission with optimal asynchronous fallback guarantees. Cryptology ePrint Archive, Report 2022/1397 (2022). https://eprint.iacr.org/2022/1397

12. Dolev, D., Strong, H.R.: Authenticated algorithms for byzantine agreement. SIAM J. Comput. **12**(4), 656–666 (1983). https://doi.org/10.1137/0212045

13. Elsheimy, F., Tsimos, G., Papamanthou, C.: Deterministic byzantine agreement with adaptive $o(n \cdot f)$ communication. Cryptology ePrint Archive, Paper 2023/1723 (2023). https://eprint.iacr.org/2023/1723

14. Feldman, P., Micali, S.: Optimal algorithms for byzantine agreement. In: 20th Annual ACM Symposium on Theory of Computing, pp. 148–161. ACM Press (May 1988). https://doi.org/10.1145/62212.62225

15. Fischer, M.J., Lynch, N.A., Paterson, M.S.: Impossibility of distributed consensus with one faulty process. J. ACM (JACM) **32**(2), 374–382 (1985)

16. Fitzi, M., Garay, J.A.: Efficient player-optimal protocols for strong and differential consensus. In: Borowsky, E., Rajsbaum, S. (eds.) 22nd ACM Symposium Annual on Principles of Distributed Computing, pp. 211–220. Association for Computing Machinery (Jul 2003). https://doi.org/10.1145/872035.872066

17. Fitzi, M., Hirt, M.: Optimally efficient multi-valued Byzantine agreement. In: Ruppert, E., Malkhi, D. (eds.) 25th ACM Symposium Annual on Principles of Distributed Computing, pp. 163–168. Association for Computing Machinery (Jul 2006). https://doi.org/10.1145/1146381.1146407

18. Gao, Y., Lu, Y., Lu, Z., Tang, Q., Xu, J., Zhang, Z.: Efficient asynchronous byzantine agreement without private setups. In: 2022 IEEE 42nd International Conference on Distributed Computing Systems (ICDCS), pp. 246–257 (2022). https://doi.org/10.1109/ICDCS54860.2022.00032
19. Ghinea, D., Goyal, V., Liu-Zhang, C.D.: Round-optimal byzantine agreement. In: Dunkelman, O., Dziembowski, S. (eds.) Advances in Cryptology – EUROCRYPT 2022, Part I. Lecture Notes in Computer Science, vol. 13275, pp. 96–119. Springer, Heidelberg (May / Jun 2022). https://doi.org/10.1007/978-3-031-06944-4_4
20. Ghinea, D., Liu-Zhang, C.D., Wattenhofer, R.: Optimal synchronous approximate agreement with asynchronous fallback. In: Proceedings of the 2022 ACM Symposium on Principles of Distributed Computing, pp. 70–80 (2022)
21. Ghinea, D., Liu-Zhang, C.D., Wattenhofer, R.: Multidimensional approximate agreement with asynchronous fallback. Cryptology ePrint Archive (2023)
22. Heilman, E., Kendler, A., Zohar, A., Goldberg, S.: Eclipse attacks on bitcoin's peer-to-peer network. In: Jung, J., Holz, T. (eds.) USENIX Security 2015: 24th USENIX Security Symposium, pp. 129–144. USENIX Association (Aug 2015)
23. Karlin, A., Yao, A.: Probabilistic lower bounds for byzantine agreement. Unpublished document (1986)
24. Katz, J., Koo, C.Y.: On expected constant-round protocols for byzantine agreement. In: Dwork, C. (ed.) Advances in Cryptology – CRYPTO 2006. Lecture Notes in Computer Science, vol. 4117, pp. 445–462. Springer, Heidelberg (Aug 2006). https://doi.org/10.1007/11818175_27
25. King, S., Nadal, S.: Ppcoin: Peer-to-peer crypto-currency with proof-of-stake. self-published paper, August **19**(1) (2012)
26. Lamport, L., Shostak, R., Pease, M.: Concurrency: The Works of Leslie Lamport. Association for Computing Machinery, New York, NY, USA (2019), edited by Dahlia Malkhi
27. Momose, A., Ren, L.: Optimal communication complexity of authenticated byzantine agreement. In: Gilbert, S. (ed.) 35th International Symposium on Distributed Computing (DISC 2021). Leibniz International Proceedings in Informatics (LIPIcs), vol. 209, pp. 32:1–32:16. Schloss Dagstuhl – Leibniz-Zentrum für Informatik, Dagstuhl, Germany (2021). https://doi.org/10.4230/LIPIcs.DISC.2021.32
28. Mostéfaoui, A., Moumen, H., Raynal, M.: Signature-free asynchronous binary byzantine consensus with $t<n/3$, $\mathcal{O}(n^2)$ messages, and $\mathcal{O}(1)$ expected time. J. ACM **62**(4) (2015). https://doi.org/10.1145/2785953
29. Mostéfaoui, A., Raynal, M.: Signature-free broadcast-based intrusion tolerance: Never decide a byzantine value. In: Lu, C., Masuzawa, T., Mosbah, M. (eds.) Principles of Distributed Systems, pp. 143–158. Springer, Berlin Heidelberg, Berlin, Heidelberg (2010)
30. Mostéfaoui, A., Raynal, M.: Signature-free asynchronous byzantine systems: From multivalued to binary consensus with $t<n/3$, $\mathcal{O}(n^2)$ messages, and constant time. Acta Inf. **54**(5), 501–520 (2017). https://doi.org/10.1007/s00236-016-0269-y
31. Nakamoto, S.: Bitcoin: A peer-to-peer electronic cash system. Decentralized business review (2008)
32. Nayak, K., Ren, L., Shi, E., Vaidya, N.H., Xiang, Z.: Improved extension protocols for byzantine broadcast and agreement. In: Attiya, H. (ed.) 34th International Symposium on Distributed Computing (DISC 2020). Leibniz International Proceedings in Informatics (LIPIcs), vol. 179, pp. 28:1–28:17. Schloss Dagstuhl–Leibniz-Zentrum für Informatik, Dagstuhl, Germany (2020). https://doi.org/10.4230/LIPIcs.DISC.2020.28

33. Patra, A., Rangan, C.P.: Communication optimal multi-valued asynchronous byzantine agreement with optimal resilience. In: Fehr, S. (ed.) ICITS 11: 5th International Conference on Information Theoretic Security. Lecture Notes in Computer Science, vol. 6673, pp. 206–226. Springer, Heidelberg (May 2011). https://doi.org/10.1007/978-3-642-20728-0_19

34. Pfitzmann, B., Waidner, M.: Information-theoretic pseudosignatures and byzantine agreement for $t \geq n/3$. IBM Research, Armonk, NY, USA (1996)

Author Index

M. Joye and G. Leander (Eds.): EUROCRYPT 2024, LNCS 14655, p. 463, 2024.
https://doi.org/10.1007/978-3-031-58740-5

Printed in the United States
by Baker & Taylor Publisher Services